D1515247

Railroads in the Nineteenth Century

Encyclopedia of American Business History and Biography

Railroads in the Nineteenth Century

Edited by

Robert L. Frey
Wilmington College of Ohio

A Bruccoli Clark Layman Book

 Facts On File®
New York·Oxford

Encyclopedia of American Business History and Biography:
Railroads in the Nineteenth Century

Copyright © 1988 by Bruccoli Clark Layman, Inc., and
Facts on File, Inc.

ISBN 0-8160-2012-4

Full CIP information available on request
British CIP information available on request

Designed by Quentin Fiore

Printed in the United States of America

10 9 8 7 6 5 4 3 2 1

To Patricia and Brenda

Contents

Foreword

The Encyclopedia of American Business History and Biography chronicles America's material civilization through its business figures and businesses. It is a record of American aspirations—of success and of failure. It is a history of the impact of business on American life. The volumes have been planned to serve a cross section of users: students, teachers, scholars, researchers, government, and corporate officials. Individual volumes or groups of volumes cover a particular industry during a defined period; thus each *EABH&B* volume is freestanding, providing a history expressed through biographies and buttressed by a wide range of supporting entries. In many cases a single volume is sufficient to treat an industry, but certain industries require two or more volumes. When completed, the *EABH&B* will provide the fullest available history of American enterprise.

The editorial direction of *EABH&B* is provided by the general editor and the editorial board. The general editor appoints volume editors, whose duties are to prepare, in consultation with the editorial board, the list of entries for each volume, to assign the entries to contributors, to vet the submitted entries, and to work in close cooperation with the Bruccoli Clark Layman editorial staff so as to maintain consistency of treatment. All entries are written by specialists in their fields, not by staff writers. Volume editors are experienced scholars.

The publishers and editors of *EABH&B* are convinced that timing is crucial to notable careers. Therefore, the biographical entries in each volume of the series place business and their leaders in the social, political, and economic contexts of their times. Supplementary background rubrics on companies, inventions, legal decisions, marketing innovations, and other topics are integrated with the biographical entries in alphabetical order.

The general editor and the volume editors determine the space to be allotted to biographies as major entries, standard entries, and short entries.

Major entries, reserved for giants of business and industry (e.g., Henry Ford, J. P. Morgan, Andrew Carnegie, James J. Hill), require approximately 10,000 words. Standard biographical entries are in the range of 3,500-5,000 words. Short entries are reserved for lesser figures who require inclusion and for significant figures about whom little information is available. When appropriate, the biographical entries stress their subjects' roles in shaping the national experience, showing how their activities influenced the way Americans lived. Unattractive or damaging aspects of character and conduct are not suppressed. All biographical entries conform to a basic format and have the same rubrics.

A significant part of each volume is devoted to concise background entries supporting and elucidating the biographies. These nonbiographical entries provide basic information about the industry or field covered in the volume. Histories of companies are necessarily brief and limited to key events. To establish a context for all entries, each volume includes an overview of the industry treated. These historical introductions are normally written by the volume editors.

We have set for ourselves large tasks and important goals. We aspire to provide a body of work that will help redress the imbalance in the writing of American history, the study of which too often slights business. Our hope is also to stimulate interest in business leaders, enterprises, and industries that have not been given the scholarly attention they deserve. By setting high standards for accuracy, balanced treatment, original research, and clear writing, we have tried to ensure that these works will commend themselves to those who seek a full account of the development of America.

—William H. Becker
General Editor

Acknowledgments

This book was produced by Bruccoli Clark Layman, Inc. James W. Hipp was the in-house editor.

Production coordinator is Kimberly Casey. Art supervisor is Cheryl Crombie. Copyediting supervisor is Joan M. Prince. Typesetting supervisor is Kathleen M. Flanagan. Michael D. Senecal is the editorial associate. The production staff includes Rowena Betts, Charles D. Brower, Joseph Matthew Bruccoli, Patricia Coate, Mary Colborn, Holly Lynn Deal, Mary S. Dye, Sarah A. Estes, Cynthia Hallman, Judith K. Ingle, Maria Ling, Warren McInnis, Kathy S. Merlette, Sheri Neal, Joycelyn R. Smith, and Virginia Smith. Jean W. Ross is permissions editor. Joseph Caldwell, photography editor, and Penney Haughton did photographic copy work for the volume.

Walter W. Ross and Rhonda Marshall did the library research with the assistance of the staff at the Thomas Cooper Library of the University of South Carolina: Daniel Boice, Cathy Eckman, Gary Geer, Cathie Gottlieb, David L. Haggard, Jens Holley, Dennis Isbell, Jackie Kinder, Marcia Martin, Jean Rhyne, Beverly Steele, Ellen Tillett, Carol Tobin, and Virginia Weathers.

Introduction

Era of Growth and Acceptance: 1825-1850

By 1815 there were few nations in the world with a greater need for an effective transportation system than the United States. With the uncertainties of national survival overcome, Americans were beginning to move to the west over the Allegheny Mountains. Although most of the nation's population lived near the seaboard, and the rivers draining into the ocean provided adequate local transportation, the need to travel inland was increasing, and the lack of transportation across the mountains was a major hindrance.

The first idea of a railroad in the United States had been advanced before the revolutionary war when the great American inventor Oliver Evans suggested the construction of a steam-powered railroad between Philadelphia and New York. Evans, who was not adequately appreciated by his contemporaries, had been experimenting with steam engines to power millstones. By 1801 Evans had constructed an amphibious steam carriage that chugged around Philadelphia convincing people that Evans really was deranged. Unfortunately, Evans's inventions were ahead of their time, and he was unable to secure funds to perfect them. He died in 1819 convinced that future steam locomotives would pull passenger trains up to 300 miles per day. Most of his contemporaries continued to derive great mirth from Evans's predictions, but many of them lived to see him vindicated.

Probably the first known transportation system to actually use rails in the United States was constructed in 1795 to transport rock and cement in the Boston area. In 1807 another railway was constructed in Boston by Silas Whitney. Two years later Thomas Leiper built a railroad to a stone quarry near Philadelphia, and in May 1827 a 9-mile line was constructed from a coal mine at Summit Hill to Mauch Chunk, Pennsylvania. The longest early railroad was the Delaware & Hudson (D&H) Canal Company's 29-mile gravity railroad from its Honesdale, Pennsylvania, coal mines to the D&H canal at Roundout, New York. All of these railroads, however, used wooden rails and horse or mule power. Most of the lines were gravity lines where the cars coasted downgrade with loads and were drawn back to the mine or oven by animal power. With the exception of the D&H line they were also quite short. These lines were designed to haul a single cargo to the point where it was to be used or to haul it to a better developed and more efficient source of water transportation.

The first incorporated railroad in the United States was the Granite Railway Company of Massachusetts, which was chartered by the state on March 4, 1826. Its purpose, hauling blocks of granite for the construction of the Bunker Hill Monument, was similar to that of the earlier railroads. The Granite Railway was only three miles long and was powered by horses. It was also the first railroad to utilize wooden rails overlaid with iron. The line eventually became part of the New York, New Haven & Hartford Railroad.

The first known charter for an intercity railroad in the United States was granted by New Jersey in 1815 to Col. John Stevens. Stevens had been attempting to secure this charter since 1811, and in 1812 he petitioned Congress to support a national railroad. Since Colonel Stevens was not as eccentric as Evans, he was regarded more seriously, but it is difficult to escape the conclusion that the charters granted by New Jersey in 1815 and Pennsylvania in 1823 were intended more to humor the revolutionary war veteran than to sanction a railroad. In 1825 Stevens operated one of the first live-steam model railroads—a locomotive that ran around a loop of track on his lawn.

One of the major reasons people were unwilling to back Colonel Stevens was that most Americans believed the effective transportation system the country needed had already been developed. The same year Colonel Stevens first operated his live-steam model on his lawn, the great engineering marvel of the new nation, the Erie Canal, had been opened. The canal opened the West to New York City and, furthermore, provided a laboratory for the training of many American civil and mechanical engineers, such as John Jervis. Until the 1840s canals remained competitive with railroads in the question over which could provide better transportation. Eventually, the high initial cost of canals, the fact that they froze over in the winter in many parts of the country, and the slow speed of the boats allowed the railroad to win out. Canals continued, however, to transport bulk commodities, such as coal, that did not require speedy or timely delivery. Canals never were able to overcome their problems dealing with mountainous terrain. Railroads again proved to be more adaptable to the severe grades faced by projects moving to the west.

The successful development of the railroad was inevitably related to developing a more effective form of motive power than the horse or mule. Various techniques were attempted, such as the sail car, but the steam locomotive soon dominated the field. Stationary steam engines had existed for over a century when the first successful locomotive was operated by Richard Trevithick in South Wales in 1804. The development of railroads received a tremendous boost with the opening in England of the Stockton & Darlington Railroad on September 27, 1825. Although it was only twelve miles long and usually operated with horse-drawn cars, it opened with a steam locomotive, the Locomotion, pulling more than thirty cars. Some of these were coal cars, others carried flour, and one was the first passenger car in history, in this case reserved for the directors of the railroad.

The Stockton & Darlington helped to garner support for the much more important Liverpool & Manchester (L&M) Railroad. By 1830, against tremendous opposition from the British gentry and canal interests, George Stephenson and his son Robert had succeeded in constructing the L&M. Before the line was finished the famous Rainhill Trials were held in October 1829 to identify the most effective steam locomotive. At the age of twenty-six Robert Stephenson constructed the Rocket, the locomotive that won the trials. At the trials it operated at a top speed of twenty-nine miles per hour and clearly demonstrated the promise of steam locomotion. The development of these early British railroads and locomotives was extremely important for the United States. Many fledgling American mechanical and civil engineers journeyed to England to see the new railroads and to study the machinery, including locomotives like the Rocket. They returned to

the United States to put their newfound ideas into practice. The fact that American railroads turned out to be quite different from British railroads has led some historians to conclude that the influence of British practice was not significant on early American railroads. Such a conclusion has been shown to be incorrect. Not only in railroading, but in canal building, textile manufacturing, paper making, tanning, powder making, bridge construction, and many other areas, the rapid industrial progress of the United States is attributable, at least in part, to lessons and technologies learned from the British and the French.

The first steam locomotive to operate on American rails was the British-built Stourbridge Lion. It was constructed prior to the Rocket and proved to be too heavy for the line on which it was to operate—the Delaware & Hudson Canal Company railroad from Honesdale to Carbondale, Pennsylvania. After several failures, the seven-ton locomotive was set aside, used as a stationary boiler, and dismantled.

Thus by the late 1820s railroads clearly promised to be one facet of a transportation system which the new nation could utilize to, in the words of John C. Calhoun, "bind the Republic together with a perfect system of roads and canals." Although railroads were in their infancy when Calhoun made his statement in 1817, by 1830 railroads would already loom as a major factor in interstate transportation. Two major factors combined in the 1820s to increase the need for all forms of transportation. One was the tremendous population growth of the states west of the original thirteen states (Kentucky, Tennessee, Ohio, Louisiana, Indiana, Mississippi, Illinois, Alabama, and Missouri). In 1810 these states or territories contained 15 percent of the total U.S. population, but by 1830 this figure had grown to 28 percent. Trade with this increasingly populous region was extremely important for the East. The topography of the Midwest provided adequate river transportation down the Ohio and the Mississippi rivers to New Orleans. Early efforts were made to improve transportation by connecting the Great Lakes and the Ohio River by canal. If the East did not develop an effective transportation link with these western states, the western people would be forced to trade primarily with New Orleans. By 1825 a significant number of steamboats were already competing to make the best time to and from New Orleans.

The second major factor was the rivalry that developed between the major eastern cities for dominance in the western trade. There were five major American coastal cities in the early nineteenth century: Boston, New York, Philadelphia, Baltimore, and Charleston. New York and Philadelphia had populations that were approaching 100,000, while the other three had populations between 25,000 and 35,000. New York and Philadelphia had the initial edge for the western trade because of their size and huge financial resources. Baltimore's convenient and strategically located harbor allowed it to join the "big two." Both Boston and Charleston gradually fell behind in the battle for the western trade, Boston because it was located farther from the western states than the other cities, and Charleston because it did not have the capital base of the merchant-oriented northern cities. Boston, in particular, still attempted to gain its share of the western trade indirectly by trading through New Orleans but was less and less successful as the century progressed.

New York decisively grabbed the lead in this competition with its bold 364-mile Erie Canal project. The city had already experienced phenomenal growth between 1812 and 1825; the dollar value of its international trade in the latter year was three times greater than Philadelphia's. The Erie Canal had a more favorable location than any possible canal constructed west from Philadelphia or Baltimore, and this might have been the major factor that delayed the other two cities from matching New York's gambit. The canal was an immediate success and further supported New York City in its position as the premier trading center in the country.

But Pennsylvania did not totally surrender. The state had been a leader in the turnpike movement and by the mid 1820s had several that ran between Philadelphia and Pittsburgh. Turnpikes, however, were no match for a canal like the Erie. While four to six horses were required to pull about four tons in a Conestoga wagon, a canal boat with one horse could pull eight to ten tons. Thus, about the time the Erie Canal was completed Pennsylvania began the construction of a complex canal and horse-drawn railroad system to cover the 394 miles between Philadelphia and Pittsburgh and the Ohio River. Partially completed in 1830 and totally completed in 1834, the Pennsylvania system did not experience the financial success of the Erie

Canal because of the time consumed while transferring from one form of conveyance to another.

Baltimore also attempted to gain access to the western trade via the turnpike (the National Road, eventually Route 40) and the canal (Chesapeake & Ohio Canal). Because Baltimore was about 200 miles closer to the western waters than New York and 100 miles closer than Philadelphia, it had a slight advantage. Furthermore, Baltimore's leaders were the first to envision a railroad system to the west without any canal components or sections. The corporate title, Baltimore & Ohio (B&O), made the final destination of the line clear. It was chartered in 1827, and the cornerstone was laid on July 4, 1828, the preferred month and day for the beginning of auspicious transportation projects.

Since the Baltimore & Ohio was the first major American railroad, it served as a type of laboratory. Many prominent civil engineers were involved in the construction of the B&O, including Jonathan Knight, who was the chief engineer, Stephen H. Long, George W. Whistler, William G. O'Neill, and Benjamin H. Latrobe. Knight, McNeill, and Whistler made an important trip to England in 1828 and 1829 to study the construction of the Stockton & Darlington and the Liverpool & Manchester and also to examine locomotives and other rolling stock. When they returned to build the B&O they essentially attempted to duplicate British construction efforts.

The initial section of the Baltimore & Ohio was built to last for the ages—British style. The Carrollton and Thomas viaducts, used by freight trains today, are examples of this sturdy construction. Although initial operation to Ellicott's Mills, a distance of thirteen miles, was by horse-drawn vehicles, several other methods of locomotion were attempted. One of the most interesting was the wind-powered sail car, which would only work if the wind was blowing briskly from the rear and in a quartering direction. Wind from the port or starboard sides threatened to overturn the car, and wind blowing directly toward the car sent it in a direction opposite to that desired. A horse-powered treadmill car also ran into difficulties when it collided with a cow. Clearly a new type of motive power was necessary.

Efforts to purchase steam locomotives from England were stymied by a curve on the main line 150 feet in radius. Robert Stephenson did not recommend any of his locomotives for operation over curves with a radius sharper than 900 feet. In 1830 Peter Cooper, a self-taught mechanic who dabbled in a number of trades in Baltimore, attempted to show the directors of the B&O that a steam locomotive could be designed for the main line. The result was the famous Tom Thumb, which lost a race with a horse. Although Cooper went on to be one of the most famous mechanics in American history, he was merely a popularizer of the steam locomotive and not a significant contributor to the technology. Nonetheless, his experimental locomotive began a B&O commitment to steam locomotives that lasted for more than 100 years.

Charleston, left behind in the race to open trade with the west, nonetheless figured prominently in the early railroad history of the country. Construction of a rail line from Charleston to Hamburg, directly across the river from Augusta, Georgia, began in 1830. Attempts to use horsepower and windpower were no more successful on this railroad than they had been on the Baltimore & Ohio. Horatio Allen had been brought from the north to be the chief engineer of the railroad. Having seen steam locomotives successfully operating in England and having been the first engineer of the Stourbridge Lion, Allen was a strong proponent of steam locomotion. He convinced the directors of the South Carolina Railroad to order a locomotive from the West Point Foundry in New York City. The company constructed its, and the nation's, first locomotive, the Best Friend of Charleston. The Best Friend's initial trip on December 25, 1830, established two firsts for the South Carolina Railroad: operation of both the first American-built steam locomotive and the first scheduled steam railroad train in the nation.

The life of the Best Friend of Charleston was short. It ended on June 17, 1831, when the fireman tied down the safety valve. The thin iron boiler could stand little excess pressure and, in an act that would be repeated many times during the days of steam engines, it burst. The boiler was hurled 25 feet, the fireman was killed, the engineer and another individual were badly scalded, and the traveling public was terrified.

Allen moved quickly to quell the fears of the public. Another steam locomotive, the West Point, was already in operation on the line. Allen relocated the safety valve so that only the engineer could reach it, and he put a "barrier car," piled high with bales of cotton, between the tender and the first passenger car. The barrier car was intended to protect passengers from the steam and boiling water should another boiler explosion occur. In 1833 the South Carolina Canal & Railroad Company main line was completed to Hamburg. Its length of 136 miles qualified it as the longest single railroad in the world, a record it did not hold for long.

Neither the Baltimore & Ohio nor the South Carolina Railroad was constructed into areas where a successful transportation system already existed. Thus the citizens of both cities were strongly behind these two railroads, and there was little resistance from canal, stagecoach, or turnpike operators, or tavern and inn keepers. The third public railroad in this country was denied such luxury. The Mohawk & Hudson (M&H) was completed in 1830 by John B. Jervis to join the central New York cities of Albany and Schenectady. Because the state was still deeply in debt for constructing the Erie Canal, the M&H, which threatened competition with the canal, faced strong opposition. Laws were drawn in such a way that only short lines connected end to end across New York could be constructed before about 1850. It was not until 1851 that the railroads paralleling the Erie Canal were freed from paying tolls to the canal. The Erie Canal interests had done their best to ensure a monopoly, but eventually the M&H was linked with other lines to form the New York Central System.

Early railroads had one of three purposes. First, there were the short lines, like the Granite Railway of Massachusetts, whose major purpose was to carry a single product a short distance. Second, there were the intercity railroads or western lines that attempted to link up cities or markets in a linear fashion, the Baltimore & Ohio being a primary example. Finally, there were railroads designed to provide transportation to local markets in a major city. Such cities usually had lines radiating out from them like the spokes on a wheel. Boston was the primary example of this type of railroad system with lines running to Lowell, Fitchburg, and Worcester, Massachusetts; Norwich, Connecticut; and Providence, Rhode Island.

With the success of railroads like the Baltimore & Ohio, the South Carolina, and the Mohawk & Hudson, a type of "railroad fever" swept many parts of the nation. Opposition to the railroads came from people who stood to lose business and money because of their introduction. Sometimes railroad workers were shot at and beaten up, sections of railroad were torn up, and locomotives and rolling stock damaged. But such opposition did not last long. Railroads were infinitely superior to canals and turnpikes, and the feared displacement of workers did not occur.

The Baltimore & Ohio had reached Harpers Ferry, Virginia, in 1834. Here the railroad had to cross the Potomac River; the line was delayed while Benjamin H. Latrobe designed and constructed a covered wooden bridge 800 feet long. By 1837 the line had spanned the Potomac and a branch had been built from Baltimore to Washington, despite the opposition of local turnpike companies. The construction cost of the inclined planes at Parr's Ridge (near Mount Airy, Maryland), the branch to Washington, the rugged line from Point of Rocks to the Potomac crossing at Harpers Ferry, and the wooden bridge there strained the finances of the railroad uncomfortably.

The economic difficulties faced by the nation in 1837 reduced traffic on the B&O and made it impossible to do necessary rebuilding. Most of the stone supports for rails needed replacing with wooden ties. While the Washington branch was laid with "T" rail, the remainder of the line had wooden rails overlaid with iron straps. These straps were dangerous because they would sometimes break loose from the rail and protrude through the bottoms of passing cars. Called "snakeheads," they frequently caused personal injury or death to passengers and crew members. In 1839 westward construction and rebuilding were resumed, and the line was completed to Cumberland, Maryland, 181 miles from Baltimore. The addition of "T" rails, wooden ties, and heavier locomotives improved the operation of the B&O and allowed it to yield modest dividends during most of the 1840s.

West of Cumberland the Baltimore & Ohio had three alternatives to reach the western waters. It could build in a northwesterly direction to Pittsburgh, which was the shortest route and the easiest to build. The line could be built in a more westerly direction to Parkersburg, Virginia, on the Ohio River, which proved to be the shortest direct route to the rapidly developing city of Cincinnati. Finally, the line could be built between the two other routes to Wheeling, Virginia, also on the Ohio River and the beginning of the National Highway, later Route 40, in Ohio. Either Virginia or Pennsylvania had to grant the B&O permission to build across its state.

Virginia did so but Pennsylvania did not, yielding to pressure from the new Pennsylvania Railroad by including conditions in Pennsylvania's charter which appeared to give the B&O the right to build to Pittsburgh but actually blocked the B&O from that city if the Pennsylvania Railroad met the state's requirements. The Pennsylvania met its obligations, and the B&O built to Wheeling, the line being completed on the last day of 1852. The length of the line from Baltimore was 379 miles, and a passenger train made the run in about eighteen hours–a speed of slightly over twenty miles per hour.

The Baltimore & Ohio was not the first railroad to reach the western waters from one of the three competing eastern cities; rail service between the Hudson River and the Great Lakes had been available since the 1840s. About ten short connecting railroads, including the Mohawk & Hudson, constituted an unincorporated "Central Line," but the trip from New York to Albany had to be made by riverboat until 1852, when it was possible to travel from New York to Lake Erie by rail. An alternate route, the Erie Railroad, had been completed in 1851. In many ways this was a remarkable railroad. Constructed to a gauge of 6 feet, the widest ever used in the United States, the line wound through New York State, crossing numerous mountain ranges and deep valleys. One of its viaducts, the Starucca Viaduct near Lanesboro, Pennsylvania, is still used by trains and is one of the most impressive stone-arch structures in the world.

Philadelphia businessmen began a western railroad late compared to Baltimore, but, once started, they pushed construction of a railroad across Pennsylvania with vigor. The Pennsylvania Railroad was incorporated in 1846, and by 1852, also a little ahead of the B&O, the line was completed to Pittsburgh. This line until 1854 had to use inclined plains to reach over the Allegheny Mountains. Thus, interestingly enough, rail lines from all three cities reached western waters at Buffalo, Pittsburgh, and Wheeling at about the same time.

Another early railroad associated with Philadelphia and New York was the Camden & Amboy (C&A), built by Robert L. and Edwin A. Stevens, the sons of Col. John Stevens. After acquiring a charter in 1830 the C&A was constructed from Camden, New Jersey, across the river from Philadelphia, to South Amboy, New Jersey, on the ocean thirty miles south of New York City. Final connections to both cities involved ferry boats. Direct connections on rails leased or owned by the Pennsylvania Railroad from west of Philadelphia to New York were not obtained until after the Civil War. From the 1850s to 1863 New York-bound traffic on the Pennsylvania had to be turned over to the Philadelphia & Reading at Harrisburg. The C&A dominated transportation between Philadelphia and New York for over thirty years. It was one of the best built early American railroads, being partially equipped with Robert L. Stevens's "T" rail.

Railroad construction in New England did not lag behind that in the Middle Atlantic states merely because Boston appeared to be out of the race for western trade. Eventually the railroads radiating out of Boston made efforts to connect with key markets in three specific directions. First a series of lines, including the Fitchburg and the Vermont Central, attempted to link Boston with eastern Canada, thus directing Canadian trade to and from Boston. Second, attempts were made, primarily through the Western Railroad of Massachusetts, to link Boston with Albany and the "Central Line" to Buffalo and the western trade. Third, via predecessors of the Boston & Maine and the New York, New Haven & Hartford, efforts were made to link Boston with New York. All of these efforts succeeded to some degree, but they were unable to restore Boston to the economic preeminence it enjoyed in the eighteenth century.

Until the 1850s the financing of railroads involved a combination of private and public capital. The quarry or coal mine lines were low-cost affairs financed by the owners of the mines and quarries themselves. The Baltimore & Ohio and the South Carolina Railroad were essentially city projects and most of the money came in the form of municipal bonds or other forms of public support. Exceptions such as the Camden & Amboy were financed primarily by individual investors, who also played a minor early role in the B&O and the South Carolina Railroad. The Pennsylvania Railroad, during the late 1840s and early 1850s, was heavily financed by state and local commitments; in 1857, however, an amendment to the Pennsylvania state constitution made it illegal for counties, municipalities, or townships to invest public funds in railway construction. Thereafter, the issuance of stocks and bonds formed the basis for financing Pennsylvania's railroads. Several other states developed similar prohibitions on using public money to support what were

frequently dubious railroad construction projects. Prior to the Civil War little capital to support railroad construction came from outside the United States.

In 1830, 23 miles of railroad were in operation. This figure grew to 2,818 miles in 1840 and to 9,021 miles in 1850. The year in which the greatest mileage was put into service was 1850 with 1,261 miles added. By 1860, 30,626 miles of railroad were in operation. Part of the reason for the success of railroads was the speed and relatively low cost of the transportation. In 1853 the cost of moving a ton of freight 1 mile by turnpike was approximately $15, while the rate on most railroads ranged between $1 and $2. River transportation, costing about $0.37, was the least expensive, but rivers did not always flow where freight had to go.

The Era of War and Western Expansion: 1850-1870

By the time of the Civil War an extensive network of railroads covered New England, the Middle Atlantic states, Ohio, Indiana, Illinois, and southern Michigan and Wisconsin. Lines in the South were less frequent, but all states had at least one rail line. In states like Texas, Florida, Louisiana, and Alabama, many of the lines were isolated with no outside connections, which was seldom the case in the North. The South had little of what could be termed a railroad system, but the North had already progressed a long way toward developing such a system.

When the fighting began with the attack of Fort Sumter, the North held a great advantage because of its superior railroads. Early in the war the South attempted to reduce this advantage by constantly attacking a crucial border state railroad–the Baltimore & Ohio. Baltimore was a city with divided loyalties, as were many of the cities along the main line to Wheeling. But the many attacks by the South, and Stonewall Jackson in particular, drove the railroad to a strong support of the Union.

The B&O continued under attack many times during the war, but, despite the intermittent destruction, the line showed steady profits. In 1861 the net receipts stood at $1.8 million while in 1865 that figure had improved to $4.4 million. Dividends of 6 percent were paid from 1861 to 1863 and were increased to 7 percent in 1864 and 8 percent in 1865. The central location of the B&O made it valuable to the Union, which channeled heavy freight and troop traffic over the line. Other railroads that suffered extensive damage during the war included the Orange & Alexandria (later part of the Southern Railway System), which ran south from Washington to Lynchburg, Virginia; the Virginia Central (later the Chesapeake & Ohio), which ran west from Richmond; the predecessors of the Norfolk & Western, which ran from Petersburg, Virginia, to Bristol, Tennessee; the Richmond, Fredricksburg & Potomac, which ran north from Richmond; the Louisville & Nashville; the Western & Atlantic (the line of the Andrews Raid); and the Nashville & Chattanooga. Almost all Virginia railroads suffered extensive damage because the state changed hands about sixty times during the war. Each side took turns destroying railroad equipment.

Not only did the Baltimore & Ohio make money during the war but so did other northern roads. The Erie paid its first dividend during the war, and the land-grant Illinois Central, although forced to give low rates to government traffic, still paid 8 percent dividends in 1863 and 10 percent in 1865. Even the Wilmington & Weldon Railroad in North Carolina declared a 31 percent dividend as late as 1863. The few southern railroads operating in 1865 did not declare dividends.

The Civil War was the first major war in which railroads were a prominent factor. Early in the war southern commanders Stonewall Jackson, Robert E. Lee, and Braxton Bragg appeared to use railroads more effectively than did their northern counterparts. But in 1863 the Union moved 25,000 troops over a roundabout route from south of Washington to the middle of Tennessee in about twelve days. By that time the number of southern railroads in operating condition had deteriorated to the point where they could not be used effectively. As northern troops moved in they were followed by Herman Haupt's U.S. Military Railroad, which rapidly rebuilt the railroads, changing them to standard gauge if necessary. Because of their adequate supplies of locomotives, rolling stock, rails, ties, and copper wire, the North could rebuild where the South could only watch.

Many later railroad builders learned their trade with the U.S. Military Railroad during the Civil War. Some even came out of the Confederate ranks, such as Gen. Thomas Lafayette Rosser, later a civil engineer on the Northern Pacific under the direction of chief engineer Haupt. At the hands of the U.S. Military Railroad personnel, destroyed bridges

were reconstructed in remarkably short time out of "beanpoles and cornstalks," President Lincoln thought. The Civil War was an excellent training ground for civil engineers, some of whom later helped to construct the major transcontinental railroads.

With the Civil War over, the thoughts of many railroaders turned to the construction of a transcontinental railroad to link the Atlantic and Pacific oceans with bands of steel. An amendment to the Army Bill of 1853 had authorized the survey of three routes to the Pacific. Under the direction of Jefferson Davis, then secretary of war, the surveys were carried out. The northernmost route followed what eventually became the Northern Pacific. The central route followed what eventually became the Union Pacific-Central Pacific. The southern route was the only one not later used by a transcontinental line. A dispassionate examination of the three routes would probably suggest the central route as the best for a transcontinental route because of established trails, a greater population, and the shortest route from the eastern population centers to California. In the 1850s members of Congress were not dispassionate about such matters, and internal battles by proponents of the different routes prevented any initiation of a transcontinental railroad.

In 1854 Asa Whitney, a railroad promoter, proposed a generous land-grant program, a 60-mile-wide swath of land to the railroad that built to the Pacific. Whitney's idea was that the railroad could pay for its construction by selling land. The use of land grants to encourage railroad construction was not new with Whitney. The Illinois Central had been constructed in the 1850s with a 2.5 million-acre land grant from the federal government. That the Central was constructed to a length of 700 miles, then the longest railroad in the world, in six years convinced many people that the land-grant idea was successful in speeding construction. The Mobile & Ohio was also constructed with the aid of a federal land grant in the 1850s.

The major issue remained the route over which the government should sponsor the transcontinental railroad. As long as the southern states remained in Congress they, voting together, could block the choice of the northern or central route. The northern states could in return block the choice of the southern route for the railroad. With the South out of Congress after 1861 the Congress quickly acted to support the first transcontinental railroad. On July 1, 1862, the first Pacific Railroad Bill was passed, mandating the Pacific Railroad to be constructed by two companies. The Central Pacific, which was to build east from the western terminus of Sacramento, had been organized in 1861. The Union Pacific, to build west from Omaha, was an entirely new company, initially capitalized at $100 million. According to the bill each railroad was to receive ten square miles of land for each completed mile of track. In addition a government loan, in the form of U.S. bonds, was to be issued to the two companies. For each mile completed on level terrain (the plains), the companies were to receive $16,000 worth of government bonds. In the foothill or plateau areas the amount was increased to $32,000 per mile and in the mountainous areas to $48,000 per mile.

That initial grant was far from the end of the federal government's support for transcontinental railroads. On July 2, 1864, a second Pacific Railroad Bill was passed, chartering the Northern Pacific Railroad to build from the Great Lakes to Puget Sound along the route surveyed in the 1850s as the northern route. The bill also increased the land grant of the Pacific Railroad to match the twenty square miles of land per mile of completed rail given to the Northern Pacific. In addition to federal land grants, states also pledged territory for the construction of railroads.

The construction of a railroad across 1,800 miles of basically unsettled territory in six years was remarkable. And when, on May 10, 1869, the golden spike ceremony took place at Promontory Point, Utah, linking the two railroads and the Atlantic coast with the Pacific coast, it was a time of national celebration. Over 15,000 people helped to construct the Union Pacific-Central Pacific line, many of them Civil War veterans. They had to be supplemented, however, by Irish and Oriental immigrants and sometimes by convicts. Difficulty with Indians was a constant concern, and the government provided inadequate protection for the construction crews. Nonetheless, the completed line was a triumph in engineering skill.

It has been much easier to see the negative side of the Pacific Railroad project. From the beginning there was a substantial amount of corruption in the project particularly on the Union Pacific (UP). The Crédit Mobilier (a separate company of UP stockholders who made huge profits by inflating construction and supply contracts) became a na-

tional scandal that implicated members of Congress and U.S. vice-president Schuyler Colfax. The small towns established in the wake of the construction gangs were notorious for their crude lifestyle. Treatment of the Indians and the decimation of the buffalo population have also been the objects of severe criticism over the past century. Eventually, it took the intervention of Congress to mark the point where the two railroads were to meet. Left to their own devices the Union Pacific would have built to the Pacific and the Central Pacific to the Missouri, or perhaps the Mississippi, River.

Furthermore, the haste with which the project was completed led to a poorly constructed railroad that eventually had to be rebuilt at a tremendous cost. For many years the Union Pacific, running from a relatively insignificant eastern terminal, Omaha, to an even less significant western terminal, Ogden, was dependent on its connecting railroads for adequate traffic. Little traffic was generated along its own lines, and in the 1880s the Union Pacific was regarded as a weak line. The Central Pacific fared much better because it had a more settled traffic base. It was also increasingly less dependent on the Ogden gateway to the east because the Southern Pacific built east from California along what was the southern route in the army survey of the 1850s. By construction and by merger the company was able to create an alternate line to eastern markets. That made the Union Pacific more vulnerable until, by construction of the Oregon Short Line and by acquisition of the Oregon Railway & Navigation Company, the UP fashioned access to the key city of Portland, Oregon.

The construction of the second transcontinental, the Northern Pacific (NP), was also fraught with difficulties. Adequate capital to begin the project was the first problem. Eventually the NP convinced Congress to allow it to mortgage its land grant in order to raise the capital for initial construction in 1870. The attempt to raise money for another transcontinental line at about the same time as the completion of the Pacific Railroad (with understandable opposition from the Union Pacific and Central Pacific) was a factor. Investors were also skeptical of the practicality of building a railroad in such a northern section of the country. Success appeared certain when Jay Cooke & Company, the nation's largest banking house, agreed to market NP bonds. The always optimistic Cooke made such an excellent effort to convince prospective investors of the ideal nature of the climate of the Northwest that the area became known, in jest at least, as Cooke's "banana belt." The bonds did not sell as easily as Cooke had hoped. In addition, the officers of the NP, including Pres. J. Gregory Smith, were New Englanders who attempted to manage the railroad from afar. The failure of Cooke to sell the NP's bonds led to the collapse of Jay Cooke & Company and the panic of 1873. Construction on the NP stopped, locomotives had to be sold, and employees were laid off. Eventually the NP was completed under the direction of Henry Villard in 1883, but it took longer to complete the NP than it took to complete the Union Pacific-Central Pacific.

The Golden Age of Railroads: 1873-1893

The decades following the panic of 1873 and prior to the panic of 1893 mark the golden age of railroad building and operation. By the onset of the depression of the 1890s more than a dozen trans-Mississippi River lines were in existence.

In 1870 the Kansas Pacific was completed from Kansas City to Denver, and in 1871 the Denver Pacific was completed from Denver to a connection with the Union Pacific at Cheyenne, Wyoming. These two lines were acquired by the Union Pacific, then being run by Jay Gould. The Oregon Short Line, connecting with the UP west of Green River, Wyoming, and running northwest to the Idaho-Oregon state line, was completed in 1882, and the Oregon Railway & Navigation Company, connecting the Oregon Short Line with Portland, was completed in 1884. Both of these lines also became a part of the Union Pacific under Gould and formed its outlet to the Pacific Coast. The Denver & Rio Grande was completed in 1883 from Denver via Pueblo, Colorado, to Ogden, Utah. Thwarted in its efforts to build south into Texas and New Mexico by the Atchison, Topeka and Santa Fe (ATSF), the Denver & Rio Grande (D&RG) had turned west to tap coal mines near Carson City. In 1881 the D&RG leased the Denver & Rio Grande Western (D&RGW), which was building southeast of Salt Lake City. Two years later a connection between the two lines completed the narrow gauge line from Denver to Salt Lake City and later to Ogden. The D&RGW strongly supported the construction of the Western Pacific in an attempt to gain a West coast connection, which would allow

the D&RGW to compete more effectively with the Union Pacific.

Also in 1883 the Southern Pacific was completed from San Francisco and Sacramento to New Orleans. One year earlier the Texas & Pacific (T&P) was completed from New Orleans to El Paso, Texas, via Shreveport, Louisiana, and Dallas, Texas. The T&P was located closest to the southern route surveyed by the army in the 1850s and had been chartered in 1871 to build to California. Although the line was completed by Jay Gould, the construction of the Southern Pacific east from California effectively and permanently limited the western terminus of the Texas & Pacific to El Paso. The Atchison, Topeka and Santa Fe, which proposed to connect Kansas with Santa Fe, New Mexico, was chartered in 1859. The ATSF opened much of Kansas to settlement, but by 1887 it had expanded well beyond its original goal, owning a line from Chicago to California. Because it was the only trans-Mississippi railroad to have its own line into the key rail hub of Chicago, the ATSF was one of the most successful of the western roads.

Along with the Southern Pacific, the third successful western road of the golden age was the Great Northern (GN). Put together carefully by one of the most impressive railroad builders in a century of great builders, James Jerome Hill, the GN was completed to the Pacific at Seattle in 1893. Although it was completed ten years later than its rival the Northern Pacific, the Great Northern had been built more conservatively and over a more advantageous route. Eschewing construction solely to block other lines, a practice common on the Northern Pacific and the Union Pacific, Hill built his traffic base carefully. The result was a railroad that weathered the frequent financial panics of the late nineteenth century to emerge by the turn of the century as the flagship railroad of the Northwest.

A final trans-Mississippi line worthy of mention is the Missouri Pacific. On July 4, 1851, ground was broken for the Pacific Railroad at St. Louis. This line was to build through Jefferson City, Missouri, to the Pacific Ocean long before the Central Pacific or the Union Pacific was considered. The intentions of its builders were far greater than their performance. The line did not reach Kansas City until 1865, and then much of its emphasis was shifted toward Texas and Memphis because of the acquisition of lines in those areas. The Missouri Pacific spent most of its existence competing with the

Missouri-Kansas-Texas, the St. Louis Southwestern, and the Frisco for traffic from St. Louis to Texas rather than competing with the Union Pacific and the Santa Fe for traffic to the Pacific. In 1879 the Missouri Pacific was acquired by Jay Gould. He expanded it to Pueblo, Colorado, Omaha, Nebraska, and across most of Texas to El Paso and the Mexican border. With the Wabash and other railroads he was attempting to control, Gould hoped to have a true transcontinental railroad. Financially overextended, his empire did not survive the depression of 1893.

Connecting the trans-Mississippi River railroads with key rail centers like Chicago and St. Louis were a group of railroads that attained great significance during the golden age of railroading. They were originally organized in the 1850s and were combined into regional systems by 1890. The Chicago & North Western (C&NW), originally the Galena & Chicago Union (G&CU), was Chicago's first railroad. Built west to a connection with the Illinois Central at Freeport, Illinois, the G&CU reached the Mississippi River in 1855. Eventually the G&CU, renamed the Chicago & North Western in 1859, connected Chicago with Milwaukee, Wisconsin, St. Paul, Minnesota, and Omaha, Nebraska, in the last city interchanging with the Union Pacific to give that road a Chicago outlet.

The Chicago & Rock Island was built from Rock Island eastward to Chicago and was opened for the entire distance in 1854. Eventually the Rock Island was extended to Omaha and into Kansas, Oklahoma, and northern Texas, but it never reached the Pacific destination that was attached to the corporate title in 1866. By the turn of the century the Rock Island was one of seven major railroad systems in the nation. Overexpansion and intense competition led to its demise in 1980, although the majority of the physical plant continues to operate under the ownership of other railroads.

The Chicago, Burlington & Quincy (CB&Q) became, perhaps, the most prosperous of these Granger, or midwestern, agricultural railroads. It began as a short line connecting the city of Aurora with the Galena & Chicago Union in 1849. This short line was eventually linked to similar lines to form a continuous railroad named the CB&Q by 1865. Under the direction of the cautious Boston financier John Murray Forbes, the line grew encouragingly, but by 1875 its western lines were virtually surrounded by Jay Gould-controlled properties.

Moving more aggressively, by 1890 the CB&Q had pushed its own or partially owned lines to Omaha, Kansas City, Denver, and St. Paul-Minneapolis. Mergers were contemplated with many different railroads, and several times a Pacific extension was considered (the line eventually did reach Billings, Montana, by two routes), but in 1901 most of its stock was purchased by James J. Hill's Great Northern and Northern Pacific railroads.

The Chicago, Milwaukee & St. Paul (CM&St.P) was chartered in 1847 as the Milwaukee & Mississippi Railroad. By 1874 its name had been changed to the CM&St.P, and it had a line from Chicago into Minnesota. By 1887 it had extended to Kansas City and Omaha. Although the Milwaukee Road was the smallest of the Granger roads, it played a major role in the twentieth-century railroad picture by building the last transcontinental line to the Pacific and becoming one of the most dynamic and well-known railroads in the early twentieth century. By the 1980s it had fallen into the same difficulties faced by the Rock Island and, although still in existence as a corporation, the Milwaukee operates less than half the mileage it did at its peak.

Several key railroads operated north and south roughly parallel to the Mississippi River, the two most important being the Illinois Central (IC) and the Mobile & Ohio. The IC was the more successful of the two and by 1881 had a line from Chicago to New Orleans. In that year the entire 550-mile main line was converted by 3,000 men in one day from wide gauge to standard gauge. The Mobile & Ohio did not prosper as well, primarily because of the destruction and lack of capital caused by the Civil War. The line did eventually link Birmingham, Montgomery, and Mobile, Alabama, with St. Louis and was one of the most successful southern railroads. A few additional lines, such as the Alton Railroad, the Wabash, and the Frisco were of lesser significance, as were more local roads like the Minneapolis & St. Louis.

Across the states of the old Northwest Territory, the Middle Atlantic, and New England, several major railroad systems were developing during the late nineteenth century. Linking Chicago with New York were three major systems: the New York Central (NYC), the Pennsylvania, and the Erie. The weakest of the three was the Erie, primarily because of its unfortunate history of mismanagement. By 1874 Hugh Jewett became president and reorganized the railroad as the New York, Lake Erie & Western Railroad. The line was converted to standard gauge in 1880 and that same year gained access to Chicago. Some stability allowed the company to prosper until the depression of 1893.

The two most impressive railroad systems in the United States from 1870 to 1890 were undoubtedly the Pennsylvania Lines and the New York Central System. The latter was consolidated into its final form by Cornelius and William Vanderbilt and included the Mohawk & Hudson River, the other "Central Line" railroads from Albany to Buffalo, the New York & Hudson, the Lake Shore & Michigan Southern, the West Shore, the Ohio Central, the Michigan Central, and the Big Four. Several of these railroads, such as the Big Four, were neither owned nor leased by the New York Central until well into the twentieth century. Instead they operated in the confederation known as the New York Central (NYC) System as a result of interlocking directorates, minority stock ownership by the New York Central, and favorable traffic connections afforded by cooperation with the NYC. The New York Central Railroad, not the system, included virtually all lines east of Buffalo, as well as the Buffalo to Chicago line via Cleveland and Toledo (the Lake Shore & Michigan Southern). Over the New York Central System operated some of the best passenger trains the country had to offer. A significant portion of the freight and mineral products of the rapidly industrializing nation also passed over the lines of the NYC.

The Pennsylvania was larger and more successful than the NYC. The Pennsylvania was originally chartered to construct a line between Philadelphia and Pittsburgh. After this was accomplished in 1861 the line expanded by leasing and purchasing already constructed railroads. Corporate names like the Cumberland Valley, the Northern Central, the Philadelphia & Erie, and the Allegheny Valley allowed the new line to build throughout Pennsylvania and into Maryland and Virginia. The Pittsburgh, Fort Wayne & Chicago, and the Pittsburgh, Cincinnati, Chicago & St. Louis (both including many earlier Ohio and Indiana railroads) were added to the Pennsylvania in the 1860s.

With more than 3,000 miles of track west of Pittsburgh, the Pennsylvania system was divided into two sections, the Pennsylvania Company to manage the lines west of Pittsburgh and the original company to manage the lines east of Pittsburgh.

Although the arrangement remained extant through the century, it frequently created coordination problems in the Pittsburgh area where the two systems came together under dual management. After 1870 the Pennsylvania extended to New York City and further into Maryland, Delaware, and Virginia as well. With lines from New York through Pittsburgh to Cincinnati, Chicago, and St. Louis, the Pennsylvania was more than a match for the New York Central. At the turn of the century the Pennsylvania also controlled two key border state lines, the Baltimore & Ohio and the Chesapeake & Ohio. At the same time the New York Central dominated the Chicago & North Western.

Other significant lines developed in the East despite the dominance of the Pennsylvania and the New York Central. In New England the Boston & Maine (B&M) and the New York, New Haven & Hartford (NYNH&H) systems had emerged to dominate the railroad scene by 1890. The Vermont Central (later the Central Vermont), a major early force, had suffered irreparable damage in the panic of 1873 and in 1890 could no longer challenge the B&M or the NYNH&H. Smaller railroads like the Maine Central, the Rutland, the Boston & Albany, and even the Delaware & Hudson played significant roles from time to time. None of the New England railroads was ever able to assemble a system that transcended the region. Blocked to the west by the New York Central, the New England railroads attempted with limited success to tap the Canadian trade, but they were never able to build systems beyond Lake Ontario, the easternmost of the Great Lakes. Nonetheless, struggle for control of the railroads and street railway systems in New England was as fierce as in any part of the country between 1880 and the early years of the twentieth century.

The coal-producing anthracite region of northeastern Pennsylvania generated several significant railroads. The Delaware & Hudson (D&H) eventually built north from the northeastern part of Pennsylvania to the Canadian border at Rouses Point, 190 miles north of Albany. In the 1880s it appeared poised to become a major New York-New England railroad system because of the iron foundries along its route, and because the extension of the railroad had opened the door to increased Canadian trade. It did not happen. Many of the iron foundries were driven out of business by the emerging steel industry while others moved south into Virginia. Also the D&H failed to make significant inroads into the American-Canadian traffic that traveled over the already existing railroads connecting the two countries. Plenty of coal continued to move northbound on the D&H rails, and enough Canadian goods moved southbound to allow the railroad to remain reasonably prosperous, but it did not become a major interregional railroad as many had hoped in the 1870s.

Two other significant railroads, the Delaware, Lackawanna & Western and the Lehigh Valley, also developed out of the northeastern Pennsylvania coal region. Both of these railroads were the products of consolidating smaller lines, each acquiring its name in 1853. Both also eventually expanded to compete for their traffic in the New York to Buffalo route, thus creating competition among four railroads between those two cities. As long as coal was the major industrial and domestic fuel, as was the case throughout the nineteenth century, there was enough business for all of these lines, including smaller bridge lines from the Lehigh River to New England like the Lehigh & New England and the Lehigh & Hudson River. The introduction of inexpensive oil by the 1920s sounded the death knell for these lines. Other lines in the area such as the Central of New Jersey and the New York, Ontario & Western struggled to survive the nineteenth century and only did so because of the lack of adequate motorized competition. By the Great Depression both were redundant systems. Neither played a major role at any time in the nineteenth century.

Probably the most significant anthracite road of the nineteenth century was the Philadelphia & Reading (P&R). Tapping the coalfields from the south and being one of the best built of early American railroads, the P&R had much in its favor. Its expansion between 1850 and 1870 was controlled and sound. After 1870 the P&R president, Franklin B. Gowen, aggressively purchased coal land for the railroad—eventually acquiring ownership of about 30 percent of the anthracite land in Pennsylvania. In the 1880s and 1890s the railroad suffered three financial failures, one after it attempted to put together a coalition of lines linking Pennsylvania and New England. It was too late for this type of expansion, however, and the two existing giants, the New York Central and the Pennsylvania, blocked the P&R.

The Baltimore & Ohio, the third railroad to attain western waters in the 1850s, continued to expand in the years after the Civil War. By 1874 it had constructed a line to Chicago and also had leased a line into Pittsburgh. Unfortunately, this created a "war" between the B&O and Pennsylvania that eventually led to the construction of a good deal of redundant trackage between Washington and New York. Continued construction extended the B&O from Cincinnati to St. Louis, but the debt incurred by the extensive construction between 1870 and 1890, in conjunction with increased competition on all sides, drove the railroad into receivership in the depression of 1893.

Southern railroads did not begin to combine into regional systems until the final decade of the nineteenth century. It took many years for most southern railroads to recover from the effects of the Civil War; the lack of adequate capital and the limited need for a heavy transportation system in a lightly industrialized area retarded the growth of most southern railroads. For instance, although several local Virginia and North Carolina railroads were under the ownership of a single individual and were known locally as the Atlantic Coast Line, they were not actually combined into a system of that name until 1893. Although John S. Williams had under his ownership a group of railroads informally known as the Seaboard Air-Line by 1881, the railroads were not combined until 1900. The Southern Railway System, a combination of more than thirty independent railroads, did not come into existence until 1894.

Another factor that retarded the development of southern railroads was the corruption that took place during Reconstruction. North Carolina and Georgia, in particular, were victimized by people from the North, along with some natives as well, who promised to build railroads in exchange for financial support from the state. Milton S. Littlefield of Illinois and Hannibal I. Kimball of Connecticut joined hands with W. W. Holden of North Carolina and Rufus B. Bullock of Georgia to line their pockets, but to build few miles of railroads. Certainly the dollar value of the corruption on northern and western railroads was far greater than was the case in the South, but the South could ill afford such a misuse of its meager resources. Nonetheless, for most of the late nineteenth century the southern economy was local rather than regional or national, and the railroad organization reflected this fact. Only in the last decade of the century did this condition appear to change significantly.

There were three railroads in the South that did grow large enough from 1870 to 1890 to be considered interregional lines atypical of the local railroads of the day. One was the Chesapeake & Ohio (C&O), which by 1900 extended from tidewater at Newport News, Virginia, to Cincinnati. In the last twenty years of the century the C&O became one of the major bituminous-coal hauling railroads in the country. Under the leadership of C. P. Huntington for a time, the C&O was reorganized by Vanderbilt interests in 1888 but fell into the hands of the Pennsylvania interests in the early part of the twentieth century.

The other interregional southern railroad system prior to the 1890s was the Louisville & Nashville (L&N), which had constructed a line between its namesake cities before the outbreak of the Civil War. After the war expansion to Memphis, New Orleans, Mobile, Montgomery, Atlanta, Cincinnati, and East St. Louis made the L&N the biggest single southern railroad system by 1890. Finally, another southern railroad which expanded rapidly from 1880 to 1900 was the Norfolk & Western (N&W), so named in 1881. Under the direction of its energetic president, Frederick J. Kimball, the N&W reached the Ohio River in 1892 where it connected with existing roads to Columbus, Ohio. The N&W built its own line into Cincinnati in 1901. With a line from tidewater at Norfolk to Cincinnati and Columbus, the N&W provided stiff competition for the C&O.

The corruption and dishonesty that accompanied railroad construction in the years after the Civil War was not restricted to railroads alone. The corruption, resulting in the era's being known as the Gilded Age or the Great Barbeque, has distorted the modern view of the times. Despite the questionable practices of the era, the nation succeeded in constructing the most impressive railroad system in the world. Great fortunes were made, and many were critical of those who made them. The honest were unjustly condemned as easily as the dishonest. Just as it is easy to condemn the Erie war, as well as several similar escapades, not all railroads were constructed by corrupt means. Sometimes actions that appeared to be dishonest or corrupt were mere incompetence. Railroads such as the Northern Pacific appeared to have suffered more from the latter than the former.

Nonetheless, increasingly serious problems with the American railroad system were becoming apparent in the years after the Civil War. The problem of rate schedules, for freight primarily but also for passenger travel, was one of the greatest. The art or practice of setting rates became increasingly complicated as the century progressed. Furthermore, to many people it appeared as if the rates had no logical basis behind them, and worse, that they were blatantly discriminatory. Shippers soon discovered that rates for shipping a product depended on where the shipper was, who the shipper was, and what was being shipped. With each of these questions there corresponded reasonable and defensible answers and unreasonable and indefensible ones. The nature of those answers depended heavily on the perspective of the person asking or answering the questions.

Certainly where the shipper was located could logically explain a rate differential. If the shipper were located on a new line with relatively little traffic, as opposed to an established route with substantial traffic, a higher rate could be justified. Such was the case with rates in 1880, for instance. The New York Central and the Pennsylvania east of Chicago charged 0.81 cents per ton per mile on agricultural products compared with 1.40 cents charged by the Burlington west of Chicago and 2.50 cents by the Union Pacific west of Omaha. Whether the differential should have been that great was debatable, but most shippers admitted that some difference was justifiable based on the amount of traffic and the construction costs of a line. Since railroads like the Union Pacific, however, had been aided substantially by government land grants and bonds, many shippers in Nebraska were not willing to concede that a difference of 1.69 cents per ton-mile between the Pennsylvania and the Union Pacific was justifiable.

Shippers usually agreed that the distance the item was to be transported should have the greatest bearing on the rate. But increasingly in the years after the Civil War the distance had an inverse relationship to the rate, and the long-haul/short-haul discrimination became one of the most highly criticized aspects of railroad rate making. To illustrate, it was often cheaper to ship an item over a long distance between two points where there was competition than over a shorter distance where there was no competition. It cost about $0.13 per hundred pounds to ship grain from St. Paul, Minnesota, to Chicago in the 1890s, but farmers living en route in Wisconsin commonly had to pay $0.25 per hundred pounds. There were at least three railroads from the Twin Cities to Chicago operating through Wisconsin: the Burlington, the Chicago & North Western, and the Milwaukee Road. In an effort to gain more business one or all three of the lines often shipped freight at less than cost between these two cities. For shippers living at Black River Falls, Wisconsin, however, the C&NW had a monopoly. At Black River Falls, and similar locations, the C&NW charged higher rates in an attempt to recoup its losses on freight shipped at low rates, or at less than cost, from the Twin Cities to Chicago.

One of the ways in which railroads attempted to avoid or reduce the excessive competition that led to the long-haul/short-haul discrepancy was by the pool. A pool was an agreement between railroads to divide the traffic between locations. One of the earliest pools, the Iowa Pool, was created in 1870 by the Burlington, the Rock Island, and the Chicago & North Western. Since each road had approximately equal capabilities to handle traffic between Omaha and Chicago, they agreed to divide all through traffic between them, thus maintaining rates acceptable to each company. Pools were, of course, opposed by shippers in Omaha and Chicago who had benefited by the low rates created by competition. Since the rates at places like Black River Falls did not decline significantly when pools were in effect, there was little support among shippers for pools no matter where they were located. Pools were also disrupted by new railroads building into the territory of companies in a pooling arrangement. Not bound by the rates of the pool the new line could gain a foothold by pricing its services under those of the railroads in the pool. The result was either the destruction of the pool or its absorption of the new line.

In an effort to control rates states began in the 1870s to pass laws regulating passenger fares, requiring freight rates based exclusively on distance, and creating regulatory commissions to oversee the railroads. Illinois, the first state to take such action, was followed by other midwestern states such as Iowa, Wisconsin, and Minnesota, as well as by a few southern states like Georgia. Because most of these legislative actions were backed by an organization of farmers known as the Grange, the resulting laws were often known as Granger laws.

Railroads in states where Granger laws were enacted resisted the new laws in a variety of ways. Some fought them in the courts arguing that char-

ters allowing railroads to set rates and tariffs once given could not be violated by subsequent laws regulating rates. In Iowa, where railroad charters were granted with the expressed right on the part of the state to regulate rates at a later date, railroad lawyers could not use this tactic. In Iowa the railroads used the argument that the state of Iowa could not regulate a railroad chartered in another state. Another common form of resistance was to reduce the quality and quantity of service to customers, a tactic practiced most frequently in Wisconsin. In states like Iowa some railroads worked out compromises with shippers and legislators that temporarily improved relations. The U. S. Supreme Court in *Munn* v. *Illinois* (1876) upheld the Granger laws, thus making such accommodations desirable.

But the issue of regulation did not remain at the state level. In the 1880s efforts to create railroad regulatory commissions moved to the national level. The rapid expansion of railroads was creating a crisis for the federal system. Steamboat travel had first highlighted the crisis which eventually required a broadening of the interpretation of the "commerce" clause of the United States Constitution in *Gibbons* v. *Ogden* (1824). Railroads were proving to be too big for regulation by individual states. Merging into ever larger systems, speeded by the depression of 1884-1885, railroads appeared immune to local and state government efforts to control them. The number of voices demanding federal regulation was also increasing. Historians in the 1960s discovered that many railroad executives and bankers of the late nineteenth century were interested in some form of national regulation. Competition was becoming too cutthroat. Bankrupt railroads with nothing to lose were often initiating rate wars that endangered stable and well-managed lines. Pools, interlocking directorates, traffic agreements, and voting trusts were not stabilizing the railroads to the extent anticipated even by people like James J. Hill, E. H. Harriman, J. P. Morgan, and other major figures in the business.

The Supreme Court opened the way to the creation of a national regulatory commission by reversing *Munn* v. *Illinois* in *Wabash* v. *Illinois* in 1886 and deciding that an interstate railroad could only be regulated by the federal government. This decision struck down the Granger laws for most railroads, at least the larger ones. Now there was no choice but to enact federal regulation, at least in the eyes of most members of Congress and the public. The result was the creation of the Interstate Commerce Commission in 1887. In the wake of the creation of the ICC came many years of wrangling over what the words "reasonable and just" meant when applied to railroad rates. The controversial issue did not recede as a major irritant in the eyes of railroads until after World War II. In the long struggle agreement was seldom reached. Initially, railroads successfully resisted or circumvented rate decisions unfavorable to them. After the passage of the Hepburn Act of 1906 and the Mann-Elkins Act of 1910, government regulatory agencies frequently dictated rates to railroads in an intensely political and often unrealistic manner. It was this action, asserts the prominent business historian Albro Martin, that eventually brought about the decline of America's railroads. Probably, but the public image of people like J. P. Morgan, William H. Vanderbilt, Daniel Drew, and Jim Fisk did much to destroy public confidence in railroad leadership and create the atmosphere in which the ICC had to make its judgments.

The status of a person also determined the rate paid for freight and whether or not a passenger fare was collected. The extensive use of passes, granting free transportation to prominent people, was a major tactic used by railroads to influence and reward friendly government officials and shippers. These passes were so widely dispersed that they clearly affected passenger tariffs. One of the most onerous tactics used by railroads, but actually forced on them by powerful shippers, was the rebate. Here a shipper paid the same rate everyone else paid, but at the end of a period–a month or a year–the railroad gave the shipper a rebate. The person who best utilized rebates in creating and maintaining a fortune was John D. Rockefeller, who had the foresight to locate his oil refinery in Cleveland where he had access to several railroads. He was able to play one railroad off against another by demanding a rebate in return for all of his considerable business. Rebates were difficult to detect because it appeared as if the favored shipper (Rockefeller in this case) was charged the same rate as any other oil shipper.

Finally, what was being shipped (agricultural products, livestock, coal, lumber product, etc.) was a significant factor affecting rates. Here there was no objective basis, other than profit, for calculating a rate considered fair to both the shipper and the railroad. But there were many other factors affecting the definition of a fair rate. For instance, if the Northern Pacific Railroad charged a Minnesota wheat farmer $1 to ship a ton of grain to Chicago in 1890, the same rate the following year might be considered unfair by the farmer because his price per bushel of wheat declined by 30 percent over the preceding year, not an uncommon occurrence in the deflationary 1890s. If a railroad was having a difficult year at the same time shippers were having a difficult year, also common because of the turbulent economic conditions of the period, an attempt by the railroad to increase its income by raising rates was understandably met with anger. In addition, the seeming arrogance and lack of public concern evidenced by many railroad owners and managers was a strong reason behind public anger and demands for regulation. The fundamental question remained: What was a reasonable profit for a railroad? Some balance between the corporate interest and the public interest had to be achieved, and it was this compromise that the ICC and state regulatory commissions were designed to achieve. That they were not successful in achieving such a balance should hardly be a surprise considering the complex variables that had to be taken into account.

In recent years efforts have been made by business and economic historians to present the railroad side of the story in the debate over what motivated railroad owners and managers. Several general conclusions have emerged. First, it is difficult to describe the railroad owners and managers as a group uniformly opposing all forms of government regulation. Some were opposed to any form of regulation at all. Others were convinced that federal regulation was a positive necessity. Most of them appeared to have been somewhere in the middle, either realizing federal regulation was an idea whose time had come and attempting to influence the legislation in ways least offensive to the railroads, or being moderately opposed, but willing to make the best out of the situation if regulation was approved. There is little doubt that an undetermined, but not insubstantial, number of managers viewed state regulation and the ICC as a way to control cutthroat competition in an industry that had failed to do so on its own.

A second conclusion is that despite the fact that railroad owners and managers, like Jay Gould, James J. Hill, and J. P. Morgan, were perceived and portrayed as not working "in the public interest," they were not all greedy, dishonest characters only "in it for the money." Recent studies by Maury Klein, Albro Martin, and Vincent Carosso successfully present a different, and more realistic, view of these "robber barons." Unlike the late twentieth century, the nineteenth had not developed a strong concept of the public interest. The survival of the fittest was a concept well suited to the business philosophies of Gould, Hill, and Morgan. The same concept was supported by religious and social institutions which accepted its validity. Perhaps people like Gould, Hill, and Morgan carried the concept too far, but they were more often the heroes, rather than the villains, of the day. On the other hand there is probably little that any historian can do to justify some of the practices of Daniel Drew, Jim Fisk, and Calvin Bryce, for instance.

Furthermore, "progressive" historians and popular journalists have long overstated the profits men such as Gould and Morgan reaped from their business dealings. The hatred of the rich and the dislike of big business led to charges of irresponsibility to the public. But Morgan and Hill, particularly, perceived their loyalty and accountability to lay, not with the public, but with the stockholders. Their seeming disdain for stockholders was often the result of a struggle for control of the company or control of the direction of the company in which some of the opposing stockholders were far from innocent of using questionable tactics. Men like Morgan and Hill possessed the confidence, the decisiveness, and the spirit (bred in part by the age), not to yield or back down.

A third conclusion has already been set forth. Despite the seeming lack of public concern evidenced by the worst of the "robber barons," comparative history shows that there was certainly no more, and almost as certainly a great deal less, social dislocation and damage to the public interest in the development of the American railroad system than that in any other nation of the world. The result of that development, furthermore, was a railroad network of slightly more than 193,000 miles, which by 1900 laced the country so well that people in all but the least-populated areas of the country were within earshot of the steam locomotive's whistle. Some parts of the system were overbuilt, to be sure, and some parts did not enjoy state-of-the-art technology, but American railroads, in general, were acknowledged to be equal to the world's most advanced railroad technology. In fact, the nation was on the verge of world leadership in mechanical and civil engineering technology.

Another major development in the American railroad scene from 1870 to 1890 had a profound, yet often unnoticed, impact on the country. This was the development of standard and uniform parts, practices, and procedures necessary to turn the railroads of the country into a national system. The best examples of uniform parts were the acceptance of the standard gauge of 4 feet 8½ inches and the introduction and acceptance of the air brake and the automatic coupler.

At the outbreak of the Civil War about 46 percent of the railroad mileage in the country was built to other than standard gauge. In the years after the war most new railroads were built to standard gauge, but the changeover was not complete until 1886, when most of the southern railroads changed to standard gauge. In the period from 1865 to 1886 interchange of freight traffic was made difficult because of the gauge differences. Several devices were used to effect necessary interchange. The most common method was to have a crane lift a freight car off its trucks (wheels), roll the trucks out from under the car, and substitute trucks of the correct gauge. This was a time-consuming practice that required a crane, dual-gauge track, and a substantial amount of manpower. It was only manageable because the number of cars to be interchanged was not large. As the economy became more national in scope, that is, as raw materials and manufactured products were distributed over greater distances, the need for more frequent interchange of cars necessitated gauge standardization. After the conversion of the southern railroads in 1886 the only significant nonstandard gauge railroads were the narrow-gauge lines in the Colorado Rocky Mountain area and in a few other locations where narrow-gauge railroads served primarily local markets.

Probably the two most significant inventions in railroad history after the 1850s were the air brake and the automatic coupler. The use of hand brakes and the link and pin coupling system were responsible for thousands of deaths and hundreds of thousands of injuries to employees and the public alike in the nineteenth century. Until the introduction of George Westinghouse's air brake in the 1870s, braking was accomplished by reversing the locomotive, hand braking each car, or a combination of the two. Some locomotives were equipped with steam-actuated brakes that were a definite improvement, but an effective continuous brake that could be set by the engineer on the entire train simultaneously had eluded inventors. Using compressed air and a device known as the triple valve, Westinghouse succeeded in making his brake the standard for American railroads. Because of its clearly demonstrated superiority the Westinghouse brake was installed on the passenger cars of most railroads within a few years after its successful introduction. Railroads were reluctant to go to the expense of installing air brakes on freight trains, however, and there were some railroads that resisted putting them on passenger trains. It was eventually necessary for the Congress of the United States to mandate such installations through passage of the Railroad Safety Appliance Act of 1893.

The link and pin coupling system was the other device responsible for killing and maiming many people. As with the air brake, an improved coupling system was attempted by many inventors. Some of these devices were reasonably successful but none as much so as the coupler devised by Eli Janney. Based on the principle of curving the fingers of the human hand and sliding them past each other into a locked position, Janney's coupler had the added advantage of not requiring the brakeman to step between the cars to couple and uncouple them. Invented about the same time as the air brake, the automatic coupler did not gain quite as rapid an acceptance as did the air brake. Part of the reason was the existence of effective competitors. Once again it was the Railroad Safety Appliance Act of 1893 that forced many railroads to install the Janney automatic coupler on locomotives and rolling stock. The installation of these two devices went a long way to reduce deaths and injuries among train crews and passengers.

One other type of technology that should be mentioned at this point, but has little to do with standardization or uniformity, is bridge building. Bridge building was a crucial factor in the creation of major rail systems. Prior to the Civil War rivers often blocked the crossing of railroads. The Mississippi River was the most prominent example, but the Ohio River, the Missouri River, and the Tennessee River were also large physical barriers to railroads. Bridge construction had been a problem for American railroads from the outset. Several railroads, like the Baltimore & Ohio, had constructed sturdy stone viaducts, but they were often built only over small rivers and creeks. Ferry boat companies benefited from these river barriers, but it was obviously a slow, expensive, and time-consuming practice to transfer freight from a railroad car to a boat and then again to a railroad car. It did, of course, provide work for teamsters and riverboat captains, but it also slowed down the movement of freight and passengers and prevented the creation of an integrated national rail system. From the late 1860s efforts began to span these great rivers with equally impressive bridges. By 1870 four railroad bridges spanned the Mississippi north of St. Louis; the Missouri had been spanned at both Kansas City and Omaha; and the Ohio was bridged at both Cincinnati and Louisville.

Probably the most famous bridge across any of these rivers was the steel-rib arch bridge completed at St. Louis by Captain James B. Eads in 1874. It established a nonsuspension bridge record for its span. Constructed of hollow-tube chromium steel (expensive and little used at that time) the center span was 520 feet with connecting side spans of 502 feet each. The bridge rested on four masonry piers built up from bedrock inside pneumatic caissons. It remains in use today. The first of John August Roebling's famous suspension bridges was the double-decked railroad bridge spanning the Niagara River at Niagara Falls—the first successful railroad suspension bridge—completed in 1855. An even more spectacular bridge, with a record span of 1,057 feet, was completed in Cincinnati in 1867. This bridge, although no longer used for rail traffic, is still used by automobiles. The construction of bridges by civil engineers like Eads and Roebling caught the imagination of many Americans. Furthermore, these bridge projects helped to train an entire group of civil engineers, much as the Erie Canal and the B&O Railroad had a generation earlier. With towering railroad bridges spanning the greatest rivers of the nation, the American railroad system took one more significant step toward being an integrated, unified national transportation network.

Of the practices and procedures developed between 1870 and 1890 to turn the American railroads into a national system, several others deserve mention. One was the creation of standard time. As long as the United States was a nation composed primarily of semi-isolated, autonomous, agricultural communities, with little need for extensive contact and coordination on any schedule, the time of day was not critical. The advent of railroads, as long as schedules were loose, connections were casual, traffic was sparse, and speeds a minor consideration, did not immediately make time a critical factor. It did not matter that when it was noon in Chicago it was only 11:50 in Aurora, a town only fifty miles west. By the 1850s cities like Pittsburgh, where many railroads came together, found it a minor irritant that each railroad had a different time. Some stations had three or more clocks, each one displaying the time of a different railroad. A passenger had to take care to look at the correct clock or the train might be missed. Since schedules were only haphazardly followed in the 1850s it probably did not make much difference at which clock one looked.

In the years after the Civil War business leaders began to see the country in a different way. As manufacturing gradually became dominant over agriculture the relatively isolated autonomous communities gave way to a network of cities and towns made more and more interdependent by industry and transportation. Railroads were seen as the link between cities and also as the means to transport raw materials to the factory. Consequently, schedules and their maintenance as well as the frequency of interchange between railroads became more important. Increasingly the time differences, often within a small area, became more irritating. Furthermore, as new methods of operating trains became more time dependent, it was critical that engineers had identical time. Ten minutes difference could cause disastrous train wrecks.

The problem was how to ensure a standardization of time in such a way that it would be realistic in New York, Chicago, and San Francisco. Immediately after the Civil War there were some proposals for a uniform national time. This gained little support because of the tremendous distance across the nation. Eventually, other proposals incorporating time zones were put forward. William F. Allen, who was the editor of *The Official Guide of the Railways* (a national listing of all railroad schedules), popularized the concept of four time zones. Most railroads put this system into effect in November 1883. Congress did not adopt standard time until 1918, and by then they had complicated the issue with "daylight saving" time, a device standardized to an even greater degree today.

Other organizations that worked to create standardization were the associations of car builders and master mechanics, the General Time Convention, the Association of American Railway Accounting Officers, the American Railway Engineering Association, the American Railway Association, and many others. Recognizing the need for standardized practices and procedures, these voluntary organizations appointed special study committees and held meetings from which statements of standards were formulated. They devised ways to put these standards into practice on their own roads and, in some cases, attempted to gain popular support for them.

The car builders and master mechanics associations were influential in standardizing track gauge and in gaining acceptance of the air brake and the automatic coupler. The General Time Convention was important in developing the standard time system, but it also established uniform train signals, train orders, and car movement reports. The association of accounting officers set uniform accounting standards and the Railway Engineering Association established basic civil engineering standards for American railroads. With the exception of the Railway Safety Appliance Act, these voluntary groups did not need the support of the federal government to gain acceptance of their reforms. In most cases they were in a position to enact them on their own and should get a significant amount of recognition for the valuable service they performed in the late nineteenth century in improving the reliability, safety, and efficiency of the American railroad system.

Further examination of the car movement system shows how important it was to resolve a relatively minor matter before a national railroad system could emerge. If a load of freight in a Pennsylvania Railroad boxcar was bound for Omaha, Nebraska, it had to change to the Burlington at Chicago. Unless some business arrangement could be designed to allow the PRR boxcar to operate over the Burlington, the entire contents of the car would have to be unloaded at Chicago and reloaded into a Burlington car, a costly and time-consuming practice. The method eventually formulated was a mileage-based rental charge of $0.75 per mile. To make this system work a great deal of standardized "paperwork" was necessary. Although the per-mile rental charge worked reasonably well it did allow railroads to use foreign road cars for storage purposes. If the car was not moved (and there were priorities for car movement, but they were difficult to enforce), no rental fee was paid. In the twentieth century the rental fee was changed to a per diem basis. This meant a railroad paid a fee as long as a foreign car was on its property regardless of whether the car was moved or not.

Another way in which railroads improved interchange service was by the creation of fast freight lines. Developed toward the end of the Civil War, these companies did a great deal to make feasible through-freight service over several railroads. By the mid 1870s most through-freight was carried by the Star Union Freight line or the Empire line (both Pennsylvania Railroad-sponsored companies), the Great Western Dispatch (Erie), the Continental Fast Freight Line (Baltimore & Ohio), or the Red Line (New York Central). Each company was jointly owned by the railroads that were part of the system, and each company supplied cars roughly in proportion to the amount of traffic carried. Because the boxcars used in the fast-freight service were among the first standardized by the installation of air brakes and automatic couplers, the fast-freight system underscored the importance of standardization in facilitating a profitable service.

Railroads were also influential in the actual creation and destruction of many towns and cities. Not only were towns created because railroads crossed at that point or locomotives had to be fueled and watered every so many miles, but many towns were cut off before they could grow because the railroad chose not to build through them. The most prominent example of an American city made by railroads is Chicago. Starting as a small town, its location at the western end of the Great Lakes proved to be a natural terminus for railroads from the East. St. Louis, likewise, proved to have an advantageous location for railroads, although in the 1850s it appeared that towns like Cairo, Illinois, Hannibal, Missouri, and Duluth, Minnesota, would have greater growth potential than either Chicago or St. Louis. The railroad changed such expectations. Towns like Brainerd, Minnesota, and Livingston, Montana, on the Northen Pacific were created almost entirely by the railroad. Many years later, in the 1950s, when diesel-electric locomotives replaced steam locomotives, these towns and many others like Altoona, Pennsylvania, Marion, Ohio, Peru, Indiana, Centralia, Illinois, Oelwein, Iowa, Grand Island, Nebraska, and Auburn, Washington, suffered tremendous dislocation. Many of them have never recovered a strong economic base.

In the years after the Civil War the railroad had an important social as well as economic impact. The railroad, for instance, loomed large in popular art and literature. The famous Currier & Ives prints are just one example of the manner in which railroads caught the national attention. Such popular ditties as "The Charming Young Widow I Met in the Train," "Asleep at the Switch," "In the Baggage Car Ahead," and "The Message of a Dying Engineer," while hardly classics, are also representative of the impact of railroad images on the people. Railroads carried young men off to careers in the city, to battle at Shiloh, Cold Harbor, and San Juan, brought products from Sears & Roebuck to small towns in Minnesota, and brought politicians, visitors, and immigrants. The railroad provided a connection to the outside world for many people that no other technology, until the development of the telephone and the automobile fifty years later, could provide. Indeed the sight of smoke, the sound of the whistle, and the clanging of the bell were invitations to excitement and expectation for almost all Americans. Small wonder that people were moved to sing, paint, and write about the railroad and its locomotives.

The Era of Merger and Monopoly: 1890-1900

One result of the successful efforts toward standardization and uniformity on American railroads from the Civil War to 1890 was a significant reduction in rates for freight and passengers. Some of these reductions were caused by state and federal government efforts to regulate rates, but those efforts were far less a factor than were the techniques that allowed railroads to operate more efficiently and less expensively. For instance the development of the heavy consolidation (2-8-0) freight locomotive and the ten-wheeler (4-6-0) general-purpose locomotive allowed the weight of trains to increase from about 650 tons in the late 1860s to about 1,800 tons in the early 1890s. Heavier trains at faster speeds allowed a reduction in the number of locomotive crew members. Automatic air brakes and couplers also allowed a reduction in the number of brakemen. The actual number of railroad workers did not decline in the period, but the number of ton miles each worker produced increased at least fourfold from 1865 to the turn of the century.

The decade of the 1880s witnessed the greatest construction of railroad mileage in the history of the country: 71,000 miles. In the year 1887

Encyclopedia of American Business History and Biography

Railroads in the Nineteenth Century

Charles Francis Adams, Jr.

(May 27, 1835-March 20, 1915)

by Don Snoddy

Union Pacific Museum

CAREER: Lawyer, investor (1856-1861); soldier, Union Army (1861-1865); writer, investor (1861-1915); member (1869-1872), chairman, Massachusetts Board of Railroad Commissioners (1872-1879); member, Board of Arbitration, Eastern Trunk Line Association (1879-1884); president, Union Pacific Railroad (1884-1890); historian, reformer (1890-1915).

Charles Francis Adams, Jr., attained status as a railroad figure in two distinct areas: first as an architect and member of the Massachusetts Board of Railway Commissioners, and second as president of the Union Pacific Railroad. Despite what is usually termed his failures in both creating an effective and equitable regulatory mechanism and in running a major transcontinental railroad system, Adams remains an important figure in the history of the last half of the nineteenth century. His career, with its successes and failures, amply illustrates several of the most important challenges faced by the railroads and American society during the former's period of growth and consolidation.

Born on May 27, 1835, Adams was a member of one of the most respected and powerful families in the United States. His great-grandfather was John Adams, a signer of the Declaration of Independence, vice-president under George Washington, and the second president of the United States. Adams's grandfather was John Quincy Adams, the sixth president of the United States and a staunch foe of Andrew Jackson. Adams's father, Charles Francis Adams, was a politician and diplomat who, as ambassador to Great Britain during the Civil War, was instrumental in reducing England's support for the Confederacy. Adams's legacy from such a lineage was wealth, privilege, connections, influence, and, most of all, opportunity. What was not received was a sense of purpose and direction and a guarantee of success. As were his two famous

Charles Francis Adams, Jr. (courtesy of Union Pacific Railroad Museum)

brothers, Henry and Brooks (John Quincy Adams II was the fourth brother), Charles Adams, Jr., was led to regard the rich Adams heritage as both curse and blessing. For Brooks and Henry, both of them, like Charles, historians, the burden of their ancestry manifested itself in a pessimistic view of history as decay. Charles Adams, Jr., on the other hand, was marked by a curious mixture of decisive action and confused indecision, especially early in life. Given Adams's background, Edward Kirkland's assertion that Adams's greatest contribution as a historian was his "campaign against fileopietism" is instructive. Rather than an inevitable product of privilege, Adams seemed to view his achievements apart from the legacy of his family. Regardless of his views, Adams's life was inextricably linked with who he was and what his family represented.

Adams's education was typical of that commonly received by aristocratic Bostonians, consisting of private schools and a time at the Boston Public Latin School. As did his brother, Henry, Adams disliked the education to which he was exposed. He entered the Boston Latin School at thirteen, but soon came to hate the traditionalist manner and curriculum of the institution. Adams performed poorly and was finally taken out of school in 1851 to complete his final year under a private tutor.

Entering Harvard as a sophomore, Adams found the college to be an improvement over Boston Latin but still not without problems. Throughout his life Adams complained of the impersonal and distant manner of his Harvard instructors. As do many students who are disenchanted with academics, Adams concentrated on activities outside the classroom. He finished in the lower half of his class but was a member of the Institute of 1770, president of Alpha Delta Phi, and a leader in the Hasty Pudding Club. More important to his later career, Adams spent much of his time reading and writing, devouring Thackerey, Emerson, Tennyson, and Carlyle; writing for the *Magazine*; and winning a Bowdoin Prize for an essay on Juvenal.

After his graduation in 1856 Adams entered the Boston law firm of Dana and Parker, which was headed by Richard Henry Dana, the author of *Two Years Before the Mast* (1840). Adams read law for two years before attempting the bar examination. He was not taken with the law, feeling he had little affinity for its principles, but, nevertheless, passed a one-page exam proctored and graded by the Adams family friend, Judge George T. Bigelow. For the next several years Adams worked half-heartedly as a lawyer, invested in real estate, lived at his father's home, and cultivated a social life. While he was uneasy with his career and life as a lawyer, Adams lacked even an inkling of an idea for an alternative profession. He feared the uncertainty in which his situation placed him, writing in his diary that an "objectless life is more bitter than death."

In 1858 Charles Adams, Sr., was elected to the U.S. House of Representatives, the family moving to Washington the next year. Adams remained in Boston to take care of his work and the family possessions, but in 1860 he visited the capital for the first time. On his trip Adams was able to pick some of the fruit of his family's influence, meeting and talking with many of the most powerful men in the country. One of these, William Henry Seward, a failed Republican candidate for president, took Adams on a trip to the West to campaign for Abraham Lincoln. His experiences in Washington and the West fanned Adams's interest in public affairs, and he began to formulate a direction for his life.

With Lincoln's victory in 1860, the die had been cast for war, and Adams's father was appointed as minister to the Court of St. James, his express responsibility to lessen English support for the South. On April 12, 1861, hostilities broke out, and Adams's life was radically changed. Despite the fact that his first published article, "The Reign of King Cotton," appeared in the April 1861 *Atlantic Monthly* to a generally good reception, Adams still felt aimless. He noted that the article marked him "as a young man of somewhat nebulous promise," but that was inadequate praise for him at the time. Adams desired a complete break with his present life, a break which came in October 1861 with his enlistment in the Union army.

He was commissioned a first lieutenant in the First Regiment of Massachusetts Cavalry Volunteers and was immediately sent to South Carolina, where Union troops occupied Hilton Head Island and Beaufort. The conditions there were comfortable and nothing like the sacrifices Adams expected. The regiment did, however, see action at Antietam and Gettysburg, and by this time Adams was becoming disenchanted with army life. By war's end he had been breveted a brigadier general, but ill health caused him to relinquish his command and to be discharged. On November 8, 1865, he married Mary Hone Ogden, whom he had met on furlough, and with whom he later had three daughters and twin sons.

The war had radically changed the direction of Adams's life, and he ended any pretense of returning to the practice of the law. Instead, he decided to strike out in a completely new direction and to make for himself "a specialty in connection with the development of the railroad system." The condition of the railroads in the post-war years was desper-

Adams in his senior year at Harvard (courtesy of Harvard Archives, Harvard University)

ate, with massive destruction, heavy traffic, and little capital to build and repair the lines. The growth of the industry had been phenomenal during the 1850s, and the performance of the railroads during the war, especially in the North, had convinced nearly all of their importance to the growth and prosperity of the nation. But there was little money, construction standards were lax, corruption was common, and there was no regulation or guidance of the development of the rail network. Adams saw the railroads as an example of what was needed in the way of reform in the United States; he also saw himself as an agent of that reform.

Adams knew that he could use his writing skills as a means of establishing himself as an expert in the field of railroad operation and reform. His first salvo was published in the April 1867 *North American Review* and was entitled "The Railroad System." Adams was still ignorant of the de-

tails of railroad operation, and this article, like others from this period, is long on generalities and short on specifics. By 1869 Adams had progressed far enough to develop his most important idea, that of the railroad commission. The notion of an appointed body to oversee railroad operations on a state level, safeguarding the rights and interests of both railroads and railroad customers, appealed to Adams as a positive step for the railroads and also as an opportunity for himself to gain influence in his chosen field.

Adams lobbied the Massachusetts state legislature for creation of such a board. He also continued his railroad writings, concentrating specifically on the 1868 "Erie wars." In June 1869 Adams was appointed to the newly created Massachusetts Railroad Commission. In July 1869 his article, "A Chapter of Erie," appeared in the *North American Review,* a publication which cemented his reputation as a journalist and railroad reformer. His portraits of Cornelius Vanderbilt, Jay Gould, James Fisk, Jr., and Daniel Drew, and his narratives of their exploits made him a public figure and no doubt enhanced his position on the railroad board. The commission consisted of three members, had no enforcement powers, but had the power to subpoena and disseminate information. It was this mixture of powerlessness and public visibility which both doomed the Massachusetts model of railroad regulation and made it the most popular form to copy in other states.

Adams's experience on the commission, of which he was a member from 1869 to 1879, led him to formulate several ideas about the nature of railroad operations. First, Adams realized that railroads, because of their high fixed costs in plant and equipment and their relatively low variable costs, would always tend toward a seemingly discriminatory rate structure. Railroads preferred to carry large cargoes long distances; consequently they constructed their rate structures to lure and reward such loads. The problem arose when those with small cargoes or short hauls were charged higher per-ton-mile rates. Adams observed that "it is an undisputed law of railroad economics that the cost of the movement is in direct inverse ratio to the amount moved."

This first discovery led him to see that railroads would also tend toward large systems, a tendency which he believed, with proper regulation, would decrease costs and minimize rates. He was

Portrait of Adams by Francis Millet, completed in 1876 (courtesy of Adams National Historical Site)

among the first regulators to postulate the particularly negative effects of intense competition on railroads. This belief led him to write that "competition and the cheapest possible transportation are wholly incompatible." The only problem with this vision of railroads and their regulation was the question of how to determine rates that were equitable to customers and that would still provide railroads with adequate revenues to fund needed expansions and repairs. This problem, of course, would not be solved during Adams's lifetime.

Adams's tenure on the commission must ultimately be deemed a failure. The vision of a regulatory mechanism fair to both customer and railroad vanished in the Gordian Knot of the rate question. The ultimate failure of regulation would occur in the deflationary early 1890s and the progressive 1900s. Adams's commission did accomplish some improvements. The board convinced the state to codify existing rail regulations, enact uniform charter laws, recommend uniform safety and equipment standards, and mandate the use of the telegraph and the standard railroad uniform.

The commission also further improved Adams's image as a fair and informed railroad regulator. He was asked to arbitrate a settlement in the 1877 strike on the Boston & Maine Railroad. His re-

port, which was accepted by both management and labor, underscored Adams's strengths and weaknesses as a railroad thinker. Adams proposed that railroads, as a vital public enterprise, must always be kept running, preferably with labor and management joining in an appropriate *esprit de corps*. For labor, Adams recommended gradual increases in wages, protection against arbitrary dismissals, and insurance against death, disability, and old age. These reasonable suggestions, able to be accepted in principle by all, were useless unless ways could be found to implement them.

It was this last difficulty that led Adams to refuse reappointment to the commission in 1878. Lacking the enforcement powers needed to place his ideas into action, Adams was frustrated in relying on good will and public pressure to ensure the success of his proposals. In 1879 Adams accepted an appointment to the Board of Arbitration of Albert Fink's Eastern Trunk Line Association. He served for five years as chairman and as a single arbitrator for the association which attempted to ally all the major railroads east of the Mississippi. His tenure in this position tended to lessen Adams's faith in the potential of railroad cooperation. It did nothing, however, to lessen his reputation as an honest man.

In 1884 Adams assumed the presidency of the tortured and weighty Union Pacific (UP) Railroad. The UP had undergone a tumultuous birth and an even more troubling childhood. In 1884 the railroad was bending under the burden of an almost incredible government debt and a negative public image brought about by the revelations of the Credit Mobilier scandal. Adams brought to the UP his spotless reputation as an honest man and administrator. What he did not possess was experience in actually running a railroad. Adams's tenure as the UP president was a failure. Besides the fact that the UP was torn by several factions with competing interests, it was subject to varying whims and statutes of the federal government. As a result, the UP stands as one of the first case studies which provide evidence against government subsidy. In addition, there was Adams himself. The characteristics which served him so well as a scholar and arbitrator were negatives when placed in a railroad administrator. Maury Klein, in his *Union Pacific: The Birth of a Railroad, 1862-1893*, explains Adams's deficiencies in more detail:

Charles Francis Adams, Jr., third from the left, with the officers of his Union Army regiment (courtesy of Massachusetts Historical Society)

Adams also suffered grievously from that ancient disease of his family, chronic introspection, which transformed every decision into a torment of the soul. In the business arena he was a nervous Nellie, an incessant worrier who shrank from conflict and could not stand fire in battle. Finally, for all his insight into the vagaries of human nature, he was a poor judge of men. Ultimately this proved to be his Achilles heel.

Adams's first real test at the helm of the UP was a serious labor problem. In winter 1884 the UP had attempted to increase production at the company-owned coal mines at Rock Creek, Wyoming. The workers, represented by the Knights of Labor, refused the extra work; the company hired Chinese workers to increase production. Tension mounted, and on September 2, 1885, violence flared between the Chinese and the other workers. Scores of Chinese were killed, and the rest were chased out of the mining settlement. Adams investigated and published a report highly critical of the Knights of Labor, recommending prosecution of the guilty parties. Anti-Chinese sentiment, however, insulated the miners from censure. Adams was able to bar some of those responsible from reemployment.

The floating debt, which amounted to over $6 million, was a constant pressure to both the stock price and the operations of the UP. Adams was able to pay this off in 1886 but immediately after was led into a program of expansion which promised more financial problems. In addition to replacing the hastily and poorly built original track, Adams was led into a mind-boggling network of alliances, pools, and expansions, which strained both Adams's nerve and the UP's resources. The crucial acquisition was the Oregon Railroad & Navigation (OR&N) Company, a line previously associated with Henry Villard and a point of chaos in the railroad situation in the Northwest for many years. The UP leased the OR&N in 1886, but Adams's plans went awry when the Northern Pacific completed a branch in the same area which siphoned off the OR&N traffic. The expansion into the area put $10 million of debt back on the books and eventually left the UP and Adams in an uneasy partnership with the Great Northern of James J. Hill. The final stress on the UP was soon to follow.

The passage of the Interstate Commerce Act in 1887 had opened the door to federal regulation of the railroads. Unfortunately, it also closed the door to cooperation among the railroads. However imperfect were the traffic pools, their operation had at least been a first line of defense against the deadly rate wars. The 1887 act outlawed this technique but provided no alternative. As early as 1888 the railroads were feeling the evil effects of rates spiraling downward. Attempts by Adams, coordinated by J. P. Morgan, to create an alternative system failed in 1889. Financial conditions on the UP and in the rest of the industry worsened, and on November 26, 1890, Adams was forced out as president. Although he was bitter at being removed, Adams was most likely blessed by being out of the company before its impending collapse could come to fruition.

The years after his presidency of the UP were spent writing, managing his impressive fortune, traveling, and agitating for reform. He was a respected speaker and historian and served on Harvard's Board of Overseers from 1882 to 1907, playing a leading role in the movement to modernize the curriculum he had found so distasteful. He lived to see the debacle of railroad regulation which occured in the first fifteen years of the twentieth century, coming to believe that no system could approximate the complexities and sophistication of the market. As did his brother, Henry Adams, Charles Francis Adams, Jr., seemed an anachronism in a world careening toward world war. He had a brilliant mind, yet was somehow out of step with the demands of the world he inhabited. He died of pneumonia in Washington, D.C., on March 20, 1915.

Publications:

Conservatism and Reform (Philadelphia: Congressional Republican Committee, 1860);

"The Reign of King Cotton," *Atlantic Monthly*, 7 (April 1861): 451-465;

The Erie Railroad Row Considered as an Episode in Court (Boston: Little, Brown, 1868);

Railroad Legislation (Boston: Little, Brown, 1868);

"A Chapter of Erie," *North American Review*, 109 (July 1869): 30-106;

A Chapter of Erie (Boston: Fields, Osgood, 1869);

The Double Anniversary: '76 and '63 (Boston: W. P. Lunt, 1869);

The Senatorial Term (Boston: Little, Brown, 1869);

Chapters of Erie and Other Essays (Boston: J. R. Osgood, 1871);

The Government and the Railroad Corporations (Boston, 1871);

Railways and the State (Boston, 1871);

The Regulation of all Railroads Through the State-Ownership of One (Boston: J. R. Osgood, 1873);

The Vienna Exposition and the Philadelphia Centennial (Boston: Estes and Lauriat, 1874);

The Grangers (Cambridge, Mass.: 1875);

The Railroad Problem (New York: The Railroad Gazette, 1875);

Charles Francis Adams (N.p., 1876);

The May-Pole of Merrymount (Boston, 1877);

Railroads: Their Origin and Problems (New York: Putnam's, 1878);

Communication on the "Old Planters," so called, about Boston Harbor (Boston, 1879);

The New Departure in the Common Schools of Quincy and other papers on Educational Topics (Boston: Estes and Lauriat, 1879);

Notes on Railroad Accidents (New York: Putnam's, 1879);

The Public Library and the Common Schools (Boston: Estes and Lauriat, 1879);

The Federation of the Railroad System (Boston: Estes and Lauriat, 1880);

Individuality in Politics (New York: Independent Republican Association, 1880);

Taxation of Railroads and Railroad Securities (New York: The Railroad Gazette, 1880);

"The Canal and Railroad Enterprise of Boston," in *The Memorial History of Boston*, volume 4, edited by J. Windsor (Boston, 1881), pp. 111-150;

State School Supervision (Boston, 1881);

A College Fetich (Boston: Lee and Shephard/New York: C. T. Dillingham, 1883);

Address of Charles Francis Adams, Jr. and Proceedings at the Dedication of the Crane Memorial Hall, at Quincy, Mass., May 30, 1882 (Cambridge, Mass.: J. Wilson and Son, 1883);

A Few Observations on the Prince Society's Edition of The New English Canaan (New York, 1883);

Episodes in New England History (Cambridge, Mass., 1883);

Sir Christopher Gardiner, Knight (Cambridge, Mass.: John Wilson, 1883);

The Chinese Massacre at Rock Springs, Wyoming Territory, September 2, 1885 (Boston: Rand, Avery, 1886);

The Interstate Commerce Law (Boston, 1886);

The Case of the Union Pacific Railway Company (Boston: R. A. Supply, 1888?);

The Interstate Commerce Act: Its Operation and its Results (Boston: Rand, Avery, 1888);

Mr. Arthur and the Strike of Engineers on the Boston & Maine Railroad in 1877 (Chicago, 1888);

Richard Henry Dana: A Biography (Boston & New York: Houghton, Mifflin, 1890);

History of Braintree, Massachusetts (1639-1708) (Cambridge, Mass.: Riverside Press, 1891);

Some Phases of Sexual Morality and Church Discipline in Colonial New England (Cambridge, Mass.: J. Wilson, 1891);

Three Episodes of Massachusetts History (Boston: Houghton, 1891);

The Centennial Milestone (Cambridge, Mass.: J. Wilson, 1892);

Columbus and the Discovery of America (Cambridge, Mass.: J. Wilson, 1892);

The Genesis of the Massachusetts Town and the Development of Town Meeting Government (Cambridge, Mass.: J. Wilson, 1892);

Massachusetts: Its Historians and Its History (Boston & New York: Houghton, Mifflin, 1893);

Address Delivered before the Students of the Veterinary School of Harvard University, September 27, 1894 (N.p., 1894);

Antinomianism in the Colony of Massachusetts Bay, 1636-1638 (Boston: The Prince Society, 1894);

Reform in City Government (Chicago, 1894);

The Emancipation of the Voter, the Free List and Proportional Representation (Boston, 1895);

The Journeyman's Retrospect (Cambridge, Mass.: J. Wilson, 1895);

Addresses of Hon. Charles Francis Adams and Hon. George G. Crocker Delivered before the Legislative Committee on Taxation, in March 1893, and the letter of Enoch Ensley (Boston: Anti-Double-Taxation League, 1898);

Historians and Historical Societies (Cambridge, Mass.: J. Wilson, 1899);

"Imperialism" and "The Tracks of our Forefathers" (Boston: D. Estes, 1899);

Charles Francis Adams, by his son, Charles Francis Adams (Boston & New York: Houghton, Mifflin, 1900);

The Sifted Grain and the Grain Sifters (Cambridge, Mass.: The Riverside Press, 1900);

The Confederacy and the Transvaal: a People's Obligation to Robert E. Lee (Boston: Houghton, Mifflin, 1901);

An Underdeveloped Function (New York, 1902);

Before and After the Treaty of Washington: The American Civil War and the War in the Transvaal (New York: New York Historical Society, 1902);

Charles Sumner and the Treaty of Washington (Cambridge, Mass., 1902);

The Civil War Pension Lack-Of-System (Washington, 1902);

Horace Gray (Cambridge, Mass.: J. Wilson, 1902);

Investigation and Publicity as Opposed to "Compulsory Arbitration" (Boston, 1902);

Lee at Appomattox and other papers (Boston & New York: Houghton, Mifflin, 1902);

Memoir of William C. Endicott, LL.D. (Cambridge, Mass.: J. Wilson, 1902);

"Shall Cromwell Have a Statue?" (Boston: C. E. Lauriat, 1902);

The Constitutional Ethics of Secession and "War is Hell" (Boston & New York: Houghton, Mifflin, 1903);

Memoir of George Bigelow Chase, A.M. (Cambridge, Mass.: J. Wilson, 1903);

A Milestone Planted (Lincoln, Mass., 1904);

An Account of the Celebration by the town of Lincoln, Mass., April 24, 1904 (Lincoln, Mass., 1905);

Some Phases of the Civil War (Cambridge, Mass.: J. Wilson, 1905);

John Quincy Adams, and Speaker Andrew Stevenson, of Virginia (Cambridge, Mass.: J. Wilson, 1906);

Theodore Lyman (1833-1897) and Robert Charles Winthrop, Jr. (1834-1905) (Cambridge, Mass.: J. Wilson, 1906);

Lee's Centennial (Boston & New York: Houghton, Mifflin, 1907);

"The Solid South" and the Afro-American Race Problem (Boston, 1908);

"The Campaign of 1777," Proceedings of the Massachusetts Historical Society, 43 (1910): 13-65;

"Address at the laying of the Cornerstone," Proceedings of the American Antiquarian Society, 20 (1911): 8-16;

The Panama Canal Zone (Boston, 1911);

Studies Military and Diplomatic, 1775-1865 (New York: Macmillan, 1911);

Seward and the Declaration of Paris (Boston, 1912);

The Trent Affair: An Historical Retrospect (Boston, 1912);

"The Negotiation of 1861 Relating to the Declaration of Paris of 1856," Proceedings of the Massachusetts Historical Society, 46 (1913): 23-84;

Trans-Atlantic Historical Solidarity (Oxford: Clarendon Press, 1913);

Commerce of Rhode Island, 1726-1800 (N.p., 1914);

The Crisis of Foreign Intervention in the War of Secession, September-November, 1862 (Boston, 1914);

The Monroe Doctrine and Mommsen's Law (Boston & New York: Houghton Mifflin, 1914);

The Railroad Rate Case (Boston, 1914);

Railroads' Position Critical (Boston, 1914);

"The British Proclamation of May, 1861," Proceedings of the Massachusetts Historical Society, 48 (1915): 190-241;

Increase of Taxation (Lincoln, Mass., 1915);

Charles Francis Adams, 1835-1915; an Autobiography; with a Memorial Address delivered November 17, 1915, by Henry Cabot Lodge (Boston & New York: Houghton Mifflin, 1916).

References:

Charles Edgar Ames, *Pioneering the Union Pacific: A Reappraisal of the Builders of the Road* (New York: Appleton, Century, Crofts, 1969);

Edward Chase Kirkland, *Charles Francis Adams, Jr., 1835-1915: The Patrician at Bay* (Cambridge, Mass.: Harvard University Press, 1965);

Maury Klein, *Union Pacific: The Birth of a Railroad, 1862-1893* (New York: Doubleday, 1987);

Thomas K. McCraw, *Prophets of Regulation* (Cambridge, Mass.: Harvard University Press, 1984).

Archives:

Materials relating to Charles Francis Adams, Jr., are in the Union Pacific Railroad Company Collection at the Nebraska State Museum and Archives, Lincoln, Nebraska; and in the Charles Francis Adams, Jr., papers of the Massachusetts Historical Society, Boston, Massachusetts.

Horatio Allen

(May 10, 1802-December 31, 1889)

by F. Daniel Larkin

State University College, Oneonta, New York

CAREER: Resident engineer, Chesapeake & Delaware Canal (1824-1826); assistant engineer, Delaware & Hudson Canal (1826-1829); chief engineer, South Carolina Railroad (1829-1834); principal assistant engineer, New York City Water Works (1838-1842); president, Novelty Iron Works (1842-1870); president, New York & Erie Railroad (1844-1851); president, American Society of Civil Engineers (1871-1873).

Horatio Allen was born on May 10, 1802, in Schenectady, New York. His mother, Mary Benedict Allen, was a woman of high culture and social standing, and his father, Dr. Benjamin Allen, was a professor of mathematics at Union College at Schenectady. In 1802 Schenectady still contained less than 2,000 people. The most important attribute of the town, and the one which would contribute most to Allen's career, was the fact that it stood at the gateway to the Mohawk Valley and the water-level route through the Appalachian Mountains. As Allen was growing up the War of 1812 highlighted the need for improved transportation to the West. His youth was spent in the heady days of growth in the region.

In 1823 Allen graduated from Columbia College with high honors and a mathematics degree. After spending almost one-and-a-half years in a half-hearted study of the law, Allen joined the Chesapeake & Delaware (C&D) Canal Company in 1824 as a resident engineer. While working for the C&D Allen became acquainted with Benjamin Wright. In 1826 Allen left the C&D to join the Delaware & Hudson (D&H) Canal Company as an assistant engineer to chief engineer Wright.

The D&H position was important to Allen in several respects. First, it provided Allen with his first experience in railroad construction. The D&H project, in addition to constructing a canal, also built a 16-mile railroad to assist in hauling freight up the waterway. Second, the position marked the beginning of a long association with John B. Jervis, who replaced Wright as chief engineer of the D&H in 1827. Although only twenty-six years old, Allen apparently impressed Jervis with his aptitude and resourcefulness. When the time came to purchase locomotives for the railroad, Jervis sent Allen to England to procure them.

The railroad portion of the canal works was designed to use steam engines on the level portions of the route and a system of inclines to overcome the steeper parts of the terrain. Because the wood stringer and iron rail construction was quite fragile Jervis provided Allen with very precise specifications concerning locomotive weight. The locomotives, in order to work on the rails, were to be limited to five-and-a-half tons on four wheels. Six-wheel locomotives were dismissed because of their inability to negotiate the tight turns of the route. On February 24, 1828, Allen wrote to Jervis to inform him that "I am at length in the land of railroads and in the atmosphere of coal smoke." The young engineer was delighted to be in England and wasted little time in contacting Robert Stephenson, the expert builder of steam engines. He was delayed until July, however, in contracting for four locomotives, one from Stephenson and three from the Foster, Rastrick Works at Stourbridge.

All four locomotives arrived in New York City between January and September 1829 and were tested at foundries in the city. For reasons still unclear, only Foster, Rastrick's Stourbridge Lion arrived at the head of the D&H Canal at Honesdale, Pennsylvania.

The Stourbridge Lion, the first commercial locomotive to be run on an American railroad, worked well but was unusable because of its weight, its seven tons exceeding the maximum the rails could bear by at least one and one-half tons. The wheels were removed from the frame and the lo-

Horatio Allen

comotive was used as a stationary steam engine on one of the inclined planes. The other engines were apparently cannibalized for their excellent English wrought iron. But Allen's failure to follow instructions did not prevent a lasting friendship with Jervis. The two corresponded while working on their subsequent separate projects and later worked together on the great Croton waterworks.

In 1829 Allen left the Delaware & Hudson to become the chief engineer of the South Carolina Railroad. The line from Charleston to Hamburg was designed specifically for locomotive engines and Allen ordered one from the West Point Foundry in New York City. When the Best Friend of Charleston was put into service in December 1830, it was the first American-built locomotive in regular use.

Allen's contract with the South Carolina road permitted his absence during the "unhealthy" summer season. During the summers of 1830 and 1831 he visited his parents in Schenectady, where he compared notes with Jervis, who was in charge of building the Mohawk & Hudson Railroad. Both engineers were seeking to develop a locomotive that could negotiate curves at high speeds. Jervis's Experiment was a six-wheeled swivel truck engine on a single frame. Allen's South Carolina was an eight-wheeled, double-truck machine created by connect-

ing two frames to a single boiler and firebox. Allen felt it necessary to take this approach to provide for an adequate number of drive wheels. Both engines were built by the West Point Foundry and put into service in 1832. The simpler Jervis design worked well and became the standard for locomotive builders. Allen's more complex machine was subject to many breakdowns, due in part to the two frames constantly varying their parallelism while traveling over uneven track. The Allen design was not utilized by other manufacturers.

Allen resigned from the South Carolina Railroad in 1834 and returned to New York. He married Mary Moncrief Simons of Charleston that same year, and they spent the next three years abroad. On their return in 1838 the Allens settled in New York City, and he was soon appointed principal assistant to John Jervis on the Croton Aqueduct project. The aqueduct posed new challenges to Allen's engineering ability, particularly in the construction of the High Bridge across the Harlem River. Allen was in charge of testing the bridge piles to determine the amount of weight they could support. The experiment was one of the first of its kind in the United States, and Allen's technique became an accepted method for calculating such figures. Allen remained with the Croton project until 1842.

On his return from Europe in 1838 Allen had been hired as a consultant to the New York & Erie Railroad; after his departure from the Croton Aqueduct Allen became the railroad's president in 1843. Much of Allen's administration was occupied with attempts to raise funds for the completion of the financially overburdened project. Failing in this, Allen resigned as president in October 1844, though he remained with the railroad as chief engineer.

The rest of Allen's career was taken up with the management of the Novelty Iron Works, in which he had invested in 1842. This successful enterprise, located in Manhattan on the East River, was one of the principal producers of engines and boilers for steamships during the nineteenth century, employing over 15,000 people during the Civil War.

While a resident of New York City, Allen helped to found the Union League Club. He held a

membership in the American Society of Mechanical Engineers and from 1871-1873 was president of the American Society of Civil Engineers. Later in his life he developed strong interests in both astronomy and the valve mechanisms of steam engines. Allen died in East Orange, New Jersey, on December 31, 1889.

Publication:
Astronomy in its General Facts and Relations, Taught by Aid of Mechanical Presentation and Illustration (New York: E. D. Jenkins, 1877).

References:
J. K. Finch, *Early Columbia Engineers* (New York: Columbia University Press, 1929);

John B. Jervis, "Facts and Circumstances in the Life of John B. Jervis," handwritten autobiography, Jervis Public Library, Rome, N.Y.

Archives:
Material concerning Horatio Allen is located in the John B. Jervis Papers of the Jervis Public Library in Rome, N.Y.

Oakes Ames

(January 10, 1804-May 8, 1873)

by James W. Hipp

Columbia, S.C.

CAREER: Laborer, superintendent, vice-president (1820-1844); co-president, Oliver Ames & Sons (1844-1873); member, executive council of Massachusetts (1860-1862); member, U.S. House of Representatives (1863-1873); director, Crédit Mobilier of America (1865-1873); director, Union Pacific Railroad (1870-1873).

Oliver Ames

(November 5, 1807-March 9, 1877)

CAREER: Laborer, manager (1807-1844); co-president (1844-1873); president, Oliver Ames & Sons (1873-1877); state senator, Massachusetts (1852, 1857); director, Crédit Mobilier of America (1865-1873); director (1865-1877); acting president (1866-1868); president, Union Pacific Railroad (1868-1871).

Oakes Ames (courtesy of Library of Congress)

Oliver Ames (courtesy of Union Pacific Railroad Museum)

Oakes and Oliver Ames were among the key figures in the construction of the Union Pacific (UP) Railroad. Respected and successful manufacturers in New England, the Ameses have long been painted as villains as a result of their involvement in the 1872 Crédit Mobilier scandal. Recent scholarship, such as Maury Klein's *Union Pacific: The Birth of a Railroad* (1987), shows that the Ameses were more foolish and ineffectual than venal. Rather than illustrating a moral truism about nineteenth-century business ethics, the story of Oakes and Oliver Ames underscores the challenges and difficulties faced by the men who built the transcontinental railroads.

Oakes Ames was born on January 10, 1804, in Easton, Massachusetts. Oliver Ames was born in Plymouth, Massachusetts, three years later, on November 5, 1807. Their father, Oliver Ames, was a manufacturer of shovels, a business which Oakes and Oliver joined when they were able. Both boys received adequate, if not spectacular, educations before entering their father's business as common laborers. Learning each phase of the company's operation, Oakes and Oliver advanced slowly in the firm until 1844, when their father retired and turned control of the newly renamed Oliver Ames & Sons over to them. The company was quite successful, and, because of the gold rushes in California and the rest of the world in the late 1840s and 1850s, the Ames shovel became internationally known. At the beginning of the Civil War the firm was valued at $4 million.

The Ameses, in addition to their own manufacturing concerns, were active in Republican and Whig politics and also in railroads. Oliver Ames was elected to the Massachusetts State Senate in 1852 and 1857 but did not seek office again. Oakes Ames was elected to five terms in the U.S. Congress, serving from 1863 to 1873. Oakes's position in Washington played a crucial role in the government's policy toward the Union Pacific. The Ameses first became involved in railroads in 1855, when they joined together to build the Easton Branch Railroad from their shovel works to Stoughton, Massachusetts, where the line linked with the Boston & Providence Railroad. They also invested in four Iowa railroads, including the Cedar Rapids & Missouri, which later became part of the Chicago & North Western.

Their greatest railroad investment, however, was in the Union Pacific. The struggle to authorize, build, and finance a transcontinental railroad had been raging for decades in the U.S. Congress. Because the secession of the Southern states resolved the sectional differences over route selection, momentum for a Pacific railroad built rapidly until 1862 with the passage of the Pacific Railway Act. The Pacific Railroad project was so large that sufficient capital was not available through normal channels, and the line languished until the Pacific Railway Act of 1864 enlarged the available land grant.

As was the case with most railroads during the period, the Union Pacific formed a separately incorporated construction company to finance and build the line. In addition to the limited liability a corporation offered investors, the construction company offered near-term profits on a project that was risky and unprofitable except in its long-term prospects. The construction company for the Union Pacific was known as the Crédit Mobilier. It was through the Crédit Mobilier that the Ameses became involved in the Union Pacific. Their initial investment in April 1865 was $100,000, a figure that would grow enormously over the years. Yet even more than their money, the Union Pacific and the Crédit Mobilier needed the Ameses' reputation. Oakes Ames's position in Congress and their stature as respected Eastern businessmen made the brothers invaluable in attracting new investors.

From the beginning the Ameses clashed with Thomas C. Durant, the vice-president of the Union Pacific and the architect of the Crédit Mobilier. Durant was obsessed with reaping short-term profits while the Ameses, while definitely not averse to making money, sought a more practical balance between construction profits and the long-term wealth of the line.

From 1866-1868 Oliver Ames was the acting president of the UP. Oakes Ames oversaw the affairs of Crédit Mobilier. By 1867 Durant had been forced off the board and the UP, which was rapidly becoming a financial sink hole, was under the aegis of the Ameses. On August 16, 1867, Oakes Ames signed contracts to build over 600 miles of track for the UP for upwards of $47 million. The contracts and the profits they generated were to be paid to the shareholders of Crédit Mobilier stock.

Because of the delicate nature of these arrangements and the fact that the UP was starving for capital, Oakes Ames sold shares of Crédit Mobilier stock to some of his fellow members of Congress. Ames knew the UP was in a fragile financial condition and was at all times subject to the whims of Congress. While he always denied these sales were meant as a bribe, he did recognize their positive influence on the UP's interests.

The arrangement remained relatively secret until September 4, 1872, when the New York *Sun* printed letters from Ames concerning the distribution of the stock in Congress. The uproar was intense and instantaneous. By this time Oliver Ames had left the presidency of the UP in which capacity he had served from 1868-1871. He was never directly implicated in the scandal but his indecisive leadership had contributed to many of the railroad's problems. Oakes Ames did not escape from the firestorm of criticism so easily. Two separate Congressional investigations subjected Ames and the Crédit Mobilier to intense scrutiny. In 1873 he was censured by Congress, an action which many now view as undeserved. Oakes Ames died on May 8, 1873, merely days after his public disgrace.

Oliver Ames returned to the ailing Oliver Ames & Sons after his resignation in 1871 as UP president. He died on March 9, 1877. The UP did not forget the input both Ameses gave to the construction of the line; a monument to them both stands on what once was the highest point on the route. When E. H. Harriman oversaw the rebuilding of the line at the turn of the century, the memorial was abandoned. In many ways the fate of the monument mirrors that of those it memorialized. But then, the Ameses' true monument was the Union Pacific itself.

In retrospect it is quite easy to moralize about the behavior of Oakes Ames and other UP and Crédit Mobilier figures. It is not quite so simple to realize the great struggle it was in the 1860s to initiate and build such a huge project as the UP in a country so capital-starved as the United States. The achievement of Oakes and Oliver Ames was not that the UP was completed in spite of the corruption; their achievement was that the railroad was completed. Despite their failures, Oakes and Oliver Ames deserve to be known as, in Maury Klein's words, "neither heroes nor villains but merely figures in a complex drama. . . ."

References:

Charles Edgar Ames, *Pioneering the Union Pacific* (New York: Appleton, Century, Crofts, 1969);

Maury Klein, *Union Pacific: Birth of a Railroad, 1862-1893* (New York: Doubleday, 1987).

Archives:

Materials concerning Oakes and Oliver Ames are located in the Charles E. Ames papers of Baker Library, Harvard Business School, Boston, Massachusetts; in the Oliver Ames papers of the Arnold B. Tofius Industrial Archives, Stonehill College Library, North Easton, Massachusetts; in the Union Pacific Railroad Company Collection of the Nebraska State Museum and Archives, Lincoln, Nebraska; and in the records of the Union Pacific Railroad at the Union Pacific Offices, Omaha, Nebraska.

Atchison, Topeka and Santa Fe Railway

by William S. Greever

University of Idaho

In 1900 the Atchison, Topeka and Santa Fe (ATSF) Railway, commonly called the Santa Fe, extended from Chicago to Kansas City and from there to Denver, San Francisco, Los Angeles, and Houston. The Santa Fe was founded by Cyrus K. Holliday in 1859 when the Kansas legislature granted the company Holliday's written and promoted charter. Holliday also authored a law, passed by the United States Congress in 1863, which established a land grant, eventually consisting of almost 3 million acres, to be turned over on completion of a line from Atchison to the Colorado boundary. Construction of this line by Holliday and the ATSF began westward from Topeka in October 1868 and was completed in December 1872, just two months before the land grant was due to expire. The track ended "nowhere" but was completed to Pueblo, Colorado, in 1876. That same year the ATSF purchased the Kansas Midland line, which gave it access to Kansas City.

In addition to the nearly 3 million acres of land acquired through the federal grant, the ATSF also owned almost 300,000 acres which it had purchased from the Pottawattomie Indians in 1868. In order to sell these federal and tribal tracts the railroad initiated a vigorous colonization program. The program was especially successful in attracting members of the Mennonite community in Russia, and by 1883 almost 15,000 of the sect had fled religious persecution in their homeland to settle along the ATSF lines. By the time its parcels of land were depleted in 1886 the ATSF had netted profits of nearly $9.5 million on the sales of its lands. In addition to selling its land the ATSF financed itself by selling first-mortgage bonds, common stocks, and other securities at a discount to investors. How deep a discount investors required from the risky project is revealed by the fact that in 1870 notes and stock carrying a face value of $1.35 million were sold for only $800,000 in cash.

The ATSF used this capital to finance its expansion. Seeking an opening into New Mexico in 1878, the ATSF secured possession of the crucial Raton Pass only thirty minutes before forces from the rival Denver & Rio Grande (D&RG) attempted to claim it. In 1880 construction reached Albuquerque and, by a short branch line, Santa Fe. The next year the Santa Fe entered El Paso and connected with the Southern Pacific (SP) line from Los Angeles at Deming, New Mexico. Anxious to reach the Pacific over its own rails, the ATSF extended its line to Guaymas, Mexico, in 1882, but the port generated little traffic and the spur was sold to the SP in 1897.

One of the ATSF expansions became one of the most famous stories in railroad lore. When in 1878 the silver mines at Leadville, Colorado, became extremely productive, both the ATSF and the D&RG planned new lines there. Unfortunately, any line to Leadville had to pass through Royal Gorge, a pass so narrow that it allowed room for only one set of tracks. The tense situation between the two lines, neither having forgotten the Raton Pass controversy earlier in the year, soon degenerated into violence as both lines hired gunmen and built rock fortresses in the gorge. The most important battles, however, were fought in the state and federal courts. The outcome was finally settled in 1880 when the United States Supreme Court ruled that the D&RG possessed the legal rights to the gorge; the decision gave the ATSF priority in the state of New Mexico.

Still determined to reach the Pacific Coast, and in order to earn over 13 million land grant acres, the ATSF teamed with the St. Louis & San Francisco Railroad during 1880-1883 to build the Atlantic & Pacific (A&P) Western Division from Albuquerque to the California border at Needles. The SP built a spur east from Mojave, California, to Needles, but diverted most of its transcontinental traffic

The Atchison, Kansas, law office in which the ATSF was organized September 15-17, 1860

to its own tracks elsewhere. Starved for traffic, the A&P threatened to build a parallel line to Mojave. The SP quickly settled the conflict in 1884 by means of a lease-sale of the Mojave-Needles route to the A&P for a price of $30,000 per mile. The Santa Fe reached San Diego in 1885 by purchasing the California Southern and extending it to the A&P line at Barstow. In 1887 the ATSF finally gained access to Los Angeles over its own rails. The previous year the ATSF had bought the Gulf Colorado & Santa Fe in order to obtain a route into Houston and Galveston. The year 1887 saw ATSF expansion into Denver and, to obtain a longer haul on its western traffic, from Kansas City to Chicago.

During the 1870s the ATSF hauled cattle from "cow towns" such as Dodge City and Wichita and did a brisk business in tanned buffalo robes. In the 1880s and 1890s most of its important freight traffic was linked to agriculture. The ATSF was not entirely successful in staying out of traffic pools and rebate plans. In fact an 1886 rate war with the SP was so severe that, for a few hours on March 8, a ticket from Kansas City to Los Angeles cost only $1.

The ATSF initiated its first program to im-

prove its existing lines in 1881, replacing iron rails with steel, ballasting important tracks, reducing grades, and straightening curves. But the condition of its physical properties did not cause the ATSF its later problems. The too rapid expansion and an overly generous dividend program led to financial difficulties and a voluntary reorganization in 1889. The plan succeeded in reducing interest charges by 1.35 percent but increased bonded debt by one-third and failed to provide additional working capital. The ATSF was further burdened by the ill-advised purchase of the shaky St. Louis & San Francisco (Frisco) and Colorado Midland lines. The 1893 depression shattered the system into bankruptcy. Even worse, investigators proved that profits for the years 1891-1894 had been overstated by over $7 million.

The railroad's reorganization in 1895, arguably the most successful ever designed for an American railroad, greatly reduced debt and cut interest payments in half. The new president of the ATSF, Edward P. Ripley, quickly earned his road a reputation for adhering to the highest standards of business ethics. Shorn of the Frisco and the Colorado

Midland, but retaining the A&P, the ATSF operated 6,435 miles of track in 1895. By 1986 this had almost tripled to 19,160 miles. By lease, construction, and purchase of the San Francisco & San Joaquin Valley Railway, the ATSF during 1898-1900 obtained a line from Mojave to San Francisco. With the last of its strategic routes in place, the ATSF was well equipped to begin its twentieth-century growth.

References:

Glenn Danford Bradley, *The Story of The Santa Fe* (Boston: Badger, 1920);

Keith L. Bryant, *History of the Atchison, Topeka and Santa Fe Railway* (New York: Macmillan, 1974);

James H. Ducker, *Men of the Steel Rails: Workers and the Atchison, Topeka and Santa Fe Railroad, 1869-1900* (Lincoln: University of Nebraska Press, 1983);

William S. Greever, *Arid Domain: The Santa Fe Railway and its Western Land Grant* (Stanford, Cal.: Stanford University Press, 1954);

James Marshall, *Santa Fe: The Railroad that Built an Empire* (New York: Random House, 1945);

L. L. Waters, *Steel Rails to Santa Fe* (Lawrence: University of Kansas Press, 1950).

Archives:

The railroad retains its own records at its offices at Chicago, Illinois, and Topeka, Kansas. There is also a small collection at the Baker Library of Harvard University at Boston, Mass.

Matthias W. Baldwin

(December 10, 1795-September 7, 1866)

by Alec Kirby

George Washington University

CAREER: Jeweler's apprentice (1811-1817); jeweler, Fletcher & Gardiner (1817-1819); jeweler, self-employed (1819-1828); partner, Mason and Baldwin (1828-1831); president, Baldwin Engine and Locomotive (1831-1866).

Matthias Baldwin, locomotive builder, was born on December 10, 1795, in Elizabethtown, New Jersey, into a well-to-do family. His father, William Baldwin, was a successful carriage maker who left a considerable estate in 1799. Poor management on the part of his executors, however, resulted in the virtual bankruptcy of the family, and Baldwin grew up in near poverty. His mother supervised his education, although from a young age Baldwin demonstrated little enthusiasm for school. Mechanical devices were his particular interest, and at age sixteen he was apprenticed to the Woolworth Brothers in Frankford, Philadelphia County, Pennsylvania, to learn the jeweler's trade. His mother, meanwhile, moved to Philadelphia.

His family's decision to move to Philadelphia proved to be very important to Baldwin's later career as a locomotive builder. By the time he reached adulthood, the city had already become a center for railroading. In 1809 Thomas Leiper of Philadelphia built a model railway with a wooden track in the Bull's Head Tavern Yard. Shortly thereafter he constructed a small railroad at the Leiper quarries, near Chester, to haul rock from the quarries to a dock on Ridley Creek. The road, which ran about three quarters of a mile, was in use for twenty years, becoming one of the first useful railroads in America. It was also within sight of where Baldwin would later have his first workshop. In 1823 the General Assembly of Pennsylvania approved a petition for the construction of a railroad from Philadelphia to Columbia, in Lancaster County. The railroad was completed the year after Baldwin completed his first locomotive.

In 1817 Baldwin completed his apprenticeship and became a journeyman jeweler for the Philadelphia firm of Fletcher & Gardiner. He quickly developed a reputation among customers for his craftsmanship and ingenuity. After three years with the firm, Baldwin began his own business as a jeweler. Success came shortly in an extremely crowded market. He later described his nine years as a self-employed jeweler as the low point in his life, although he acknowledged the experience taught him how to manage a business.

Matthias W. Baldwin

At age thirty Baldwin decided to change his trade, and three years later he entered into a partnership with Peter Mason, a machinist and wood engraver. At that time the tools and machines used for bookbinding were virtually all imported. The two men began the manufacture of these machines themselves, as well as the construction of copper cylinders for printing calico. Although Baldwin is not remembered as an inventor, he developed a process for rolling designs onto the surface of cylinders. He etched the calico design onto a soft steel surface, which was then hardened and used as a "mill" to roll its design onto the copper cylinder. Baldwin's method revolutionized the industry.

The growing success of the Baldwin-Mason partnership required a larger workshop. The move to new quarters was to prove of signal importance to Baldwin's career. The new shop housed numerous machines that required a great deal of power. Older hand machines and foot lathes the partners had used previously were no longer satisfactory for the expanding firm. They tried horsepower, but found it inadequate. Mason and Baldwin purchased a steam engine to provide power, but the engine

did not perform well. After a few unsuccessful attempts to improve it, Baldwin decided to build his own engine. His machine delivered five horsepower and attracted the attention of other machine shop owners. After receiving offers to purchase the engine, the partners began to manufacture them for sale. Steam engines quickly became the firm's primary business. Within three years Baldwin bought out Mason's interest in the partnership and became the sole owner of the burgeoning firm.

Meanwhile, the steam locomotive was being developed rapidly in England. In 1829 Horatio Allen of New York imported an English engine for use on the Delaware & Hudson Railroad at Carbondale, Pennsylvania. The next year a steam locomotive was built in New York for the South Carolina Railroad. This was the first locomotive made in America for commercial use.

Locomotives clearly fascinated Americans. In 1830 Franklin Peale of the Philadelphia Museum approached Baldwin about constructing a model locomotive, which would be large enough to run on a circular track at the museum and to haul two small cars carrying four passengers. To build this locomotive, Baldwin studied the plans of engines built in England, adapting them to fit the requirements of the Museum. His locomotive was completed in April 1831.

The small novelty engine attracted large crowds. Early in 1832 the Philadelphia, Germantown & Norristown Railroad Company asked him to build a full-sized locomotive to replace horse traffic on the railroad. Under the circumstances at the time, the project proved extremely difficult to carry out. There were few experienced mechanics and adequate tools available. Cylinders, for example, had to be bored by a chisel fixed in a block of wood and turned by hand. Although Baldwin developed and perfected some details, the locomotive shared basic characteristics of the engines of the period. Old Ironsides, as it was called, had a wooden frame with wooden wheels and tires of wrought-iron. The locomotive made its first test run on November 24, 1832.

Old Ironsides received a great deal of attention in the press, and most observers called it a success. The railroad company, however, was skeptical, announcing it would use the locomotive only in good weather. Indeed, the company refused to pay Baldwin the full $4,000 cost of the engine, claiming that it did not perform according to contract.

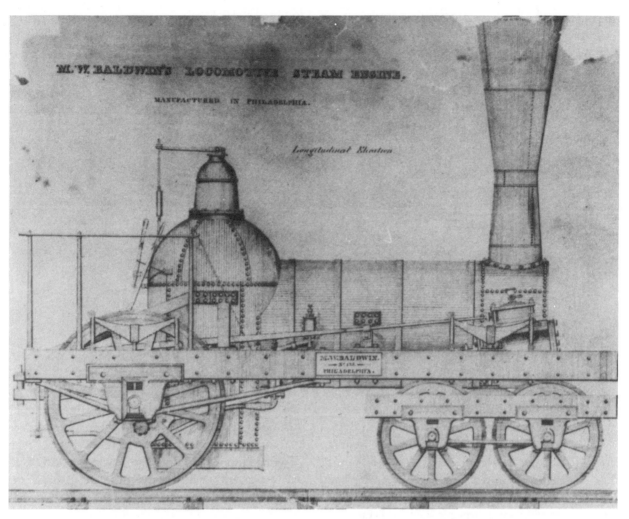

The Baldwin-designed-and-built Martin Van Buren, delivered in 1839 to the Philadelphia &
Columbia Railroad

The dispute eventually was resolved by an arbitration committee, but Baldwin was so upset that he reportedly vowed never to build another engine.

He quickly changed his mind. Railroad companies more impressed with Old Ironsides than the Germantown road expressed interest in obtaining a Baldwin locomotive. Baldwin constructed ten more engines before moving to larger facilities in 1837. In his new plant he was to build 1,500 locomotives before his death in 1866. Although locomotives were to remain his primary business, he occasionally undertook other projects, such as constructing an ice-breaker for the city of Philadelphia. However, by concentrating on engines, he expanded his market to include a sizeable export trade, beginning with a shipment to Cuba in 1838.

Despite Baldwin's success in developing markets, his firm did not grow without interruption. In 1837, immediately after moving to his new plant,

he was reduced to bankruptcy by the economic panic of that year. Baldwin, negotiating with his creditors, convinced them not to seize his property, pledging to pay off the debts—with interest—within three years. Actually, it took him five years to pay off his obligations. Yet even in the face of this financial crisis, Baldwin continued to develop the locomotive. By 1842 he had constructed a six-wheeled gear locomotive capable of hauling a much heavier load than any engine then available.

Baldwin became a prominent figure in Philadelphia and was active in public affairs. In 1837, for example, he was elected to the convention called to amend the Pennsylvania State Constitution. Baldwin gained public attention when the convention considered a proposal to restrict suffrage to "free male white citizens." He forcefully opposed the restriction. But philanthropy took more of his time than political pursuits. He gained a reputation as the "church builder" of Philadelphia, funding, mostly himself, the construction of five churches. He was also a family man. In 1827 he married Sarah C. Baldwin (no relation), and the couple had five daughters, one of whom was adopted.

While Baldwin was not a skilled inventor, he excelled at refining and improving the ideas of others. Baldwin, to be sure, did not invent the steam locomotive, but he did more than any other American to make locomotives available to a growing railroad industry.

Unpublished Document:
Wolcott Calkins, "Memorial of Matthias Baldwin"; available in the Library of Congress.

References:
Edward Cressy, *A Hundred Years of Mechanical Engineering* (New York: Macmillan, 1937);
Ralph Kelly, *Matthias W. Baldwin: Locomotive Pioneer* (New York: The Newcomen Society of England, American Branch, 1946).

Baltimore & Ohio Railroad

by John F. Stover

Purdue University

Receiving a charter from Maryland in 1827, the Baltimore & Ohio Railroad (B&O) was the first railway projected westward over the Allegheny Mountains to the Ohio Valley. The businessmen of Baltimore were worried about the increased western trade that New York City was gaining from the Erie Canal. They feared that the National Road could not successfully compete with either the Erie or a projected canal system planned by Pennsylvania. The Baltimore leaders soon decided that a railroad to the west was the answer to the commercial competition from the north. Of the $3 million of capital stock issued by the company under the charter, the state of Maryland took $1 million, the city of Baltimore $500,000, and the remainder was made available to individuals and corporations. The company was organized in April 1827, and a merchant-banker from Baltimore, Philip E. Thomas, was elected president. Surveying parties were sent out to seek a route to the Potomac, and the first stone for the new railroad was laid on July 4, 1828.

The first track was laid in the English standard gauge of 4 feet, 8½ inches in October 1829; in May 1830 daily passenger service was started from Baltimore to Ellicotts Mills, thirteen miles west of Baltimore. Horses pulled the first trains on the B&O even though some experts thought steam locomotion was practical. A small experimental steam engine, the Tom Thumb, built by Peter Cooper, convinced the B&O directors that steam power was possible; in 1831 they ordered steam locomo-

tives for their road. B&O officials soon learned that steam locomotives could pull moderate loads up a 2-percent inclined plane, an important ability considering the mountainous terrain of western Maryland and Virginia. In fact, the multitude of engineering problems faced and solved by B&O officials was so great that D. Kimball Minor, the editor of the *American Railroad Journal*, described the Baltimore & Ohio as the Railroad University of the United States. The B&O reached Frederick, 61 miles west of Baltimore, late in 1831 and Harpers Ferry in 1837. A 32-mile branch to Washington, D.C., was opened in 1835. By 1836 the revenue on the 84-mile Main Stem to Harpers Ferry was $281,000, more than 40 percent of which came from passenger service.

Under the presidency of Louis McLane (1836-1848) much of the original line of the B&O was upgraded, and the line was pushed westward to Cumberland. Both the city of Baltimore and the state of Maryland subscribed to $3 million of new B&O stock. Late in 1842 the line to Cumberland, the eastern terminal of the National Road and 128 miles west of Baltimore, was opened to service. Important coal mines were located in the Cumberland area, and by 1848 coal moving to Baltimore made up 40 percent of eastbound tonnage. Thomas Swann, succeeding McLane as president from 1848 to 1853, financed the building of the B&O over the mountains of Western Virginia to Wheeling by obtaining new stock subscriptions and selling bonds

The Washington, D.C., station of the Baltimore & Ohio Railroad (courtesy of the Baltimore & Ohio Railroad)

in England. The last rails of the new line to Wheeling were laid on December 24, 1852. Between 1851 and 1857 a second route to the Ohio River (the B&O-controlled Northwestern Virginia Railroad) was built. This 104-mile road ran from Grafton, 100 miles west of Cumberland, to Parkersburg, 90 miles downstream from Wheeling. By 1860 B&O revenue on the 379-mile Main Stem from Baltimore to Wheeling amounted to $4 million. The economic importance of the growing B&O was reflected in the population of the city of Baltimore, which climbed from 80,000 in 1830 to 212,000 in 1860.

John W. Garrett, a Baltimore commission merchant and banker, became the B&O president in 1858, a position he would hold until his death in 1884. He was a champion of the individual shareholder and successfully pushed for more frequent dividends on the common stock. He also ran the company during the crisis of the Civil War, which came early to the Baltimore & Ohio when John Brown stopped a B&O passenger train during his raid on the United States arsenal at Harpers Ferry in October 1859. Because of its location in a border state, the B&O was destined to experience far more than its share of violence and destruction in the Civil War. Early in the conflict Garrett spoke of his line as a "Southern" railroad, but the increasing destruction of B&O property by Colonel Thomas J.

(Stonewall) Jackson made Garrett speak of Confederates as "rebels." Because of the destruction, portions of the B&O in the mountains of Virginia could not be fully restored for weeks and months at a time. In the early fall of 1863 Garrett played a major role in helping direct the rail movement of 25,000 Union troops from Washington, D.C., via the B&O and other lines in Ohio, Indiana, Kentucky, and Tennessee, to the aid of General Rosecrans near Chattanooga. Throughout the war the Baltimore & Ohio line to Washington, D.C., was the only rail connection to the nation's capital. Despite the destruction it suffered, the B&O prospered during the war years. By 1865 annual revenue on the Main Stem was up to $10 million and 8 percent dividends were being paid on the common stock.

In the years after the Civil War John Garrett greatly expanded his railroad. Between 1868 and 1873 he built the Metropolitan Branch northwest of Washington and linked it to the Main Stem near Point of Rocks. In the late 1860s Garrett started to build two giant wrought-iron bridges across the Ohio River, one at Benwood, just below Wheeling, and the other downstream at Parkersburg. In 1866 the B&O leased the 137-mile Central of Ohio, which ran west from near Wheeling to Columbus, Ohio. In 1869 the Central of Ohio leased the Sandusky, Mansfield & Newark, which gave the B&O a line north to Lake Erie. By 1871 he had also completed a new line from Cumberland to Pittsburgh. In the early 1870s Garrett built a 263-mile line west from the Sandusky line to Chicago, which was opened to traffic late in 1874. South of Harpers Ferry in Virginia a branch was built in the Shenandoah Valley which reached Staunton in 1874 and Lexington in 1883. In the early 1880s Garrett began to build a line into Philadelphia, a line which was finished by Robert Garrett, who was president from 1884-1887.

The B&O, which was operating only 520 miles of line in 1865, had grown to a rail network of 1,700 miles by 1884. Most of the expansion had been paid for with borrowed money rather than new share capital. During the postwar years, Garrett's railroad had engaged in several rate wars with the Pennsylvania, the New York Central, and the Erie, with the final result being a general lowering of freight rates. Despite the lower rates, the annual revenues of the B&O by the early 1880s were above $18 million a year. Garrett's rather harsh views on the rights of railroad labor resulted in the 1877 railroad strike, which started on the Baltimore & Ohio because of a reduction in wages.

In the decade and a half between 1884 and the turn of the century, four different men were president of the Baltimore & Ohio. Robert Garrett, not nearly as talented as his father, was president until 1887. Samuel Spencer, who was elected president in 1887, sought to reform the accounting procedures followed by the B&O and to reduce the floating debt by selling off the telegraph and sleep-ing-car services operated by the railroad. His reforms were not welcomed by his board of directors, and, after one year, Spencer was replaced by Charles Mayer, a Baltimore coal merchant. If Spencer's proposals had been accepted, the B&O might have escaped its later receivership. During the late 1880s and the early 1890s, operating expenses on the B&O climbed faster than the total revenue, resulting in a marked reduction and often elimination of dividends. There was little money available for repairs or improvements, and the depression of the mid 1890s further reduced revenue. Early in 1896 Charles Mayer resigned as president and was replaced by John K. Cowen, longtime general counsel of the B&O. On March 1, 1896, the Baltimore & Ohio was placed in the hands of receivers. A successful and orderly reorganization plan was accepted by shareholders and bondholders, and on July 1, 1899, the receivers officially surrendered control of the B&O. The success of the reorganization was aided by the return of prosperity in the late 1890s. By 1899-1900 the B&O had a yearly revenue of $42 million and was able to pay a 2 percent dividend on its common stock.

References:

Edward Hungerford, *The Story of the Baltimore & Ohio Railroad: 1827-1927* (New York: Putnam's, 1928);

John F. Stover, *History of the Baltimore & Ohio Railroad* (West Lafayette, Ind.: Purdue University Press, 1987).

Archives:

The records of the Baltimore & Ohio are located at the Baltimore & Ohio Museum in Baltimore, Maryland.

William Darius Bishop

(September 14, 1827-February 4, 1904)

by George M. Jenks

Bucknell University

CAREER: Superintendent (1850-1855), president, Naugatuck Railroad (1855-1867, 1883-1903); member, U.S. Congress (1857-1859); U.S. Commissioner of Patents (1859-1860); member, Connecticut House of Representatives (1866, 1871); president, New York & New Haven Railroad (1867-1871); president, New York, New Haven & Hartford Railroad (1871-1879); member, Connecticut State Senate (1877, 1878).

William Darius Bishop was a prominent railroad official and Democratic politician in the state of Connecticut. Born in Bloomfield, New Jersey, on September 14, 1827, to Alfred and Mary Ferris Bishop, Bishop moved with his parents to Connecticut in 1836. He entered Yale in 1845 and graduated in 1849, distinguishing himself as a political debater and as president of the Linonia Society.

Bishop's career is notable because of the high level of responsibility he attained at a young age. His father was a railroad contractor in charge of the construction of both the Naugatuck Railroad and the New York & New Haven (NY&NH). Upon his father's death in 1849 the younger Bishop, just out of Yale, was hired to complete the projects. From this beginning he worked on a series of railroad construction jobs, including building a line from Saratoga Springs to Whitehall in New York, the Milwaukee & Chicago, and the Milwaukee & Watertown, the last two located in Wisconsin.

In addition to this construction activity Bishop also served as superintendent of the Naugatuck Railroad from 1850 to 1855 when he became president of the line. At twenty-eight years of age, Bishop was the head of a not insubstantial railroad and a member of its board of directors, a position he held until his death.

Bishop's early success was not unique to members of his social class, which was privately

William Darius Bishop

schooled, Ivy League, Episcopal, and which supplied a large percentage of the business and political leaders of the day. Bishop's entrance into politics was therefore not surprising. In 1856 he ran for and won a Democratic seat in Congress. When he failed in a reelection bid in 1858, Bishop was appointed United States Commissioner of Patents by President Buchanan. He served only from 1859 to 1860 but in that time reorganized and systematized the work of the office.

After 1860 Bishop confined himself to political affairs in Connecticut, serving twice in both the state House of Representatives, in 1866 and 1871, and the state Senate, in 1877 and 1878. Other than trying a few patent law cases (he had been admitted to the Connecticut bar in 1870), Bishop devoted most of his energies to railroads.

Bishop resigned as president of the Naugatuck in 1867 to take the same position at the New York & New Haven. As president of the NY&NH, Bishop transformed the line through consolidation into one of the most powerful in the region. He was not above using his political influence to accomplish this feat. When state law forbade the NY&NH from merging with the Hartford & New Haven, Bishop, a member of the 1871 Connecticut House of Representatives, pushed through a law permitting the 1872 creation of the New York, New Haven & Hartford (NYNH&H). Under Bishop's management until 1879, the NYNH&H expanded toward its goal of becoming the major line between New York and Boston.

After his retirement from the NYNH&H in 1879, Bishop was not actively involved in railroads until 1883 when he was renamed to the presidency of the Naugatuck Railroad. He remained in this post until his final retirement in 1903.

Bishop died on February 4, 1904. At the time of his death he still served on the board of directors of the Naugatuck and as president of the Eastern Railroad Association, which he had helped to form in 1884. He was reputedly a man of few words but was remembered as a suave and accomplished orator with a keen sense of humor. Other than railroads and politics, Bishop's interests included hunting and fishing.

Publications:

Speech on the Admission of Kansas under the Lecompton Constitution (Washington, 1858);

Argument Delivered before the Legislative Committee on Railroads at New Haven, Conn., June 9, 1874, on the Petition of the New York and Eastern R.R. Co. for Authority to Bridge the Housatonic River (New York: Van Kleeck, Clark, 1874);

Letter in Reply to Hon. Oliver Hoyt, April 3, 1882, Showing What It Was Mr. Joseph A. Pool, a Promoter and Corporator of the "Parallel Charter," Proposed . . . (Hartford: Case, Lockwood & Brainard, 1882).

References:

Biographical Directory of the American Congress, 1774-1971 (Washington: U.S. Government Printing Office, 1971);

Thomas C. Cochran, *Railroad Leaders, 1845-1890* (Cambridge, Mass.: Harvard University Press, 1953);

William Richard Cutter, *Genealogical and Family History of the State of Connecticut* (New York: Lewis Historical Publishing, 1911);

Edward Chase Kirkland, *Men, Cities and Transportation* (Cambridge, Mass.: Harvard University Press, 1948);

Dwight Lewis and J. Gilbert Calhoun, *The Judicial and Civil History of Connecticut* (Boston: Boston History, 1895);

N. G. Osborn, *Men of Mark in Connecticut*, volume 4 (Hartford, Conn.: William R. Goodspeed, 1908).

Boston & Maine Railroad

by Charles J. Kennedy

University of Nebraska

In most histories of New England railroading the Boston & Maine (B&M) Railroad ranks as the second most important system in the region, being placed behind only the New York, New Haven & Hartford (NYNH&H) system. The earliest manifestation of the B&M was chartered in 1833 as the Andover & Wilmington Railroad, an 8-mile line intended to link Andover, Massachusetts, with Boston over the tracks of the Boston & Lowell (B&L) Railroad. The line was opened in 1836, its largest stockholder being the Andover Academy and Theological Seminary. Almost immediately plans were made to extend the line to Haverhill, Massachusetts, and from there to Portsmouth, New Hampshire, and the Maine border. The Haverhill branch was completed in 1837 but the extension to New Hampshire and to Maine did not materialize because of strained finances. The company had acquired a New Hampshire charter in 1835, incorporating as a separate entity known as the Boston & Maine. A Maine charter for the rest of the planned extension was also procured, this section being known as the Maine, New Hampshire & Massachusetts Railroad. The strategy of incorporating separately in three states, seemingly a product of chance, would prove crucial in the future of the Boston & Maine.

In 1842 the line, which extended into the states of Massachusetts, Maine, and New Hampshire, was merged into the Boston & Maine Railroad; the company retained its separate charters in the three New England states. The newly consolidated Boston & Maine expanded rapidly. Not content any longer to rent access to Boston over the tracks of the Boston & Lowell, the B&M completed its own line to the city in 1845. In 1847 the B&M gained access to Portland, Maine, by jointly leasing the Portland, Saco & Portsmouth Railroad with the Eastern Railroad, a line which for many years was the B&M's most intense competitor.

The Boston & Maine was known throughout the nineteenth century as one of the most conservatively run railroads in the nation. The management, also regarded as among the finest in the region, concentrated on maintaining the quality of its physical plant, improving its community image through superior service and attractive rates, minimizing costs, and retaining stable and fair rate relations with the Eastern. These policies enabled the B&M to remain virtually debt-free through the 1860s and to maintain its 10-percent stock dividends.

This comfortable and profitable state of affairs ended in 1870 when the Portland, Saco & Portsmouth canceled its lease with the B&M and the Eastern. The B&M was forced to construct its own 44-mile line into Portland, using the opportunity to extend its service to six cities not previously on the route. While the new line endangered cooperation with the Eastern, the B&M was able to convince its competitor, which at the time was heavily in debt, to maintain stable rates. But for the first time the B&M took on significant debt and lowered its dividends.

The 1880s saw the B&M move to become a dominant system in the region. The B&M's most important aquisition was the 1884 lease of the Eastern, an agreement which saved the Eastern from bankruptcy and the B&M from the Eastern's destructive competition. The lease of the Eastern came about as a result of an attempt by the Eastern to forcefully lease the B&M. Each railroad had come to realize that their almost parallel routes were detrimental to both. Yet the B&M intensely resisted the Eastern strategy. The original strategy of incorporating separately in three states enabled the B&M to take control of the situation and gain a favorable position. The B&M signed a 54-year lease for the Eastern but was able to consolidate the line completely into the B&M in 1890.

The 1884 lease of the Eastern also had the effect of bringing several members of the Eastern board of directors into similar positions on the B&M. These directors, led by Frank Clark, helped to engineer the B&M's 1886 lease of the Worcester, Nashua & Rochester (WN&R) Railroad. Clark had consolidated the Worcester & Nashua Railroad, which began operations in 1848, and the Nashua & Rochester Railroad, which opened in 1874, into the WN&R in 1883. The WN&R added little to the B&M except protection of its Portland traffic, but the lease did greatly remunerate Clark and his fellow investors.

In 1887 the B&M successfully negotiated the lease of the Boston & Lowell Railroad and its associated lines. The B&L, under the leadership of Charles S. Mellen, later the president of the New York, New Haven & Hartford, had formed an extensive system of railroads in New England. In March 1887 the New Hampshire Supreme Court ruled against the B&L in a lawsuit concerning the railroad's lease of the Northern Railroad. The effect of the ruling was to dismember the B&L system and to force the constituent lines to seek affiliation with the B&M.

In 1893 A. Alexander McLeod was hired away from the Philadelphia & Erie Railroad to assume the presidency of the B&M. McLeod quickly managed to lease the Connecticut River Railroad, a line which was coveted by the NYNH&H and J. P. Morgan. Morgan, his plan for a railroad monopoly in New England thwarted, imposed a settlement between the B&M and the NYNH&H which stabilized the situation and also removed McLeod from the B&M presidency. Lucius Tuttle, formerly of the NYNH&H, became the new B&M president.

Tuttle was able to lease two large lines before the end of the century: the 424-mile Concord & Montreal in 1895 and the 478-mile Fitchburg System in 1900. With these two acquisitions the B&M reached a size which enabled it to compete more effectively with the other large systems in the region. In 1900 the B&M operated 2,324 miles of track, the product of consolidating forty-seven major and minor regional lines. The only real cause for concern was that the railroad owned only 519 miles of that track, the rest being leased. The high costs associated with the leases caused trepidation over the possible effects of an economic downturn. But optimism ran high at the turn of the century that the B&M would continue to prosper.

References:

Charles J. Kennedy, *Chapter on the History of the Boston and Maine Railroad*, 2 volumes (Lincoln, Neb.: University of Nebraska-Lincoln College of Business Administration, 1978-1979);

Edward Chase Kirkland, *Men, Cities, and Transportation, 1820-1900* (Cambridge, Mass.: Harvard University Press, 1948).

Archives:

The largest archive of Boston & Maine materials is in the personal collection of Charles J. Kennedy, Lincoln, Nebraska.

Brakes

The earliest railroads used brakes similar to those on horse-drawn wagons. A lever by the driver's seat was attached to a pivot and positioned in such a way that when pushed or pulled by the driver it pressed on the wagon wheel and slowed the vehicle. As long as railroads employed horses for motive power and wooden rails, this type of braking device proved adequate for most circumstances. This was particularly true in England where relatively few steep grades were encountered. With the coming of the steam locomotive, however, such crude brakes were clearly inadequate.

Most early locomotives pulled short trains at slow speeds, and stopping them was often accomplished by allowing the locomotive and train to drift to a stop. If necessary, lever-type hand brakes could be pushed against the wheels of the locomotive and cars to slow the train. This required several additional employees, brakemen, to operate the levers on each car, an expense on which many railroads looked unfavorably. Some railroads, however, did not even bother with brake levers. One account tells of a South Carolina railroad which stopped its trains by having passengers jump to the ground and hold onto the cars while crew members attempted to jam pieces of cordwood between the spokes of the wheels.

The earliest steam locomotives were not much help in braking trains. The drop hook form of link motion, which allowed the locomotive to be operated in reverse, was of little help in braking trains. Neither the drop hook nor the "V" hook (another early form of reversing link motion) was capable of engaging and reversing the mechanism of the locomotive unless it was stationary. Consequently, the crude brake lever continued to be used into the 1840s and in some cases until the Civil War.

With the advent of the Stephenson linkage in 1842 it became possible to reverse the locomotive while operating at speed. Until the Civil War this method of braking, reversing the engine, was supplemented with improved brakes on individual cars. In the 1840s a double-acting brake was developed, which allowed a brakeman to simultaneously set the brakes on all the wheels of a car with a single brake wheel. As the brake wheel was turned, chains or levers pressed the "shoes" against the wheels. These shoes, originally of wood, were eventually leather lined and finally replaced by iron brake shoes. When the engineer whistled "down brakes," brakemen would scramble to the brake wheels and "tie down" two to four cars. If additional braking power was necessary, the locomotive could be reversed. The double-acting brake was invented by Willard J. Nicholls, a car shop foreman on the Hartford & New Haven Railroad. Nicholls failed to patent his invention, however, and it was later claimed by H. S. Tanner, of whom little is known.

The double-acting brake, because of a continued reliance on reversing, did not solve every problem. Reversing the locomotive caused tremendous wear and tear on the reversing linkage and the driving tires, and slipped driving tires often resulted if the locomotive had to slide any distance forward with the mechanism in reverse. Damage to the rails was also a constant danger, particularly near stations where stops were frequently made. Furthermore, reversing the locomotive was of little value in holding a train in check while descending a significant grade. In such a case the brakes on individual cars had to be used.

In any case, the life of a mid-nineteenth-century brakeman was difficult. In the best of weather conditions it was difficult to stand on top of a swaying boxcar even at slow speeds and turn down the brake wheels. If the weather was cold, rainy, or snowy, the situation was even worse. Between the hazards of the brakes and the couplers there were few brakemen who lasted more than a few years without some type of serious injury. Because of these difficult conditions railroads could not recruit the best men to be brakemen. Many deserted their posts when the weather got bad, often leading to disastrous results when the engineer whistled "brakes down" only to find that half his brakemen had deserted at the last fueling stop.

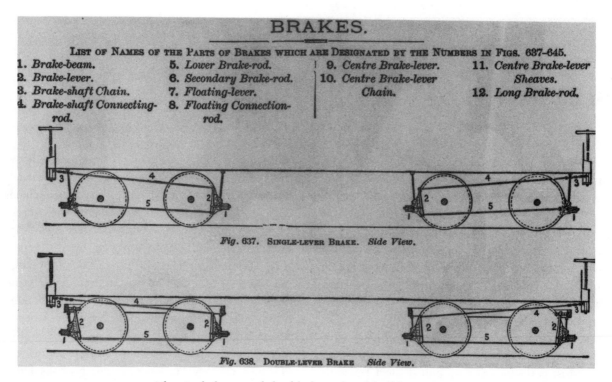

BRAKES.

LIST OF NAMES OF THE PARTS OF BRAKES WHICH ARE DESIGNATED BY THE NUMBERS IN FIGS. 637–645.

1. *Brake-beam.*
2. *Brake-lever.*
3. *Brake-shaft Chain.*
4. *Brake-shaft Connecting-rod.*
5. *Lower Brake-rod.*
6. *Secondary Brake-rod.*
7. *Floating-lever.*
8. *Floating Connection-rod.*
9. *Centre Brake-lever.*
10. *Centre Brake-lever Chain.*
11. *Centre Brake-lever Sheaves.*
12. *Long Brake-rod.*

Fig. 637. SINGLE-LEVER BRAKE. *Side View.*

Fig. 638. DOUBLE-LEVER BRAKE. *Side View.*

The single-lever and double-lever hand braking systems

Despite the problems associated with these primitive braking systems, braking technology advanced slowly. There were railroad owners who were not willing to expend money which would not yield immediate profit. But the better explanation for the slow advance in technology is that there was little demand for improved brakes, there being few serious accidents in the first decade of American railroading. Trains were short, thus allowing the crude, individually braked cars to meet the braking needs. In addition, speeds seldom exceeded over twenty miles per hour, and traffic density was low. Angus Sinclair, a prominent locomotive journalist of the late nineteenth and early twentieth century, suggested that several serious accidents in the first decade of American railroading would have generated a more effective train brake. As rail technology increased, however, accidents began to increase. In the late 1840s and the 1850s, with train travel, train frequency, and train speeds all increasing, the growing number of serious accidents began to alarm the public. In 1853, for instance, a train approaching Norwalk, Connecticut, at a speed of about fifteen miles per hour, was unable to stop short of an open drawbridge. The train plunged into about 12 feet of water and forty-six people died.

The public's fear forced the railroads to pay more attention to the matter of adequate brakes. Clearly a need existed for a better braking system, but the cost appeared prohibitive even before one had been developed. Many systems, however, were tried. By 1870 more than 300 patents for train brakes had been granted in the United States alone. The most concerted efforts involved attempts to develop a continuous train brake, that is, one that would allow all the brakes on the locomotive and cars to be applied at the same time. Many forms of power were contemplated, including compressed air, steam, hydraulic, vacuum, spring, and inertia. Many early efforts attempted to use the inertia of the moving train to provide braking power. Others attempted to use the power resulting from the compression of the cars against the locomotive when it was reversed. Still other momentum systems attempted to use a clutch and windlass, which could be engaged only when the engineer wanted to stop the train. None of these systems was reliable enough to gain acceptance beyond a limited area.

George S. Griggs did devise a momentum brake in 1839 that was used on several New England railroads for a short time. William G. Creamer of New York invented a spring brake in 1853 that was applied rather widely. Each brake wheel was outfitted with a spiral spring, and brake

Advertisement for one of Westinghouse's rivals

wheels were roped together to the cab of the locomotive. Before the train departed from each station the wheels were wound up and the springs set. If no emergency stop was necessary it was still possible to stop the train by using the brake wheel and by reversing the locomotive. If an emergency stop was necessary, however, the engineer could pull the rope and all the springs were supposed to apply the brakes. In several widely publicized cases during the 1860s the Creamer spring brake failed to prevent serious accidents and was eventually discarded.

Steam was tried as a braking mechanism as well. While it proved to be a successful method for braking a locomotive, it was inadequate for an entire train. Flexible couplings were necessary for transmitting the steam from car to car, and it was not possible in the mid nineteenth century to develop a coupling that did not leak profusely. It was thus impossible to push the steam for more than about two or three cars before condensation took place, eliminating the steam power that was intended for braking. As the technology evolved it became clear that the air brake and the vacuum brake were the only two braking systems to meet the demands of a continuous train brake. Both were marketed successfully until the final decade of the century, when the air brake became universal.

The development of the air brake is linked to George Westinghouse (1846-1914), one of the most innovative American mechanical minds of the nineteenth century. Westinghouse was moved to design a brake because of a terrible railroad accident he witnessed as a young man. Unaware of the work that had already gone on in the field he began with technology already tried and discarded. He eventually settled on the use of compressed air, after first having attempted brakes powered mechanically by the train's momentum transmitted through chains and by steam. Several air brakes had been attempted as early as 1845, and the first air brake patent in the United States was issued in 1852. In 1860 an air brake was demonstrated in England but, while not substantially different from Westinghouse's, was never successful in becoming the standard brake for British railroads.

Westinghouse's first version of an air brake was tested in April 1869 on the Pennsylvania Railroad. Known as a straight air brake, it operated only when air from a storage tank on the locomotive was admitted into a series of pipes and hoses running the length of the train. When released this air activated the brake cylinder under each car, and its piston moved rods and levers which pressed the brake pads against the wheels. A steam-driven pump on the locomotive compressed the air for storage in the tank. The major problem with this brake was the fact that it took air to set the brakes. If a serious leak occurred in the train-length lines that transmitted air to the cylinders on each car, there might not be adequate air pressure to actuate the brakes. If a coupler failed and the train separated, the cars not coupled to the engine had no brakes. Despite the drawbacks of Westinghouse's new brake its reception was dramatic. Within the decade more than 3,000 locomotives and about 10,000 passenger cars were equipped with the brakes.

In 1873 Westinghouse introduced the triple valve, a device that eliminated the problems of the straight air brake, which was part of a system eventually called the automatic air brake. It was different from any other air brake system and rightfully set Westinghouse apart as the man who invented the modern railroad brake. A special valve, called the triple valve, was applied to each car and locomotive. The triple valve was designed so that it could monitor the air pressure in the entire train line. Each car was also outfitted with an auxiliary air reservoir, which enabled it to apply its own brakes without being dependent on the locomotive to supply the compressed air necessary to set the brakes.

The triple valve was so named because it could carry out three functions. It could sense low pressure in the auxiliary reservoir and divert air from the train line to refill the reservoir in the car. If the pressure in the train line dropped too far, either because the train had separated or the engineer had reduced the air pressure in the train line for braking purposes, the triple valve could set the brakes for that particular car in proportion to the amount of reduction–a slight setting of the brakes for a "five pound reduction," or a total setting of the brakes if the pressure dropped suddenly. Finally, if the pressure in the train line was adequate and if the auxiliary reservoir was filled, the triple valve released the brakes or, if already released, did nothing.

The automatic air brake revolutionized the operation of American trains. The automatic coupler and the automatic air brake were the two most dramatic safety improvements in the history of American railroads. Together they allowed the operation of longer and heavier trains with greater safety and reliability. In 1886 and 1887 the Master Car Builders Association held tests near Burlington, Iowa, to determine the best type of braking system. The triple value proved to be somewhat of a disappointment in that it was unable to brake a fifty-car train

Advertisement listing the wide range of brake products offered by Westinghouse

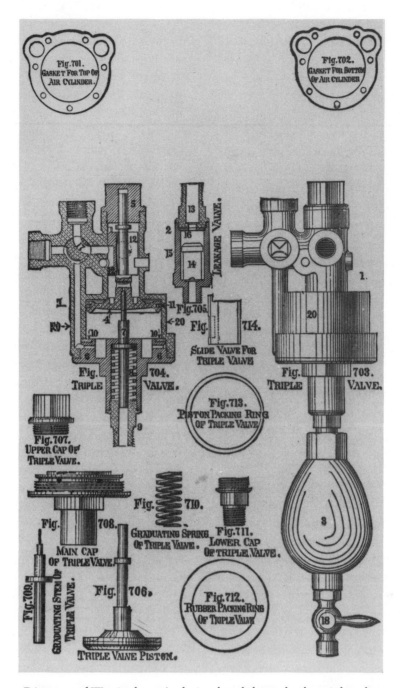

Diagram of Westinghouse's design breakthrough, the triple valve

smoothly and evenly because of the length of time it took for the brakes to be set at the rear of the train. Westinghouse immediately redesigned the triple valve with new vent pipes on each car, which increased the speed of the system by sixfold. A hand-braked fifty-car train took almost 800 feet to stop from a speed of twenty miles per hour. With Westinghouse's new triple valve the same train could be stopped in 166 feet.

Only one competitor seriously challenged the Westinghouse brake. In 1874 Frederick W. Eames

of Watertown, New York, had patented a vacuum brake. He did not immediately develop the brake for commercial production, but by the early 1880s the Eames Vacuum Brake was on the market. It was a straight brake which used a steam ejector to develop the vacuum needed in the train lines for braking. It was a simple brake to operate and maintain because it had few moving parts. Braking was created by a pulling action opposed to the pushing action of the Westinghouse automatic air brake. All cars and locomotives had to be equipped with vacuum "pots," an addition which restricted the interchange of cars once most railroads adopted the Westinghouse brake. The Eames brake was used extensively by the Northern Pacific Railroad, particularly on its more mountainous routes.

Northern Pacific locomotives operating in mountainous areas were also equipped with LeChatelier Water Brakes, a steam locomotive version of the dynamic brake on a diesel-electric locomotive. The LeChatelier brake was used primarily to ease the effects of heat on the brake shoes of cars descending long grades. It consisted of a regulating valve which diverted hot water from the boiler into the exhaust passages of the cylinders. The water changed into hot vapor which was immediately sucked into the cylinders by the action of the pistons. The reverse lever could be positioned to allow the desired amount of vapor to enter the cylinders to act as a cushion, thus slowing piston travel. Of course this action slowed down the speed of the locomotive and train as well, saving wear and tear on the brakes and the braking system. It did not, however, necessarily save wear and tear on the cylinder heads and packings.

The water brake worked reasonably well when handled correctly. An engineer who allowed too much water to get into the exhaust passages applied too much vapor to the cylinders, allowing the possibility that the cylinder packing might be blown out or the cylinder heads might be damaged. In most cases cylinder-head relief valves were installed on locomotives with the water brake in order to absorb an engineer's mistake. Both the Eames and the LeChatelier brakes had serious weaknesses because of their inability to brake trains of significant length and weight. The Eames brake was considered adequate only for trains of about twenty cars on the Northern Pacific's 2.2 percent grades over the Rocky and Cascade mountains. The water brake did not increase braking capacity but only provided a reserve braking force. The Eames Company did not give up, however; in 1890 it stopped producing the vacuum brake, reorganized as the New York Air Brake Company, and developed its own air brake. It continued to service railroads like the Northern Pacific, which continued to make limited use of the vacuum brake until the mid 1890s. In the twentieth century the New York Air Brake Company remained Westinghouse's only rival.

Usage of Westinghouse automatic air brakes continued to spread rapidly in the years following the successful redesign of the triple valve in 1887. So clearly was the automatic air brake the best braking system for American railroads that the Congress of the United States passed the Safety Appliance Act in 1893. Since most main line passenger trains were already equipped with air brakes (by 1876 almost 75 percent of American passenger cars had air brakes, and by 1890 the number was almost 100 percent), this act concentrated primarily on freight cars, requiring the adoption of air brakes within a certain time span. By 1900 the locomotives and cars of all Class I railroads were equipped with air brakes. Safety on American railroads had been a common public concern since the 1840s. The government had reacted to steam boiler explosions on riverboats by requiring regular boiler inspections by government inspectors. Likewise, the numerous railroad accidents led Congress to force railroads to install such an obviously effective safety device as the automatic air brake.

In 1894 a high-speed brake for passenger trains was introduced. A 30 percent increase in the train line air pressure allowed a six-car passenger express moving at 60 miles per hour to be stopped within 1,200 feet. Improved rubber connections between the cars and better coupling devices between the air hoses allowed the air brake line pressure to be increased without leakage. No additional changes were made in the automatic air brake in the nineteenth century. About 1905 an improved "K-type" brake was introduced for freight trains that made possible effective braking on trains of 100 cars in length. At about the same time an improved "LN" brake was introduced for passenger cars. In the early 1930s the "AB" brake, the one currently in use on American railroads, was introduced, which was able to brake trains of more than 200 cars and weighing more than 15,000 tons.

References:

Alfred E. Bruce, *The Steam Locomotive in America: Its Development in the Twentieth Century* (New York: W. W. Norton, 1952);

Angus Sinclair, *Development of the Locomotive Engine* (Cambridge, Mass.: The M.I.T. Press, 1970);

John H. White, "A Short History of Railway Brakes," *The Bulletin of the National Railway Historical Society*, 40, no. 5 (1975): 6-17.

—Robert L. Frey

John Woods Brooks

(August 2, 1819-September 16, 1881)

by John Lauritz Larson

Purdue University

CAREER: Chief engineer, Boston & Maine Railroad (1839); superintendent, Auburn & Rochester Railroad (1843-1845); superintendent, Michigan Central Railroad (1846-1855); director, Aurora Branch Railroad (1852); director, vice-president, St. Mary's Ship Canal (1852); director, Great Western Railway (1852-1854); director, Central Military Tract Railroad (1852-1856); director, Chicago & Aurora Railroad (1853-1856); director (1853-1876), president, Burlington & Missouri River Railroad (1853-1855, 1864-1865, 1867-1875); president, Central Military Tract Railroad (1854-1856); director, president, Michigan Central (1855-1867); director, Chicago, Burlington & Quincy (1857-1876); director, Hannibal & St. Joseph Railroad (1857-1870); commissioner, Hoosac Tunnel (1863-1866); director, president, Burlington & Missouri River Railroad, Nebraska (1869-1876); president, Omaha & Southwestern Railroad (1872).

John Woods Brooks

John Woods Brooks entered business through the technical side of railroading. Born in Stow, Massachusetts, on August 2, 1819, Brooks followed his academy education with a practical study of engineering under Laommi Baldwin, one of America's premier railroad engineers. After this apprenticeship young Brooks worked for the Boston & Maine Railroad, becoming its chief engineer in 1839. On April 21, 1842, he married Charlotte Louisa Dean, and the next year the young couple removed to upstate New York, where John became superintendent of the Auburn & Rochester (A&R) Railroad.

The Auburn & Rochester was one of several small roads that, if consolidated, had the potential to form a parallel route to the Erie Canal. Such a consolidation was prohibited by laws protecting the state's interest in the canal, but Albany iron merchant Erastus Corning wished to change all that. While working for the A&R, Brooks learned firsthand both the evils of fragmentary railroading and

the advantages of integrated long lines. Searching for feeder lines for the New York Central route that Corning was creating, Brooks journeyed to Detroit in 1845 to look at Michigan's bankrupt Central Railroad. Brooks realized that if he could find investors to buy the road, it would create an important line to the West.

Brooks took his investment proposal to Albany, Boston, and New York, where it met with cautious interest among capitalists such as Corning, John Murray Forbes, John E. Thayer, and Michigan creditors like the Farmers Loan & Trust Company of New York. Detroit attorney James F. Joy helped steer a charter through the Michigan legislature while Brooks prepared a systematic *Report on the Merits of the Michigan Central Railroad, as an Investment for Eastern Capitalists* (1846). This masterpiece of persuasion demonstrated Brooks's particular talents as an engineer-promoter in a world where technical expertise was becoming crucial to entrepreneurial decision making. Brooks envisioned not a discrete local road but rather a railroad system encompassing roadbed, rails, rolling stock, stations, warehouses, fuel, passengers, shippers, and connections at both ends. Forbes and his friends founded the Michigan Central (MC) Railroad in 1846, with Brooks becoming superintendent and Forbes occupying the presidency.

Superintendent Brooks at once began rebuilding stations, roadbed, and track, replacing old strap-iron rails with modern "T" rails and extending the line westward. In 1849 the railroad reached Lake Michigan. Brooks's improvements to the line, including faster passenger trains, tighter schedules, longer freight trains, and fewer stops, benefited shippers and passengers but laid waste to both ambling country habits and wandering country livestock. That winter angry farmers struck back with violence by burning woodpiles, derailing trains, engaging in gunplay, and finally burning the company's Detroit depot. Brooks and his backers fumed at this rural ingratitude and successfully prosecuted the "conspirators."

The Michigan Central cost 50 percent more to perfect than Brooks had predicted, but investors saw rewards rather quickly, and all parties learned valuable lessons about this new railroad business. For the year ending May 31, 1850, earnings reached $692,000 and two years later passed the $1 million mark. During this period Brooks gathered into his own hands, in his position as the engineer and manager on the property in Michigan, control over purchasing, construction, and operations—matters that untrained entrepreneurs in Boston could not fully understand. He acquired in these years a lifelong hatred of cutthroat competition, urging his allies back East and his competitors to the south to cooperate and maintain rates. He ran an innovative railroad, experimenting with passenger conveniences like sleeping cars, through tickets, baggage service, and close connections. In 1855 Forbes retired, and Brooks became president of what had been *his* railroad all along.

Brooks recognized that Chicago, and not the lakeshore, should be the one western terminus. At Chicago many railroads would feed the Michigan Central, just as it fed the New York lines. By 1852 Brooks and legal counsel James F. Joy had persuaded a reluctant Forbes to build into the Windy City. Brooks and Joy combined several small Illinois roads into the Chicago, Burlington & Quincy (CB&Q), which by 1856 touched the Mississippi River at two points. As the eastern trunk lines took shape in that decade, Brooks, Joy, and Forbes took financial interests in, and then control of, the Hannibal & St. Joseph (H&StJ) in Missouri and the Burlington & Missouri River (B&MR) in Iowa—both land grant roads too important to leave to competitors. Through the Civil War decade and into the 1870s this remarkable team of technician, politician, and financier played a central role in railroad development across the nation's midsection.

Railroad development naturally stimulated ancillary investment opportunities for John W. Brooks and his colleagues. One such investment was the Sault Ste. Marie ship canal between Lakes Michigan and Huron. In 1852 Congress offered free lands to encourage this project, and the Michigan Central group seized the bait. Brooks was no hydraulic expert himself and intended to play only an investor's role, but in 1854 skyrocketing costs and technical blunders forced him into the northern wilds of Michigan to personally oversee construction. The canal was finished in 1855, but the investment proved disappointing.

A similar temptation in the next decade caused Brooks even more grief. The state of Massachusetts had extended $2 million toward a project to construct a railroad tunnel under Hoosac Mountain. After years of waste Gov. John A. Andrew fired the original contractor, Herman Haupt, and in 1862 named Brooks to head a commission to examine the tunnel and recommend a course of action. Brooks's commissioners believed the tunnel could be built in eight years, and they urged the state to proceed. From 1863 to 1866 Brooks personally managed the Hoosac Tunnel project, unfortunately accomplishing little more than had his predecessor. Inadequate technology, imperfect science, and an uncharacteristic lack of systematic direction frustrated his intentions. In May Brooks collapsed in a state of paralysis that nearly cost him his life and caused him to drop the Michigan Central presidency and all his other enterprises.

While Brooks slowly recovered, railroad competition west of the Mississippi steadily grew more intense. In 1867 Brooks gradually returned to duty as the nominal head of the Burlington road in Iowa, and in 1869 he assumed the presidency of a new land grant extension, the Burlington & Missouri River in Nebraska (B&MR-N). It was during this period that Joy offered Brooks shares in several Iowa construction companies that promised good returns with little risk, and Brooks invested with little forethought. As president of the CB&Q, Joy later extended liberal credits to those companies to protect his investment, and Brooks did not object. Tragically, these "River Roads" investments collapsed in the panic of 1873, and two years later Forbes discovered Brooks's and Joy's inside dealing. The confidence and friendship of thirty years exploded. Angry at the embarrassment, Forbes purged his friends from the CB&Q board; bitter at Forbes's self-righteousness, Brooks would not repent. "We who do not claim to be immaculate," Brooks protested, "are content with right intentions and good results."

Before the two men could repair the damage to their friendship, Brooks was stricken once more with illness and began a slow decline toward death. He repaired to his home in Boston, where he had lived since 1857, and languished in unhappy retirement. Despairing of recovery, in May 1881 he tried an ocean cruise and took up residence at Heidelberg, Germany, hoping that somehow a change of air might do him good. On September 16 he died.

Despite the "river roads" scandal and the partisan attacks surrounding the Hoosac Tunnel, Brooks impressed most observers with his competence and integrity. Charles Francis Adams once called him "the most thoroughly competent man in the United States," and John Murray Forbes (whose loyalty was exceeded only by his wrath) declared him "a perfect Napoleon in his way." From very common beginnings Brooks had used his engineering training first to guide investors and then to elevate himself into a position of wealth and entrepreneurial leadership in the fast-moving railroad industry.

Publication:

Report on the Merits of the Michigan Central Railroad, as an Investment for Eastern Capitalists (Detroit: Charles Willcox, 1846).

References:

Thomas C. Cochran, *Railroad Leaders, 1845-1890: The Business Mind in Action* (Cambridge, Mass.: Harvard University Press, 1953);

John M. Dickinson, *To Build a Canal: Sault Ste. Marie, 1853-1854, and After* (Columbus: Ohio State University Press, 1981);

Alvin F. Harlow, *Road of the Century* (New York: Creative Age Press, 1947);

Harlow, *Steelways of New England* (New York: Creative Age Press, 1946);

Edward C. Kirkland, *Men, Cities and Transportation*, 2 volumes (Cambridge, Mass.: Harvard University Press, 1948);

John Lauritz Larson, *Bonds of Enterprise* (Cambridge, Mass.: Harvard University Press, 1984);

Irene D. Neu, "Building the Sault Canal," *Mississippi Valley Historical Review*, 40 (June 1953): 25-46;

Robert J. Parks, *Democracy's Railroads* (Port Washington, N.Y.: Kennikat Press, 1972).

Archives:

Material concerning John Woods Brooks is located in Michigan Central Railroad Archives of the New York Central System, Detroit, Michigan; in the Erastus Corning Papers of the Albany Institute of History and Art, Albany, New York; and in the Chicago, Burlington & Quincy Railroad Archives of the Newberry Library, Chicago, Illinois.

Alexander Johnston Cassatt

(December 8, 1839-December 28, 1906)

by Michael Bezilla

Pennsylvania State University

CAREER: Civil engineer, Pennsylvania Railroad and subsidiary lines (1861-1866); superintendent of motive power Philadelphia & Erie Railroad (1866-1867); superintendent of motive power (1867-1870), general superintendent, Pennsylvania Railroad (1870-1871); general manager, Pennsylvania Railroad Lines East (1871-1874); third vice-president (1874-1880), first vice-president (1880-1882), director, Pennsylvania Railroad (1883-1906); president, New York, Philadelphia & Norfolk Railroad (1885-1889); president, Pennsylvania Railroad (1899-1906).

Alexander J. Cassatt led the Pennsylvania Railroad (PRR) to become, in fact as well as in slogan, "the standard railroad of the world." As a mechanical and operating officer, he made the PRR a leader in the adoption of the air brake and interchangeable parts for locomotives. As president, he launched one of the largest capital improvement projects in railroad history, designed to anchor the eastern end of the Pennsylvania in the heart of New York City. As a railroad statesman, he was among the first leaders in the industry to advocate federal regulation of railroads to benefit both the public and the carriers.

Alexander Johnston Cassatt was born on December 8, 1839, in Pittsburgh, Pennsylvania, one of six children of Robert and Katherine Johnston Cassatt. The Cassatt forebears were French Huguenots who had immigrated to America in the 1650s. Robert Cassatt's success in banking and other commercial ventures in western Pennsylvania provided the family with a more than comfortable existence. In 1848 the Cassatts moved to Lancaster and two years later to Philadelphia. By that time Robert Cassatt had begun to devote increasing amounts of time to travel and other leisure activities. In 1851 the Cassatts took up full-time residence in Europe, first in Paris and then in Heidelberg, Germany.

Alexander Johnston Cassatt

Alexander enrolled at a private academy at Darmstadt, Germany, and remained there until he graduated in 1856, a year after his father had returned with the rest of the family to the Philadelphia suburb of West Chester. Alexander's German education reinforced a childhood interest in technological subjects, and, upon his own return to the United States, he enrolled at Yale. Dissatisfied with the school's engineering curriculum, he soon transferred to Rensselaer Polytechnic Institute and graduated as a civil engineer in 1859.

Cassatt immediately accepted a job as a rodman, or surveyor's assistant, in the construction of the Georgia Railroad. The uncertainties of the political situation–the southern states were threatening secession–brought this work to a halt by the end of the year, and Cassatt returned home to Pennsylvania.

In April 1861 he became a rodman on the Philadelphia division of the Pennsylvania Railroad. Within two years he was promoted to assistant civil engineer in charge of constructing a link between the PRR at Philadelphia and the United Railroads of New Jersey near Trenton, a connection designed to give the Pennsylvania access to the New York metropolitan area. The competence with which he performed his tasks caught the attention of Col. Thomas A. Scott, a PRR vice-president who would eventually head the road. Scott was instrumental in Cassatt's promotion in 1864 to resident engineer (chief civil engineer) of the middle division of the Philadelphia & Erie Railroad, a PRR subsidiary serving the oil and timber lands of northwestern Pennsylvania.

Cassatt was headquartered in the mountain outpost of Renovo. In 1866 he moved from there to equally remote Irvineton to become resident engineer of the Warren & Franklin Railroad, a PRR-controlled feeder of petroleum products to the Philadelphia & Erie. In spite of the community's isolation and its lack of social and cultural amenities, Cassatt was joined in Irvineton by his parents. Robert Cassatt by then exercised only a passive interest in his business holdings, preferring to encourage the fledgling careers of his children. Alexander and his sister Mary, in Paris studying painting, were the elder Cassatt's favorites.

In 1866, still under Tom Scott's patronage, Cassatt was made superintendent of motive power for the Philadelphia & Erie and was transferred to Williamsport. The move brought him into the mechanical department and helped broaden his experience as both an engineer and a manager. Cassatt spent barely a year in Williamsport before being named superintendent of motive power for the entire Pennsylvania Railroad Lines East (of Pittsburgh and Erie), which was headquartered in Altoona. The advancement was remarkable, considering the brevity of his tenure as a mechanical officer, and was a tribute to the thoroughness of his formal education and the skill with which he had mastered previous assignments. The promotion also reflected the personal esteem in which he was held, not only by Scott but also by J. Edgar Thomson, PRR president since 1852 and one of the ablest railroad men of the era.

The move to the bustling shop town of Altoona brought Cassatt literally into the heart of the sprawling PRR system. He was responsible for overseeing the maintenance and operation of the existing locomotive fleet as well as for the design and construction of new power, a task the railroad largely handled itself at the Altoona works.

Cassatt saw the need for standardization–that is, the development of a few basic classes of locomotives that could be used systemwide and whose uniformity of design would permit the maximum use of interchangeable parts. Heretofore, locomotives had been designed without much regard for the economies of scale inherent in mass production, resulting in an expensive proliferation of classes and designs.

By 1873, six years after Cassatt's promotion, the PRR classified 373 locomotives–nearly half its fleet–as standard. Most were home-built; those that were manufactured by commercial builders met rigid PRR specifications. The adherence to standard designs and the preference for building its own engines were characteristics that were to continue from Cassatt's era on through to the end of steam locomotive construction on the Pennsylvania in the 1940s.

Cassatt also witnessed the introduction of the air brake, an invention that revolutionized railroading. The brake's inventor, George Westinghouse, persuaded him to have the PRR sponsor the first practical trials of the device in April 1869. Cassatt quickly realized the air brake's potential for increasing the safety and efficiency of train operations. A few months later he ordered the PRR to begin equipping its passenger trains with the appliance. Freight trains began to be so equipped in 1878.

Cassatt's stay in the mechanical department was not a long one. In April 1870 he was promoted to general superintendent, an Altoona-based operating position. One of his first assignments, however, was to act in place of an ailing President Thomson in negotiating the purchase of a controlling interest in the Camden & Amboy Railroad, which would assure the PRR of undisputed access to the New York area. The New York Central and the Erie railroads tried to thwart the PRR, but Cassatt outmaneuvered them. Impressed with this feat, Thomson elevated his protégé in 1871 to the newly created position of general manager and moved him to Philadelphia.

Cassatt had married Maria Lois Buchanan, niece of President James Buchanan, on November 25, 1868. Three years later, when the couple moved east to the PRR's headquarters city, they had two children, Edward and Katherine. The Cassatts purchased fifty-six acres of land near Haverford, located in the suburbs west of Philadelphia, and built Cheswald, the family estate. Two more children, Robert and Eliza, were born there.

As general manager Cassatt became acquainted not only with motive power and operations but also with finance, law, and nearly every other aspect of the business of railroading. His most difficult assignment came in 1877 when a series of trainmen's strikes curtailed operations on the PRR and other eastern lines. Discontent centered on wage reductions, which the railroads insisted were necessary because of the prolonged economic recession. Pittsburgh was a hotbed of labor unrest, and Cassatt was dispatched to that city in July to represent Scott, who had succeeded Thomson as president in 1874. Cassatt's job was to protect company property from destruction by the angry workers. But he was too much the patrician to sympathize with workingmen, and, in any case, the situation in Pittsburgh was beyond control. Rioting broke out, the passenger station was burned, and damages to PRR property and equipment totaled $2.3 million. As the road's senior executive present at the Pittsburgh riots, Cassatt became the target of long-lasting labor hostility.

After the Pittsburgh strike Cassatt turned his attention to the oil fields of northwest Pennsylvania and northeast Ohio, where John D. Rockefeller's giant Standard Oil Company was skimming PRR profits by demanding rebates, or kickbacks, on its shipments of petroleum products. President Scott attempted to set up a PRR subsidiary, the Empire Transportation Company, in the refinery business to draw enough oil from Rockefeller's refineries to pressure Standard Oil into withdrawing its demands for rebates. When Rockefeller countered by ceasing all shipments via the Pennsylvania Railroad, Scott caved in and sent Cassatt to make peace with the oil baron. To retain Standard's business, Cassatt had to agree to give Rockefeller rebates on all petroleum products the railroad carried, regardless of who owned them.

The defeat—the one time a major rival got the better of the mighty Pennsylvania—left Cassatt with a hatred of rebates. It also hastened Scott's departure as president. There was much speculation that Cassatt would be the next chief executive, but in June 1880 the PRR's directors instead chose first vice-president George B. Roberts. Cassatt had never gotten along personally with Roberts and regarded him as being too cautious in expanding the railroad and generating new sources of revenue. For his part, Roberts thought Cassatt's proposal for a federal ban on rebating would lead to further government regulation that would ultimately stifle the railroad industry.

Nevertheless, Roberts welcomed Cassatt's assistance in obtaining permanent control over the PRR's primary southern link, the Philadelphia, Wilmington & Baltimore (PW&B) Railroad. Robert Garrett, president of the B&O, was attempting to purchase enough PW&B stock to wrest control of the line from the PRR. He nearly succeeded until Cassatt discovered a group of shareholders Garrett had overlooked. The PRR paid $14.9 million in 1881 for their stock, a block of sufficient size to assure the Pennsylvania of continued control over this vital property.

Cassatt mounted the canceled check in his office, ostensibly as a symbol of his triumph over the renowned Garrett. The check also reminded other PRR executives that Cassatt had been arguing for years that the Pennsylvania should secure ownership of the PW&B and that it could have done so for a relatively small sum had it not waited for the B&O to force the issue. Disagreements with the Roberts administration convinced Cassatt to retire in 1882 at the age of forty-two. He remained staunchly loyal to the Pennsylvania, rebuffing countless job offers—including presidencies—from other railroads. In the manner of his father, he preferred to devote his time to family and leisure activities, especially the breeding and raising of horses.

Cassatt thus occupied himself for the next seventeen years, during which time he also traveled throughout Europe and spent time with his sister Mary, then emerging as a famous artist. Only two business ventures distracted him. First, in 1883, he returned to the PRR as a director. Second, in 1885, he became president of the New York, Philadelphia & Norfolk (NYP&N) Railroad, a new line in which he was a major stockholder. The NYP&N gave the PRR a southern connection at Norfolk, Virginia, via a route down the Delmarva peninsula and across the Chesapeake Bay via ferry at Cape Charles. Only mildly interested in this venture, he retired from the presidency in 1889.

Following George Roberts's death in 1897, Cassatt's name was again among those most frequently mentioned for the PRR presidency. He did not actively seek the post, however, and it went to Frank Thomson, nephew of the legendary J. Edgar Thomson. But Frank Thomson died suddenly in June 1899. First vice-president John P. Greene, an attorney, lacked the engineering experience the Pennsylvania preferred its presidents to have. Thus the board of directors turned to Cassatt, who professed reluctance to take the job but nonetheless accepted on June 9, 1899. Cassatt's presidency, while brief by PRR standards, was nevertheless eventful and set the foundation for the railroad's prosperity in the twentieth century.

Cassatt first directed his attention to the practice of rebating, which he said was still sapping the strength of the Pennsylvania and other roads. He entered into an informal accord with William K. Vanderbilt of the New York Central to form what he called "a community of interest," by which the PRR and the NYC purchased controlling shares in smaller and weaker eastern lines. The two giants were thus able to nullify the "divide and conquer" strategy that Standard Oil and other large shippers had been using to win rebates. These shippers could no longer play railroads against one another in their search for the largest kickbacks.

When steel king Andrew Carnegie encouraged George Jay Gould to drive his Wabash and its affiliated railroads east to Pittsburgh to offer competition to the PRR and the NYC-controlled Pittsburgh & Lake Erie, Cassatt retaliated vigorously. Gould also owned the Western Union Telegraph Company, which, by contract, had located its poles along the PRR right-of-way. Cassatt refused to renew the contract in 1901, and then—by way of warning Gould away from Pittsburgh—proceeded to cut down Western Union's poles from one end of the PRR to the other, an action later upheld by the courts.

But Cassatt's community-of-interest plan also drew fire from the public and government officials who regarded the scheme as monopolistic. President Theodore Roosevelt branded Cassatt as another "malefactor of great wealth." But Cassatt regarded the community-of-interest plan as a temporary expedient. He spoke out more vigorously than

ever in favor of additional federal regulation of railroads, arguing that court decisions had robbed the Interstate Commerce Commission of the power to forbid rebates and bring order and fairness to rate-making. Without a community-of-interest or some similar plan, he contended, railroads would still find themselves at the mercy of large shippers. Cassatt thus joined with President Theodore Roosevelt in supporting both the Elkins Act (1903) and the Hepburn Act (1906).

The Elkins Act prohibited rebates, while the Hepburn Act—which Cassatt reputedly helped draft—gave the ICC power to set rates. Many railroad executives branded the Hepburn Act a dangerous restriction of free enterprise. They feared that it would restrict investment in the railroad industry and set a precedent for even more restrictive regulation.

Cassatt's actions on other fronts were far less controversial. After years of hesitant expansion under George Roberts, the PRR undertook extensive improvements of many kinds under Cassatt. For example, the railroad widened its busy main line between Harrisburg and Pittsburgh from two tracks to three and four, while at the same time reducing curvatures, easing grades, and replacing worn-out iron trusses with massive stone arch bridges. A new freight yard—one of the nation's largest—was constructed at Enola, across the Susquehanna River from Harrisburg. In southeastern Pennsylvania, a low-grade freight line was built between the Susquehanna and a point near Philadelphia, relieving congestion on the main passenger line between Harrisburg and eastern cities.

Handsome new passenger stations were erected at Pittsburgh, Washington, D.C., and other cities. In 1902 the Pennsylvania Special, the predecessor of the famed Broadway Limited, was inaugurated. This flagship of the PRR passenger fleet was soon traversing the New York to Chicago route in eighteen hours, offering stiff competition to the NYC water level route. Powerful new locomotives of the Atlantic, or 4-4-2 type, were built to pull the PRR's passenger and express trains. The Pennsylvania became one of the first roads to adopt all-steel construction for its passenger and freight car fleet, which, at more than a quarter-million units, was the nation's largest.

The most heavily publicized improvement project also happened to be the most expensive yet undertaken by an American railroad. The Pennsylvania had long been in an inferior position in the New York metropolitan area relative to the New York Central. The Vanderbilt road terminated in Manhattan, while the PRR lines ended at Jersey City, on the west bank of the Hudson River. The Pennsylvania's passengers thus faced the inconvenience and delay of a ferry ride between PRR trains and Manhattan. This situation also made the NYC the preferred road for passengers traveling between New England and midwestern points.

The Pennsylvania had studied the problem for decades but had always been stymied by the costs and engineering problems associated with building a bridge across the Hudson. When Cassatt became president, he saw that the technology of electric traction—as demonstrated in Europe—had advanced sufficiently to allow trains to use subaqueous tunnels rather than a bridge to reach Manhattan. The financial hurdles still existed, but Cassatt was prepared to borrow heavily—in spite of his road's ultraconservative fiscal heritage—to assure the project's successful completion.

Accordingly, the PRR launched a $115-million project in 1901 to make Manhattan its eastern terminus. Two tunnels were bored beneath the Hudson to Manhattan, where the ornate Pennsylvania Station was to be erected as the centerpiece for the entire project. Continuing eastward, four tunnels beneath the East River linked Manhattan with Long Island, and through them ran the hundreds of daily commuter trains of the Long Island Rail Road (LIRR). Electric locomotives were used exclusively, putting the PRR in the lead among American railroads in this form of motive power. By the 1930s the Pennsylvania would operate the nation's largest electrified system, stretching south to Washington, D.C., and west to Harrisburg. The PRR also used the project to improve its freight service to and from New England. A new yard at Greenville, New Jersey, was built, from which cars were floated across New York Harbor to Long Island. Trains eventually used LIRR rails to reach the New York, New Haven & Hartford's line, which crossed the East River at Hell Gate. The New Haven made direct, all-rail connections with New England points.

Cassatt never lived to see the completion of what literally would be his most monumental work. He died of heart failure on December 28, 1906, nearly a year before the first trains began using the new Pennsylvania Station. In the seven years before his death, Cassatt had essentially rebuilt the Pennsyl-

vania. He accomplished the rebuilding by using a managerial style that differed radically from that of George Roberts, who had consulted frequently with the company's directors before going ahead with even modest expenditures. Cassatt was more impulsive, acting first and informing the directors afterward. It is unlikely that the Pennsylvania would have undertaken improvements on such a massive scale had not a man such as Cassatt been chief executive. Yet, as events of subsequent decades attest, Cassatt's rebuilding of the railroad was crucial in its ability to remain profitable for many years and to meet the transportation demands of the nation's industrial heartland. Cassatt did substantially increase the PRR indebtedness. Funded debt stood at a record $191 million in 1906 and had more than doubled over the previous ten years. This was of no small consequence to a railroad so imbued with conservative instincts, as shown by the directors' choice of a successor to Cassatt. The new president was James McCrea, a Lines West executive with a reputation for frugality.

After his death Cassatt was forgotten, ultimately overshadowed by the fame of his sister Mary. When New York's Pennsylvania Station was razed in 1963, the bronze statue of Cassatt that had rested there for more than a half century was carted to a New Jersey dump along with the rubble from the structure.

Alexander Cassatt nevertheless ranks among the ablest of the Pennsylvania's long line of distinguished presidents. His call for increased government railroad regulation did not produce the results he envisioned, although he could not have recognized that in his lifetime. On the other hand, the physical improvements he oversaw paid for themselves many times over and continue to benefit PRR successors, Amtrak and Conrail.

References:

"Alexander J. Cassatt," *Railway Age* (January 4, 1907): 6-7;

Annual Reports of the Pennsylvania Railroad Company (Philadelphia, 1899-1907);

George H. Burgess and Miles C. Kennedy, *Centennial History of the Pennsylvania Railroad* (Philadelphia: Pennsylvania Railroad Co., 1949);

Patricia T. Davis, *End of the Line: Alexander J. Cassatt and the Pennsylvania Railroad* (New York: Neale Watson Academic Publications, 1978);

H. W. Schotter, *The Growth and Development of the Pennsylvania Railroad Company* (Philadelphia: Allen, Lane & Scott, 1927).

Archives:

An undetermined quantity of Cassatt's personal and family papers is in the hands of various descendants. Letter books and other materials relating to Cassatt's presidency and possibly his earlier activities with the Pennsylvania Railroad form part of a larger collection of PRR records held by the Pennsylvania Historical and Museum Commission at Harrisburg.

Chesapeake & Ohio Railway

by John F. Stover

Purdue University

The Chesapeake & Ohio was the product of an 1868 consolidation of the Covington & Ohio Railroad and the Virginia Central Railroad. The Covington & Ohio had been chartered by the state of Virginia in 1853 as a westward extension of the Virginia Central to the Ohio River, but only limited surveying had been completed by 1861. The Virginia Central was an 1850 reorganization of the Louisa Railroad, which was chartered by Virginia in 1836. The standard-gauge Louisa was named for an interior county northwest of Richmond and had 40 percent of its capital supplied by the state of Virginia. The first 21-mile segment of the new road, from Hanover Junction on the Richmond, Fredericksburg & Potomac (RF&P) westward to Frederick's Hall, was built by 1837. A contract with the older RF&P provided that line with the mandate to supply the equipment and operate the Louisa Railroad. By 1840 the Louisa was built twenty-seven miles farther west to reach Gordonsville. In 1845 a prosperous planter, Edmund Fontaine, was elected president of the Louisa, a position he would hold until 1865. President Fontaine had several new ideas for his railroad, and in 1847 the Louisa purchased motive power and cars and started to operate its own lines. It also projected construction to the west and south to Richmond.

In 1850 the Louisa was reorganized as the Virginia Central Railroad. By 1851 the road was operating ninety-seven miles of line, including new extensions from Gordonsville to Charlottesville, and from Hanover Junction south to Richmond. Between 1850 and 1858 the state of Virginia built for the Virginia Central the 18-mile Blue Ridge Railroad over and through the Blue Ridge Mountains from Mechum's River to Waynesboro. The four tunnels needed for the project were constructed under the direction of Colonel Claudius Crozet. West of Waynesboro the Virginia Central was built via Staunton on west to Jackson's River, now Clifton Forge. On the eve of the Civil War the 195-mile Virginia Central was the second longest line in the state and had an equipment roster of 27 locomotives, 34 passenger cars, and 210 freight cars.

During the Civil War the Virginia Central was an important rail route both for the shipment of Confederate supplies and also for the movement of troops. Gen. Stonewall Jackson used the line several times, especially when his army came to the aid of Robert E. Lee in the defense of Richmond in the summer of 1862. Because of its location the Virginia Central was frequently subjected to raids by federal troops. Repairs were difficult since the Confederacy was so short of railroad supplies. With the great inflation of the Confederacy currency the railroad was forced to push up both passenger fares and freight fares, which by 1865 were ten times higher than the prewar figures. When the war ended the Virginia Central had only $100 in gold in its treasury.

With the end of the Civil War the Virginia Central at once started to rebuild its lines. Limited service was restored in a few weeks, and the entire road was in operation by the spring of 1866. In 1865 Gen. William C. Wickham, a former Confederate cavalry officer, was elected president of the Virginia Central. Wickham managed to extend the road ten miles west to Covington by July 1867. The unbuilt Covington & Ohio lay almost entirely in the new state of West Virginia. On August 31, 1868, the Virginia Central and the Covington & Ohio were merged into the Chesapeake & Ohio Railroad, chartered concurrently by Virginia and West Virginia. General Wickham was the president of the new company, and he at once started seeking financial support for the extension of the line to the Ohio River. When he found no financial help in Europe Wickham turned to the New York banking firm of Fisk and Hatch. Wickham was introduced to Collis P. Huntington, fresh from his laurels of completing the Central Pacific. Huntington and his associates proposed to build and equip the 200-mile extension for $15 million. Huntington became the C&O president with Wickham as vice-president. Using as many as 7,000 men the road was built west from the Virginia line and east from the newly platted Ohio River town of Huntington, West Virginia. Enroute vast new coal deposits were discovered in the mountain counties of West Virginia. Officials drove the final spike on January 29, 1873, completing the 428-mile road from Richmond to Huntington. The C&O had cost much more to build than Huntington had estimated, and capital structure increased fivefold to $38 million. Total revenue in 1873-1874 was only $1.5 million. The road was in default by the end of 1873, and Wickham was appointed receiver in 1875.

The C&O was reorganized as the Chesapeake & Ohio Railway by a committee headed by Huntington and A. S. Hatch. At the foreclosure sale April 2, 1878, A. S. Hatch purchased the road for $2.75 million. In the reorganization Huntington remained as president, Hatch became first vice-president, and Wickham the second vice-president. In 1879 the revenue amounted to $1,891,000 with expenses of $1,507,000, figures quite low when generated out of a capital structure of $57 million. The rolling stock in 1879 consisted of 81 locomotives, 51 passenger cars, and 2,300 freight cars. More than half of the C&O freight cars were used for hauling coal. But the reorganized line still lacked adequate connections in the west and a deep-water port in the east. In 1879 Huntington obtained permission from Virginia to extend the C&O seventy-five miles from Richmond down the Virginia peninsula to the great natural harbor at Newport News on Hampton Roads. This line was completed and in operation by 1882 and gave the C&O access to both coastal and ocean commerce. Huntington made arrangements with the Old Dominion Steamship Company for a daily line of steamers between his new port and New York City. In the early 1880s the C&O also extended its service west of Huntington, West Virginia, over the tracks of the Elizabeth, Lexington & Big Sandy Railroad to Winchester, Kentucky.

The Kentucky Central gave service north to Cincinnati. Both of these Kentucky lines were controlled by Huntington. In 1886 more than 40 percent of the freight carried by the Chesapeake & Ohio consisted of coal. In that year the revenue of the road had climbed to $4,096,000 with expenses of $2,867,000. This was still a very small return on a total capital investment of $73 million. In 1887 Huntington applied for the appointment of a receiver for the Chesapeake & Ohio, but Drexel, Morgan & Company worked out a plan of reorganization and the road escaped a foreclosure sale.

The C&O was reorganized in 1888 by the Vanderbilt interests, and a trusted Vanderbilt lieutenant, Melville E. Ingalls, replaced Huntington as president. Ingalls remained president of the Chesapeake & Ohio until 1900, and during much of that time was also president of the Cleveland, Cincinnati, Chicago & St. Louis Railway. With Ingalls's strong management, supported by the financial backing of Morgan, the C&O expanded and prospered during the decade of the 1890s. The mileage operated by the Chesapeake & Ohio grew from 667 miles in 1889 to 1,425 miles in 1900. By 1891 the C&O had acquired the 231-mile Richmond & Allegheny Railroad, which gave a new direct route along the James River from Clifton Forge to Richmond. During the 1890s several new lines and branches were acquired in West Virginia and northeastern Kentucky. By 1900, through ownership, leases, or trackage rights, the C&O was operating a system serving Newport News, Richmond, Washington, D.C., Cincinnati, and Louisville. During the decade the entire road was ballasted with stone and relaid with heavier 70- to 100-pound rails, many new bridges were replaced, tunnels enlarged, and new equipment added. The C&O equipment roster in 1900 consisted of 375 locomotives, 216 passenger cars, and 16,600 freight cars. Total revenue increased from $4,314,000 in 1889 to $13,402,000 in 1900, with the operating ratio declining from 82 percent to 65 percent. The hauling of coal increased and accounted for 50 percent of all freight ton-mileage by 1900-1901. Annual dividends of $1 were paid from 1889 to 1900, and by the turn of the century the C&O was becoming the prosperous road its founders had dreamed of in earlier decades.

References:
John F. Stover, *The Railroads of the South, 1865-1900:*

A Study in Finance and Control (Chapel Hill: The University of North Carolina Press, 1955);

Charles W. Turner, Thomas W. Dixon, Jr., and Eugene L. Huddleston, *Chessie's Road* (Alderson, W.Va.: Chesapeake & Ohio Historical Society, 1986).

Archives:

Some material is located at Chesapeake & Ohio Historical Society in Alderson, W.Va.

Chicago & North Western Railway

by H. Roger Grant

University of Akron

During the decades after the Civil War the Chicago & North Western (C&NW) Railway emerged as one of the mighty "west of Chicago" railroads. At the turn of the twentieth century the C&NW system operated 9,336 miles of line and, according to the investment firm of Schmidt & Gallatin, was "remarkable and impregnably entrenched in the territory it occupie[d]." During this period the C&NW absorbed a host of independent roads, including the Fremont, Elkhorn & Missouri Valley; the Sioux City & Pacific; the Milwaukee, Lake Shore & Western; and the Winona & St. Peter. It also acquired stock control over the Omaha Road, the strategic 1,706-mile Chicago, St. Paul, Minneapolis & Omaha. Thus the C&NW and its affiliated properties bound together nine midwestern and Great Plains states and operated "speedways" that linked Chicago with Omaha–the famed "Overland Route"– and the Twin Cities.

Resembling contemporary giant carriers, the Chicago & North Western evolved out of modest beginnings. The corporation came into being on June 6, 1859, with the reorganization of the failed Chicago, St. Paul & Fond du Lac Railroad Company. This property consisted of 177 miles of line between Chicago and Fond du Lac, Wisconsin.

Blessed with honest and dynamic leadership, most notably the creative efforts of William Butler Ogden (1805-1877), the infant Chicago & North Western expanded steadily. A key acquisition occurred in 1864–"the Grand Consolidation"–when the company joined with the Galena & Chicago Union, Chicago's pioneer railroad which was once headed by Ogden. The Galena extended from Chicago to the Mississippi River at Clinton, Iowa, and operated additional lines north and west of Chi-cago. It fit the C&NW well. The combined C&NW totaled 860 miles in 1864, making it one of the largest railroads in the country.

The Chicago & North Western grew dramatically in the 1870s and 1880s. Additional acquisitions and new line construction pushed the road into the treeless prairies of the Great Plains, often preceding settlement. In fact, the company's wholly owned subsidiary, the Dakota Central Railway, which hammered down 185 miles of track between Volga and Pierre in the Dakota Territory in 1880, did much to spur agricultural and town development in the eastern area of what in 1889 became South Dakota. Soon trainloads of wheat rumbled eastward to Minneapolis, Milwaukee, and Chicago, and carloads of merchandise, farm machinery, and lumber rolled westward.

Business on the Dakota Central and other portions of the Chicago & North Western system became brisk, and income rose rather steadily. Gross earnings from freight and passenger traffic increased from $1,915,566 in 1864 to $42,950,000 in 1900. Of course the devastating depressions of the mid 1870s and mid 1890s hurt the road, decreasing earnings and slowing construction. Hard times, nevertheless, did not force the company into the hands of court-appointed receivers. By the turn of the century the C&NW's securities became especially popular with investors; the combination of handsome dividends and overall safety made these shares appropriate for "widows and orphans." Only the Delaware, Lackawanna & Western, "the Road of Anthracite," paid higher returns.

Unquestionably, superb management explains much of the financial prowess of the Chicago & North Western. Marvin Hughitt (1837-1928), who became general manager in 1872 and the road's sixth president in 1887, sought to create a strong and efficient regional carrier. This vision, coupled with a basic conservatism, achieved considerable profitability. Direct ties to the Vanderbilt family and other capitalists provided ample pools of investment dollars.

The financially vibrant Chicago & North Western gave the traveler and shipper the "Best of Everything." In the fall of 1887, for example, the C&NW, Union Pacific, and Southern Pacific launched the Overland Flyer, a train which offered daily first-class passenger service with through cars between Chicago and San Francisco. This run, which became the Overland Limited after November 1896, in time gained a reputation "with the single exception of its eastern counterpart, The Twentieth Century Limited, for being the most radiant and celebrated train in America."

Somewhat less appealing to the public was the Chicago & North Western's involvement in the "Iowa Pool" during the 1870s and early 1880s. To minimize costly competition the company entered into an informal "gentlemen's agreement" with the Chicago, Rock Island & Pacific and the Chicago, Burlington & Quincy during the summer of 1870 to share traffic generated by the opening of the "Omaha Gateway." These three rival roads "shared" business created by completion of the Union Pacific-Central Pacific between Council Bluffs, Iowa, and Sacramento, California. Yet, unlike some competitors, the C&NW never committed blatant acts of "corporate arrogance," and generally the railroad experienced good relations with patrons, even during the Populist revolt of the 1890s.

Labor relations, too, went smoothly. The Chicago & North Western encountered little trouble with its workers during either the bitter unrest of 1877 or the Pullman strike of 1894. Marvin Hughitt lacked the intense, even vicious anti-union feelings of several contemporary presidents, most notably Charles E. Perkins of the Burlington. Hughitt believed strongly that employees should earn a living wage and that compensation should not depend upon any "law" of supply and demand. That is why the C&NW paid trainmen on a mileage basis rather than by the unpopular "classification system" that meant lower pay for many runs. As the paternalistic Hughitt wrote in 1895, "The Chicago & North-Western Ry. must always be a friendly family of adults, who should want to make the Co. the best possible. . . ."

The Chicago & North Western functioned well and demonstrated its dedication to serving its service territory. Wrote a South Dakota newspaper editor in 1898, "The Northwestern [*sic*] is a friend of the public . . . [and] we are fortunate to be able to say that we are a city on the Northwestern [*sic*] line."

References:

Robert J. Casey and W. A. S. Douglas, *Pioneer Railroad: A Story of the Chicago and North Western System* (New York: Whittlesay House, 1948);

W. H. Stennet, comp., *Yesterday and To-day: A History of the Chicago & North Western Railway System* (Chicago: Rand McNally, 1910).

Archives:

The principal papers of the Chicago & North Western are located in the general offices of the Chicago & North Western Transportation Company, Chicago, Illinois, and in the archives of Northern Illinois University, DeKalb, Illinois.

Chicago & Rock Island Railroad

by F. Daniel Larkin

State University College, Oneonta, New York

The decade of the 1850s was a time of feverish railroad building in the United States. It was as though the delay in the beginning of the massive conflict between the states, a delay brought about by the fragile Compromise of 1850, was solely for the benefit of the railroad builders. Prior to 1850 construction had brought the iron roads to the eastern Great Lakes and to the headwaters of the Ohio River. During the ten years that followed, the Mississippi River and beyond became the goal. Although railroad construction continued in the East, it was the Midwest that gained much of the new track. One reason for this was the terrain. Engineers and construction men had little trouble pushing the rails across the relatively level land. Certainly it was easier than building railroads through the Appalachians. A second reason was that by the 1850s bankers and stock promoters had joined the merchants in helping to finance the roads. The influx of eastern capital succeeded where local money failed. Railroads linked the Atlantic Ocean and the Mississippi River.

A perfect example of the railroad building energy of the pre-Civil War decade was the Chicago & Rock Island. Chartered in February 1851 by the Illinois legislature, the approved route was between Chicago and the Mississippi River town of Rock Island. The backers of the road, especially its first president, Judge James Grant of Davenport, Iowa, projected a line across the mighty river into Iowa. But at the time no railroad bridge spanned the river. Construction of a bridge, in addition to building the road into Iowa, called for more funds than the original backers of the Rock Island could raise. This provided an opportunity for a powerful group of New York capitalists to take over the railroad.

The Michigan Southern & Northern Indiana was controlled by New York financiers. It was nearing Chicago from Lake Erie, but lacked a right-of-way into the city and negotiated with the Rock Island for the use of the latter's route into Chicago. In return new capital became available to the Rock Island, and Michigan Southern directors George Bliss, John Stryker, Elisha Litchfield, and John B. Jervis were added to the railroad's board. Grant willingly stepped out of the Rock Island presidency in order to permit the experienced railroad builder Jervis to assume leadership of the company.

Unlike his practice on previous roads, Jervis did not also serve as chief engineer. His brother William took over the chief engineer's job, and the firm of Farnam and Sheffield was hired as sole contractor for the line. The firm's senior partner, Henry Farnam, like Jervis, was a New Yorker who had worked on the Michigan Southern. The energetic Farnam completed the 181 miles of railroad from Chicago to the Mississippi by 1854.

When the Chicago & Rock Island reached the great river, Farnam organized the Mississippi Bridge Company to span the river and link with a railroad that he already was building in Iowa. On April 22, 1856, the structure, the first of the railroad bridges across the Mississippi, was opened to traffic. The Chicago & Rock Island was thus connected to the existing sixty miles of Farnam's Mississippi & Missouri. The Rock Island was on its way across Iowa toward the Missouri River and the "Great American Desert."

Unfortunately the opening of the bridge between Rock Island, Illinois, and Davenport, Iowa, was not without incident. Two weeks after Rock Island trains began passing over the span, the bridge was hit by a steamboat and partially destroyed. Even though the boat, the *Effie Afton,* had caused the fire that burned the bridge supports, the owners of the steamer sued the bridge company on the grounds that the structure was an artificial hazard to river transportation. The bridge company hired Abraham Lincoln to represent them and retained Jervis as their engineering expert. Lincoln put together a successful defense that cleared the way for future railroad spans across the rivers of the West. The bridge was rebuilt and the Rock Island Railroad was able to resume its trans-Mississippi trade.

Henry Farnam succeeded Jervis as the Rock Island president in 1854 and remained in charge of the railroad until 1864. He was followed by John F. Tracy who, with renewed financial backing from New York capitalists, succeeded in finishing the line across Iowa to Council Bluffs on the Missouri. Earlier the track of the Mississippi & Missouri had been added to the main line of the Rock Island. Once at Council Bluffs the Rock Island gained a connection to the Far West via the Union Pacific.

Tracy was a skilled railroad manager whose wise policies placed the Rock Island on firm financial ground. His leadership made it possible for the railroad to continue to pay dividends even during the panic of 1873. But Tracy himself was not as fortunate. He had taken substantial personal loans to purchase stock in the Chicago & North Western Railroad and was a victim of the panic. Tracy's financial collapse forced him to resign as Rock Island president, and Hugh Riddle, the road's general superintendent, took over leadership of the company. Riddle ushered in an era of a conservative approach to the railroad's expansion.

During the remainder of the 1870s the railroad experienced a steady growth of business and a corresponding soundness in its securities. Despite such stability the Rock Island under Riddle followed a building policy limited only to a number of short branch lines in Iowa. In 1879, however, a bout with the Burlington and the North Western over control of the Cedar Rapids Railroad caused the Rock Island to depart from this conservative strategy. The Cedar Rapids ran north from Burlington, Iowa, through Cedar Rapids to southern Minnesota. At about the time that the Rock Island gained control of the disputed property, some of its major stockholders carried off a second coup by buying ownership of the Minneapolis & St. Louis. By using portions of both the newly acquired lines, the Rock Island was in a position to wrest trade between Chicago and the twin cities of Minnesota from the St. Paul and the North Western railroads.

The relatively short burst of buying activity of the early 1880s marked the end of Riddle's administration. In 1882 he was replaced by Richard R. Cable, an ardent expansionist. The new era of building activity of the Rock Island was due, in part, to disappointing returns from a pact with Jay Gould's Union Pacific. What was supposed to offer great business rewards resulted only in a small increase in traffic at the price of rate wars with other Iowa railroads. The Rock Island was forced into new construction to connect with the Southern Pacific and the Rio Grande in order to reduce its reliance on the Union Pacific as its connection to the West. The Rock Island also sought to improve its position in its own area by joining in a pool arrangement with its Iowa competitors. The pool proved unworkable, and the Rock Island withdrew from the agreement after little more than a year.

By the end of the 1880s the Rock Island abandoned its ideas of construction across the Rockies, which had been formulated in another attempt to reduce its reliance on other roads, and also halted its construction activity east of the mountains. The struggle to make dividend payments was largely responsible for the cutbacks. Even so the railroad ended the decade with two and one-half times the track mileage that it possessed in 1880. During the remainder of the nineteenth century, the Rock Island's halt in new construction turned out to be a wise and timely decision. It was a major factor in enabling the company to avoid collapse in the panic of 1893. In fact the Rock Island was so financially secure that is continued to pay dividends throughout the depression-ridden 1890s.

References:

Julius Grodinsky, *Transcontinental Railway Strategy, 1869-1893* (Philadelphia: University of Pennsylvania Press, 1962);

William E. Hayes, *Iron Road to Empire: The History of 100 Years of the Progress of the Rock Island Lines* (New York: Summers-Boardman, 1953);

John B. Jervis, *Report in Relation to the Railroad Bridge over the Mississippi River at Rock Island* (New York: William Bryant, 1857);

Arthur M. Johnson and Barry E. Supple, *Boston Capitalists and the Western Railroads: A Study in the Nineteenth-Century Railroad Investment Process* (Cambridge, Mass.: Harvard University Press, 1967).

Chicago, Burlington & Quincy Railroad

by John Lauritz Larson

Purdue University

The Chicago, Burlington & Quincy (CB&Q) system began as a collection of tiny railroads conceived by local Illinois promoters: the Aurora Branch, chartered in 1849; the Northern Cross (NC), chartered in 1849; the Peoria & Oquawka (P&O), chartered in 1849; and the Central Military Tract (CMT), chartered in 1852. By 1852 only the Aurora boasted any operating track. Farther west the Hannibal & St. Joseph in Missouri, chartered in 1847, and the Burlington & Missouri River (B&MR) in Iowa, chartered in 1852, promised land-grant subsidized railroads beyond the Mississippi.

Money and competition quickly forced these fragments into a network. Already in 1851 the eastern trunk lines were racing around Lake Michigan toward Chicago, and, to secure future traffic for these roads, eastern capitalists were shopping for connections. Michigan Central investors, led by John Murray Forbes of Boston and guided by James F. Joy and John W. Brooks in Detroit, quietly bought interests in all of these local roads. Joy became president of the Aurora, and, through this tiny functioning line, he built the constituent parts of what would become the CB&Q. The CMT linked Aurora with Galesburg in 1854, the P&O connected Galesburg with the Mississippi River at Burlington in 1855, and the NC did the same at Quincy in 1856. The Chicago, Burlington & Quincy was officially born in 1856, when the Aurora, headed by James F. Joy, changed its name and absorbed the CMT. The merger complete, Joy installed local engineer John Van Nortwick as president, turning his own attention to new growth in the West. The panic of 1857, fluctuating income, heavy debts, and aid to the still-independent Northern Cross and Peoria & Oquawka railroads marred the first years of CB&Q operations; but in 1860 the 210-mile CB&Q, with a capital stock of $4.6 million and a funded debt of $5.1 million, generated revenues of $1.5 million, a net income of $63,000, and paid its first 5 percent dividend.

The Civil War was good for business at the CB&Q. Revenues tripled, mileage doubled, and, while inflation drove up operating costs, net income at the end of the war topped $1.5 million–twenty-four times the prewar figure. The Illinois property was secure, but the same could not be said for the trans-Mississippi extensions in Missouri and Iowa. In 1865 James F. Joy again became president of the CB&Q and made expansion in the West his top priority.

From the beginning the Hannibal and the Burlington & Missouri River had competed for the interests of CB&Q investors. Forbes favored the B&MR as the short line toward the Pacific Railroad terminus at Council Bluffs. Joy, on the other hand, thought the Hannibal, completed to the Missouri River in 1859, offered the quickest, if not the most direct, route to a transcontinental interchange. Joy quickly moved to acquire interests in Kansas City area properties that, by late 1869, formed an all-rail link from Chicago to the Union Pacific, including Mississippi and Missouri river bridges. With his own line finally finished in 1869, Charles E. Perkins, Forbes's young cousin and superintendent of the B&MR, grabbed for this western traffic only to find his advantage blunted by pooling arrangements made with the other Chicago roads while Joy's Missouri connections remained free to compete. The directors of the CB&Q became divided over *where* to invest in connections and *whether* to strike for Joy's quick profits or Forbes's long-run developmental gains.

In 1871 Joy's loss of the Hannibal to Jay Gould and his overextension in his other Missouri investments cost him the presidency of the CB&Q. Under the new leadership of James M. Walker, the company focused on building its network of branches in Illinois and Iowa and pushing west into

Nebraska. To meet cutthroat competition, financial stringency, and "Granger" rate regulations, the CB&Q leased the B&MR in 1872 and sought to economize on expenses everywhere. It was while investigating an unexplained hemorrhage of funds in 1875 that Forbes discovered that certain CB&Q directors, led by Joy and Brooks, were paying themselves as contractors out of funds advanced by the CB&Q to the so-called Iowa "River Roads," which now stood bankrupt and unfinished. Reminded of the "Crédit Mobilier" scandal, Forbes pounced on his former allies and purged them from the board. In 1875 the reorganized CB&Q absorbed the B&MR, and the next year Forbes named Robert Harris president of the consolidated company. Two years later he took the presidency himself while he prepared Charles E. Perkins (and the Boston directors) for a new generation of leadership.

When Perkins claimed the CB&Q presidency in 1881 the environment of midwestern railroading had changed dramatically. The company now operated over 2,700 miles of track and carried $20 million worth of passengers and freight. Capital stock and funded debt together equaled almost $100 million. This enormous property paid dividends of 8 percent or better, but it operated in an increasingly crowded field where equally large systems competed on declining margins of profit. In most states laws had been passed to control rates or regulate commercial operations, while cutthroat pricing and competitive construction repeatedly threatened railroad war. Confident in his company's strength and his own strategic sense Perkins opened his administration with a burst of expansion.

The first project on Perkins's list was to build his own line to Denver, which he completed in 1882. In 1883 he repurchased the Hannibal and in 1886 built the Chicago, Burlington & Northern to connect with St. Paul and the lines to the Pacific Northwest. By 1888 branch development in Nebraska, Colorado, Kansas, and elsewhere had increased the system to 4,900 miles, but the value of business increased much more slowly and net income leveled off at about $7.5 million. In this overheated environment Perkins worked and reworked the internal structures and procedures of the CB&Q to economize in every way.

The year 1888 brought the first real setback to Perkins's CB&Q. A prolonged and bitter strike by locomotive engineers and firemen drove up the costs of operations just as regional revenues declined. To compound the problem the Interstate Commerce Act, passed in 1887, prohibited pooling among the Chicago lines, and new regulations in Iowa further limited ratemaking freedom. In 1888 the CB&Q lost money for the first time, but, to stabilize the stock price, the directors paid a 5 percent dividend anyway. From 1888 to 1893 the Burlington struggled to recover in a hostile and saturated market, but the 1893 depression plunged many railroads into receivership and placed interest-paying roads like CB&Q at a new disadvantage.

The CB&Q managed to pay dividends each year from 1893 to 1896, but, to remain viable in the face of huge new reorganized systems of railroads, it faced the choice of either assembling a much larger system or being swallowed up by another. Restrained by his conservative directors from constructing a grand consolidation of western and intermountain lines, Perkins maneuvered instead to sell the CB&Q to the first buyer who offered $200 cash per share. In 1901 E. H. Harriman and James J. Hill battled for control of the CB&Q, with Hill, backed by J. P. Morgan, meeting Perkins's asking price. Hill immediately merged the Burlington with his Great Northern and Northern Pacific lines in the ill-fated Northern Securities Company. When the United States Supreme Court dissolved this holding company in 1904, the Burlington returned to independent status within Hill's northwestern empire. Already fifty years old in 1905 and one of the soundest survivors from the pioneer era, the Burlington continued to develop to be one of the leading railroads of the twentieth century.

References:
John Lavritz Larson, *Bonds of Enterprise: John Murray Forbes and Western Development in America's Railway Age* (Cambridge, Mass.: Harvard University Press, 1984);

Richard C. Overton, *Burlington Route: A History of the Burlington Lines* (New York: Knopf, 1965);

Overton, *Burlington West: A Colonization History of the Burlington Railroad* (Cambridge, Mass.: Harvard University Press, 1941);

Overton, *Perkins/Budd: Railway Statesmen of the Burlington* (Westport, Conn.: Greenwood Press, 1982).

Archives:
Records of the Chicago, Burlington & Quincy are located in the Burlington Railroad Archives of the Newberry Library, Chicago, Illinois. The author is indebted to Richard C. Overton for the use of a manuscript statistical appendix prepared for *Perkins/Budd*.

Chicago, Milwaukee & St. Paul Railway

by R. Milton Clark

Missoula, Montana

The Chicago, Milwaukee & St. Paul (CM&StP) Railway Company, known informally as the "St. Paul," was in 1900 a 6,347-mile regional system serving the midwestern states of Illinois, Iowa, Michigan, Minnesota, Missouri, North Dakota, South Dakota, and Wisconsin. The important gateway cities of Chicago, Minneapolis, St. Paul, Omaha, and Kansas City were linked by main lines, and the railroad had an extensive network of branch lines. The CM&StP operated 837 locomotives and a fleet of 833 passenger and 36,337 freight cars. The St. Paul was in a period of growth and prosperity, having experienced a 77-percent increase in gross ton miles and a 25-percent increase in passenger miles since 1891. The carrier was also earning about three times the amount needed to service its debt and, after paying dividends of 7 percent on preferred stock and 5 percent on common, there was money to reinvest for such projects as improving grades and alignment, laying new passing tracks, and building passenger and freight stations.

The Milwaukee & St. Paul (M&StP) Railway, the original name of the CM&StP, was chartered in Wisconsin on May 5, 1863, as a result of the foreclosure and reorganization of the bankrupt La Crosse & Milwaukee (L&M) Railroad, which had been incorporated in 1852 to build from La Crosse to Milwaukee via Portage and Horicon. The L&M had consolidated in 1854 with the Milwaukee, Fond du Lac & Green Bay, a line chartered in 1853 to build between its namesake points via Iron Ridge. From this beginning thirty-six railroads were consolidated into the CM&StP system by 1900 and included Wisconsin's first line, the Milwaukee & Prairie du Chien, organized as the Milwaukee & Mississippi Rail Road in 1847.

Alexander Mitchell and Sherburn S. Merrill were elected president and general manager, respectively, of the Milwaukee & St. Paul in 1865. Mitchell, a Scottish immigrant and banker, came to

America in 1838 and arrived in Milwaukee in 1839. For twenty years, 1867-1887, he was the dominating force behind the development of the St. Paul. Merrill was a railroad manager of considerable ability who began his career in 1850 as a grading gang foreman with the Milwaukee & Mississippi. Except for a brief absence in 1873 while serving another carrier, he ran the railroad until felled by a stroke in 1884.

During the 1870s and 1880s the St. Paul expanded rapidly, reaching Omaha, Fargo, and Kansas City by means of new construction and acquisition of existing railroads. With these important gateways attained, the railroad began to extend branch lines and further develop the system as the region served grew in population and prosperity, a process that would be repeated again and again over the years. Because of Chicago's increasing prominence as the crossroads of the nation and the opening of a line there from Milwaukee in 1873, the name of the M&StP was officially changed to the Chicago, Milwaukee & St. Paul Railway in 1874.

In 1881 the CM&StP established the Milwaukee Land Company to manage properties not required for operating purposes. The subsidiary came to hold many thousands of acres, including timberlands in the Pacific Northwest, and was an important asset of the railroad in financing the purchase of new locomotives and the rebuilding of freight cars.

During the 1870s powerful industrial dynasties had begun to buy into the St. Paul, and by the middle of the 1880s, the board of directors included Chicago meat packer Philip D. Armour, William Rockefeller of Standard Oil, and Henry Flagler, who represented the interests of financier Charles W. Harkness. With the deaths of Merrill in 1885 and Mitchell in 1887, control of the railroad passed to this new group which remained dominant into the twentieth century.

Because the Missouri River was the western limit of its operation, management became concerned about the St. Paul's ability to compete with other transcontinental railroad systems. In 1896 James J. Hill, builder of the Great Northern (GN) Railway, and financier J. Pierpont Morgan gained control of the Northern Pacific (NP) Railway. Hill and Morgan wanted access to Chicago and were negotiating for control of the Chicago, Burlington & Quincy to attain it. Were this to happen, the CM&StP traffic interchange at Minneapolis, St. Paul with the GN and NP would be adversely affected. The Rockefeller interests wanted to keep the Morgan-Hill combination out of Chicago, a goal shared by Edward H. Harriman of the Union Pacific Railroad. The acquisition of the CB&Q by Morgan and Hill had a profound impact on the St. Paul, which was felt to the end of its corporate existence on December 31, 1985, when it was acquired by the Soo Line Railroad Company.

The Hill Lines amalgamation was a factor in causing the St. Paul to construct the expensive Puget Sound Extension (completed in 1909) in an attempt to gain new long-haul traffic. The cost of this construction contributed to the bankruptcy of the CM&StP in 1925, the largest business failure in the history of the United States at that time. Although it became a "transcontinental" carrier, the St. Paul was never able to make advantageous rates and routes because most industries in the Pacific Northwest were captive to the Hill lines (GN, NP, CB&Q, and SP&S later merged as Burlington Northern [BN]), which would not cooperate with Milwaukee. The Milwaukee objected to the BN merger and successfully delayed it for years. However, the Milwaukee finally agreed to it in 1970 in exchange for certain traffic concessions (new routes and rate-making capability), but by that time it was in such poor shape physically that it was not a competitive

force and it declared bankruptcy again on December 19, 1977, the third time this century.

The Chicago, Milwaukee & St. Paul can be credited with several significant achievements in the nineteenth century. It pioneered the development of grain elevators and the movement of bulk grain by rail. It opened the first rail route between Milwaukee and St. Paul in 1867 and was in the forefront of the railroad industry fight to overturn the so-called Granger laws of the 1870s. It was the first railroad to equip all of its passenger cars for steam heating in 1887 and, in 1888, was the first to operate electrically lighted passenger trains west of Chicago. Of less technological importance, yet in a sense heralding the independent and progressive spirit that characterized the St. Paul, it introduced in 1898 a newly re-equipped passenger train, the Pioneer Limited (operating between Chicago and Minneapolis and one of the earliest named trains in the U.S.), with equipment painted a striking orange which was in marked contrast to the standard drab green livery of the era. The color orange became a CM&StP tradition and was used on many types of equipment and structures for more than eighty years.

References:

Arthur Borak, *Financial History of the Chicago, Milwaukee & St. Paul Railway* (Minneapolis: University of Minnesota, 1929);

John W. Cary, *History of the Chicago, Milwaukee & St. Paul Railway Co. and Representative Employees* (Chicago: Railway Historical, 1901);

Cary, *The Organization and History of the Chicago, Milwaukee & St. Paul Railway Company* (Milwaukee, Wis.: Cramer, 1892);

August Derleth, *The Milwaukee Road: Its First 100 Years* (New York: Creative Age, 1948);

Arthur D. Dubin, *Some Classic Trains* (Milwaukee, Wis.: Kalmbach, 1964);

H. H. Field, *History of the Milwaukee Railroad, 1892-1940* (Chicago: Gunthorp-Warren, 1941);

Herbert William Rice, *Early History of the Chicago, Milwaukee & St. Paul Railway* (Iowa City: University of Iowa, 1938).

Charles Peter Clark

(August 11, 1836-March 21, 1901)

by George M. Jenks

Bucknell University

CAREER: Foreign trade business (1855-1862); Ensign, U. S. Navy (1862-1865); foreign trade business (1866-1870); clerk, Board of Receivers, Boston, Hartford & Erie Railroad (1870-1872); general manager (1873-1879), president, New York & New England Railroad (1879); vice-president, New York, New Haven & Hartford Railroad (1882); president, New York & New England Railroad (1883); receiver, New York & New England Railroad (1883-1885); president, New York & New England (1885-1886); president, New York, New Haven & Hartford Railroad (1887-1899).

Charles Peter Clark had a career at sea in the U. S. Navy and as a foreign trader before beginning his life's work as a railroad official. He has been referred to by Edward C. Kirkland in *Men, Cities, and Transportation* as "one of the most distinguished railroad presidents of New England."

Clark was born in Nashua, New Hampshire, on August 11, 1836, to Peter and Susan (Lord) Clark. His father was a graduate of Yale University, a lawyer, and, at one time, treasurer of the Concord Railroad. Clark's grandfather, Peter Clark, Sr., had also been a railroad man in New Hampshire, where he had been a director on the Concord Railroad, the Boston, Concord & Montreal, the Boston & Lowell, and the Troy & Greenfield. Charles Clark attended Phillips Academy in Andover, Massachusetts, and entered Dartmouth College in 1852, leaving after a year because of poor health. Some accounts of his withdrawal from Dartmouth also allude to religious doubts. He went to sea for a year and returned to Dartmouth in 1854. After another year he left college for good in 1855 and spent time learning the business of the merchant marine. Clark bought a small ship, began a business in foreign trade, and became quite successful. In 1857 he married Caroline Tyler, with whom he would have six children. In 1862 he gave up his Boston-based busi-

Charles Peter Clark

ness to participate in the Civil War as an ensign in the U. S. Navy. He commanded various ships on operations in the Gulf of Mexico, the Mississippi River, and the Tennessee River.

After the war Clark entered the mercantile business in St. Louis, but after a brief time returned to Boston and became a partner in the West India trading firm of the Dana Brothers. He left the firm in 1870 to take his first railroad job as clerk of the Board of Receivers of the Boston, Hartford & Erie Railroad. The corporation was reorganized as the New York & New England Railroad (NY&NE),

and he was appointed general manager in 1873. He was elected president of the line in 1879.

After only a few months Clark resigned and left to spend two years in Europe with his family, enjoying what he considered a well-earned rest. In early 1882, shortly after his return from Europe, he was named second vice-president of the New York, New Haven & Hartford (NYNH&H) Railroad. In 1883 he and Francis L. Higginson solicited proxies and defeated the management of the financially troubled NY&NE. Clark took over the presidency of the NY&NE, although he was reluctant to leave the New York, New Haven & Hartford. The NY&NE soon became insolvent, and Clark was appointed receiver. He quickly made the road solvent again and, in 1885, was re-elected president. He retired from the NY&NE in 1886 after a change in ownership.

In 1887 he was renamed as president of the New York, New Haven & Hartford Railroad and remained in that post until 1899. Clark was an able and vigorous man who appointed capable and talented men to carry out his policies. During Clark's tenure the NYNH&H grew into the most important transportation system in New England. The line expanded into Rhode Island and Massachusetts and built the famous South Station in Boston, then the largest railroad terminal in the world. The NYNH&H was also the first line to use the third-rail system to run trains electrically on tracks designed for steam-driven locomotives. While president, Clark mandated the installation of block signals, heavier rails, crushed rock for ballast, and also eliminated grade crossings. By the time Clark resigned from the presidency in 1899 for health reasons, he had increased the NYNH&H mileage from 265 to 2,047, total assets from nearly $22 million to over $100 million, and capital stock from $4 million to over $15 million.

Clark was one of that group of able New England railroad executives who were educated in private schools and the Ivy League colleges and were born to a certain amount of wealth and status. Although he never graduated from Dartmouth, the college granted him an honorary degree in 1871. He was a Congregationalist and a Republican and was regarded as an honest, able, and intelligent man. Although he had considered both the law and the ministry as careers, Clark saw the railroad as a consummate challenge. In an 1899 letter to G. A. Warburton, Clark said of railroad men: "But there are so many kinds of service that special qualifications are requisite for each department, although honesty, without adjective or adverb, and greater or lesser intelligence, must be everywhere at the foundation." After retirement he was a delegate to the 1900 International Railway Congress in Paris. Clark continued to serve as a board member of the Boston Terminal Company, which oversaw the operations of the South Station, and he was also elected to the board of the Shipany, Litchfield & Northern Railroad. He died in Nice, France, on March 21, 1901.

Publication:

Charles P. Clark, Receiver, *Henry A. Brassey vs. New York and New England Railroad Co. et als. in the Circuit Court of the United States . . . Receivership Proceedings* (Boston: Cashman, Keating, 1884).

References:

Thomas C. Cochran, *Railroad Leaders, 1845-1890* (Cambridge, Mass.: Harvard University Press, 1953);

Edward Chase Kirkland, *Men, Cities, and Transportation* (Cambridge, Mass.: Harvard University Press, 1948);

John L. Weller, *The New Haven Railroad* (New York: Hastings House, 1969).

Archives:

Material concerning Charles Peter Clark is located in the Records of the New York, New Haven & Hartford Railroad in the Baker Library of the Harvard Graduate School of Business Administration, Boston, Massachusetts; in the Clark Papers of the G. W. Blunt Library at the Mystic Seaport Museum, Mystic, Connecticut; in the New York, New Haven & Hartford ledgers at the Wilton Historical Society, Wilton, Connecticut; and at the Railroad Collection of the New Haven Colony Historical Society, New Haven, Connecticut.

Lorenzo S. Coffin

(April 9, 1823–January 17, 1915)

by Roger B. Natte

Iowa Central Community College

CAREER: Farmer (1854-1915); land agent, Des Moines River Navigation Company and the Des Moines & Fort Dodge Railroad (1870s); farm editor, *Fort Dodge Messenger* (1872-1880?); Grange agent (1873-1877); immigration agent, Iowa State Immigration Board (1873-1875); president, Iowa Farmers' Alliance (1880-1883); director, Iowa State Agricultural Society (1880-1886); commissioner, Iowa Railroad Commission (1883-1885); lobbyist for railroad safety legislation (1889-1893).

Lorenzo Stephen Coffin, farmer, farm leader, humanitarian, and promoter of railroad safety legislation, was born on April 9, 1823 in Alton, New Hampshire, and died near Fort Dodge, Iowa, on January 17, 1915. He was the son of Stephen Coffin, a Baptist minister and farmer.

Little is known of Coffin's parents or of his childhood except that his early education was limited to what he could receive at home. In 1835 his family moved from Alton to Wolfsboro, New Hampshire, where Coffin had the opportunity to receive his first formal education at Wolfsboro Academy, an opportunity which was interrupted two years later by the death of his mother. At fourteen Coffin returned home to help on the farm and remained there until he was twenty-one.

Coffin's early life had a decided impact on the development of his later ideas and attitudes: the Yankee emphasis on hard work and thrift was to help him to succeed and prosper in the frontier economy of Iowa; the religious atmosphere of a clergyman's home created an adult whose future action was dictated by Christian ideals; and his thorough, if limited, education gave him an abiding faith in the value of education.

In 1844 Coffin left his father's farm and, although limited in his finances, managed to work his way through one year of a school in Boston. He then traveled to Oberlin Collegiate Institute, now

Lorenzo S. Coffin

Oberlin College, in Ohio where he entered the preparatory department with the intention of becoming a teacher. At this time Oberlin was one of the most progressive schools in the nation; not only was it one of the first colleges to open its doors to women but, much more important to Coffin's future, its faculty and students were actively involved in the spirit of reform which was so strong in the pre-Civil War period. Coffin was exposed to many of the major reform causes, especially prohibition, woman's rights, and abolition, all of which were to be key elements in his later humanitarian efforts. Coffin reached two other milestones at Oberlin, becoming a preacher and marrying Cynthia T. Curtis, a fellow student at the college.

The financial burden of married life forced the couple to terminate their formal education after a year and a half in favor of seeking employment. From Oberlin they moved to Chester, Ohio, where they were both hired as teachers in the Geauga Seminary, a Freewill Baptist institution. Among their students at the seminary was future president James A. Garfield.

After one year the failing health of Mrs. Coffin induced the couple to give up teaching, and in the winter of 1854 Coffin went west to survey the opportunities in north central Iowa, an area just opening for settlement. Impressed with the possibilities, Coffin borrowed $500 from a brother, returned to Iowa the next year with his wife, and purchased 160 acres.

Initially, the new area was not kind to Coffin; he experienced all the difficulties generally associated with the frontier. The change of climate did not bring the anticipated relief for his wife and in 1856 she died. Prairie fires swept over his farm, destroying his improvements, his crops, and some of his livestock. Later his crops were destroyed by grasshoppers, and in 1857 the area felt the full brunt of the nationwide depression. For seventeen years Coffin was to live in a small log cabin not much different from those of his less educated neighbors.

In 1857 Coffin returned east to marry Mary Chase of Orleans County, New York, returning to Iowa after the wedding. While working his farm, Coffin did not lessen his interests in religion and preaching. Even though he was never associated with any particular denomination, Coffin served as a circuit rider in the area from 1859 to 1876 and filled vacant pulpits on a temporary basis for the rest of his life.

Coffin also held a lingering interest in government and politics. In 1861 he was elected to two county offices which, surprisingly, were the only elected offices he was to occupy. When his chances for popular election were the greatest, he was too deeply involved in his reform causes to be interested. When he did become interested, he was too old to be considered seriously by a major party.

Ironically, Coffin never completed his terms in office, as the Civil War interrupted them. Once the war began, Coffin, moved by the abolitionist zeal which he had acquired while at Oberlin, rushed to the colors and was assigned to the Iowa 32nd Infantry on the Missouri-Arkansas border. His abilities were readily recognized, and he moved up rapidly in the ranks. He advanced from private to sergeant and was later promoted to regimental chaplain, receiving special recognition for his bravery and leadership. It appears, however, that his dedication to his position as chaplain and his interest in the welfare of the men overrode his commitment as a soldier. While serving as chaplain, he frequently searched the area for reading material for the men and luxury items for the hospital. On one of his forays he was declared absent without leave and dismissed from the service.

The discharge apparently had little practical effect upon Coffin's future. He was held in as high regard as any returning veteran and was elected as an officer of the county Soldier's Union. Nevertheless, the discharge was a personal burden which was not lifted until Congress passed legislation in 1891 that led to President Benjamin Harrison's issuance of an honorable discharge.

On his return to Iowa Coffin resumed his farming. His farm, which he called Willowedge, became one of the showplaces of Iowa and he achieved great success in raising stock. Instrumental in introducing purebred varieties of hogs, horses, sheep and cattle into the state, Coffin had one of the finest herds of blooded cattle in Iowa. He wrote extensively about stock raising and was recognized for his efforts by being elected president of the Iowa Breeders Association. He experimented with cheese and butter making and attempted to establish a butter and cheese factory as a method of increasing the income of local farmers. In 1891 Coffin was named the Iowa representative to the National Dairy and Food Commission and was chosen that same year to serve as the treasurer of the organization, enabling him to travel extensively throughout the nation.

Coffin was deeply involved in efforts to promote agriculture. In 1872 he became one of Iowa's first farm editors for a general newspaper, *The Fort Dodge Messenger,* and used his column to help educate his fellow farmers. When the state organized farm institutes, Coffin was recruited to travel around the state lecturing on agricultural matters. In the post-Civil War period, when farmers began to organize politically, Coffin was to exercise considerable influence, first in the local and state agricultural societies, and later in the Grange and Farmers' Alliance movements, holding leadership positions in all of them. A promoter of the cooperative movement, he helped organize cooperative creameries, a farmers' mutual insurance company, a farmers' consumer cooperative, of which he was to serve as the agent, and a farmer-owned barbed wire factory.

When the Farmers' Alliance was organized in Iowa in the 1880s, Coffin was elected its first president and, as such, became a key figure in the Farmers Protective Association, a regional organization established to fight monopolies in the industries on which the farmers depended.

Coffin's interests broadened when the state, in an attempt to attract settlers and to encourage economic growth, established an immigration board in 1870 and chose Coffin as one of the recruiting agents. His trips to the East opened his eyes to new economic possibilities and made him increasingly a proponent of industrialization as the key to progress. In his reports and letters he urged Iowans to adopt policies which would attract manufacturers. Even more important was the impact of the trips on his humanitarian spirit and ideas. For the first time his writings began to show an interest in the unfortunate: homes for the elderly, an orphanage, free schools, and low-cost housing for worthy working women.

In the 1870s Coffin's personal financial interests were extended beyond farming when he became a land agent for the Des Moines River Improvement Company and later the Des Moines & Fort Dodge Railroad. It was in these positions that Coffin first became acquainted with railroads, seeing the safety problems which the railroad employees faced and which gave impetus to his crusade for railroad safety laws. It was for this crusade to make railroads safer that he was to receive his greatest recognition.

Railroading was, in the postwar period, one of the nation's most hazardous occupations. The loss of life and limb on the railroads during the period was appalling. In 1881 over 30,000 men were either killed or maimed in rail accidents, most of which were due to two types of primitive equipment: the pin and link coupler and the handbrake. To make matters worse, there were no railroad liability laws and an injured worker usually faced release from his job with no compensation. By the 1880s these conditions were no longer necessary since technological improvements, although not yet perfected, had been made in both systems. Implementation was slowed largely because of lack of interest by the railroads.

Coffin was brought face to face with the problem in 1874 when he personally saw a brakeman lose several fingers while switching cars. Subsequent investigation indicated to Coffin the frequency of this type of occurrence and he soon became the self-proclaimed spokesman for the workers' interests. His crusade led to his appointment in 1883 to the Iowa Railroad Commission. His first goal was to arouse the public to the extent of the problem. He wrote thousands of letters, including one to every religious and family newspaper in the country. He took to the speaker's platform and traveled at his own expense to all parts of the nation to speak to any group which would hear him. He attended and spoke at the National Convention of Master Car Builders and met with the Railroad Master Mechanics at their annual convention for six consecutive years. He spoke to the national conventions of the railroad brotherhoods and frequently attended state and regional meetings. He also took his cause to the pulpits, and, whenever there was a major meeting of any religious organization, he sought a place on the program. Finally, he went directly to the railroad management.

Coffin's initial success came in 1885 when the Master Car Builders and the Master Mechanics Association agreed to encourage the development of a practical air brake, test its effectiveness, and, if successful, recommend its adoption by the railroads. The tests were run and in 1887 the two groups recommended the adoption of both the Westinghouse air brake and the Janney automatic coupler.

Installation of the new devices did not take place immediately. Few railroads were willing to incur the expense of adopting the new devices so Coffin continued his crusade by promoting the passage of state and federal mandatory safety appliance acts. For four years, from 1889 to 1893, Coffin virtually was a full-time lobbyist of Congress. Railroads were either apathetic or opposed to a mandatory bill. Coffin was aided in his efforts when he succeeded, through the intervention of influential friends, in gaining the ear of President Harrison, who included a call for the passage of such an act in his inaugural address and his subsequent State of the Union address. The bill requiring air brakes and automatic couplers was finally passed and signed into law in March 1893. Coffin's almost 20-year campaign was ended.

Although the railroads did manage to get extensions on the date that the requirements would go into effect, the impact of the law was dramatic. The accident rate for employees was reduced by 60 percent, and the passenger injury rate from coupling and braking accidents was reduced to near zero. In addition the law proved to be financially advantageous to the railroads themselves since the new devices reduced the wear and tear on the equipment.

Coffin's railroad reforms did not stop with the safety laws. He pushed for, but failed to achieve, a Sunday no-work law for railroad employees. He started and supported a Railroad Temperance Association, its white button campaign financed almost entirely by himself. Through his efforts a railroadmen's retirement home was established in 1890 at Highland Park, Illinois, and he served as its president until his death in 1915. Finally, he worked to create YMCAs for railroad men as an acceptable social and recreational alternative to the saloons and street life generally available to the railroader away from home.

The focus of Coffin's reform work extended beyond the railroads. For example, the Railroad Temperance Movement was simply part of his general temperance work, which he pursued on both the local and state levels. In 1893 he was offered the Prohibition Party's nomination for governor but rejected it out of loyalty to the Republican Party. In 1907, after being elected president of the Iowa Anti-Saloon League in 1903, he accepted the Prohibition Party's nomination to be governor.

In the 1890s Coffin, inspired by the work of Maude Ballington Booth, daughter-in-law of the founder of the Salvation Army, became interested in the problems of ex-convicts. This was a time in which the state did little for the released convict; parole was in its experimental stage and the recidivism rate was very high. In 1901 Coffin organized the Iowa Benevolent Association which intended to assist newly released convicts to readjust to life outside prison walls. In accordance with this purpose, Coffin contributed land and money for the construction of Hope Hall. The Hall, which would accommodate forty men, served as a halfway house where a man released from a prison could learn a useful occupation and get a new start. The home was one of three established in the United States and was administered by the Prison Volunteer League of which Mrs. Booth was the head. Reform of the state prison system, with increased rehabilitation programs, lessened the need for such a home, and in 1910 it was reorganized under the direction of the Women's Christian Temperance Union as a home for unwed mothers.

Coffin's last philanthropic project was his involvement in the Progressive Movement's "rural life" or "back to the farm" program. He sought to establish a rural YMCA program and an agricultural school for girls, both of which he hoped would help to instill Christian and rural values. Nothing resulted from either of these proposals.

With Coffin's interests and involvements, it was virtually impossible to escape some ties with political parties. Except for the last ten years of his life, Coffin, like most Iowans of the period, was a staunch Republican. In each election, even after the turn of the century, he was an ardent campaigner for the party and a much-sought-after political speaker, traveling across the state in the party's service. In spite of being mentioned frequently for major political office, and enjoying considerable popular support, Coffin showed little interest in running until his reform crusade was completed. When he did show an interest in public office, he was over seventy years old, an age which prevented him from being seriously considered. In 1907 the Prohibition Party did nominate Coffin for governor, and the following year he was the nominee of the United Christian Party for vice-president. The last was more symbolic than serious and no one, including Coffin, saw it as anything other than an honor for his past efforts.

Coffin's last years were marked by mental decline. He became unable to handle his own personal and financial affairs and became a target for those who wished to take advantage of his humanitarian spirit. Involved in a third marriage, a subsequent divorce, and several sensational lawsuits, he was finally placed under guardianship. He passed away at his home near Fort Dodge on January 17, 1915, at the age of ninety-two.

Lorenzo Coffin was a product of the nineteenth century, a true microcosm of his age. In his life can be seen the movements and attitudes of that period; the settlement of the frontier, pre-Civil War reform, the war itself, industrialization, the agrarian protest movement, and American's problems coming to grip with a new industrial society. Coffin reflected the traditional American belief in the individual and the individual's ability to make a difference. A self-made man who acquired a relatively modest fortune in farming and land speculation, he took on the cause first of the farmer and then of the railroader against the forces of modern industrial society. He then turned to the less fortunate members of society, the unwed mother and the convict, and sought to open to them America's opportunities. He acted, not as a radical, but within the traditional framework of democratic change and achieved a surprising amount of success.

Publication:

Lorenzo S. Coffin, "Safety Appliances on the Railroads,"

Annals of Iowa (January 1903): 561-582.

References:

"Justice to Mr. Coffin," *Annals of Iowa* (January 1902): 308-310;

"Lorenzo Coffin, Farmer," *Palimpsest* (October 1941): 289-292;

"Mr. Coffin's Great Reforms," *Annals of Iowa* (January 1903): 626-629.

Jay Cooke

(August 10, 1821-February 16, 1905)

by Robert L. Frey

Wilmington College of Ohio

CAREER: Clerk, Hubbard & Lester, Sandusky, Ohio (1835-1836); clerk, Seymour & Bool, St. Louis, Missouri (1836-1837); clerk and office manager, Washington Packet Line, Philadelphia, Pennsylvania (1838); clerk, Congress Hall Hotel, Philadelphia (1838); clerk, E. W. Clark & Company, Philadelphia (1839-1842); partner, E. W. Clark & Company (1842-1858); managing partner, Jay Cooke & Company (1861-1873).

Jay Cooke was born on August 10, 1821, in a frontier town which is now Sandusky, Ohio. He was one of the first children born in this fledgling town on the banks of Lake Erie. His father, Eleutheros, was a prominent lawyer, businessman, and politician and descended from a family whose presence in America goes back to Salem, Massachusetts, in 1638. Later members of the family moved west and Eleutheros finally settled in the Western Reserve where Jay Cooke was born. Jay's mother, Martha Carswell, was the daughter of a Revolutionary War veteran who had been imprisoned in Canada during the war.

Eleutheros Cooke's difficult first name had been the source of some confusion about him, including causing him to lose an election. He did not want his sons to suffer the same confusion. Jay Cooke's older brother was named Pitt, after the English statesman William Pitt, and Jay was named after the first chief justice John Jay, whom Eleutheros admired. Jay Cooke, his two brothers, and his two sisters grew up in a substantial stone

Jay Cooke

house in Sandusky. Years later, Cooke recalled his happy childhood and recounted stories of his youth in diaries and letters now housed in the Historical Society of Pennsylvania.

In his fourteenth year young Jay Cooke began to seek his fortune. He was hired by a Mr. Hubbard in 1835 to clerk in his Sandusky dry-goods and grocery store and, within a year, was being paid at the rate of $250 a year. This salary was surpassed handily by the company of Seymour & Bool, also dry-goods merchants, who offered him $600 a year in 1836 to come to St. Louis and clerk for them. Cooke's memoirs claim the primary reason for this offer was Mr. Seymour's romantic interest in one of Cooke's cousins. Cooke did his best to fulfill the role of a young gentleman in St. Louis, attending dancing classes and taking French lessons, but he had little respect for the frontier citizens of the city: "There is but few respectable persons in St. Louis. It is dangerous for a person to go out after dark, for persons are often knocked down at the corners of streets and robbed and frequently killed." No such fate befell him, fortunately, but when the panic of 1837 wiped out his employer, Cooke returned to Sandusky.

William C. Moorhead, the husband of Cooke's older sister Sarah, offered him a position with his new Washington Packet Line canal boat company in Philadelphia. Accepting the job in 1838, Cooke handled the booking of passengers, the newspaper advertising, and a wide range of secretarial duties. Canal competition was stiff, however, and the packet line failed. After working for a short time as a hotel clerk, Cooke returned for the second time to Sandusky to ponder his future career. Few seventeen-year-old men had such a varied geographical and vocational experience as had Jay Cooke. Despite lacking a job, Cooke appeared satisfied with the course of his career to that point.

An offer was not long in coming. While in Philadelphia, Jay Cooke had encountered many young businessmen and had impressed most of them with his efficiency, friendliness, and competence. The banking firm of E. W. Clark & Company offered him a position in 1839, and Cooke readily accepted. He developed his skills rapidly, writing to his older brother at one point, "I am getting to be a good judge of bank notes, can tell counterfeits at sight, and know all or nearly all the broken banks in the United States of America." In the unstable banking world of the 1840s, a person with these abilities was extremely valuable. By the age of twenty-one Cooke was a full partner in the banking house which expanded rapidly during the 1840s, opening houses in St. Louis, New Orleans, and New York. In addition to being a partner in the banking house, he also wrote a regular financial column in

the *Philadelphia Inquirer*—a newspaper that supported him editorially all of his life.

At this stage of his burgeoning career, Jay Cooke met the young woman who was to become his wife. Dorothea Elizabeth Allen was the sister of the president of Allegheny College in Pennsylvania, and Cooke met her while visiting his brother Henry, who was a student at the college. When Miss Allen returned home to Baltimore, Cooke regularly traveled to visit her. These visits were interrupted, however, when she moved to Lexington, Kentucky, with her brother, who had taken a position with Transylvania University. Despite the separation, their relationship continued, and on August 21, 1844, Jay and Libby (as he called her) were married by Dr. Henry S. Bascom, president of Transylvania University. Cooke, his bride, and his brothers, Henry, who graduated from Transylvania about the time of Jay's wedding, and Pitt, who had been married a few weeks earlier, all traveled from Lexington to Sandusky for a visit after the wedding. After a short time in Sandusky, Cooke and his wife returned to Philadelphia, where he once again plunged into the banking business.

E. W. Clark & Company was heavily involved in the development of many of the early railroads in the East. The company was also involved in the marketing of bonds during the Mexican War. Both of these ventures gave Cooke valuable experience which he used later in his career. But the panic of 1857, coming on the heels of the death of the founder of E. W. Clark & Company, brought the house to its knees. During this period of difficulty, which was compounded by internal conflicts within the Clark family, Jay Cooke acted as the mediator. Cooke retained the trust of the Clark family and remained neutral in the conflict. When the company was eventually reorganized as two separate houses in 1858, Cooke was asked to remain with both of the firms, but he refused.

Jay Cooke spent the next three years in partial retirement. Hunting and fishing expeditions were interspersed with efforts to oversee some of the Clark investments, including the Vermont Central Railroad and the Franklin Railroad, which eventually became a part of the Western Maryland. Cooke's desire to reenter the banking business, however, led to the founding of Jay Cooke & Company in 1861. He was a two-thirds partner, and his brother-in-law William G. Moorhead was a one-third partner. Cooke remained the managing partner throughout the history of the company. It seemed an inauspicious time to open a banking firm. With the election of Lincoln, the secession movement, and the Civil War looming, the future seemed uncertain at best.

But the unsettled financial conditions of the country in 1861 and the challenges of the Civil War provided an opportunity for Jay Cooke & Company. Cooke's first step in attaining fame and fortune was the successful marketing of Pennsylvania's $3 million bond issue. Because the state was $40 million in debt, the banking community thought it impossible to sell the bonds at par value as the state legislature required. An amendment in the legislature to allow sale of the bond issue at less than par was found to be illegal by the state supreme court on the suggestion of Jay Cooke, who was convinced that he could market the bonds at par on patriotic pride alone. Sending agents to all parts of the state and carefully drafting circulars, pamphlets, and posters emphasizing the patriotic need for the successful subscription of the issue, Cooke managed to oversubscribe the issue in less than a month. News of this effort was carefully disseminated by Cooke to influential people throughout the North, to Jefferson Davis in the Confederacy, and to newspapers in England. His achievements did not go unnoticed.

With the inauguration of Abraham Lincoln came a new secretary of the treasury, Salmon P. Chase, former governor of Ohio and friend of Henry D. Cooke, Jay's brother and a journalist and editor. The new secretary faced a treasury with no reserves at the same time that a tremendous amount of money was needed to finance the war. Chase, acting on advice from financiers like Jay Cooke, decided to raise the money by borrowing from the people in a variety of bond issues, by increasing direct taxes, and by instituting a special direct tax—the income tax. Cooke & Company became deeply involved in the bond sales.

An early issue of twenty-year bonds, or "81s" as they were called because of their 1881 maturity date, were sold at approximately an 8 percent discount, yielding about ninety-two cents on the dollar. These were followed by the "7-30s," sold at par. The "7-30s" were twenty-year convertible bonds yielding 7.3 percent interest per year and payable in gold. Cooke & Company was involved in the sale of both issues but was not the exclusive agent for either. Early in 1862 the famous "5-20s"

Portrait of Cooke by William M. Chase

were authorized to the amount of $500 million. Less desirable than either of the earlier issues, these bonds yielded only 6 percent and the principal could be repaid any time between five and twenty years (thus the name "5-20") at the pleasure of the government. Efforts to dispose of this bond issue were remarkably unsuccessful for a full year after their authorization because of the lack of adequate resources in the New York, Philadelphia, and Boston banks. The only solution appeared to be popularizing the loan and attempting to sell it directly to a wide range of citizens. Unfortunately, the U.S. Treasury Department was not organized for such an effort. Jay Cooke & Company was, and it became the primary agent for the disposition of the bond issue. Cooke organized 2,500 agents to sell the bonds all over the North. The keystone of Cooke's technique was advertising: newspapers, pamphlets, and circulars. Despite the fact that Secretary Chase allowed little money for advertising and allowed an extremely low sales commission, Cooke and his associates threw their entire energies into the loan. Because they emphasized patriotism, Cooke and his agents were remarkably successful at selling the issue. The "5-20s" were eventually oversubscribed when the drive ended in January of 1864. While Cooke and his people congratulated themselves, jealous competitors and political opponents began to criticize the government for relying on a private banking house. They also criticized Cooke for the perceived fortune he made. Actually, Cooke's commission was never more than three-eighths of one percent, and Cooke shared two-thirds of this commission with the agents who sold the bonds. Cooke eventually reported to Secretary Chase that his net profit from the sale of the "5-20s" was slightly over $220,000, or somewhat less than one-twentieth of one percent.

Cooke was also instrumental in gaining support for the development of a national banking association to voluntarily regulate the confusing American money supply. He was also involved, to some degree, in the less-than-successful marketing of the "10-40" loan and in a totally unsuccessful attempt to discourage the government from issuing additional greenbacks. Nonetheless, he helped to support the greenback in 1863 by persuading the government to sell U.S. gold in the face of rapidly escalating gold prices that threatened to make the greenbacks virtually worthless. There is little doubt that Jay Cooke deserved his title as "the financier of the Civil War," especially when Chase was secretary of the treasury. In 1864, however, Chase resigned and was replaced by William Pitt Fessenden of Maine.

Although his relationship with Cooke was not as close as Chase's, Fessenden, too, came to rely on Cooke's advice. The cost of the war was tremendous, and by mid 1864, when Fessenden became secretary, the national debt stood at $1.7 billion, and the treasury needed almost $100 million to meet the budgeted expenditures for the remainder of the year. Earlier bond issues, such as the "81s" and the "5-20s," were periodically reauthorized and marketed. Once again, Jay Cooke came to the aid of the North by agreeing to sell more "5-20s" at a time when bond sales were depressed. Cooke's agents turned to their time-tested methods to publicize and sell the loans. The successful outcome of the operation was never in doubt. Shortly thereafter, Cooke & Company also became agents for the languishing "7-30" loan. At the time only $133 million worth of these bonds had been sold, primarily by the national banks. In less than six months,

Cooke and his organization sold $830 million worth of them.

Building on the techniques used in the 1863 distribution of the "5-20s," Cooke brought the mass marketing of bonds to a high point not reached again until World War I. Journalists like Horace Greeley and Whitlaw Reid were enlisted to spread the praises of the "7-30s." Many of the same problems that plagued the "5-20" sales still existed. The government could not keep up with the demand for bonds, and frequently months passed before Cooke received enough bonds for distribution. Cooke's commission varied from one-quarter to three-quarters of one percent, but the tremendous cost of the 1864 bond campaigns far exceeded that of the 1863 effort. When the war ended and Lincoln's assassination occurred, Cooke ordered government bonds already on the market to be bought up in order to maintain the stability of the nation's credit. In his memoirs Cooke considers this step, in which he used his own financial resources, to be the most important service he gave his country.

As the nation recovered from Lincoln's assassination, the sale of bonds increased in a dramatic and unexpected fashion. Goals were reached well ahead of schedule, and many people in government and finance were amazed by the success of Cooke's efforts. Some of Cooke's methods, however, were questionable. He was frequently able to gain favorable editorial support in newspapers by giving the editor a 60-day option on as much as $50,000 of government bonds. If the option was utilized, the purchaser received the profit minus the prorated interest. The option could be renewed, and Cooke usually used the less salable "10-40s" for this purpose. Clergymen were encouraged to advise their parishioners to buy bonds. Even the Quakers were encouraged to buy bonds by the unfulfillable promise that their money would go directly to the support of hospitals and the wounded rather than be used to buy weapons and ammunition. Night clerks were available to receive the subscriptions of working people who could not adhere to bankers' hours. As soon as Southern areas were secured militarily, Cooke's agents descended on the people with the intent to play on any fears that their loyalty might be questioned by encouraging them to buy bonds. As troops were mustered out of the military, Cooke's agents were there to offer safe financial investments for each soldier's hard-earned pay. There is no doubt that Cooke's agents used high-pressure tactics.

As peacetime conditions returned, the activity in bond sales diminished. Washington also declined as a banking center, and Jay Cooke opened a New York branch of his company. Although this strained some of Cooke's New York contacts, the new branch became an important part of Cooke's empire and turned in an unexpectedly good first year. Other groups approached Cooke frequently to market bonds or to invest in the projects. He was reluctant to take part in these enterprises without careful investigations of their financial potential. Although railroads were his favorite investments, he involved himself in only a small number of them, primarily because he liked to have total control over the projects he joined. Because of pressure from some of his partners, as well as outsiders, Jay Cooke eventually became interested in the upper Midwest. His interest centered on the possibility of a rail line from Duluth, Minnesota, to the Pacific Ocean. He was asked to consider marketing the $100 million in bonds of the Northern Pacific (NP) Railroad–the second land-grant railroad and a project languishing since 1864. At first he resisted but soon began to purchase extensive acreage in northeastern Minnesota.

After Grant's election to the presidency in 1868, it was widely rumored that Cooke would be the next secretary of the treasury. When this appointment did not materialize, Cooke apparently decided to support the Northern Pacific venture and undertook extensive research. Parties composed of engineers and friends of Cooke traveled over many miles of the proposed NP route. Construction costs of the Union Pacific were taken into consideration, and all available information was gathered before a final decision was made. Journalists in the exploration parties returned with descriptions of the Northwest that were so overstated as to eventually lead to the area being derisively called "Jay Cooke's banana belt." Cooke, however, gave closest attention to the report of engineer W. Milnor Roberts. Roberts thought it possible to build the road from Duluth to the Pacific in three years at a cost of less than $100 million. Despite Roberts's widespread reputation as a cautious engineer, this estimate proved to be far off the mark.

On January 1, 1870, an agreement was signed linking Jay Cooke & Company to the Northern Pacific. Cooke received one-half ownership in the en-

Jay Cooke at eighty

terprise, eventually expanded this to thirteen twenty-fourths, and became the sole fiscal agent of the company. Efforts to raise an initial amount of $5.6 million to begin construction of the railroad proved deceptively easy. Cooke and his agents called on such prominent people as Henry Ward Beecher and Horace Greeley to invest in the enterprise and to encourage others to do so. In fact, there was a tremendous scramble for these initial shares among a wide range of people. On February 15, 1870, work on the NP's main line began near Duluth.

On January 1, 1871, after only about sixteen miles of track had been completed, Cooke had to market $100 million worth of NP bonds to continue construction of the railroad. These bonds, payable in gold, were to be sold at par and were to bear 7.3 percent interest per year. Certain banking houses were assigned as regional agents, but traveling agents, similar to the system Cooke used during the Civil War, were also employed. All of these agents were loaded with numerous pamphlets, circulars, maps, posters, and placards. Even traveling lecturers, frequently with impressive academic credentials, were used. Many of the pamphlets were in Jay Cooke's favored question-and-answer format. Although the quality of these publications was outstanding for their day, the public response to the bond-marketing effort was disappointing. Diligent efforts had to be made to discourage agents from selling the bonds at a discount. Efforts to increase the number of agents and the amount of advertising did not bring an appreciable increase in sales, but it did tremendously increase the cost of marketing the bonds. Overseas efforts to sell bonds were frustrated at one juncture after another, partially because most of Jay Cooke's minority partners in the London and Paris offices were opposed to his involvement with the NP.

Cooke never tolerated what he perceived to be dishonesty. As rumors of corruption in the construction of the NP reached him, he acted quickly. W. Milnor Roberts was hired as chief engineer to replace the aging Edwin Johnson. By December 1871 the line had been pushed to the Red River in North Dakota, 238 miles from Duluth. About twenty-five miles of the West Coast line, located slightly north of Portland, Oregon, had also been completed.

One of the most attractive aspects of the NP was its potential in attracting immigrants to settle along its new line. To this end, Cooke hired Henry Villard, a young German journalist, to help stimulate German immigration, but he attempted to channel Cooke's interest to the economically depressed Scandinavian countries instead. Settlement was delayed, however, because of the difficulty in securing title to the government land. NP president J. Gregory Smith, whom Cooke disliked and distrusted, played a large part in the delay by failing to request the government to inspect the railroad. The inspection was a necessary step in the process of transferring the grant land from the government to the NP. Since the first transfers did not occur until late 1872, settlement on railroad land could not begin until early 1873. Frederick Billings oversaw the Land Department and was heavily involved in the settlement program.

In 1872 Cooke finally succeeded in ridding the Northern Pacific of J. Gregory Smith. Cooke had been irritated with him for some time because he remained in Vermont and managed the NP through people Cooke perceived to be inept. Gen. George W. Cass, closely allied with the Pennsylvania Railroad, became president. The management of the NP now took a more Pennsylvania orientation rather than a New England one; and Cass's first effort was to reduce as many unnecessary costs as possible, an effort which proved to be a case of too little, too late.

In mid 1873 the NP main line reached the Missouri River town site of Bismarck, named after the German chancellor. Missouri River steamboats could now link up with the NP to improve the movement of people and cargo through the upper Midwest. Cooke also attempted to expand the NP influence and business potential by acquisition. In November 1870 controlling interest was purchased in the St. Paul & Pacific Railroad, which was extended to Brainerd on the NP main line. The Lake Superior & Mississippi Railroad between St. Paul and Duluth, Cooke's first rail acquisition in the area, also was leased to the NP in 1872 because of its failure to develop the traffic and income originally expected.

By late 1872, however, financial problems had already begun to mount. Since the sale of Northern Pacific bonds had been slow while the costs of construction were high, Cooke regularly advanced cash to the NP. Eventually payments to NP employees were delayed. The bonds of the St. Paul & Pacific had been selling at less than par, which further depressed sales of NP bonds. Jay Cooke continued to advance additional funds from his own house to cover the shortfalls in NP financing–a practice viewed with alarm by his partners. Cooke's long line of successful ventures stretching back to 1861 perhaps convinced him that he would be able to overcome the financial drain caused by the NP. Public confidence, however, was definitely on the decline, not only in Minnesota but also in Chicago, Philadelphia, New York, and London. Moreover, the entire national situation was not encouraging. Serious fires in Chicago and Boston, unenlightened federal money management, and scandals like the Crédit Mobilier on the Union Pacific created uncertainty and caution among investors. Sales of NP bonds continued to decrease. Nonetheless, Jay Cooke attempted to put together a syndicate to purchase the NP 7.3 percent bonds and give the public the impression that the company was sound. Efforts to this end had not gone far when the collapse occurred.

On September 18, 1873, after attempting to call in all possible loans, Cooke & Company was unable to meet its obligations and closed its doors, first in New York, then Philadelphia, and finally in

Washington. The closing came as a tremendous shock to the public and caused pandemonium in financial circles as the word of Cooke's closing spread. In succeeding days a review of the company's finances did not indicate a hopeless financial situation. There appeared to be no major "runs" on the company, nor were there any major upcoming encumbrances that would have been catastrophic. It was the minority managers in New York who had initiated the closing without consultation with Jay Cooke. Once the closings had taken place, however, they led to a national collapse of grave proportions as most American people lost confidence in the banking system (Cooke & Company in particular) and attempted to withdraw their investments.

The liquidation of the company took place slowly and was a severe disappointment to Cooke. Always sensitive to public criticism, he felt betrayed by many people whom he considered friends or had assisted in earlier years. He was forced to move out of his magnificent house and into a small cottage. Since his wife had died in 1871 and his children were grown, this did not present a serious hardship. He was not allowed to participate in the breakup of his firm, but his son-in-law and son opened a reorganized Cooke & Company under the name of Charles D. Barney & Company. Cooke refused all of the many offers to return to the banking business that came his way, being content periodically to provide advice to his sons.

Cooke gradually became more active. After the bankruptcy proceedings were behind him, he invested a small amount in Utah silver mines, a type of investment he had earlier discouraged. He traveled to Utah to inspect the properties and enlisted the assistance of Jay Gould and the Union Pacific in building a branch line to the mines. These mines produced significant amounts of silver, and Jay Cooke eventually sold his share of the company for about $1 million. With this money, he repurchased both his Lake Erie island resort, Gibraltar, and Ogontz, his large estate near Philadelphia. The latter he converted into a prominent school for young ladies, while he lived a short distance away with his daughter, Mrs. Charles D. Barney, and her family.

Cooke resumed his interest in the Northwest by reinvesting in land in Minnesota. He thought himself vindicated when the Northern Pacific was fi-

nally completed from Lake Superior to the Pacific in 1883. Although invited by Henry Villard to the golden spike ceremony, he did not choose to attend. Several years later, however, he did journey to Duluth and was received warmly as the "Daddy of Duluth." He then continued to the West Coast on the main line of the NP, stopping frequently to examine the line. At all points, including the terminal city of Tacoma, he was greeted by enthusiastic crowds who honored his role in the building of the NP.

Cooke continued to live with his daughter, visiting Gibraltar twice each year until February 16, 1905, when he died peacefully at age eighty-four. He was a man of strong, traditional, but moderate, evangelical Protestant beliefs. He remained a loyal churchgoer throughout his life, did not tolerate profanity, and frowned on business or social activity on Sundays. For instance, he stopped Sunday railroad excursions and lectured his partners frequently about keeping the Sabbath holy. He was perceived as an honorable businessman by his colleagues and was less interested in power for its own sake than such contemporaries as J. P. Morgan. Cooke made significant efforts to provide as much assistance as he could to people who needed help and was known by employees and associates alike as a kind man and good friend.

Publication:

The Northern Pacific Railroad: Its Route, Resources, Progress, and Business; The New Northwest and Its Great Thoroughfare (Philadelphia: J. Cooke, 1871).

References:

John L. Harnsberger, *Jay Cooke and Minnesota: The Formative Years of the Northern Pacific Railroad* (Ann Arbor, Mich.: University Microfilms, 1958);

Matthew Josephson, *The Robber Barons* (New York: Harcourt, Brace & World, 1934);

Ellis Paxson Oberholtzer, *Jay Cooke, Financier of the Civil War* (Philadelphia: George W. Jacobs, 1907; reprinted, 1970).

Archives:

The papers of Jay Cooke may be found in the Jay Cooke Correspondence, Papers, and Memoirs, Library of the Historical Society of Pennsylvania, Philadelphia; the Ohio Historical Society in Columbus, Ohio; and the Baker Library, Harvard University at Boston, Massachusetts.

Erastus Corning

(December 14, 1794-April 9, 1872)

by F. Daniel Larkin

State University College, Oneonta, New York

CAREER: Merchant, Albany, New York (1820s-1860s); partner, Albany Nail Factory (1826-1837); president, Albany City Bank (1830s); president, Mutual Insurance Company (1830s); vice-president, Mohawk & Hudson Railroad (1833-1835); president, Utica & Schenectady Railroad (1833-1853); mayor, City of Albany (1834-1838); partner, Albany Iron Works (1837-1872); member, New York State Senate (1842-1845); president, Erastus Corning & Company (1848-1866); president, St. Mary's Falls (Sault St. Marie) Ship Canal Company (1853-1863); president, New York Central Railroad (1853-1864); member of Congress from New York State (1857-1859, 1861-1863).

Erastus Corning represents the ideal of the complete nineteenth-century man. That is, he was involved in many career activities and succeeded in nearly all of them. Corning, as were many of his contemporaries who rose to fame and fortune during that vibrant period of national growth, was involved in a leadership role in several diverse activities. He, like many of the successful men who shared his time, remained active in his career until the end of his life.

Corning was born in Norwich, Connecticut, on December 14, 1794. His family's American roots can be traced to the early 1640s. Corning's father, Bliss Corning, was not a particularly energetic or successful man but managed to send his son to school at a time when it was necessary to pay a tuition for even a basic education. When about 1805 the family moved to Chatham, New York, southeast of Albany, young Corning was given the opportunity to complete his common school (elementary) education. This was largely due to the generosity of his mother, Lucinda Corning's, brother, Benjamin Smith. Smith, a bachelor and a successful merchant in Troy, New York, paid Corning's tuition when it became beyond the means of Corning's father to do

Erastus Corning in a portrait by Charles Loving Elliot (courtesy of the Albany Institute of History and Art)

so. Bliss and Lucinda Corning, by then, had ten other children to support. In part Smith's special interest in one of his sister's many children probably stemmed from the fact that Corning had been crippled. Due to an injury during infancy Corning was forced to rely on crutches much of his life. In any case, at about age thirteen, Corning ended his formal schooling, journeyed the twenty miles to Troy, and started work in his uncle's hardware business.

Troy, where Corning spent the next seven years, was a fortuitous location for the budding merchant. Situated on the east bank of the Hudson River a few miles north of Albany, the newer village was much closer to the confluence of the Hudson and Mohawk rivers than its older and larger neighbor to the south. The Mohawk River flowed from central New York eastward to its junction with the Hudson. In doing so, it carved a deep, narrow valley through the Appalachian Mountains. As the only water-level route from east to west through the long mountain barrier, the Mohawk Valley was the easiest route from the Atlantic Coast west to the Great Lakes and beyond.

Beginning at about the time of Troy's founding in 1789, thousands of emigrants from New England began to funnel through Troy into the Mohawk Valley. These Yankees were the vanguard of an "invasion" which lasted nearly a half century. Migrants from an agriculturally overcrowded New England sought the open, fertile, inexpensive lands of western New York, the Ohio country, and the upper Midwest. It was not surprising that in such a favorable economic climate Corning's uncle's business prospered. So did Corning, who dabbled in some mercantile activities of his own.

In 1814, with the small amount of capital he had saved, Corning moved eight miles downriver to Albany. Albany in 1814 was not only the capital of New York and its second largest city but was also a commercial and political center already 200 years old by the time of Corning's arrival. Within a decade of Corning's move to the city, Albany became the eastern terminus of the Erie Canal, which added to its importance as a transfer point for trade between New York City and the West. On arriving in Albany, Corning became a clerk in a hardware firm that had done business with his uncle. So placed, the young man began in earnest his rise to success.

In 1825 Corning rose to partnership in the firm in which he was employed. A few months later, on the death of the senior partner, Corning purchased his partner's share to become sole owner. During the time that he was advancing in the mercantile firm, the twenty-five-year-old Corning wed Harriet Weld, whom he had met while living in Troy. Married in 1819, by 1836 the couple had five boys, of whom only Erastus, Jr., and Edwin lived to adulthood. Corning's mercantile business was so successful during the Erie Canal boom of the 1820s that he was able to diversify his holdings. In 1826 he purchased an ironworks and began the manufacture of nails. Soon there emerged from it the much larger and more diversified Albany Nail Factory. Corning also began to invest in banks and insur-

ance companies. By the 1830s he held directorships in many of them and was president of both the Albany City Bank and the Mutual Insurance Company. Corning had become a prominent citizen of Albany and, as such, entered politics.

As the seat of government Albany was one of the state's top two political centers, the other being New York City. By 1830 political power in Albany and, to a large extent, the rest of the state was in the hands of the Democrats. New York's principal Democrat during this period was another Albany resident, Martin Van Buren. In the 1820s Van Buren had fashioned a machine called the Albany Regency to insure control of his home base. By the early 1830s Corning was a key member of the Regency. Initially a Jeffersonian Republican, Corning affiliated with the Jacksonian Democrats when the old Jeffersonians split into two party groups in the late 1820s. Once he became a Democrat, Corning remained one throughout his life, even when a number of his fellow northern Democrats left the party as a result of the sectional upheavals preceding the Civil War. Prior to 1834 Corning limited his political activities strictly to participation within the party. In that year, however, he was elected mayor of Albany and was subsequently reelected for three additional one-year terms.

Shortly before he became mayor, Corning was elected to a corporate position which foreshadowed another phase of his complex career. In 1833 he became vice-president of the Mohawk & Hudson Railroad. The company was incorporated in 1826 but did not begin operations until 1831 on its 15-mile line constructed between Albany and Schenectady. The short line was built for the passenger trade and was intended to complement, not compete with, the immensely successful Erie Canal. By canal, the 26-mile trip between the two cities took as long as ten hours. The trip by rail between Albany and Schenectady could be made in less than an hour. The Mohawk & Hudson Railroad was the first railroad in New York State and second in the country to successfully utilize locomotive power. It also was the first of the several roads that Corning later brought together to form the New York Central. Another and longer link in the New York Central chain was the Utica & Schenectady.

Within three months of becoming Mohawk & Hudson vice-president, Corning was named president of the recently organized Utica & Schenectady Railroad. Incorporated in 1833, the Utica & Schenectady, unlike its much shorter predecessor, was constructed in direct competition with the Erie Canal. Its track closely paralleled the canal for eighty miles through the narrow Mohawk Valley. Corning led the Utica & Schenectady throughout its twenty years as an independent company. Testimony to his leadership skill was the fact that the railroad prospered despite state government opposition. Because the New York legislature saw the Utica & Schenectady as a potential threat to the state-owned Erie Canal, laws were enacted to limit the railroad's competitiveness. For example, freight hauled by the railroad during the winter when the canal was closed was subject to an added charge equivalent to the amount of toll due if it were shipped on the canal. Despite the burden of the additional rate charges, the railroad continued to operate and to withstand the low-cost water transportation advantage of the Erie Canal. Obviously it was necessary for Corning to keep railroad operating expenses to a minimum in order to remain competitive with the canal. Eventually, partly as a result of Corning's growing political influence in the legislature, the restrictions placed on the Utica & Schenectady were removed. The Utica & Schenectady provided Corning with experience for his later railroad ventures, and it offered an additional market for the goods produced by another of Corning's businesses.

The output of Corning's Albany Nail Factory consisted largely of nails, iron rods, and plate iron. With the coming of the railroads, however, the factory began producing iron products for the new roads. Demand became strong enough by 1837 for Corning to bring a partner into the business who was skilled in iron making and who could supervise production of a more diverse product line. When John Winslow joined Corning in the manufacture of iron, the name of the Albany Nail Factory was changed to the Albany Iron Works in order to reflect the product line expansion.

One of the chief products turned out by the renamed factory was railroad spikes. Not only was Corning's Utica & Schenectady a customer for the spikes but the burst of railroad-building activity in the 1840s and 1850s provided a ready market for the output of the Albany Iron Works. When the earliest roads had been constructed it was the practice to use only a thin strip of wrought iron nailed to a long "rail" or stringer usually made of oak or white pine. The reason for this technique was the rel-

atively high cost of the iron strips, or straps as they were called at the time. When the train passed along the track, its wheels rested on the iron strap. Although saving on cost, the practice had a very dangerous shortcoming. With the passage of trains over the strap rails, the nails holding the straps in place tended to work loose. In time the ends of the straps would begin to curl, the loose ends would be pushed up and, once high enough, would catch on the underside of the passenger cars and rip through the wooden floors. The "snake heads," as they were called, were responsible for maiming and death among the railroad passengers. Because of this, eastern railroads began converting to the new, all iron "I" and "T" rails by the mid 1840s. These heavy rails were fastened directly to the wooden cross ties by means of heavy spikes. Of course, the heavier rails could also support heavier train loads. The Albany Iron Works manufactured railroad spikes, and Erastus Corning & Company, the mercantile firm, arranged for the importation of some of the new rails from England, the primary source at the time.

By 1860 the Albany Iron Works employed about 750 workers. With the outbreak of the Civil War the following year Corning's company bid for government war contracts, even though its senior partner was an anti-administration Democrat initially opposed to the conflict. In any case Corning, as a member of Congress during the first two years of hostilities, did not personally seek Union government contracts. His partner John Winslow did so instead. Winslow's success was demonstrated by the fact that iron from their factory went into the manufacture of cannons, railroad equipment, and other war material. The most notable contribution made by the Albany Iron Works to the United States government war effort was toward the building of the USS *Monitor*. Iron plate for the novel vessel was produced by Corning's company in cooperation with three other iron manufacturers. The *Monitor* contract led to the company's furnishing plate for several other ironclads during the war years.

The Albany Iron Works was a very successful enterprise. This fact notwithstanding, Winslow decided to sell his holdings in the company shortly after the close of the war. In 1867 Corning bought Winslow's interest and became sole owner of the works. Of additional interest in the senior Corning's iron manufacturing ventures was his financial involvement in the nearby Rensselaer Iron

Works. During the final months of the Civil War the Rensselaer Works was among the pioneers of the improved Bessemer steel-making process in the United States.

Even though Corning was involved in iron manufacture he continued to invest in railroads. As the rail lines began to push west beyond Buffalo, Corning looked to the new railroads and to the western lands as an outlet for his capital. As he had already invested in Michigan lands it was logical that his attention was attracted to the Michigan Central Railroad. The Michigan Central had been taken over by the state of Michigan at about the time of the panic of 1837. The state continued construction on the line running west from Detroit, but the economic hard times made progress very slow. By the mid 1840s the road was little more than halfway across Michigan's lower peninsula. Agitation began to develop, spurred on by James Joy, a Detroit attorney, for the state to sell the Central in order that it could be speedily completed by private capital. When the act for the sale of the road passed the Michigan legislature in March 1846, Erastus Corning's name appeared on the list of buyers along with that of the great Boston railroad financier John Murray Forbes.

Within three years of the sale of the Michigan Central the railroad reached Lake Michigan. In 1849 the company began operating ferry service to Chicago and also began a steamboat service to Buffalo from the eastern terminus at Detroit. The boat across Lake Erie to Buffalo connected with the railroads which crossed central New York State. The water link was satisfactory for a time, but the leaders of the Michigan Central began to search for a land route between Buffalo and Detroit. This was needed in order for the Central to compete with its principal rival for the Buffalo to Chicago trade, the Michigan Southern Railroad. The land link for which the Central managers were searching was found in an underdeveloped Canadian line called the Great Western. This road followed a straight line route through Ontario's lower peninsula from Niagara Falls to Windsor, across the international border from Detroit. Corning assisted in improving the Canadian road by using his influence in New York to help convince the state's legislature to pass a law allowing railroads in the state to invest in Great Western stock. Additional funds were pumped into the Great Western by American private investors, among them Corning and Forbes.

Both men were added to the line's board of directors. Corning served from 1851 until 1854, when he resigned because of a dispute over company policy. Although Corning left the Great Western's board, the railroad remained the connecting road between the Michigan Central and the New York Central, the amalgamation of New York railroads achieved by Corning in 1853.

In addition to his investments in factories and railroads, Corning also speculated in land. Corning's largest land purchases were located in four states: New York, Iowa, Michigan, and Wisconsin. The New York venture commenced in 1835 with purchases in Steuben County, approximately eighty miles west of Binghamton. Corning, in partnership with eight other men, bought nearly 2,000 acres of land along the Chemung River. The area was connected to the Erie Canal, about seventy miles to the north, by a waterway system involving the Chemung Canal, Seneca Lake, and the Cayuga & Seneca Canal. A village was planned at the Chemung River end of this waterway, and it was named Corning. The community prospered and currently is best known for its major industry, Corning Glass.

Erastus Corning's interest in Steuben County land was not solely for its speculative value. The county was adjacent to Pennsylvania's Tioga County and its coal deposits. In 1840 Corning bought shares in the Arbon Coal Company in Tioga County, and a railroad was built to carry coal from the Tioga village of Blossberg to Corning, New York. From there Corning marketed the coal to his Albany Iron Works and to the Utica & Schenectady Railroad, as well as to other factories and rail lines. The coal-carrying rail line also helped stimulate the growth of the village of Corning, as did the arrival of the Erie Railroad. The Erie reached Corning in 1849 on its way from New York City to Lake Erie. Two years later it was completed to the Lake Erie port of Dunkirk, New York. The growth generated by the Erie Railroad in Corning and the surrounding area was enough to augment the value of Erastus Corning's real estate holdings, which were worth five times their original cost of $53,000 by the time of Corning's death in 1872.

In addition to his land purchases in Steuben County, Corning bought property in Chautauqua County in 1835. The tract was at the mouth of the Cattaraugus Creek on Lake Erie, thirty miles south of Buffalo, New York. He also invested in real estate in Auburn, New York, the county seat of Cayuga County, twenty-five miles west of Syracuse. Including Corning, sixty-five persons were involved in the purchase of 400 acres in and around Auburn. One of the investors was Martin Van Buren, then vice-president of the United States. Neither the purchase at Auburn nor the land on Lake Erie was as profitable as the property at Corning. Although the Cattaraugus Creek property was improved by the dredging of a harbor and the construction of a shipyard, the further growth of the community was diminished by the selection of Dunkirk, fifteen miles to the south, as the Erie Railroad's western terminus. By 1845 lots in the harbor village that once sold for $200 each dropped to a mere $6. Eventually the small village on Cattaraugus Creek was abandoned, and Corning suffered a loss on his Lake Erie speculation.

The land in Auburn turned out to be more financially rewarding than the Lake Erie property. Soon after the purchase was made, however, the panic of 1837 and the depression which followed led to foreclosure on the land by the mortgage holder, the Farmer's Loan & Trust Company of New York City. Corning anticipated the foreclosure and took steps to secure sole ownership of the property when it was put on sale to settle the mortgage. As a result of an arrangement with fifty-nine of his partners, Corning was the only bidder when the sale took place in August 1843. He paid the bank $17,350 for the 400 acres. Corning immediately began the sale of small parcels of his purchase. Within five years he had recovered nearly twice the purchase price on sales of only about half of the 400 acres. Almost thirty years after his purchase of the entire parcel, Corning continued to receive an income from the Auburn land.

Corning's speculative ventures were not limited to New York real estate. In 1835 he was among the organizers of the American Land Company. The list of original investors included United States Attorney General (and former Regency member) Benjamin F. Butler, United States Senator from New York Silas Wright, and Amos Kendall, a close advisor to then-President Andrew Jackson. During the speculation fever that swept the United States in the years preceding the panic of 1837, the American Land Company bought land in nine states, mainly in the Midwest and South. In the depression years following 1837 land sales declined, but by

1845 they were again on the rise due to the continuation of westward migration. Between 1845 and 1861 Corning received regular dividend payments of 5 percent or more on his investment. But the outbreak of the Civil War abruptly ended the flow of dividends, since all remaining company land was in Alabama and Mississippi. After the war a final settlement was made to stockholders amounting to little more than $3 per share, much less than 1 percent of their prewar value.

Another of Corning's investments was the New York Land Company. By the time of the Civil War he owned 25 percent of the company. Many of the company's holdings were in the present state of Iowa, therefore less affected by the war. However, the extent of Corning's gain or loss in the New York Land Company remains obscure. Sources indicate that he probably did not lose on the venture and continued to invest in the company well into the 1860s. But by then he was far more involved in land speculation in Michigan and Wisconsin. In 1855 Corning was a principal in the purchase of the Fox and Wisconsin Improvement Company. The Improvement Company itself was a failure, due in part to the hard times brought on by the panic of 1857. However, Corning's involvement in the Improvement Company paved the way for his role in the St. Mary's Falls Ship Canal Company. This company was formed to build a canal around the falls in the St. Mary's River, the water passage between Lakes Superior and Huron. Corning joined the company and was elected its president in 1853. The canal was built in three years, and, under the terms of the company charter, the man-made waterway was turned over to the state of Michigan in return for 750,000 acres to be claimed from any public land in Michigan. The company took approximately three-fourths of their award in timberlands and much of the remainder in iron range in the state's Upper Peninsula. In September 1863 the company was dissolved, and it was decided that the land should be sold to enable the directors to divide the holdings. Corning traveled to Detroit to attend the public auction where he purchased nearly 100,000 acres to be added to the nearly 2,700 acres he already owned in Michigan. It was little wonder that the Albany merchant was keenly interested in improving rail connections between his home city and the Middle West.

In 1842, with the completion of the Attica & Buffalo Railroad, Albany was finally linked to Buffalo by rail. It had taken eleven years to complete construction of the seven rail lines that crossed central New York. Still for the next eleven years it was necessary to change railroads five times in making the 300-mile trip across New York. In some instances this was not a relatively simple matter of going from one station to an adjacent one, but traveling from one side of a city to the other. There was no question that a consolidation was needed and that Corning was the man to accomplish it. Actually the trend toward a union of all the roads across New York began in 1850 with the joining of the Auburn & Syracuse with the Auburn & Rochester to form the Rochester & Syracuse Railroad. Later in 1850 the roads between Rochester and Buffalo combined into the Buffalo & Rochester. It now remained for Corning, as president of the Utica & Schenectady, to play the leading role in bringing the several roads across New York together.

The chief factor in bringing about consolidation of the central New York roads was the completion in the early 1850s of a number of railroads that could compete for the western traffic. The New York & Erie was completed to Lake Erie in 1851, the Pennsylvania Railroad was built to Pittsburgh by 1852, and the Baltimore & Ohio was opened to the Ohio River in 1853. There was no question that the central roads of New York State had to act or lose their share of the western trade to these new rivals. At Corning's urging a meeting of the central New York lines was held in Albany on February 12, 1851. It was decided to ask the state legislature for permission to combine into a single railroad company. During the two years that it took to convince the state's lawmakers, Corning was the leading lobbyist for the railroads. As it happened, the Whig party, not Corning's Democrats, was the majority party in the legislature. But Corning was able to call successfully upon his old friend and Whig leader Thurlow Weed to achieve passage of the bill. The New York Central Consolidation Act was passed on April 2, 1853.

At the first meeting of the stockholders of the new corporation in July, Corning was elected president of the New York Central, Dean Richmond of the Buffalo & Rochester was named the new firm's vice-president, and John V. L. Pruyn, secretary-treasurer of the Utica & Schenectady, was elected to that same post with the Central. With this act Corning became head of a $23 million corporation and one of the leading railroad men in the country.

Because of purchases of stock in the old member companies by the new corporation, Corning netted an estimated $100,000 profit from the merger. In addition the New York Central almost immediately began construction of a second track between Albany and Buffalo. Nearly $700,000 was spent for the purchase of the rails, the agent for which was Erastus Corning & Company of Albany. Spikes, followed by wheel sets, were purchased from Corning's Albany Iron Works for the sum of $155,000. The man who spearheaded the consolidation of the railroads between Albany and Buffalo made out very well from the union.

Erastus Corning continued in New York Central's presidency until April 1864 when he resigned in favor of Dean Richmond. During the years between 1853 and 1864 Corning was unable to devote full time to the affairs of the railroad. He spent two terms in Congress and several months in Europe while president of the Central. Although no longer Central president after 1864, Corning remained a member of the road's directorate. He also remained actively interested in other roads during the late 1860s. Besides the New York Central and the Michigan Central, Corning had investments in eleven other roads at the time of his death. But the rigors of managing so large a portfolio composed of such diverse interests began to tell on the man already seventy-five years old. In 1869 Corning fell ill and was bedridden for several months. In 1870, however, he experienced a recovery and was able to travel with his wife, Harriet, to their favorite summer haunt, Newport. But with the death of his son Edwin in 1871, Corning's health once again declined. This time he did not recover and died at his home in Albany on April 9, 1872.

References:

Codman Hislop, *Albany, Dutch, English, American* (Albany: Argus Press, 1936);

Edward Hungerford, *Men and Iron, The History of the New York Central* (New York: Crowell, 1938);

Joel Munsell, *Annals of Albany* (Albany: Munsell & Rowland, 1854-1859);

Irene D. Neu, *Erastus Corning, Merchant and Financier, 1794-1872* (Ithaca, N.Y.: Cornell University Press, 1960);

Frank W. Stevens, *The Beginnings of the New York Central Railroad* (New York: Putnam's, 1926).

Archives:

Material concerning Erastus Corning is located in the Erastus Corning Papers of the Albany Institute of History and Art at Albany, N.Y.

Charles Henry Coster

(July 24, 1852-March 13, 1900)

by Albro Martin

Bradley University

CAREER: Clerk and partner, Aymar & Company (1867-1872); partner, Fabbri & Chauncey (1872-1884); partner, J. P. Morgan & Company (1884-1900).

Charles Henry Coster, private banker, was a leading architect of the American railroad system as it existed in the first half of the twentieth century. During the hectic years of the 1880s, when railroad mileage in the U.S. grew at a record rate, and in the crisis years of the 1890s, Coster became the chief railroad expert in the firm of J. P. Morgan & Company, conceiving and executing dozens of railroad and industrial financings, mergers, and reorganizations which helped to make his firm the unchallenged leader in corporate finance.

Coster was born in Newport, Rhode Island, during the summer of 1852, into a family of New York merchants, a class of businessmen that had led the economic development of the city and the nation in the era before the rise of big business. He was the grandson of John Gerard Coster, who had emigrated, with his brother, from Haarlem, The Netherlands, at the end of the eighteenth century. Coster's grandfather, a doctor, gave up the profession on discovering that the booming mercantile world of New York offered better opportunities. With his brother, J. G. Coster founded a firm that specialized in importing Dutch specialties and eventually owned numerous vessels trading with the East and West Indies. He had three sons, one of whom, Gerard H., married a daughter of Nathaniel Prime, a leading New York banker. They were the parents of Charles Henry Coster.

Young Coster knew the mercantile, insurance, and banking worlds from childhood, since his uncles and in-laws were prominent in all three. He attended private schools until he was nearly fifteen, at which point he had received the firm grounding in reading, writing, arithmetic, spelling, and book-

Charles Henry Coster (courtesy of the Pierpont Morgan Library)

keeping that was all a career in business then required. In 1867 he climbed the traditional high stool in the counting room of Aymar & Company, importers, remaining with that firm in 1872 when it was taken over by Fabbri & Chauncey. The takeover proved a felicitous one for Coster, as Egisto P. Fabbri was a close associate of J. P. Morgan, then beginning to make himself known in the infant world of investment banking. In 1884, at the age of thirty-two, Coster accepted a partnership in the firm of Drexel, Morgan & Company, the predecessor of J. P. Morgan & Company. Coster found his desk piled high with work when he arrived, and the flow never let up.

By 1884 J. P. Morgan was already front-page news. The journalists of that era saw in the Wall Street "crowd" a fat target for their alternating attacks and adulations, which they used to sell papers in an age when politics and diplomacy had lost much of their luster. It was front-page news when Morgan undertook to settle the rate wars between the New York Central and Pennsylvania railroads that repeatedly demoralized eastern railroads and their customers. William H. Vanderbilt, president and major owner of the usually very profitable Central, had come to lean heavily upon Morgan for business advice, and Morgan was able to persuade him to buy the New York, West Shore & Buffalo Railroad, which rival interests, by then bankrupt, had constructed to parallel the Central's main line. Drafting a plan of reorganization, which included the floating of a 400-year first mortgage gold bond, was one of Coster's first major assignments, and he brought it off beautifully in 1885. Until the Central itself fell on hard times and merged with the Pennsylvania in the ill-fated Penn Central, these West Shore "Gold 4s" were classic gilt-edged securities, reposing comfortably in the strongboxes of the widows and orphans of three continents.

There followed a series of major railroad reorganizations, interspersed with untold numbers of smaller assignments. Coster quickly came to be the person Morgan and the other partners turned to when railroad assignments posed knotty problems. While railroad receiverships were not unknown at that time, virtually all of what came to be "standard" business procedure in reorganizations, including the body of legal precedent and statutory law that would embody it, was still unformulated. Coster invented many of the techniques the next generation of investment bankers would take for granted. It was a risky business for those who knew what they were doing; for those who did not, it frequently proved fatal; e.g., the unsuccessful early efforts to reorganize the Richmond Terminal Company, the Northern Pacific, and the Erie. Coster made it his business to learn everything he could about the affairs of a troubled railroad enterprise on his own, for he had long since learned that

no businessman's assessment of his own condition or prospects could be taken at face value.

When Coster arrived on the scene in 1884, the venerable Philadelphia & Reading Railroad, which had been hauling the highly prized anthracite coal of eastern Pennsylvania to urban markets for nearly half a century, was up for reorganization. The experience was invaluable to Coster for, in his daily contacts with Morgan, he learned those elements of financial success that were not obvious. Among the most important of these was post-reorganization management, which called for the banker to take the initiative in bringing the best operating men into the picture to run the railroad efficiently and to keep it free from outside interference. Another element was the need to assure timid investors that *this time* the newly reorganized railroad would be operated efficiently and profitably, meet its interest payments on time, and ultimately pay a dividend. The key that unlocked investor confidence was the famous "voting trust," wherein the banker who floated the new securities replacing the old would retain voting control of the property until its performance was assured. No innovation was ever more controversial in principle–it seemed so undemocratic and does so to this day–or more successful in practice. The idea of the voting trust was probably Morgan's; his longtime legal counsel, Francis Lynde Stetson, probably found the way to make it stick in court; but it was Charles Coster who best put it into practice throughout the hectic years of the dying century.

In the decade before the 1893 depression, Coster worked out reorganization plans for the Baltimore & Ohio (B&O), securing the removal of Robert Garrett, the incompetent son of the famous John W. Garrett; the Cleveland, Columbus, Cincinnati & St. Louis ("Big Four") Railroad, an important midwestern carrier being acquired by the New York Central to round out its system southwest of Cleveland to St. Louis; the Chesapeake & Ohio, Collis P. Huntington's foray into eastern railroading, which had lacked an eastern port for coal exports until Coster's plan secured it a connection to Newport News; and the Chicago & Atlantic, which was placed in the hands of the Erie Railroad as the Erie's logical extension to Chicago.

Corporate reorganizations, contrary to much of American folklore, were anything but "make-a-killing-and-get-out" deals. The fees which Morgan & Company and other prominent investment bankers charged for reorganizing America's railroads and introducing modern corporate structure were not particularly impressive. These men knew that the real rewards were in creating a continuing relationship between the bank and the new firms. They knew that in the economically and technologically dynamic fin de siècle world, their creations would be making repeated trips to the well to tap the western world's savings, and such enduring relationships were what made a great bank even greater.

To the casual observer, the American railroad map seemed complete by 1890, but men like Coster and Morgan knew better. In the previous two decades, the price of nearly everything had declined, including the price of money. Railroad corporations that had financed construction at high real interest rates (as opposed to the 5 and 6 percent figures that decorated the handsome bond certificates) watched helplessly as freight rates dropped year after year until their railroads were desperate to earn enough money to pay their fixed charges. Contrary to the opinion of "experts" then and now, it was not only a monetary deflation at work. While real factor costs of production on railroads, and elsewhere, had declined dramatically, overcapacity in the railroad system also contributed to the vicious struggle for traffic, the collapse of tariff schedules, and the return of rate discrimination. The "smart money" saw trouble ahead, and it came quickly. The cruel depression of the 1890s–the first since America had become largely a society of industrial wage earners–placed a record number of railroads in receivership. The final hour had struck for the Victorian railroad corporation.

To the surprise of very few who had followed closely the development of railroads in the postbellum South, the onset of the depression served as the last straw for the Richmond and West Point Terminal and Warehouse Company. This shaky holding company had brought together in the 1880s several large southeastern railroads, including the Richmond & Danville, the railroad backbone between Washington, D.C., and Atlanta, Georgia; the East Tennessee, Virginia & Georgia, which ran southwest to Memphis; and a host of smaller railroads, most of which were poorly built and unprofitable. The principle of trying to create strength by combining weakness had proved disastrous and was further complicated by the southern individualism that had hampered cooperation between the states of the Confederacy. The attitude

manifested itself in the refusal of the holders of the constituent lines' securities to agree on a plan of reorganization. While everyone felt that his securities were being asked to make a larger sacrifice than the other fellow's, no one was willing to accept Wall Street's firm opinion that while the lines might yet be made to hang together, they would certainly hang separately.

Southern railroads had been woefully backward at their prewar best and, by the end of the Civil War, were barely in business. Physical damage had been devastating, and such lines as did operate regularly made do with facilities that were obsolete even by 1860 standards. More significantly, the outlines of a coordinated through-route system of railroads had not begun to appear when the South went to war. All of these shortcomings had been attacked energetically by the postbellum generation, but progress had been slow. Capital was at a premium throughout the nation, for the North was also building and rebuilding railroads furiously. The South could only offer investors (most of them, perforce, northerners) a slim chance that their interest would be paid, since southern agriculture (there was no industry to speak of) remained depressed, and cotton output, which did not return to prewar levels until the mid 1880s, languished for lack of transportation facilities. Southern state legislatures, corrupt and incompetent, distorted railroad builders' plans to fit political expediencies. By the end of the 1880s it was obvious that however much assistance the South had received from the North in creating a transportation system from which the entire nation could benefit, it would require much more in the future. In addition to money, the South needed northern planning and management. It was a tall order for anybody who would tackle it.

When the first overtures were made to Morgan & Company by the men who controlled the Richmond Terminal Company, Coster went to work on a plan that would completely dismantle the old amalgamation and create an entirely new railroad system. Coster's plan would not immediately enrich either speculator or investor but would create a corporation which took as its objectives improving the physical plant, installing modern management, and generating profits for improvement, not distribution. This meant that every investor except those holding the senior securities of the few independently viable constituent lines could expect his bonds to be replaced by new ones paying a lower rate of return. Reducing fixed charges—what a railroad had to pay month in and month out whether it operated or not—was always Morgan's first objective. In return for sacrifices in the present, he was always willing to promise rewards in the future. Bondholders who consented to lower interest rates or had their bonds obliterated were usually soothed by receiving preferred stock which might conceivably pay a dividend in the near future. Holders of common stock in the old companies had the choice between paying a cash assessment per share to provide money needed to carry out the reorganization, or forfeiting their shares, which in any case promised dividends only in the dim future, if ever. Morgan & Company was not interested in merely keeping sick railroads alive; it proposed to make them vigorous, growing enterprises whose securities would be eagerly bid for in the future. In the rapidly expanding environment of fin de siècle America, such optimism was the only realistic attitude.

All of this was too much for the men who, for the moment at least, controlled the companies making up the Richmond Terminal. They tried to take their business elsewhere but were aghast to find that no other Wall Street house would touch them. When the depression worsened, the realization dawned on them that no simple receivership could save the southeastern railroads. Back they came to Morgan & Company, and Charles Coster met them politely at the door, his conditions unchanged. He and his colleagues were not sure that tackling the project was prudent, but the work was necessary, and Morgan & Company was best prepared for the job. Coster jocularly compared the men of the Richmond Terminal to the man who, after a night on the town, showed up at his own house at three in the morning. Asked sarcastically by his wife why he had not stayed out all night, he replied that he would have, but hers was the only place in town still open.

Notwithstanding the great complexity and vast amount of detail the reorganization entailed, Coster was as deliberate and thorough as ever. He insisted on an independent financial audit of the client's firm, an equally independent evaluation and appraisal of its physical plant, and, of course, a survey of its present and future business prospects. Such data would govern the issuance of the tiers of securities, from senior bonds to common stock, which by their priority and amount implied various expectations as to conservatively estimated present earnings, near-term earnings, and long-term earnings. Coster was an expert, like Morgan, in finding expert help. In this case he tapped Samuel Spencer, one of the most knowledgeable railroad operating men in the nation. Spencer, who did not suffer fools gladly any more than a Morgan or a Coster would, had not lasted long as president of the Baltimore & Ohio, a position gained when Morgan & Company reorganized the line. He had challenged the B&O directors' policies and their misleading way of reporting net earnings and was replaced after one year. Coster could afford no major mistakes and only a few minor ones. What seemed to outsiders as sheer brilliance, if not superhuman powers, on his part was, in great measure, simply an unlimited capacity for absorbing and analyzing detail and an ability to choose qualified associates.

The reorganization was an outstanding success. From the ashes of the Richmond Terminal arose the phoenix of the Southern Railway; Samuel Spencer became its first president. Coster's program for the steady reinvestment of net income into the improvement of the railroad and its rolling stock, structures, shops, and terminals did more to bring the South into the twentieth century than almost any other single factor. The railroad was never again insolvent, and owners of its securities, while they did not become rich quickly, watched it grow with the New South and become one of the strongest railroad properties in the nation.

"No other private banking house presided over so many major rescues as did Morgan's New York firm," declares Vincent Carosso in his history of the company. Coster's preeminent role was unquestioned. While managing the Southern Railway reorganization, which would have fully occupied a lesser man, he also took a major hand in reorganization of the Northern Pacific (NP) Railroad, which Morgan had helped finance in the years when Frederick Billings and Henry Villard were extending it to Puget Sound. Then, as now, transcontinental railroads were more likely to catch the imagination of men than the grim eastern workhorses that trooped through the Morgan offices. Morgan himself was no exception, and he savored the NP reorganization as his crowning achievement. While Coster did most of the planning and execution of the reorganization, Morgan had his hands full fending off a number of parties who were already deeply involved with the faltering railroad. Chief among them was Morgan's ally in the West, James J. Hill, who had already been blocked by the Minnesota courts in an attempt to add the NP to his efficient and profitable Great Northern Railway system.

Even so, Hill was Coster's main source of information and counsel on the true potentialities of the NP under efficient management, which it had theretofore lacked. Morgan had agreed with Hill and Hill's chief associate, George Stephen (Lord Mount Stephen, the first colonial raised to the peerage for his leadership in building the Canadian Pacific), to place the NP under Hill's management as quickly as possible, but either out of concern for public opinion or pride in his own stewardship, Morgan put Hill off year after year. Coster proved himself as unimpressed by Hill's indignant letters to him and to Morgan as he was by all other interests who had chafed under the autocratic rule of a Morgan voting trust. Not until late 1900, when Morgan no longer had the services of Coster, was the trust terminated.

During the 1890s both the Reading and the Erie again trudged through the process of "Morganization," this time so effectively that they had relatively smooth sailing until the Great Depression of the 1930s. But Coster did not deal exclusively in railroads. In spite of the depression, or perhaps because of it, the 1890s saw the first big wave of corporate mergers. What many have called the "second industrial revolution" was under way, as the scientific breakthroughs of the nineteenth century bore fruit in a host of new industries that demanded financing, organizing, and management. Electricity—its generation, transmission, and consumption—was creating an entirely new field for investment banking. In the late 1880s Morgan had helped Thomas A. Edison set up the Edison General Electric Company, with only lukewarm success. Edison was an inventor but electricity as a business was being practiced more impressively by Thomson-Houston Electric. In a merger plan that was the work of Coster, Thomson-Houston took over the Edison concern, Henry Villard (who was promoting the merger while neglecting the Northern Pacific) was replaced as president, and a new $50-million industrial giant, General Electric, was born.

By no means were all of Coster's undertakings a success. In 1896 Coster reported favorably on the prospects for the Studebaker Company, long the nation's leading farm wagon manufacturer and a player in the barely emergent automobile business. Morgan & Company took a $2-million participa-

tion in the financing, but the horseless carriage was still little more than a toy, and the offering failed. But in 1898 and 1899 Morgan & Company laid the foundations for what was long the largest industrial corporation in the world–U.S. Steel–when it began the process of restructuring the chaotic American steel industry with the formation of Federal Steel and National Tube. Coster worked closely with another up-and-coming Morgan partner, Robert Bacon, on steel matters; if Coster had lived, he would doubtless have played a major role in the critical first decades of U.S. Steel.

The social cost of all this complicated financial maneuvering, which must have seemed like priestly mumbo jumbo to most Americans, and the huge fortunes which a few privileged men amassed in the process, have long been the stuff of American mythology. Economic ruin, however, found little favor as an alternative among Americans who valued the freedom with which these men faced and solved awesome problems affecting millions of their fellow citizens. More than a few hoped someday to emulate them on a smaller scale. To be sure, these gentlemen did not work for nothing, nor were all their rewards in the future. Their life-styles were baronial by the standards of modern financial geniuses, whose dollar incomes are many times greater: such has been the result of inflation, steep progressive income taxes, and the extinction of the domestic servant class. To state their firms' fees in terms of simple dollar amounts, however, has led to major misunderstanding. Generally little cash payment beyond a fee for professional services was involved, which was approximately equal to what a first-class law firm would have charged. A share in the future profits of the reorganized enterprises was another matter, and strikingly large amounts of common stock, if valued at par, were taken by Morgan & Company for little or no cash payment. The market value at the time and for years after seldom reached "par" (today recognized as a meaningless term for a share of equity), but the partners had the choice of selling their stock at the small market advance that usually followed reorganization or of waiting for the long-term appreciation upon which they were betting the firm's reputation.

Coster's career ended on the eve of the great prosperity of the "Progressive" era, in which the bankers shared mightily. At his death, however, he and the considerably older George C. Thomas, each with a 12 percent share in the profits of the firm, were second in importance only to Morgan himself, who took 35 percent. Coster's capital account was closed out at $300,000. Between 1886 and 1894 his annual share varied from nothing in 1893 to $57,000 in 1894. Some data exist for individual reorganizations. Coster's share of the profits for the General Electric financing, for example, was $47,000; the same amount for the Chesapeake & Ohio job; but only $5,800 for the "Big Four," the New York Central being a particularly close association.

What men like Coster brought to J. P. Morgan & Company, and to the restructuring of the American industrial economy that was proceeding apace in his day, is almost impossible to state in monetary terms: his profound knowledge of banking and extensive experience in all aspects of business affairs; an unbelievable capacity for long hours of grueling work; and, most important—or so Morgan himself believed—"character," which was the first thing Morgan looked for in an associate. Men like Coster were rare, at once objects of awe and admiration, and of criticism and abuse which more often than not bore a tinge of sour grapes. John Moody's description of Coster stuck: "a white-faced, nervous man, hurrying from meeting to meeting and at evening carrying home his portfolio." Louis D. Brandeis, a bitter foe of big business, spoke darkly of men who created havoc by trying to manage enterprises that were far too great for one man's talents, and he could well have been thinking of Coster, who was said to have served on more boards of directors than any other man in history. James J. Hill, after years of frustration with Morgan and Coster's reluctance to terminate the Northern Pacific voting trust, wrote George Stephen in 1898 that "Mr. Coster, who is the active man in Morgan's house, has practically broken down and may never do hard work again."

Morgan and his firm eventually gained a reputation for bringing the best men into the firm and then "using them up" with man-killing work loads. The careers of Robert Bacon, George Perkins, and, a generation later, Dwight Morrow contributed to this judgment in the years following Coster's death in 1900. The truth is that Coster contracted a very bad cold in the raw March days, insisted upon going to the office and putting in his usual day's work, and soon was put to bed by his doctor. Years of sedentary work and lack of exercise probably were factors in his death, but his photographic portrait reveals a vigorous clear-eyed man in the prime of life. In those days, the pneumococcus struck down young and old, strong and feeble, rich and poor, and on March 13, 1900, it claimed Charles Henry Coster. His loss was keenly felt in informed circles, who suspected that Coster's talents would be needed more than ever in the years ahead. They were entirely right. Between 1900 and 1929 the American people poured more billions into all kinds of long-term investments than anyone could have foretold. The railroads were extensively rebuilt and their capacity enlarged; huge new factories sprang up, turning out goods virtually unheard of in 1900; millions of residential units were built for a population that increased by nearly 50 million souls; and the modern, high-rise city replaced the grubby urban centers of old. Coster, only forty-seven when he died, would certainly have made a telling contribution to this great transformation of material America.

Coster was the ideal Victorian businessman, father, and pillar of the community, but he did not fit the stereotype of the bourgeoisie as anti-intellectual. Studious, even scholarly, he was an expert philatelist in the years before he became too busy for stamps and, in 1876, published *United States Locals and Their History*, long considered a standard work by stamp collectors and today a valuable rare book. The Coster family, consisting of his wife, Emily Pell Coster, whom he married in 1886, three daughters, and a son, did not follow the uptown movement to the more fashionable Murray Hill and Fifth Avenue residential districts but remained at 27 West Nineteenth Street. His accomplishments entitled him to a prominent place in history, but, like Morgan's other partners, he has been forgotten in the brilliant glare of J. P. Morgan's fame, thus demonstrating the idea that Americans do not deserve to have great men. He lived in times that were not merely interesting but also of singular opportunity. James J. Hill had told a friend a few years before that he did not believe any subsequent generation would have the opportunity to do what they had done on such an imperial scale. Charles Henry Coster might have said the same.

References:

Vincent P. Carosso, *The Morgans: Private International Bankers, 1854-1913* (Cambridge, Mass.: Harvard University Press, 1987);

Commercial and Financial Chronicle, 70 (March 17, 1900): 502;

Maury Klein, *The Great Richmond Terminal* (Charlottesville: University of Virginia Press, 1970);

Albro Martin, *James J. Hill and the Opening of the Northwest* (New York: Oxford University Press, 1976);

John Moody, *The Masters of Capital: A Chronicle of Wall Street* (New Haven: Yale University Press, 1921);

Moody, *The Railroad Builders* (New Haven: Yale University Press, 1921);

Lyman Horace Weeks, ed., "Charles Henry Coster," *Prominent Families of New York* (New York: The Historical Company, 1897).

Archives:

There are no Charles Henry Coster papers, as such, although the archives of J. P. Morgan & Company, in the Morgan Library, contain thousands of items bearing on his business career. No biography, and apparently not even a historical essay, has ever been published on Coster. Contemporary and later works on American railroads betray little awareness that there was such a person, although a fleeting glance appears now and then. For that matter, there has never been a good biography of J. P. Morgan, although potboilers come out regularly every few years. In writing this essay, however, permission was granted to read in draft the pertinent chapters of Vincent P. and the late Rose Carosso's magisterial history, *The Morgans*, which was then in press. This generous favor is deeply appreciated. The book, and especially the copious footnotes, are rich in detail. The Carossos knew their subject, understood the characters, and devoted long years to archival research. Maury Klein's history of the Richmond Terminal provides much detail on this outstanding episode in Coster's career.

Couplers

For a train to be a train, some method of coupling locomotives and cars is necessary. Coupling devices, or couplers, on early railroads were either of the crudest type or were not used at all. On railroads where horses provided the motive power, often only one cart was hauled by each horse. If more than one cart were hauled, a wooden tongue, a leather strap, or a chain was used to hitch the cars together. These makeshift devices, installed by local mechanics at the rear of each car to accommodate the coupling device, underscored the poor technology; also, there was little or no standardization as there was little, if any, interchange of equipment.

While steam locomotive technology appeared and developed rapidly, coupling technology changed only slowly. Simple chain couplers continued to connect most cars in England and the United States for many years after locomotives appeared. These couplers utilized significant amounts of slack between cars which ran out when the train was started and ran in when the train stopped. Consequently, stopping and starting on early trains, both in England and the United States, was a jolting experience for passengers and freight alike. Because speeds were not high and the weight of trains not great, such discomfort was dismissed as mere inconvenience.

Over the years the slow but inexorable development of coupling devices in England differed from that in the United States. The British gradually developed a screw and turnbuckle system of coupling. This system was located at the center line of each car and used buffers on the outside extremes of the end sills of each car. The coupling held the cars together, while the buffers, which contained heavy springs, prevented the cars from crashing together when the train was stopping. It was not until the 1850s, however, that buffers to control slack were installed with regularity and then only on the cars of a few railroads.

In the United States adequate coupling devices developed even more slowly than they did in England. Consequently, until after the Civil War a passenger in an American train was advised to be seated securely while holding onto something sturdy when the "all aboard" call was given. Stopping was an even greater adventure as the point at which brakes would be applied was always guesswork. Conditions actually worsened when locomotives were equipped with steam brakes while cars still lacked automatic couplers and adequate buffers. From 1840 through the end of the Civil War that was the case on most American railroads.

American railroads did not adopt the screw-type couplers and the buffers common in England. The link and pin coupler system gradually replaced chains as the preferred American coupling device and lasted until the 1890s on some railroads. The

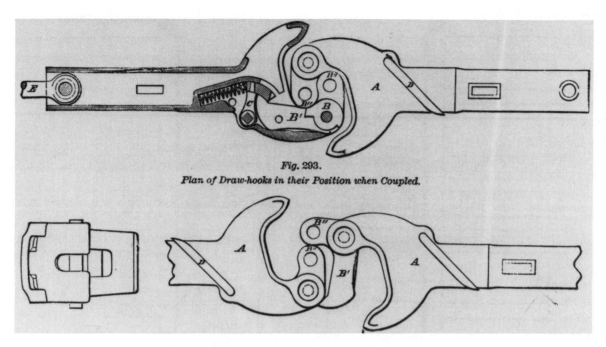

Fig. 293.
Plan of Draw-hooks in their Position when Coupled.

Diagram of the mechanism of the Janney Coupler

link and pin system was composed of an iron box, called the draft box, mounted in the center of the end sill of each car and extending a foot or so beyond it. The iron box was open only on the end facing away from the car. A hole in the top and the bottom of the box accepted an iron pin with a collar that would prevent it from slipping through the box and a round or cylindrical-shaped head to make it easy to hold. The link was an iron ring in the shape of a squared oval. The dimensions and exact form of the link varied from railroad to railroad, but it averaged 18 to 24 inches in length and 8 to 12 inches in width. Although the link and pin system was a definite advance over any previous coupling system, the lack of standardization caused problems.

The major problem with the link and pin system, however, was the actual process of coupling the cars, which was laborious, complex, and dangerous. The brakeman was required to step between the cars as they were about to hit, lift the link that was already in the draft box of one car, and guide it into the draft box of the car to which it was to be coupled. He then had to drop the pin to hold the link and couple the cars. As many of the locomotives did not have precise brakes and there was an unpredictable amount of slack between the cars in a train, the amount of movement that took place after the link was slipped into the draft box of the receiving car was difficult for the engineer and brake-

man to predict. Brakemen all too often were run over or had their hands or fingers smashed in the process of coupling. As train frequency, speed, and weight increased in the years after 1840, the number of brakemen injured and killed on the job increased dramatically.

Many efforts were made to develop a safer and more efficient automatic coupler. The trade magazines of the day show at least forty-two different types of couplers developed from about 1840 to the early 1890s. About a dozen of these were adopted by the Master Car Builders Association in the 1870s. These couplers appear to fall roughly into three types.

First were the types that were variations of the link and pin coupler. The Marks, Perry, McKeen, Archer, and Gifford couplers were all adopted by the Master Car Builders Association, and each of them used varying systems to guide the link into the draft box without requiring the brakemen to do it by hand. Each of them also used some kind of metal buffer mounted on the end-sill near the draft box in order to reduce slack and its consequent danger to passengers, freight, and brakemen.

A second group of couplers used some type of metal "tongue" mounted in the draft box and equipped with a hook or catch that engaged the "tongue" from the car being coupled to it. A similar device was used by the American Flyer toy train company on its model trains of the late 1940s and early 1950s. The Ames and the Fitzgerald & VanDorn were two adopted couplers that followed this pattern. Other couplers with names like LeRoux & Van Aarle, Meadows & Meade, and the Morgan used the same method. Once again, the "tongue" was fixed and with luck would slide into the draft box of the mating car and engage without the digital assistance of the brakeman.

The third type of coupler was the one that eventually emerged as the standard American model. This type abandoned the link and pin concept in favor of designing a conceptually new coupler. A Confederate army veteran, Maj. Eli H. Janney (1831-1912), was responsible for inventing it several years after the end of the Civil War. While he was clerking in a dry goods store near Alexandria, Virginia, Janney whittled a model of his proposed coupler. The design of the coupler was similar in concept to curving the fingers of each hand slightly and then sliding them together to hook the hands. Just as the knuckles or joints of the fingers allow the fingers to bend in order for them to slip past each other and lock, Janney developed a swinging or pivoting metal "knuckle" that allowed the two couplers to slide past each other. A spring actuated by the force of the contact between the two cars closed the "knuckles," thus coupling the cars. Best of all, a bar extending to the side of the car allowed the "knuckles" to be released, thus uncoupling the cars without the brakeman having to step between the cars.

Janney secured a patent in 1868, produced an improved design in 1873, and shortly thereafter arranged a trial of his coupler on the Pennsylvania Railroad. Despite the successful demonstration of the coupler, Janney's product was not an immediate commercial success. Several factors contributed to the railroads' refusal to adopt the system. First, the cost of converting cars and locomotives to the Janney coupler from the link and pin, or any other semiautomatic coupler then in use, was considerable. Most railroad companies did not see the new coupler as such a significant improvement that it justified the cost of conversion. Second, there were similar couplers on the market, and some of them

worked quite well. The Downing, Hills, Thurmond, Muller, Boston Automatic, and Simpson couplers were all similar to Janney's. Several of them were already in use on major railroads, and these companies were not easily convinced that Janney's coupler was superior.

Lorenzo Coffin, an Iowa farmer and safety activist, was primarily responsible for the acceptance of Janney's coupler and, to some extent, for the air brake. Appalled by the number of deaths and injuries caused by railroads (in 1881, 30,000 railroad employees were killed or injured in accidents), Coffin mounted a vigorous national crusade for the installation of the Janney coupler and the Westinghouse air brake. As a railroad commissioner for Iowa, Coffin was successful in encouraging the state to mandate the use of air brakes and couplers when operating in Iowa. His ultimate victory came in March 1893 when the United States Congress approved the Railroad Safety Appliance Act mandating the use of Janney couplers and air brakes on all American interstate railroads.

By 1900 all major American railroads and many local and short-line railroads had equipped locomotives and rolling stock with Janney couplers. Improved versions of the coupler have been developed in the twentieth century to cope with the 15,000-ton, two-mile-long coal trains operated by railroads like the Chessie System, the Burlington Northern, and the Norfolk Southern, but the basic design of the Janney coupler has stood the test of time amazingly well. Although not widely copied by other national railroad systems, the Janney coupler has met the needs of American railroads.

References:

Thomas M. Cooley, *The American Railway* (New York: Scribners, 1897);

Stewart H. Holbrook, *The Story of American Railroads* (New York: Crown, 1947);

Larry Kumferman, "Railroad Oddities," *Model Railroader*, 19 (January 1952): 75;

John F. Stover, *American Railroads* (Chicago: University of Chicago Press, 1961).

–Robert L. Frey

Eugene Victor Debs

(November 5, 1855-October 20, 1926)

by W. Thomas White

James Jerome Hill Reference Library

CAREER: Locomotive paint-scraper, Vandalia Railroad (1870-1871); locomotive fireman, Terre Haute & Indianapolis Railroad (1871-1874); grocery clerk (1874-1879); Terre Haute city clerk (1880-1883); general secretary and treasurer, Brotherhood of Locomotive Firemen (1880-1892); assistant editor and editor, *Locomotive Firemen's Magazine* (1880-1892); Indiana state assemblyman (1885-1887); president, American Railway Union (1893-1897); presidential candidate, Social Democratic Party of America (1900, 1904, 1908, 1912, 1920); associate editor, *Appeal to Reason* (c. 1904-1906).

Eugene Victor Debs was a nationally significant figure in organized labor during the late nineteenth century and one of the nation's preeminent voices of radical protest during the Progressive Era. As grand secretary and treasurer of the Brotherhood of Locomotive Firemen and as editor of its official magazine, Debs was able to publicize his views on worker solidarity and cooperation within the railroad industry and the general work force. Failing to convince other railroad labor leaders on the need for mutual cooperation, he organized the American Industrial Union along industrial, rather than craft, lines. After the destruction of the American Railway Union in the Pullman Strike of 1894, Debs became a central figure in American democratic socialism. An eloquent speaker, he was a perennial presidential candidate on the Socialist Party ticket from 1900 to 1920.

Eugene Victor Debs was born on November 5, 1855, in Terre Haute, Indiana, the first son of Jean Daniel, a local businessman, and Marguerite Marie Bettrich Debs. His parents, of Alsacian lineage, were poor but attained middle-class status by operating a successful store specializing in fine foods and liquors. Consequently, as a youth Debs was able to attend both private schools (Old Semi-

Eugene Victor Debs (Gale International Portrait Gallery)

nary School) and Terre Haute's first public schools. After graduating from grade school he attended one year of high school with the children of the town's leading families. In 1870 he left school and took an unskilled job as a locomotive paint-scraper in the maintenance shops of the Vandalia Railroad. Within a year he left the Vandalia to take a position as a fireman, an apprentice locomotive engineer, on the Terre Haute & Indianapolis Railroad, a job which became available when the regular fireman reported for work while intoxicated.

In 1874 the full force of the panic of 1873 was unleashed on rural Indiana, and the nineteen-year-old Debs was laid off. He moved to St. Louis in search of employment, instead finding the Victorian Age's harsh version of urban poverty. Unable to find work Debs returned to Terre Haute and, with his father's help, obtained a position as clerk in a local grocery. He remained a clerk until 1879, when he was elected city clerk on the Democratic ticket.

During that time Debs remained active in railroad labor affairs. In February 1875, inspired by Brotherhood of Locomotive Firemen founder Joshua Leach during the labor leader's visit to Terre Haute, Debs played an important role in organizing the local Vigo Lodge of the Brotherhood; he was elected its secretary. He became increasingly active in railroad affairs in that capacity despite his continuing employment as a retail clerk.

In the wake of the traumatic nationwide railroad strikes in 1877, Debs delivered an important speech at the Brotherhood of Locomotive Firemen's annual convention at Indianapolis. In marked contrast to his later views and actions, he criticized the use of strikes for seeking redress of labor's grievances. Debs counseled strict adherence to the rule of law and decried the violence that accompanied the 1877 turmoil on the roads. While he noted the justice of the strikers' demands, he nonetheless delivered a comparatively conservative speech, one that urged moderation and restraint. The assembled delegates enthusiastically applauded the address—itself indicative of the Brotherhood's cautious approach at the time—and the occasion proved an important benchmark in Debs's career.

Consequently, he was appointed assistant editor and, shortly thereafter, editor of the *Locomotive Firemen's Magazine*, the Brotherhood's official journal. In 1880 his rise to prominence continued, and Debs was named general secretary and treasurer of the national organization. Meanwhile, he continued to be active in Terre Haute's lodge, serving as secretary and master of the Firemen's local that he had helped to establish. Following his 1881 reelection as city clerk, he married Katherine Metzel in 1885 and successfully ran for the Indiana state assembly as a Democrat with cross-class support.

Increasingly, labor organizational affairs occupied Debs's attention. He remained reluctant to recognize unbridgeable class differences; persisting in his belief or hope, shared by most Americans of the time, that cross-class, community loyalties, and values would shape the emerging urban, industrial society. Accordingly, he was sympathetic neither to the American Federation of Labor nor to the Knights of Labor in the 1880s. Indeed, along with other railroad Brotherhood officials, Debs encouraged the rank and file not to recognize the Knights' strike against Jay Gould and the southwestern lines in the mid 1880s.

His conservative approach to labor conflict began to change as a result of the 1888 strike by the locomotive firemen and engineers against Charles Perkins and the Chicago, Burlington & Quincy Railroad. The thundering defeat dealt the strikers in that conflict convinced Debs of the inadequacy of his earlier views when faced by intransigent employers, internal disunity, and hostile public opinion. Consequently, he worked hard during the next four years to create unity among the railroad brotherhoods and to transcend craft and institutional differences in order to create a solid, unified front that could work effectively for the welfare of all railroad workers.

When it proved impossible to forge a meaningful alliance among the existing railroad brotherhoods, Debs led a faction of like-minded dissidents out of the brotherhoods to create the American Railway Union (ARU) in 1893. Under his leadership the industrially organized ARU weathered the opposition of both the skilled, craft-based brotherhoods and James J. Hill in the 1894 Great Northern (GN) Strike. During the conflict on the GN Debs had unsuccessfully urged ARU locals to avoid a strike, but once called, the conflict was resolved by an arbitration committee in St. Paul. Although the Great Northern strikers had, in reality, won only parity with their counterparts on other northwestern lines, a myth, carefully nourished by the ARU, grew that they had won a smashing victory. As a result of this illusory victory previously organized and unorganized railroaders eagerly joined the American Railway Union.

At the ARU's first annual convention, held in Chicago in 1894, the delegates ignored Debs's repeated counsels for restraint and declared a sympathy boycott to support employees of the Pullman Palace Car Company. That otherwise local dispute rapidly escalated as railroad managers attached Pullman cars to as many trains as they could, while their own employees, furious over repeated wage cuts and layoffs resulting from the depression, declared boycotts and strikes on all transcontinental railroad lines except the Great Northern. One of the greatest strikes of the nineteenth century, the Pullman Strike pitted Debs's American Railway Union against the Chicago-based General Managers' Association and, ultimately, the full force of the federal government, which, at President Grover Cleveland's order, deployed soldiers in what was, as Secretary of War Daniel Lamont reported, the largest troop movement since the Civil War.

With the collapse of the strike Debs and other ARU leaders were arrested on conspiracy charges and were later charged with contempt of court for ignoring federal injunctions issued to enjoin strike activity. Despite the best efforts of defense attorney Clarence Darrow, Debs was sentenced to six months in the Woodstock County Jail. That experience, which allowed him ample time to read and reflect upon his personal experiences in the labor movement, proved important in Debs's evolution as a democratic socialist.

Upon his release Debs was accorded a warm and large reception in Chicago and his native Terre Haute. In 1896 he campaigned hard for William Jennings Bryan and the Populist platform. The following year he announced himself a socialist in an address entitled "Present Conditions and Future Duties," a speech given to the remnants of the American Railway Union at the convention where it merged with the Social Democratic Party of America. Debs remained active in labor affairs, supporting insurgent West Virginia miners, the formation of the Western Federation of Miners, and in 1905, the Industrial Workers of the World.

However, he was best known for his long-term political activities and his eloquent, rousing speeches, the latter often delivered from the Red Special train which traversed the entire nation. The socialist candidate for president in five out of the six contests between 1900 and 1920, Debs seemed the embodiment of democratic socialism for many Americans in the Progressive Era. In 1900 he made a modest showing and polled only a little more than 96,000 votes as a presidential candidate.

Four years later, however, Debs attracted over 400,000 votes and became associate editor of the prominent socialist weekly *Appeal to Reason*, which was published in Girard, Kansas. That position and his ongoing lecture tours earned Debs a living and widened the outlets for his views. Although he drew large crowds in 1908, he was able to improve only slightly over his 1904 popular vote. The 1912 contest, fought in the midst of growing domestic unrest as well as the disarray within the Republican Party, marked a dramatic increase in socialist

sentiment. During that election Debs garnered over 900,000 votes (roughly 6 percent of the total), an amount which surprised the many observers who had forecast that the progressive appeals of Woodrow Wilson and Theodore Roosevelt would impinge sharply on the socialist vote.

Weakened by two physical collapses, Debs did not enter the presidential race in 1916, although he did run unsuccessfully for the House seat representing Indiana's Fifth Congressional District. Suffering another attack of illness, he was confined to his bed for most of 1917 as the United States entered World War I. Shortly after the Bolshevik Revolution Debs rose from his sickbed and delivered a series of antiwar speeches denouncing the Wilson Administration's campaigns to suppress dissent.

At a particularly noteworthy speech at Canton, Ohio, Debs denounced corporate leaders for their superpatriotism and the general war hysteria that was sweeping the nation. Two weeks later he was arrested for alleged violations of the Espionage Act of 1917. A Cleveland federal jury found Debs guilty and sentenced him to ten years in prison. From his jail cell in the Atlanta Federal Penitentiary, the aging and ill Debs conducted his last presidential campaign in 1920. Despite his incarceration, poor health, and the general disarray of the socialist movement following the Palmer Raids, Debs received nearly 1 million votes.

Just before Christmas, 1921, President Warren G. Harding, in a surprise move, pardoned Debs and two dozen other political prisoners and released them from prison. Debs remained frail and bedridden much of the time, however, and on October 20, 1926, Eugene Debs died of a massive heart attack in the Lindlahr sanitarium near Chicago. He remains one of the greatest leaders the American left has produced.

Publications:

"Confederation of Labor Organizations Essential to Labor's Prosperity," *American Journal of Politics* (July 1892): 63-71;

"Robert G. Ingersoll," *American Journal of Politics* (February 1893): 198-202;

Liberty (Terre Haute, Ind.: E. V. Debs, 1895);

Tribute of Love to His Father and Mother (Terre Haute, Ind., 1899);

The American Movement (Chicago: C. H. Kerr, 1900);

"The Social Democratic Party," *The Independent* (August 23, 1900): 2018-2021;

The Growth of Socialism (Chicago: C. H. Kerr, 1902);

Labor In Politics (St. Louis, 1903);

Debs addressing workers of the New York, New Haven & Hartford Railroad in 1908 (courtesy of Brown Brothers)

"The Social Democratic Party's Appeal," *The Independent* (October 13, 1904): 835-840;

The Socialist Party and the Working Class (Chicago: National Committee of the Socialist Party, 1904);

Unionism and Socialism (Terre Haute, Ind.: Standard Publishing, 1904);

Class Unionism (Chicago: Industrial Workers of the World, 1905);

Craft Unionism (Chicago: Industrial Workers of the World, 1905);

Debs: His Life, Writings, and Speeches (Girard, Kans.: Appeal to Reason, 1908);

The Federal Government and the Pullman Strike (Chicago: C. H. Kerr, 1910);

Unity and Victory (Chicago: C. H. Kerr, 1910);

Riley, Nye and Field (N.p., 1914);

Labor and Freedom (St. Louis: P. Wagner, 1916);

Labor and Socialism: The Voice and Pen of Eugene V. Debs, edited by Phil Wagner (St. Louis, 1916);

The Debs Trilogy: Man, Woman, Child (Girard, Kans.: Appeal to Reason, 1917);

The Fight for Liberty (Chicago, n.d. [c.1918]);

Pastels of Men (New York: Pearsons, 1919);

The Negro Workers (New York: Emancipation Publishing, 1923);

Walls and Bars (Chicago: Socialist Party, 1927);

Jesus, the Supreme Leader (Girard, Kans.: n.d.);

Woman . . . Comrade and Equal (Girard, Kans.: n.d.);

You Railroad Men (Chicago: C. H. Kerr, n.d.).

References:

Bernard J. Brommel, *Eugene V. Debs: Spokesman for Labor and Socialism* (Chicago: C. H. Kerr, 1978);

Milton Cantor, *The Divided Left: American Radicalism, 1900-1975* (New York: Hilland Wang, 1978);

Ray Ginger, *The Bending Cross: A Biography of Eugene Victor Debs* (Brunswick, N.J.: Rutgers University Press, 1949);

David F. Karsner, *Debs Goes to Prison* (New York: I. K. Davis, 1919);

Karsner, *Debs: His Authorized Life and Letters* (New York: Boni and Liveright, 1919);

Karsner, *Talks with Debs in Terre Haute* (New York: The New York Call, 1922);

Ira Kipnis, *The American Socialist Movement, 1897-1912* (New York: Columbia University Press, 1952);

Aileen S. Kraditor, *The Radical Persuasion, 1890-1917: Aspects of the Intellectual History and Historiography of Three American Radical Organizations* (Baton Rouge: Louisiana State University Press, 1981);

Donald L. McMurry, "Federation of the Railroad Brotherhoods, 1889-1894," *Industrial and Labor Relations Review*, 7 (October 1953): 73-92;

H. Wayne Morgan, *Eugene V. Debs, Socialist for President* (Syracuse: Syracuse University Press, 1962);

Nick Salvatore, *Eugene V. Debs: Citizen and Socialist* (Urbana: University of Illinois Press, 1982);

Salvatore, "Eugene V. Debs: From Trade Unionist to Socialist," *Labor Leaders in America*, edited by Melvyn Dubofsky and Warren Van Tine (Urbana: University of Illinois Press, 1987), pp. 89-110;

David A. Shannon, "Eugene V. Debs: Conservative Labor Leader," *Indiana Magazine of History*, 47 (1951), 357-364;

Shannon, *The Socialist Party of America: A History* (New York: Macmillan, 1955);

James Weinstein, *Ambiguous Legacy: The Left in American Politics* (New York: New Viewpoints, 1975);

Weinstein, *The Decline of Socialism in America, 1912-1925* (New York: Monthly Review, 1967).

Archives:

Materials concerning Debs are widely dispersed and may be found in the Brotherhood of Locomotive Firemen and Enginemen Papers of the Labor-Management Documentation Center, Catherwood Library, Cornell, University, Ithaca, New York; the Theodore Debs Scrapbook of the Fairbanks Memorial Library, Terre Haute, Indiana; the Eugene V. Debs Collection of the Tamiment Institute, New York University; the Eugene V. Debs Papers of the Houghton Library, Harvard University, Cambridge, Massachusetts; the Eugene V. Debs Collection of the Debs Foundation, Terre Haute, Indiana; the Eugene V. Debs Collection of the Fairbanks Memorial Library, Terre Haute, Indiana; the Adolph Germer Papers of the Wisconsin State Historical Society, Madison; the Morris Hillquit Papers of the University of Wisconsin, Madison, the Morris Hillquit Papers of the Tamiment Institute, New York University; the Department of Justice Files of the National Archives, Washington, D.C.; the Henry Demarest Lloyd Collection of Wisconsin State Historical Society, Madison; the Socialist Party Papers of the Perkins Library, Duke University, Durham, North Carolina; the Eugene V. Debs Collection of the Indiana State Library, Indianapolis; and the Eugene V. Debs Collection of the Cunningham Library, Indiana State University, Terre Haute.

Delaware & Hudson Railroad

by Katherine E. Larkin

Oneonta, New York

The history of the Delaware & Hudson (D&H) Railroad began in 1823 with the birth of the Delaware & Hudson Company, originally incorporated to build a canal to carry coal from northeast Pennsylvania to New York City. In 1898 the canal was closed due to the more efficient transportation provided by the company's railroads, the first of which was begun in 1827.

In the early 1800s two Philadelphia merchants, William and Maurice Wurts, bought land in the Lackawanna Valley of Pennsylvania and planned to mine the anthracite coal that existed there in large deposits. With much difficulty they managed to transport to Philadelphia, via the Lackawaxen and Delaware rivers, approximately 100 tons of stone coal. Although the Wurts brothers sold their coal in Philadelphia, they had to compete with coal merchants from the Lehigh Valley, which is closer to the city. Because of this competition the Wurtses decided to look for other markets, in particular, New York City.

During the 1820s the people of New York City and the surrounding area primarily heated their homes and powered their factories with wood. Many factories also were powered by water, the supply of which was then so abundant in the New York City region. The Wurts brothers had to convince New Yorkers that coal was more economical than wood. One fact in their favor was that a small amount of coal will provide as much heat as a much larger amount of wood. The Wurtses' plan was to find a way to transport coal more efficiently to New York City in order to be able to sell it there more cheaply than a comparable energy-producing amount of wood.

The Wurts brothers faced quite a task in finding an inexpensive way to get their coal to New York City. The terrain between northeastern Pennsylvania and the city was crisscrossed by steep ridges and no direct water route existed. It was finally decided that a canal could be built along the Lackawaxen River to the point it joined the Delaware River, then southeasterly along the river to the place where Pennsylvania, New Jersey, and New York come together. It would then continue in a northerly direction through the Rondout Creek Valley approximately 55 miles to the Hudson River at Kingston, New York. The total length of the canal would be 105 miles.

On March 13, 1823, the Delaware & Hudson Company was incorporated by the State of Pennsylvania. Six weeks later a similar act of incorporation was passed in New York. The company was authorized to build a canal between the Delaware and Hudson rivers in order to transport coal to markets in and around New York City. By November 1823 Benjamin Wright, chief engineer of the Erie Canal, had completed a survey of the canal route for the Wurts brothers. As the Delaware & Hudson's first chief engineer, Wright started construction and supervised the project until his resignation in 1827. John B. Jervis, Wright's assistant, took over as chief engineer of the project, and in December 1828 the entire length of the canal was placed in operation.

Meanwhile, another important part of the project had been authorized by the Pennsylvania legislature in 1826. Permission was granted to build a railroad from the coal mines at Carbondale over the Moosic Mountains to Honesdale, the new village at the head of the canal and named for Philip Hone, first president of the company. Jervis proposed the railroad, the first of its kind in the United States, after it was decided that it would be prohibitively expensive to build a canal over the mountains. Construction on the railroad commenced in 1827; it was designed to use five inclined planes as a method of overcoming the steepest grades in its 17-mile-long route.

John B. Jervis chose as his assistant a young engineer named Horatio Allen. Jervis instructed Allen to go to England and purchase the thin strap iron rails and to arrange for the manufacture of the required locomotive engines. He contracted with two companies to build four engines. One engine, the America, was built by Robert Stephenson and Company of Newcastle. The other engines, the Delaware, the Hudson, and the Stourbridge Lion, were built by Foster, Rastrick and Company of Stourbridge. Only the Stourbridge Lion ever reached Honesdale and when tested was found to be too heavy for use on the light-rail line. Allen had not followed Jervis's instructions concerning maximum locomotive weight, and, though the railroad was operational by the end of 1829, horsepower was substituted for locomotives. Finally, in 1860 two 4-foot, 3-inch gauge engines were put into use.

Passenger service was introduced on the line in the summer of 1860 and was available on the entire line by 1877. This service was mostly local at first, but by the turn of the century was used by large numbers of excursionists who visited the scenic countryside during summer months. An amusing incident connected with the passenger service happened in 1869 with the birth on the train of two new passengers, christened Dinah Delaware and Catherine Hudson Richards.

During the Civil War the mines in the Lackawanna Valley were busier than ever due to a great increase in the demand for coal. By 1863 the demand was greater than the D&H Company's production and transportation facilities had the power to supply. As a result the price of coal went up. Also during this time, Pres. George T. Olyphant, Vice-Pres. Thomas Dickson (who later succeeded Olyphant as president in 1869), and the other managers of the company began to look toward the "creation of new channels of supply." In December 1863 the D&H began negotiations with the Erie Railroad in order to obtain access to western markets over the Erie and its connections. The D&H still had to find some way to connect with the Erie at Lanesboro. In 1864 talks were begun with the Jefferson Railroad over the building of a line from Carbondale to Lanesboro. Because the Civil War was still in progress, nothing came of the conferences until many years later.

After the boom period of the Civil War the Delaware & Hudson Company decreased coal production and therefore suffered a drop in earnings. However, after the war, the D&H began to expand its railroad connections in an effort to tap a wider market. The years between 1866 and 1873 were a time of great railroad expansion for the D&H Company.

In 1868 the company contracted with the Erie Railroad to transport coal west to Binghamton,

New York, and to ship coal to the New York City and the New Jersey areas during winter when the frozen canal was closed. Thus began the first of many agreements negotiated to allow the D&H Company to reach markets all year long.

By 1867 the D&H had received railroad rights in New York State. In 1870 the D&H and the Albany & Susquehanna (A&S) Railroad, built between Albany and Binghamton, signed a contract for continuous lease of the A&S. The D&H first connected with the A&S at Binghamton and later farther north in the Susquehanna Valley at Nineveh, New York. The acquisition of the A&S provided the D&H with a route to Albany. In the last years of the 1870s the D&H leased the Rensselaer & Saratoga Railroad, allowing the company to extend its interests up into the Adirondack Mountains.

The 1880s and 1890s saw further expansion by the D&H Railroad into the northeast, although not to such a great extent as before. This period was one of good business that led the managers of the D&H Company to believe that their policy of railroad expansion had indeed been a success that had benefited the company greatly. In 1899 the D&H sold the canal, it no longer being relied upon for the transportation of coal. The Delaware & Hudson Company now relied exclusively on the railroad for the transport of its product.

References:

A Century of Progress, 1823-1923 (Albany, N.Y.: J. B. Lyon, 1925);

Jim Shaughnessy, *Delaware & Hudson* (Berkeley, Cal.: Howell-North Books, 1967).

Delaware, Lackawanna & Western Railroad

by James W. Hipp

Columbia, S. C.

The Delaware, Lackawanna & Western (DL&W) Railroad had its earliest beginnings in the Cayuga & Susquehanna (C&S) Railroad, a line which ran between Owego and Ithaca, New York. The C&S, chartered in 1828 as the Owego & Ithaca (O&I) Railroad, was completed in 1834 but was never able to generate sufficient revenues to become profitable. By 1842 the O&I had sunk into receivership and had ceased operations. The line was purchased that year for $18,000, but neither new ownership nor a name change to the Cayuga & Susquehanna could save the moribund line. In 1848, after operating for an additional six unspectacular years, the line was purchased by William Earl Dodge, the famous New York merchant, and George Scranton, the nascent iron and coal magnate. In less than a year Dodge and Scranton had transformed the C&S into a reliable and efficient means of transporting Scranton's iron and coal. But the line would be leased to the DL&W in 1853.

The corporate heart of the DL&W was the Liggett's Gap Railroad, which had been chartered in 1832 but never built. Scranton arranged for the charter to be reactivated and the road to be built, beginning operations on the line, renamed the Lackawanna & Western Railroad, in 1852. In 1849 another future part of the DL&W, the Delaware & Cobb's Glen (D&CG) Railroad, was chartered to build from the Delaware River to a point near Scranton, Pennsylvania. By the time of its official incorporation in 1850 the D&CG was under the control of many of those who were building the Lackawanna & Western, including Scranton, Dodge, John I. Blair, and George D. Phelps. On March 11, 1853, the state of Pennsylvania approved the merger of the Lackawanna & Western with the D&CG, officially marking the birth of the Delaware, Lackawanna & Western. Phelps was elected the line's first president.

From the beginning the DL&W's greatest strength was its wealth, provided both by the seemingly limitless amount of cargo represented by the Scranton interests and by the financial capital provided by Moses Taylor, the prominent New York banker and member of the DL&W board. Taylor played a principal role both in acquiring and leasing new lines and also in promoting the railroad's main cargo, anthracite coal. In 1853 the C&S was leased, and in 1869 the DL&W leased the Morris & Essex, a line which extended from Morristown, New Jersey, to the New York Harbor. When the Morris & Essex was connected with the former D&CG line, the DL&W gained access to the trading center of New York City.

The same year that the Morris & Essex was leased the DL&W bought the Syracuse, Binghamton & New York, leased the Oswego & Susquehanna, and built the Valley Railroad from Great Bend to Binghamton. With the lease in 1870 of both the Chenango & Susquehanna and the Greene railroads, the DL&W had succeeded in extending its lines to western New York state and Lake Ontario. Prior to these acquisitions the DL&W had been dependent on the Erie Railroad and its 6-foot gauge track for transporting its cargoes to the West. As a result, much of the DL&W's track was also 6 feet wide, easing transfer woes between the two railroads. On March 15, 1876, the DL&W converted its track to the standard gauge of 4 feet 8½ inches.

The large supply of coal, much of it produced by company-owned mines, provided the railroad with a relatively stable financial picture. The line's rapid and extensive improvements and expansions stretched the company's resources in the wake of the panic of 1873; dividends were suspended from 1876-1880. The DL&W escaped receivership, but its depressed stock price enabled the indefatigable Jay Gould to gain a position in the railroad. Although Gould was denied control of the company, he did convince the DL&W to build in 1880 the New York, Lackawanna & Western (NYL&W) Railway, a 207-mile connection from Binghamton to Lake Erie. In 1882 the DL&W signed a perpetual lease for the NYL&W.

In 1890 the late Moses Taylor's National City Bank was acquired by the Standard Oil Company. The purchase also placed Rockefellers and their proxies on the board of the DL&W, continuing the road's heritage of great capital wealth. During the 1890s, but beginning especially in 1899 with the elevation of William H. Truesdale to the road's presidency, the DL&W underwent a massive program of physical improvement. Lines were straightened, equipment and track replaced, and bridges were improved, all meant to improve the efficiency of its coal-hauling business and the newly burgeoning eastern passenger trade.

At the turn of the century the DL&W, as a result of its ample and consistent financing and its wise leadership, was one of the most efficient and technologically advanced railroads in the United States. It would remain so until the decline in the 1940s of anthracite coal as a major fuel source.

References:

Robert J. Casey and W. A. S. Douglas, *The Lackawanna Story* (New York: McGraw-Hill, 1951);

Thomas Townsend Taber, *The Delaware, Lackawanna & Western Railroad in the Nineteenth Century* (Muncy, Penn.: Thomas T. Taber III, 1977).

Archives:

The corporate records of the Delaware, Lackawanna & Western Railroad are located at the Syracuse University Library, Syracuse, New York, and at the Eleutherian Mills Historical Library, Wilmington, Delaware.

Denver & Rio Grande

by Jackson C. Thode

Denver & Rio Grande Western Railroad

The Denver & Rio Grande Western Railroad of today is the successor to the original Denver & Rio Grande (D&RG) Railway. As a common carrier railroad serving the states of Colorado and Utah, with operating rights over another line across the state of Kansas, it survives as an independent transportation enterprise whose corporate name perpetuates that of the original company.

Formally organized in the Colorado Territory on October 27, 1870, by Gen. William Jackson Palmer and several of his Civil War comrades, the Denver & Rio Grande was an out-of-the-ordinary concept in several respects. Neither its title nor its charter indicated any interest in becoming a Pacific railroad. Colorado was seen as being isolated from the eastern United States by 400 miles of the "Great American Desert" and from the West by the largely unexplored wilderness of the Rocky Mountains. Thus the new railroad was premised on a north-south location extending from Denver south along the eastern mountain base by way of the few small settled communities there and along the Rio Grande del Norte and from there to El Paso, Texas, and on to the city of Mexico, capital of a nation of then some 10 million inhabitants, a potential market of large proportion.

A brand new, untried idea of a narrow track gauge (3 feet between the rails) was adopted. Such an arrangement promised reductions of more than one-third in initial construction costs compared with standard-gauge lines, accompanied by similar savings in locomotive and rolling stock investment without loss of comfort, speed, capacity, or safety. Furthermore, any extensions into the mountains could be more easily adapted to the terrain, with tighter curves and heavier grades than standard-gauge construction, resulting in lower outlays of money.

General Palmer also visualized his new enterprise as an organization of friends and associates with "no jealousies and contests and differing policies . . . carry(ing) out unimpeded and harmoniously one's view in regard to what ought and ought not to be done . . . and all would work heartedly and unitedly towards the common end. . . . " With every employee having a stake in the "friendly little road," financial success was more assured, and management-labor conflicts were less likely to develop. Within a decade most of the concepts would be found to be less than wholly realistic.

Lacking any form of government subsidy the D&RG initially found it very difficult to finance its visionary project. Promotions in Britain and Holland, however, were more effective in gathering enough funds to warrant the start of construction. Grading south from Denver was begun in March 1871, and the first rails were laid on July 28 of that year. The narrow-gauge track reached Colorado Springs that fall, was pushed on to Pueblo the next summer, and, by November 1, 1872, was extended west along the Arkansas River another 36 miles to the coal mines in Fremont County. The main line then totaled 155 miles.

The financial panic of late 1873 delayed the D&RG's expansion, and only nine more miles of rail westward to Cañon City were completed in 1874. Not until late 1876 was it possible once again to forge ahead; that year the southward thrust was renewed with ninety-three miles of new road built from Pueblo to near Trinidad. Divergence westward from the north-south trunk line into the mountains toward that prime objective–the Rio Grande del Norte–also was accomplished, with twenty-two additional miles of track spiked down. In 1877 and 1878 another fifty-eight miles of road were completed over the Sangre de Cristo range to the legendary Rio Grande at Alamosa. In crossing the Veta Pass, the D&RG used the sharpest curve (thirty degrees) and heaviest grade (4.5 percent) to reach the highest altitude (9,393 feet above sea

The 2-6-0 locomotive Shou-wa-no was one of the D&RG's first freight locomotives (courtesy of Colorado State Historical Society)

level) encountered by any American railroad to that time.

During 1878 the fabulous mineral riches of Leadville, Colorado, were discovered. General Palmer, whose "Baby Railroad" now comprised 337 miles of main line, promptly sought additional funds to undertake construction, not only west from Cañon City along the Arkansas River to the new Golconda but also southward over the Raton mountains from the end of line near Trinidad. This time, however, an obstacle more formidable than financing barred the way. When the D&RG men arrived to start work on February 27, 1878, the Raton Pass was in possession of the construction forces of the rival Atchison, Topeka & Santa Fe (ATSF).

Acknowledging defeat, Palmer and his men quickly diverted their efforts to the extension westward toward Leadville from Cañon City. As suggested by its name, Cañon (Canyon) City lies at the mouth of the Royal Gorge of the Arkansas River where the chasm, in places little more than 30 feet wide with vertical walls more than 1,100 feet high, affords the only feasible entrance through the Front Range into the mountains. On the morning of April 19, 1878, D&RG crews started their work at Cañon City. Forewarned by the preliminaries to

this D&RG activity, the Santa Fe, on the same day, managed to recruit a ragtag local force and put it to work inside the mouth of the gorge. Thus began one of the classic battles in railroad history. Armed men manned stone forts and breastworks along the route; opposing engineering and grading crews challenged each other face to face or surreptitiously outflanked each other; receiverships ensued, and the legal complexities over priority rights of the contending companies were thrown upon the courts.

The Royal Gorge War, involving a decision favorable to the Rio Grande by the U. S. Supreme Court in 1879, endured for two years. But at last, on February 1880, the long, exhausting, and expensive conflict between the D&RG and the ATSF was resolved by the court-motivated Treaty of Boston; and on April 5, 1880, General Palmer and his associates finally regained possession of the property to which they had so doggedly devoted ten years of their lives. Under the terms of the treaty the D&RG agreed to a southern limit at the 36th parallel (Española, New Mexico), which effectively eliminated the original north-south concept. And the "friendly little road" envisioned in the early days also became a thing of the past; to finance the additional construction mandated by the Leadville boom, Jay Gould entered the scene and gained three of the five positions on the D&RG directorate.

But with its credit thus bolstered, the railroad now spread throughout western Colorado and into Utah during a three-year period of extraordinary expansion. In the remaining nine months of 1880 alone, 347 miles of new track (ten miles more than were built in the previous nine years) were added to the system. In 1881 another 381 miles were laid down; and in 1882 an additional 216 miles, including an extension to the Colorado-Utah border aimed at Ogden, Utah, were constructed.

Because its charter in Colorado did not authorize construction in Utah, a separate company under the name of the Denver & Rio Grande Western (D&RGW) Railway was organized by General Palmer in the Utah Territory on July 21, 1881. Building southeast from Salt Lake City, the D&RGW completed 155 miles of line in 1882. In 1883 79 miles were built east to connect with 97 miles of trackage laid by D&RG crews west from the Colorado-Utah border. The last spike was driven on March 30, 1883, at Desert Switch, Utah. Construction crews immediately began work on the 40-mile stretch from Salt Lake City to Ogden, and they connected with the Central Pacific on May 16, 1883. Thus a new link, albeit entirely of narrow 3-foot gauge, was forged in the transcontinental railroad chain.

The extraordinary monetary outlays consumed in carrying out this monumental expansion and the vicious antagonism by the Union Pacific toward this competitive upstart caused many problems within the Rio Grande management. General Palmer resigned as president of D&RG on August 9, 1883, and reorganization of both the Colorado and Utah companies ensued. New managers took over the Denver & Rio Grande, although Palmer successfully retained control over the D&RGW.

When additional lines using the standard gauge of 4 feet 8½ inches reached Colorado during the 1880s—the Burlington at Denver, the Rock Island at Colorado Springs, the Missouri Pacific at Pueblo, and the Denver, Texas & Fort Worth (DT&FW) at Trinidad—the physical disadvantages and economic handicaps of the Rio Grande's narrow gauge became more apparent. As early as 1881 an outside third rail to accommodate standard-gauge equipment had been spiked down along one side of the narrow gauge between Denver and Pueblo. The same scheme was adopted between Pueblo and Trinidad in 1887 to preclude construction of a competing line by the DT&FW. When the standard-gauge Colorado Midland in 1887 forced its way into the remote mountain areas that had been the exclusive province of the Rio Grande, regauging could be avoided no longer. Between 1888 and 1890 the main line of the Denver & Rio Grande was revised, relocated, and rebuilt to standard gauge. In Utah the story was the same; by mid November 1890 both the D&RG and the newly named Rio Grande Western (RGW) were able to proclaim standard-gauge service over the entire 778 miles of their combined main lines.

The final decade of the nineteenth century for the two railroads saw none of the frantic pace of the preceding twenty years. The silver panic of 1893 devastated the economies of Colorado and Utah, with a corresponding effect on the two Rio Grandes. By radical retrenchment in every branch of their service, both companies escaped bankruptcy; and with the economic recovery of the late 1890s, new records were again being set in revenues and net earnings. Gen. William Jackson Palmer, still at the head of the Rio Grande Western, relinquished his position in 1901 and sold out to George J. Gould, who had acquired the D&RG that same year. Many of Palmer's long-time, faithful RGW associates and employees were granted shares in the profits from the sale, showing that his early theme of a "friendly little road" had never been allowed to die through all the years of struggle.

Unpublished Document:

Arthur O. Ridgway, Denver & Rio Grande, Development of Physical Property in Chronological Narrative (Denver: I.C.C. Valuation Records, D&RGWRR, 1921).

References:

Robert G. Athearn, *Rebel of the Rockies, The Denver & Rio Grande Western Railroad* (New Haven: Yale University Press, 1962);

Herbert O. Brayer, *William Blackmore: Early Financing of the Denver & Rio Grande Railway and Ancillary Land Companies 1871-1878* (Denver: Bradford-Robinson, 1949);

John S. Fisher, *A Builder of the West, The Life of General William Jackson Palmer* (Caldwell, Idaho: The Caxton Printers, 1939);

Robert A. LeMassena, *Rio Grande . . . to the Pacific!* (Denver: Sundance, 1974);

O. Meredith Wilson, *The Denver and Rio Grande Project, 1870-1901* (Salt Lake City: Howe Brothers, 1982).

Archives:
"The Archive of the Denver and Rio Grande West-ern Railroad Company, Denver, Colorado, was established in 1941 (and since disbanded). . . . Much of the archive is now in the Colorado Historical Society Library, Denver. Other portions are in the Colorado Railroad Museum, Golden, and the Denver Public Library," in the words of Dr. O. Meredith Wilson.

Chauncey Mitchell Depew

(April 23, 1834-April 5, 1928)

by E. Dale Odom

North Texas State University

CAREER: Yale graduate (1856); admitted to New York Bar (1858); state legislator and secretary of state, New York (1861-1865); president, New York Central & Hudson River Railroad (1885-1898); chairman of the board, New York Central (1898-1928); candidate, Republican presidential nomination (1888); Republican senator, New York (1899-1911); practicing attorney; and board member of several corporations (1911-1928).

During his more than nine decades of life, Chauncey Depew made significant contributions in four different fields. First, he was an able attorney and talented legislative lobbyist. Second, although he was never a railroad man, *per se*, as vice-president and president of the New York Central & Hudson River Railroad for fourteen years and chairman of the board for an even longer time, Depew was an important railroad businessman. Third, as a state legislator, United States senator for twelve years, candidate for other national offices, and a power in the New York Republican party for over fifty years, he made an important mark as a politician. Finally, he was an internationally known orator, after-dinner speaker, wit, and raconteur. If Depew had confined his efforts to one, or even two fields, he most likely would have been an even more noted man. He was, however, the recipient of good fortune throughout his career. Everything appeared to come easily for him and his career is commonly viewed as having followed the path of least resistance.

Chauncey Mitchell Depew was born at Peekskill, New York, on April 23, 1834, the son of Isaac and Martha Mitchell Depew. His father was of

Chauncey Mitchell Depew

French Huguenot descent while his mother came from a Connecticut family related to Roger Sherman. Isaac Depew was a successful businessman engaged in river transportation, but most of the Depew ancestors had been farmers, and young Depew considered becoming one early in life. Martha Depew was a well-educated woman at a time when that was a rarity, and she gave her son a strong beginning in education by teaching him at home and by placing him, at five years of age, in a school conducted by the wife of the minister of the Dutch Reformed Church in Peekskill. Depew later gave the minister, Dr. Westbrook, considerable credit for instilling in him at an early age an avid and lifelong interest in the classics, great literature, politics, and history. As a young boy he devoured all the books in the local circulating library and considered Charles Dickens as his particular favorite.

From the age of nine to eighteen Depew was schooled at the Peekskill Military Academy. The curriculum must have tended toward the utilitarian for Depew later maintained that he would have preferred a better preparation for Yale. His father originally did not consider college for his son; he expected him to join him in his business after he had finished at the academy. But Depew wanted a higher education, and his mother and Dr. Westbrook prevailed on the elder Depew to send the young man to Yale. Although the Yale College *Catalogue of the Officers and Students, 1851-1852* claimed that its subjects offered preparation for careers in "higher mercantile, manufacturing or agricultural establishments," the training Depew received at Yale between 1852 and 1856 was in the classics. Of course, a classical education in that era was considered appropriate to success in any of those fields. The young New Yorker not only obtained a good classical education, but also received excellent preparation for his political and public-speaking career. Almost as important as his classroom work were his extracurricular activities, particularly the discussions and debates of his literary society, where he honed his talent to both entertain and persuade.

Although he won awards for composition and oratory, Depew finished near the middle of his class at Yale. More important than his class standing was that Yale was the site of the beginning of Depew's lifelong association with the newly organized Republican party. He came to Yale a Democrat; his father had been one and had defended slavery. But Depew, although never an abolitionist, became strongly antislavery and in 1856 supported John Fremont, the Republican candidate for the presidency.

After graduation from Yale in 1856 Depew, at the age of twenty-two, returned to Peekskill where he studied law in the office of William Nelson and was admitted to the New York Bar in 1858. His

zeal in denouncing slavery and in supporting the Republican party quickly drew him into active politics. A delegate to the 1858 state convention and an important campaigner for Lincoln and Hamlin in the 1860 presidential contest, in 1861 he was elected by a comfortable margin to the New York legislature to represent a district that for years had voted Democratic. Depew's personality and his skill as an orator rapidly boosted the young man to prominence in New York politics. His greatest asset, as it was throughout his life, was his ability to express ideas clearly and precisely and with great wit and fluency. He was a genuinely likable, naturally charming man who rarely made political enemies, primarily because he tried to keep personalities out of politics. Furthermore, although he was obviously ambitious, he was not ruthlessly so, and often sacrificed, or seemed to, his personal interest for the good of his party. In business he often asserted that making money was never his objective, and at his death his fortune, estimated to be between $5 million and $15 million, was considered by the *New York Times* not to be half of what he might have amassed.

After serving one term in the New York legislature, Depew, at the age of twenty-nine, won a statewide election in 1863 to the office of secretary of state. After two years in that position Depew was offered a presidential appointment to be United States ambassador to Japan. He refused the post and its $7,500 salary, instead joining Cornelius Vanderbilt as an attorney and lobbyist for the Vanderbilt railroads. Depew's salary was far less with Vanderbilt than with the government, but he must have been influenced by Vanderbilt's advice: "Railroads are the career for a young man; there is nothing in politics. Don't be a damn fool." Depew was the attorney for the New York & Harlem and the New York Central & Hudson River railroads until 1875 when he was named general counsel to the newly consolidated New York Central (NYC). In 1882 he became the second-vice-president of the NYC.

During the many years that Depew served Vanderbilt and the New York Central, he made his main contribution as a legislative lobbyist. Until the late 1870s Depew was almost always successful in that capacity. By 1880 railroads were drawing increased criticism from many of their patrons. The basic problem was that both New York City merchants and western farmers and businessmen were upset at any rate discrimination that favored the other. Both were selfish in their interests and each would often condemn the railroad and Depew as he sought to conciliate each group, find grounds for compromise, and at the same time protect the best interest of the New York Central. In 1877 the *Husbandman* accused Depew of employing "obvious untruths and unpleasant innuendos" that were proof of the railroad's "arrogance and deceit." Yet Depew's charm, wit, and talent as a public speaker caused him to draw less vituperation than did most railroad lobbyists. This, of course, was part of the reason why he was so valuable to the Vanderbilts and the New York Central.

Furthermore, his connections with the Republican party did nothing to diminish his usefulness to the NYC. As a leader of the reformist Halfbreed faction of the party, however, Depew came into conflict with the famous Roscoe Conkling. In New York politics it was Depew, the corporate politician, against Conkling, the machine politician. Conkling won re-election in 1881, but the corporate political leaders won in the long run. They won not only because the Pendleton Act of 1883 began to take away patronage as leverage for the machine politician, but because the corporate politicians, whom Depew epitomized, were more willing to make concessions to public opinion and to compromise on issues. For instance, Depew fought state regulation of railroads in New York up until 1882, but when regulation became inevitable he switched to supporting a New York railroad commission based on the less radical and less hated Massachusetts model.

Both Commodore Vanderbilt and his son William often paid attention to Depew's advice on how to improve the image of the NYC. In the early 1880s the attorney persuaded William Vanderbilt to sell some of his stock in the New York Central. The argument that any legislation that might threaten railroad dividends would harm the poor widows who owned the stock had become untenable when Vanderbilt owned almost all the stock in the New York Central. Furthermore, when the Vanderbilt family resigned all of their railroad presidencies and vice-presidencies in 1885, it was apparently Depew's idea to remove them from any public connection with the road. The increasing virulence of public criticism of the railways partly accounts for Depew's rapid rise in the bureaucracy of the New York Central. The times called for executives who could deal with public wrath, and so

when NYC President Rutter died in the summer of 1885, Depew replaced him as chief executive and remained in that office until 1898.

The fact that Depew was not actually a railroad man at all, but a skillful lawyer and politician was indicative of the growing size and sophistication of railroads and their management. Depew's appointment also fit the administrative history of the New York Central, where top executives usually had not been closely involved in actual railroad operations. Depew continued that tradition, concentrating the use of his tact and diplomacy on trying to improve his company's image. He maintained that as chief executive he listened to all complaints and that his door was always open to any employee, to the public, and to the press. His talent for defending the NYC's position continued in evidence, and a conciliatory labor policy, begun in the 1870s, contributed to good labor relations. Only one strike marred Depew's tenure as president and it took place while he was on one of his frequent trips to Europe.

It was during the years that he was rising to prominence as a railway attorney and executive that Depew had become devoted to his avocation of public-speaking. He called it his recreation, a way of resting his brain cells that were tired from long hours spent on railroad business. But his public speaking, like his other avocation, politics, must have been quite useful to the New York Central. Most of his speeches—he often spoke three to five nights a week—were at dinners closing the annual meetings of various trade associations. Such exposure helped the New York Central to obtain more business and better its image.

Late in his life Depew was often asked about his recipe for longevity. He said "work, temperance, and fun, the ability to laugh [and] refusal to worry" had prolonged his life. He seldom drank alcohol, did not smoke, and was usually home in bed by eleven. He continued his seemingly exhaustive public speaking schedule throughout his career as a railroad president, United States senator, and on to his ninetieth year in 1924. In the last four years of his life he attended few dinners but did give reporters annual interviews on his birthday right up to his last in 1927. When he was ninety-two, he told reporters that he expected to live to a hundred, at which time he expected to have time to "take up golf."

As a speaker Depew was more than just an entertaining humorist. The *New York Times* called him "a philosopher, and one of the wise men of the Western world." The fact that he was chosen to give the speech at the 1886 ceremony dedicating the Statue of Liberty indicates his reputation as an orator. Lee Benson asserts in *Merchants, Farmers, and Railroads* that "Depew's richly imaginative style is impossible to recapture by paraphrase or by illustration, and only a reading of the original does full justice to his talents." But no characterization can truly indicate the effectiveness of a speaker who was quick-witted, well-informed, and obviously relished regaling an audience.

While his public-speaking avocation developed and his career as president of the New York Central continued, Depew still pursued his strong interest in politics. In 1888 he was a serious candidate for the Republican nomination for the presidency. Depew eventually withdrew from the race because, among other reasons, the western Republicans were hostile to anyone associated with the railroads. The eventual winner, Benjamin Harrison, offered to make Depew his secretary of state but was refused. During these years and throughout his life, Depew served as a member of a large number of public service organizations; for example, he served on the board of the University of the State of New York from 1877 to 1904. His political career peaked in 1899 when he was chosen United States senator from New York, a position that he occupied for two six-year terms until he retired in 1911 at the age of seventy-seven.

Although as a senator Depew was important, respected, and even feared by his colleagues because of his sharp tongue and oratorical power, he never stood out as the leader his age and his fame would seem to have merited. Several factors may explain why. Reform was popular and, outside New York, he could never be considered a reformer. His popularity was hurt particularly when, during the famous investigation of the New York life insurance industry, it was revealed that Depew had been receiving an annual retainer of $20,000 from the Equitable Life Assurance Company. After the retainer was exposed, he quickly gave it up and later returned to his usual popularity, at least with easterners. Depew also lacked the seniority to contend with the likes of Senate fixtures Thomas Collier Platt, Mark Hanna, and Nelson Aldrich. Furthermore, by the time he rose to the Senate, he seems

to have been considered something of a dilettante. Senate leaders and the public may have had some trouble taking him seriously because of his colorful dress which, at times, bordered on the outlandish. Depew understood that his image adversely affected his political career. He was fond of quoting President James A. Garfield, who had one time told Depew that he might have been president if he had not told funny stories. He thus tended to blame his lack of higher political achievement on the fact that he was prominent as a witty public speaker. Unlike most opponents of progressive reform Depew was an advocate of expansion overseas, and spoke eloquently on behalf of acquiring the Philippines. In the Senate he considered himself, and was considered, as something of an authority on foreign affairs, but during his tenure foreign affairs were orchestrated by Theodore Roosevelt, who tended to overshadow all New York politicians.

From the time of his retirement as NYC president in 1898 until his death in 1928, Depew continued as chairman of the NYC board. He also continued to serve until his death on the boards of several other corporations, including Western Union. Although he was a busy man, he found time for marriage and family. He married Elise Hegemann in 1871 and they had one son, Chauncey M. Depew, Jr. She died in 1893. In 1901 Depew married May Palmer, who survived him.

Depew retained an active interest in politics until shortly before his death. His last quotes in the press include a report that he thought President Coolidge should be drafted to run for another term in 1928. From 1860 to 1920 he attended every Republican national convention as a delegate, and was chosen to go in 1924, but became ill and was unable to make the trip. He was an intimate friend of every Republican president from Lincoln to Harding, and it was Lincoln, he said, who first convinced him of the effectiveness of using humorous anecdotes to make his points in public speaking.

The old New Yorker remained in reasonably good health and clear mind until shortly before his death from bronchial pneumonia on April 5, 1928, eighteen days short of his ninety-fourth birthday. He left an unappraised fortune estimated to be worth between $5 million and $15 million. Yale University was a large beneficiary, receiving $1 million. He was buried in Hillside Cemetery in his native town of Peekskill, New York.

Publication:

Chauncey Mitchell Depew, *My Memories of Eighty Years* (New York: Scribners, 1922).

References:

Howard K. Beale, *Theodore Roosevelt and the Rise of America to World Power* (Baltimore, Md.: Johns Hopkins University Press, 1956);

Lee Benson, *Merchants, Farmers and Railroads* (Cambridge, Mass.: Harvard University Press, 1955);

Edward Hungerford, *Men and Ideas: A History of the New York Central* (New York: Thomas Y. Crowell, 1938);

Walter Licht, *Working for the Railroad* (Princeton, N.J.: Princeton University Press, 1983);

New York Times, April 5, 1928, p. 5;

Willard Hayes Yeager, *Chauncey Mitchell Depew, The Orator* (Washington, D.C.: George Washington University Press, 1934).

Archives:

A collection of Chauncey Depew's speeches and papers are located in the library of George Washington University, Washington, D.C.

Grenville Mellen Dodge

(April 12, 1831-January 3, 1916)

by John F. Due

University of Illinois

CAREER: Railway surveyor (1852-1854); merchant, real estate broker, banker, freighter (1854-1862); officer, ending with rank of major general, Union Army (1862-1866); chief engineer, Union Pacific Railroad (1866-1870); chief engineer, Scott and Gould lines (1871-1881); cofounder, Cuba Railroad (1900-1903).

Grenville Mellen Dodge was born on April 12, 1831, in Danvers, Massachusetts, to Sylvanus and Julia Phillips Dodge, a family that had been in Massachusetts since 1638. His father was a butcher and, later, village postmaster. Grenville worked at a number of jobs as a teenager, graduated from Norwich University in engineering in 1850, and received a diploma as a civil and military engineer from the Partridge School in 1851. As did many college students of the period, Dodge developed a great enthusiasm for railroad construction. After graduation he went west to Peru, Illinois, where two of his college classmates had settled, and found work as a surveyor laying out city lots. But Dodge was primarily interested in a railway survey position and received such an appointment in 1852 with the Illinois Central (IC), then building south from Chicago. Dodge was not happy with his superior on the IC, returned to Peru in 1852, and soon obtained a position with the Mississippi & Missouri Railroad (M&M), a subsidiary of the Rock Island, as chief assistant to Peter Dey on the survey being

Grenville Mellen Dodge (courtesy of Union Pacific Railroad Museum)

made across Iowa. Thomas C. Durant, with whom Dodge would clash later in their careers, was also involved in the construction of the M&M.

Progress on the survey was slow, and construction of the M&M was seriously delayed. After Dodge married Anne Brown, whom he had met in Peru, on May 29, 1854, he acquired land on the Elkhorn River, twenty-five miles west of Omaha, and farmed for a time, hoping the railroad would build through his land. But when the railroad did not come and Indians returned to the area, the Dodges moved in 1855 to Council Bluffs. Until 1861 Dodge did railroad survey work in Iowa and engaged in various forms of business, including real estate, banking, freighting, and merchandising. He also formed a local militia company, an activity with which he had been involved in Peru. But his interest in railroad development remained. In 1857 he met Abraham Lincoln, an acquaintance that would aid Dodge in subsequent years, and spoke with him about possible transcontinental railroad routes. Dodge had become convinced that the only feasible route for a transcontinental line was up the Platte Valley. After Lincoln was elected and inaugurated, Dodge joined other groups in lobbying for a bill authorizing a transcontinental railroad using the Council Bluffs-Platte Valley route. Before the Civil War the political strength of the South, which favored a southern route, had blocked legislation. But once the South seceded, enactment of the legislation favoring a northern route became possible.

As soon as the Civil War began, Dodge placed his militia company at the disposal of the governor of Iowa, who placed it in the Fourth Iowa Division, and appointed Dodge a colonel. The division was sent to Rolla, Missouri, as part of the Army of the Southwest, and Dodge had his first task of rebuilding and operating a railroad, the Pacific, which ran between St. Louis and Rolla. Dodge played a part in the major campaign of the Army of the Southwest, which defeated the Confederate forces of Sterling Price and Earl Van Dorn at Pea Ridge, Arkansas, in 1862. Shortly thereafter Dodge was promoted to brigadier general and placed in charge of the forces that were rebuilding the railroad lines destroyed by the Confederates in Tennessee and Mississippi. General Grant thought highly of his work and ordered Dodge, among other activities, to organize what became a successful secret service for the army in the west. In 1863 he was summoned to Washington by President Lincoln to discuss rail routes to the Pacific.

In 1864 Dodge was promoted to major general. As the Battle of Atlanta began in 1864, Dodge suffered a severe head wound and returned to Council Bluffs for several months of recovery. He was then given command of the Army Department of Missouri with the thankless tasks of trying to pacify the population of that severely divided state and ending the extensive guerrilla warfare. During 1865 and 1866 Dodge was in command of the campaign against the Indians, in the area between the Missouri and the Rockies, who were blocking supply and travel routes to the west and delaying the commencement of the building of the Union Pacific. Despite inadequate numbers of troops he succeeded in bringing the Indians under control. Forced to use such drastic measures as killing the Indians, Dodge's techniques were roundly criticized by the Department of the Interior and other groups. Dodge responded that the Indian problem was the product of the failure of the government to live up to its treaty obligations and of the actions of various persons, military and civilian, in unnecessarily slaughtering Indians.

In 1866 he made the decision to leave the army permanently. Thomas C. Durant, the vice-president of and leading figure in the Union Pacific Railroad, had encouraged Dodge to leave the army to become chief engineer of the railroad as early as 1863. Dodge was not willing to do so as long as the war continued, but in 1866 he accepted the position. Durant's interest in Dodge was twofold, prompted by Dodge's capacity as a railroad engineer and his relationship with President Lincoln. Already Durant and Dodge had differed over the starting point of the railroad, the latter favoring Council Bluffs-Omaha, while Durant favored other points. The government, possibly because of Dodge's 1857 meeting with Lincoln, forced the acceptance of Council Bluffs.

When Dodge took over as chief engineer the railroad was moribund; construction had stopped; the track was in bad shape; and Durant was under fire for his financial dealings. Dodge accepted the job of chief engineer with some reluctance because of his concern about Durant, whom he knew from M&M days, and did so only after he was assured complete authority over building. He reorganized the operations, brought in the Casement brothers to head actual construction, and pushed construction ahead rapidly.

He was confronted, however, with serious obstacles. Because there was no railroad to Council Bluffs, supplies, including locomotives, had to be brought up from St. Joseph by water. Even though the Chicago & Northwestern did reach Council Bluffs in 1867, all supplies had to be ferried across the Missouri River until a bridge was completed in 1872. More serious obstacles were Indian raids. On many occasions Indians attacked the line, damaged trestles, and sometimes killed workers. But probably Dodge's chief obstacle was the endless difficulty with the devious Durant. Part of their disagreement centered on the selection of the route. Dodge was convinced that only Lone Tree Pass, which was west of Laramie and which Dodge had discovered when scouting Indians in 1866, was a feasible route, while Durant refused to be nailed down on his preference. Disagreement was also fomented because of Durant's refusal, despite his promises, to grant Dodge full autonomy. For example, on one occasion Durant spread rumors, without Dodge's knowledge, that the construction shops would be transferred from Cheyenne to Laramie. The most serious cause for disagreement between Dodge and Durant, however, was their differing attitudes toward the Ames brothers. Durant, locked in a battle over control of the Union Pacific, was highly critical of the two men's leadership, while Dodge was generally more supportive of the Ameses.

It was not until 1868, at a meeting involving presidential candidate Ulysses S. Grant, Sidney Dillon, Dodge, and others, that Dodge's authority in engineering matters was confirmed, a confirmation that prevented his resignation. There remained, however, the disagreement with the Central Pacific (CP) over where the two lines would join their rails. Each railroad, of course, wanted to build as far as possible in order to maximize its subsidy benefits. The original legislation had authorized the CP to build to the California-Nevada border, but this restriction was later removed. Subsequent legislation specified that each railroad should build until they met, and did not specify an exact location. Because this same law allowed the railroads to survey 300 miles past the end of construction, in 1868 the UP and the CP were grading past each other. Dodge finally managed to persuade C. P. Huntington of the CP to agree to a junction at Promontory Point, Utah, and the two lines were officially joined on May 10, 1869. As part of the agreement the UP sold the Promontory-Ogden segment of the line to the CP, allowing the CP access to Ogden. With all these accomplishments, Dodge was only thirty-eight years old in 1869.

In 1870 Dodge resigned as chief engineer and urged the directors to fire Durant, which eventually they did. Dodge was elected a director of the UP in 1871. He was involved in the investigation by the government of the role of the Crédit Mobilier, which technically did the contracting for the building of the railway and which was widely criticized for bribery and misuse of federal funds. Dodge was not directly involved in the contract dealings, but his wife did have Crédit Mobilier stock.

In the decade from 1871 to 1881 Dodge was not involved with the Union Pacific but instead in the building of railways in the Southwest. In 1871 and 1872 he was chief engineer of the Texas & Pacific, headed by Thomas Scott of the Pennsylvania Railroad. But the panic of 1873 and the failure of Jay Cooke and Company brought construction to an end and led to strong criticism of the projects. For the next seven years Dodge worked with Jay Gould in the development of a number of lines in the Southwest, in the process becoming president of the Missouri, Kansas & Texas. Dodge thought better of Gould than did others but found him too willing to take risks, especially in regard to a planned venture for building into Mexico, which turned out to be a complete fiasco.

Gould, meanwhile, had obtained control of the UP in 1874 and dominated it until 1883. When he gave up control in that year, the UP was burdened with an even heavier load of debt and a worse public image than it had before Gould's arrival. Charles F. Adams, Jr., who succeeded Gould, brought Dodge back into the company as an adviser on the best way to extend the road to tidewater. The UP was successful in this goal by gaining control of the Oregon Railway & Navigation (OR&N) Company and then in 1884 building the Oregon Short Line to connect with the OR&N at Huntington. Gould regained control of the UP in 1890, but the road sank into receivership during the 1893 depression. The bankruptcy forced the UP to give up the OR&N and the Oregon Short Line, depriving the line of its outlet to the Pacific Coast. When the UP passed into the control of Edward Harriman in 1897, Dodge ended his over thirty years of affiliation with the road.

In his later years Dodge maintained his home in Council Bluffs, overlooking the river valley. He

Dodge (center, right, facing camera) congratulates his Central Pacific counterpart, Samuel S. Montague, on the completion of the Pacific railroad, May 10, 1869 (courtesy of Union Pacific Railroad Museum)

was active in various veteran and military groups. He joined with Sir William Van Horne, president of the Canadian Pacific, in building the Cuba Railroad between 1900 and 1903. He also became interested in building railroads in South America, but health reasons prevented his doing so. Earlier both Russia and China had expressed interest in his aiding railroad construction. In 1906 he resigned from the board of directors of four railroads for reasons of health. In 1913 and in 1915 Dodge underwent treatment for cancer, and he died in Council Bluffs on January 3, 1916.

Basically Dodge was a builder of railroads, not a financial promoter, and his success in building the Union Pacific under most adverse circumstances was one of the greatest accomplishments in United States railroad history. He was also an effective lobbyist, and his long friendship with Presidents Lincoln and Grant stood him in good stead.

He was an active Republican and served a term as congressman from Iowa in 1867-1868, while simultaneously supervising construction of the railroad. As with everyone involved with the Union Pacific in the earlier years, Dodge was subjected to criticism with regard to the contracting system and the role of the Crédit Mobilier, but he came out relatively unscathed. The Union Pacific, over most of its first forty years, built up an unparalleled record of bad public relations and scandal, and it is surprising that Dodge was able to complete the railway with his reputation intact.

Publication:

How We Built the Union Pacific Railway, and Other Railway Papers and Addresses (Washington, D.C.: U.S. Government Printing Office, 1910).

References:

Robert B. Athearn, *Union Pacific Country* (Chicago: Rand McNally, 1971);

Wesley S. Griswold, *A Work of Giants: Building the First Transcontinental Railroad* (New York: McGraw Hill, 1962);

Stanley P. Hirshson, *Grenville M. Dodge: Soldier, Politician, Railroad Pioneer* (Bloomington: Indiana University Press, 1967);

James McCague, *Moguls and Iron Men: The Story of the First Transcontinental Railroad* (New York: Harper & Row, 1964);

J. R. Perkins, *Trails, Rails and War: The Life of General* *G. M. Dodge* (Indianapolis: Bobbs Merrill, 1929).

Archives:

There are several collections of material relating to Dodge in the Iowa State Department of Archives and History at Iowa City, Iowa, and at Des Moines, Iowa. Additional material is located in the Grenville M. Dodge Papers of the Western History Collection in the Denver, Colorado, Public Library.

William Earl Dodge

(September 4, 1805-February 9, 1883)

by Richard Lowitt

Iowa State University

CAREER: Partner, Phelps Dodge & Co. (1832-1878); director, New York & Erie (1845-1857); founder and director, Central of New Jersey (1849-1868); director, Lackawanna Iron & Coal (1853-1883); United States Congressman (1865-1867); member, Board of Indian Commissioners (1868-1874); president, Houston & Texas Central (1870-1877).

William Earl Dodge, prominent New York merchant and contributor to the development of the lumber industry and railroads, chiefly in the anthracite regions of Pennsylvania and post-Civil War Texas, was born on September 4, 1805, in Hartford, Connecticut, and died in New York City on February 9, 1883. His father, David Low Dodge, was an enterprising businessman and a prominent pacifist who argued that war was inconsistent with the religion of Jesus Christ. His mother, Sarah Cleveland, was the daughter of a hat manufacturer turned Evangelical minister who preached that slavery was an anomaly in a supposedly Christian country. While William Dodge became neither a pacifist nor an abolitionist, religious stewardship, manifested in varied philanthropic activities, was a central theme in his adult life.

In the course of his first year, William was moved to New York City, where his father tried to establish himself as the New York partner of S. and H. Higginson, a large importing and jobbing firm with branches in Boston, Baltimore, and New Orleans. British interference with American commerce

William Earl Dodge

prior to the War of 1812 caused the firm severe losses and ultimate bankruptcy. In 1813 the family moved to Bozrahville, Connecticut, where David Low Dodge became the general manager of one of the first New England cotton mills.

In 1815 the family again returned to New York City where David Low Dodge launched his own commission business. Though successful at the outset, he gave up the venture after the panic of 1819 and returned to Bozrahville as the general superintendent of the cotton mill. There the family remained until the spring of 1825, when David Low Dodge again returned to New York City which remained home to him and his son William for the rest of their careers.

Because of the family's frequent moves, William's formal education was haphazard and ended at age thirteen. Dodge, however, was an avid and lifelong reader of mercantile, philanthropic, and religious materials. He launched his business career in 1818 as a clerk in a wholesale dry goods store, where he remained for one year. Returning with his family to Bozrahville in 1819, he took a position in a country store where his increased responsibilities led to a bout of nervous prostration from which he slowly recovered after the family returned to New York City in 1825. Starting anew, Dodge worked as a clerk in his father's dry goods store, and took over the business when David Low Dodge retired in 1827. The following year, the twenty-three-year-old William Earl Dodge married eighteen-year-old Melissa Phelps, the daughter of a leading New York merchant, Anson G. Phelps.

Phelps's firm, Phelps & Peck, was mainly involved in the importation and domestic sale of metals, primarily tinplate. The business, however, entailed much more than that. From the United States, Phelps would export cotton to Liverpool where his partner Elisha Peck directed the European trade. In addition to the import-export business, Phelps & Peck was heavily involved in metal processing in New York and also in the purchasing of large amounts of real estate. Basic business strategy did not change in 1832 when Dodge retired from his own mercantile business to join his father-in-law in a new firm called Phelps Dodge & Company.

The new firm consisted of three partners: Anson G. Phelps, William E. Dodge, and Daniel James, also a son-in-law of Phelps, who replaced the retired Elisha Peck. The firm quickly became the leading metal import firm in the country and, by the 1870s, according to the *New York Times,* had the "largest business in metals probably of any mercantile house in the world." Besides tinplate, the firm imported sheet iron, zinc, copper nails, riv-

ets, lead, solder, antimony, and other items to be sold to merchants throughout the United States. Prior to the Civil War, Phelps Dodge & Company shipped cotton from New York, New Orleans, and other ports to Liverpool for sale in Europe, the proceeds being used to purchase the metals shipped back to New York.

While playing an active role in the mercantile affairs of Phelps Dodge & Company, William E. Dodge, because he had able younger partners, was able to expand both his and the company's areas of interest. The white pine trees of Pennsylvania timberlands along the west branch of the Susquehanna River first attracted his attention. The company entered the lumber business in the 1830s with its own sawmills, rafting operations, and marketing of the lumber felled from trees on its lands. Besides Pennsylvania, Phelps Dodge & Company engaged in lumbering activities on pinelands in Canada, Wisconsin, Michigan, Georgia, and Texas. Aside from Pennsylvania, the company's operations in the Georgian Bay area of Ontario were the most extensive.

In addition, Phelps Dodge & Company sponsored manufacturing, including the production of sheet copper and copper wire in the Naugatuck River valley in Connecticut. Anson G. Phelps was most interested in this endeavor. The town of Ansonia in the Naugatuck valley was named after him, but the company did not operate in its own name. Instead it either purchased existing companies or established new ones, turning out brass and copper items which were then marketed by Phelps Dodge & Company. The largest purchaser of metal products from the Connecticut mills owned by Phelps Dodge & Company during the antebellum period was the United States government.

While Dodge never took an active interest in this phase of the company's affairs, he did give his attention to its small but profitable copper mining interests in Ontonagon County, Michigan. By 1850 he was a leading stockholder and director of the rich Michigan copper mine. His involvement was almost unique, since the development of the Michigan copper industry until then had been dominated by Boston firms and investors. Closer to home, he was also involved in the Weldon iron mine in New Jersey. Mining, however, was a minor interest. During the Civil War, Dodge sold his stock in the Michigan copper mine, and the company stayed out of mining until shortly before his death, when Dodge was no longer active in business.

Even before the death of Phelps in 1853, Dodge was the dominant figure in the firm. While Phelps was interested in railroad development, Dodge played a prominent role in the organization of several major railroads. He quickly realized that railroads would be of prime importance to Phelps Dodge & Company in marketing the materials the firm imported or produced and in bringing goods to port areas for shipment abroad or for sale in urban areas. As a mercantile capitalist whose wealth was derived basically from trade and commerce, railroad development offered Dodge a lucrative investment opportunity that could strengthen both the primacy of the port of New York and his business.

The first railroad with which Dodge became involved was the New York & Erie. Over its tracks western shippers would be able to ship their produce to New York City faster than by any other route, and New York merchants could ship their products to the West before merchants of any other city. Moreover, since the road would pass close by some of the best coalfields in Pennsylvania, the Erie could supply the city of New York and the eastern market with fuel more cheaply than any other competitor.

So convinced was Dodge of the benefits of the Erie railroad to New York merchants that he personally solicited subscriptions. In the summer of 1845 he was named a director of the railroad; it was through his influence that the New York & Erie contracted with the Scranton brothers to manufacture rails at their Slocum Hollow foundry, thereby breaking American dependence on imported rails. In addition, Dodge and other New York merchants loaned the Scrantons $100,000 to equip their mills with new machinery. The Erie contracted for 12,000 tons of rails at $46 a ton, little more than half the cost of the English rails previously used. The contract opened the way for the transformation of Slocum Hollow into the city of Scranton, Pennsylvania.

The high point of Dodge's twelve years as a director of the New York & Erie occurred on May 15, 1851, when, on behalf of the officers and directors of the company, he addressed the throngs of people assembled at Dunkirk to celebrate the completion of the road connecting the Atlantic with the Great Lakes. In 1859 the road went bankrupt, and Dodge was no longer a director. He had resigned from the board and disposed of his stock in the summer of 1857 because the New York & Erie Railroad broke one of his basic tenets as a devout Christian moralist; it violated the Sabbath by operating seven days a week.

Dodge was one of the founders of the Central Railroad Company of New Jersey (CNJ) and for twenty years served as a director. The road survived the panic of 1857 and thereafter prospered because it connected the port of New York at Jersey City with the Delaware River at Easton, Pennsylvania. At the outset, the road's income was derived from passenger traffic; after 1854 it came from coal carried by the Delaware, Lackawanna & Western to a terminal on the Delaware River from whence the CNJ carried it to its facilities in Jersey City for sale in the New York market.

Dodge served briefly in the 1850s as a member of the road's finance and executive committees but did not play a large managerial role. On resigning his directorship in 1868 because of Sunday running, Dodge disposed of his stock at $116 to $118 a share. Two years later the CNJ was bankrupt, a development which gave Dodge much satisfaction. He had proclaimed upon resigning as a director that on every locomotive should be placed a banner bearing the legend, "We break God's law for a dividend."

His interests in the Erie and the CNJ railroads had brought Dodge into contact with the Scranton brothers and led him in 1853 to play a prominent role in organizing the Lackawanna Iron & Coal Company. He helped raise funds for the company and served as a director for the rest of his life. As in his railroad ventures, Dodge did not play an active role in the day-by-day management of the company. His role was to help provide capital and, as a devout Sabbatarian, to insist that the Lord's Day not be violated. His precept proved profitable. Whenever he sold his railroad stock, he did so at a profit; and by 1880 the Lackawanna, which did not run on Sunday, was one of the largest and most profitable steel works in the world

Dodge's association with the Scrantons led him to invest with Seldon Scranton in other ironworks in New Jersey and, on his own, in Illinois and Virginia. With George Scranton he became involved with the founding in 1851 of the Delaware, Lackawanna & Western Railroad Company, a major anthracite carrier. The road, among other things, allowed the Scrantons to market effectively the rails and pig iron produced at their works and to carry coal to the port of New York. Overall, the Delaware, Lackawanna & Western provided an outlet for the vast mineral resources of the Wyoming and Lackawanna valleys in Pennsylvania. By absorbing other roads in Pennsylvania, New York, and New Jersey, it was able to tap western trade because of an outlet to Buffalo. Dodge was a director of several of these smaller lines, playing, as always, no active role in their management but making sure that the system maintained high rates and was profitable.

And profitable it was. By 1880 the Delaware, Lackawanna & Western owned more than 18,000 acres of coal lands, worth at least $1,000 an acre and with an annual productive capacity of more than four million tons. The road also owned numerous coal deposits and real estate in New York City, Buffalo, Syracuse, Rochester, and Chicago. Being an anthracite railroad, it concentrated on coal shipments more than passenger service and was able to avoid Sunday operations, thereby enabling Dodge to continue in good conscience as a director and large stockholder.

Dodge's name also appeared among the men of national prominence listed as incorporators of the Union Pacific. He subscribed to twenty shares of stock at a cost of $2,000 and received seventy votes in the election of directors held on October 29, 1863, not enough to secure a seat on the board but enough to indicate that Dodge was recognized as a prominent railroad promoter. Earlier and closer to his home base Dodge through both his own name and that of Phelps Dodge & Company, invested in several New England railroads, the Long Island Railroad Company, and an Indiana railroad, which reinforced his stature as a leading promoter of the railroad age. Surplus capital from the profits of Phelps Dodge & Company were invested in America's first big business and helped in the transformation of the American economy.

Dodge, however, can best be considered a mercantile capitalist. As a prominent merchant, Dodge was invited to serve on the board of several insurance companies. In addition, he heavily subscribed to the stock of the Atlantic Cable Company and became a director of the United Telegraph Company (later known as Western Union Telegraph Company) in 1863. Like many merchants, including Phelps who, at the time of his death in 1853, was one of the largest property owners in New York, Dodge invested in real estate. The combined interests of the Phelps and Dodge families made them one of the largest holders of real estate in New York City before the Civil War.

By the late 1850s Dodge was devoting less of his time to business and more to charitable and public affairs. The emergence of modern America, with its rapid growth in population and wealth, its corporate and bureaucratic structure, and its excesses and corrupt activities, offended his sense of mercantile honor which, along with his concern for Christian virtue, guided his views and outlook. A devoted family man, Dodge was always concerned about what he considered the right and wrong ways of earning and spending money.

His spending, namely his charitable activities, was cast within a religious mold. A Calvinist, though not a dogmatist, Dodge by the time of his marriage associated himself with the Presbyterian church and after its split sided with the evangelical "New School" group. But religion for Dodge was not so much a matter of theology as of faith willingly embraced and good deeds gladly done. Toward his employees and those of the companies he served, Dodge felt a responsibility for their spiritual, if not their material, welfare. Through liberal donations he saw to it that all had access to a church and, whenever possible, tried to speak at a Sunday school attended by the families of the workers.

Though not a friend of slavery, Dodge thought that the abolitionists often went to extremes. The problem, he insisted, could be solved peaceably through colonization. As a vice-president of the American Colonization Society for over twenty years, Dodge handled business affairs for the society and its New York branch. Throughout his life he remained convinced that "this country is not the place for the colored man." Africa was his true home. These views insulated Dodge from any conflict with his associates and customers in the South, and some of his charitable contributions went to aid blacks in their efforts to improve their lot. In the postwar years he served as a director of the Slater Fund, which spent $1 million to improve education for freed men and women.

A good portion of his charitable contributions were for beneficent work of a religious nature. At the time of his death he was granting an average of $1,000 a day to such enterprises. Seminaries and religious societies received his benefaction as did cultural institutions, libraries, and museums. By the end of the Civil War his conversion to total abstinence was complete and from 1865 to 1883 Dodge was president of the National Temperance Society.

Though a Whig in his political convictions and an admirer of Henry Clay, it was municipal corruption rather than ideology that finally led Dodge to enter the political arena. His views on national and municipal issues were no different from the majority of New York merchants. In 1855 he became a member of the Chamber of Commerce of the State of New York, later serving as its first vice-president. As its president from 1867 to 1875, Dodge was the chief spokesman of the New York mercantile community. It wasn't until late in the 1860 presidential campaign that he joined the Republican party, having previously endorsed John Bell and Edward Everett at a Cooper Union rally. Dodge was appalled by the possibility of civil war and the devastation it would heap on a New York mercantile community with strong southern business ties. He participated as a member of the New York delegation to the Peace Conference that met in Washington in February 1861 to seek to resolve the sectional crisis. Though it accomplished nothing, the conference gave Dodge an opportunity to speak forcefully as a businessman, "a merchant of New York, the commercial metropolis of the nation," for the reconciliation he hoped would save the nation from destroying its commerce through war.

When war came Dodge played a role in the activities of numerous committees and organizations supporting the war effort, most notably the Christian Commission and the Loyal Publication Society. However, he only very reluctantly endorsed Lincoln's reelection. He believed the president was so fully committed to the abolition of slavery as a condition of peace that the end of the conflict would be delayed longer than if the defeated states were allowed to resolve the matter for themselves. He finally endorsed Lincoln's reelection in October 1864 because of his nomination as the Republican candidate for Congress from the Eighth District. In a contested election that finally was resolved in April 1866, Dodge was declared the winner over the incumbent James Brooks.

As a representative Dodge served mainly as a spokesman for the New York mercantile community; however, his endorsement of higher tariff rates on manufactured items indicated his divided loyalties between his roles as head of a metal-importing firm and as director of several railroads and a coal

and iron company. Whenever the opportunity arose, he favored federal aid to railroads, strongly endorsing it for the Northern Pacific Railroad. As a merchant, he expressed the hostility of the mercantile community to greenbacks and other forms of currency devaluation. On the major issues of the Thirty-ninth Congress, Dodge, again reflecting the views of the New York mercantile community, opposed Radical Reconstruction by arguing for reconciliation so that business conditions could settle into their former prosperous pattern. He achieved one notable success. In February 1867 he helped organize a Congressional Temperance Society.

Dodge, after the end of his term in Congress, quickly recognized that the end of the war meant new investment opportunities. While there was no marked change in the business of Phelps Dodge & Company, he became associated with new business ventures and expanded his investments in railroads. The most notable venture was the creation of the Georgia Land & Lumber Company in 1868 with him as president and largest stockholder. The expenditure of northern capital in central Georgia was met with favor. In 1870 the Georgia legislature honored Dodge by creating a new county in the area and naming it after him.

Railroads in Texas also attracted his attention after the Civil War. The Houston & Texas Central (HTC) and the system that by 1870 came to be known as the International & Great Northern were controlled by eastern merchants including Dodge. He served as president of the former for seven years during which the road prospered. He changed the gauge of its tracks and insisted that it not operate on Sunday. In 1877, however, the HTC was on the verge of bankruptcy and Charles Morgan, a New York shipping magnate, gained control and deprived Dodge of the only railroad presidency he ever had. About a year before the shake-up on the H&TC, Dodge severed his connection with the International & Great Northern. By 1880 these roads were already under the aegis of leading railroad entrepreneurs: the H&TC under Collis P. Huntington and the International & Great Northern under Jay Gould. In addition to railroads, Dodge also heavily invested in Texas real estate both in the Panhandle and the western part of the state.

Railroad enterprises in Wisconsin, Iowa, New York, North Carolina, and elsewhere attracted his interest and those of fellow New York merchants. In most instances he served as a director of the lines as they were absorbed into the larger railroad systems developed in the postwar years. He was also an early purchaser of stock in the New York Elevated Railroad Company in 1872, but when the line began running on Sunday he promptly withdrew.

The year 1873 brought Dodge to national attention when Phelps Dodge & Company was accused of defrauding the government of $1 million by undervaluing metal imports coming through customs in New York. While the revenue system and corrupt custom officials were more at fault than the company, the dispute was widely noted. Press coverage on the whole was unsympathetic, but New York merchants expressed their support in 1873 by unanimously reelecting Dodge as president of the Chamber of Commerce. In 1874 Congress modified the revenue law to remove the confusion that prompted the dispute. Despite his concern about this controversy and the notoriety it brought Phelps Dodge & Company, the postwar years found him less occupied with business affairs. He saw to it that his sons were given an opportunity to engage in the management of the enterprise and, by the end of 1878, he was no longer an active partner in the company he had helped to organize in 1832.

The most notable manifestation of his interest in public affairs was his service as a member of the newly created Board of Indian Commissioners. Appointed in 1869 by President Grant, Dodge served until 1874 when he resigned because of differences with the secretary of the interior pertaining to personnel involved with Indian affairs. In addition, through his service as president of the Chamber of Commerce of the State of New York, Dodge maintained his role as a leading spokesman of the New York mercantile community and its concerns of maintaining and strengthening the city as the major commercial metropolis in the world. Dodge was much concerned that railroad regulation in western states could interfere "with the great channels through which commerce is now, to a large extent, carried on." He bitterly protested what his fellow merchants considered discriminatory freight rates levied by railroads against New York shippers.

While critical of the harsh views of Thaddeus Stevens, Benjamin F. Butler, and the other Radical Reconstructionists, Dodge, nevertheless, was a devoted supporter of Ulysses S. Grant, serving as a delegate to the national Republican convention and as a presidential elector in 1872. Yet, at the same

time, he objected to further interference by the federal government with the legislatures of southern states. What the South needed, he maintained, was capital to develop its resources, which could not occur until confidence in southern state governments could be restored. What Dodge and his associates in the New York mercantile community most desired was for the South to regain its former position in the commercial economy of the country.

For the remainder of his life Dodge retained an active interest in public affairs. Endorsing Republican candidates, Dodge felt he was no longer outside the main current of Republican policies once federal troops were removed from the South. Dodge did become distressed when Chester A. Arthur came to the presidency following the assassination of James A. Garfield in 1881. Arthur had been the collector of the Port of New York when Phelps Dodge & Company was accused of defrauding the government. Interest in national affairs, of course, did not preclude concern for local politics. Dodge was a consistent opponent of "Boss" Tweed and played a minor but not negligible part in his undoing. Thereafter, he opposed the leadership of "Honest John" Kelly and his Tammany Hall associates.

As important as public affairs in Dodge's later years were his philanthropic concerns. Widely known as "The Christian Merchant," he believed no social or industrial system could ever replace individual accountability. A sense of Christian stewardship as a practical working force in every vocation or avocation was a dominant trait of his personality. Recognizing that he was engaged in a losing battle, he nevertheless continually waged war against "Sunday Railway Desecration," insisting that railroads were violating the moral law, driving away their best workmen, and making it impossible for Christians to "invest in roads that disregard the Sabbath."

Though Dodge sold most of the stock he owned in railroads, he was almost alone in doing so. With values rooted in a strong sense of Christian ethics and virtue that fit easily into the antebellum New York mercantile community, Dodge was distressed at the changes in public life and business conduct he witnessed in post-Civil War America. Through his generous philanthropic activities, both at home and abroad, he believed that he could help perpetuate his sense of Christian ethics.

In 1866 Dodge became president of the American branch of the Evangelical Alliance, a post he retained until his death. Colleges, seminaries, missions, both at home and abroad, benefited from Dodge's philanthropy during his later years and in his will. While he still believed colonization in Africa offered the best solution to the race problem, in his later years, he saw Christian education as a chance to better the race in America and also as an opportunity to prepare blacks for missionary work in Africa. He contributed to several black colleges and was consulted by John F. Slater before Slater contributed $1 million for the education of freedmen. He bequeathed $20,000 to the National Temperance Society and Publication House, having served as its president until his death in 1883. Temperance was at all times part of his religion and prohibition was his ultimate goal.

In his will, as throughout his career, Dodge called himself a merchant. To his wife and sons, he recommended that a portion of their annual income always be employed "for the promotion of the Kingdom of Christ." His wide-ranging bequests further indicated his belief that "the real security, under God, is in the virtue and intelligence of the people."

References:

D. Stuart Dodge, *Memorials of William E. Dodge* (New York: Anson D. F. Randolph and Co., 1887);

Phyllis B. Dodge, *Tales of the Phelps-Dodge Families* (New York: New York Historical Society, 1987);

Richard Lowitt, *A Merchant Prince of the Nineteenth Century* (New York: Columbia University Press, 1954).

Archives:

The papers of Phelps Dodge & Company are available in the Manuscript Division of the New York Public Library. There are small collections of William E. Dodge papers in both the New York Historical Society and the New York Public Library.

Francis Marion Drake

(December 30, 1830-November 20, 1903)

by H. Roger Grant

University of Akron

CAREER: Store clerk (1854-1859); storekeeper (1859-1861); Union Army (1861-1865); attorney (1866-1903); railroad investor (1866-1903); president, Iowa Southern Railroad (1866-1870); president, Missouri, Iowa & Nebraska Railroad (1870-1881); president, Indiana, Illinois & Iowa Railroad (1881-1898); governor, Iowa (1896-1898).

Francis Marion Drake was an obscure, yet representative, nineteenth-century American railroad figure. Born in the western Illinois hamlet of Rushville on December 30, 1830, Drake was the son of John Adams Drake, a merchant and small-time capitalist. In 1837 the senior Drake moved his wife, Harriet Jane O'Neal Drake, whom he had married in 1826, and their flock of children (ultimately fourteen) to the raw frontier settlement of Fort Madison, Iowa, then part of the Wisconsin Territory. The Drakes stayed in this Mississippi River community until March 1846 when they moved to inland Davis County. There John Drake founded the town of Drakesville and pursued agricultural and banking interests.

Like his brothers and sisters Francis received rudimentary formal education, attending public schools in Fort Madison. Although he never graduated from high school Drake expanded his knowledge through his own initiative; he read widely and enthusiastically and associated with "learned" people.

In the early 1850s Francis Drake revealed his love for adventure and risk-taking. In 1852 he organized a wagon train from southern Iowa to the gold fields of northern California. Once there, however, Drake turned to raising cattle, remaining in the Sacramento area for about a year. He returned to the Midwest in 1854 but soon set out again for the Golden State, this time driving a herd of dairy cows. While Drake arrived successfully in California, he nearly lost his life on the trip home, surviving both a shipwreck and a shipboard fire. Once safely back in Iowa Drake worked for his father and brothers in their Drakesville-based business en-

Francis Marion Drake (courtesy of State Historical Society of Iowa–Special Collections)

terprises. On December 24, 1855, Drake married Mary Jane Lord. In 1859 he entered business on his own and settled in the nearby Appanoose County village of Unionville, where he operated a general store.

During the Civil War Francis Drake rallied to the Union colors. He raised a company of volunteers for an Iowa infantry unit and saw combat. In 1863 the Iowa governor commissioned him as a lieutenant colonel and asked him to recruit additional troops. Once again Drake endured hostile fire, being wounded severely and captured by Confederate forces. Later he won parole and rejoined his regiment. When Drake left the service in 1863 he wore the uniform of a brigadier general.

After the war Drake abandoned his occupation as a small-time merchant. He studied law, won admission to the local bar, and left Unionville for neighboring Centerville, the bustling seat of Appanoose County. The quintessential community booster, Drake became keenly interested in improving his region's transportation, meaning, of course, railroads. In 1866 he launched the Iowa Southern Railroad, which in 1870 joined the Missouri, Iowa & Nebraska (MI&N) Railway, a road that by

1872 linked Keokuk, Iowa (via Alexandria, Missouri), with Centerville, a distance of ninety miles. Eight years later the MI&N, under Drake's direction, reached Van Wert, Iowa, fifty-eight miles west of his adopted hometown. Drake also saw need for better rail service to the north of Centerville. In 1880 he spearheaded construction of the 24-mile Centerville, Moravia & Albia Railroad that tied Centerville with the strategically located Monroe County seat of Albia, situated on the Chicago, Burlington & Quincy (then the Burlington & Missouri River Railroad) and the Iowa Central lines.

There were other railroad projects. Drake assisted in the development of two central Iowa branchlines for the Iowa Central (then the Central Iowa). Built under the corporate banner of the Iowa Central & Northwestern Railway in 1881 and 1882, these pikes connected Hampton with Belmond and Minerva Junction with Story City. A much larger undertaking involved constructing the 110-mile Indiana, Illinois & Iowa Railroad, commonly called the "Three I." Opened between Streator, Illinois, and North Judson, Indiana, in 1883, this surprisingly profitable road within a decade reached South Bend, Indiana, forty miles east of its original terminus. Drake would serve as "Three I" president from its inception to his retirement in 1898.

In all likelihood Francis Drake represented various investors in his railroad schemes. Evidence suggests that Drake worked closely with Russell Sage, the shrewd Wall Street financier. Yet Drake's business activities made him a millionaire, and thus he possessed the financial means to expand independently his railroad holdings.

By the time of his 1903 death, due to the complications of diabetes, Francis Marion Drake was a household name to Iowans. Rather than for his railroad exploits, Drake was known primarily as the principal benefactor of Drake University in Des Moines, and as the Republican governor of Iowa between 1896 and 1898. Equally as important, though, was Drake's role in creating modest-size railroads during the nineteenth century. Indeed, such railroads became vital building blocks for twentieth-century railroad systems. In Drake's case the Chicago, Burlington & Quincy acquired the MI&N, which had changed its name to Keokuk & Western in 1886; the Iowa Central leased the Centerville, Moravia & Albia (it later became an independent electric road); and the New York Central absorbed the

"Three I." As this shows, Drake had a significant part in establishing constituent roads of several of the largest twentieth-century lines.

References:
Des Moines Register and Leader, November 20, 1903, 1;

Des Moines Register and Leader, November 21, 1903, 1; S. Thompson Lewis, *Biographical and Genealogical History of Appanoose and Monroe Counties, Iowa* (Chicago: Lewis Publishing, 1903); *New York Times*, November 21, 1903, IX:5.

Daniel Drew

(July 29, 1797-September 18, 1879)

by Charles B. Weinstock

Pittsburgh, Pennsylvania

CAREER: Drover (1815-1834); steamboat operator, Wall Street speculator and financier (1844-1875); director, Erie Railroad (1854-1868).

Daniel Drew was, for most of his life, a financier and Wall Street speculator who specialized in conducting stock manipulations, most often on shares of the Erie Railroad. His methods were seldom ethical, even by the loose standards of his day. Along with Jay Gould and Jim Fisk he was a mastermind behind the infamous Erie War, besting Cornelius Vanderbilt in a contest for control of the railroad and collecting a substantial portion of Vanderbilt's fortune at the same time. Caught short by the deft stock manipulations of Jay Gould, Drew lost his fortune and declared bankruptcy in 1876. At the time of his death in 1879 he was dependent on the charity of his family.

Daniel Drew was born on July 29, 1797, on the family farm near Carmel, New York, to Gilbert and Catherine Muckleworth Drew. Because the farm was not profitable, young Drew was required to help work it and as a result did not receive much education as a child. His family raised cattle, and Drew learned the business thoroughly. When his father died, Drew's older brother Tom took charge of the farm. Drew decided to leave the farm and make his own way. When the War of 1812 broke out, Drew used the opportunity to make $100 by substituting for a draftee. Despite the fact that he was underage, Drew convinced the military to accept him and in 1814 was stationed at Fort Gainesvort, New Jersey. The Treaty of Ghent was signed shortly after he entered the military, and he saw no fighting. Drew was out of the army in three months and $100 richer.

Daniel Drew (courtesy of Brown Brothers)

Drew returned to the family farm, but he soon became restless and decided to become a cattle driver. His capital was limited, so he was forced to specialize in calves. Although not strictly legal at the time, Drew's calf business suffered more from the problem of getting the animals to market before they became sick and died.

During those years Drew interrupted his career as a drover to join a circus. At the time several circuses wintered near Carmel, and Drew joined one as a jack-of-all-trades, doing everything from raising the canvas to appearing as a clown. He was successful and was offered part ownership but decided instead that there was more money in the cattle business. He married Roxana Mead, the sister of his brother Tom's wife, on March 5, 1820, and settled back into the cattle business. Although a drover again, Drew was now able to deal in fully grown cattle. His usual method of operation was to convince farmers to give him animals on consignment for sale in New York City. In this manner he would collect several hundred head, drive them to the city, and sell them at a good price. He would seldom pay the farmers what he owed them, preferring to move along to other areas for his next herd of cattle.

Always a schemer, Drew soon developed a technique to make an even higher profit on the cattle he was driving. Henry Astor, the brother of John Jacob Astor, was a thriving butcher in New York. To get a jump on his competitors, Astor was in the habit of riding uptown from his store in the Bowery to meet the drove coming in. This allowed him to purchase the choicest animals. Drew, knowing this, fed his herd salt the night before and kept them from water during the drive into town. He sent word ahead for Astor to meet him at the Bull's Head Tavern, then a favorite meeting place for cattlemen. Just before Astor arrived, the cattle were allowed to drink all the water they wanted. The weight of the water added about fifty pounds per head. Since he sold the beef by the pound, this "watered stock" made a tidy profit for Drew. Henry Astor was furious when he discovered the deception but not so furious that he did not recommend Drew to his competitors. Astor's cooperation allowed Drew to continue to sell watered stock.

These trips were quite profitable, and by 1829 Drew was able to lease the Bull's Head Tavern, which he operated for many years. It was not long before "Uncle Dan'l," as he came to be called, found another opportunity for profit. Word had reached him of exceptionally fine cattle available at low prices in the Ohio Valley. With the help of a heavily collateralized loan from Henry Astor, Drew brought the first herd from Ohio to New York. Of over 2,000 head, he lost nearly a fourth of the herd to sickness, wolves, and other maladies, but still managed to clear over $30 per head at the market. Drew conducted several more long-distance droves

before leaving the cattle business in 1834 to make his fortune in operating steamboats.

The operation of steamboats on the Hudson River had been a monopoly since the state of New York had granted a license to Robert Fulton and Robert Livingston in 1807. In 1824 the United States Supreme Court, in *Gibbons* v. *Ogden*, overturned the monopoly. By 1834 Cornelius "Commodore" Vanderbilt was making his fortune running steamboats on the Hudson. One of the routes served Peekskill and was used by Drew on his trips back to Carmel. In what was to become the first of many associations and conflicts between Drew and Vanderbilt, Drew decided to enter the steamboat business. He became a partner in the *Water Witch*, operated by a competitor of Vanderbilt on the Peekskill to New York route. After losing $10,000 the first season, Drew convinced the people of Putnam and Westchester counties to provide financing and help him fight Vanderbilt's near monopoly. Drew immediately slashed the fare. Soon everyone was losing money, and, before long, Vanderbilt bought Drew's business to rid himself of the nuisance. The other investors complained, but Drew was content with his profit.

Drew then turned his sights on the Hudson River Association (HRA), which ran steamboats from Albany to New York City. Through ruthless fare-slashing using his boat, the *Westchester*, and others, Drew aggravated the HRA. As a result the HRA took him in on a pooling arrangement in 1836. Drew quickly saw an opportunity to make more money and, while still in the HRA, became the silent partner in a competing line. The competitor cut prices, and Drew convinced the HRA that they must buy it out. Acting for both sides, Drew conducted the negotiations and pocketed a large amount of the association's cash.

In 1839 Drew saw that he could make more money on his own and broke with the association. He established the People's Line, which dazzled travelers with floating palaces like the *Isaac Newton*, a 300-foot, 500-berth ship put into service in 1845. The People's Line dropped fares so low that the association, already weakened by the loss of money from buying out Drew's phony competitor, collapsed. Drew bought them out and immediately raised the fare to Albany. Being well financed, the People's Line allowed no competition. When a poorly financed competitor opened, the People's

Line would carry passengers for free until the other line went out of business.

To help finance his growing empire, Drew founded the Wall Street firm of Drew, Robinson and Company. The brokerage bought and sold railroad and steamboat stocks and soon convinced Drew that he could make more money at speculation than by running a steamboat line. When Vanderbilt eventually left the steamboat business for railroading, Drew followed. In 1850 Drew and George Law established a steamboat line from New York up Long Island Sound to Stonington. Drew and Vanderbilt together bought a controlling interest in the connecting Boston & Stonington Railroad.

Since his base of operations was now Wall Street, Drew moved to New York City to 52 Bleecker Street at the corner of Mulberry Street. A Methodist, he attended the Mulberry Street Church every Sunday and spent a good deal of his time outside business hours attending church functions. Around the time of the Civil War he moved again, this time to a house on Seventeenth Street at Union Square, and helped his church to build a new building nearby. During his life he also financed the construction of a church in Carmel and pledged money to endow both the Drew Theological Seminary and Wesleyan University in 1867.

In 1854 Drew became associated with the Erie Railroad. The New York & Erie Railroad, as it was first known, ran from Dunkirk on Lake Erie to Piermont on the Hudson when it was first completed in 1851. Piermont was some twenty-four miles from New York City, and a ferry service between the two points was instituted. Drew decided that a place as an insider on the Erie would lead to profitable stock manipulations, so he set about to become a director. His manipulations would earn him the nickname "Speculative Director." At the time there was a chain of small railroads which together formed a line from Lake Erie to Albany and would later form the basis of Vanderbilt's New York Central. Drew was in a position to favor these lines on steamboat rates for through traffic from New York at the expense of the Erie. He also bought a controlling interest in a Lake Erie steamboat line, which was the Erie Railroad's major connection. Finally, he bought a controlling interest in the Buffalo & State Line Railroad, which connected to both the Central and Erie. Drew then let it be known to the Erie board that he planned to give the New York

Central a better deal on both ends and hinted that he wanted a bigger share of the through rate involving the Lake Erie steamers. To buy him off, the Erie made him a director and its treasurer.

Drew almost immediately used his position as a director to force the Erie to borrow money from him. Piermont was an inconvenient eastern terminus, and the directors decided to push through to Jersey City, a project which involved boring an expensive tunnel through Bergen Hill. By manufacturing political and construction problems, Drew managed to make the job more expensive than it already was. He also started rumors on Wall Street that the tunnel was in trouble. The Erie's stock price dropped, and it had trouble raising money to meet payroll and operating costs. Drew loaned the railroad $1.5 million, taking a chattel mortgage on the line's rolling stock as security; the Erie was firmly in his control.

Drew and Vanderbilt soon began to tangle again. Although Vanderbilt was not naive concerning Drew he did seem to be unable to stay away from him. He did not seem to realize that to Drew there was little difference between antagonist and partner. For instance, when Vanderbilt invested in the Harlem Railroad, a line that extended from the Harlem Valley to a depot at Fourth Avenue and Twenty-sixth Street, in 1857, Drew joined him. They extended the line through the Harlem Valley, and it became a money-maker. Both knew that it would be even more profitable if the line could be extended down Broadway to the Battery. Without Vanderbilt's knowledge Drew purchased a large block of Harlem stock and then, with the help of Boss William Tweed, got the Common Council to pass an ordinance allowing Vanderbilt to lay rails down Broadway. The stock soared. At this point Drew began a bear campaign on the stock. That is, he sold shares short and then manipulated events to cause the market price to drop, allowing him to purchase the shares for delivery at a price less than he sold them for. When he had completed making his short sales Drew had Tweed and the council reverse itself and disallow the construction. An injunction was obtained to stop the laying of rails on Broadway. Drew's plot should have caused the stock to plunge, but it didn't. From its high at 75 Drew and his friends had hoped to get it down to 50 before covering their shorts. Instead the price would not fall below 73 because Vanderbilt convinced another court to dissolve the injunction. Drew was able to cover his shorts with the stock he already owned and came out with little damage. Some of the politicians involved in the campaign were not so lucky.

Not being one to give up, Drew tried again to manipulate the stock, this time in Albany. A favorable report was given out by the legislature on the prospects of a Broadway franchise for the Harlem Railroad. The stock shot up to 150. Again Drew sold short, as did members of the state legislature in Albany. Almost immediately they defeated the Broadway franchise and expected the stock to fall. It did, to 100 in two days, but then it ran up to 185 and beyond. In their greed Drew and the others had sold short more shares of stock than were available, leaving no way to cover their short sales. Drew, looking out for himself, went to Vanderbilt, admitting that he couldn't deliver the shares, and begged for leniency. After some haggling he was able to persuade Vanderbilt into settling for about $500,000, a small amount since otherwise Drew faced bankruptcy. The members of the legislature were not so lucky, and reputedly many of them left Albany at the end of the session with unpaid rooming bills.

In 1863 Drew sold his Stonington Railroad shares, using the services of James Fisk, Jr., a salesman who had worked for Jordan, Marsh in Boston. Fisk's work was apparently satisfactory because, in 1865, Drew helped Fisk set up the Wall Street firm of Fisk and Belden. Drew and Fisk were to be involved in business together until Fisk's murder in November 1871.

Drew's takeover of the Erie had caught the attention of Commodore Vanderbilt. Vanderbilt wanted to strengthen his control of rail transport in New York and in June 1866 tried to purchase control of the Erie. Drew, seeing an opportunity to profit, persuaded the railroad to issue convertible bonds and 28,000 shares of previously unissued stock as security for a $3 million loan to be used for improvements. After converting the bonds Drew had in his possession 58,000 shares of Erie stock that Wall Street knew nothing about. Erie was then selling at 95, and Drew began to sell borrowed shares. When he released his own 58,000 shares on the market, Erie stock fell to 47, and Drew was able to cover at a nice profit.

In response Vanderbilt started buying up Erie stock and joined forces with a group of Boston investors led by John L. Eldridge, who himself owned a large block of Erie. Together, in October 1867,

they arranged to throw Drew off the board. Seeing that he was about to lose control of his profit center, Drew went to Vanderbilt and persuaded him to let Drew stay on as a director. To assuage the feelings of the Boston crowd, one of Vanderbilt's men was elected to the board. This "dummy" resigned the following day, paving the way for the appointment of Drew. In the same election John Eldridge was elected president of the Erie, and Jay Gould and Jim Fisk became directors. Drew, Fisk, and Gould immediately plotted to manipulate Erie stock.

The Erie's charter prevented it from issuing stock to increase its capitalization. However, it could issue bonds convertible to shares of stock at par value. On February 18, 1868, Drew had the board authorize $10 million in improvements and issued bonds in that amount. This gave Drew the ability to create 100,000 new shares of Erie stock. Drew immediately began to sell tremendous quantities of Erie stock short, making everyone certain that he would be unable to cover. To help this come true, on March 3 Vanderbilt got a New York City court to issue an injunction against the Erie issuing any additional shares of stock. On March 5 Drew got a judge in Binghamton to require the issuance of more stock. Vanderbilt thought he was on solid ground even as Drew continued to sell short. As delivery time neared Drew, Fisk, and Gould converted the bonds and printed up the 100,000 new shares.

Worried that Vanderbilt would be able to enforce his injunction and destroy the new shares, the three arranged to have the shares "stolen" on March 9. The same afternoon the shares turned up in Drew's broker's office and were placed on the market the next day. Vanderbilt supported the market until he discovered the new certificates. The price had been 83 but soon dropped to 71, enabling Drew and friends to cover their shorts and walk away with $7 million of Vanderbilt's money. On March 11, 1868, an angered Vanderbilt swore warrants for the arrest of Drew, Gould, and Fisk. Before the warrants could be served, the Erie headquarters was moved across the Hudson River to Taylor's Hotel in Jersey City. Vanderbilt was at great risk for he had staked a good part of his fortune on the Erie. The $7 million being hoarded by Drew and friends was withdrawn from Wall Street, causing money to tighten, interest rates to rise, and stocks to fall. Margin calls followed, but to Drew's chagrin, Vanderbilt managed to survive.

With Vanderbilt in control in New York, and the Erie gang firmly ensconced in "Fort Taylor," the situation was at a stalemate. To enhance its position the Erie convinced the New Jersey legislature to charter the railroad in that state and then counterattacked. The Erie cut rates by one-third on the New York to Buffalo route. The passenger fare dropped from $7 to $5. Vanderbilt's New York Central could not meet the slashed rates; the Erie could not afford them either, but Drew, Fisk, and Gould were willing to sacrifice the line to defeat Vanderbilt.

The Erie then introduced a bill in Albany which legalized the $10 million of stock. Vanderbilt fought hard to keep the bill from passing. At the risk of arrest Gould went to Albany to "convince" the legislators to pass it. The Erie dollars outweighed the New York Central dollars, and the law passed. As the New York Central's stock slipped from 132 to 109, Vanderbilt sent a private note to Drew asking for his terms. Drew saw him on a Sunday when the process servers weren't allowed to arrest him. After preliminary discussions Drew returned to New Jersey, and a second conference was scheduled. During this second conference, Gould and Fisk walked into the room and demanded participation in the settlement. In October 1868 the Erie bought the stock back from Vanderbilt by using corporate funds; Drew was allowed to keep his personal profits. Before they would agree to this settlement, Gould and Fisk demanded that Drew leave the Erie forever. Drew is quoted as telling Vanderbilt, "There ain't nothin' in Ary no more C'neel."

Gould and Fisk thought Drew wrong and started a new bear campaign involving the locking up of greenbacks in November 1869. Drew got wind of their plans and on his own sold 70,000 shares of Erie short at 40. The price soon dropped to 35, and things looked momentarily bright for Drew. However, Gould and Fisk had turned bullish upon learning that the federal government was going to put additional greenbacks into circulation and the price soon rose to 52. Drew found himself in the unenviable position of being unable to cover his shorts. Along with August Belmont and other investors, he formed a committee which attempted to get an injunction restraining delivery of the short shares until a large consignment of shares could arrive from England. In an attempt to save his own skin at the expense of others on the committee, Drew warned Gould and Fisk of the injunction in time to have it vacated. In return he wanted access to newly printed shares. When Gould and Fisk refused, Drew exposed their attempt to lock up money, hoping to get Gould and Fisk ousted from the Erie. His duplicity discovered, Drew was treated as an informer by his fellow bears. The price climbed to 61 as he tried to cover. Just before the delivery date, many small investors sold their shares, and Drew was able to cover at 57, a loss of $1.5 million and a large amount of prestige.

In September 1870 Gould was caught without enough Erie shares to cover his short sales, while Drew held the floating supply of the stock. Drew loaned Gould the stock at a rate that allowed him to make back some of his earlier losses. Then the two joined together in holding Erie shares for a price rise. The stock climbed to 56, and all of a sudden shares started appearing on the market. In order to support the price Drew continued to buy even as Gould was secretly selling. Gould also talked Drew into short selling Chicago & North Western stock, which was at 75. At the same time Gould was engineering a pool to bull the same stock, which had come under the eye of Vanderbilt. The stock climbed, eventually to 230. In the ensuing settlement everyone except Drew was allowed to buy at 150. Drew was forced to pay market for the shares and lost $750,000 on the deal. Thereupon the North Western plummeted to 75.

This last debacle, coupled with some other reverses and the panic of 1873, drove Drew to leave Wall Street in March 1875 and to file for bankruptcy on March 11, 1876. His assets were listed at $746,459.46, and his liabilities at $1.09 million. The newspapers of the day thought that the endowments of the Drew Theological Seminary and of Wesleyan University would be safe, but such was not the case. Drew had held onto the capital and merely paid the interest. When he declared bankruptcy, the capital for the endowments became another asset claimed by creditors.

Daniel Drew died on September 18, 1879, dependent on the charity of his family. He was buried in the family burial ground in Carmel on September 23, 1879.

References:

Charles Francis Adams, Jr., and Henry Adams, *Chapters*

of Erie and Other Essays (New York: Henry Holt, 1886);

Clifford Browder, *The Money Game in Old New York* (Lexington: University Press of Kentucky, 1986);

Maury Klein, *The Life and Legend of Jay Gould* (Balti-

more: Johns Hopkins University Press, 1986);

Edward Harold Mott, *Between the Ocean and the Lakes, the Story of Erie* (New York: John S. Collins, 1899);

Bouck White, *The Book of Daniel Drew* (New York: Doubleday, Page, 1910).

Thomas C. Durant

(February 6, 1820-October 5, 1885)

by Alec Kirby

George Washington University

CAREER: Partner, Durant, Lathrop and Company (1843-1850); partner, Durant and Farnam (1850-1863); vice-president, Union Pacific Railroad (1863-1869); president, Crédit Mobilier of America (1865-1867).

Thomas C. Durant, executive of the Union Pacific Railroad and a major figure in the building of the first transcontinental railroad, was born on February 6, 1820, in Lee, Massachusetts. His parents, Thomas and Sybil (Wright) Durant, were wealthy and of colonial ancestry. Early in life Durant chose surgery as a profession and at age twenty graduated *cum laude* from Albany Medical College. But he soon found himself restless for a more profitable career and at age twenty-three joined his uncle's trading firm of Durant, Lathrop and Company of Albany, exporters of flour and grain. Durant was put in charge of the firm's office in New York City. During the next several years Durant became an avid speculator, widely known in financial circles for his prowess. It was during this period—in 1847—that he married Heloise Hannah Timbel, with whom he had a son, William West, and a daughter, Heloise.

By 1850 transportation companies were increasingly obvious and attractive investments. In the East, canals, especially the Erie Canal, and railroads had already helped to transform the economy of the Atlantic seaboard states. Durant saw an opportunity in providing similar transportation benefits to the West. In 1851 he joined with Henry Farnam, a railroad engineer from Connecticut, in constructing the Michigan Southern Railroad. This railroad was the first to connect Chicago with the East and is credited—along with the Michigan Central—with helping dramatically to stimulate the economic

Thomas C. Durant (courtesy of the New York Public Library, Astor, Lenox and Tilden Foundations)

growth of Chicago. Yet the Michigan Southern turned out to be merely a prelude to Durant's later railroad speculation. Continuing his association with Farnam, Durant contracted to build the Chicago & Rock Island. Work began on the road on April 10, 1852, and was completed on February 22, 1854, eighteen months before the completion date specified in the contract. Nevertheless, while construction was in progress, Durant and Farnam began planning an expansion of the Chicago & Rock Island. This expansion was organized separately as the Peoria & Bureau Valley Railroad and joined the Rock Island at Bureau Junction. The two companies were merged in July 1854.

By the middle of the 1850s Durant had already influenced the development of the railroad industry. His projects had linked Chicago to the East, a road had been constructed to the Mississippi, and a branch had been run as far as Peoria. In May 1855 Durant and Farnam contracted for the construction of the Mississippi & Missouri Railroad. But Durant's speculations nearly ruined the partners in 1857. The firm, however, managed to recover, and the railroad was later expanded several times.

The Mississippi & Missouri reflected the partners' growing interest in a railroad link to the West Coast. While the road was still under construction Durant and Farnam sent Peter Dey and Grenville M. Dodge to survey possible cross-country routes. In 1863 Durant, at his own initiative and expense after Farnam's retirement, sent three survey teams, including a geologist, to report on coal and iron. Durant continued to lobby President Lincoln and Congress to pass legislation to provide federal aid to construct a railroad to the Pacific.

For at least a decade there had been mounting public pressure for such legislation. During the 1850s the increasing tension between the North and the South made agreement on a bill impossible. It was not until the southern delegations left Congress at the start of the Civil War that Congress was able to pass the legislation. The Pacific Railway Act of 1862 had as its goal the building of a road to connect the eastern railways with the network which was being constructed on the Pacific coast. The act created the Union Pacific Railroad Company, which was to provide the eastern portion of the line, from Omaha to the borders of California. The western part of the line, from the eastern border of California to San Francisco, was to be built by the Central Pacific Railroad Company, a California corporation.

The act also provided the Union Pacific with financial resources to help attract further investment from the private sector. The authorized federal aid consisted of land grants plus the loan of government bonds. For each mile of track completed the company was to receive 3,200 acres for a total land grant of about 33 million acres. Government bonds would amount to $60 million. To secure the bonds, the government retained a first-mortgage lien on the line and all company property. The capital stock of Union Pacific was set at $100 million, which was divided into 100,000 shares of $1,000 each. When 2,000 shares had been sold, stockholders were to elect thirteen directors, who in turn would appoint the officers of the new company.

Durant was among the individuals authorized in the legislation to obtain subscriptions to Union Pacific stock. The task, as Durant soon discovered, was enormously difficult. With the Civil War raging and the fortunes of the Union army deteriorating, it is remarkable that he was able to sell any subscriptions at all. Construction costs were spiraling with inflation, while the purchasing power of fixed government subsidies was shrinking. Few prominent Boston investors demonstrated any interest in the project, and their absence only fueled the skepticism of other potential backers. Durant, eagerly pushing the project, purchased 50 shares himself. He later claimed that he attracted enough investors to reach the necessary 2,000 mark only by personally loaning money to investors so they would be able to make the initial payment on their stocks. When the first 2,000 shares had been sold, Durant claimed that he had furnished three-fourths of the money himself. Whether or not Durant's claim was true, the formal organization of the Union Pacific was possible. Durant was among the directors elected at the first stockholders' meeting on October 29, 1863. The directors subsequently chose Durant to serve as vice-president of the Union Pacific.

As vice-president Durant was to assume control and responsibility for the railroad. The Union Pacific president, Maj. Gen. John Dix, was, at age sixty-five, in command of the Union Army's Department of the East. Because of his military duties he never took active charge of the railroad's affairs, although he remained its titular head until 1866. Durant had promoted Dix for the Union Pacific presidency because of the reputation that the military man enjoyed. The arrangement allowed Durant to control the corporation with a free hand.

Difficulties in selling the initial 2,000 shares of Union Pacific stock showed that the incentives offered by the 1862 Act were insufficient to attract adequate investment. What was particularly discouraging to potential investors was the federal government's first claim on assets. Also, due to the volatile wartime economic climate, government bonds were selling at a discount, while construction costs were rising. The obvious solution was to persuade Congress to amend and liberalize the 1862 Act. During the winter of 1863-1864 Durant, assisted by two influential businessmen, Henry S. McComb and Cornelius S. Bushnell, urged Congress to revise the act. They were remarkably successful, having the Pacific Railroad Act of 1864 on the president's desk by late spring. Despite the weak state of the company's finances, Durant spent $435,754.21 in Washington to promote the bill. Charges of bribery were never proved, although a complete accounting of how these funds were spent was never provided.

The new bill increased the amount of government aid and eased the conditions for obtaining it. The par value of Union Pacific stock was reduced to $100 per share. The government's lien was subordinated to first-mortgage bonds that the company could issue up to an amount equal to that of the government bonds. Finally, the land grant was doubled.

In the fall of 1864 Durant arranged the first Union Pacific construction contract in New York with H. C. Crane, an attorney for Herbert Hoxie. Crane was a Union Pacific stockholder, while Hoxie was an employee of the railroad. Under the contract Hoxie was to construct 247 miles of road, for which he was to be paid $50,000 per mile. This was considerably above the cost predicted by Peter Dey, a longtime Durant associate who resigned from the Union Pacific to protest the contract. Hoxie—who had no personal wealth and no experience in the construction industry—soon announced that he was unable to carry out the construction, whereupon the contract was promptly transferred to Durant and his associates.

Durant's actions in taking over the construction of track for the railroad company of which he was vice-president revealed much about his faith in the viability of the transcontinental railroad. Durant had little if any conviction that such an enterprise could make money. It was in the construction of the road that Durant saw potential profits.

Despite such designs, the construction plans required enormous financial commitments, and Durant had difficulty persuading investors to accept the risk entailed in the project. Their concern was understandable. Durant and his associates stood in the relation of partners, liable not only for their investments but also for the extent of their personal wealth. At this point Durant formed a construction company, Crédit Mobilier of America, to shield the investors with limited liability. With this mechanism Durant was able to obtain enough backing to

continue to construct—albeit at a high cost—the Union Pacific road.

One of the new investors was Oakes Ames, a wealthy New England shovel manufacturer and member of Congress. He and his brother Oliver bought $1 million worth of Crédit Mobilier stock and provided the firm with a loan of $600,000. Durant and the Ames brothers, however, were soon furiously battling with each other for control of Union Pacific and Crédit Mobilier. In 1866, when Oliver Ames became president of the Union Pacific, Durant began to lose control. For the next three years the Durant and Ames factions, or the "New York crowd" and the "Boston crowd," continued their battle. The Ameses ultimately triumphed. In part, Durant's opposition to the "Boston crowd" may have been the result of simple jealousy. Durant was the original author of the Union Pacific construction plan. He had established Crédit Mobilier, invested his own funds, negotiated the first contract, and worked to attract other investors. It is understandable that he would be reluctant to yield control.

A more substantive explanation for the dispute is that Durant and Ames had fundamentally different visions of the Union Pacific. While Durant doubted that the transcontinental line could ever be profitable, and thus put a premium on making a financial success of its construction, Ames believed that the railroad could be a financial success in the long term. Ames and his supporters thus insisted on higher quality construction—at a more reasonable cost—than Durant felt wise. On May 18, 1867, Durant was forced out as president, director, and member of the executive committee of Crédit Mobilier. As a result, the direction and control of the organization fell to the "Boston crowd." Durant still remained as vice-president of Union Pacific, although his authority was clearly in eclipse.

Nevertheless, he used what influence he could still command to complete the Union Pacific as rapidly as possible, insisting that construction proceed regardless of cost. He spent most of his time at the point of construction, urging and demanding greater speed. This haste probably doubled the cost of construction. Yet Durant knew that the Ames group would eventually force him out of the Union Pacific, and he was determined to finish the project before they succeeded.

The haste and, indeed, recklessness with which Durant completed the railroad is illustrated

Durant inspecting a Union Pacific roadbed in August 1866 (courtesy of Union Pacific Railroad Museum)

by an event which occurred as he was traveling westward in May 1869 for the ceremony signaling the linkage of the Union Pacific with the Central Pacific. Durant's train was stopped by ties piled on the track. A mob of some 300 armed men waited alongside the track. They were all employees of Union Pacific, and they demanded their back pay, overdue for months. Durant telegraphed Oliver Ames in Boston to send the money, and the payroll was met. Yet the event was a symptom of the persistent mismanagement the railroad suffered.

On May 10, 1869, at Promontory, Utah, Durant joined with Leland Stanford of the Central Pacific in driving the "last spike." Fifteen days later Durant, knowing that the Ames group was finally

poised to oust him from the Union Pacific, resigned as vice-president of the railroad and declined reelection as director.

By this time Durant was in poor health. After his resignation he moved to the Adirondack mountains, where he had extensive land holdings. Although he lost much of his fortune in the panic of 1873, he promoted a plan to develop the iron and timber resources of the Adirondacks. He was particularly interested in promoting a railroad from Saratoga across the St. Lawrence into Canada. But Durant's poor health and reduced financial circumstances prevented him from pursuing the project. He died in North Creek, New York, on October 5, 1885.

Unpublished Document:
Henry W. Farnam, *Henry Farnam*. Biography. Available at Yale University and the Library of Congress.

References:
Charles Edgar Ames, *Pioneering the Union Pacific* (New York: Meredith Corp., 1969);
Robert G. Athearn, *Union Pacific Country* (Lincoln: University of Nebraska Press, 1971);

Arthur M. Johnson and Barry E. Supple, *Boston Capitalists and Western Railroads* (Cambridge, Mass.: Harvard University Press, 1967);
Maury Klein, *Union Pacific: The Birth of a Railroad, 1862-1893* (New York: Doubleday, 1987);
Henry K. White, *History of the Union Pacific Railway* (Clifton, N.J.: Augustus M. Kelley, 1973).

Erie Railroad

by F. Daniel Larkin

State University College, Oneonta, New York

In New York State in 1832 steam locomotive power was being used on only 16 miles of railroad. All 16 miles were the property of the Mohawk & Hudson Railroad, a line founded in 1826, opened in 1831, and which would later form the miniscule beginnings of the massive New York Central rail empire. When completed and combined in 1869 the New York Central & Hudson River Railroad linked the port of New York with the Lake Erie port of Buffalo by means of 450 miles of track via the state capital at Albany. But as the tiny Dewitt Clinton, the Mohawk & Hudson's single locomotive, was making its short run between Albany and Schenectady, much grander railroad planning was in progress. In 1832 promoters from New York City and several counties across the state's southern tier applied to the legislature for a charter to build a railroad to connect New York City with Lake Erie by way of a direct southern route.

The bill cleared the legislature in April 1832 and chartered the New York & Erie Railroad with a capital limit of $10 million. But the powerful Erie Canal interests had succeeded in including several restrictive clauses in the charter which severely hampered the railroad. One clause required that 5 percent of the capital had to be raised before the company could be organized and another mandated legislative approval for connections to railroads in neighboring New Jersey and Pennsylvania. Despite the 5 percent rule and other restrictions the company was capitalized rapidly. Among the original directors elected in July 1833 were Eleazar Lord, an early advocate of the road, and Benjamin Wright,

chief engineer on the Erie Canal and, during its early construction, the Delaware & Hudson Canal. Lord was named as the company's first president, and Wright was appointed to the chief engineer's post. Wright's survey, completed in 1834, proposed a rail line beginning on a point on the west bank of the Hudson River "twenty-four miles north of the City Hall of New York" and running a total of 483 miles through the village of Binghamton to Dunkirk on Lake Erie.

Prior to the start of construction the directors decided to build a 6-foot-wide track instead of the 4-foot 8½-inch width that was becoming standard for American railroads. One of the arguments in favor of the wide gauge was that it would permit the use of the larger engines needed to overcome the numerous steep grades on the railroad route. By 1841 construction on the line had progressed from Piermont-on-Hudson to Goshen, New York, a distance of forty-six miles, and that section was opened by September. Another 117 miles of the line were graded during 1841, but the railroad finances were in such a dismal state that the future of the road and the investment it represented appeared bleak. As a result the Erie Railroad became an issue in the gubernatorial election of 1842. The incumbent governor, William Seward, and his Whig party advocated saving the Erie through state loans. The Democrats countered that the state should take over and complete the line. Both parties used the unfinished railroad as leverage in the campaign. Although the Democrats triumphed in 1842, a special session of the legislature held after the election postponed the question of the Erie's fate by delaying the sale of the road under state foreclosure for six months.

Although the first grace period expired in April 1843, the legislature granted an extension until 1850 under the condition that work on the Erie be resumed by 1845. Horatio Allen was elected president of the Erie in 1843 in order to give the project credibility. Allen, an engineer who had worked on the Delaware & Hudson project in 1827-1829 and had built the South Carolina Railroad in 1829-1834, called for a renewal of public faith in the Erie project. He noted that although nearly $4.75 million had been spent, almost sixty-four miles of track, a large amount for that time, were in operation. Allen attempted to raise the estimated $7 million necessary to finish the line by trying to persuade the city of New York to contribute nearly half the amount, but the Common Council turned a deaf ear to the proposal. When all other attempts to raise the funds failed Allen resigned as president in October 1844; he remained with Erie as chief engineer.

The financial problems which beset the Erie slowed construction to a crawl. When the railroad finally reached Binghamton in 1848, it was still less than halfway to Lake Erie. The project had already cost $8 million, and only three years remained to complete it before the legislative extension expired. Finally, in 1851, the line, under the direction of president Benjamin Loder and chief engineer Allen, reached Dunkirk to satisfy the deadline. At the time of its completion the Erie was the longest railroad in the United States. As befit the occasion a special ceremonial train carried dignitaries to Dunkirk on May 14. President Millard Fillmore and four of his cabinet, including Secretary of State Daniel Webster, were on the train that helped dedicate the $20 million undertaking. After nearly two decades of financial, managerial, political, and construction problems, the Erie became a reality.

The opening, which should have marked a lessening of the Erie's difficulties, turned out to be only the end of one phase of problems and the beginning of another. In 1853 the seven railroads on the other route between Albany and Buffalo combined to form the New York Central. This consolidation caused rate competition to develop between the Central and its ally, the Hudson River Railroad, and the Erie. The Erie's earnings were further pressured in 1857 by massive physical destruction caused by

winter floods. Engineers' strikes compounded the problems. Added to this was the panic of 1857, which depressed railroad earnings in general. As a result of the pressures the Erie was forced into receivership in 1859; it was reorganized as the Erie Railway Company. The next decade or so was disastrous to Erie operations as the reorganization had opened the company to the manipulations of three of the most ruthless operators on Wall Street: Daniel Drew, James Fisk, and Jay Gould. As if those three were not enough for any organization to bear, Cornelius Vanderbilt also became involved in the railroad. He had temporarily controlled the Erie in 1867 but had lost it to Drew, Fisk, and Gould. After he completed his takeover of the New York Central in 1867 Vanderbilt returned his attention to the Erie. Fisk and Gould provided the opposition during this foray. When Vanderbilt attempted to buy enough Erie stock to regain control Fisk and Gould printed phony stock to sell to Vanderbilt. The two men pulled in almost $7 million of Vanderbilt's money before he figured out their plan. Both Gould and Vanderbilt went to Albany in order to bribe the legislature to rule on the legality of the stock. After spending large amounts in bribes Vanderbilt abandoned the fight and left the Erie to Gould and Fisk.

While the Erie "war" generated much public outrage, notoriety, and excitement, the only real outcome of the conflict was to leave the Erie in poor operating condition and heavily burdened with some $5 million in debt. These encumbrances led to a second reorganization, and the company was reformed in 1878 as the New York, Lake Erie & Western Railroad.

The new company began energetically by double-tracking its entire 472-mile length and replacing iron rails with steel. The unconventional 6-foot gauge was reduced to standard, and the rolling stock was modernized. The Erie also bought the Atlantic & Great Western and built the Chicago & Atlantic Railroad, thus attaining access to Chicago over its own rails.

Despite the brisk start the New York, Lake Erie & Western Railroad sank into receivership within seventeen years. The company's debt burden increased far beyond the railroad's ability to pay the fixed charges associated with it. The costs associated with the modernization and the expansion, along with the costs of the Erie's checkered past, were too heavy to bear during the 1893 depression.

Demand for its business remained strong, but the company's transportation rates were kept low due to competition with rival railroads.

In 1895 the company succumbed to its third reorganization of the nineteenth century and became the Erie Railroad Company. Eden B. Thomas took over as president and began a program aimed at consolidation and fiscal responsibility. But by the end of the century, the Erie remained burdened with a bonded indebtedness of more than $137 million. In addition to the debt the Erie carried stock totaling over $146 million. The railroad's annual fixed charges, including interest and dividend payments, amounted to more than $8 million in 1898. But the Erie's officers were optimistic about the future since net income for 1898 reached nearly $650,000. It ap-

peared that the bad management and manipulation of the road which so characterized the nineteenth century might be undone in the twentieth.

References:

Charles Francis Adams, Jr., and Henry Adams, *Chapters of Erie* (Boston: James R. Osgood, 1871);

Frederick C. Hicks, ed., *High Finance in the Sixties* (Port Washington, N.Y.: Kennikat Press, 1966);

Edward Hungerford, *Men of Erie* (New York: Random House, 1946);

E. H. Mott, *Between the Ocean and the Lakes: The Story of Erie* (New York: Collins, 1899).

Archives:

Records concerning the Erie Railroad are located at the Erie-Lackawanna Historical Society, Inc. at Wayne, Pennsylvania.

Henry Farnam

(November 9, 1803-October 4, 1883)

by Alec Kirby

George Washington University

CAREER: Surveyor, Erie Canal (1821-1824); assistant engineer (1825-1827); chief engineer, Farmington Canal (1827-1846); chief engineer and superintendent, Farmington Railroad (1846-1850); partner, Sheffield & Farnam (1850-1854); partner, Farnam & Durant (1855-1863); president, Chicago & Rock Island Railroad (1855-1863).

Henry Farnam, engineer, railroad builder, and philanthropist, was born in Scipio, Cayuga County, New York, on November 9, 1803. His parents, Jeffrey Amherst Farnam and Mercy Tracy, traced their family roots to eighteenth-century settlers in eastern New York. Farnam's parents were farmers, but from an early age Farnam demonstrated little interest in agriculture. He was, however, an exceptional student. Despite limited access to books and formal schooling, Farnam taught himself trigonometry and surveying before he was sixteen. He studied in the evening by firelight to save on the expense of candles. Because of his distaste for farm work, his parents sent him at a young age to live with a local physician, Dr. Phineas Hurd, so that he might learn medicine. He quickly lost interest in the medical profession and returned to his father's farm. There he

Henry Farnam (courtesy of The New York Public Library, Astor, Lenox and Tilden Foundations)

completed his schooling and briefly taught in the local school.

Farnam began his career as an engineer on the Erie Canal, the great project to link East to West. Work on the Erie Canal began in 1817, and the chief engineer of the section west of Rochester was David Thomas, a Quaker whom Farnam had met through a relative. In 1821 Farnam applied to Thomas for a job in a surveying party. Camp cook was the only position available and Farnam took that job. He progressed quickly and several months later he became an assistant engineer. His work on the canal was a success, but Farnam's health was seriously affected by the climate. By the time he left the canal after its completion in the fall of 1824, he had nearly died of malaria. In search of a healthier climate, he accepted a position as assistant engineer on the Farmington Canal and in 1825 moved to Connecticut.

Working on the Farmington Canal and the Farmington Railroad between 1825 and 1850, Farnam mastered the skills he later used to construct the first network of railroads to the West. Connecticut chartered the Farmington Canal in 1822, although construction did not begin until 1825, when Davis Hurd became chief engineer. It was Hurd who selected Farnam to serve as his assistant. Farnam quickly earned Hurd's confidence and respect, and Hurd successfully urged the canal's directors to promote Farnam to chief engineer when Hurd retired in 1827. Farnam held this position for as long as the canal was in operation.

The Farmington Canal was in fact only the southern part of a water system that extended from Long Island Sound northward into Massachusetts, eventually connecting with the Connecticut River. The Farmington Canal Company operated the distance from New Haven to the state line; the Hampshire & Hampden Canal Company operated the rest. The two companies merged in 1826. By 1828 construction took the canal to Farmington; within a year continuous navigation was possible to Westfield. The canal reached Northampton in 1835. Despite constant expansion, the canal proved unprofitable in part because it was capable of accommodating only boats of twenty to twenty-five tons. In 1836 the New Haven & Northampton Canal Company took over the canal, but the new owners were unable to turn the operation around.

Throughout the expansion and corporate change, Farnam served as chief engineer and superintendent. The work proved to be particularly difficult, since to cut costs the company skimped on construction. As a result the canal was of poor quality. Two-thirds of the sixty locks were made of wood. With constant breaks in the banks of the canal, Farnam constantly traveled in his buggy to make repairs. Years later, after he retired, he still had nightmares about breaks in the canal walls.

By 1845 it was clear that the canal would never be a financial success. Farnam, recognizing the impact of the railroad on transportation, proposed that a railroad be built along the canal and that the canal be abandoned. He made this proposal to Joseph E. Sheffield, the principal stockholder and president of the company. Through his work at the canal Farnam had developed a close relationship with Sheffield. The two had made plans to build a railroad from New Haven to New York and obtained a charter in 1844. They had dropped the proposal when they could not interest enough investors to begin work. After Farnam proposed the railroad along the Farmington Canal, Sheffield, in spring 1845, anonymously promoted the idea in a New Haven newspaper. The directors voted to adopt the plan in February 1846, and they selected Farnam to serve as chief engineer and superintendent of the project. Work was begun in January 1847. The first leg to Plainville was completed in January 1848, and in 1850 the road was extended to Tariffville and Collinsville.

With the railroad completed, Farnam resigned from the New Haven & Northampton Company. He had gained valuable experience in engineering and business. Also during this period, in 1839, he married Ann Sophia Whitman of Farmington and began a family which was to include five children.

Farnam had been quick to appreciate the importance railroads were to play in the economic development of the country. He had seen the potential of the New Haven & Northampton Railroad as a substitute for the canal. He demonstrated equal prescience in recognizing the opportunity for building railroads in the West. In 1850 Farnam and Sheffield—who had sold his stock in the New Haven & Northampton Company—organized the firm of Sheffield and Farnam. They began to construct the Michigan Southern Railroad, which connected Chicago with the East. This marked the beginning of Farnam's association with Thomas C. Durant, who after Farnam's retirement played an important role in the construction of the Union Pacific Railroad. The Michigan Southern—along with the subsequently constructed Michigan Central Railroad—is credited with dramatically stimulating the economic development of Chicago.

With the completion of the Michigan Southern in March 1852, Farnam began to make plans for a road from Chicago to the Mississippi. This road, the Chicago & Rock Island, was begun in April 1852 and completed in February 1854, eighteen months before the completion date in the contract. Even while construction was still in progress Farnam began organizing for a railroad south to Peoria and Bureau Valley. This road was completed in mid 1854.

As the next step Farnam envisioned bridging the Mississippi River. These plans were blocked, however, by various financial interests along the river. Conflict centered on a contest between the two modes of travel available at the time—waterways and railroads. Most of the large natural waterways in the United States run from north to south, while most of the railroads ran from east to west. Building a bridge across the Mississippi River brought these two means of travel into open conflict. Heightening the battle was the sharp economic rivalry between St. Louis and Chicago. St. Louis, with its investments in steamship navigation, vigorously opposed the construction of the bridge; Chicago, which saw its economic growth tied to the railroad, placed a high priority on the construction of the bridge. To counter lawsuits Farnam hired Abraham Lincoln, whose arguments won the famous Rock Island Bridge case. Farnam, while head of the Chicago & Rock Island, also became president of an independent company that constructed the bridge across the Mississippi. He himself designed the bridge and superintended the construction, which was completed in April 1855.

By this point Sheffield retired, and Farnam and Durant organized a partnership to build a railroad across Iowa to Grinnell.

This road, the Mississippi & Missouri, was met with great investor skepticism. Moreover, Durant's financial speculation nearly destroyed the firm of Farnam & Durant during 1857. The firm survived, and the Mississippi & Missouri was ultimately extended to the Missouri River, although that was not achieved until after Farnam had retired. In the last several years before his retirement, Farnam continued to serve as president of the Chicago & Rock Island. In these years he also assumed the presidency of the Merchant's Loan and Trust Company, a bank which he helped form as an original stockholder.

On June 4, 1863, Farnam resigned the presidency of the Chicago & Rock Island Railroad. One month later he began his retirement by boarding a steamer for Africa. For the next five years Farnam traveled through Africa, the Middle East, and Europe, accompanied by his wife and three youngest children. In 1868 he returned to the United States and settled in New Haven. He devoted the rest of his years to philanthropy. As early as 1863 he had donated $30,000 to Yale College; after 1868 he doubled this sum, as well as providing smaller gifts to individual departments within the college. On September 30, 1883, Farnam suffered a stroke, and he died on October 4, 1883.

Unpublished Document:

Henry W. Farnam, "Henry Farnam." Biography. Available at Yale University and the Library of Congress.

Reference:

Charles Edgar Ames, *Pioneering the Union Pacific* (New York: Meredith Corp., 1969).

Albert Fink

(October 27, 1827-April 3, 1897)

by E. Dale Odom

North Texas State University

CAREER: Graduate in architecture and engineering, Darmstadt, Germany (1848); engineering assistant, Baltimore & Ohio Railroad (1849-1857); chief engineer and superintendent (1857-1865), general superintendent and vice-president, Louisville & Nashville Railroad (1865-1875); executive director, Southern Railway & Steamship Association (1875-1877); executive director, Trunk Line Pool (1877-1889); retirement (1889-1897).

Albert Fink is generally regarded as the originator of railway economics and statistics and was also a brilliant engineer who invented a railway bridge truss and supervised the construction of some of the largest railroad bridges of his time. He devoted roughly the first half of his life to engineering and the second half to the study of the economics of profitable and stable railroad operation.

Albert Fink was born in Lauterbach, Germany, on October 27, 1827, the son of Andres S. and Margaret (Jacob) Fink. He attended a polytechnic institute at Darmstadt and graduated in engineering and architecture in 1848. Because of the turbulent German politics of 1848, Fink immigrated to the United States in 1849 and settled in Baltimore, Maryland. He went to work for the Baltimore & Ohio (B&O) Railroad as an assistant in the engineering department. By 1857, at the age of thirty, he had also become a consulting engineer for the Norfolk & Petersburg Railroad. That same year Fink left the B&O and moved to Louisville, Kentucky, to become construction engineer of the Louisville & Nashville (L&N) Railroad. Fink advanced gradually in the L&N bureaucracy, becoming chief engineer and superintendent in 1859, general superintendent in 1865, and a vice-president in 1870.

His tenure as superintendent included the years of the Civil War, which certainly tested Fink's capability as an engineer, as the Louisville & Nashville suffered considerable destruction at the hands

Albert Fink

of the warring armies. It was during his years at the L&N that Fink also found time to practice architecture, designing and constructing a new courthouse for Louisville in the late 1850s. His crowning achievement as an engineer was supervising the building of the railway bridge across the Ohio River at Louisville, which, when completed, was the longest truss bridge in the world.

During his later years as an executive of the Louisville & Nashville, Fink began to become more interested in the economics of profitable railway operation than in engineering. In 1874 he submitted a report to the board of directors entitled "The Fink Report on the Cost of Transportation" that is generally regarded as the foundation of railroad economics. In 1875 Fink resigned his position with the L&N. He helped to organize, and accepted a position as the executive director of, the Southern Railway & Steamship Association. This Atlanta-based organization was intended to stabilize transportation rates across the South.

Fink's growing reputation as an advocate of cooperation rather than competition among railroad companies attracted the attention of Cornelius Vanderbilt and the operators of the big trunk line roads in the East. Consequently, when the New York Central, the Erie, the B&O, and the Pennsylvania railroads created the Trunk Line Pooling Association in 1877, they recruited Fink to direct it. The pool grew from four railroads to forty by 1883, and Fink's small staff of a few clerks had grown to several hundred. The pool embraced almost all the railways north of the Ohio River and east of the Mississippi River. Fink had grandiose ideas of such associations controlling railroad rates throughout the country. He and George Blanchard, a vicepresident of the Erie Railroad, were mostly responsible for advocating the principle of federal government aid in strengthening railroad pooling machinery.

Fink argued that the main complaints about railroad services came from merchants who used the railways, and that these complaints stemmed mainly from instability, disorder, numerous rate changes, all of which were products of intense competition. Therefore, Fink argued, pooling and railroad cooperation should be carried out under the authority and direction of the United States government in order to promote stability, order, and efficiency. Fink became noted for his testimony before the numerous congressional committees examining railway problems and considering railroad regulation legislation during the early 1880s. Without any actual models to follow, Fink had made himself an expert on railroad costs and the problems of rendering railroad service to the various kinds of users. Yet until the Railway Transportation Act of 1920, legislators refused to follow Fink's recommendations. His counsel, and that of several others who

were seen as too closely connected with the railroads, was not taken into account by the Congress when they created the Interstate Commerce Commission (ICC) in 1887. In fact, Fink's success in holding the large trunk line pool together until his retirement in 1889 may well have hurt his chances of obtaining legislation to facilitate railroad cooperation. The *New York Times* actually blamed the "autocratic sway of that pool" for the passage of the Interstate Commerce Act, an act that forbade pooling and gave the ICC the mandate to force railroads to compete.

Charles Francis Adams, and many others, gave Fink most of the credit for holding the trunk line pool together. A very large, tall man of imposing appearance, Fink was usually described as brusque and autocratic, but those who knew him well describe him as a kind and warmhearted man who had many friends among railroad men. His first wife, whom he married in Baltimore as a young man, died at a young age. He married Sarah Hunt in Louisville on April 14, 1869, and they had one daughter, Ellen. In 1889 Fink, who was in poor health, resigned his $25,000-a-year position as director of the trunk line pool. His income was supplemented by the considerable revenue he received from a bridge truss he invented and patented in the 1850s while with the Baltimore & Ohio. Although a relatively young man of sixty-two at his retirement, Fink, apparently due to poor health, did not achieve much in the remaining eight years of his life. He died of pneumonia at a sanitarium in Sing Sing, New York, on April 3, 1897, at the age of sixtynine. He left most of his estate, which was not appraised, to his daughter. He was buried in Louisville, Kentucky.

Publications:

An Investigation into the Cost of Transportation on American Railroads, with Deductions for its Cheapening (Louisville, Ky.: J. P. Morton, 1874);

The Cost of Railroad Transportation, Railroad Accounts, and Governmental Regulation of Railroad Tariffs (Louisville, Ky.: J. P. Morton, 1875);

Investigation into the Cost of Passenger Traffic on American Railroads with Special Reference to Cost of Mail Service and its Compensation (Louisville, Ky.: J. P. Morton, 1876);

Are the New York Railroads Discriminating Against the Commerce of this City? (New York: Russell Brothers, 1878);

Commissioner's Report upon Resolutions Offered by Hon. J. W. Garrett, at a Meeting of Presidents of

Trunk Lines, on December 5, 1878 (New York, 1878);

Argument Before the Committee of Commerce for the Senate of the United States, on the Reagan Bill, for the Regulation of Interstate Commerce (New York: Russell Brothers, 1879);

Argument Regarding the Division of East Bound Freight from Chicago, between the Terminal Roads, Submitted to the Board of Arbitration, August, 1879 (New York: Russell Brothers, 1879);

Argument Before the Committee of Commerce of the House of Representatives of the United States, on the Reagan Bill, for the Regulation of Interstate Commerce (New York: Russell Brothers, 1880);

The Railroad Problem and its Solution (New York: Russell Brothers, 1880);

The Railroad Problem (New York, 1881);

Why Railroad Tariffs are not Maintained (New York: Russell Brothers, 1881);

Report upon the Adjustment of Railroad Transportation Rates to the Seaboard (New York: Russell Brothers, 1882);

Report upon the Relative Cost of Transporting Live Stock and Dressed Beef (New York: Russell Brothers, 1883);

Statistics Regarding the Movement of Eastbound and Westbound Traffic over the Trunk Lines and Connecting Roads (New York: Russell Brothers, 1884);

Measures for Securing Stable, Equitable & Indiscriminating Railway Tariffs (New York: Russell Brothers, 1885).

References:

Lee Benson, *Merchants, Farmers and Railroads* (Cambridge, Mass.: Harvard University Press, 1955);

Alfred D. Chandler, *The Railroads: Pioneers in Modern Management* (New York: Arno Press, 1979);

New York Times, April 4, 1897, pp. 4-5.

James Fisk, Jr.

April 1, 1835-January 7, 1872)

by Charles B. Weinstock

Pittsburgh, Pennsylvania

CAREER: Peddler (1853-1860); salesman, Jordan, Marsh and Company (1860-1864); broker (1863-1872); partner, Fisk & Belden (1865-1869); director (1867-1872); vice-president and comptroller, Erie Railroad (1868-1871); partner, Brooklyn Oil Refinery (1869-1870).

James Fisk, Jr., lived a life of almost surreal cunning and vulgarity and in the process provided many of the stereotypes disseminated by late nineteenth- and early twentieth-century critics of business and businessmen. During his brief and brilliant career as a stock speculator and railroad official of sorts, Fisk used his outrageous personality and ruthless business skills to shock and entertain those who came into contact with him and to fund an extravagant lifestyle. Known primarily for his roles in the "Erie war" of 1867-1869 and the Jay Gould "gold corner" of 1869, Fisk's excessive behavior in both business and social affairs obscured his very real business talents and marked him as a prime example of the perceived depravity of laissez faire capitalism.

The circumstances of Fisk's birth and upbringing were more typical of the new breed of western

James Fisk, Jr. (courtesy of Brown Brothers)

businessmen which emerged in the middle and late nineteenth century than of the New England scions which had dominated American business from the beginning of the Republic. James Fisk, Jr., was born on April 1, 1835, in Pownal, Vermont, the son of a peddler. His mother died in 1843, and his father, James Fisk, Sr., remarried soon after, moving his family to Brattleboro, Vermont. Fisk, Sr., opened an inn in Brattleboro where Fisk honed his nascent skills as an entertainer and a wit. In 1850 Fisk followed in the footsteps of his fellow rogue speculator Daniel Drew by joining a circus. Fisk spent approximately two years in Van Amberg's Mammoth Circus and Menagerie, working as an animal tender, roustabout, and ticket clerk. While it might be dangerous to place too much importance on his experience in the circus, there can be little doubt that much of Fisk's manner and business style was formed during his carnival years.

When Fisk returned to his father's peddling business in 1853, he was intent in applying to sales the techniques he had learned in the circus. Against the wishes of his skeptical father, Fisk painted the peddling wagons in garishly bright colors, adopted the dress of a gentleman, and mixed entertainment with his sales talk. The quickly increasing sales resulting from these changes soon convinced his father that Fisk had indeed learned valuable techniques in the circus. In 1854 Fisk married Lucy Moore, a fifteen-year-old girl from Springfield, Massachusetts. Because he was often traveling and away from home, Fisk spent little time with his wife. He would not change this as his career advanced. And advance it did. When his father retired, Fisk expanded the business to five wagons and also became a jobber, buying merchandise from the Boston firm of Jordan, Marsh and reselling to smaller retailers in the area. This arrangement did not satisfy Fisk's growing ambition, however, and in 1860 he went to work in Boston as a salesman for Jordan, Marsh.

When the Civil War broke out Eben Jordan, president of Jordan, Marsh, sent Fisk to Washington, D.C., to try and sell textiles to the government. Fisk lobbied congressmen and military officials in a hospitality room he set up in a hotel, soon signing a contract to provide the government with thousands of blankets which had been mildewing for years in a Jordan, Marsh warehouse. This and other similar sales to the government were so successful that Jordan, Marsh was required to buy more textile mills to meet the increased demand. Fisk was soon made a partner in the firm.

Fisk was clearly, and admittedly, a war profiteer. Yet he was comparatively honest and reliable, delivering good quality merchandise at the agreed upon price on the agreed upon date. This tension between the shady and the honest was at the center of Fisk's business career. In 1862 this tension was most clearly seen. In the war-torn and blockaded South thousands of tons of cotton were rotting in warehouses and in the fields. In the North textile mills were sitting idle because of a lack of raw material. Fisk saw the opportunity to profit from this situation while giving benefit to all sides, providing the Union army with needed uniforms, the South with desperately needed foreign exchange, and, of course, himself with profits. His many trips southward to buy contraband cotton violated numerous laws, but Fisk easily rationalized any moral difficulties.

As the war began to wind down in late 1864, the needs of the government also began to decline. Jordan bought Fisk's interest in the firm for $65,000, and Fisk used the money to open his own textile jobbing house in Boston. Business conditions continued to worsen, and the firm closed its doors after a few months. In what must be seen as the beginning of his true career, Fisk left for New York and Wall Street in late 1864. He opened a brokerage firm upon his arrival, but a bear market soon depleted his funds. As the end of the war approached Fisk's imagination once again asserted itself. He realized that the end of the war would cause a collapse in those Confederate bonds held in England. He also realized that the news of a Confederate surrender would be delayed by the trip across the ocean. Fisk concocted a scheme whereby he would telegraph the news of Lee's impending surrender to a compatriot in Canada who would speed to England and sell Confederate bonds short. All worked as planned, and Fisk's agent reached London two days before the first official word arrived from New York. Confederate bonds, which had been selling at 80, collapsed to 22 on the news from America. Had not one of Fisk's partners secretly placed a $5 million limit on the amount of bonds to be sold, the profits on the scheme would have been tremendous. Still, the transaction was rewarding to the participants.

Fisk, using these and other, borrowed funds, was able to return to Wall Street in late 1865. His

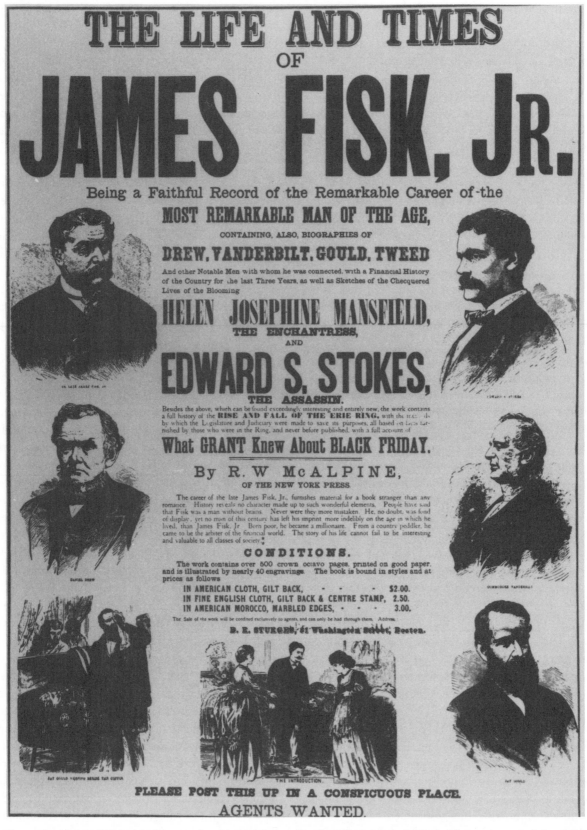

Flyer advertising R. W. McAlpine's book on Fisk produced in the wake of the Gold Corner scandal in 1869

first break had occurred in 1863 when he was able to broker the sale of the Stonington steamboat line by Daniel Drew to a group of Boston investors. Fisk secured a good price for Drew, who repaid him by financing the new brokerage firm of Fisk & Belden. The firm enabled Fisk to reap large profits, especially from the stock manipulations of Drew. In late 1867 two events occurred which were to dominate the rest of his life: first, in October 1867, Fisk, along with Jay Gould, was elected to the board of directors of the Erie Railroad; second, in November 1867, he met Josie Mansfield, an actress and reputed prostitute, who was to become Fisk's mistress and the agent of his downfall.

The years Fisk spent involved with the Erie formed the centerpiece of his career and were also the basis of one of the greatest railroad legends. The "Erie war" had its beginnings in 1859 when Drew persuaded Cornelius Vanderbilt to join the Erie board. Vanderbilt had many previous dealings with Drew but differed from the grizzled, old speculator in one important characteristic: whereas Drew always saw his involvement in a company as an opportunity for speculation, Vanderbilt was ever intent on running his acquisitions as enterprises. As would seem inevitable, the differing investment goals of Drew and Vanderbilt eventually boiled over into open conflict. The role of Fisk and Gould in the Erie was, in the beginning at least, as brokers and tacticians of Drew's strategies.

The strategy of choice was in this case, and most others, the bear campaign. In such schemes Drew would sell at a high price large amounts of borrowed stock, which would depress the stock's price. When the stock was sufficiently low, Drew would replace the borrowed stock and reap his profits. Drew's only problem was that the Erie's charter prevented the issuance of new stock which could then be used to drive down the price. It did, however, permit the issuance of convertible bonds which could then be exchanged for new stock. On February 18, 1868, Drew had the board secretly authorize $10 million in convertible bonds supposedly earmarked for improvements to the railroad. With these bonds in their possession Drew, Fisk, and Gould had the ability to create 100,000 shares of Erie stock which no one would know existed. The three speculators began to sell stock at a such a pace that many thought it impossible for them to replace it at any cost. This was certainly Vanderbilt's opinion. In order to assure this outcome Vanderbilt obtained a

court order restraining the Erie from issuing any further stock. At the same time he was buying Erie stock to support the price.

Drew, in response to Vanderbilt's moves, obtained a court order to *require* the Erie to issue more stock. Fulfilling their obligations Drew, Fisk, and Gould converted the bonds and printed the new shares. Worried that Vanderbilt would be able to enforce his injunction and destroy the new shares, the three partners arranged to have the shares "stolen," to turn up in their broker's office, and to be placed on the market the next day. Vanderbilt continued to buy the shares until he realized the scam. By this time the price had plummeted from 83 to 71, and Drew, Fisk, and Gould were able to transfer over $7 million in Vanderbilt's money to their own accounts. On March 11, 1868, Vanderbilt obtained warrants for the arrest of Drew, Fisk, and Gould. The three fled New York jurisdiction by crossing the Hudson River into New Jersey, where they set up headquarters in a hotel dubbed by the press as "Fort Taylor." This event marked a new phase in the Erie war and also began the ascendancy of Gould and Fisk in its operation.

Gould and Fisk were content to be safely across the river from the authorities. Fisk, in fact, had installed Josie Mansfield in an adjoining room in the hotel. Drew, on the other hand, became desperately homesick for his family. When Vanderbilt was able to survive the margin calls which resulted from the Erie panic, the war seemed to change from cavalry attacks to trench maneuvers. Gould engineered a plan whereby the state legislature would pass a bill legalizing the 100,000 shares of converted stock. Simultaneously, the Erie slashed rates in order to further the financial pressure on Vanderbilt through his New York Central Railroad. At the risk of his own arrest Gould traveled to Albany to lobby, through any and all means, the legislature. Despite the presence of a large amount of Vanderbilt money attempting to gain the same measure of influence, Gould's interests prevailed.

The passage of the bill caused Vanderbilt to seek a settlement in October 1868; he sent a private note to the miserable Drew requesting terms. During their second meeting Drew and Vanderbilt were interrupted by Fisk and Gould demanding inclusion in the deal. The settlement involved the Erie buying Vanderbilt's stock at a still substantial profit to the speculators, the banishment of Drew from the Erie, and the passage of control of the fragile and ravaged Erie to Fisk and Gould. The two rising speculators now had control of a railroad which they used for dual purposes. Gould had dreams of efficiently running the Erie, but he also shared with Fisk the desire to further manipulate the stock. Ironically, a new bear campaign in November 1869 snared Drew. By the end of this episode Drew had lost $1.5 million and not a little prestige. After they gained control of the Erie, Gould and Fisk began to exert an influence on the style of the line. Fisk had purchased the opulent Pike's Opera House in 1868 for the railroad's future use. In August 1869 the Erie offices were moved to the new location. For convenience sake Josie Mansfield was installed in an opulently furnished house close to the Erie offices, an arrangement which did not seem to affect Fisk's relationship with his wife, who was cloistered away in Boston. But Fisk's private life and his extravagant vision for the Erie did not prevent him, along with Gould, from engaging in several less than ideal manipulations.

On January 15, 1869, the Albany & Susquehanna (A&S) Railway opened between Albany and Binghamton, a route which Gould and Fisk regarded as well-suited to provide the Erie with access to New England. The road was already very nearly bankrupt when it caught the attention of Gould and Fisk, theoretically making it simple to acquire. But there were several factors which complicated the transaction. For one, most of the railroad's capital stock was owned by the townships along the route, and they were forbidden to dispose of their stock at less than par. Secondly, the stock which was able to be traded on the market was priced at less than 20, which showed that par stock was not a good value. Gould and Fisk instead used their notable and noted lobbying skills to try and convince the town leaders to place their proxies behind the Erie management. In a move reminiscent of the Erie war, A&S president Joseph Ramsey ruled in August 1869 that any transfer of stock to Erie was illegal. A flurry of court injunctions followed, the outcome being that Ramsey was removed from the A&S. While this technically placed the A&S in Erie hands, Ramsey managed to foil the scheme and in effect drove the A&S into chaos.

But this merely placed another opportunity before Fisk and Gould. With the A&S technically insolvent, a friendly judge appointed Fisk as a receiver for the company. When Fisk arrived at A&S headquarters with a group of armed men from the Erie,

Artist's rendering of Fisk's murder in 1871

he was met by an equally armed contingent from the A&S. This confrontation was followed by a more serious battle for the railroad itself, which the Erie had seized. The two armies, the Erie group more a drunken mob, fought at the Long Tunnel, fifteen miles east of Binghamton. Although no one was killed the A&S troops prevailed. Legal maneuvers followed, and Ramsey was able to retain control of the road. Knowing that Gould and Fisk would probably never cease in their struggle for the line, Ramsey placed the A&S beyond the pale of the Erie by leasing it to the Delaware & Hudson Canal Company.

Fisk also engaged in several other investments during the hectic years he was in control of the Erie. One of his favorites was his interest in the Narragansett Steamship Company. In 1869 he expensively refurbished two large steamships, the *Providence* and the *Bristol*, placing a live canary in each of the 250 staterooms. He also purchased a garish uniform which he wore every time he went sailing. Fisk also entered into a contractual relationship with Edward Stokes, with whom Fisk formed the Brooklyn Oil Refinery Company. The refinery received favorable rates from the Erie while supplying the Erie with constant traffic. Needless to say, it also gave Stokes and Fisk large profits.

It is clear from this review of Fisk's activities that he was a tireless worker. Amazingly, 1869 also was the year of the famous gold corner, which Fisk engineered with Jay Gould. Both Gould and Fisk maintained that their involvement in the gold corner was as much a product of their patriotic urge to increase the value of the country's gold stock as it was a profit scheme. To ensure that the plan would succeed, which involved preventing the government from selling gold, Gould involved Able Corbin, President Ulysses S. Grant's brother-in-law. It was Corbin's job to convince Grant to hold onto the government's gold and thereby support the price.

Fisk sank at least $8 million into the plan, and the price of gold began to climb. As the price rose above $150 per ounce, the country's economic situation began to tighten. Complaints to the president poured in from all over the country. On September 22, 1869, Corbin let Gould know that the government was soon going to sell gold. Gould kept this information to himself, quietly selling his over $50 million in gold. Fisk continued to buy, though Gould was keeping the interests of his partner in mind. On September 24, 1869, known as Black Friday, the price of gold hit $164 before news of the government gold sales was released. Almost immediately the price plummeted to $134, wiping out many investors. Fisk's brokerage firm, Fisk & Belden, went bankrupt, though again Gould made provisions. Fisk, though really a peripheral player in the scheme, was publicly thought to be its leader because of his visibility.

During this time, possibly because of his busy work schedule, Josie Mansfield was becoming disenchanted with Fisk and interested in Edward Stokes. In January 1870 she left him, but a month later Fisk was actively pursuing her. By fall 1870 Fisk was aware of Stokes's involvement with Josie, and he canceled the Erie's contract with the Brooklyn Refinery. Stokes became desperate for money. When Josie refused to choose Fisk over Stokes, Fisk charged his rival with embezzlement from the refinery. Lawsuits, recriminations, and other tactics dragged on for over a year, with the final result that by December 1871 a legal stalemate had been reached. At the end of that month Fisk resigned from the vice-presidency of the Erie, remaining as comptroller and director.

On January 6, 1872, Stokes cornered Fisk in the Grand Central Hotel. In a rage over the legal struggles, Stokes mortally shot Fisk. Fisk survived until the next day, identifying Stokes as his assailant. On January 7, 1872, with his wife at his side, Fisk died. In the end he was a victim of the style he had cultivated so carefully. Clearly the flamboyance and vulgarity for which he is remembered still obscure the nature of his business career. It may be that Fisk, unlike Jay Gould, is finally inseparable from the myths which surround his life.

References:

Charles Francis Adams, Jr., *A Chapter of Erie* (Boston: Fields, Osgood, 1869);

Maury Klein, *The Life and Legend of Jay Gould* (Baltimore, Md.: The Johns Hopkins University Press, 1986);

Edward Harold Mott, *Between the Ocean and the Lakes: the Story of Erie* (New York: John S. Collins, 1899);

W. A. Swanberg, *Jim Fisk: The Career of an Improbable Rascal* (New York: Scribner's, 1959).

Archives:

Materials relating to James Fisk, Jr., and his association with the Erie Railroad are located in the Erie Railroad Records at the Pennsylvania Historical and Museum Commission, Harrisburg, Penn.

John Murray Forbes

(February 23, 1813-October 12, 1898)

by John Lauritz Larson

Purdue University

CAREER: Clerk, J. & T. H. Perkins, Boston (1828-1829); clerk, partner, Russell & Company, China (1830-1838); merchant, Boston (1838-1846); director and president, Michigan Central (1846-1855); director (1857-1898), president (1878-1881), chairman, Chicago, Burlington & Quincy (1881-1898); chairman and treasurer, Chicago, Burlington & Northern (1885-1892).

John Murray Forbes was born on February 23, 1813, in Bordeaux, France, where his merchant father, Ralph Bennet Forbes, was waiting for the end of the Napoleonic wars. The elder Forbes was unsuccessful in business, but John Murray's mother, Margaret Perkins Forbes, was a younger sister of Boston's merchant prince Thomas Handasyd Perkins. When Ralph Forbes died in 1824, his two oldest sons entered the China trade with the Boston firm of J.&T.H. Perkins to help their mother support John Forbes and his five sisters at home. Through the generosity of his brother Thomas, John Murray Forbes enjoyed five years of formal schooling at Round Hill School in Northampton, Massachusetts. He relished the intellectual freedom as well as the physical exercise that marked this experimental school, but by his fifteenth birthday Forbes knew he must take up the mercantile life to achieve independence and repay his debts.

In 1828 John Murray Forbes entered the Perkins firm, assuming that he would be sent to China. Two years later the seventeen-year-old Forbes shipped out to replace his late brother Thomas as the Perkins man in the Canton firm of Russell & Company. Nominally an apprentice clerk, Forbes also inherited the confidential duties his brother Thomas had performed for the leading Chinese hong merchant, Howqua, a task which gave him extraordinary responsibility for thousands of dollars of other people's money. He met the challenge well for over two years but took sick in 1833

John Murray Forbes

and returned home to recover.

On his return to Boston Forbes set about finding a wife. The isolation in China and his heavy responsibilities there had left the youth anxious for security, and in February 1834 he married Sarah Hathaway of New Bedford, Massachusetts. Of course, marriage only increased his need for a career, and since the China business was all he knew, Forbes once more sailed for Canton. Arriving at Russell & Company in the summer of 1834, Forbes learned for the first time that he had been made a secret partner during his first tour of service and that his share of the profits already amounted to $14,000. Furthermore, Howqua wanted him back as his personal agent and offered as an incentive a 10 percent share in his business. Disinclined to stay away from his bride so long, Forbes nevertheless accepted this promise of certain fortune and settled in for another three-year term.

Before 1834 legitimate trade at Canton belonged to the British East India Company, and American firms like Russell & Company worked the opium networks on the fringes of the old British monopoly. However, with the 1834 opening of the market, British and American ships crowded the Canton wharves, flooding the market with Western goods and driving the price of teas out of sight. While Forbes's old correspondents still expected personal attention and favor, cutthroat competition in China forced commission merchants to do an efficient, regular, high-volume business on very small margins of profit. Scrambling to endure what now became a chaotic, year-long trading season, Forbes complained to a correspondent in London "that the China Trade is not subject to the rules of commerce elsewhere & that no calculation can be made in it." This speculative free-for-all in an exotic and unfriendly land impressed upon Forbes the "evils" of unrestrained competition and the need for system in business, principles he took to be axiomatic during the rest of his career. It was here in the Celestial Empire that he first glimpsed the meaning of the commercial and industrial revolutions that were changing his own Western world.

Forbes left China again in December 1836, hoping to salt down his fortune at home and take up those domestic luxuries denied a resident merchant in China. Instead he landed in New York in March 1837 in the midst of a banking panic. Forbes fell to work at once covering his own obligations and those of Russell & Company. When the emergency had passed Forbes realized that Boston was slipping out of the mainstream of the China trade and that better investment opportunities existed elsewhere in the rapidly expanding American economy. Once settled in Milton, Massachusetts, he cautiously took up investments in fields central to American industrial development: land, iron, steam, and railroads. Passive investments in the coal lands and iron works never served him well, nor did his many plunges into steamships designed by brother Bennet ever pay what he expected. In railroads, however, John Murray Forbes found profitable investments and a career worthy of his ambitions.

The Michigan Central Railroad caught Forbes's attention just as railroads generally were capturing the imagination of the American nation. Planned in 1837 as part of a statewide system of internal improvements, the Central Railroad languished into the 1840s, crippled by inadequate funding, mismanagement, and more traffic than the road could bear. In 1846 Detroit businessmen, led by attorney James F. Joy and Internal Improvements Commissioner George F. Porter, spearheaded a movement to sell the Central Railroad which attracted New York railroad engineer John W. Brooks, Boston financier John E. Thayer, and finally John Murray Forbes. The company named Forbes as president in order to draw investments from conservative Boston families; Forbes accepted, he said, to "get things going & keep it warm" as a retirement sinecure for his seafaring brother, Bennet.

Instead of a sinecure Forbes found serious work to be done. The Michigan Central purchase called for a $500,000 payment, due September 30, 1846, and Forbes scrambled for funds, raising the required amount one week before the deadline. He and Brooks then set to work rebuilding the road's physical plant, while investors watched eagerly for signs of early returns. Engineer Brooks took charge of construction and operations while Forbes handled the business and fund-raising matters. The two leaders blended their expertise on matters of strategy, where Forbes's conservative temper and his China experience played a major part. Forbes intended a "trim" and efficient company doing only the "usual business of railroad transportation," but competition combined with frontier conditions made it unclear just what that necessarily entailed. Reluctantly, Forbes sanctioned steamships to ply the lakes connecting his Michigan line with Chicago and New York cars. Brooks insisted on large, slow trains, heavy track, sturdy warehouses, and first-class facilities along the main line. Both men hoped to leave feeder lines to the enterprise of ambitious local interests.

Forbes saw his role in Michigan as a regional developer, not an agent for petty local enterprise, and he felt little sympathy for small merchants and farmers who were injured by the march of progress. He believed his railroad provided the framework for central Michigan's developing economy, and whatever profits he could glean were small compensation for the great benefits that followed. However, local interests bristled at the prospect of "foreign" monopoly influence in their markets, and while Forbes poured money into a first-class developmental railroad, his future customers encouraged investment in a rival Michigan Southern line to Chicago that would seriously threaten Forbes's profits.

James F. Joy was the first to see the danger. As early as 1848 he lined up a charter to build an extension to Chicago that Forbes, preoccupied with the high costs of construction in Michigan, refused to pursue. When the race to Chicago took shape the next year Forbes was denied an Indiana charter by friends of the Michigan Southern, and he finally bought rights in October 1851 for ten times the earlier price. Working straight through the winter his crews succeeded in reaching Chicago on May 21, 1852, just one day ahead of the Michigan Southern. The Michigan Central had become an interregional line, and Forbes found himself at the center of the transportation revolution in the West.

Forbes's Michigan experience reminded him of the reckless days in Canton just after the collapse of the old British monopoly. Hoping to prevent that kind of chaos, he envisioned a rational, systematic process of frontier railroad investment that would just keep pace with pioneer settlement and help the country grow into itself. Unfortunately, other railroad promoters, more speculative than Forbes, saw quick profits in rapid thrusts into the frontier, which forced Forbes and his associates to do the same.

The Chicago, Burlington & Quincy (CB&Q) Railroad, the company in which Forbes labored for the balance of his years, sprang from this westward movement. The Michigan Central's legal expert, James F. Joy, and its technical expert, John W. Brooks, studied the many small projects afloat in the Illinois countryside, and in 1852 they recommended a group of four properties to Forbes and the eastern investors. The Aurora Branch Railroad ran twelve miles west from a junction with the Galena & Chicago Union. The Aurora planned to connect with the as yet uncompleted Central Military Tract, which would run to Galesburg, where the equally hypothetical Peoria & Oquawka and the Northern Cross lines would offer links to the Mississippi River in Iowa and Missouri. The Forbes group—leading Michigan Central stockholders in Boston and New York together with Brooks and Joy—took

control of these local fledglings and by 1856 forged a new consolidated CB&Q. Even before this work was completed the Forbes group extended additional financial aid to the Hannibal & St. Joseph in Missouri and the Burlington & Missouri River (B&MR) in Iowa to secure feeders in the coming race for traffic. The West was in a hurry and Forbes instinctively resisted, but congressional land grants to the Hannibal in 1852 and the B&MR in 1856 prematurely forced him to invest ahead of demand.

Such intense speculation in western railroads produced the overextension Forbes had often predicted, and by 1857 a banking panic sent the Boston financier once more racing to cover the obligations of his many frontier lines. Never wanting a manager's job, Forbes had surrendered the Michigan Central presidency to Brooks in 1855, and after a major capital campaign for the CB&Q in early 1857, he retired to his new island retreat, Naushon, at the mouth of Buzzard's Bay, where he copied the leisured habits of Boston's gentry. The crisis came in October, and in twenty-four hours Forbes boarded a steamer for England, hatching a plan to raise $1.5 million to save the Michigan Central from default. Plunging all his resources (including his house) and the funds of his kinsmen in China (who, because of the distance, could not repudiate their investment in less than three months) into a syndicate to buy Michigan Central bonds, Forbes guaranteed the sale of the issue and then resold the paper in London to investors who trusted *him*, but not his railroads. Within a month he had formulated a similar deal to save the CB&Q, but still the Missouri and Iowa lines remained vulnerable. As these frontier investments increased Forbes exacted greater control over the local companies, which secured his railroad connections but laid the foundations for future hostility between the investor and his constituents.

Before the pressure of the competition in Mississippi Valley railroading could be resolved, the sectional conflict in national politics exploded in civil war. John Murray Forbes had played no active part in politics before 1850, and he, like most Americans, felt no particular embarrassment about the compromise with slavery in the South. Still, Forbes noticed that where slavery existed, industrial development seemed to lag behind, and he concluded that the free labor system was the key to capitalistic success. Not surprisingly, then, when the Compromise of 1850 threatened to limit the free labor field for development, Forbes's interest in antislavery began. Polarization steadily destroyed national political discourse, and Forbes sharpened his critique of the "slave power conspiracy," which he believed would spread slavery throughout the nation and crush the poor whites of the South beneath an arrogant slaveholding class. His personal investments in Iowa and Missouri lent an urgency to his analysis, and his enthusiasm for confrontation swelled. He contributed to the Kansas Emigrant Aid Society of Amos A. Lawrence and to John Brown's violent exploits in Kansas. Forbes even claimed to have entertained Brown at his home in Milton sometime before the Harpers Ferry raid. Thrilled by Lincoln's election he momentarily disbelieved the secession that followed. With the attack on Fort Sumter, however, Forbes plunged into war like a zealot.

Forbes performed many services during the war. In the first days he purchased supplies and transportation for Massachusetts troops bound for the Union army. He showered Washington officials with advice ranging from naval procurement to wartime finance. He launched a privateering vessel, mounted a recruiting scheme that bordered on headhunting, pushed for emancipation, and encouraged the use of black troops against the Confederacy. His most unusual effort came in 1863 at Port Royal, South Carolina, where he shared in a successful 8,000-acre plantation intended to prove the value of free contract labor as a substitute for slavery. Finally, he poured money and energy into the Loyal Publication Society, nationalistic Union Leagues, and the postwar-Republican mouthpiece, *The Nation*. Experiencing war as a free agent, Forbes assigned to the conflict his own peculiar interpretation, and he celebrated in the Union victory the founding of "a nation . . . instead of the mere confederacy these people pretend we have been."

The Civil War brought both good and ill to midwestern American railroads. Frontier lines like the Hannibal in Missouri and the Burlington in Iowa marked time uncertainly through the years of conflict, while the federal Pacific Railroad acts of 1862 and 1864 laid the bait of generous subsidies in the path of such western lines. Forbes felt personally exhausted after the war, and, leaving James F. Joy in charge of westward railroads, he retired again from business. Social pursuits—the Saturday Club of Boston, riding, hunting, sailing, and entertaining friends (such as Ralph Waldo Emerson) at

Milton or Naushon—preoccupied him. Before long, however, Joy became deeply involved in a speculative circus at Kansas City which contradicted Forbes's own commitments to Iowa and Nebraska and also his vision of sequential east-west development. Awakened to the danger in 1867 by his young cousin Charles E. Perkins (then superintendent of the B&MR), Forbes demanded a commitment to the Iowa extension as the CB&Q's *main* line in a confrontation that eventually wrecked his long-standing friendship with Joy. He pressed for the completion of the B&MR in 1869 and for its continuation into Nebraska as an independent branch of the transcontinental Union Pacific line.

John Murray Forbes hated government subsidies to railroads, but in the postwar West he found them everywhere, luring speculative investors and aggravating tensions between himself and James F. Joy. Joy, then president of the CB&Q, dealt with the pressures by trying to seize the prize ahead of the enemy. Forbes denounced all such games as blackmail, preferring a mind-your-own-business conservatism upon which he sold bonds with his personal guarantee. Speculators like Jay Gould, he reasoned, cared nothing for development and therefore would ruin any property for a quick paper gain. Local farmers and merchants, on the other hand, cared only for their own low rates and encouraged just such speculators in the name of competition.

By 1874 maximum rate Granger laws threatened revenues for legitimate midwestern carriers, while cutthroat competition produced wreckage in the capital market. Forbes's defense against the Grangers depended on *not* being guilty of graft and abuses. Therefore, when he discovered in 1875 that Joy had led the CB&Q directors into scandalous investments in the so-called Iowa River Roads, Forbes exploded in self-righteous anger. Marshaling his considerable fortune and influence he staged a takeover of the CB&Q, drove Joy and his friends from the board, and seized once more an active role on the moving railroad frontier.

Forbes's reorganized CB&Q enjoyed an uneasy peace in the 1870s based on the pooling of transcontinental traffic between Chicago and the West. Hard times kept all parties in line, but economic recovery late in the decade promised a return to competitive construction. Any regional struggle was bound to pit that volatile gamesman, Jay Gould, against Forbes's dogmatic young cousin, Charles E. Perkins of the Burlington. The aging Boston financier found himself caught between styles and generations. He wanted "peace and pools," but he could not lay down with the likes of Gould. "Must we grow in branches & feeders as the Devil fish grows & as Joy believed in growing," he queried Perkins, "or can we take a breathing spell and perfect our own line?" There was to be no rest. In 1878 Forbes took the presidency himself while he groomed Perkins for leadership. By 1881 competitive construction broke out anew, and Forbes handed Perkins the reins for a wide ride of expansion that carried the Burlington route to Denver and into the far Northwest, and north to Minneapolis-St. Paul via the Chicago, Burlington & Northern.

After 1881 Forbes served as chairman of the board of the CB&Q, but for another decade Perkins still described him as "the head man." Financial policy remained firmly in Forbes's hands, while his conservative sense and long experience permeated all other aspects of operations and strategy. Often posing as a timid old man ("I should wish you to the Old Harry if you led my crutches into any hobbly places"), he continued to plot defensive and offensive moves in the Northwest and to dream of assembling huge end-to-end systems by merging with the Pennsylvania Railroad. He opposed the Interstate Commerce Act of 1887, but he knew in part how the reckless policies of railroad developers had brought it about. Having been present at the creation of industrial America he felt more comfortable than younger men measuring laissez-faire theory against observable results. (He once proposed converting Jay Gould's giant Western Union into a public monopoly like the post office!) He found more time in the 1880s for tangential issues, like civil service reform, Republican party politics, and the perennial battle against "money heretics." Finally, he indulged his lifelong passion for leisure with long vacations all over the country and long hours sailing and riding at Milton or Naushon.

Forbes remained alert and active into his eighth decade, long enough to see one more disastrous financial panic (1893) and the major reorganization of railroads that followed. He scratched off letters in a now-shaky hand to "gold bug" editors, condemning William Jennings Bryan's 1896 silver campaign. By then, however, he was visibly failing, and on October 12, 1898, he died. John Murray Forbes was mourned by Sarah, his wife of sixty-four years, and five surviving children (one pre-

ceded him in death), who remembered more a gentle, doting father than a powerful man of business. His colleagues of a lifetime on the CB&Q eulogized him as "among the first to see the possibilities" in railroad development and one of the few such pioneers to "share in its realization." More at home among Boston's literati than Wall Street's magnates, Forbes used rules of business laid down in the age of sail to help invent corporate America, and he tried to set a high standard for capitalist integrity. Equally creative and conservative, he fascinated those who knew him, even though his career quickly slipped from view as the new generation took hold of the instruments of progress he had fashioned for them.

Publications:

Letters and Recollections of John Murray Forbes, 2 volumes, edited by Sarah Forbes Hughes (Boston: Houghton, Mifflin, 1899);
Reminiscences of John Murray Forbes, 3 volumes, edited by Sarah Forbes Hughes (Boston: Geo. H. Ellis, 1902);
Letters of John Murray Forbes, 3 volumes, edited by Sarah Forbes Hughes (Boston: Geo. H. Ellis, 1905).

References:

Thomas C. Cochran, *Railroad Leaders, 1845-1890: The Business Mind in Action* (Cambridge, Mass.: Harvard University Press, 1953);
Arthur M. Johnson and Barry E. Supple, *Boston Capitalists and Western Railroads* (Cambridge, Mass.: Harvard University Press, 1967);
John Lauritz Larson, *The Bonds of Enterprise: John Murray Forbes and Western Development in America's Railway Age* (Cambridge, Mass.: Harvard University Press, 1984);
Richard C. Overton, *Burlington Route: A History of the Burlington Lines* (New York: Knopf, 1965);
Henry Greenleaf Pearson, *An American Railroad Builder: John Murray Forbes* (Boston: Houghton Mifflin, 1911).

Archives:

Materials pertaining to John Murray Forbes are located in the John Murray Forbes Papers of the Baker Library, Harvard Graduate School of Business Administration, Boston, Massachusetts; in the Forbes Family Papers (microform) of the Massachusetts Historical Society, Boston, Massachusetts; in the James F. Joy Papers of the Michigan Historical Collections, Ann Arbor, Michigan; in the Erastus Corning Papers of the Albany Institute of History and Art, Albany, New York; in the Burlington Railroad Archives of the Newberry Library, Chicago, Illinois; and in the Michigan Central Railroad Archives of the New York Central System, Detroit, Michigan.

John Work Garrett

(July 31, 1820-September 26, 1884)

by John Stover

Purdue University

CAREER: Partner, Robert Garrett & Sons (1839-1858); president, Baltimore & Ohio Railroad (1858-1884).

John Work Garrett, businessman and railroad president, was born July 31, 1820, in Baltimore, Maryland, the third son of Robert Garrett and Elizabeth Stouffer Garrett. His father, who immigrated with his parents to America from Ireland in 1790, moved from Pennsylvania to Baltimore in 1819 and established a commission house. His business prospered by selling flour to customers in Boston and New England fish and South American coffee to customers in the western areas of Virginia and Pennsylvania. John Garrett and his brother, Henry, enjoyed life in the lively harbor town in the 1820s. They kept busy by attending school and performing frequent chores in their father's store and warehouse. Each attended Baltimore's Boisseau Academy from the age of twelve. At age fourteen John was transferred to Lafayette College in Easton, Pennsylvania, but left after two years to work in his father's commission house.

In the fall of 1836 Garrett made his first business trip to western Virginia and western Pennsylvania for his father's produce and commission house. He arranged for the purchase of pork, flour, and butter and collected business debts owed to his father. For the next several years John continued to gain experience on these western trips while his brother spent more of his time in Baltimore helping his father with contracts and correspondence. Their father was proud of the enterprising spirit shown by his two sons and in 1839 recognized the growing role they played by changing the name of his firm to Robert Garrett & Sons. The firm continued to prosper and Henry and John began to purchase and speculate in small lots of state and railroad securities. They generally were discerning in their investments and more often than not turned a fair profit for the firm.

John Work Garrett

In the summer of 1846 Garrett married Rachel Anne Harrison, the daughter of the Baltimore merchant Thomas Harrison. The young couple settled in a house not far from the senior Garretts, and they also set up a summer home southwest of Baltimore on a farm that his parents owned. John and Rachel Garrett had four children: Robert, Thomas Harrison, Henry S., and Mary Elizabeth.

During the late 1840s the firm became involved more deeply in finance when it started to discount commercial paper and deal in British sterling bills of exchange. The Garretts also were increasing their purchases of Baltimore real estate, including two small hotels. The family prospered and, before the Civil War, probably had total holdings of nearly a million dollars. Robert Garrett had been an early investor in the Baltimore & Ohio (B&O) Railroad, and in 1846 the firm owned eleven shares of stock. This B&O investment would later greatly increase, and Henry became a B&O director in 1852. John became a member of the B&O board in 1855, helping to elect his friend Chauncy Brooks to the presidency a few weeks later.

Granted a charter in 1827, the B&O was the first railway projected westward over the Allegheny Mountains to the Ohio Valley. It was Baltimore's answer to the Erie Canal, which was expanding the western trade of New York City. A line to Frederick, Maryland, was opened in 1831 and one to Washington, D.C., in 1835. The 178-mile route to Cumberland was finished in 1842, and Wheeling, on the upper Ohio, was reached late in 1852. In the early 1850s the 30-member B&O board of directors consisted of the private stockholders group of twelve directors and the eighteen directors who represented the city of Baltimore and the state of Maryland. The private interests, including Garrett, felt that freight rates should be high enough to produce a profit that would permit dividends, while the city and state directors felt the rates should be low enough to bring prosperity to the city and state, with dividends being only of secondary importance.

With Garrett and Johns Hopkins (a major stockholder) both on the board and Brooks in the president's chair, the private interests were ready for battle. With some support from the Baltimore directors the private interests soon succeeded in increasing freight rates on coal by fifty cents a ton. The private interests gained a second victory in December 1856 when, by a margin of seventeen to twelve, they voted a 30 percent stock dividend payable after January 12, 1857, in certificates of debt paying 6 percent and convertible into stock after five years. A year later, with the retirement of Brooks, Garrett was elected B&O president at an annual salary of $4,000 by a vote of sixteen to fourteen.

On his election in 1858 Garrett was president of a railroad with 500 miles of line, representing an investment of $26 million with annual revenues of about $4 million and a roster of 4,500 employees. The traffic on the B&O consisted largely of coal, flour, grain, livestock, and manufactured goods,

with the coal traffic from the mines of western Virginia producing about a quarter of the total revenue. The city of Baltimore had grown and prospered since the laying of the first stone on the B&O in 1828. The city's population of 80,000 in 1830 had grown to 212,000 by 1860. During the 1850s the B&O and other new trunk lines had created a strong east-west axis of domestic trade between the mid-Atlantic states and the Old Northwest. By the mid 1850s there was also a growing political alliance between the western states and the Northeast which would help determine loyalties in the Civil War. Because of its location in a border state, the B&O was destined to experience far more than its share of violence and destruction in the war.

The first violent preview of the future conflict came in mid October 1859, when John Brown's raid on Harpers Ferry resulted in the stopping of a B&O express train, the wounding of a porter, and the cutting of telegraph wires. As war drew closer Garrett's railroad was in the unenviable position of being located in a slave state but with much of its traffic moving to and from free states. Garrett, who was a moderate southern Democrat, spoke in early 1861 of the B&O as a "southern" railroad and called Confederate leaders "our Southern friends." As the two sides armed themselves in the days after the surrender of Fort Sumter, both the Confederacy and the Union regarded Garrett and the B&O with suspicion. The eastern end of the line came fully under Union control in May 1861 when Gen. Benjamin F. Butler and his troops occupied Baltimore and the surrounding area. Further west in the region around Harpers Ferry, the Confederate colonel Thomas J. "Stonewall" Jackson was in control of the B&O line. By June 1861 Jackson had captured more than 50 B&O locomotives and some 300 freight cars, put the torch to many railroad bridges, and destroyed miles of track. Jackson's actions closed down the main line of the B&O for ten months. By the early summer of 1861 John Garrett was not thinking of Confederates as "misguided friends" but rather as "rebels." The B&O had become a Union railroad.

During the war Confederate destruction and occupation of the B&O line was far more common on the eastern slopes of the Alleghenies than on the western since pro-Confederate feelings were fairly rare in western Virginia. Whenever the Confederate forces were pushed well south of the B&O the work crews moved in to repair the broken road. Of course, the Confederate northern campaigns of September 1862 and June and July of 1863 again brought great destruction to the B&O. But every attack, broken bridge, or torn up rail line had taught the repair crews and construction workers new techniques for speedy repair and renewal. The repaired B&O lines were used in September and October 1863 for a massive movement of Union troops to break the siege of Chattanooga. Some 25,000 Union troops in more than thirty trains of 700 cars were moved 1,200 miles from northern Virginia via Harpers Ferry, Grafton, Wheeling, Columbus, Indianapolis, Louisville, and Nashville to Bridgeport in northeastern Alabama. Secretary of War Edwin M. Stanton gave Garrett the responsibility for the troop movement from Washington, D.C., to Jeffersonville, Indiana. Tom Scott of the Pennsylvania Railroad directed the troop movement south of the Ohio River.

The Civil War brought prosperity as well as destruction to the B&O. Total revenue on the 379-mile Main Line from Baltimore to Wheeling climbed from $3,211,000 in 1861 to $10,096,000 in 1865. During the four years of war passenger revenue climbed more than fourfold, while freight revenue nearly tripled. The 40-mile Washington branch also saw a great increase in traffic. In the late 1850s a single daily freight train of no more than ten cars satisfied the rail freight needs of the nation's capital. With the coming of war, as many as 200 freight cars arrived daily in Washington from Baltimore. Between 1861 and 1865 the passenger revenue more than doubled on the Washington branch. Passenger traffic out of Washington reached a record volume in the weeks of demobilization in the spring of 1865, with nearly 14,000 troops a day leaving Washington in early June. The B&O declared good dividends during the war, with the 6 percent rate of 1861 climbing to 7 percent in 1864 and to 8 percent in 1865. President Garrett's reference to the four years of the Civil War in the last paragraph of the 1865 annual report was one of understatement:

> The Board again acknowledges with satisfaction their appreciation of the vigor, skill, and fidelity of the officers and men ... by which the business of the Company was successfully conducted during periods of frequent danger and embarrassment.

In the late fall of 1865 Garrett was reelected for the seventh time to the presidency of the B&O. In the 1865 election John Chapman, a longtime political foe of Garrett, was also nominated but received only one vote. In subsequent years Garrett was easily returned to office, generally by a unanimous vote. Garrett had come to the presidency in 1858 as a still fairly young man of thirty-eight. He knew the Baltimore commission business, was well versed in the banking and financial affairs of the city, but was still much of a neophyte in the management of an expanding railroad. The four difficult years of the Civil War had done much to improve the polish of the railroad president. In the postwar 1860s and early 1870s the portly and urbane Garrett was confident of the future of his railway and also certain of his political skill with both his B&O subordinates and the political leaders of his city and state. Physically a large man, he gave the impression of both determination and vigor that was steady and methodical. At times he could be autocratic, but those close to him knew him as a kindly and often affectionate man.

In the postwar decades Garrett expanded his railroad while simultaneously facing economic depression, rate wars, and labor violence. Between 1865 and his death in 1884 the B&O expanded from 520 miles to about 1,700 miles, with new mileage in Pennsylvania, Delaware, Virginia, Ohio, Indiana, and Illinois. Some of the earliest expansion after the war took place in Maryland, Pennsylvania, and Virginia. At the end of the Civil War Garrett began to fear that if he did not build a line northwest out of Washington toward Harpers Ferry, some other road would come forward to undertake the project. In 1866 he began to survey a route out of Washington well northeast of the Potomac toward his own main line. The survey was slow, and construction was not pushed until after 1870. The 43-mile metropolitan branch from Washington to the B&O Main Line east of Point of Rocks was completed in 1873 at a cost of more than $3 million. Soon most passenger service west of Baltimore used the new line via Washington instead of the older original line. Also during the early postwar years, Garrett succeeded in completing a line northwest from Cumberland via Connellsville to Pittsburgh. This 150-mile line, known as the Pittsburgh, Washington & Baltimore, was opened for through traffic in May 1871. In the same years the B&O was slowly extending its service south from Harpers

Ferry into the lower Shenandoah Valley. The 32-mile line from Harpers Ferry to Winchester was leased in 1867 and extended to Strasburg in 1870, Staunton in 1874, and Lexington in 1883.

Garrett realized that any major expansion of rail traffic west of the Ohio River depended upon replacing the car ferries at Wheeling and Parkersburg with bridges across the Ohio. Plans for building both bridges were drawn early in the postwar years. The Parkersburg Bridge was opened in January 1871 and the Wheeling Bridge in June 1871. Each of the bridges, including approaches, was about a mile and a half in length, and the two wrought-iron truss bridges cost a combined total of more than $2 million. West of the new bridges the B&O connected with two Ohio lines, the Central Ohio at Bellaire and the Marietta & Cincinnati at Belpre. The B&O would not obtain complete control over the Marietta & Cincinnati until the turn of the century. However, in November 1866 the B&O obtained a twenty-year lease to the Central of Ohio and its 137-mile route west to Columbus. Three years later the Central of Ohio leased the 116-mile Sandusky, Mansfield & Newark, which ran from Newark on the Central Ohio north to Sandusky on Lake Erie. By 1871 Garrett was eagerly planning the construction of a new line from a point on the Sandusky road west to Chicago. The 263-mile road to Chicago, known as the Chicago Division, was completed by November 1874, at a cost of $7.8 million. By 1874 Garrett's B&O Railroad was a railroad of 1,166 miles, more than twice the length of the line in 1865.

The rail system of the whole nation had expanded during the same years as the B&O had grown. Between 1865 and 1873 the iron and steel network had doubled, growing from 35,000 to 70,000 miles of line. Shippers, farmers, manufacturers, and merchants all seemed eager for more railroad mileage. However, when Jay Cooke, the Philadelphia banker, sought to build the Northern Pacific across the prairies of Minnesota and North Dakota, he strained his resources so greatly that his bank failed in September 1873. Other banks soon shut their doors, and the New York State Stock Exchange was closed for ten days. Soon bankruptcies became commonplace, factories shut down, and many railroads were forced into receivership. In the spring of 1873 the fifty-two-year-old Garrett had become ill and his doctors suggested an extended tour of Europe for the restoration of his health. Thus

Garrett was in Europe when the panic started. Vice-president John King urged Garrett to return home, but Garrett felt the B&O was not threatened and replied to King:

> Reduce purchases to judicious minimum, using materials closely. Cease buying engines. Reduce constructing cars to company's economical capacity. . . . Maintain revenues granting safe indulgences. . . . Panic must be brief country being sound. . . .

The B&O did weather the panic but suffered substantial losses of traffic and revenue. Total revenue on the B&O had climbed from $8.6 million in 1866 to $15.7 million in 1873 but then declined to a low of $13.2 million in 1877. The operating ratio climbed from 61 percent in 1872 to 69 percent in 1875.

In the decades of the 1870s and after, Garrett was faced with a series of rate wars with his rival trunk lines to the north: the Pennsylvania, the New York Central, and the Erie. These rate wars were so frequent that the *Commercial and Financial Chronicle* claimed they happened as often as "small pox or the change of seasons." The four longest were: January 1874 to December 1875; April 1876 to April 1877; June 1881 to January 1882; and March 1884 to December 1885. The first of these started as Garrett was completing his line to Chicago. The appearance of another line to the east from Chicago pleased farmers and grangers, especially after they heard Garrett claim that his line to Chicago would, like the biblical Samson, pull down the temple of high freight rates upon the heads of rival carriers. The rival trunk lines quarreled as they tried to set fair freight rates between Chicago and the Atlantic Coast. The New York Central claimed its lower grades and easier curves offset the fact that the B&O route to Baltimore was shorter. In 1876 Garrett told his board that the New York Central was overlooking the crucial factor: "The fact that on the Baltimore and Ohio line for three hundred miles coal literally crops out . . . more than compensates for the difference in grades and curves." After each rate war the new stabilized rates were generally a bit lower than the "normal" rates that had existed before the rate conflict. Average freight rates across the nation had declined from just over two cents a ton-mile at the end of the Civil War to about one cent a ton-mile in the mid 1880s.

The last major problem facing Garrett during the postwar years was the labor violence caused by the railroad strike of 1877, which started with a labor dispute on Garrett's own road in mid July 1877. Despite the depression of the mid 1870s and the resulting decline in traffic, Garrett continued in the 1870s to pay annual dividends of $8 to $10 on each share of B&O common stock. In 1877 Junius Morgan urged Garrett to reduce his dividend rate, but the B&O president had a different plan in mind—a cut in wages. Early in July the B&O board of directors decided on a 10 percent wage reduction for all employees earning more than a dollar a day to be effective on July 16. Many B&O workers had recently read the optimistic company reports that were given the stockholders as another 10 percent dividend was declared. The workers knew that Garrett would bring in strikebreakers to defeat any strike. They resolved to seize the trains and yards and scare off scabs with violence, if necessary. On July 16 the B&O workers deserted their trains in the Baltimore yards and also stopped trains and blockaded the yards at Martinsburg on the Main Line 100 miles west of Baltimore. Violence in Baltimore between workers and the Maryland National Guard resulted in ten dead and several dozen injured. Eventually, the arrival of federal troops brought peace to Baltimore and opened the rail lines to the west, but not before the strike had spread to Buffalo, Chicago, St. Louis, Omaha, and, with the greatest violence and property loss, Pittsburgh. By early August the strike had been broken, but an editorial in the *Nation* described the 1877 labor violence as the most extensive in the history of the nation.

Later in 1877 Garrett approved some concessions in the work rules for train crews, and in 1880 he established the B&O Railroad Employees' Relief Association for the purpose of "protecting and promoting the interests of the employees of the Baltimore and Ohio Company and of their families in cases of accident, sickness and death." About the same time, major improvements were added to the Locust Point Terminal in Baltimore, such as the building of a tobacco warehouse and additional grain elevators. In 1881 a new seven-story fireproof Central Headquarters Building was completed in downtown Baltimore. Earlier in the 1870s the B&O had built and operated resort hotels along the line at Cumberland and Oakland in Maryland, and in Newark and Chicago Junction in Ohio. By the early 1880s the B&O was also building and operating its own sleeping cars and had organized its own independent telegraph organization.

Garrett was planning an extension of the B&O to Philadelphia in the early 1880s, but the new line to Philadelphia would not be fully in operation until 1886, two years after Garrett's death. Traffic on the B&O continued to grow in the late 1870s and early 1880s, climbing from $13.2 million in 1877 to $18.3 million in 1880 and $19.4 million in 1884. Between 1877 and 1884 the operating ratio was never above 62 percent. Between 1859 and 1884 Garrett's railroad paid cash dividends to the shareholders every year, ranging in amount from $6 to $10 and averaging over $8 a year. By 1884 the B&O was a trunk line of more than 1,700 miles, but a smaller and weaker system than either the New York Central or the Pennsylvania. Garrett had expanded his railroad more with borrowed money than new share capital. During his 26-year presidency, the share capital increased by less than half, while the bonded debt more than tripled. This trend toward larger and larger debt would clearly contribute to the financial crisis and receivership of the 1890s.

Garrett prospered during his long tenure as president of the B&O. He had refused to take more than $4,000 a year as president but, of course, had received far more than that as a major stockholder. In mid 1867 the Garrett family owned 14,500 shares of B&O stock. While Garrett's attitude toward labor, as shown in the 1877 strike, was generally tough and unbending, he was frequently a generous man with gifts to his church, Lafayette College, the YMCA, and other worthy projects. Throughout the postwar years Garrett and his family found time to travel. They made several trips to Europe, including the extended trip of 1873 and 1874, and shorter trips in 1878 and 1881. Garrett's long years with the B&O—extending well past that of his early rivals, Commodore Vanderbilt and J. Edgar Thomson—had made his name a household word in much of the nation by the 1870s. Garrett had a new county in western Maryland named for him in 1872, and in West Virginia a company of militia volunteers was named "The Garrett Rifles." Along the line of the B&O several local newspapers suggested Garrett should be the Democratic nominee for president in 1872 and 1876 and later suggested that he represent Maryland in the U.S. Senate.

In November 1883 Mrs. Garrett was fatally injured. The sixty-three-year-old Garrett never really recovered from his wife's death and soon lost all interest in life. Within a few months his eldest son, Robert, became acting president of the railroad. John Garrett died at his cottage at Deer Park, Maryland, on September 26, 1884. The B&O board of directors praised Garrett for his persistent energy in giving Baltimore the unequaled advantages of its geographical position. The *Railroad Gazette* endorsed this viewpoint when it claimed: "No man in Baltimore has been so closely or so extensively identified with the progress of the city." Certainly John

W. Garrett had succeeded in giving Baltimore a major trunkline railroad to the west.

References:

Edward Hungerford, *The Story of the Baltimore & Ohio Railroad: 1827-1927* (New York: Putnam's, 1928);

John F. Stover, *History of the Baltimore & Ohio Railroad* (West Lafayette, Ind.: Purdue University Press, 1987).

Archives:

The Robert Garrett family papers are located in the Manuscripts Division of the Library of Congress in Washington, D.C. Additional materials are located in the Baltimore & Ohio Museum in Baltimore, Maryland.

Jay Gould

(May 27, 1836-December 2, 1892)

by Maury Klein

University of Rhode Island

CAREER: Director, Erie Railroad (1867-1872), president (1868-1872); director, Union Pacific Railroad (1874-1884, 1890-1892); director, Kansas Pacific Railroad (1875-1880); director, Chicago & Northwestern Railroad (1878-1884); director, Chicago, Rock Island & Pacific Railroad (1878-1884); director, Wabash Railroad (1879-1884), president, (1881-1884); director, Hannibal & St. Joseph Railroad (1879-1881); president and director, Missouri Pacific Railroad (1880-1892); director, St. Louis, Iron Mountain & Southern Railroad (1881-1892); president (1882-1892); president and director, Missouri, Kansas & Texas Railroad (1880-1888); director, Texas & Pacific Railroad (1880-1892), president (1880-1887, 1890-1892); director, International & Great Northern Railroad (1881-1892), president (1882-1892); director, Delaware, Lackawanna & Western Railroad (1881-1889); director, Central Railroad of New Jersey (1880-1882); director, New York & New England Railroad (1881-1884); director, New York, Lackawanna & Western Railroad (1881-1883); director, Louisville & Nashville Railroad (1883-1884); director, Richmond & West Point Terminal Railway and Warehouse Company (1890-1892); director, Atlantic & Pacific Telegraph (1875-1877); director, American Union Telegraph (1879-1881); director, Western

Union Telegraph (1881-1892); president and director, Manhattan Elevated (1881-1892); president, New York Elevated (1881-1890); president, Metropolitan Elevated (1885-1892).

Jason Gould was born on May 27, 1836, on a farm in Roxbury, Delaware County, New York. He was the fifth and final child of John Burr and Mary More Gould. As the only son he was pampered by his older sisters, but his childhood was rendered insecure by the deaths of his mother, two stepmothers, and a sister before he was ten. His last stepmother, Mary Ann Corbin, produced a stepbrother to Jay named Abram. Adversity forced on Jay (as he was called in childhood) and his sisters large responsibilities at an early age.

A small, frail, sickly child, Jay seemed unlikely to survive life on a harsh upcountry farm, much less take his father's place someday. But he showed early in life the characteristics that would make him so formidable in business: a quick mind, love of learning, perseverance, an indomitable will, remarkable self-control, and a shrewd disposition for the practical. Quiet and unfailingly polite, he matured far more quickly than most boys and learned to push himself constantly against whatever limits life and his own stamina imposed.

*Jay Gould (courtesy of New-York
Historical Society)*

Jay took eagerly to education in a local school
and a nearby private academy. His father grudgingly accepted that the boy would never be a
farmer and traded the family farm for a tin store in
Roxbury, where the family moved in 1852. Jay
helped tend the store and at night taught himself
mathematics and surveying with the help of borrowed instruments. At age sixteen he was running
his own survey operation with several hired hands
while still hoping to attend college. A series of near
fatal illnesses slowed him for nearly two years. He
taught surveying briefly and wrote a history of Delaware County remarkable in its scope and grace for
one so young.

In 1856 Jay formed a partnership with
Zadock Pratt, one of the best known tanners of his
age, and went to build a tannery in the virgin forests of eastern Pennsylvania. At age twenty he supervised construction of all the facilities and a small
village named Gouldsboro in his honor. The enterprise was dogged by bad luck and misunderstand-
ings that led Pratt in 1859 to sell his interest in the

tannery to Gould and two new partners, Charles
M. Leupp and his brother-in-law, David W. Lee.

Leupp's firm was one of the most prominent
in the "Swamp," New York City's tanning district.
Unfortunately, disagreements arose between the
new partners and were compounded by Leupp's mental illness, which grew so severe that in October
1859 he shot himself. His death threw the tannery's
affairs into dispute between Gould and Lee, who
tried clumsily to seize the place by force and was
routed. The matter lingered in court for several
years and cost Gould most of the capital he had accumulated. Even worse, the popularity of Leupp led
to hard feelings against Gould in the Swamp and deprived him of a future in tanning. In later years critics twisted the episode into a grotesque myth that
Gould had driven Leupp to kill himself.

Prior to Leupp's suicide Gould had formed
other partnerships in tanning and opened an office
in New York. Although he left tanning, he remained in New York and turned instead to one of
the nation's most dynamic growth industries, Wall
Street. These years of apprenticeship remain the
most obscure period of Gould's life, but there is no
doubt he again displayed a phenomenal capacity
for growth. Lacking both money and connections,
the surest avenues to success on Wall Street, he survived the turbulent Civil War years as an outsider,
mastering the intricacies of finance with a swiftness
and thoroughness that would later astonish business rivals who made the mistake of underestimat-
ing his ability.

During these years Gould also met Helen Day
Miller, the daughter of a prominent merchant who
had retired and taken an office on Wall Street.
Reared in the strict, staid conservatism of Murray
Hill, Helen became the one and only love of
Gould's life. They were married on January 22,
1863, and had six children: George Jay (1864),
Edwin (1866), Helen (1870), Howard (1871), Anna
(1875), and Frank (1877). For the rest of his life
Gould devoted most of his considerable energy to
business and family. No figure of raging controversy such as Gould became ever lived a quieter or
more proper domestic life.

In 1867 Gould first thrust himself into the public eye by gaining a seat on the board of the Erie Railroad, an enterprise so tainted that it was known as
"The Scarlet Woman of Wall Street." The notorious
financial scavenger Daniel Drew had been feasting
on the Erie for years. Aware that his old rival, Cornel-

ius Vanderbilt, wanted control of the Erie, Drew joined forces with Gould and another director, James Fisk, Jr., in resisting Vanderbilt's efforts. There followed the infamous Erie War, a circus of outrageous events that became a cornerstone of Wall Street lore and stigmatized Gould with a reputation he was never to escape.

The fight brought Gould and Fisk together for the first time. While Drew garnered most of the headlines, they did most of the hard and dirty work. Ultimately Drew sold out to Vanderbilt, leaving Gould and Fisk with little to show for the struggle except precarious control of the looted Erie Railroad. The two young financiers proved a brilliant team and, to the astonishment of the business world, secured their hold on Erie through a series of controversial moves including an alliance with Boss Tweed, the political chief of Tammany Hall, who furnished the Erie with two state supreme court judges among other services.

They were the oddest couple ever to hit Wall Street, the perfect match of Apollonian and Dionysian energies, and for five years their antics sent shudders of indignation through the financial establishment. While Fisk delighted the press with his Falstaffian antics, the meek, quiet Gould startled rivals with his bold attempt to transform the Erie into a major rail system.

In 1869 Gould tried to forge a consolidated route from the Erie to Chicago by snatching control of lines on which the mighty Pennsylvania and New York Central depended for their connections. His attempt failed for want of sufficient resources, but the episode forced the two strongest railroads in the nation to reverse past policies and embark on expansionist programs to assure their hold on western routes. Even at this early stage in his career Gould revealed an ability to conceive plans far in advance of the conventional wisdom and to move with startling imaginativeness to realize them—only to fail when, as was often the case, his resources were not equal to his vision.

Nothing better illustrates this tendency than the fact that during 1869 he found himself enmeshed in a scheme even greater than the attempt to transform the Erie into a major rail system. A succession of events linked to his rail campaign led Gould into a brazen effort to corner the nation's gold supply. This spectacular episode touched off an unprecedented feeding frenzy on the gold exchange that climaxed in the infamous Black Friday,

September 24, which paralyzed New York's financial institutions for several days. Gould emerged from the debris with serious losses on several fronts, including a fatal blow to his budding rail system.

In the long run Black Friday inflicted its worst damage on Gould's reputation. Together with the Erie War, the gold corner fixed the image of Gould as financial predator for generations to come. Charles Francis Adams, Jr., and his brother Henry created unforgettable portraits of Gould and Fisk in their scathing *Chapters of Erie*. From this influential work emerged the legend of Jay Gould, the ultimate robber baron. Never in his lifetime would Gould shake free of the reputation given him by the Adams brothers. Like the Erie he became the Scarlet Woman of Wall Street, doomed forever to be haunted by a past that in print contained as much fiction as fact.

During the next two years Gould's hold on the Erie weakened as criticism mounted, his opponents gained strength, and Fisk became less an asset than a liability because of his personal excesses. In January 1872 the lover taken by Fisk's mistress shot the clown prince of finance dead, depriving Gould of his closest friend and most trusted ally. A few months earlier Boss Tweed had been routed by reformers, stripping Gould of his power base in New York. Taking advantage of these setbacks, Gould's foes within the Erie conspired to oust him from the road. Their efforts met with success after a comic opera chase through the company's offices that added yet another colorful chapter to the Gould myth.

In March 1872 Gould found himself once again a trader on Wall Street. The brokerage firm of Smith, Gould & Martin had dissolved in August 1870, and Gould never attached his name to another house, preferring instead to operate as a special partner in other firms. This fueled the image of him as a lone wolf who held no corporate office, belonged to no house, and did not even have a seat on the New York Stock Exchange. For the next two years he enhanced his already formidable reputation as a trader. Some of his deals became the stuff of legend on Wall Street, notably his corner of Chicago & Northwestern stock and his capture of Pacific Mail Steamship Company. The latter fight brought him together with the man who became his lifelong associate and close friend, Russell Sage.

Despite his genius at trading, Gould was never content to operate merely as a speculator. His instinct was always to take hold of a property, usually one in deplorable shape because it was all he could afford, and transform it into a viable enterprise through efficient and imaginative management. Although few people realized it, he had tried to do this with Erie only to be thwarted by a combination of circumstances. His control of Pacific Mail gave him entry into a coming arena of business struggle, transcontinental traffic. In March 1874 he solidified his place in that tempestuous arena by gaining control of the first transcontinental railroad, the Union Pacific.

Like the Erie, the Union Pacific prior to Gould's appearance was a moribund property tainted by scandal, riddled with inefficiency, and cursed with a weak, inept management and a stormy relationship with the federal government that had worsened since the infamous Crédit Mobilier scandal of 1872-1873. It had gone through three presidents in four years and in 1873 hovered again at the brink of bankruptcy. The man and the company were well matched: he was a financier looking to rise above his reputation as a trader through some genuine achievement in business; the Union Pacific was a promising enterprise desperate for someone to redeem it from past sins.

Gould turned the demoralized company around, straightened out its tangled finances, and two years later paid its first dividend despite the depression. Even critics of the dividend agreed that Union Pacific finances had undergone a striking transformation. Besides putting its financial house in order, Gould brought harmony to the strife-torn management, waged its competitive wars, captained its political battles, revamped its internal structures, constructed branches, formulated rate policies, and developed resources along its lines. He accomplished these things by immersing himself in every aspect of the road's affairs until his knowledge of them was encyclopedic in breadth and detail.

His style of management bordered on the unique. Gould held no office except member of the executive committee, with the venerable Sidney Dillon as president and Silas H. H. Clark as general superintendent. Dillon made no decisions without consulting Gould; in the field Clark received orders officially from Dillon and privately from Gould. This triangular arrangement might have been a disaster, yet Gould made it work through a mixture of tact, patience, and close friendship with Dillon and Clark.

In an age of outsized egos, Gould was content to dwell in the shadows and let others take credit. For a man so consumed with ambition, he was strikingly free of vanity; he liked to tell reporters that he was a mere passenger in his corporate vehicles. His intellect was cool and precise, almost mathematical, and his manner diffident and soft spoken, geared always to the task at hand. He never dictated but suggested politely, and in meetings let others drone on before expressing succinctly the point for which they groped. Setbacks only spurred him to look ahead to the next obstacle; he never blamed others for failures or made excuses for himself.

Older Union Pacific investors like Oliver Ames, who feared Gould had come in simply to make a killing in the stock, soon learned to trust and admire his ability. For six years Gould grappled with the problems facing the road. He made great strides in developing the resources along the line, especially coal and land. His eager eye looked constantly for fresh sources of business that might give the road a long haul. The origins of the Union Pacific as a powerful and diversified company owe much to Gould's vigorous work during these early years.

At the same time Gould tried to settle the host of long-standing differences between the company and the federal government. The road was unique in possessing a federal charter, which made it a creature of Congress and therefore subject to shifts in the political winds. Bitter disputes over the government loan to build the road, the land grant, payments for mail and other government services, and other issues had raged for years. The Crédit Mobilier scandal had destroyed the Union Pacific's credibility in the public eye and left the road even more at the mercy of speculators, lobbyists, venal congressmen, and other predators who tried to wring some advantage from its political vulnerability.

Gould toiled long and hard to resolve these controversies and remove the company from the political arena. He did not want to share control of the road with Washington, but his efforts to settle the government debt and other issues ultimately failed for reasons beyond his control. The passage of the punitive Thurman Act in 1878 helped convince him

Jay Gould's home, Lyndhurst (courtesy of Lyndhurst Archive)

that his future lay elsewhere than with the Union Pacific.

During these same years Gould also emerged as the dominant player on the chessboard of railroad strategy west of the Missouri River. In 1874 the Union Pacific and Central Pacific remained the only overland route, but new competitors had begun to appear. To the west Gould made his peace with a wary Collis P. Huntington of the Central Pacific and subdued attempts by Pacific Mail to cut transcontinental rates. At the Omaha gateway the Iowa roads combined in a pool to maintain their share of the through rate, prompting Gould to search for ways to smash their united front or seek new routes to Chicago. By 1878 he had managed only a tenuous truce with his most implacable enemy, the Burlington.

Gould also recognized the need for the Union Pacific to secure its territory by building branch lines. Through his vigorous prodding the company developed a north-south feeder system in Utah, a series of roads in Colorado, and a major branch line in the Republican Valley of Nebraska. These branches were crucial to his plan of developing local business all along the road, especially in the

mineral-rich mountain region where ores promised a long haul. He looked eagerly toward Idaho and Montana as well and negotiated tirelessly to bolster the Union Pacific's place in the treacherous rail scene of Colorado.

The Colorado intrigues led Gould in 1875 to absorb the rival Kansas Pacific, which owned the best line from Denver to Cheyenne. However, the road went bankrupt before the merger could take place, forcing Gould to thread his way through a complex reorganization fight that lasted five years. During that time Gould's own position underwent a profound change. He had failed to resolve the conflicts with the government or break the Iowa pool. New competitors threatened Union Pacific territory, and a speculative miscalculation in 1878 jeopardized his own solvency at a time when his chief asset was a large and unwieldy block of Union Pacific stock.

In this dangerous position Gould essayed a bold gambit that was to transform his role in the business world. He sold off a major part of his Union Pacific holdings and used the proceeds to cover his losses and buy into new operations. Although he remained active in Union Pacific, which his friends still dominated, the gambit allowed him to strike out in new directions, to build a system of his own without shared control.

During the years 1879-1881 Gould unleashed a series of lightning moves that forged a business empire of staggering proportions at a speed that simply dazzled observers. The impact was all the more devastating for being so unexpected; the little man who had but recently elevated himself from speculator to businessman, and who even more recently seemed at the brink of failure, soared to even more dizzying heights before his earlier accomplishments had been digested.

In rapid succession Gould gained control of the Kansas Pacific reorganization, bought the Wabash Railroad and a road between Kansas City and St. Louis, acquired a half interest in the Denver & Rio Grande, and picked up the Missouri Pacific along with several minor roads in Kansas. These holdings created a line capable of competing with the Union Pacific. To avert this possibility Gould's friends in that road agreed to purchase the Kansas Pacific and merge it with the Union Pacific. Although harshly criticized, the consolidation was a logical step for the Union Pacific, which has retained the Kansas road ever since.

The move made even more sense for Gould. Besides giving him handsome profits, the consolidation allowed him to move nimbly into another arena of rail development where he did not compete with his longtime associates. Conventional wisdom dictated that only a trunk line should serve as parent to a major system, but convention was for Gould always a point of departure. Instead he transformed the Missouri Pacific, a simple line from St. Louis to Kansas City, into the nucleus of a giant system in the Southwest, adding to it in rapid order control of the St. Louis, Iron Mountain & Southern, the Texas & Pacific (which Gould had to complete from New Orleans to El Paso), the Missouri, Kansas & Texas, and the International & Great Northern.

Once in possession of these roads, Gould launched ambitious expansion programs on each one. At the same time he extended his campaign into other regions. In the East Gould bought into the Lackawanna and helped extend it to Buffalo, gained control of the New York & New England, joined the board of the Central of New Jersey, and loaned money to the Philadelphia & Reading. He pushed the Wabash into Detroit and Chicago,

forged an epochal peace treaty with Huntington in Texas, and eyed extensions into Mexico. To baffled analysts he seemed intent on nothing less than a transcontinental system of gigantic proportions. By the winter of 1880 he dominated 8,160 miles of road, more than any other individual in the world.

Impressive as this rail empire was, Gould did not confine his energies to it alone. During these same years he also fashioned brilliant coups in the telegraph and mass transit fields, giving him a dominant position in the two most vital areas of the industrial economy: transportation and communications. Here as with the railroads he entered the field in the guise of a speculator and proceeded to gain control of major companies that he retained as profitable enterprises under his management.

Even before acquiring control of the Union Pacific Gould learned that it owned a sizable block of stock in the small telegraph company that served the Pacific roads, Atlantic & Pacific (A&P). The railroad's managers thought so little of this asset that they had granted a banker an option to take half of it at 12. Gould got the option waived, gained control of A&P, provided it with vigorous management and new technology, and launched a rate war with the industry's giant, Western Union. Through complex and ingenious tactics he forced Western Union to absorb A&P at a hefty profit for Gould and his associates, several of whom were the Boston investors in Union Pacific.

Analysts dismissed the episode as a hit-and-run affair, but in March 1879 Gould formed a new telegraph company, American Union, which built lines and took some railroad business away from Western Union. While the new telegraph war raged, Gould commenced work on two overseas cables. In a brilliant market coup he hammered down the price of Western Union and then bought heavily until he was its largest stockholder. Since he had used this tactic before, Wall Street assumed that Gould was angling to unload his latest company on Western Union.

Wall Street was wrong, as it was so often about Gould. The little man did force a merger in January 1881, but when the smoke cleared he proved to be astride the largest communications company in the world. Although several smaller firms fought him bitterly for a few years, none challenged the domination of Western Union. To Wall Street's surprise Gould stayed with the company for the rest of his life, giving it sound, efficient management that reaped large dividends for himself and investors.

A similar pattern unfolded with the elevated railroads in New York City, which possessed a brief and stormy history like so many of the ventures he undertook. In 1879 the two major lines, Metropolitan Elevated and New York Elevated, stopped fighting each other and leased their lines to Manhattan Elevated, a holding company which held the lease as its only asset. During the next two years, however, the bickering between different interests in the companies grew worse and were compounded by financial problems and clashes with the city over several issues.

By 1881 default loomed unless someone could intervene to straighten out the elevateds' tangled affairs. Russell Sage decided to try, and it was evidently his plea that drew Gould into the fray. There followed one of the most bizarre episodes in Gould's long and controversial career, one that ultimately raised charges that he had used a major newspaper, the state attorney general, and a state supreme court judge to realize his goals. The Manhattan Elevated caper became another cornerstone of the Gould legend even though the charges were never substantiated. Although the behavior of both officials was curious in the extreme, the charges that Gould had corrupted them do not bear close scrutiny.

Through another of his patented market maneuvers, Gould emerged in October 1881 with control of Manhattan Elevated and through it the leased companies. After fending off several suits he reorganized the management, improved operations, and transformed the floundering elevateds into a sound and profitable enterprise. They became, like the telegraph, one of the pillars of his fortune. Although their very nature made them controversial in New York, the elevateds provided good service through an era of explosive population growth.

By 1882 Gould had put together a business empire centered around three major properties: the Missouri Pacific system, Western Union, and Manhattan Elevated. He devoted himself to their management and development for the next decade and succeeded in leaving each one considerably stronger than he had found it. Unlike many businessmen who amassed great wealth, Gould never considered retirement or diverted his fortune into safe investments in order to live off the proceeds. Like so many great entrepreneurs, he was a driven man for

Cartoon reflecting the seeming defeat of Gould's interests in the presidential election of 1884

whom business was a creative act that obsessed him as art did the painter or music the composer.

Genius has at bottom but two qualities: a gift or talent for something and the drive or obsession to fulfill it. By this measure Gould was a genius. Although his fortune was estimated at $75 million or more, he could have made two or three times that amount had he been content merely to pile up money. The urge in him was to develop virgin country, to lay rail and piece together systems where little business yet existed and where settlement was still sparse. Nothing energized him more than a challenge or a knotty problem to solve, and no problem intrigued him more than bringing farms or industry to untapped regions. Gen. Grenville M. Dodge, no slouch himself at this work, understood this element of Gould better than most:

There is no man ... who risked so much credit and so many millions, and got so little return as Jay Gould, in trying to develop the country from the Mississippi River to the Pacific Coast. ... [H]e will stand in history as having risked and planted his millions in developing a new country, while others merely risked and planted their millions in a country already developed ... where there was no risk as to returns.

Gould influenced railroad development as a builder and organizer of systems and as a promoter of local resources and industry along the lines he controlled. No one did more to reshape the railroad map of America in the late nineteenth century, both in the amount of track his companies laid and in the mileage constructed by other companies responding to his lightning moves. As the driving force behind first the Union Pacific and then the Missouri Pacific, Gould became the catalyst for the expansion wars of the 1880s. Just as earlier he had forced the Pennsylvania and New York Central to abandon their conservative policies in favor of expansion, so did he compel the Burlington and ultimately all the Iowa roads to follow the same course.

Gould's policy of development thrived on an expanding economy and a bullish market that buoyed the price of stocks in his roads, many of which were marginal investments. These conditions prevailed until the summer of 1881, when the assassination of President Garfield signaled a downturn that continued for three years. Gould found himself thrown on the defensive, forced to defend the massive empire he had erected with such swiftness. Like many great generals, he conquered more than he had the resources to protect, and the ensuing struggles took a heavy toll on both his financial and his physical resources.

This long struggle climaxed in May 1884, when a brief but severe panic rocked Wall Street. For the next several months Gould bent grimly to the task of salvaging his imperiled fortune and shoring up his battered empire. Although he succeeded, the ordeal nearly broke his health. After 1884 his stamina was never the same, and he acknowledged his growing limitations by leaving Wall Street once he was safely out of danger. Although critics never believed that he had quit the market, Gould apparently kept his vow except when necessity forced him back in 1890.

For the remainder of his life Gould devoted himself to his business interests. Despite massive evidence to the contrary, few observers were convinced that he had left the market, and fewer still were willing to accept him in his new role. During these years Gould tried with only marginal success to escape the reputation born of his early years on Wall Street. The gap between the reality of his business career and the legend of his activities widened steadily until it became a fixed part of the national folklore.

Aware that settlers were pouring into the plains states, Gould patched up his damaged rail empire and embarked on a program of expansion and reorganization. Between 1885 and 1887 the Missouri Pacific-Iron Mountain system increased from 1,960 to 4,150 miles, most of it new construction. Other transcontinental roads followed suit, triggering the most prolific decade of rail expansion in American history. Gould was the man most responsible for the outburst, as even conservative roads felt obliged to add mileage lest they be outstripped by rivals.

At the same time Gould threaded his way patiently through the maze of three complex reorganization fights lasting most of the decade. Although the Missouri, Kansas & Texas slipped from his grasp, he retained control of the Texas & Pacific and Wabash. In 1888 he acquired the St. Louis, Arkansas & Texas or "Cotton Belt" road which paralleled the Iron Mountain for a considerable distance. It too underwent reorganization but remained in Gould's hands. Together these lines constituted what became popularly known as the "Gould roads."

During the years 1880-1890 Gould also devoted considerable time and energy to integrating the rail empire he had fashioned and developing business along its lines, essentially repeating what he had done with the Union Pacific but on a grander scale. Although his resources were never equal to his ambitions even at this late date, he managed to turn the Missouri Pacific into a sound, reasonably efficient system. The reputation of Gould's roads for poor service and undermaintenance was undeserved, belonging rather to the later era when his son George was in charge than to this earlier period. Gould worked tirelessly to improve service, upgrade facilities, and bring more efficient management to his system.

But he was a man torn in too many directions. Apart from his rail enterprises, there were important developments in Manhattan Elevated and Western Union to look after, the residue of fights that had dragged on since he first seized command of those companies. Even worse, the little man's health, always fragile, had begun to fail, undermining the seemingly bottomless reservoir of energy on which he had always drawn. Bouts of facial neuralgia tormented him with excruciating pain, and exhaustion forced him to take more frequent vacations to restore his strength.

Sometime in 1888 Gould learned he had tuberculosis, the scourge that had killed his father and several other relatives. He swore the doctor to secrecy and continued at his work for four years without anyone, including his own family, knowing of his affliction. The ordeal of hiding his condition gradually took its toll on his nerves, yet he did not complain or ask for sympathy but simply toiled until he had to rest and then rested only until he could toil again. It was a profile in courage few Americans have matched.

To make matters worse Gould became during the late 1880s the target of constant, biting criticism from the press, especially the New York dailies that feared his power over the telegraph and cable lines. Wild charges that he held a stranglehold on the Associated Press, and that half a dozen major newspapers were under his thumb, flew about repeatedly, intermixed with vicious personal attacks on the "Wizard of Wall Street" or "Mephistofeles" or several other epithets that were routinely hurled at him. He became known as the most hated man in America, the victim in part of his past reputation and in part of the changing nature of New York journalism, which was caught up in circulation wars as savage as the rate wars plaguing railroads.

Those rate wars concerned Gould deeply in his twilight years because their growing intensity threatened to drag all the systems into ruin. To a large extent the relentless rate-slashing was the result of the expansion wars for which Gould had served less as creator than as catalyst. As once isolated roads evolved into sprawling systems, they found themselves clashing on several fronts and unable to keep disputes in one region from spilling over into other arenas. The attempt to forge self-contained systems had not bred security, instead it had merely enlarged the scale of battle.

Gould pondered this irony at great length. The rate wars were a boon for shippers but disaster for the carriers. Their effect on income accounts made it difficult for them to carry the added costs of expansion, let alone provide adequate funds for maintenance, equipment, and betterments. Dividends were curtailed, the value of rail securities shrank steadily, and new capital grew ever harder to secure. A host of weaker roads slid into bankruptcy before the depression of 1893, exposing their inability to compete without scaling down their bloated capital structures.

By 1888 the competitive arena was in shambles. The Interstate Commerce Act had prohibited pools without providing any substitute mechanism for maintaining order. Railroad managers, deprived of their most familiar vehicle for adjusting differences, watched helplessly as pools and associations collapsed. The Transcontinental Pool, which in five years had grown from two to thirteen members, was but one casualty of this new and most ferocious round of rate wars. Thoughtful rail executives recognized the need for some power greater than themselves to staunch the bloodletting, but few were willing to surrender any part of their own domain to an outsider.

To the surprise of many people, the figure who emerged as a leader in the search for stability was none other than Gould, the man who had for years been castigated as a wrecker of values. He was the driving force behind the well-publicized meetings of railroad presidents at the home of J. P. Morgan in 1888 and again in 1890. On both occasions he advocated far more sweeping proposals than most of the other presidents were willing to consider, including a central association with the power to set through rates, manage all competitive business, operate joint agencies for procuring traffic, and determine routing over member roads. Another pet idea of Gould would have prohibited any road from building into the territory of another road without the latter's permission.

To put more teeth in his arguments Gould stunned Wall Street one last time in the fall of 1890 with a lightning stroke reminiscent of his old campaigns. Before anyone divined what had happened, he recaptured the Union Pacific, snatched Pacific Mail back from a group that had taken it from him, bought a large block of Santa Fe stock, and acquired enough shares in the Richmond Terminal to give him four seats on its board. For a brief time rumors of impending combinations on a gigantic scale flooded Wall Street, but none of them materialized, and the organizations created to bring harmony collapsed with unceremonious haste.

In peace as in war Gould proved a man ahead of his time. Unlike many rail leaders he understood that conditions were changing and, as always, was ready to move with them. Unfortunately, he could not carry enough of his peers with him, partly because many of them could never look past his reputation as a wrecker. Death claimed him before he could achieve his loftier goals, leaving much of the work he had started to be finished by the man who would dominate the next era of railroad history, E. H. Harriman.

Personally, Gould was a small, dark man with an oversized head, delicately shaped hands and feet, and dark piercing eyes. His voice was soft and musical, his manner courteous and quiet. He seldom spoke and listened intently to whatever he wished to hear. His powers of concentration awed those who knew him. Among the business titans of his age Gould was the most inconspicuous in appearance and unassuming of manner. He preferred it that way; part of his trouble with the press was his inability to deal with them in a comfortable way.

Apart from business, Gould's passions were books and flowers. He assembled a large library, read voraciously from the volumes, and even devised his own catalogue for them. At Lyndhurst, his magnificent estate in Irvington-on-Hudson, he owned the largest private greenhouse in America. Orchids were his specialty, but Gould both grew and studied a wide variety of plants to the point where his knowledge of horticulture may have rivaled his understanding of finance. He also loved horses but never involved himself in racing like so many Wall Street men.

All these interests paled before his family, which remained always the polar opposite of business in competing for his attention. Gould was devoted to his wife and children with a rectitude that made even Victorians blush. The point at which these polar extremes joined was his fervent wish that the boys follow him in business, that the empire he had fashioned be not only his legacy to them but also the instrument that would bind them together in later years.

The death of his wife in January 1889 after a series of strokes left Gould crushed with grief. His eld-est daughter, also named Helen, had always been devoted to her father and moved at once to fill the vacuum in his life, but Gould's own health began to deteriorate as the disease gradually worsened and the efforts to conceal it grew ever more difficult. He required longer and more frequent vacations, often in the guise of lengthy inspection tours of his Southwest railroad system that was conveniently located in the dry desert climate he needed.

By 1892 Gould had come to feel a prisoner of his private railway car and that fall put off the usual trip to the Southwest. In November he fell desperately ill as the disease entered its terminal phase. He died on the morning of December 2 at his Fifth Avenue home in New York City. His will proved as remarkable as its author and confirmed to critics his reputation as a selfish, grasping predator. It left not one cent to anyone outside the family and included an intricate trust arrangement designed to force the children to manage the fortune together for their common interest.

For ninety years Gould remained the archetypal villain of American history during the industrial age. As the quintessential robber baron he served as a convenient stereotype for a turbulent and confusing period of American history. Only in recent years has modern scholarship restored to Gould the broader canvas of his achievements, which are matched by only a handful of entrepreneurs of that era.

Publication:

History of Delaware County (Roxbury, N.Y.: Keeny & Gould, 1856, reprinted New York: Polyanthos, 1977).

References:

Julius Grodinsky, *Jay Gould: His Business Career, 1867-1892* (Philadelphia: University of Pennsylvania, 1957);

Maury Klein, *The Life and Legend of Jay Gould* (Baltimore: Johns Hopkins University Press, 1986);

Maury Klein, *Union Pacific: The Birth of a Railroad, 1862-1893* (Garden City: Doubleday, 1987).

Archives:

Records concerning Jay Gould are located in the Union Pacific papers of the Nebraska State Department of Archives and History, Lincoln, Nebraska.

Franklin Benjamin Gowen

(February 9, 1836-December 14, 1889)

by George M. Jenks

Bucknell University

CAREER: Manager, Shamokin Furnace Colliery (1857-1858); partner, Turner & Gowen (1858-1859); lawyer (1860-1862); district attorney, Schuylkill County, Pennsylvania (1862-1864); counsel (1865-1866), head of legal department (1867-1869), acting president (1869), president, Philadelphia & Reading Railroad (1870-1880, 1882-1884, 1886); delegate, Pennsylvania Constitutional Convention (1872-1873); counsel, Commonwealth of Pennsylvania (1876-1877); lawyer (1886-1889).

Franklin Benjamin Gowen was born in Mount Airy, Pennsylvania, on February 9, 1836, the fifth child of James Gowen and Mary Miller Gowen. Gowen's father was an Irish immigrant, and his mother was from an old Germantown family. The elder Gowen was a successful businessman who retired at age fifty-nine to live the life of a gentleman farmer.

James Gowen, though Irish, was Episcopalian, not Roman Catholic. He was a tolerant man religiously, having once opposed an attempt by missionaries to convert Jews living in the United States to Christianity, seeing such an attempt as an insult. Gowen sent the eight-year-old Franklin Benjamin (named after Benjamin Franklin, but with the names reversed) to a Catholic school in Emmitsburg, Maryland, where he remained for about a year until his two elder brothers left to study law. He was then sent to Beck's Boys Academy in Lititz, Pennsylvania, a Moravian school attended by the sons of many well-to-do eastern families.

Gowen's father took him out of school in 1855 before he graduated and apprenticed him to a storekeeper in Lancaster. The storekeeper, Thomas Baumgardner, was kind to Gowen and encouraged him to continue his studies. Gowen was next sent to manage his father's Shamokin Furnace Colliery

Franklin Benjamin Gowen (courtesy of the Hagley Museum and Library)

for about a year, and then, in 1858, he and James G. Turner from Pottsville joined in partnership as coal mine operators. Coal prices were low, the money ran out, and the partnership was dissolved. Creditors moved in, and Gowen was out of business the next year. Gowen eventually paid all the creditors.

In 1858 he married Esther Brisben of Sunbury, a lasting but not particularly happy union. Gowen gained some notoriety in Pottsville for his speaking ability and helped found the Pottsville Literary Society in 1857, where he participated in debates and poetry readings. He began studying law in the office of a Pottsville attorney; he was admitted to the bar in 1860 and began his practice in Pottsville. Gowen was a loyal Democrat and in 1862 was elected district attorney of Schuylkill County. He did not, however, show much enthusiasm for prosecution and resigned the position in 1864. His third child, Franklin Benjamin, Jr., was born in 1863, and when Gowen was drafted in 1864 he instead paid a substitute to take his place in the Union army. He could well afford it since by then his law practice was paying handsomely. In 1865 both his sons died, and Gowen's brother, George, was killed in the war. However, Gowen turned to his work with his usual zeal and paid off his debts remaining from his partnership with James Turner. In the same year the Philadelphia & Reading (P&R) Railroad picked him to serve as its counsel in Pottsville. He was successful in this position and in 1867 was made head of the P&R's legal department. In this new position he moved to Philadelphia, the headquarters of the railroad.

The Reading was dependent on the anthracite coal traffic, its lines stretching out of Philadelphia eastward to Jersey City and westward to Reading and from Reading to Lancaster, Harrisburg, Sunbury, Wilkes-Barre, Williamsport, Easton, and other points. This dependency on the coal trade meant that the price of coal, and, therefore, the wages paid to the miners, was of crucial importance to the railroad. In 1867 the Workingmen's Benevolent Association (WBA) was formed and by 1869 it had become a powerful force in the coal regions. The Reading watched the growth of the union very carefully. Reading President Charles E. Smith's health was failing, and in 1869 he left the firm to take an extended vacation and recommended that Gowen, only thirty-three years old, serve as acting president in Smith's absence. Smith's health did not permit his return, and Gowen was officially elected president in 1870.

Gowen fought the WBA in a battle over control of coal production and wages. By raising freight rates Gowen found he could control the supply to distributors and the wages of the miners. In response the Pennsylvania Senate Committee on the Judiciary investigated the charge that the railroads had increased freight rates in violation of their charters. Gowen's eloquence and skill in the Reading's defense convinced the committee that the railroads were not in such violation. He spent perhaps $4 million to break the union, money wasted in paying interest on funds borrowed to maintain operations;

replacing equipment and facilities damaged in the strike; paying for the Coal and Iron Police; and other expenses associated with the "long strike." He held the views one might expect of a corporate executive of the time, believing that the corporation had almost unlimited power to act as it pleased. However, he was not a cruel man and was more sensitive than many executives to the workers' needs. He, for instance, did not pay wages in the form of barter from a company store, but in cash, and he also provided benefits to workers that others did not.

Gowen thought that the way to successful railroading in the coal regions was to own the coal lands and thereby control production and transportation. However, the Reading's charter forbade the railroad from owning or operating coal mines. To remedy this inconvenience he had introduced into the legislature in 1871 an act which had buried within it a clause permitting ownership of mines by the Reading. The clause was discovered, however, and the bill died. Gowen then had a bill introduced permitting the Reading to borrow large amounts of money. When this law passed, Gowen bought coal lands, developed and undeveloped, in the name of the Laurel Run Improvement Company. In 1871 the name was changed to the Philadelphia & Reading Coal and Iron Company. By 1874 the company had acquired about 100,000 acres of land.

But coal prices were unstable, and the Reading's debts increased. McCalmont Brothers & Company of London, the largest stockholder in the company, was becoming worried over Gowen's management. To assuage their fears Gowen went to London in 1873 to float a loan, using his enthusiasm and eloquence to soothe the McCalmont Brothers.

In 1872 Gowen was named by the Democratic party as a delegate to the constitutional convention called to amend the state constitution. He was mainly interested in matters pertaining to the railroads, and when he had said all he had to say on the matter, he resigned from the convention to devote his time to the Reading.

Gowen's place in history has long been the product of his prosecution of the Molly Maguires, a secret organization made up of Irish-Americans and associated loosely with the Ancient Order of Hibernians. The organization was thought to be responsible for the murder of several people, for incidents of arson in the coal regions, and was regarded by some as a terrorist group supporting the mine workers.

In 1873 Gowen wrote to the Pinkerton National Detective Agency and asked for their services in ridding the coal fields of the Molly Maguires. The agency sent James McParlan, one of its agents, to Pottsville to infiltrate the organization. He was successful in this strategy and gave evidence in a series of nationally reported sensational trials. Gowen took a leave of absence from the Reading and served without pay as an assistant to the Schuylkill County District Attorney to take part in the prosecution. By 1877 twenty members of the Molly Maguires had been hanged and twenty-six others sent to prison. Whether they were all guilty remains in doubt.

In his management of the Reading Gowen was ambitious but occasionally used poor judgment. His acquisition of coal lands and dependence on one product proved a burden. He was opposed to monopoly and thought that regulation of public utilities was necessary. At the same time he felt that regional monopolies were justifiable and opposed "interference" from other corporations. He thought that public utilities had a responsibility to the public, unlike many of his contemporaries, and he was evidently not corrupt. Gowen did not bribe officials or legislators as other railroad heads did, even abolishing free passes, a form of bribery generally used by railroads to encourage important people to look favorably on them. Unopposed to workmen's benefits, and even to unions, Gowen did oppose what he saw as "militant" unions. In hiring he was not prejudiced against ethnic groups as was common in the coal regions.

Gowen did, however, transfer funds between the Philadelphia & Reading Railroad and the Philadelphia & Reading Coal and Iron Company to make the books and annual reports look good. But by 1880 his bad management and decisions were catching up with him; the railroad was declared bankrupt and receivers were appointed. In 1881 Frank S. Bond was elected president, but in 1882 Gowen was returned to the office. He continued in an attempt to build a parallel line competing with the Pennsylvania Railroad, but, when the New York Central withdrew its support, the project died. In 1884 he resigned the presidency. In 1886 he was again elected president, but after another bankruptcy that same year was forced out by J. P. Morgan. He resigned and sailed for Europe.

On his return to America Gowen resumed his law practice. He argued before the U.S. Senate Interstate Commerce Committee against discriminatory freight rates. In 1889 he was in Washington again to argue a case before the Interstate Commerce Commission. He bought a revolver from a hardware store and on December 14 went to his hotel room and shot himself. His suicide was a shock for there seemed to be no reason for it. There was an unfounded rumor that he was killed in revenge for his prosecution of the Molly Maguires.

Gowen was a complex man. He was well-traveled, making several trips to Europe, and was also an avid translator of German poetry. He was a handsome, intelligent, sensitive man, but impetuous and egotistical. Although he was not happy in his marriage, Gowen was a faithful husband to his wife and a loving father to his children. He was not ostentatious as were other moguls of his time, but he lived well. He once ranked near the Morgans and Vanderbilts in reputation, but his fame was not lasting, perhaps because the Reading was a regional road, and his life was very much tied up with that company. His most lasting legacy may be Gowen City, a village of 300 inhabitants in Northumberland County, Pennsylvania, renamed for him, and which for years had a historical sign stating that the village was named for Francis B. Gowen. The sign was later changed to "Franklin I. Gowen, Capitalist and landowner."

Publications:

Argument in the Cases of the Philadelphia and Erie Rail Road Co., et al., vs. the Catawissa Railroad Co., the Atlantic and Great Western Railway Co., et al., and Andrew Scott vs. the Same Defendants, Delivered June 21st and 22d, 1886, before the Supreme Court of Pennsylvania at a Special Session Held at Wilkesbarre (Philadelphia: H. G. Leisenring's Steam Printing House, 1866);

Argument before the Judiciary Committee of the Senate of Pennsylvania on Behalf of the Railroading and Mining Interests of Pennsylvania, March 30th, 1871 (Philadelphia: Leisenring Steam Printing House, 1871);

The Coal Monopoly: Correspondence between B. B. Thomas, President of the Thomas Coal Company, and F. B. Gowen, President of the Philadelphia and Reading Railroad Company, with the Charter of the Laurel Run Improvement Company, Now the Philadelphia and Reading Coal and Iron Company (New York: Coal Trade Circular Print, 1873?);

Argument before the Joint Committee of the Legislature of Pennsylvania, Appointed to Inquire into the Affairs of the Philadelphia and Reading Coal and Iron Company and the Philadelphia and Reading Rail-

road Company, at Atlantic City, New Jersey, July 29th and 30th, 1875, on Behalf of Said Company (Philadelphia: Press of Helfenstein, Lewis & Greene, 1875);

Argument als Anwalt fuer den Staat in dem Prozess gegen Thomas Munley, angeklagt in der Court der Common Pleas von Schuylkill County, Pa., wegen Ermordung des Thomas Sanger, eines Minen-Aufsehers in Raven Run, am 1. September 1875 Aus dem Englischen uebersetzt von J. Wm. Schrader (Pottsville, Pa.: Jefferson Demokrat, 1876);

Argument des Staatsanwaltes. Mordprozess des Thomas Munley (Pottsville, Pa.: Jefferson Democrat Druckerei, 1876);

Argument of Counsel for the Commonwealth in the Case of the Commonwealth vs. Thomas Munley, Indicted in the Court of Oyer and Terminer of Schuylkill County, Pa., for the Murder of Thomas Sanger, a Mining Boss, at Raven Run on September 1st, 1875 (Pottsville, Pa.: Miners' Journal Book and Job Rooms, 1876);

To the Public: Statement of Franklin B. Gowen, President of Philadelphia and Reading Railroad Company, Regarding Threatened Strike by the Brotherhood of Locomotive Engineers, March-April, 1877 (Philadelphia: 1877);

Argument before the Committee on Commerce of the House of Representatives upon Bill No. 1028 to Regulate Interstate Commerce, Washington, D.C., January 27th, 1880 (Philadelphia: 1880);

Argument in Case of the Commonwealth vs. Petroff, Indicted in the Court of Quarter Sessions of Dauphin County for Corrupt Solicitation of Members of the Legislature, Delivered March 10, 1880 (Philadelphia?: 1880);

Statement of the Present Condition of the Philadelphia & Reading Railroad Co. and the Philadelphia & Reading Coal and Iron Co., with Plan for Their Financial Re-organization (Philadelphia: Jackson Bros., Printers, 1880);

Mr. Gowen's Defense: Speeches of Mr. Franklin B. Gowen (ex-President) and Others Concerning the Philadelphia and Reading Railroad Company, Delivered at a Public Meeting Held by Mr. Gowen at the Cannon Street Hotel, London, on Thursday, the 10th of November, 1881 (London: 1881);

Philadelphia & Reading Railroad Company: Address of Mr. Franklin B. Gowen, President of the Company, to the Share and Bondholders at the Academy of Music, Philadelphia, on Saturday, April 23, 1881 (Philadelphia: Jackson Bros., Printers, 1881);

The Railway Problem: Address on the Position which the City of Philadelphia Should Occupy to the Commonwealth of Pennsylvania to Its Transportation Lines and to the Railway Problem of the Day, Delivered upon the Invitation of Citizens of Philadelphia at the Academy of Music, June 16, 1881 (Philadelphia: Jackson Bros., Printers, 1881?);

Argument before the Committee on Railroads of the House of Representatives of Pennsylvania upon the Bill Presented by Mr. Hulings of Venango County, to Prevent Unjust Discrimination by Railroad Companies, Delivered in the Hall of the House of Representatives, Harrisburg, February 13th, 1883 (Philadelphia: Allen, Lane & Scott's Printing House, 1883);

Argument before a Committee of the Legislature of Pennsylvania Appointed under a Joint Resolution Approved June 2d, 1883, to Inquire into the Legal Relations of the Standard Oil Company to the State; into Its Conduct as to the Payment of Taxes to the State, &c, &c. (Philadelphia: Allen, Lane & Scott's Printing House, 1884);

Address to the Share and Bondholders of the Philadelphia & Reading Railroad Company at the Academy of Music, Philadelphia, Friday Evening, December 11th, 1885 (Philadelphia: Allen, Lane & Scott, 1885);

Argument before the Committee on Interstate Commerce, U.S. Senate, Saturday, March 24th, 1888, on Amendments Suggested by Him to the Interstate Commerce Act, Giving Exemplary Damages for Its Violation, and Authorizing United States Courts to Issue Writs of Mandamus against Common Carriers (Philadelphia: Allen, Lane & Scott, 1888);

Argument delivered before the Interstate Commerce Commission, Washington, D.C., January 17th, 1888, in the Cases of George Rice vs. the Railroad Companies: Known as the Standard Oil Monopoly Cases (Marietta, Ohio: G. Rice; Philadelphia: Allen, Lane & Scott, 1888);

Argument in the Matter of the Investigation of the Standard Oil Trust by the Committee on Manufactures of the House of Representatives (Philadelphia: Allen, Lane & Scott, 1889).

References:

Harold Aurand and William Gudelunas, "The Mythical Qualities of Molly Maguire," *Pennsylvania History*, 49 (April 1982): 91-105;

Biographical Encyclopaedia of Pennsylvania of the Nineteenth Century (Philadelphia: Galaxy, 1874), p. 627;

James Walter Coleman, *Molly Maguire Riots: Industrial Conflict in the Pennsylvania Coal Region* (Richmond, Va.: Garrett and Massie, 1936);

"Gowen's Tragic Death," *New York Times*, December 15, 1889, pp. 1-2;

Jay V. Hare, *History of the Reading* (Philadelphia: John Henry Strock, 1966);

Philip S. Klein and Ari Hoogenboom, *A History of Pennsylvania*, second enlarged edition (University Park: Pennsylvania State University Press, 1980);

Arthur H. Lewis, *Lament for the Molly Maguires* (New York: Harcourt, Brace & World, 1964);

Marvin Wilson Schlegel, *Ruler of the Reading: The Life of Franklin B. Gowen, 1836-1889* (Harrisburg: Archives Publishing Company of Pennsylvania, 1947);

Anthony F. C. Wallace, *St. Clair: A Nineteenth-Century Coal Town's Experience with a Disaster-Prone Industry* (New York: Knopf, 1987);

C. K. Yearley, Jr., *Enterprise and Anthracite: Economics and Democracy in Schuylkill County, 1820-1875* (Baltimore: Johns Hopkins University Press, 1961).

Archives:
Materials relating to Franklin B. Gowen are located in the Reading Collection of the Hagley Museum and Library, Wilmington, Delaware; and in the Baltimore & Ohio Collection and the Garrett Papers of the Maryland Historical Society Library, Baltimore.

Great Northern Railway

by Don L. Hofsommer

Augustana College

The Great Northern Railway, like so many other of the nation's large roads, survived a difficult birth and evolved from a troubled childhood. Its earliest predecessor, the Minnesota & Pacific, chartered in 1857, implied important long-range strategy in its very name, but by summer 1862–and now restyled the St. Paul & Pacific–it had managed to link only the ten miles between St. Paul and St. Anthony, part of present-day Minneapolis. Expansion followed, in a halting way, toward the northwest. Specifically, the road's promoters hoped to forge a transportation bridge of sorts between the Mississippi River (the falls at St. Anthony) and the fertile Red River Valley of Minnesota, Dakota, and Manitoba. In doing so they would gather a large overhead traffic (business moving to and from points beyond the St. Paul & Pacific), open a huge and potentially productive territory, and earn for the road a vast grant of land. But the panic of 1873, a plague of locusts, and other misfortunes impaired success. In 1878 James J. Hill and others (the "associates") combined to acquire the property; under their aegis requisite lines were completed and the grants obtained. The timing was propitious. Prosperity returned, and Hill, who emerged supreme among the associates, embraced a dream of expansion.

Hill looked west, toward Montana and beyond. Under the flag of the St. Paul, Minneapolis & Manitoba (successor to the St. Paul & Pacific and named thus in 1878), rails reached Helena in 1887. By that time Hill was also looking eastward, buying lines and building others in Minnesota, and establishing the Northern Steamship Company to provide a friendly water route all the way to Buffalo. His thirst for expansion remained unslaked. Out of the St. Paul, Minneapolis & Manitoba emerged the Great Northern (GN) Railway in 1881, which pushed an impressive road across the Rockies and the Cascades to tap Puget Sound in 1893.

The timing now, it seemed, was awful. A new and devastating financial panic was sweeping the land, and bankruptcies among western railroads were nearly epidemic. Yet the Great Northern survived. Hill had insisted on rigorous engineering standards that gave the road easier grades and curvature than the competition, and the company's financial condition was comparatively healthy. Thus when the panic lifted in 1898 the Great Northern was well positioned to take advantage of burgeoning opportunities.

Hill's devotion to operating efficiencies was matched by his devotion to the colonization and the improvement of economic and cultural conditions in the road's service area. There was, he clearly understood, a symbiotic link between the company and its customers; the GN would profit only if its patrons prospered. Consequently, Hill authorized an endless list of projects ranging from irrigation to plant breeding. All of it represented benign self-interest yet resulted in shared progress. Small wonder that even before Hill died in 1916, he was hailed as "The Empire Builder."

Hill had tried twice during his lifetime to merge the Great Northern with other roads to form a much larger system and thus enjoy the economies of scale, but he was rebuffed by a variety of political forces. The most famous of Hill's attempts was the 1901 formation of the Northern Securities Corporation, a holding company which bought and held the stock of the Great Northern and the Northern Pacific, and through those two roads controlled the Chicago, Burlington & Quincy. Although the merger was declared invalid in 1904, the railroads continued to maintain a close relationship. Hill's successors mounted another abortive campaign during the late 1920s, but it was not until March 3, 1970, that the 8,000-mile Great Northern became an integral part of the Burlington Northern Railroad.

References:
Ralph W. Hidy, Muriel E. Hidy, Roy V. Scott, with Don L. Hofsommer, *The Great Northern Railway: A History* (Boston: Harvard Business School Press, 1988); Albro Martin, *James J. Hill and the Opening of the North-*

west (New York: Oxford University Press, 1976).

Archives:
Material concerning the Great Northern Railway is located at the James Jerome Hill Reference Library, St. Paul, Minnesota; and in the Great Northern Railway Company Records of the Minnesota Historical Society, St. Paul, Minnesota.

James Theodore Harahan

(January 12, 1841-January 22, 1912)

by John F. Stover

Purdue University

CAREER: Employed on several railroads (1864-1890); second vice-president, Illinois Central Railroad (1890-1906); president, Illinois Central Railroad (1906-1911).

James Harahan, railroad official and president of the Illinois Central Railroad, was born on January 12, 1841, in Lowell, Massachusetts, the son of Thomas and Rose (McCurn) Harahan. He attended the public schools of Lowell until the age of seventeen, when he became a freight clerk for the Boston & Providence Railroad in Boston. In 1861, at the age of twenty, he enlisted in Company G of the First Massachusetts Infantry. He remained in the army for three years, was wounded at Gettysburg, and was mustered out on May 25, 1864. In 1866 he married Mary Kehoe, with whom he had four children: William J., James T., Jr., Anna, and Mary.

After the Civil War Harahan filled a variety of positions on several different railroads. He was a switchman on the Orange & Alexandria in Virginia and later worked from 1864 to 1865 in Nashville on the Nashville & Decatur. From 1870 to 1872 he was in charge of the 18-mile Shelby Railroad in Kentucky and from 1872 to 1879 was roadmaster of the Nashville & Decatur. For four years Harahan was divisional superintendent on the Louisville & Nashville (L&N), first on the Memphis line and then the New Orleans line. In 1883 he was named general superintendent on the L&N lines south of Decatur, and in 1884 became general manager of the entire railroad. Briefly in 1885 Harahan was general superintendent on the Pittsburgh divi-

James Theodore Harahan

sion of the Baltimore & Ohio but after three months returned to the Louisville & Nashville as assistant general manager. In April and May 1886 he was in charge of planning the change of gauge of the entire 2,000-mile L&N system from its 5-foot width to the standard 4-foot 8½-inch gauge. Road and track crews numbering 8,000 men moved 2,000 miles of rail a little over 3 inches closer together during the daylight hours of Sunday, May 30, 1886. Between 1889 and 1890 James Harahan was successively assistant general manager of the Lake Shore & Michigan Southern, general manager of the Chesapeake & Ohio, and general manager of the Louisville, New Orleans & Texas.

In 1890 Harahan moved to the Illinois Central (IC) Railroad, where he would remain for the rest of his career. In the fall of 1890 Edward H. Harriman, who had a large investment in the Illinois Central, resigned as vice-president of the railroad to concentrate on his other investments. At once the board elected John C. Welling, the IC comptroller, to be first vice-president, and James Harahan to be second vice-president in charge of operation and traffic. Harahan would retain that office until his elevation to the presidency in 1906. Harahan had made himself a master of every position he had held on the several lines he had served since the Civil War. He had a genius for grasping and retaining detail. He never allowed himself to forget the dictum of Michelangelo that "trifles make perfection." Harahan was solicitous for the welfare of his employees and also believed that the public should be kept informed of the problems and difficulties of railroad operation.

In 1890 the Illinois Central Railroad was a 2,900-mile line in ten states extending west of Chicago to Sioux City, and south to Cairo, Memphis, and New Orleans. It had annual revenues of more than $15 million, assets of over $100 million, and had paid regular dividends since 1861. Since the IC's president, Stuyvesant Fish, was more interested in rail finance than operation and spent much of his time in New York City, Harahan oversaw most of the day-to-day operations of the IC from his Chicago office.

In July 1894, during the Pullman strike, an IC train was derailed and dozens of freight cars were burned. Without the good services and personal popularity of vice-president Harahan, the Illinois Central might have had far more trouble during the strike. Many of the IC workers felt a personal loyalty to Harahan for they knew he had once worked at the tasks they were performing. In 1901 he was elected to the IC board of directors, a position he

would retain until 1911. During his decade and a half as vice-president, the IC increased its mileage by nearly half, while the freight and passenger traffic expanded about fourfold. Much of the added mileage was the result of the acquisition in the early 1890s of two lines in southern states: the Louisville, New Orleans & Texas, and the Chesapeake, Ohio & Southwestern.

In 1905 and 1906 a quarrel over Fish's investments of IC funds developed between Edward Harriman, the dominant IC stockholder, and Fish, the IC president. When peacemaking efforts failed, Harriman moved to oust Fish and select a new president. Harriman decided that the man who was in charge of IC operations in Chicago should be the new president, and James Harahan was elected to succeed Fish on November 7, 1906. During his struggle with Harriman, Fish had argued that a Harriman victory would mean that the IC would lose its independence and come under the control of the Union Pacific, a line fully controlled by Harriman. Once in the presidential chair, Harahan assured his staff and employees that he had no intention of allowing the Illinois Central to lose its independence or be merged with the Harriman-controlled lines. No such control of the IC did develop, a fact made the more certain by Harriman's death in 1909. Shortly after taking office, Harahan convinced the board of directors that the president's office should be moved to Chicago from New York City, where Fish had maintained his office. Much smaller offices were retained in New York City, and the third vice-president, Alexander G. Hackstaff, became the top official in New York. The shift from New York to Chicago reflected the fact that Harahan was essentially an operations man, while Fish had always been first a financier.

During the presidency of Harahan, the Illinois Central system added only about 300 miles of new line to the 4,400 miles in operation in 1906. Much of the new mileage was a 216-mile extension from Jackson, Tennessee, to Birmingham, Alabama, added in 1906-1908. At about the same time Edward Harriman, who had a controlling interest in the Central of Georgia, sold his Central of Georgia stock to the Illinois Central. The IC and the Central of Georgia connected at Birmingham, but the Central of Georgia continued as an independent road. In the first decade of the new century, the Illinois Central remained prosperous, with annual revenues above $50 million, an operating ratio of about

70 percent, and annual dividends of $7. About four-fifths of the revenue came from freight, with mine products producing a third of the tonnage, followed by farm products, manufactured goods, and forest products. The last year of the Harahan presidency was blemished by the revelation of a scandal concerning fraud and corruption in the repair of Illinois Central freight equipment. Several officials in middle management were involved, and losses to the railroad were estimated to be near $1 million.

On his seventieth birthday, January 12, 1911, James Harahan retired as president of the Illinois Central Railroad. During his more than four years as president, and sixteen years as second vice-president, he had been an extremely industrious and conscientious railroad official. After leaving the Illinois Central, Harahan became the president of the Memphis Bridge & Terminal Company, which was planning a railroad bridge across the Mississippi River. Harahan was killed in a railroad wreck near Kinmundy, Illinois, on January 22, 1912.

References:

Carlton J. Corliss, *Main Line of Mid-America: The Story of the Illinois Central* (New York: Creative Age, 1950);

John F. Stover, *History of the Illinois Central Railroad* (New York: Macmillan, 1975).

Edward Henry Harriman

(February 25, 1848-September 9, 1909)

by Lloyd J. Mercer

University of California, Santa Barbara

CAREER: Partner, E. H. Harriman and Company (mid 1870s to 1885); vice-president and president, Sodus Bay & Southern Railroad (1882-1884); board of directors and chairman of the finance committee, Illinois Central Railroad Company (1883-1909); vice-president, Illinois Central Railroad Company (1887-1890); chairman board of directors and executive committee, president, Union Pacific Railroad Company (1897-1909); chairman board of directors and executive committee, Chicago & Alton Railroad Company (1899-1907); board of directors, Baltimore & Ohio Railroad Company (1899-1909); chairman board of directors and executive committee, Kansas City Southern Railway (1900-1905); chairman board of directors and executive committee, president, Southern Pacific Company (1901-1909); board of directors, Northern Pacific Railway Company (1902-1904); board of directors, Chicago, Burlington & Quincy Railroad Company (1902-1904); board of directors and executive committee, Erie Railroad Company (1903-1909).

Edward Henry Harriman, a leading figure in American railroading from the late 1890s until his death in 1909, was born in the Episcopal rectory at Hempstead, Long Island, on February 25, 1848. He died at his mansion, still under construction, at Arden, New York, on September 9, 1909. Harriman, a man of perhaps 5 feet 4 inches and 130 pounds, was known as the "little giant" of Wall Street. During his peak period of influence, from 1898 to 1909, he controlled the Union Pacific (UP), the Southern Pacific, and the smaller Chicago & Alton Railroad while continuing to be a director and major force at the Illinois Central and several other important railroads.

Harriman's father, the Reverend Orlando Harriman, had been a prize-winning scholar at Columbia University. His mother, Cornelia Neilson Harriman, was a member of an old and distinguished New Jersey family. In 1850 the Reverend Harriman received a call from a mountain parish in California. On his way to California, via the Isthmus route, he became ill in Panama and arrived in California a month late to find his parish taken and no others available. After a year of wandering in California he returned to New York and moved to Jersey City. Orlando Harriman's career was financially unsuccessful but a small inheritance received by his wife eased financial pressures in later years. Henry Harriman grew up in this poverty-stricken en-

Edward Henry Harriman (courtesy of Sherer)

vironment and experienced firsthand the problems of never having enough money. With the church support provided to clergymen's sons, his father sent Harriman and his three brothers to Trinity School in New York City. In 1860 Harriman won the top prize for scholarship at Trinity School.

In 1861 Henry left school to start work as an office boy but soon advanced to messenger clerk on Wall Street. His experiences in the rough and tumble of the street provided an education in the rudiments of finance and monetary affairs. In 1868 or 1869 he became the managing clerk for D. C. Hayes Company. In the summer of 1870, at the age of twenty-two and with a loan from an uncle, Harriman bought a seat on the New York Stock Exchange. Harriman was successful both as a commission broker and as a trader for his own account. In the mid 1870s he allowed his friend James B. Livingston an interest in the business, and the firm became E. H. Harriman & Company.

Harriman's first big success came in 1874 when he produced a $150,000 profit by selling short as "Deacon" White attempted to corner the "anthracite" stocks. In 1875 Harriman took a

short position in Delaware & Hudson stock while John Jacob Astor was buying all he could. The price rose steadily, and short-sellers were obliged to cover at a loss; much of Harriman's anthracite profits were swept away.

Over the span of his career Harriman was a successful stock market investor and became one of the dominant figures on Wall Street. No less a financial expert than Bernard Baruch, who also had humble beginnings, wrote of Harriman that "he was the man I did my best to emulate when I first entered Wall Street." Baruch also wrote that Harriman seemed to him "to be the epitome of all that was dashing."

But Harriman did have interests outside his work. He was a director of the Traveler's Club and a member of both the Union and Racquet clubs. Early in his Wall Street career Harriman belonged to the Seventh Regiment of the National Guard which was considered the best militia organization in the state of New York. He drilled with August Belmont, Jr., and other Wall Street associates and is reported to have been an excellent marksman. He was early attracted to the Adirondacks for outdoor activities including fishing and hunting. Boxing and raising trotting horses were other avocations. The latter became his primary hobby in later years.

Harriman was instrumental in the opening of the Tompkins Square Boys' Club in New York City in 1876. This resulted from his friendship with George C. Clark; the influence of the Clark family led Harriman to take an interest in social betterment work on the East Side. A similar institution, the Wilson Mission School for girls, gave Harriman the idea for organizing the Boys' Club. By 1907 the Boys' Club had 6,000 members, its own building (five stories and a basement) which Harriman paid for entirely, and a camp on Long Island. Harriman provided continual direction and financial support for the Boys' Club from 1876 to his death in 1909. In fulfillment of a Harriman promise made in 1907 Mrs. Harriman continued to match 50 percent of the annual contributions obtained by the club from all other sources.

In the late 1870s Harriman met Miss Mary Williamson Averell at the Clarks' home. Miss Averell's father, William J. Averell, was the leading banker of Ogdensburg, New York, and president of the Ogdensburg & Lake Champlain Railroad Company. Harriman and Mary Averell were married on September 10, 1879, at Ogdensburg. Over the next sixteen years three sons and three daughters were born to the couple.

Harriman's entrance into railroad management came in 1880 when he was elected a director on the board of his father-in-law's railroad. The railroad directorship and the experience it provided turned Harriman's attention to the potential of railroads as a business and investment vehicle. In the fall of 1881 he and several partners bought controlling interest in the Lake Ontario Southern Railroad.

The 34-mile-long Lake Ontario Southern was a reorganization of the Ontario & Southern, which had begun business in the early 1870s. The road ran from the town of Stanley to a harbor on Lake Ontario known as Great Sodus Bay; it connected with the Pennsylvania Railroad at Stanley and the New York Central at Newark. The road's physical condition and equipment were poor, and it was regarded as an unprofitable and undesirable property.

In 1882 the Lake Ontario Southern was reorganized as the Sodus Bay & Southern with S. J. Macy as president and Harriman as vice-president. In an action which would become his hallmark Harriman vigorously pushed the improvement of the physical condition and equipment of the road. At a board meeting in October 1883 Harriman named a price at which he would either sell his stock or buy that of the other owners. He became almost the sole owner of the property, and the board was reorganized with him as president.

Improvements in the road were continued, and in the spring of 1884 Harriman offered the road for sale to both the Pennsylvania and the New York Central. He exploited both the strategic location of his road and the competition between the larger roads. The New York Central took an option on the road until noon on July 1, but a few days after the New York Central took the option, the Pennsylvania expressed a desire to buy the road. At the last moment the New York Central decided to renew its option, but Harriman was conveniently absent from his office and the road was sold to the Pennsylvania. This first excursion into railroad finance was apparently quite profitable for Harriman. His strategy was based on principles that he would employ often in his later career as a railroad magnate. First, Harriman believed that a railroad's physical condition and equipment must be excellent and well maintained. Second, he believed that location and strategic position were important considerations and valuable assets.

A rising force in the Illinois Central in the early 1880s was Stuyvesant Fish, a member of a wealthy New York family and the son of ex-President Grant's secretary of state. Fish, a long-standing friend of Harriman, was also a director of the Ogdensburg & Lake Champlain. Fish's ascendancy at the Illinois Central piqued Harriman's interest in that road, and in 1881 he purchased bonds of one of its subsidiaries, the Chicago, St. Louis & New Orleans. The combined influence of the Boissevain Brothers firm, which held the proxies for Illinois Central stock held in Holland, and Fish, who had become vice-president of the Illinois Central, led to Harriman's election in 1883 as an Illinois Central director. On the board he exerted his influence to institute a bold policy of improvement and expansion. He also became closely associated with Fish in the management of the road, serving as chairman of the finance committee of the board of directors. His work on that committee became well known and laid the groundwork for his later accomplishments with his own railroads. In 1885 Harriman retired from the firm of E. H. Harriman & Company to concentrate on railroads.

A struggle, the first of many, between J. P. Morgan and Harriman over control of a railroad occurred in 1886-1887. The Illinois Central leased the Dubuque & Sioux City in 1867, but continued profitable operation of the railroad required significant investment which would pay only if the Illinois Central owned the line. With some adroit legal maneuvering by Harriman concerning the voting of proxies held by Drexel, Morgan & Company, a board favorable to the Illinois Central purchase was elected at the Dubuque & Sioux City annual meeting early in 1887. Litigation over the matter continued for some months until Drexel, Morgan & Company accepted a compromise offered by the Illinois Central. Soon after this victory Harriman was elected vice-president of the Illinois Central in place of Fish, who had been elevated to president.

Fish and Harriman were appalled by the slipshod administrative methods and internal financial procedures they found and in 1888 set out to reform Illinois Central management. To do so they instituted a highly centralized management structure. The two key departments, transportation and traffic, remained completely separate, and their managers reported directly to officials at Chicago. The president and vice-president personally coordinated the activities of the other departments of the railroad. Harriman and Fish preferred the centralized structure because its fewer administrative personnel reduced complexity and expenses. Over the next two decades this structure became the common management style of American railroads. Harriman used it with his later railroads, and it is undoubtedly why he complained of being overworked and tired.

While Fish was in Europe during the summer of 1889, Harriman, as acting president of the Illinois Central, had his first major conflict with a high official of the road. At the time the general manager or traffic manager generally had discretion regarding rate making. In April 1889 the Illinois Central board had amended one of its bylaws to make rate reductions contingent on the approval of the president, who was to report his decision in such cases to the board. E. T. Jeffrey, a respected and able railroad executive, was then general manager. Jeffrey disagreed with this new bylaw, and Fish had promised Jeffrey he would not be deprived of his rate-making power if he stayed with the road. In a conversation with Jeffrey in early September, Harriman reminded him of the bylaw amendment. Jeffrey objected strongly to Harriman's insistence on carrying out the instructions of the bylaw and resigned the same day. Because he was fairly new as an officer of the company and not widely regarded as an experienced railroad man, Harriman was placed in a difficult position by Jeffrey's resignation. He stuck to the principle involved and named a new general manager, his action being approved by the board of directors and Fish. This incident increased Harriman's standing and power at the Illinois Central. While remaining on the board Harriman resigned as vicepresident in 1890 and moved to New York to give time to his other activities.

In 1885 Harriman had bought at auction the 7,863-acre Parrott estate in the Ramapo Highlands about forty-five miles north of Jersey City and ten miles west of the Hudson River. Over the years Harriman added land to the estate at every opportunity. By 1905 the purchase of about forty wooded tracts and farms had enlarged the estate to almost thirty square miles, making it one of the most extensive country estates in the New York City vicinity. The Harrimans made it their permanent summer home, giving it the name of Mrs. Parrott's family, Arden.

The Parrott homestead was reserved in the sale, but the reservation did not include a cottage formerly occupied by a married daughter. After it was enlarged and improved, the former cottage became the Harrimans' residence at Arden. Construction of the Harriman mansion at Arden did not begin until 1905 and was not completed until after Harriman's death in 1909. The family did not move into the new home until the summer of 1909.

Harriman became interested in the development and extension of the dairy industry in the Ramapo Valley. In 1896 he organized a company, Arden Farms Dairy Corporation, to manage the agricultural development of the estate. A portion of the Harriman lands was given to the state of New York after his death and became Harriman Park. Arden House now belongs to Columbia University and is a meeting place for scholars.

Harriman's greatest business achievement was the reorganization and rebuilding of the Union Pacific Railroad. In October 1893 the Union Pacific, along with many other roads, went into bankruptcy and the hands of receivers. For two years the original reorganization committee struggled to find an acceptable plan to revive the railroad, a major obstacle being the UP's large government debt that exceeded $58 million. The reorganization effort was placed in the hands of Jacob Schiff of Kuhn, Loeb & Company in the fall of 1895. Schiff's committee developed a reorganization plan, but it ran into opposition, led by Harriman, at all points. In an interview Harriman informed Schiff that his purpose was to reorganize the Union Pacific himself, the original intention being to unite the Illinois Central and the Union Pacific. He opposed Schiff's plan because he feared it would give control of the Union Pacific to the New York Central and the Chicago & North Western, effectively shutting out the Illinois Central. Harriman's price for peace was chairmanship of the executive committee of the reorganized Union Pacific. Illinois Central credit finally convinced Schiff to compromise. With Illinois Central credit Harriman was able to obtain the funds necessary for the Union Pacific reorganization at 3 or 3.5 percent versus the 4 to 5 percent Kuhn, Loeb & Company would have to pay for them. Schiff proposed a settlement which, if Harriman accepted, would make him a director of the reorganized company and a member of the executive committee. Harriman agreed and assumed those posts in December 1897. Just short of the age of fifty Harriman began the great works of his railroading career. Collaboration between Harriman and

Schiff would continue for the remainder of Harriman's life and pay handsome dividends to both. Harriman became chairman of the board of directors of the Union Pacific and chairman of its executive committee on December 1, 1898, and Kuhn, Loeb & Company became the company's primary bankers.

In addition to his genius Harriman brought tremendous financial resources to the Union Pacific. These included the support of the New York City Bank and its president, James Stillman. From his stock market years and the Illinois Central, Harriman also brought connections with the Goulds and Vanderbilts. In 1902 William Rockefeller and Henry Rogers of Standard Oil, and in 1904 H. C. Frick of U.S. Steel joined the financial combination built by Harriman. These substantial financial resources were necessary because the reorganization, with the repayment of the government debt, required $75 million to be raised.

The key to the Union Pacific reorganization was the agreement on repayment of the railroad's government debt and accumulated interest. The reorganization proceeded only when the committee agreed to pay the government debt, both principal and interest, in full and in cash. The reorganization plan was a strong one which considerably reduced fixed charges and laid the foundation on which Harriman built his control of the Union Pacific and, from that, the Southern Pacific.

In the summer of 1898 Harriman took his two older daughters and several Union Pacific officials for a daylight examination of the Union Pacific line from the Missouri River to the Pacific. He sent a telegram from Portland to the board of directors asking them for authority to spend up to $25 million for improvements and equipment for the road. By 1904 over $50 million had been invested in rebuilding and new equipment. Between 1898 and 1907 the average capacity of the railroad's freight cars was raised from 20 to 34 tons. The average Union Pacific locomotive weighed 37 tons in 1898 but by 1909 had increased to 68 tons. In addition to reconstruction and new equipment Harriman insisted on adequate maintenance. He saw to it that maintenance expenditures were sufficient to keep his roads in first-class condition. From the operational point of view, the Union Pacific was a great success under Harriman. The railroad also poured out a flood of earnings, an investment in the Union

Pacific during the Harriman years paying a handsome return.

In 1899 major stockholders of the Chicago & Alton, who later became members of Harriman's Chicago & Alton syndicate, proposed that Harriman acquire the road. S. M. Felton, a well-known expert and railroad manager, made a thorough examination of the property for Harriman, satisfying him that the Chicago & Alton could be bought for less than its potential value.

The Chicago & Alton was, under its president, T. B. Blackstone, a conservatively managed road which had for thirty years or more paid 8 percent dividends on its stock, which was selling at seventy-five to one hundred points above par. For many years the Chicago & Alton had not spent enough to provide extensions, betterments, and the additional equipment necessary to serve its territory. The road's physical condition had also declined as the line aged. Several opportunities for merger with larger roads had been rejected.

During Harriman's control of the Chicago & Alton a $22.3 million program of physical improvements was undertaken. Although expensive the program brought improvements in performance. In the 1890s the earnings of the Chicago & Alton had been declining. Under Harriman gross earnings rose from $6.3 million in 1898 to $12.8 million in 1907 (Harriman's last year with the Chicago & Alton), and net earnings rose from $2.7 million to $4.4 million. This appears to be evidence of good management. Despite this evidence of good management Harriman's control of the Chicago & Alton was a major focus of the Interstate Commerce Commission (ICC) investigation of the Harriman lines in 1906 and the source of violent and serious charges against Harriman. The principal issue of concern was the financial manipulations of the Harriman syndicate.

The syndicate initially acquired 97 percent of the stock of the Chicago & Alton. New 3 percent bonds worth $32 million were offered to stockholders at sixty-five soon after the reorganization. The new directors then declared a cash dividend of 30 percent, worth $6.7 million, on the stock of the Chicago & Alton. In 1900 the Chicago & Alton Railway Company was formed as a holding company. The holding company sold its stockholders $22 million of 3.5 percent collateral trust bonds at sixty. The old preferred stock of the Chicago & Alton was purchased with the proceeds of this sale, and, in exchange for $18.3 million of old common stock of the Chicago & Alton, the holding company issued $19.5 million of its own common and $19.5 million of its own preferred. The holding and operating companies were consolidated in 1906.

The substantial increase in the nominal capitalization of the Chicago & Alton, which added about $54 million in bonds and $39 million in stock and resulted in only $25 million spent in betterments and extensions, caused Harriman's control of the railroad to be severely criticized. Also of concern was the rise in fixed payments, with interest due on about $12 million in 1899 and $70 million in 1907.

There is no doubt that Harriman's management improved the profitability of the Chicago & Alton. He also significantly improved the road's physical condition, an improvement which was reflected in a rise in both passenger and freight productivity that was greater than the national average over the period. The financing undertaken by the Harriman syndicate did increase the fixed charges on the road from about $1.4 million per year to $3.3 million, but, contrary to Prof. William Z. Ripley of Harvard, Harriman's severest critic, Harriman's actions did not make the stock of the Chicago & Alton worthless. In 1909 the average New York Stock Exchange bid for Chicago & Alton common varied from 57 7/8 to 74 3/4 and preferred from 70 to 78 1/2. While this was much less than the Harriman syndicate had paid for the stock, it was far from worthless. Harriman's management of the Chicago & Alton improved the road rather than looting it as charged by critics.

In spring 1899 Harriman agreed to join the New York reorganization committee of the Kansas City, Pittsburgh & Gulf Railroad. In November 1899 a reorganization plan was adopted creating a new company, the Kansas City Southern. Harriman was elected a director of the reorganized company and chairman of the executive committee. Beginning April 1, 1901, control of the road was passed for a five-year period to a votingtrust equally representing Harriman and his associates and a group of steel manufacturers headed by John W. Gates. During the voting trust period significant improvements and equipment additions were made. Gross earnings rose from $4.1 million to $6.6 million, and passenger and freight productivity rose at a rate exceeding the national average. A new board of directors was elected on May 17, 1905, with Harriman

and Gates offering no opposition. The American representative of the line's Dutch stockholders became chairman of the new board of directors, which then made a sweeping change in the company's officers. Harriman soon disposed of his interest in the road.

By 1901 the Union Pacific's competition with the Great Northern and the Northern Pacific focused on the Chicago, Burlington & Quincy and access into Chicago. In 1899 Harriman offered to purchase the Burlington on behalf of the Union Pacific, and several conferences with Charles E. Perkins, president of the Burlington, followed in early 1900. Harriman offered $140 a share in cash while Perkins adamantly held out for $200 a share. Harriman considered this an impossible figure and formed a syndicate with Jacob Schiff of Kuhn, Loeb & Company, James Stillman of National City Bank, and George J. Gould to purchase Burlington stock. The price of the Burlington stock rose in the market, alerting the Great Northern and Northern Pacific interests to the Harriman attack. James Hill of the Great Northern entered into negotiations with Perkins and eventually capitulated to Perkins's price. Perkins issued a call for the stock to be sold, and 97 percent of it was presented. The Northern Pacific and Great Northern had won the battle for the Burlington. But the war was not over.

Harriman and Schiff urged Hill to give them a one-third interest in the Burlington for which they offered one-third of the purchase price. Hill rejected their offer. Harriman then decided on a counterattack; he would purchase a majority interest in the Northern Pacific, which would give him a half-interest in the Burlington.

By the close of the market on May 3, 1901, Kuhn, Loeb & Company had amassed a majority of total Northern Pacific stock but lacked about 40,000 common shares. Since the common stock could vote to retire the preferred stock this posed a potential problem. James Hill by this time had become aware that something was afoot and, upon questioning Schiff, discovered Harriman's plan. Hill cabled J. P. Morgan in Italy for authority to purchase at least 150,000 shares of Northern Pacific common after the close of business on May 4. With the pressure of the Morgan purchases Northern Pacific common advanced from 110 to 130 on May 6 and reached 149 3/4 the next day. Morgan bought no more stock after May 7. A panic in Northern Pacific stock occurred in the market during the following two days, many brokers selling stock which

Harriman during his tenure at the Union Pacific (courtesy of Union Pacific Railroad Museum)

they did not have and could not buy. Disaster was averted on May 9 by an agreement between Schiff of Kuhn, Loeb & Company and Robert Bacon of J. P. Morgan to settle with the "shorts" for $150 a share.

On the morning of May 4 Harriman was ill at his home and concerned about the shortfall in Northern Pacific common. He gave a Kuhn, Loeb & Company partner (Heinsheimer) an order to purchase 40,000 shares of Northern Pacific common. With the substantial trading in the stock that day Harriman assumed his order had been filled. On Monday he discovered that Schiff had countermanded his order, believing it unnecessary. Those 40,000 shares cost Harriman control of the Northern Pacific.

Rather than costly litigation Hill suggested a compromise which was signed May 31. Harriman and some of his associates were to be placed on the boards of the Burlington and the Northern Pacific. To prevent recurrence of the Northern Pacific struggle, Hill decided on the formation of a giant holding company for the stocks of the Great Northern, Northern Pacific, and Burlington. This was the Northern Securities Company, incorporated November 12, 1901, with a capitalization of $400 million.

Both the state of Minnesota and the federal government filed suit against the Northern Securities Company on antitrust grounds, the state losing its case and the federal government winning. Both cases were appealed to the Supreme Court. The state case was dismissed for lack of jurisdiction, but the federal case was decided against the Northern Securities Company by a vote of five to four. The Northern Securities Company was ordered to divest itself of Great Northern and Northern Pacific stock.

Divestiture could be accomplished either by returning exactly the shares originally surrendered to the Northern Securities Company or by a pro rata distribution of shares. Harriman desired the first which would leave him in control of the Northern Pacific while Hill, of course, wanted the second. With control of the Northern Securities Board Hill got his way. Harriman appealed all the way to the Supreme Court, but lost.

Harriman had lost the war for the Burlington, but with a sharp rise in stock prices in 1906 he won a great fortune. The cash realization from the stock transactions was $116.8 million on stock which had cost only $76.9 million. The Union Pacific's cash profit was $39.99 million. The profit from the stock transactions was invested by the Union Pacific in several other railroads. While this did not give the Union Pacific majority control in any case, these purchases were viewed with alarm by many. Although the purchases sharply increased the investment income of the Union Pacific, Harriman's main purpose appears to have been to forward what he called a "community of interest," whereby he could open connections or modify competition. Out of apparent defeat Harriman reaped a fortune for himself and his stockholders.

The Central Pacific Railroad between Sacramento and Ogden, built in 1869, posed an obstacle to the increased efficiency Harriman sought with reconstruction of the Union Pacific. Repeated attempts to buy the road were rebuffed by the Southern Pacific. The death of Collis P. Huntington in August 1900 presented an opportunity for Harriman to achieve his end by gaining control of the Southern Pacific.

Early in 1901 Harriman obtained authorization from the Union Pacific board of directors for issuance of $100 million of 4 percent, first mortgage, convertible bonds, which provided the means to buy control of the Southern Pacific. By mid 1901 the Union Pacific owned 45.5 percent of the outstanding Southern Pacific shares and had effective control.

Reconstruction of the Central Pacific was soon begun and completed within three years at a cost of around $22 million. Another $30 million was spent on betterments for the Southern Pacific and $41 million on new equipment. The implicit merger of the Union Pacific and Southern Pacific was widely regarded as detrimental to society because of the increased monopoly power of the combined lines. The Interstate Commerce Commission argued that the Union Pacific's control of the Southern Pacific eliminated competition and recommended that such stock ownership control of one railroad by another not be permitted and that such lines should not have common directors or officers. The government litigated Union Pacific control of the Southern Pacific and eventually won a judgment in the Supreme Court with the Union Pacific eventually being forced to divest itself of Southern Pacific stock in May 1913.

The Southern Pacific was profitable in the pre-Harriman years but was significantly more profitable during Harriman's control. In terms of passenger and freight productivity the Southern Pacific far outpaced both its pre-Harriman record and the national averages.

Harriman's attention turned from the United States to the world stage in 1905. Kuhn, Loeb & Company's floating of Japanese war bonds and Harriman's connection with the Pacific Mail Steamship Company attracted his attention to the Orient. Lloyd C. Griscom, the American ambassador to Japan, invited Harriman to visit Japan in the spring of 1905. Because of his curiosity to see the Orient and his vision of an around-the-world transportation line, Harriman accepted this invitation. The globe-belting line would include the Pacific Mail steamships from America to Japan and Port Arthur; the railroad across Manchuria, China, and Russia to a Baltic port; and steamship to New York.

The South Manchuria Railroad, the Chinese Eastern, and trackage rights on the Trans-Siberian Railway to the Baltic comprised the railroad portion of Harriman's vision. The grand plan failed in part because of popular reaction in Japan to President Roosevelt's role in the negotiations to end the war with Russia. The Japanese public felt its army had won the war but that everything was given away in the peace treaty. Also, the transfer of the South Manchuria Railroad to Japan required the consent of China, which was not forthcoming. Opposition to American influence by Baron Komura, Japanese minister of foreign affairs, was the final blow to Harriman's plans, Komura convincing his colleagues to break off negotiations with Harriman. Jacob Schiff of Kuhn, Loeb & Company visited Japan in 1906 and attempted to revive the negotiations, but Komura's opposition again carried the day.

Long-term friendly relations between Harriman and President Roosevelt soured in the fall of 1906 apparently due to Harriman's refusal to aid in Republican party fund-raising and Roosevelt's reneging on a promise made to Harriman with regard to his fund-raising for the 1904 election. This break led to Roosevelt's letter characterizing Harriman as an "undesirable citizen." It also led to the ICC investigation of the Harriman lines that concentrated on the Chicago & Alton. No charges were forthcoming from the rather sensational investigation, but Harriman's reputation was blackened in the public's eye. On Wall Street and among railroad men, there was a concern that the government would pursue a similar course with regard to other railroads. This did not happen, further supporting the appearance that this investigation was an attempt to "get" Harriman.

In 1906 one of the most dramatic episodes in the history of the Illinois Central unfolded with a contest between Harriman and his longtime friend Stuyvesant Fish. In the end Fish was ousted from the Illinois Central and Harriman's candidate, James T. Harahan, was elected president of the road.

Dissatisfaction with Fish among the directors dated from the spring of 1903. Fish had deposited $500,000 of Illinois Central money in the Trust Company of the Republic, a small and weak bank of which he was a trustee. Harriman had the money returned to the Illinois Central and smoothed over the relations with Fish.

In the summer of 1903 Fish again deposited a large sum of Illinois Central money in the Trust Company of the Republic. Fish apparently was trying to provide support for the firm which was in trouble partly because of its financing of an industrial corporation, the United States Shipbuilding Company, in which Fish also had an interest. In addition to his deposits Fish also loaned himself $1.5 million of Illinois Central money with inadequate collateral.

When Harriman returned from Europe that summer, several directors brought these matters to his attention and asked his help in deposing Fish. Harriman did not agree with the directors and loaned Fish $1.2 million to enable him to resolve his financial difficulties.

In 1904 Fish again deposited Illinois Central funds in a bank in which he was interested, the Commonwealth Trust Company, which was a successor to the Trust Company of the Republic. Harriman again counseled forbearance on the part of those directors seeking to oust Fish.

Matters came to a head in 1906 over an election to fill a vacancy on the board. Fish opposed any new director with connections to the Union Pacific. Henry W. De Forest, a director of the Southern Pacific, was nominated on October 9 by enough of the board members (seven) to fill the vacancy. Fish protested this election and at the annual meeting of October 17 voted enough proxies to elect his own choice. At the next directors' meeting, on November 7, Harahan was elected president in place of Fish.

Fish was greatly embittered by what he considered the great injustice done to him. He campaigned strongly for an investigation of Harriman's management of the Illinois Central during the next year and a half. The stockholders of the road provided the final verdict on March 3, 1908, when Fish was defeated for reelection as a director. This defeat ended Fish's more than thirty years with the Illinois Central.

In the spring of 1908 it appeared that a receivership for the Erie Railroad Company was inevitable, and a conference was held on April 7 in J. P. Morgan's library to discuss what could be done. Harriman was concerned that receivership for the Erie would precipitate a new Wall Street panic, causing failure of other companies and prolongation of the business recession. He offered to put up half the $5.5 million needed if the others, which included J. P. Morgan & Company, would put up the remainder. The others refused to put up any part of the funds. Harriman offered to put up the entire amount if the others would lend it to him. This was also refused. The next day Harriman put up the entire amount which he borrowed from the National City Bank.

When news of Harriman's action became known, the stock market rallied strongly with Erie stocks leading the way. Harriman's role in saving the Erie was widely hailed by the financial community and eventually by the general public. His action led to the improvement of his public image during the remainder of his life.

Harriman was seriously ill in the summer of 1909 when he went to Europe. He returned in early September to his new mansion at Arden where he died on September 9, the day before his thirtieth wedding anniversary. The cause of death is thought to have been cancer of the stomach.

Harriman was a devoted family man, his children, especially Mary, traveling with him on many of his trips. He instilled a sense of public service in his children; his daughter Mary served in the Franklin Roosevelt administration, and his son Averell worked as a distinguished diplomat under several presidents. His relationship with his wife, Mary, was also very close. Business was interrupted on many occasions to send a message or flowers to Mary. His estate of around $70 million was left entirely to her by a simple will of about eighty words.

Edward Henry Harriman was the greatest railroad rebuilder and organizer of his (and probably any) age. He left a railroad system with significant improvement in capacity and productivity. His ideas about competition and organization of the nation's railroads were eighty years ahead of the time. In the 1970s and 1980s the nation's railroads are being reorganized, with the blessing of the ICC, in the fashion prescribed by Harriman eighty years ago.

References:

Bernard Baruch, *Baruch: My Own Story* (New York: C. G. Buroyne, 1911);

James C. Bonbright, *Railroad Capitalization* (New York: AMS Press, 1969);

Carlton J. Corliss, *Main Line of Mid-America: The Story of the Illinois Central* (New York: Creative Age Press, 1950);

Stuart Daggett, *Railroad Reorganization* (Boston: Houghton Mifflin, 1908);

Daggett, *Chapters on the History of the Southern Pacific* (New York: Ronald Press, 1922);

H. J. Eckenrode and Pocohontas Wight Edmunds, *E. H. Harriman: The Little Giant of Wall Street* (New York: Greenberg, 1933);

Samuel Morse Felton, "He Never Commanded–Yet He Never Forgot Good Work," *System* (March 1923);

William H. Goetzman and Kay Sloan, *Looking Far North* (New York: Viking Press, 1982);

Jonathan Hughes, *The Vital Few* (Boston: Houghton Mifflin, 1966);

Edward Hungerford, *The Story of the Baltimore & Ohio Railroad*, vol. 2 (New York: Putnam's, 1928);

Hungerford, *Men of Erie: A Story of Human Effort* (New York: Random House, 1946);

Interstate Commerce Commission, "The Consolidation and Combination of Carriers: Relations Between Carriers and Community of Interest Therein: Their Rates; Facilities and Practices," *Interstate Commerce Commission Reports*, vol. 12 (Washington, D.C.: U.S. Government Printing Office, 1908);

Interstate Commerce Commission, *Report on the Statistics of the Railroads of the United States* (Washington, D.C.: U.S. Government Printing Office, annual volumes);

Otto H. Kahn, *Edward Henry Harriman* (New York: C. G. Buroyne, 1911);

Kahn, *Of Many Things* (New York: Boni & Liveright, 1926);

George Kennan, *Edward Henry Harriman: A Biography* (Boston: Houghton Mifflin, 1922);

Kennan, *The Chicago & Alton Case: A Misunderstood Transaction* (Garden City, N.Y.: Country Life Press, 1916);

Kennan, *E. H. Harriman's Far Eastern Plans* (Garden City, N.Y.: Country Life Press, 1917);

Kennan, *Misrepresentation in Railroad Affairs* (Garden City, N.Y.: Country Life Press, 1916);

Kennan, *The Salton Sea: An Account of Harriman's Fight With the Colorado River* (New York: Macmillan, 1917);

Julius Kruttschnitt, "Three Business Giants for Whom I Worked," *American Magazine*, 921 (November 1921): 36-37;

Robert A. Lovett, *Forty Years After: An Appreciation of the Genius of Edward Henry Harriman* (New York: Newcomen Society, 1949);

Albro Martin, *James J. Hill and the Opening of the Northwest* (New York: Oxford University Press, 1976);

Edward S. Mead, *Corporate Finance* (New York: Appleton, 1914);

Thomas Warner Mitchell, "The Growth of the Union Pacific and Its Financial Operations," *Quarterly Journal of Economics* (August 1907): 569-612;

John Moody, *The Masters of Capital* (New Haven: Yale University Press, 1920);

Moody, *The Railroad Builders* (New Haven: Yale University Press, 1920);

John Muir, *Edward Henry Harriman* (Garden City, N.Y.: Doubleday, Page, 1912);

Richard C. Overton, *Burlington Route: A History of the Burlington Lines* (New York: Alfred A. Knopf, 1965);

Henry V. Poor, *Manual of the Railroads of the United States* (New York: H. V. and H. W. Poor, annual volumes);

William Z. Ripley, *Railroads, Finance and Organization* (New York: Appleton, 1920);

Carl Snyder, "Harriman: Colossus of Roads," *Review of Reviews*, 35 (January 1907): 37-48;

Frank H. Spearman, *Strategy of the Great Railroads* (New York: Scribner's, 1904);

Nelson Trottman, *History of the Union Pacific* (New York: Ronald Press, 1923);

Lloyd Wendt and Herman Kogan, *Bet A Million: The Story of John W. Gates* (New York: Bobbs-Merrill, 1948);

Neill C. Wilson and Frank J. Taylor, *Southern Pacific: The Roaring Story of a Fighting Railroad* (New York: McGraw-Hill, 1952).

Archives:

There is no large body of Harriman personal papers in existence. Some papers can be found at Arden Farms at Arden, New York. Another file exists at the Harriman offices at 63 Wall Street in New York City. The voluminous research papers of George Kennan are at Arden Farms under the care of the Orange County Historical Society. It has long been believed that Harriman's letters and personal papers were destroyed in the Equitable Building fire of 1912. This is not true. A considerable body of Harriman papers (including his letters from 1898 to 1909) did exist at Arden as of 1921. About 100 packages of Harriman papers were sent to storage at an unspecified garage in 1921. The present location of most of these papers is not known although a few of those sent to the garage are now at Arden Farms. Harriman letters can also be found in the Archives of the Illinois Central Railroad at the Newberry Library in Chicago and in the Union Pacific collection at the Nebraska State Archives in Lincoln, Nebraska.

Herman Haupt

(March 26, 1817-December 13, 1905)

by James A. Ward

University of Tennessee at Chattanooga

CAREER: Civil engineer, Pennsylvania Railroad (PRR) (1847-1849); transportation superintendent, PRR (1849-1850); general superintendent, PRR (1850-1852); chief engineer, PRR (1853-1855); contractor, Hoosac Tunnel (1856-1862); brigadier general, U.S. Military Railroads (1862-1863); investor, inventor, and consulting engineer (1865-1905); general manager, PRR interests in South (1872-1876); chief engineer, Tidewater Pipeline (1876-1879); general manager, Northern Pacific (1881-1883); president, Dakota & Great Southern (1884-1885).

Herman Haupt was a prominent, first-generation, formally trained engineer who helped to lead the United States to the forefront of the industrial world. He was active in railway construction and operation, became a partner of J. Edgar Thomson and Thomas A. Scott, the driving forces behind the Pennsylvania Railroad, and made a modest fortune. He relished a challenge and oversaw an attempt to bore a 4½-mile tunnel through Massachusett's Hoosac Mountain using black powder and hand drills. That effort and its ultimate failure obsessed Haupt, consumed his fortune, and occupied much of his attention for the remainder of his life; it marked his only major failure in an otherwise illustrious career. When not distracted by the tunnel, he organized the North's railways for military use and helped the Union to win its victory. Exceedingly bright, Haupt was close to being a mechanical genius; he was less skillful, however, with his financial investments.

Born to Jacob Haupt and Margaretta Wiall Snyder on March 26, 1817, Haupt entered a family of modest means. His bookkeeper and farmer father was a strict disciplinarian who died when Herman was only ten. His mother, through a family connection, won an appointment for Herman to West Point; he graduated in 1835, twenty-ninth in a class of fifty-six. By that time his personality was

Herman Haupt (Gale International Portrait Gallery)

well formed. Publicly he was brusque, oftentimes stubborn, and usually inflexible. Privately, he was often indecisive and tender to his wife, Anna Cecilia, whom he married in 1838, and their eleven children. His relationships with equals and subordinates alike were often cold, quarrelsome, and bitter.

Soon after graduation Haupt left the army and worked on location projects for various railways in Pennsylvania. After the 1837 depression halted such operations he taught at Gettysburg College until 1847. While there he wrote his famous *General Theory of Bridge Construction*, which became the standard text on the subject until the end

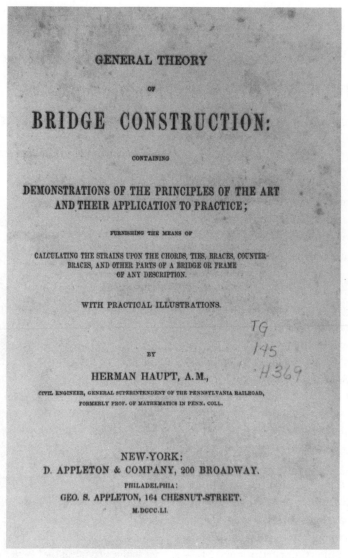

Title page of Haupt's General Theory of Bridge Construction *(1851)*

of the century. When the Pennsylvania Railroad was chartered in 1847, J. Edgar Thomson, its chief engineer, hired Haupt as an assistant engineer but named him in 1849 the company's first superintendent of transportation, with the responsibility for organizing the Transportation Department. In 1850 he was promoted to general superintendent, one of the most powerful positions in the state of Pennsylvania because of the large number of jobs it controlled. As a member of the company's inner circle, he invested in timberlands, plank roads, sawmills, and coal mines, and by 1852, when he resigned after a furious fight with the board of directors over Thomson's authority, he was a fairly wealthy man. Thomson recalled him six months later to become the Pennsylvania's chief engineer, and Haupt

finished the road to a quality that eventually earned it the sobriquet of "the Standard Railroad of the World."

Haupt left the Pennsylvania in 1856 for the Hoosac Mountain Project in Massachusetts. The venture was fraught with technical difficulties, but it was the political problems that were Haupt's undoing. Not a gregarious man and often disdainful of political niceties, he fell afoul of Hoosac opponents from the very first. Moreover, his progress through the mountain was slower than he had anticipated, which delayed the state's payments and threw him back on his own resources. For six years he assaulted the mountain, hounded by angry creditors and sniping politicians. The Massachusetts legislature finally relieved him of his contract in 1862, leaving him with a mass of debts and legal difficulties.

A bridge over the Potomac Creek, built by Haupt and his men during the Civil War in less than seventy-two hours (photograph by Mathew Brady, courtesy of the National Archives)

Ironically, Haupt achieved his greatest triumphs soon afterward when he took over the Union's military railroads, nominally under Gen. Daniel C. McCallum, organized them, and welded them into a potent fighting force. He increased the capacity of captured Southern single-track lines, developed devices for destroying track and rebuilding bridges, and forged an efficient corps of military engineers that later enabled Gen. William Sherman to wreak havoc while on his march through Georgia. His training in operations and technical matters enabled him to move masses of troops expeditiously at the Second Battle of Bull Run and to reconnect Gen. George Meade with his supply lines at Gettysburg. For his heroic service Haupt was brevetted a brigadier general, but he refused to sign his commission because he frequently needed to attend to his political and financial troubles in Massachusetts. Secretary of War Edwin Stanton insisted in 1863 that Haupt sign his commission, and when he refused Stanton ordered him out of the army. Haupt later remarked that he was the only man "ever guilty of the crime of refusing to be made a general."

The Hoosac's cloud, in the form of lawsuits and debts, hung over Haupt for the next twenty years as he moved from job to job. After the war he tried to perfect a rock drill operated by compressed air and even won a gold medal for the machine at the 1867 Paris exposition. The drill did not attain its expected financial success, however, and Haupt, instead, purchased a 108,000-acre plot in western Virginia where he operated a resort, Mountain Lake. In 1872 his old friend on the Pennsylvania, Tom Scott, tapped Haupt as general manager to complete and operate a road, the Atlanta & Richmond Air Line, between Richmond and Atlanta. Haupt fought to keep the line solvent through the 1873 depression, a Pennsylvania stockholders' rebellion, and John Edgar Thomson's death; in 1875 the Pennsylvania decided to pull out of its southern adventure. At the end of the year Haupt turned his attention to building an oil pipeline from the Pennsylvania oil fields to the Atlantic Coast in opposition to Standard Oil and the Pennsylvania Railroad. Haupt did most of the engineering, and despite a constant shortage of funds and political, and sometimes armed, opposition from entrenched interests, he completed the world's first long-distance pipeline on May 29, 1879.

Afterward he worked as a consulting engineer on compressed air trolleys, steam heating, and steam cooking devices until Henry Villard chose him in 1881 to be general manager of the Northern

Pacific. Villard's financial collapse, soon after the road's grand opening in 1883, cost Haupt his job just as he finally recovered some of his Hoosac investment at only eight cents on the dollar. For a short time he tried to build his own railroad, the Dakota & Great Southern and, failing in that, consulted with compressed air companies, proposed novel Mississippi River levees, and invested in a condensed milk process. Haupt died of heart failure on December 13, 1905, after leaving a meeting in which he had learned that he had lost his money in the condensed milk scheme; Borden later purchased the process. Haupt is buried in Philadelphia's West Laurel Hill Cemetery.

Publications:

Hints on Bridge Construction (N.p., 1842);

Patent Improved Lattice Bridge (Philadelphia, 1842);

General Theory of Bridge Construction (New York: Appleton, 1851);

Documents Referring to the Controversy Between the Canal Commissioners of the State of Pennsylvania and the Harrisburg and Lancaster and the Pennsylvania Railroad Companies (Philadelphia: T. K. and P. G. Collins, 1852);

Pennsylvania Railroad Company (Philadelphia: Collins, 1852);

Pennsylvania Railroad Company (Philadelphia: Crissy & Markley, 1854);

A Consideration of the Plans Proposed for the Improvement of the Ohio River (Philadelphia: T. K. and P. G. Collins, 1855);

The Main Line of the Pennsylvania State Improvements (Philadelphia, 1855);

The Coal Business on the Pennsylvania Railroad (Philadelphia: T. K. and P. G. Collins, 1857);

Tunnel Loan Bill (Boston: A. Mudge, 1859);

Rise and Progress of the Hoosac Tunnel (Cambridge, Mass., 1862);

Suspension of Work on the Hoosac Tunnel (N.p., 1862);

Memorial of Herman Haupt (Boston, 1863);

Military Bridges (New York: Van Nostrand, 1864);

For the Committee on Hoosac Tunnel, and Troy and Greenfield Railroad (Boston, 1866);

Tunneling By Machinery (Philadelphia: Leisenring, 1867);

Hoosac Tunnel: On What Plan, In What Time, At What Cost, and By What Means Can It Be Finished? (Boston: Wright & Potter, 1868);

Facts and Figures Concerning the Hoosac Tunnel (Boston, 1869);

The Hoosac Tunnel (Boston: Wright & Potter, 1869);

Shenandoah Valley Railroad Company (Philadelphia: Helfenstein & Lewis, 1870);

Co-Operative Colonization (Philadelphia: W. Syckelmore, 1872);

Pennsylvania Transportation Company: Its Proposed Pipe Line to Tide Water (Philadelphia, 1876);

Report on the System of the Holly Steam Combination Company Limited, of Lockport, N.Y. (Lockport, N.Y.: Union, 1879);

Report on the Meigs Elevated Railroad (Cambridge, Mass., 1881);

The Yellowstone National Park (New York: J. M. Stoddart, 1883);

Report and Estimates For an Outer Harbor at Padre Island, Coast of Texas (Washington, D.C., 1891);

Street Railway Motors (Philadelphia: Baird, 1893);

Rapid Transit in New York (Washington, D.C.: Adams, 1894);

Relative Cost of Steam, Compressed Air and Electricity For the Operation of the Railroads (Washington, D.C., 1894);

Compressed Air for City and Suburban Traction (N.p., 1897);

Reminiscences of General Herman Haupt (Milwaukee: Wright & Joys, 1901);

The Problem of the Mississippi (New Orleans, 1904);

Herman's Wooing: A Parody on Hiawatha (Philadelphia: W. Syckelmore, n.d.);

Long Distance Transmission of Power (New York, n.d.).

References:

Francis A. Lord, *Lincoln's Railroad Man: Herman Haupt* (Rutherford, N.J.: Fairleigh Dickinson University Press, 1969);

James A. Ward, *That Man Haupt: A Biography of Herman Haupt* (Baton Rouge: Louisiana State University Press, 1973).

Archives:

Material concerning Herman Haupt is located in the Herman Haupt Papers of Yale University Library, New Haven, Connecticut.

James J. Hill

(September 16, 1838-May 29, 1916)

by Albro Martin

Bradley University

CAREER: Partner, James J. Hill & Company, and other partnerships; president, Northwestern Fuel Co. (1877-1879); general manager (1879-1882), vice-president (1881-1882), and president (1882-1889) St. Paul, Minneapolis & Manitoba Railway; president, Great Northern Railway (1889-1907); chairman, Great Northern Railway (1907-1912).

James Jerome Hill, major railroad builder and contributor to the economic development of the Northwest, was born September 16, 1838, in Rockwood, Eramosa Township, about fifty miles west of Toronto, Ontario, Canada, and died in St. Paul, Minnesota, on May 29, 1916. He was one of three surviving children of James and Ann Dunbar Hill, who emigrated from Armagh, County Ulster, in 1829 and County Limerick, in what is now the Irish Republic, in 1828, respectively. Upon marriage in 1833 the elder James Hill received fifty acres of land from his father, and it was upon this farm that the family lived until his death. Young James Hill was fourteen when his father died, and it was at this time that his formal education, having been well advanced by attendance at the Reverend William Wetherald's academy and omnivorous reading on his own, stopped.

Ann Hill moved the family to Guelph, a larger town a few miles west of Rockwood. There Hill found work in a country store but three years later, having saved a few hundred dollars, he set out for the United States. Visiting the docks of New York cured him of any lingering romantic notions about going to sea, while the approach of the depression of 1857-1859 made other opportunities scarce. Rather than returning home, he said, "I took a notion to go and see St. Paul."

"Pig's Eye," as St. Paul had been called only a few years before, was a raw, wooden city of the future, mushrooming on the banks of the Mississippi River just a few miles downstream from the falls of

James J. Hill, 1910

St. Anthony, the future site of Minneapolis. Steamboats ruled transportation in the 1850s but they could not go above the falls, and communication with the northern country, including the promising but still vacant Red River valley, was by oxcart. Even before his steamboat arrived in St. Paul, the gregarious lad had secured a job with Burnson, Lewis and White, agents for the Dubuque Packet Company, which quickly recognized in his ability to write a fair hand, "cipher," and do simple bookkeeping, talents that were exceedingly rare on the frontier. No such thing as "through" freight transportation existed in the Northwest in the 1850s.

Agents at each transshipment point had to shepherd the consignee's goods from one conveyance to another. Such work occupied Hill for the next several years and taught him the practical transportation needs of the Northwest, knowledge which would gain him a respectful hearing by men with money to lend during the rest of his life. "The work is easy, all done in an office," he wrote his grandmother Mary Riggs Hill, "and I have from six o'clock every evening to walk around and enjoy myself." To Hill, that meant observing every phase of the new land's growth.

Agriculture–mainly the growing of breadstuffs–and flour milling were already beginning to replace fur trading as St. Paul's main economic base. St. Anthony, soon renamed Minneapolis, developed a renowned flour milling industry on the waterpower at the falls; river traffic grew apace, and by the end of the Civil War transfer of freight from boats at water level to wagons up on the bluff had become an expensive nuisance. (Hill was refused an active part in the Civil War owing to his blindness in one eye, a condition which resulted from a bow and arrow accident he had at the age of nine.) Always ready with liquid savings, Hill now struck out on his own, acquiring waterfront property and building on it a commodious warehouse that thrived from the beginning as the new railroads replaced the wagons, and the long process of westward railroad expansion began in earnest.

In 1867 Hill married Mary Theresa Mehegan, the devout Irish Catholic daughter of one of St. Paul's numerous Irish immigrants of the 1840s. For the next twenty years, a child would be born to the couple approximately every two years–six girls (one daughter died in infancy) and three boys.

Immigration to the rich prairie lands of the Red River valley (a river that flows northward) and the eastern counties of what would become North and South Dakota brought thousands of new settlers in the postwar years. For them the oxcarts would not do, and although the Red, a shallow stream at best and useless in the dry season, required boats that could "navigate on a heavy dew," steamboats soon made their appearance. Hill was determined to have a role in this northward expansion, but first he wanted to see for himself just what the new lands promised. Leaving behind his pregnant wife and baby daughter in 1870, Hill struck out, with a half-breed as guide, to explore the country. It was an exciting trip, full of harrowing episodes of swimming across ice-choked streams, outrunning hostile Indians, resetting his guide's dislocated shoulder, and watching the Fenian "rebellion" just over the Canadian border at Pembina. The fertility of the soil, evidenced, he said, by grass growing lushly in the previous year's oxcart tracks, convinced Hill that better transportation had to be provided and that navigation of the Red had to be an exclusively American affair.

While the railroad advanced slowly northward, Hill, in partnership with his old friend Norman Kittson, put two steamboats in regular service to Winnipeg on the Red River. Kittson, pioneer of the north country, had defied the Hudson Bay Company's monopoly by offering the Indians and half-breeds a better price for their furs at his border trading post. His prestige from St. Paul northward was incalculable, and soon the steamboat enterprise, named Kittson's Red River Transportation Company, turned aside all competition and added two more boats. The handsome profits of the enterprise would form much of the seed capital for Hill's move into railroads when their time came.

With rail transportation open between St. Paul and Duluth, on Lake Superior, at the end of the 1860s, it became feasible to import eastern coal via lake steamer from Buffalo or Cleveland, transferring it at Duluth to railroad cars. But this was a long way from creating a new business, and Hill saw a new opportunity opening up, one that would take know-how, substantial investment, and the resolution to balance volume of coal imported, number of dealers, and prices charged: in other words, organization. Hill provided it. He recognized very early that Pennsylvania anthracite, a premium heating coal, was the product that would yield the profits to support a worthwhile business. The St. Paul coal business needed sound, prosperous dealers who knew what they were doing, had the capital to provide the community with the coal-handling facilities required, and could be depended upon for a sure supply during Minnesota's subzero winters. The lure of quick profits, however, attracted dealers who cut prices and gave poor service, sometimes substituting poorer coal for the anthracite people wanted.

Meanwhile, Hill had built a strong rapport with the regional sales managers of anthracite companies like Lehigh Valley and Lackawanna in Chicago, and he got their support to meet the price-cutters head-on. When the struggle ended, most of the coal business in the Twin Cities (which in-

James J. Hill, Howard Elliott, president of the Northern Pacific Railroad, and Louis W. Hill, Sr., at Billings, Montana, October 16, 1909

cluded the hinterland for as far as the expanding railroads ran) had been consolidated into a single enterprise, the Northwestern Fuel Company, of which Hill was an important stockholder and unquestioned leader. Hill's gains in the coal business, however, would soon find their way into railroads.

The severe depression of 1873-1877 saw the nation in ferment, complicated by the indecisive election of 1876, and many railroads, especially half-completed ones like the St. Paul & Pacific and the Northern Pacific, became insolvent. Construction on the St. Paul & Pacific, Minnesota's pioneer railroad, had halted halfway down the Red River valley, and connection at the Canadian border with a line of the new Canadian Pacific slowly advancing down from Winnipeg seemed as far from realization as ever. Meanwhile, a steady influx of emigrants arrived, not only from Europe and the eastern United States but also from eastern Canada. The latter made their way through the United States south of the barrier of the Great Lakes (which deprived Canada of a midwest), on their way to the new province of Manitoba. Because the

steamboats could not go down the river until the ice was out in April, the settlers had to wait an entire year—a drain on their scarce capital—to put in a crop. Hill tirelessly explained to all who would listen, as the depression slowly gave way to better times, that a railroad would dramatically reduce the cost of populating the new land.

Making his way through St. Paul once a year en route to the Manitoba frontier was Donald Smith, a perceptive Scotsman who was head of the Hudson Bay Company in North America. Hill's ideas for taking over the St. Paul & Pacific and completing it to the border, acquiring the land grant in the process, came in part from Smith, and the two of them worked out a plan for raising the initial capital. Norman Kittson lent his prestige to the undertaking, which enhanced the chances of disarming local opposition. Smith thought his longtime friend and associate in Canadian economic development, George Stephen, could find English investors willing to put up the money on the strength of Hill's analysis of the financial opportunity before them and both men's rosy predictions of the traffic that would be

James J. Hill, 1916

they could scrape up enough collateral for a bank loan, what bank would lend on such a proposition except to an insider? Stephen was an insider, and he bravely faced the grumbling of his board of directors, who resented Stephen's cutting of the recent quarterly dividend. They approved the loan and never had cause to regret it.

Details of the financial arrangements were worked out with a vital fifth member who, because he was also trustee of the St. Paul & Pacific mortgage and representative in the United States of the Dutch investors, had to remain as inconspicuous as possible. He was John S. Kennedy of New York, yet another Scotsman, who had made his fortune in supplying railroads with the vast quantities of rails and other iron products demanded; in the Pennsylvania iron business as the Bessemer steel process appeared on the horizon; and in private banking. The four declared "associates" risked large portions of their capital in offering it as collateral for the loan; Hill risked his stock in the steamboat company and in the fuel company, which together accounted for nearly all of his estimated $100,000 net worth. But his real contribution was far more valuable. As the enormous scope of the task of completing the railroad in 1878, thereby saving the land grant, became apparent, they looked expectantly to Hill to carry it through. It was a hectic summer and fall but ultimately complete success was theirs. The Great Northern Railway, into which this "tidy little property" grew, never had a federal land grant, but the lands granted by the state of Minnesota proved a valuable asset during the early growth years of the new railroad.

The railroad was reorganized as the St. Paul, Minneapolis & Manitoba, and by the end of 1879 Hill was a rich man, the owner of a sheaf of second mortgage bonds, and one-fifth of the new common stock, securities which had claims only on the profits of the new company, which grew rapidly as prosperity returned. He became general manager at a salary of $15,000 a year and in 1882 assumed the presidency. For the rest of his life the railroad and the country through which it ran would be his main concern. The next decade was a whirlwind of activity, as he rebuilt, reequipped, and judiciously expanded the railroad.

forthcoming as prosperity returned. Stephen, also a Scotsman, had immigrated to Canada in his teens and entered the dry goods business. He reinvested his profits successively in worsted mills, rolling mills producing rails for Canada's expanding railroads, and a company that made cars and locomotives for them. As president of the Bank of Montreal when Hill first met him in 1877, he was concentrating on guiding it through the depression.

After a trip to Minnesota, and in spite of the obvious ravages of drought and grasshoppers during the summer of 1877, Stephen was convinced that Smith and Hill knew their business and agreed to put the proposition to the English branch of Morton, Rose and Company, investment bankers. But on Christmas Eve in 1877, Stephen returned with the gloomy news of the Englishmen's rejection of such a risky proposition. Thus 1878 became the year of decision for Hill and his associates. Even if

In his first years as a railroad man, Hill participated in the syndicate George Stephen had organized (at the behest of Canada's Conservative prime minister, John A. MacDonald) to complete Can-

continental U.S. freight (by means of its steamers running down from Vancouver to U.S. ports), and Hill's involvement may be considered one of his few major strategic miscalculations.

The 1880s saw the most rapid expansion of the American railroad network in our history, a near-excrescence which produced a jerry-built financial structure that Hill knew could not withstand the buffets of hard times that he saw in the near future. The decade also saw the maturing of a host of discontents arising from the dislocations brought about by the transportation revolution. Chief among the abuses of which railroads were accused were extortionate rates, sharing traffic and/or receipts to keep competing railroads profitable, inconsistent rates for long and short hauls, and discriminatory rebating which severely lowered posted rates for favored customers. Hill knew that rate levels, in fact, were in an almost uncontrollable decline due to rate cutting. (By 1890 even the Interstate Commerce Commission was alarmed at the depression in rates.) Hill sometimes participated in pools but in general believed that they were of little value even in the short run and doomed to early failure. He was right, as the crisis of the 1890s would shortly prove, and he was right about the inevitability of consolidation into strong systems. He knew the arguments in favor of charging more, sometimes, for a short haul than a longer one but wasted little time on such an emotion-charged cause. As for rebating, like most railroad men he condemned it, agreeing with Stephen that nobody wins in a rate war; but he practiced it sometimes when competition for carrying the wheat crop was intense. Although he went so far as to prepare a long, erudite statement for the Minnesota legislature on the railroad problem, he soon realized that the economic merits of such a political subject were of no consequence and thereafter seldom participated in concerted efforts by railroad leaders to influence legislation.

Much of Hill's strength came from the confidence he inspired in wealthy easterners on his frequent trips to New York. He invited men like D. Willis James, Samuel Thorne, and Jacob Schiff, of New York, and Chicago's Marshall Field to serve on his board; and was, in turn, invited to serve on the board of the Chase National Bank, soon to occupy a major role in American banking. Some of his strongest allies, however, were Bostonians like John Murray Forbes, de facto leader of the Boston State Street interests. This group controlled

Hill at Jekyll Island, Georgia, February 1916

ada's first transcontinental railroad, the Canadian Pacific. Hill, who knew the bleak, rocky country north of Lake Superior, had seen the Canadian Pacific as running through the United States from the lake to the end of the St. Paul, Minneapolis & Manitoba at the border. The extension of the Canadian Pacific westward from Winnipeg would in turn give the Manitoba road the western connection that Hill had long realized was vital. For this reason he persuaded Stephen to choose the shortest possible route, which meant one farther south than originally planned. But the Canadian Pacific was undertaken more as an instrument of Canadian statecraft than of Canadian commerce, and MacDonald insisted that every mile be on Canadian soil. Thereupon Hill bowed out, but not before he had left his mark on Canada's great project by recruiting its ultimate builder, William C. Van Horne, to be its general manager. In later years the Canadian Pacific became a serious competitor of Hill's roads for trans-

millions of dollars of railroad and industrial securities, including the Chicago, Burlington & Quincy Railroad, whose president, Charles Perkins, became Hill's close friend. In 1885 Hill, with vital help from Kennedy, persuaded the Bostonians to take a large stock interest in the Manitoba Road, and he and friends invested heavily in the Burlington's subsidiary that was building a freight line between Chicago and the Twin Cities. The alliance marks, if any one thing does, Hill's attainment of the stature and substance to become a transcontinental railroad builder.

Hill had realized almost from the beginning that a midwestern railroad, if it did not acquire absolute control of a Pacific Coast extension in those days of low construction costs, would never be able to compete in the rough days ahead. The subsequent histories of the North Western, the Milwaukee, and the Rock Island roads bear him out. He also knew it was vital to attain some degree of independence from the eastern-based railroads (chiefly the New York Central and the Pennsylvania), and some freedom from the congested rail transfer facilities at Chicago. He achieved these goals by building a direct connection to Superior, Wisconsin, on Lake Superior and establishing a fleet of lake steamers with dockage in Buffalo. But it was westward that he turned in the late 1880s.

The Pacific extension of the Manitoba Road (renamed the Great Northern in 1889 simply because Hill felt it had a solid, English ring to it) is considered the grand climax of his career, although it is as a molder of systems that he attained his most influential position in American transportation. Without a land grant beyond the boundary of Minnesota and paying market price for Indian reservation land as he went, Hill insisted upon finding the best route because, as he said, one can always improve a railroad's roadbed and rails later on, but one cannot change the route, and if someone else finds a better route and builds on it later, you will wake up to find yourself no longer the low-cost producer—and Hill was determined to be the low-cost producer come what may. The future bore him out: by 1900 rates of less than a cent per ton per mile were in sight, and Hill preached that rock-bottom transcontinental rates were more likely to be provided by rails than by a Panama Canal.

As the rails crept westward Hill agonized over the unsolved problem of where the railroad would cross the Continental Divide, the Rocky Mountains,

and Washington State's equally forbidding Cascades. A heroic young engineer, John Stevens, later to make his great mark in rescuing the faltering Panama Canal project, found an ideal pass across the divide—the Marias Pass—and a usable one in the Cascades that was named for him. (An early tunnel at the summit of the Stevens Pass, built in Hill's day, was replaced in the 1920s by one of the longest tunnels in the world.) Meanwhile, Hill sternly kept to two resolutions he had adopted years before: any man who speculated in property values along the Great Northern right-of-way, while working for the railroad, was instantly fired; and no feature of the line would be named for Hill. It was all strictly business. "We do not care enough for scenery to spend a large sum developing it," he said.

Staggering as the task of building a railroad to the Pacific Ocean was, it did not exhaust Hill's energies. Among the economic leaders of the nation in this era he is almost unique in the degree of domesticity that surrounded him. Never wishing to reside anywhere but St. Paul (although he spent a few days a year in an elegant mansion he bought at 8 East 65th Street, New York), he and Mrs. Hill reared their family of six daughters and three sons according to the standards of a prosperous midwestern businessman, and he faithfully fulfilled his vow to see that they were reared as Roman Catholics. As the Pacific extension neared completion in 1891, he finished building the largest and finest mansion in St. Paul, on Summit Avenue overlooking the city. It had cost him half a million dollars (more like $5 million now). Built like a fortress, it gave an impression of grimness outside but inside it was airy, light, and spacious. Its outstanding feature was a large art gallery wing in which Hill's fine collection of paintings was permanently displayed and open to the public on certain days.

Hill had learned early the satisfactions of acquiring and living with the rich output of the late nineteenth century's host of talented European painters. His tastes quickly settled on painters of the Barbizon school—he always had a weakness for landscapes and scenes of bucolic life—and his collection, embracing Millet, Corot, Rousseau, Troyon, Decamp, Millaise, Constable, and Renoir, was widely celebrated. Near the end of his life he was developing a taste for social realism in such acquisitions as Daumier's "Third Class Carriage."

He was also determined to improve, if not revolutionize, upper midwestern agriculture, which he considered backward. "No man can live for 12 months on seven months' work," he declared, and he tried to persuade Minnesota and Dakota wheat farmers to supplement their cereal crops with dairy farming and livestock raising. To this end he bought and donated, or sold at nominal prices, fine-blooded breeding bulls, boars, and rams to individual farmers or local livestock cooperatives, but to little avail. Equally disappointing was his brief association with the conservation movement. At a time when population growth was believed to be a threat of famine at home, Hill preached a doctrine of sensible development of western land, based on irrigation. When conservation appeared to become the plaything of impractical men like Gifford Pinchot, or the political football of celebrated reformers like Francis J. Heney, he abandoned the movement in bitterness.

A stocky man about five feet eight inches tall with a large head and grizzled beard, Hill had a vigorous, eloquent oratorical style that pleased the audiences of farmers and farmers' wives who flocked to county fairs to hear him preach his gospel of working smarter as well as harder and of cooperation between all branches of American life. His views on education are startlingly modern today. His *bête noire* was the graded system then being introduced in the public schools, which he felt smothered excellence. He pleaded for support of private colleges, which were increasingly in competition with state universities. Above all he pleaded for more trust of big business, noting that "even a barn-raising is a combination." Mutual interests, not natural antipathies, were what counted. A railroad must carry the produce of the country through which it runs, or it will have nothing to carry. Thus extortionate rates which discouraged farming made no sense to railroad men. " You and I will be rich together, or we will be poor together," he said, "and I know what it means to be poor."

No doctrinaire foe of organized labor, he was nevertheless determined not to default on his duty to keep the railroad running, and he heartily congratulated his friend, President Grover Cleveland, for breaking the Pullman strike June 21-July 20, 1894. He may not have liked the railroad men's leader, Eugene V. Debs, but he respected him as long as he fairly represented the men's interest in higher pay instead of preaching the doctrine of socialism. The railroad and the public welfare transcended the rights of both labor and capital, Hill felt, for as he told a

group of men striking his railroad in the early 1880s, "When we are all dead and gone the sun will still shine, the rain will fall, and this railroad will run as usual."

The Great Northern had barely been completed to the coast when the bitter depression of 1893-1897 struck. These four years brought a revolution in the corporate organization and financing of American railroads, largely through reorganization by bankers like J. P. Morgan and his able lieutenants Charles H. Coster, Robert Bacon, and Charles Steele, into giant systems or "communities of interest," although seldom in formal, monolithic mergers. In the process there emerged two outstanding leaders of western railroads: James J. Hill, who, with Morgan's help, gained control of the Northern Pacific (thereby ending the Northern Pacific's propensity to build parallel lines) and in 1901 startled the nation by acquiring the Burlington railroad; and Edward H. Harriman. Hill thus dominated the northwestern railroad scene, safely tucked away, he thought, north of the Columbia River. Harriman, a newcomer to the national railroad movement, who had successfully outbid Jacob Schiff for the right to reorganize the Union Pacific in 1895 and then gone on to grasp control of the Southern Pacific, had virtually dictatorial control of all the West south of the river. (There remained as independents the weak Santa Fe, newly reorganized, and the lackluster "empire" of George Gould, Jay's son, both of which Harriman admitted he would take over if the government would let him.)

Charles Perkins, longtime leader of the Burlington, had made no bones about his strong preference for Hill instead of Harriman as a merger partner. Clearly, he recognized Hill as the more constructive of the two, even though Hill was rapidly gaining the cognomen of "empire builder" among newspapermen. Hill's preference for the Burlington over the Milwaukee, a troublesome "old maid" that Morgan pressed upon him because it seemed on the point of building an unnecessary third northern transcontinental, underscores the fact that Hill was seeking far more than the "Chicago connection" that most authorities have advanced as his reason for being willing to pay twice par value for the Burlington stock. In fact, six independent Chicago railroads stood ready to exchange freight with Hill at St. Paul. The heaviest east-west traffic in the North was between Puget Sound and the Midwest, which had huge exportable surpluses of foodstuffs

240 Summit Avenue, St. Paul, Minnesota, the Hill family home from 1891 to 1921 (courtesy of the Minnesota Historical Society)

and a growing need for the lumber of the Pacific Northwest. Harriman, in fact, had bid strongly for the Burlington and deeply resented Hill's snatching it from under his nose. Thus, as the new century began, the scene was set for a battle of the Titans.

Hill had vested one-half of the Burlington stock in his Great Northern and the other half in the Northern Pacific, which he and his associates did not control nearly so firmly. Harriman undertook to get control of the Northern Pacific through his bankers, Jacob Schiff, of Kuhn, Loeb & Company, and James Stillman, of the National City Bank, which was in turn largely controlled by Rockefeller money that was flowing into a booming New York commercial banking industry. Wall Street, always ready for a good short-sell opportunity, saw what was happening, and as the price of available stock rose rapidly many traders sold short in expectation of covering at a collapsed price when the flurry

was over. But the flurry was over all too quickly as heavy purchases by Harriman and Hill's forces dried up the supply of stock and desperate brokers found themselves with their backs to the wall. Bitterly recalling old Daniel Drew's maxim, "He who sells what isn't his'n, must pay it back or go to prison," some brokers paid as much as $1,000 per share, in informal, unrecorded floor trades during the "Northern Pacific Corner" of May 9, 1901, which for a time threatened to precipitate a nationwide financial panic.

Certain provisions in the Northern Pacific's bylaws, with which Hill was more familiar than either Harriman, Schiff, or their lawyers, gave ultimate control to the common stock, not the preferred, and the Hill forces' control of the former produced victory. The parties, aware of the glares they were getting from Washington and the nation, formed a compromise settlement and allocated stock to the terrified brokers. Out of ensuing conferences came the Northern Securities Company, a pure holding company formed solely to hold the stock of the Great Northern and the Northern Pacific (and thereby the Burlington) and assure that these great properties would never suffer another such raid.

The big new "trust" attracted great attention, particularly in the Northwest. The governor of Minnesota, Samuel R. Van Sant, saw a rare political opportunity in fighting this new threat, as he supposed it to be, to competition in western railroad traffic, but governors of the other northern tier of states refused to go along with such an obvious bid for notoriety. Another politician had better luck. "His Accidency," as disgruntled old guard politicians were calling the man who had succeeded to William McKinley's presidential chair, Theodore Roosevelt, directed his attorney general to bring suit under the Sherman Antitrust Act. Determined to be the first succeeding vice-president to win nomination and election to the presidency in his own right, Roosevelt knew that to ignore the new trust was far too risky a policy.

"Great cases, like hard cases, make bad law," wrote Roosevelt's first appointee to the U.S. Supreme Court, Oliver Wendell Holmes, in his dissenting opinion in the Northern Securities case in 1904—the first of a long succession of celebrated dissents. But Holmes was in the minority. The Supreme Court's split decision (five to four) was a landmark of antitrust policy, as it removed the holding company from immunity as emphatically as earlier decisions had removed pools and trusts. Competition had nothing to do with the case; the defendants had shown that clearly. The concentration of great power was irrelevant: the three railroads were continuing to be operated as independent companies (albeit "harmoniously" as Morgan liked to say) and whenever they should cease to be independent that would be time enough to prosecute them. What the case did have to do with was politics. This was the age of the giant mergers which capped twenty years of growing discontent with the "trusts." The Republican party was showing alarming weakness along the east-west fault line of the Civil War coalition that had given it birth. Meanwhile, Roosevelt always professed to grieve at the refusal of men like Hill to recognize that Republican unity was worth more than Northern Securities. Even Morgan was willing to accept the decision of the lower court, but Hill saw the prosecution as an in-

dictment of his life's work, which would not, in the end, be the judgment of history.

As for the Great Northern, the Northern Pacific, and the Burlington, they continued under single control, composed primarily of de facto "trustees," who were determined that the prosperity of the new twentieth century would not be marred by a resumption of the destructive competition that had marked the previous quarter of a century. Old friends had helped Hill get and hold the Burlington, men like Stephen, Smith, Kennedy, Morgan, George Fisher Baker of New York's First National Bank, and many others, and they held their stock for years thereafter, meanwhile enjoying the fruits of good management. The U.S. Supreme Court ultimately made amends by approving the formal merger of all three corporations in 1970, as the Burlington Northern Railroad.

Although Hill professed to be disenchanted with the future of railroading, as the government's hand became increasingly repressive after 1906, he was loath to quit. In 1907 he took the newly created post of chairman of the board and turned over the presidency of the Great Northwest to his second son, Louis. Acquisition of the Colorado & Southern Railroad, linking the Hill lines with the Gulf of Mexico, and construction of the Spokane, Portland & Seattle quickly followed the Northern Securities defeat. The latter was built on the north bank of the Columbia River, and its superb, heavy-duty construction made it a much better line than Harriman's on the south bank. But its route to Puget Sound, although it avoided the Cascade Mountains barrier, caught on slowly, and the line was a financial disappointment in Hill's day, although later on it would prove itself mightily. Hill's last railroad venture was a final set-to with Harriman, this time in the Deschutes River Canyon of Oregon, taking Hill deep into Southern Pacific territory. It ended, though, in joint occupation of the territory.

Philanthropy was not a major interest of Hill's. Believing in the Roman Catholic church's desperate need for a learned clergy, he endowed the St. Paul Seminary in honor of Mary Theresa Hill, but he excoriated the *Encyclopaedia Britannica* for listing him as a benefactor of the monumental Cathedral, of which he did not approve. A deep believer in the power of self-education, he also endowed the Hill Reference Library in St. Paul, which remains his most notable monument. Until the end of his life, Hill was deeply immersed in regional and national affairs, counting as friends and confidants statesmen, intellectuals, and business leaders, and when he was in New York he was widely lionized by society. His attempts to influence the outcome of the elections in the Northwest yielded few successes in his efforts to keep demagogues out of office, but he savored the stunning victory that he helped his old friend Mark Hanna give McKinley over Bryan in 1896.

A strong believer in America's destiny as a major participant in world trade, Hill had tried to keep interest in the merchant fleet alive by going into the steamship business himself, but his two steamers quickly became obsolete and never proved themselves in Pacific service. Decisions of the Interstate Commerce Commission discouraged railroads and shipping companies from establishing attractive export rates from the interior of the nation. The late nineteenth-century movement away from strength on the high seas, in favor of improvement of internal rivers and harbors, depressed him. It reflected political rather than economic realities, and he accurately forecast the disaster that would strike American export industries and agriculture if war came. When it did come, Hill turned the tide of anti-Allied sentiment in the Midwest into enthusiastic support of J. P. Morgan's 1915 Allied loan, by playing a major role in the negotiations in New York and pledging the First National Bank of St. Paul, which he had acquired, to purchase a large block of bonds.

When Hill retired from active railroading in 1912 his valedictory attracted widespread attention. "Most men who have really lived have had, in some shape, their great adventure," he said. "This railroad was mine." His last year was marked by failing health, but he was still making trips east until March of 1916. He died in St. Paul on May 29 of that year of an infection that became gangrenous.

Nothing in Hill's ancestry prepares the historian for the remarkable life that he lived. Most people like Hill who "make a difference" seem to be unique in this respect. His career illustrates well the leading theories of entrepreneurship. Ideas were al-

ways his main contribution, but they were ideas that carried with them a plan for their execution. As the American railroad system approached maturity, he gave it financial and administrative stability in a part of the nation where both had been notably missing. Detractors of "robber barons," who included Hill automatically among "malefactors of great wealth," were numerous in his last years, but none deprived him of the conviction that he and his associates had played a key role in the westward expansion of the United States. Not even development of the fabulous iron deposits of the Mesabi Range had escaped his attention after 1900, although in that project more credit goes, perhaps, to his son Louis.

Hill freely forecast the eventual consolidation of American railroads into a few large systems, a transformation which was delayed but then quickly consummated between 1970 and the mid 1980s. No department of railroading escaped Hill's expertise; he was the classic "hands-on" executive who kept intimately in touch with every aspect of his enterprises (sometimes to the confusion of subordinates) while finding time for broad cultural interests, a model family life, and major contributions to public affairs. Perhaps even more so than Harriman, who did not participate in the frontier days, Hill stands out as the last and greatest American railroad leader in the heroic era.

Publication:
James J. Hill, *Highways of Progress* (New York: Doubleday, Page, 1910).

References:
Albro Martin, *James J. Hill, and the Opening of the Northwest* (New York: Oxford University Press, 1976);
Balthasar H. Meyer, *A History of the Northern Securities Case* (Madison: University of Wisconsin, 1906);
Joseph G. Pyle, *The Life of James J. Hill*, 2 volumes (Garden City: Doubleday, Page, 1916-1917).

Archives:
Hill's papers are in the Hill Reference Library, St. Paul, Minnesota. The Great Northern Railway Company Records are at the Minnesota Historical Society, St. Paul.

Ben Holladay

(October 14, 1819-July 8, 1887)

by Carlos A. Schwantes

University of Idaho

CAREER: Trader, supplier (1846-1861); owner, Holladay Overland Mail & Express Company (1861-1866); owner, California, Oregon & Mexico Steamship Company (1864-1868); owner, North Pacific Transportation Company (1868-1876); owner, Oregon & California Railroad (1868-1876).

Organizer and financier Ben Holladay was a swashbuckling financial adventurer, a transportation czar of the old West who fashioned a far-flung empire of stagecoach and freight wagon lines, river boats and coastal steamers, and railroads. Handsome, energetic, and unscrupulous, he represents the apotheosis of the stereotypical Gilded Age business baron.

Physically, Holladay was a great bull of a man who stood over six feet tall. To many he was larger than life because of his bold and autocratic business methods: he was accused of lying to investors, juggling his books, and buying political influence. He competed vigorously and was even reputed to have staged "Indian" attacks on rival stagecoach entrepreneurs. Holladay had a compulsion toward power and to that end proved a master of exploiting human weaknesses. For example, Holladay once observed of an Oregon business rival that "I think [Joseph] Gaston can be bought out, as he is a great scoundrel and very poor." Contemporaries agreed that Holladay's public and private sins were many, but those who admired him as a builder of the American West were willing to forgive his failings.

Disdained by many as a semiliterate, boorish man, Holladay lived like royalty, hobnobbing in circles of influence. He entertained in a lavish and vulgar style and was a boisterous, coarse, and crude man fond of whiskey and gambling. Nonetheless, Holladay's was the classic rags-to-riches story: born in a log cabin on October 14, 1819, he was at the height of his power in his mid fifties, maintaining

Ben Holladay

mansions in Washington, D.C.; New York City; White Plains, New York; Portland, Oregon; and Seaside, Oregon. At his sprawling White Plains estate, where he entertained the great and near-great, Holladay maintained a herd of buffalo and a narrow-gauge railroad.

Holladay was born in Blue Lick Springs, Kentucky, one of eight sons of William and Margaret Holladay. As a youngster he moved with his parents to western Missouri where he lived until young manhood, though some accounts suggest that he ran away from home. At Weston, Missouri, a bustling frontier community on the east bank of the Missouri opposite Fort Leavenworth, he engaged in a variety of occupations: saloonkeeper, postmaster, druggist, and general store and hotel operator. In Weston in 1840 he married Notley Ann Calvert, with whom he had seven children.

At the outbreak of war with Mexico in 1846 Holladay furnished supplies for Gen. Stephen W. Kearny's Army of the West. When hostilities ended he repurchased large amounts of supplies at greatly reduced prices. In 1849 he joined with Theodore F. Warner to transport fifty wagon-loads of merchandise to Salt Lake City where the two began a mercantile business. Armed with a letter of introduction to Brigham Young from Col. Alexander W. Doniphan, a Mexican War hero and a friend to Mormons during their difficulties in Missouri, Holladay was assured of business success in Utah. He and Warner made a second trip to Salt Lake City in 1850, trading goods for a herd of cattle that they drove to California and sold for a substantial profit.

During the late 1850s Holladay's developing freight transport business was under constant pressure from the large freight firm of Russell, Majors & Waddell. As a result of some poor investments the huge firm was forced to turn to Holladay in 1860 for a cash infusion. Holladay's investment made possible the legendary and short-lived Pony Express Service. But in 1861, as a result of Indian attacks and the disruptions of civil war, Russell, Majors & Waddell became insolvent. Holladay bought the firm's constituent lines, the Central Overland California and the Pike's Peak Express Company, at auction for $100,000. He renamed it the Holladay Overland Mail & Express Company and soon began the process of consolidation, improvement, and expansion of the company's business.

Holladay employed 700 men in his 4,000-mile transportation empire that operated daily stagecoach service west of Atchison, Kansas, to Salt Lake City, and less frequent service from Salt Lake City to cities in California, Idaho, Montana, Washington, and Oregon. This complex operation demonstrated Holladay's great organizational ability and knack for picking reliable personnel. His lightning-quick and ruthless expansions earned him the title of Napoleon of the West.

During the war Holladay's business was sustained by two major sources of revenue: federal mail contracts which brought in annual revenues of over $1 million, and west-bound passenger traffic which generated similar funds. Holladay lost over $1 million during the 1864-1865 Indian uprisings on the Plains. Although he petitioned the government for reimbursement of his losses, Holladay received no payment.

His stage empire reached its greatest extent in early 1866 when he acquired his competitor, the Butterfield Overland Dispatch. But only a few months later, on November 1, 1866, the shrewd Holladay sold his staging business to Wells, Fargo & Company for $1.5 million in cash, several thousand shares of Wells, Fargo stock, and a directorship in the express firm. He had correctly foreseen the demise of the overland stagecoach.

Holladay already had become heavily involved in another form of transportation; in 1861 he had acquired several ships from the Pacific Mail Steamship Company and three years later organized the California, Oregon & Mexico Steamship Company. In 1868 he merged his steamship operations into the North Pacific Transportation Company, which operated along the Pacific coast from Sitka, Alaska, to Mexico and west to Australia.

In August 1868 Holladay traveled from California to Oregon, where he used his vast financial resources to win control of several Willamette Valley railroads. He perceived an opportunity to make millions of dollars developing the remote, but resource rich, Oregon country. To that end he distributed money and favors lavishly, subsidizing newspapers, hiring lawyers, and purchasing politicians. John H. Mitchell, U.S. Senator from Oregon for twenty years, is alleged to have quipped that "Ben Holladay's politics are my politics and what Ben Holladay wants I want." Holladay, who bragged openly of his control of the press and his dominance of Oregon, introduced the Pacific Northwest to the era labeled "the great barbecue."

In 1868 two companies were competing to build railway lines on opposite sides of the Willamette River to develop the river valley's vast resources. Holladay sided with the east side company against its west side rival. During the 1868 legislative session in Salem, he entertained lavishly and used his finances to persuade the Oregon legislature; for $35,000 in graft he purchased legislation enabling him to wrest a federal grant of 3.8 million acres of public land from the west side railroad. Never had Oregon seen such a bold display of financial power. Not only did Holladay's company receive the grant, but his Oregon & California

Railroad soon acquired the defeated west side rival, the Oregon Central.

To raise money for railway construction, Holladay recklessly sold bonds at 60 to 75 percent of par value. By 1873 $11 million of these bonds had been acquired by English and German investors. With these expensive funds Holladay increased construction until 240 miles of track were built and the federal land grant secured. The Oregon & California completed a line south from Portland to Roseburg in 1873 and together with the Oregon Central settled new country by promoting immigration to Oregon.

To eliminate the threat of steamboat competition on the Willamette River, Holladay purchased the People's Transportation Company in 1871 and thus brought nine more steamships into the fold of the North Pacific Transportation Company empire, which he subsequently reorganized as the Oregon Steamship Company. This bold move gave Holladay a monopoly over transportation in the Willamette Valley. Meanwhile, he engaged in myriad dealings throughout the West, including land and mining speculations and construction of the first street railway line, in Portland, Oregon.

Holladay dominated Oregon politics and transportation affairs for nearly a decade. He stimulated the sluggish Oregon economy in the 1860s and early 1870s, yet his vast power inevitably led to public protest: "Although Oregon is noted for being ultra-democratic, and 'the people' forms the stock in trade of every village demagogue throughout her borders," observed the *Kalama Beacon* in 1871, "yet, with the exceptions of Paraguay and Utah, no other community in America has been so completely harnessed to the uses and behests of the 'one-man power' as the State of Oregon."

Holladay reached the zenith of his power in 1871, yet his great business enterprise rested upon a surprisingly shaky foundation. The panic of 1873 left his companies destitute and unable to pay interest to bondholders. Holladay was forever rearranging his holdings by creating or merging subsidiaries. His steamship and railroad interests, for example, were interlocked in a complex arrangement of pledging the securities of one to creditors of the other. The result, observed Henry Villard, the man who finally beat him at this game, was that though Holladay's creditors were among the shrewdest and most experienced bankers in Europe, they allowed themselves to be caught in his financial machinations. To untangle the snarl, German bondholders dispatched Villard to Oregon as their agent. On April 18, 1876, he took over management of the Holladay properties and eliminated the erstwhile transportation king.

With his forced retirement, Holladay's empire collapsed. More than one hundred lawsuits punctuated his final years. Holladay died in Portland on July 8, 1887, having lost his fame and good health in addition to his fortune.

References:

J. V. Frederick, *Ben Holladay: The Stagecoach King* (Glendale, Ca.: A. H. Clark, 1940);

L. R. Hafen, *The Overland Mail, 1849-1869* (Glendale, Ca.: A. H. Clark, 1926);

Ellis Lucia, *The Saga of Ben Holladay* (New York: Hastings House, 1959);

Raymond W. Settle and Mary L. Settle, *War Drums and Wagon Wheels: The Story of Russell, Majors, and Waddell* (Lincoln: University of Nebraska Press, 1966);

Henry Villard, *The Early History of Transportation in Oregon*, edited by Oswald Garrison Villard (Eugene: University of Oregon Press, 1944).

Archives:

Most of Holladay's business records were destroyed in the San Francisco earthquake and fire of 1906. Nearly two thousand letters in addition to other materials survive in the Oregon Historical Society, Portland, Oregon.

Cyrus K. Holliday

(April 3, 1826-March 29, 1900)

by William S. Greever

University of Idaho

CAREER: Partner, George W. Howard Company (1852-1853); president (1860-1864), director (1860-1865, 1868-1900); secretary, Atchison, Topeka and Santa Fe Railway (1864-1865); lawyer, Topeka, Kansas (1862-1900); president, Excelsior Gas & Coke Company (tenure undetermined); president, Merchants National Bank (tenure undetermined).

Cyrus Kurtz Holliday was a major figure in the early history of the Atchison, Topeka and Santa Fe (ATSF) Railway, commonly called the Santa Fe, as its president from 1860 to 1864 and a member of its board until his death in 1900. Born on April 3, 1826, at Kidderminster, Pennsylvania, Holliday was the seventh child of David and Mary Holliday. Cyrus's father, an accountant, died when the child was still young and left him to be raised only by his mother. The two moved to near Massillon, Ohio, where Holliday received a public school education. He graduated from Allegheny College in 1852.

After graduation Holliday became a partner in the George W. Howard Company, a firm engaged in grading railroad rights-of-way. The firm's major contract was with the Pittsburgh & Erie (P&E) Railroad, and Holliday, beginning his study of law at Meadville, Pennsylvania, assisted in drawing up the P&E charter. Within a few months after completion of the line in 1854, the P&E was sold to the Atlantic & Great Western. From this sale Holliday netted a handsome nest egg of $20,000, which opened many opportunities for the twenty-eight year old. On June 11, 1854, he married Mary Jones, a daughter of a Meadville dairyman; they had a son and a daughter.

In October 1854 Holliday went west to ponder his future and, in a letter, told of his destination: "After having traveled over Illinois, Indiana, Michigan, Iowa, Wisconsin, Minnesota, and Nebraska & Missouri, I am prepared to say that Kansas exceeds them all in point of true excellence." In December 1854 Holliday headed a group of ten men who purchased and surveyed the site of a new town they named Topeka. A Free-Soiler and anti-slavery advocate, Holliday played an active role in leading the armed combat which developed in Kansas over the issue during 1855-1856. He also appeared before the Wyandotte Constitutional Convention in 1859 and helped to pass a measure which, after Congressional approval, established Topeka as the territorial capital. Once that was approved, Holliday chose the site of the present-day state house.

Holliday was elected to the territorial council, the upper house of the legislature, in 1857. Two years later Holliday wrote, and engineered passage of, the charter for the Atchison, Topeka and Santa Fe Railway. Officially passed on February 11, 1859, the charter served the line until its bankruptcy in 1893 and reorganization in 1895. Although its charter existed in 1859, a terrible drought in Kansas delayed formation of the ATSF until September 1860. Holliday was elected president of the railroad, and his first order of business was to call a state-wide convention to petition Congress to issue land grants to assist in building four territorial railroads. The convention, which was held in Topeka on October 17, 1860, devised a plan to submit to Congress, but the Civil War delayed action in Washington. Impatient, Holliday drafted a bill granting land for two projects: first, a line south from Leavenworth to the Indian territory; and second, the ATSF, from Atchison to the Colorado border. He sent the bill to Kansas senator S. C. Pomeroy, who introduced it and secured its passage through both houses of Congress; President Lincoln signed it into law on March 3, 1863.

The territorial legislature, as expected, assigned one of the grants to the ATSF, expecting the railroad and the individual county governments to

Cyrus K. Holliday

issue bonds for construction. In 1864 Pomeroy, in recognition of his role in obtaining the land grant, was elected ATSF president, with Holliday stepping down to secretary. Both men, however, were active in seeking financial backing for the road. At first, none of the counties along the proposed route would invest money in the project. Shawnee County rejected a $250,000 bond issue, but Holliday lobbied the electors so effectively that it passed easily on the second attempt. Similar issues passed in Atchison, Osage, and Lyons counties. Holliday was also behind the 1868 decision to buy over 300,000 acres of land belonging to the Pottawattomie Indians. This land, along with the federal grant land, at first provided collateral for bonds but later was sold to settlers, yielding profits of over $9 million.

Construction of the railroad began on October 30, 1868, at Topeka. The next March, at a Wakarusa picnic celebrating the railroad's progress, Holliday predicted the line would eventually reach Chicago, St. Louis, San Francisco, Mexico City, and Galveston. Some listeners were amazed and others amused at what all took to be a flight of oratory, but by the time of Holliday's death in 1900 the ATSF served Chicago, San Francisco, Galveston,

and also Los Angeles and Denver. The original line was completed to the Colorado border in December 1872, just two months before the expiration of the land grant. When the ATSF decided against building a line from Newton, Kansas, to Wichita, Holliday and others took the opportunity; the line was profitably sold to the ATSF in 1901. In 1878 Holliday traveled into the Colorado mountains and, on his return, urged ATSF president Thomas Nickerson that great prosperity awaited the railroad which would build a line to the Colorado mining areas. How much this urging influenced the ATSF and its attempt later that same year to build through the Royal Gorge to Leadville is unclear.

Holliday remained on the ATSF board of directors until his death in 1900, but his greatest influence on the company had come during the 1860s and 1870s. His influence on the town of Topeka spanned a much longer time. He practiced law in the town from 1862 on, serving as the town's mayor for several terms. He also served as president of two of Topeka's businesses: the Excelsior Gas & Coke Company and the Merchants National Bank. He owned a large amount of farm land and several Colorado mining claims, most of dubious value.

He was meticulous in his person, rigidly correct in his business ethics, inexorably honest, reserved, a Mason, and a devout Episcopalian. In his later years he built a large house in Topeka which featured a fireplace so large a man could stand in it. When he died on March 29, 1900, his estate was worth approximately $500,000.

References:

Lea Barnes, ed., "Letters of Cyrus Kurtz Holliday, 1854-1859," *Kansas Historical Quarterly*, 6 (1937): 241-294;

Glenn Danford Bradley, *The Story of the Santa Fe* (Boston: Badger, 1920);

Keith L. Bryant, *History of the Atchison, Topeka and Santa Fe Railway* (New York: Macmillan, 1974);

Kate Holliday, "The Man Who Built the Santa Fe: C. K. Holliday and the Kansas Territory," *Mankind,* 6 (1981): 18-22, 40-43;

James Marshall, *Santa Fe: The Railroad that Built an Empire* (New York: Random House, 1945);

Frederick F. Seely, "The Early Career of C. K. Holliday, a Founder of Topeka and of the Santa Fe Railroad," *Kansas Historical Quarterly,* 27 (1961): 193-200;

L. L. Waters, *Steel Rails to Santa Fe* (Lawrence: University of Kansas Press, 1950).

Archives:

There is a small collection at the Kansas State Historical Society at Topeka.

Mark Hopkins

(September 3, 1814-March 29, 1878)

by Dan Butler

Colby Community College

CAREER: partner, Huntington & Hopkins (1855-1878); director, Central Pacific Railroad (1863-1878); director, Southern Pacific Railroad (1870-1878).

Mark Hopkins was born on September 3, 1814, in Richmond County, Virginia. Shortly after his birth, the family moved to North Carolina. Hopkins's father was a farmer of modest success, and as the size of the family grew the children were required to work on the farm. The oldest of several boys, Hopkins took an active role in helping maintain his family. One of his brothers, Moses, had a serious altercation with local authorities in North Carolina and was given the option of going to jail or moving. Moses left the area in 1845 accompanied by Mark, and the two went to live with an uncle in Kentucky.

Hopkins was never a robust individual, and farming did not appeal to him. The discovery of gold in California gave him the excuse he needed to leave, and in 1850 he and Moses headed for California. Arriving in Eldorado County in 1851, the Hopkins brothers began to mine many small streams of rivers adjacent to the town of Placerville, the county seat. The long hours and lack of success drove the brothers out of mining and into business

Mark Hopkins

within a year. Mark Hopkins began operating a grocery store in Placerville in spring 1852. He sold the store the following year and resettled in Sacramento, where he again entered the grocery business. This business flourished, and in 1855 Hopkins merged his business with that of another Sacramento merchant, Collis P. Huntington. Together they formed Huntington & Hopkins, one of the most successful mercantile houses in the city. By 1860 Huntington & Hopkins had grown into one of the largest retail, wholesale, and import firms in California.

Unlike his future railroad partners, Huntington, Charles Crocker, and Leland Stanford, Hopkins was a quiet and cautious man. He was viewed by his contemporaries as a prudent individual who could not be easily talked into risky ventures. He was also considered shrewd, industrious, and thrifty. Hopkins was never a major participant in the social life of Sacramento and was the only one of the Big Four to never move to San Francisco. Despite his vast wealth, he remained a bachelor and lived simply.

Throughout his life Hopkins had to deal with the problem of his brother Moses, whose dependence on Hopkins's guidance and protection, evident since the escape from North Carolina, continued to Mark Hopkins's death. He set his brother up in business several times and later purchased a homestead for him in Solano County, an area southwest of Sacramento. Part of Hopkins's dislike for publicity may have stemmed from his desire to protect his brother's more checkered past.

Hopkins took a much less active role in the public operation of the Central Pacific railroad than did his partners, agreeing to support the building of the railroad when it was suggested by Theodore Judah but not becoming involved with Crocker in the actual construction of the line. Instead, Hopkins chose to remain in his Sacramento office where he kept close watch over the Central Pacific ledger sheets. He supported Crocker against Judah in their conflicts during the early phases of construction; Hopkins was good-natured and quick in business dealings but refused to compromise on issues he felt were of major importance. During the building of the line he frequently disagreed with both Stanford and Crocker over both construction standards and the expenditure of company funds.

He worked closely with Stanford while the former governor of California was in Utah dealing with Brigham Young to prevent the Union Pacific from gaining complete control of that territory. Collis Huntington had been the first to realize the importance of preventing the Union Pacific from controlling the entire Mormon Commonwealth. While Hopkins moved to bolster the position of his partners in a race for control of Utah by working from his office in California, Huntington, in Washington, D.C., lobbied the outgoing Andrew Johnson administration for concessions that would allow the two lines to meet near Ogden, Utah. Huntington, Hopkins, and Stanford were successful in these efforts, but only after a bitter lobbying battle that Huntington later characterized as the most difficult he ever fought.

The completion of the Central Pacific in 1869 allowed the partners to turn their attention to consolidating their power in California. The 1868 purchase of the San Francisco & San Jose railroad and the 1877 purchase of the California Pacific Railroad gave the Big Four rail access to Oakland and San Francisco. In 1870 they established the Southern Pacific, which was to run from San Francisco to the Colorado River. During this period Hopkins remained in the background. In 1873 the general offices of the company were moved from Sacramento to San Francisco, but Hopkins chose to remain in Sacramento. Although he continued to make periodical visits to the company's headquarters, Hopkins was not frequently seen on the railroad itself. Charles Crocker later stated that he believed that Hopkins went out on the line no more than once a year.

After the company's move to San Francisco, Hopkins did begin construction of a large mansion on Nob Hill, adjacent to one owned by Leland Stanford. The large wooden structure required extensive stone work to prevent erosion. The work was completed by railroad employees, and the wall which still stands was at one point more than three stories high. Construction was slow and Hopkins worried about its cost; however, he would die before the house was completed.

Never a physically strong man, Hopkins suffered increasingly from severe bouts of rheumatism. His stays in the drier climate of Sacramento became more lengthy. In March 1888 he set out on inspection of the Sunset Route in Arizona and New Mexico. Upon his arrival in Yuma, Arizona, on March 29, 1878, only a few days after leaving San Francisco, Hopkins died. The disposition of his estate was complicated by the appearance of a woman claiming to have been Hopkins's wife, an assertion supported by Moses Hopkins. Although the woman received the bulk of Hopkins's $19 million estate, various court cases over its disposition would continue for another sixty years. A private man, Hopkins's death only increased the lack of knowledge about him, the least known of the Big Four.

References:

Matthew Josephson, *The Robber Barons* (New York: Harcourt, Brace, 1934);

Maury Klein, *Union Pacific: The Birth of a Railroad, 1862-1893* (Garden City: Doubleday, 1987);

Estelle Latta, *Controversial Mark Hopkins: The Great Swindle of American History* (New York: Greenburg, 1953);

Oscar Lewis, *The Big Four* (New York: Knopf, 1938).

Edward Hulbert

(May 21, 1823-March 28, 1888)

by George W. Hilton

University of California, Los Angeles

CAREER: Clerk, agent, roadmaster, Atlanta & West Point Railroad (1848-1857); superintendent, Adams Express Company-Southern Express Company (1857-1862, 1864-1867); superintendent, Charlotte & South Carolina Railroad (1862-1864); registrar of elections, state of Georgia (1867-1868); superintendent, Western & Atlantic Railroad (1868-1869); superintendent, Brunswick & Albany Railroad (1870-1871); convener, National Narrow-Gauge Railway Convention (1872, 1878); superintendent, Bedford, Springville, Owensburg & Bloomfield Railroad (1877-1880); superintendent, Houston East & West Texas Railway (1880); secretary, Atlanta Manufacturers' Association (1886-1888).

The principal American intellectual advocate of the narrow-gauge railway movement, Edward Hulbert was a career southern railroad executive of wide experience and excellent reputation. Born at Berlin, Connecticut, on May 21, 1823, Hulbert moved to the South at about the age of eighteen. He began his railroad career in 1848 as a freight clerk on the Atlanta & West Point at LaGrange, Georgia, and quickly rose to be an agent and roadmaster of the railroad. In 1857 he became superintendent of the central division of the Adams Express Company, South. In 1861, as a consequence of Georgia's secession from the Union, this company reorganized itself as the Southern Express Company with Hulbert retaining his position. He left in 1862 to become superintendent of the Charlotte & South Carolina Railroad but returned to the Southern Ex-

Edward Hulbert, with his wife, Anna Elizabeth Robinson Hulbert (courtesy of Georgia Department of Archives and History)

press Company in 1864 as superintendent of the central division. Toward the close of the war Hulbert served in Governor Joseph E. Brown's Home Guard in the defense of Atlanta, on the basis of which he used the title "Colonel" for the remainder of his life.

On February 22, 1867, Hulbert was one of twenty signatories to a letter to Brown asking the former governor's views on the proper course of action with respect to the federal military occupation of Georgia. Brown responded that the state was powerless to resist and counseled cooperation with the federal administrators. Hulbert was one of forty-eight men who called a convention that on March 4, 1867, endorsed Brown's view and called for the acceptance of universal male suffrage along with the rest of Congress's plan for reconstruction. Hulbert's advocacy of such policies, his Republican party affiliation, and his undoubted administrative ability made him thoroughly acceptable to the federal authorities, who appointed him registrar of the election for a convention held in March 1868 to draft a state constitution for universal male suffrage. Hulbert continued as a registrar for the election of April 1868 in which Hulbert's associate in the Southern Express Company, Rufus B. Bullock, was elected as the only Republican governor yet in the state's history. Bullock reciprocated by appointing Hulbert to be the superintendent of the state's railroad, the Western & Atlantic. Although the railroad was the state's leading source of patronage Hulbert managed it efficiently, attracting few allegations of malfeasance.

In 1869 Hulbert declined to support Bullock's call for a third intervention by federal authorities into the composition of the legislature. This breach from administration policy caused Bullock in late 1869 to replace Hulbert as superintendent of the Western & Atlantic with a more radical Republican. Hulbert became superintendent of the Brunswick & Albany Railroad, a promotion of carpetbagger and entrepreneur Hannibal I. Kimball. In that capacity Hulbert announced in February 1871, at a dinner in honor of Kimball, that he considered the common southern railroad gauge of 5 feet too broad, and that southern railroads would be more profitable if built to the 3-foot gauge recently advocated by the British engineer Robert F. Fairlie. In August 1871 Hulbert published a pamphlet, *Narrow Gauge Railways*, on the basis of which he later claimed to have been the first systematic American advocate of narrow-gauge railroads for local economic development. He became indefatigable in such advocacy. In 1872, while attempting to promote the North Georgia & North Carolina Railroad—a line projected to run from Calhoun, Georgia, east across the northern tier of the state to Clayton, Georgia—he called a convention of narrow-gauge promoters, operators, and suppliers for June 19-20 in St. Louis. The convention set forth the expectations of the narrow-gauge advocates with respect to savings in capital and operating costs and recommended uniform standards for gauge, coupler height, and the like.

The panic of 1873 slowed the building of the narrow gauges, as it did railroads generally. In 1874 Hulbert was appointed general manager of the Dayton & Southeastern, a narrow gauge being built from Dayton to the southern Ohio coalfields. In January 1877 he became superintendent of the Bedford, Springville, Owensburg & Bloomfield (BSO&B) Railroad in Indiana. Railroad construction was recovering rapidly and in July 1878 he convened a second narrow-gauge convention in Cincinnati. Oppressive heat caused Hulbert to adjourn the convention until October. The October proceedings represented negligible intellectual advance over 1872 and, in certain respects, were a rebuff to Hulbert. He had identified himself with the position that the function of the narrow-gauge railroad was local economic development. He uniformly denied the rival interpretation that the narrow gauge could provide a general transport function more cheaply and more in accord with shippers' demands than the standard-gauge railroads. The majority of the convention held the latter view, however. Partly for this reason and partly because Hulbert and Joseph Ramsey of the Bell's Gap Railroad were thought to have run the convention despotically, Hulbert was deposed as chairman of the standing committee. He refused to retain ordinary membership, and because he was the principal instigator of the conventions, his departure essentially ended any formal organization of the narrow-gauge movement. The convention planned for Chicago in 1879 was never held, nor did any later conventions reach the serious planning stage.

Hulbert resigned from the BSO&B in February 1880 to take a position as superintendent of the Houston East & West Texas, a major narrow gauge under construction between Houston and Shreveport. The promoter, Paul Bremond, also planned a line southwest from Houston parallel to the Gulf coast. This post appears to have been a failure for Hulbert as he lost his duties in May 1880.

In 1881 he oversaw the westward extension of the Bellaire & Southwestern in Ohio, and in 1882 wrote a prospectus for the company's successor, the Bellaire, Zanesville & Cincinnati. The narrow-gauge movement collapsed in 1883 with the demonstrable failure of the Toledo, Cincinnati & St. Louis and its parent line, the Grand Narrow Gauge Trunk. Although the failure of this vast project of three narrow-gauge railroads stretching from Toledo to Laredo was consistent with Hulbert's opinion that narrow gauges could not engage in successful rivalry with existing railroads, the end of the movement necessarily left him an obsolete figure. By 1883 he had left the industry in favor of a farm at Otwell, Indiana. In 1886 he returned to Georgia as secretary of the newly formed Atlanta Manufacturers' Association. Although the position was outside of railroading it was concerned with his other major interest, the economic development of the South. He died in Atlanta two years later and was buried in Oakland Cemetery.

Publications:

Remarks made before the Press Association of Georgia on August 28, 1869, on the steamer Etowah (Atlanta: Franklin Printing, 1869);

Narrow Gauge Railways (Atlanta, 1871);

An Exhibit of the Dayton & Southeastern Ry. Co. (Dayton, Ohio: United Brethren, 1875);

Bellaire, Zanesville & Cincinnati Ry. Co., Prospectus (Wheeling, W. Va., 1882);

Georgia, the Empire State of the South (Atlanta: Atlanta Constitution, 1887).

References:

John R. deTreville, "Edward Hulbert," *Dictionary of Georgia Biography,* edited by Kenneth Coleman and Charles Stephen Gurr (Athens: University of Georgia Press, 1983);

"Edward Hulbert," *Biographical Directory of the Railway Officials of America* (Chicago: Railway Age Publishing, 1885);

George W. Hilton, " 'The Well Known Narrow Gauge Railway Champion': Colonel Edward Hulbert of Georgia," *Railroad History,* 157 (1987): 16-44.

Archives:

Material relating to Edward Hulbert and his time in Georgia is located in the Genealogical File of the Georgia Department of Archives and History, Atlanta, Georgia.

Collis Potter Huntington

(October 22, 1822-August 13, 1900)

by Matthew A. Redinger

University of Montana

CAREER: Partner, Huntington-Hopkins Hardware Company (1853-1867); vice-president, Central Pacific Railroad (1861-1890); agent, Central Pacific Railroad (1863-1890); agent and attorney, Southern Pacific Railroad (1865-1890); president, Chesapeake & Ohio Railroad (1869-1889); founder, Newport News, Virginia (1879); president, Old Dominion Land Company (1880-1888); partner, over twenty railroads (1883-1900); member, New York Stock Exchange (1885-1900); president, Southern Pacific Railroad (1890-1893); president, Pacific Mail Steamship Company (1893-1900).

Collis Potter Huntington typified the American image of the "self-made man." He began his life in poverty, possessing nothing but a strong will to succeed. In his lifetime Huntington fulfilled his dream of riding from the Atlantic to the Pacific in his own railroad coach and on his own rails. Huntington earned a position among America's railroad elite and, in the process, helped mold the American transportation and industrial frontiers.

Huntington was born on October 22, 1822, in Harwinton, Connecticut, to Elizabeth Vincent and William Huntington, a tinker. The sixth of nine children, Collis began his life with what he considered "advantages"–poverty and a total lack of formal education. His boyhood acquaintances, "afflicted" with both money and education, were unwilling to do the difficult and lowly work on which he thrived.

Young Huntington began to support himself at the age of fourteen. By that time he had saved over $100 by working on a neighbor's farm for $7

Collis Potter Huntington (Gale International Portrait Gallery)

per month and board. In September 1836, while he was still fourteen, Huntington moved to New York and began a six-year career as a traveling salesman. Peddling timepieces and trinkets throughout the Midwest and the South enabled Huntington to save enough capital to open a hardware store with his older brother Solon in Oneonta, New York. The Huntingtons' store prospered despite the fact that the younger partner spent most of his time on buying or selling trips.

It was on one of these business trips that Collis met Elizabeth T. Stoddard. The two quickly fell in love and married on September 16, 1844. Elizabeth bore him no children during their forty-four-year marriage, but in early 1862 the couple did adopt Clara Prentice, the daughter of Elizabeth's deceased sister.

In March 1849 Huntington, at age twenty-seven, led an expedition of Oneontans to the gold fields of California. The already difficult trip became even more onerous because of a three-month delay in the pestilent Isthmus of Panama. Huntington turned adversity into income by seizing the opportunity to trade in commodities. He bought a boat in the Panamanian countryside loaded with

goods and sold these in Panama City for a profit. Leaving New York with only $1,200 in cash, Huntington arrived in San Francisco with over $5,000.

Upon his arrival in San Francisco in 1849, Huntington headed for "riches" in the gold fields. One day of mining, however, convinced him that his calling was in commerce. Shortly thereafter he set up a dry-goods store in Sacramento. Huntington was a consummate dealer; he kept his formula for success simple: "I kept my warehouse full when prices were low, and when they went up I sold out." He dealt in only nonperishable goods to avoid having to dump stocks of food at a loss.

In 1853 Huntington entered into a partnership with Mark Hopkins. Their store became famous as the Huntington-Hopkins Hardware Company. Like his earlier partnership with Solon, Huntington spent little time at the store. Ships passed into San Francisco Bay more often than ever to keep up with the bustling growth of the city. Huntington saw opportunity in these ships and was usually the first to evaluate and purchase their cargoes.

Collis and Elizabeth lived in an apartment above the store; it was there that he became interested in politics. He and a handful of other Whigs grew disgruntled at the Know-Nothing party's tolerance of the proslavery sentiment growing in California. These men launched the California Republican party on March 8, 1856, during the Democratic State Convention in Sacramento, and supported William Henry Seward as the first Republican presidential candidate.

Huntington developed a skill for political manipulation during his early years in California. In an 1857 attempt to bring the western terminus to a proposed stage road over Johnson Pass to Sacramento, Huntington became adept at influencing political agencies. Because of his efforts the stage company built a secondary segment of the line from Johnson Pass to Sacramento. While he lost the battle over the terminus location, Huntington did develop the ability to bend congressmen's ears his way, a necessary tool he would have to use in his struggle to build the Central Pacific Railroad.

That struggle began in 1860 when Huntington became familiar with a plan for the building of a transcontinental railroad. Huntington teamed with Leland Stanford, Charles Crocker, and his old partner, Mark Hopkins, to form the Central Pacific Railroad Company on June 27, 1861. Under Huntington's leadership, the corporation worked to make the dream of a trans-Sierra Nevada railroad a reality. The first step was to finance a survey of Theodore D. Judah's planned route over the Donner Pass. Judah, though a minor partner in the railroad, personally lobbied and solicited Congress and secured land grants for the budding enterprise. When Huntington went to Washington, D.C., in 1861, the two power-hungry entrepreneurs clashed. Judah's death in 1863 helped Huntington secure undisputed control over the railroad and removed a source of discord within it.

Huntington knew that his work in Washington would be difficult, yet important. His experiences in the capital helped him realize that his own strength and genius lay in hard-nosed business negotiations.

He was appalled at the final form of the Central Pacific land-grant bill which Judah had approved. One of his biggest worries was a provision stipulating that, if the Union Pacific Railroad failed to complete its westbound section of the transcontinental line, the Central Pacific could be held responsible for the entire road.

Each of the four major partners, Huntington, Hopkins, Crocker, and Stanford, had specific duties to perform for the company. During the road's construction Huntington remained in the East and exercised full power of attorney for the company. His old friend Mark Hopkins was the company's treasurer. Charles Crocker managed the actual construction of the railroad. Stanford acted as president of the company and used his position as governor of California from January 1862 to January 1864 to secure the loyalties of local authorities.

Although most of the partners' dealings were legal, Huntington often proved that he was not constrained by legal niceties when circumstances demanded. Laws stipulating the amounts of governmental aid to the railroads limited grading of preliminary roadbed to within 300 miles from the end of *continuous* railroad lines. So that the Central Pacific might check the record-breaking advances of the Union Pacific construction crews, Huntington intentionally misrepresented to Congress a 450-mile stretch from Humboldt Wells, Nevada (now known as Wells), to the Wasatch Mountains east of Salt Lake City. He claimed, and subsequently "proved" via a bogus map, that the distance was indeed within the 300-mile limit. Furthermore he disregarded a 7-mile gap in his "continuous" rail construction. Huntington obeyed the laws only when

they were to his own benefit, saying once that "we had better . . . confine ourselves to the law until we see where we can make more to break it than to keep it."

This approach to law seemed to have been motivated greatly by the race to get the Central Pacific to Utah. Huntington was obsessed in his battle against the Union Pacific for track miles. Although his doctors claimed that he had a dangerously "enlarged" heart, he pushed himself to his limits. He pushed his workers just as hard. He commanded Crocker to "*work on as though Heaven was before you and Hell was behind you.*" This pressure notwithstanding, the Central Pacific workers could not achieve their leader's mileage goal, which would have the junction of the two lines at the Green River in Wyoming Territory. On May 10, 1869, the two railroads met at Promontory Point, Utah, some 400 miles short of Huntington's goal.

That his railroad succeeded in preventing the Union Pacific from stopping the Central Pacific in Humboldt Wells provided little consolation to Huntington. He was not the kind to forgive and forget. While wild celebrations rocked the entire nation in honor of the completion of the first transcontinental railroad, Huntington sat in his cramped New York office brooding over the lost 400 miles. Huntington wrote a caustic note to Crocker: "I notice by the papers that there was ten miles of track laid in one day on the Central Pacific, which was really a great feat, the more particularly (since) it was done after the necessity for its being done had passed."

But the Central Pacific was not Huntington's only business interest. Even before the golden spike ceremony at Promontory Point, he had set his sights on the smaller railroads in California. Huntington, through the Central Pacific, bought outright, or acquired controlling interests in, the California Central (1864), the California & Oregon (1867), and the California Pacific (1871), among others. Huntington and his partners had incorporated the Southern Pacific Railroad Company in 1865 as a means to consolidate these smaller lines.

Huntington played the major role in the consolidation of small, independent lines into the Southern Pacific system. Thomas A. Scott of the Texas & Pacific Railroad was a major obstacle to Huntington's plans. The two battled fiercely in Washington until an 1877 stroke left Scott weak and unable to complete his own expansion plans. By 1883 a new Huntington railroad connected the oceans. In 1890, at sixty-eight years of age, Collis Huntington became the president of the Southern Pacific Railroad Company. His empire stretched from Portland, Oregon, through California and across the Southwest to New Orleans, and from San Francisco to Ogden, Utah.

Just after the completion of the Central Pacific road in 1869, Huntington expanded his interests to railroads in the eastern United States. The magnate headed a syndicate which took over the Chesapeake & Ohio Railroad on November 25, 1869. The takeover involved combining the restoration of dilapidated track in Virginia with the construction of new track through West Virginia to the Ohio River. From the beginning of his association with the Chesapeake & Ohio, Huntington had problems. In the midst of the panic of 1873, he fell on hard times, and, despite his frantic efforts, the road sank into receivership. But Huntington was not finished. In 1878, after five years of white-knuckle dealing, another Huntington syndicate repurchased the aging railroad. After regaining control, Huntington poured millions into expansion of the road, pushing westward through Kentucky then south to Memphis, Tennessee.

Huntington meant the road to cross the Mississippi River at Memphis and, eventually, to connect with the Santa Fe system, which he intended to take from Tom Scott. Huntington's partners were unwilling to finance his move across the Mississippi, so he designed an alternate plan. He persuaded Crocker and Stanford to join him in establishing the Louisville, New Orleans & Texas Railroad which connected the Chesapeake & Ohio with the Southern Pacific in New Orleans. With the completion of this line in 1884, Collis Huntington achieved his goal. He could, at last, ride his own cars on rails that he either owned or controlled, from the Atlantic to the Pacific.

Victory, though sweet, was short-lived. While attempting to break into the Great Lakes railroad system between 1886 and 1888, Huntington neglected the Chesapeake & Ohio. As track and rolling stock deteriorated, angry stockholders once again forced the Chesapeake & Ohio into receivership, and Huntington lost control of the road. By that time Huntington had other interests.

When Huntington pushed the Chesapeake & Ohio westward through Kentucky in 1878, he had also extended the road seventy-five miles south

from Richmond, Virginia. The line's eastern terminus, Newport News, lay near the mouth of Chesapeake Bay. Huntington had great dreams for his new town of Newport News. In 1872 he quietly began buying tracts of land between the Hampton Roads on the south and the James River on the east. He recognized the site's economic potential from the first time he saw it. Besides being a deepwater port, and therefore accessible to large ships, Newport News was also freer of fog and ice than ports farther north. The natural harbor offered ships protection in all kinds of weather. Huntington foresaw that the port could become a natural magnet for the products of the central interior, ensuring the success of his railroads.

Collis Huntington fell on hard times in 1883 and 1884. His wife of thirty-nine years died of cancer on October 5, 1883. He was remarried ten months later, on July 12, 1884, to the former Arabella Duval Yarrington. In addition, economic lapses threatened Huntington's fledgling city and port of Newport News in 1884. Huntington, disappointed by the slackening economy, decided to launch another commercial enterprise. Since a large number of ships frequented Newport News, he thought that a system of dry docks and a shipyard for repairing ships would stimulate the bay port.

A group of associates incorporated the Chesapeake Dry Dock & Construction Company on January 28, 1886. Although Huntington was not named in the act of incorporation, he was a member of the board of directors, the driving spirit, and holder of a commanding portion of the company's stock. He chose instead to remain just out of the limelight. Nevertheless, Huntington headed a committee which chose a site for the dry docks, wharves, and necessary buildings and prepared contracts for the facility's construction. The final site for the yards lay on land owned by Huntington's own Old Dominion Land Company. He signed the deed for the land himself. Construction crews finished the dry docks in April 1889. After only four months of operation Huntington decided that the facility should be expanded to include major shipbuilding.

As his shipyards grew, Huntington recognized the need to improve the town of Newport News itself, which had few houses and no good schools. To attract labor, Huntington financed, through his own credit, the construction of ninety-two two-story brick row houses near the shipyards which its employees could rent. He also built a four-room school where qualified teachers instructed the children of the shipyard workers. He continued to pay all of the expenses of the school out of his personal account until his death, when Mrs. Huntington took over the school's finances.

Shortly after the dry docks were completed, Huntington announced plans to sell all of his interests east of the Mississippi River except for his Chesapeake Dry Dock and Construction Company. Besides the Southern Pacific line, these yards were his most valued possessions.

In 1890 the board of directors changed the name of the yards to the Newport News Shipbuilding & Dry Dock Company. Shortly after the name change Huntington announced plans to expand the yards further. The company refused to sanction such rapid expansion, so Huntington resigned from the board of directors and contracted to finance the construction himself. The company agreed to pay Huntington in stocks and bonds. On August 17, 1891, the board of directors authorized the issue of $600,000 in bonds and $56,000 in stocks to Huntington for the finished docks.

Huntington made good use of the newly expanded yards. On July 30, 1890, he signed contracts between the Pacific Improvement Company (the Central Pacific's holding company), as its representative, and the Newport News Shipbuilding & Dry Dock Company, as its head (director?). These contracts called for the construction of a tug named *El Toro,* and two freighters named *El Sud* and *El Norte.* In 1892 Huntington repeated the agreements for two more freighters for the Pacific Improvement Company, the *El Rio* and the *El Cid.*

These four freighters received a tremendous amount of favorable press because of their superior performance and appearance. The September 23, 1893, *Marine Journal* suggested that the ships were "incomparable . . . on their speed and efficiency." After proving his yards' capabilities through these ships, Huntington began soliciting bids for government naval jobs. Before long the Newport News Shipbuilding & Dry Dock Company won contracts for three navy gunboats, the *Nashville,* the *Wilmington,* and the *Helena.*

Huntington was an active overseer of the yards. In fact he frequently reprimanded Calvin B. Orcutt, the president of the company. Before the yards received the government bids, Huntington told Orcutt that "Every ship we build . . . should be first-class in quality, in every respect whether we

make [money] or lose on her." Orcutt obviously took Huntington seriously. Between 1890 and 1900 nearly every ship built in the yards cost the company more to build than the company received for the ship. Perhaps the greatest loss was on *La Grande Duchesse.* Due to necessary repairs and improvements, the ship's total cost to the yards was $1.024 million, nearly twice the ship's original contracted price. Huntington personally covered almost all of the cost overruns incurred by the yards. In the first five months of 1897 Huntington paid the shipyards $387,000 for payroll and expenses. In 1898 he paid for the construction of Dry Dock Number 2. He was willing to dump money into the yards. He claimed in a letter to Orcutt dated October 6, 1897, that he intended to "spend considerable more money there to make it a yard that everyone connected with it will be proud of."

Collis Potter Huntington died August 13, 1900, during a visit to Pine Knot Lodge, his camp in the Adirondack Mountains and Huntington's favorite home. After a visit with friends and neighbors on his lawn, he retired at about eleven in the evening. He fell into a coma and died shortly before midnight. Reports of the cause of death vary from heart attack to cerebral hemorrhage. Regardless of the cause of his death, its impact was considerable. Telegrams of support flooded Mrs. Huntington's Fifth Avenue townhouse. In honor of Huntington's death, every wheel of the immense Southern Pacific system was still for seven minutes at 11 A.M., on Friday, August 17, 1900, the day and time of the funeral. Huntington is believed to be the only man in American railroad history so honored.

After Huntington died, numerous rumors floated around as to the size of his estate. The exact figures are still unavailable. The recipients of Huntington's generosity, however, are notable in their scarcity. Huntington looked askance at most charities. Considering the size of his estate, the number of "causes" to which he donated were few. His motives for giving were perplexing to most. While he once grudgingly gave $100 for a home for disabled miners, he completely financed the extravagant waterfall in San Francisco's Golden Gate Park. Huntington's will revealed no great outpourings of generosity. Almost all of his assets ended up in the hands of his relatives. His wife, Arabella, and his favorite nephew, Henry Edward Huntington, received the lion's share of Huntington's wealth. While few shared in Huntington's wealth, all of America is in debt to the will and drive of this pioneer in the American transportation frontier.

Publications:

Collis Potter Huntington wrote sixteen different articles for journals and papers including *Railroad Gazette, North American Review, The Wave, Commercial & Financial Chronicle,* and the San Francisco *Call.* These articles dealt with various railroads, finance, and the Newport News shipyards. Huntington is credited with eighteen major speeches and addresses between 1887 and 1900.

References:
Carinda W. Evans, *Collis Potter Huntington,* volumes 1 and 2 (Newport News: The Mariners' Museum, 1954);

David Lavender, *The Great Persuader* (Garden City: Doubleday, 1970);

Oscar Lewis, *The Big Four* (New York: Knopf, 1938).

Archives:
Materials concerning Huntington are located in his Collected Letters, Volumes 1-4, in the Mariner's Museum, Newport News, Virginia; in the Newport News Shipbuilding and Dry Dock Company Records, Newport News, Virginia; in the manuscript collections of the Stanford University Library, Stanford, California; in the Holladay Collection of Collis Huntington Holladay, San Marino, California; in the Southern Pacific Company Records, San Francisco, California; in the Henry E. Huntington Library, San Marino, California; and in the Bancroft Library of the University of California, Berkeley, California.

Illinois Central Railroad

by John F. Stover

Purdue University

In the decade of the 1840s the state of Illinois tried in vain to build a north-south railroad. Stephen A. Douglas pushed in both the U.S. House and Senate for a federal land grant to aid such a project. Finally, in the summer of 1850, both houses passed a land grant bill for the railroad, which was signed by President Millard Fillmore on September 20, 1850. The legislation, the first of its kind, gave Illinois 2.5 million acres of federal land for the building of a railroad from Cairo, Illinois, north to Dunleith in the northwestern corner of the state, with a branch from the main line to Chicago. In February 1851 the state of Illinois chartered the 705-mile Illinois Central (IC) Railroad, granting nine businessmen from New York City and Boston, including Robert Schuyler and Robert Rantoul, the right to incorporate and build the line.

The Illinois Central incorporators proposed to build the line largely with money borrowed from European bankers through a bond issue secured by the bulk of the federal land grant. About $5 million of IC bonds had been sold in England by 1852, and by 1860 the balance sheet of the company showed capital stock of $15.6 million and construction bonds amounting to $15.2 million. Completed total mileage of the road was 14 miles in 1852,

132 miles in 1853, 432 miles in 1854, 627 miles in 1855, with the last rails laid on September 27, 1856. When completed the 705-mile IC had cost $26.6 million to construct and was reported to be the longest railroad in the world. Many observers thought the new north-south line was running the "wrong way" since most roads built in the 1850s headed west toward the expanding frontier.

The construction of the Illinois Central was slowed in 1854 and 1855 by the news that Robert Schuyler, the first president of the line, had been found guilty of issuing fraudulent stock in a New England railroad. The Illinois Central was completed under the direction of William H. Osborn, who was president of the line from 1855 to 1865. Osborn reestablished the credit of his road and financed the last phases of construction with a number of short-term loans. A year after the line was finished, the IC faced the panic of 1857, which slowed western migration and also reduced traffic and revenue on the new line. Osborn at once had to deal with $4 million in short-term loans that were falling due with little chance of being renewed. He reassured the uneasy foreign investors, assessed the common stock up to par, and, with his own personal borrowing, helped maintain the credit

The Van Buren Street Station, Chicago, Illinois, of the Illinois Central in 1893 (courtesy of Illinois Central Railroad)

of the Illinois Central. Operating expenses were cut to the bone, and the railroad managed to escape receivership. By 1860 IC revenues were above the $2.4 million level of 1856.

During the Civil War the north-south direction of the Illinois Central was of great importance to the Union war effort. The location of Cairo, the IC southern terminal, at the mouth of the Ohio was like a pistol aimed down the Mississippi at the Confederacy. In 1861 and 1862 thousands of Union troops moved through Cairo as Grant started his campaign against Forts Henry and Donelson. The heavy troop movement during the war years helped increase passenger traffic more than threefold while freight revenue doubled. By 1865 annual revenue on the IC was nearly $8 million. This was true even though the Illinois Central, as a land grant road, gave all federal traffic a discount of approximately 33 percent. The IC paid its first dividends of $4 a share in 1861, a rate that was up to $10 a share by 1865. Wartime prosperity also permitted the IC to reduce its debt by $2 million during the four years of conflict.

During the 1850s and 1860s the Illinois Central, acting as a real estate agent, sold most of its 2.5 million acres of federal land to new settlers and immigrants coming into the state. The first land of-

fice was opened in 1854, and by 1860, 12,000 different units of land had been sold. The most popular size of plot was 40 acres, with an 80-acre farm next in the number of sales. By 1870 approximately 2 million acres had been sold at an average price of close to $12 an acre. The railroad was willing to extend generous credit terms to the new landowners. The $25 million of income received from land sales allowed the IC to reduce its funded debt to under $10 million by 1870.

During the postwar years the Illinois Central extended its lines both west and south. One of its acquisitions was the Dubuque & Sioux City Railroad, which by 1867 had constructed a line which stretched 142 miles west of the Mississippi River to Iowa Falls. The line was one of four Iowa land grant roads competing to be the first to reach the Missouri River. The IC leased the Dubuque & Sioux City for twenty years in 1867 and in 1868 completed a wrought iron bridge across the Mississippi River linking Dunleith and Dubuque. The Dubuque line to Sioux City was opened in 1870. The IC also expanded south during the 1870s by obtaining control of the Chicago, St. Louis, and New Orleans (CSL&NO) Railroad. Originally the CSL&NO consisted of two distinct lines: the 206-mile New Orleans, Jackson & Great Northern Railroad, which had been built up to Canton, Mississippi, in 1858; and north of Canton the 238-mile Mississippi Central, which had been completed to Jackson, Tennessee, in 1860. After the Civil War both roads came under the control of Col. Henry S. McComb, a carpetbagger from Delaware. In 1872 the Illinois Central extended financial assistance to McComb, including money to build a 104-mile connecting line from Jackson, Tennessee, up to East Cairo, Kentucky. McComb's two roads went into receivership in 1876, and the Illinois Central management bought both lines at auctions in 1877. The two southern roads were merged as the Chicago, St. Louis & New Orleans, which the IC leased in 1882 for 400 years. In 1881 the southern road was changed to standard gauge, and in 1889 a huge steel bridge was opened across the Ohio River at Cairo.

In 1883 the Illinois Central was operating 1,927 miles of road, had over 8,000 employees, and grossed $13 million of revenue, about three-quarters of which was freight. It had paid dividends for twenty-three consecutive years, with $8 per share paid in 1883. In 1883 Edward H. Harriman, a New York financier who held perhaps as many as 15,000 shares of IC stock, became a director of the line. In 1886 Harriman was elected first vice-president of the IC, just a few weeks after his good friend Stuyvesant Fish had been elected president. For the next twenty years the two New Yorkers dominated IC policy, with Harriman clearly the more powerful. In 1887 Harriman managed to wrest control of the Dubuque & Sioux City from the rival Drexel Morgan interests and add its lines permanently to the IC. About 2,000 miles of additional line were added during the Fish-Harriman years, most of it purchased rather than constructed. Short branch lines were acquired in Minnesota, Wisconsin, Indiana, and Illinois. Much of the mileage added was in the southern states of Kentucky, Tennessee, and Louisiana, a large portion being acquired from Collis P. Huntington and his associates.

Early in 1901 Illinois Central officials celebrated the golden anniversary of their line. At the time of the anniversary the IC was operating 4,200 miles of road in thirteen states, had annual revenues of $37 million, employed 32,000 people, and had paid annual dividends for forty consecutive years. President Fish proudly announced at the anniversary banquet that financial control of the IC had returned to America, since 60 percent of the common stock was held in the United States. At the turn of the century the Illinois Central was clearly the major north-south line in mid America.

References:

Carlton J. Corliss, *Main Line of Mid-America: The Story of the Illinois Central* (New York: Creative Age Press, 1950);

John F. Stover, *History of the Illinois Central Railroad* (New York: Macmillan, 1975).

Archives:

The records of the Illinois Central are located at the Newberry Library in Chicago, Illinois.

Melville Ezra Ingalls

(September 6, 1842-July 11, 1914)

by Robert L. Frey

Wilmington College of Ohio

CAREER: Attorney, Gray, Maine (1863-1864); attorney, Boston, Massachusetts (1864-1870); director, Indianapolis, Cincinnati & Lafayette (IC&L) Rail Road (1870-1873); president, IC&L (1873-1880); president, Cincinnati, Indianapolis, St. Louis & Chicago Railroad (1880-1889); receiver, Kentucky Central Railroad (1881-1883); president, Chesapeake & Ohio (C&O) Railroad (1888-1899); president, Cleveland, Cincinnati, Chicago & St. Louis Railroad (1889-1900); chairman, C&O (1899-1905).

Melville E. Ingalls was one of the most influential railroad leaders in the Midwest. A transplanted New Englander, Ingalls eventually settled in Cincinnati and master-minded the creation of the Cincinnati, Indianapolis, St. Louis & Chicago Railroad, often called "the first Big Four." He was also the major force in stabilizing and expanding the Chesapeake & Ohio (C&O), succeeding where C. P. Huntington had failed.

Born September 6, 1842, on a farm in Harrison, Maine, Ingalls was a ninth generation descendant of Edmund Ingalls of Lincolnshire, England, who immigrated to America in 1628. Ingalls's first name, Melville, was taken from Thomas Melville of Revolutionary War fame, and his middle name, Ezra, was his father's first name. He was usually called Mel by close friends and associates. Both of his brothers were trained as physicians, but he was only able to attend Bowdoin College for a short time before funds were exhausted. Returning home to Harrison he read law with a local attorney, studied at Harvard for one year, and graduated in 1863 at the age of twenty-one.

Attorney Ingalls opened a practice in Gray, Maine, but within a year joined the Boston firm of Charles Levi Woodbury, a prominent legal mind of the day. While in Gray, Mel met and later married Abbie Stimson. Ingalls rapidly gained a favorable

Melville Ezra Ingalls

reputation in Boston, being elected at age twenty-five to the Massachusetts legislature after having served on the Boston City Council for two years. Politics, however, did not seem to interest the young lawyer beyond his term in the legislature and he declined renomination in 1869.

The reason why Ingalls, at age twenty-seven, turned his back on a promising political career is unclear. He was, however, building a reputation in the Boston area as an expert on corporate law, particularly concerning railroads. In all probability this interest proved to be more intriguing, and more lucrative, than the uncertainties and compromises required in the political world. His developing interest in corporate law changed his life radically when, in 1870, Charles Woodbury sent him to Cincinnati to investigate the poor financial condition of the Indianapolis, Cincinnati & Lafayette (IC&L) Rail Road in which Woodbury had controlling interest. Ingalls lived the remainder of his life in the Queen City, assembling two of the great railroad systems of the nineteenth century in the process.

Woodbury arranged to have Ingalls appointed to a seat on the board of the Indianapolis, Cincinnati & Lafayette Rail Road and he arrived in Cincinnati in 1870 without his wife (she later joined him) and with no friends. In fact, Henry Lord, the president of the IC&L, and his associates did not greet the twenty-eight-year-old newcomer from the East warmly. Ingalls soon turned the attitude of the leaders of the IC&L and its employees in his favor. He proved to be a hard worker, and he walked all 179 route miles of track in his first few years in Cincinnati. In addition, he talked to employees, customers, and city and town leaders along the route to find out how the railroad could serve them more effectively.

Eventually Ingalls's approach succeeded in improving the financial condition of the company, but the condition of the IC&L worsened before it improved. In 1873 Ingalls was appointed receiver for the property. During the reorganization of the same year, Ingalls was appointed president, but the company slipped into receivership again in 1876. Shortly thereafter Ingalls began to turn the company around. From 1870 to 1876 Mel Ingalls had been working hard to gain the support of the key leaders of Cincinnati and some of the other towns on the railroad. He had been extolling the advantages of the IC&L to Cincinnatians, and had been actively involved in Cincinnati civic affairs in order to encourage people to think of him as a permanent citizen, not as a visiting New Englander. He was successful in these goals as in the years after 1876 the energetic young man was able to retire the debt of the IC&L by securing voluntary subscriptions, a triumph of his personal charisma. Intelligent and pleasant, he was also articulate and persuasive. But he was also a strict disciplinarian, following the familiar prescription of the day, which he repeated often to young people: work hard, be loyal to the company, and stay away from strong drink.

By 1878 the Indianapolis, Cincinnati & Lafayette began to return a dividend and Ingalls began to assemble a rail empire by consolidating small railroads in Indiana and Illinois into an 1880 merger that gained national attention. The new line was called the Cincinnati, Indianapolis, St. Louis & Chicago (CIStL&C), sometimes known as "the first Big Four." The main line of the new railroad ran from Cincinnati to Indianapolis and then through Lafayette to Kankakee, Illinois, where it used trackage rights on the Illinois Central to reach Chicago. The main line was supplemented by branches and secondary lines located primarily in Indiana. The headquarters of the new company were in Cincinnati where Ingalls served as the president of the new line.

The 1880 merger caused Ingalls's name to be counted among the most prominent forces in, not only Cincinnati, but the whole Ohio-Indiana-Illinois tristate area. About a year after the merger Ingalls was appointed receiver of the Kentucky Central, a decrepit line between Lexington and Covington, Kentucky—the latter town located across the Ohio River from Cincinnati. Also in 1881 C. P. Huntington was named to the board of the Cincinnati, Indianapolis, St. Louis & Chicago. The Chesapeake & Ohio was looking for a midwestern connection and Ingalls and the CIStL&C would become that connection.

During the 1880s Cornelius Vanderbilt II, the Commodore's grandson, gradually became a major force in midwestern railroad circles. By 1882 he had control of the Cleveland, Columbus, Cincinnati & Indianapolis Railroad, which ran east and north from Indianapolis and Cincinnati to Sandusky and Cleveland. Vanderbilt purchased controlling interest in the CIStL&C and merged the two systems into the Cleveland, Cincinnati, Chicago & St. Louis in 1889. Although Indianapolis was a key hub on the new railroad, it lost a place in the corporate title. Known as the Big Four, this line was the major rail transportation system in Ohio, Indiana, and Illinois. Vanderbilt put Ingalls in charge of the combined system and located the corporate offices in Cincinnati.

In the late 1880s Vanderbilt, who was also purchasing Chesapeake & Ohio (C&O) stock, included Ingalls in negotiations with Huntington to buy control of the C&O. Approaching seventy and desiring less activity, Huntington quickly reached an agreement to sell the railroad. Ingalls was named president of the C&O and now was president of a system with almost 3,000 miles of track and 15,000 employees. The railroads composing the Cleveland, Cincinnati, Chicago & St. Louis were generally in good physical condition with reasonably modern locomotives and rolling stock and a good traffic base. The C&O was another matter, however. It was to this line that Ingalls directed most of his attention.

During his presidency of the C&O (1888-1899) Ingalls completed the change in the nature of the C&O. The company had been shifting its effort to become part of a transcontinental system (Huntington's dream) by selling off its westernmost components (the old Kentucky Central went to the Louisville & Nashville). To get from Ashland, Kentucky, to Covington, a new line was constructed along the south bank of the Ohio River, thus avoiding the roundabout route via Lexington. Ingalls completed this line in 1888 and with his two sons rode the first train to cross the Ohio River from Covington to Cincinnati on an impressive new bridge. Earlier in 1882 Ingalls had successfully advocated the construction of a new line east of Richmond to tidewater at Newport News. Under Ingalls the C&O succeeded in connecting the Virginia tidewater to the heart of the Midwest rather than attempting to become the eastern end of a great transcontinental route.

In 1890, immediately after the Vanderbilt takeover, Ingalls managed to secure lease of the Richmond & Allegheny (later it was purchased), a water-level route following the towpath of the James River & Kanawha Canal. This line was a better route for freight traffic, particularly westbound traffic, than the steep ascent of the old C&O main line over the Blue Ridge at Afton, Va. A line was secured into Washington, D. C., via trackage rights over what became the Southern System. The two most significant improvements made by Ingalls on the C&O, however, were to repair the physical property and to exploit the coal traffic of the area. In the early 1880s the C&O was poorly constructed and maintained, and Ingalls made extensive efforts and expenditures to improve the roadbed and to put heavier rail in place on the main line. New and more powerful 4-6-0 and 2-8-0 type locomotives were purchased along with new freight and passenger rolling stock.

The heavier traffic for the new locomotives, rail, and roadbed came from a systematic and energetic effort to open coal mines along the route. Eventually the C&O became the largest carrier of "black diamonds" in the nation, and Mel Ingalls was the person most clearly able to see the value of coal as a major traffic source. *The State* newspaper of April 10, 1894, said of Ingalls: "Endowed with a robust Physique, and untiring energy, M. E. Ingalls is withal a quick perceiver, a man of enormous resources and, best of all, his soul is in the work of lifting the veil that has so long covered up the treasures [coal] of the two Virginias."

Perhaps because of his political experience, Ingalls took an active interest in political issues. He spoke out vigorously in the 1896 election campaign against William Jennings Bryan, free silver, and populism. He was not opposed to a little intimidation, stating bluntly on several occasions that a Bryan victory would result in wage reductions and delays in improvements on the C&O. Nonetheless, his relationship with labor was generally good because he advocated a "community of interest" between labor and management based on a sharing of profits. While little of this "sharing" took place, the wide dissemination of these viewpoints might have influenced C&O employees as major strikes did not occur on the C&O between 1880 and 1900.

By 1890 Ingalls was one of Vanderbilt's key railroad managers. He was, however, given a greater amount of autonomy than most Vanderbilt managers because of his success in creating and managing the first Big Four prior to Vanderbilt's involvement. Cornelius Vanderbilt II was about the same age as Ingalls, and the two of them appeared to work quite well together. Vanderbilt was forced to retire in 1896 because of poor health and William Vanderbilt, who was not vitally interested in the rail empire, allowed it to drift into the hands of J. P. Morgan and his lieutenants. This change eventually brought Ingalls's managerial career to a rather abrupt end in 1899 when he resigned as president of the C&O. The major reason appears to have been J. P. Morgan's plan to have the New York Central and the Pennsylvania Railroad purchase controlling interest in the C&O. Ingalls remained chairman of the C&O's board until 1905 when he retired at the age of sixty-three. At the testimonial dinner in his honor he is reported to have said: "I told them the sale was a mistake, and time proved I was right and they were wrong." Although he remained a director of the Cincinnati, New Orleans & Texas Pacific for several more years, he was no longer a leading force in the railroad industry.

During his sojourn in Cincinnati, and particularly after 1905, Ingalls contributed a significant amount of time and energy to civic activities. The list of organizations of which he was a member or to which he contributed is long, and there is little doubt that he was a community leader. Ingalls was president of the Cincinnati Technical School, the Cincinnati Country Club (first president in both cases), the Cincinnati Art Museum (president for twenty-six years), the Merchants National Bank, and the Commercial Club. He was a trustee of Music Hall, and he chaired the committee that remodeled the Hall in 1895. He was also a longtime trustee of the Unitarian Church on Reading Road. Throughout his life he was an advocate of physical fitness and was a pioneer in the modern playground movement. He consistently advocated the construction of adequate and spacious parks and recreational areas in the city.

In 1903 Ingalls decided to reenter politics and ran on the Democratic ticket for mayor of Cincinnati. Perhaps he picked the wrong party or the wrong issues, but his earlier political success in Massachusetts did not follow him west. He lost the election and never again attempted to run for political office. His recognition spread outside of Ohio when in 1905 he was chosen president of the National Civic Federation. Probably the most fitting memorial to him was the construction of the sixteen-story Ingalls Building located at Fourth and Vine streets in downtown Cincinnati. When completed in 1904 it was the tallest concrete reinforced building (at 210 feet) in the world, and still stands as a major office building in modern Cincinnati. Clearly Ingalls was one of the most respected and influential citizens of Cincinnati.

Mel and Abbie Ingalls had six children—four sons and two daughters. All of the sons graduated from Harvard University and two of them became executives on the New York Central Railroad. One daughter, Gladys, married a British diplomat and was still living in London as late as 1974. Ingalls always enjoyed family life, and he particularly enjoyed vacationing in the mountains of Virginia. In the 1880s he discovered some of the springs of Virginia and with several friends constructed hotels or lodges at Hot Springs, Warm Springs, and Healing Springs. Eventually a 25-mile branch line was constructed north from the C&O main line at Covington, Virginia, to serve the hotel at Hot Springs.

From this point Ingalls could travel to either end of the line in a day's journey for business purposes, but also he could spend a significant amount of time with his family at Hot Springs. It was at Hot Springs, Virginia, that Melville Ezra Ingalls died on July 11, 1914.

M. E. Ingalls was a typical nineteenth century captain of business; he was an intense, hard-driving perfectionist. His life was lived in an exceedingly disciplined manner, and he expected the same from colleagues and subordinates alike. He was a staunch opponent of any type of government interference in the operations of private corporations. From his perspective the owners and managers should be controlled only by the board of directors and the manager's own strict ethical code. At the same time he evidenced a sense of some responsibility and respect for the people working for the company. This sense did not extend to generous pay increases or an attempt to reduce the working hours of his employees, but since he often worked a twelve- to sixteen-hour day, he could not understand why others could not do the same. He took his role as a community leader seriously and embraced his adopted home with all the enthusiasm of a native-born Cincinnatian. Finally, he was a devoted family man whose disciplined child-rearing methods produced sons and daughters who also made contributions to society, although perhaps not as significant as those made by M. E. Ingalls.

References:

Account of Ingalls 1905 Banquet (Cincinatti, Ohio: Robert Clarke Company, 1905);

John Paul Jones, "The Big Man of the Big Four, M. E. Ingalls," *Railroad History*, 130 (Spring 1974): 41-50;

Charles W. Turner, et al., *Chessie's Road*, second edition (Alderson, W.V.: Chesapeake & Ohio Historical Society, 1986).

Archives:

The Chessie System corporate offices in Richmond, Virginia, and Cleveland, Ohio, have collections that bear on M. E. Ingalls. George Arents Research Library, Syracuse University, Syracuse, New York, has records on the New York Central and its subsidiaries, including the Big Four.

Interstate Commerce Commission

While the Interstate Commerce Commission (ICC) was created in 1887, making it the nation's oldest regulatory agency, its origins reach back to precolonial times and across the Atlantic.

It was from English common law that colonial America borrowed the doctrine that the state has power to regulate commerce. There is evidence that the colonies sought to establish the prices of many goods and services, although the ideas of Scottish political economist Adam Smith caused much of this early economic regulation to be repudiated.

The Founding Fathers addressed the matter of government regulation in Article 1, Section 8, clause 3 of the Constitution, providing that Congress shall have the power "to regulate commerce with foreign nations, and among the several states, and with the indian tribes." It would be a century after the writing of the Constitution before Congress turned its attention to regulating the nation's railroads.

In the aftermath of the Civil War, railroads began to cast an increasingly large shadow across the nation's economic, political, and social landscape. In terms of finance, scale of operations, employment, and annual revenues, railroads constituted America's first large industry. Though history books detail what are today considered to be outrageous acts of speculation by so-called railroad robber barons—acts that fueled demands for government intervention—such economic activity was common in most all lines of business during the later decades of the nineteenth century.

Despite the fact that after 1870 competition increased among railroads and rate levels fell rapidly, both of which contributed to many rail bankruptcies, populists in the rural Midwest and other activists sought to assert the primacy of government over industrial corporations. The size and visibility of railroads made these corporations a prime target. The struggle has been popularized simplistically in many history texts as one between large, impersonal railroad companies and small, struggling farmers.

Following the Civil War, improvements in agricultural methods and a decline in demand for agricultural commodities battered farm prices. Postwar inflation placed further hardships upon farmers, many of whom had speculated—and lost—in early railroad stocks. Out of these hardships emerged the Patrons of Husbandry, or Grange, which, among other objectives, sought political solutions to the farmers' perceived economic problems. The Grange charged that rail freight rates on farm goods were excessive and sought government assistance in reducing those prices.

Although some early railroad charters contained rate ceilings or gave states the right to restrict rail earnings, there was little uniformity in these charters and they were not considered to be effective. Galling to many smaller shippers was that the charters failed to address the matter of rate and service discrimination between persons, localities, or traffic, differences in rates based on demand rather than costs of service. So-called Granger laws passed in Illinois in 1869, in Minnesota in 1871, and later in other states, required "just, reasonable and uniform" rail rates. In some cases special rail regulatory commissions were established by state legislatures. The railroads challenged these laws, asserting a violation of economic due process under the Fourteenth Amendment to the Constitution. In two now-famous Supreme Court cases—*Munn* v. *Illinois,* 94 U.S. 113 (1877) and *Wabash Ry.* v. *Illinois,* 118 U.S. 557 (1886)—the Supreme Court established that regulation of interstate commerce is a proper responsibility of, and should be reserved to, the federal government. When property is "used in a manner to make it of public consequence, and affect the community at large," held the court, it is "clothed with a public interest" and is subject to regulation by the Congress. In the Wabash case the Supreme Court denied the states the power to regulate interstate commerce, even in the absence of federal action.

Congress was not wholly inactive during this period of state regulation of the railroads. Though no legislation was passed more than 150 bills and resolutions to regulate the railroads were introduced into Congress between 1868 and 1886. In 1872 the Senate appointed a commission to investigate various methods of reducing transportation costs. One solution cited by the Windom Commission was an end to what it termed "unfair discrimination" in rates and services by railroads, but no congressional action was taken. In 1885 Illinois senator Shelby M. Cullom led an investigation into railroad practices that identified "discrimination" in railroad rates and services as an "evil" that should be curbed through legislation.

Rail carriers, too, supported regulation, but for a different reason than rail shippers. Government land-grant promotion had encouraged excessive building of railroads. The problem of too little business for too much rail was exacerbated by economic downturns. Railroad managers were seeking a means of stemming the rapid declines in freight revenues that regularly threatened numerous roads with bankruptcy. Federal economic regulation, they believed, could serve to enforce minimum rate regulation and bring order out of competitive chaos.

On February 4, 1887, in the wake of the Cullom report, Supreme Court decisions placing the burden of interstate commerce regulation with the federal government, and supportive lobbying by the rail carriers, President Cleveland signed into law the Interstate Commerce Act. The act established a five-member Interstate Commerce Commission (ICC), whose members were to be appointed by the president of the United States with consent of the Senate. The Interstate Commerce Act became effective on April 5, 1887.

The Interstate Commerce Commission was charged with investigating complaints of violations of the Interstate Commerce Act. The act required that rail carriers establish just and reasonable rates; prohibited various forms of discrimination in rates and services, such as preference and prejudice between persons, localities, and traffic; prohibited pooling of traffic and revenues by carriers, a device devised by railroads to stem financial losses and create economic stability during recessions; prohibited carriers from charging more for shorter hauls than longer hauls over the same line and in the same direction; required carriers to make their rates public and to file rate schedules (tariffs) with the commission; and required carriers to file annual reports with the ICC.

The commission was empowered to require attendance of witnesses and testimony, to order financial documents and other papers of the carriers to be produced, to issue "cease and desist" orders to carriers, and to determine and levy damages. However, the ICC had to petition the courts to enforce its orders and levy fines, and an average case before the ICC stretched on for four years. As the commission had no authority to suspend rates under investigation, or to prescribe rates that it deemed just and reasonable, there developed agitation to put greater teeth into the Interstate Commerce Act, something not accomplished until after the turn of the century.

The first chairman of the ICC was Thomas M. Cooley, a former justice of the Michigan Supreme Court. His fellow commissioners were William R. Morrison, a former congressman from Illinois; New York lawyer Augustus Schoonmaker; Vermont lawyer Aldace Walker; and former Alabama railroad commissioner Walter Bragg.

The original Interstate Commerce Act of 1887 is most often viewed as a failure. Because it failed to provide the ICC with sufficient powers of enforcement and required it to operate through the judiciary, the Interstate Commerce Act solved few of the problems it was designed to remedy. Proponents of additional regulation argued that the ICC was unable to address rate discrimination, rebating, and maximum rates. Opponents argued that the ICC outlawed the railroads' strategies, mainly pooling, without offering an alternative plan for dealing with ruinous competition. The proponents of regulation eventually triumphed and powers deemed appropriate were added to the ICC during the early years of the twentieth century.

References:

Herbert E. Bixler, *Railroads: Their Rise and Fall* (Jaffrey Center, N.H.: Herbert E. Bixler, 1982);

Paul S. Dempsey and William E. Thoms, *Law and Economic Regulation in Transportation* (New York: Quorum Books, 1986);

Gabriel Kolko, *Railroads and Regulation: 1877-1916* (New York: W. W. Norton, 1965);

D. Philip Locklin, *Economics of Transportation*, 6th ed. (Homewood, Ill.: Richard Irwin, 1974);

Albro Martin, *Enterprise Denied: Origins of the Decline of American Railroads, 1897-1917* (New York: Columbia University Press, 1971).

—Frank N. Wilner

John B. Jervis

(December 14, 1795-January 12, 1885)

by F. Daniel Larkin

State University College, Oneonta, New York

CAREER: Chief engineer, Delaware & Hudson Canal (1827-1830); chief engineer, Mohawk & Hudson Railroad (1830-1833); chief engineer, Saratoga & Schenectady Railroad (1831-1833); chief engineer, Chenango Canal (1833-1836); chief engineer, Eastern Division, Erie Canal enlargement (1836); chief engineer, Croton Water Supply System (1836-1846); chief engineer, Hudson River Railroad (1847-1849); president and chief engineer, Michigan Southern & Northern Indiana Railroad (1850-1858); president, Chicago & Rock Island Railroad (1851-1858); general superintendent, Pittsburgh, Ft. Wayne & Chicago Railroad (1861-1864); secretary-treasurer, Rome Merchant Iron Company (1868-1885).

In 1798 Timothy Jervis moved with his wife and three-year-old son, John, from Huntington, Long Island, to land he had purchased close to what would soon become Rome, New York. Timothy and his wife, the former Phebe Bloomfield, had secured 500 acres of bottomland near the watershed between the easterly flow of the Mohawk River and the westerly meander of Wood Creek. The purchase straddled New York's water-level route through the Appalachians.

As he matured, John, the eldest of three sisters and three brothers, helped with the farming and lumbering while attending common school. At age fifteen he discontinued his formal education to devote the next seven years to the family farm and sawmill.

Construction of the Erie Canal began at Rome, New York, on July 4, 1817. Jervis was fortunate in that Benjamin Wright, the chief engineer of the waterway, was a resident of Rome and a friend of his father. Jervis was hired by Wright in 1817 to be an axeman for a survey party, his job being to clear the terrain for the survey. The industrious and

John B. Jervis

ambitious Jervis did not remain at this rather menial position for long. He was soon promoted to targetman, a position which required him to hold the surveying rod to assist in the calculations. Jervis began to learn how to use the leveling instruments themselves and how to make the complex calculations. Within a year he was made a resident engineer.

He spent the next four working seasons honing and exhibiting his engineering skills, and in 1823 he received another promotion, this time to engineering superintendent over a 50-mile section of the eastern section of the Erie. This position required not only engineering skills but also gave

Jervis the opportunity to develop his management techniques. When the Erie Canal was completed in 1825 Jervis was an experienced junior member of a profession which he had learned chiefly by observation and hands-on experience. Within two decades Jervis would move to the front rank of American civil engineers.

Shortly after Jervis left the Erie Canal project Benjamin Wright again helped to direct the course of his career. Jervis was chosen in 1825 to be Wright's principal assistant on the Delaware & Hudson (D&H) Canal project. The D&H proved to be a watershed in Jervis's career because not only did the canal, built through rough terrain, improve his engineering skills but the project also introduced him to railroad construction. The D&H project included a 16-mile railroad, the purpose of which was to transport coal from the mines in northeastern Pennsylvania to the canal for transfer to market.

Jervis enthusiastically tackled the job by immediately setting off on a survey of the canal route. Accompanied by another engineer, John B. Mills, he trekked the wilderness between Honesdale, Pennsylvania, and Kingston, New York, gaining an intimate knowledge of the country through which the canal was to be built. But as difficult as some of the canal construction was, the most challenging aspect of the assignment was the railroad which ran from Honesdale to the Carbondale mines.

Before railroad construction was started Wright resigned from the project and recommended Jervis as his replacement. So it was Jervis who was given the task of laying out the railroad route in 1827. He had almost no model to follow, as few American railroads existed. Jervis observed the operation of the Quincy Railroad, an early horse-drawn railroad in Boston, and studied works on English roads. Finally, Jervis concluded that both locomotive engines and a gravity system should be used to move the coal over the hilly terrain.

Faced with this new challenge, Jervis not only developed new technology to facilitate the movement of the coal-laden cars over the steep inclines of the gravity road but also dispatched his assistant, Horatio Allen, to purchase English locomotives. Jervis specified the maximum weight of the engines which could be borne by the wooden rails capped by wrought iron. Unfortunately, Allen sent Jervis a locomotive that was heavier than specified. The Stourbridge Lion, built by Foster, Rastrick,

and Company of Stourbridge, was a magnificent machine which ran well in its brief trials, but its weight compressed the metal cap rail into the wood. It could not be used as a locomotive on the D&H and was relegated to the less dramatic role of stationary steam engine on one of the inclined planes.

The fate of the Lion did not deter Jervis from building another railroad when he left the completed Delaware & Hudson Canal in 1830. He accepted an offer from a group of venture capitalists to construct New York's first line, a road from Albany, on the Hudson, to Schenectady, on the Mohawk River. The planned Mohawk & Hudson Railroad faced an uncertain future because of its proximity to the mighty Erie Canal. Its backers gambled that it would complement, not compete with, the Erie by providing a direct route to Schenectady where travelers could board canal packets for the trip west.

The 16-mile railroad route crossed a level, sandy plain, with inclines from the water level at both ends. The directors of the Mohawk & Hudson balked at the use of locomotives because they felt that the engines were not sufficiently reliable or powerful enough. Jervis convinced them differently and ordered the DeWitt Clinton from the West Point Foundry in Cold Spring, New York. The Clinton, although weighing approximately three tons less than the Stourbridge Lion, was of similar design and consisted of a firebox and horizontal boiler mounted on a frame powered by four fixed-position driving wheels. Considering it was one of the first locomotives built in the United States the DeWitt Clinton performed moderately well in service. But horsepower was also used on the line.

With the completion and success of the Mohawk & Hudson its directors went ahead with New York's second railroad, a connecting line from Schenectady to the mineral springs at Saratoga. Jervis, logically, was picked to engineer the project. The route he chose was, of necessity, about ten miles longer than the Mohawk & Hudson and ran through more challenging terrain. It also resulted in Jervis's most important contribution to American railway technology and one that was almost immediately adopted by locomotive builders.

The gently rolling land between Schenectady and Saratoga demanded curves on the line that had not been necessary on the Mohawk & Hudson Railroad. Locomotives with fixed wheels could not take the curves smoothly at high speeds. After careful research, particularly into the design of English railroad carriages, Jervis developed a plan to remove the front driving wheels of an engine and replace them with a four-wheel movable, or swivel, truck. The swivel truck helped to guide the locomotive into a curve, allowing for greater train speed and improved safety for the passengers. It was a simple, logical solution which was in keeping with Jervis's approach to problem solving. The less complicated the machine or structure, he believed, the less subject it would be to failure.

The new locomotive design was submitted to the West Point Foundry, where it was implemented in 1832. David Matthew, superintendent of construction of the Mohawk & Hudson, the road upon which the new, coal-burning engine was tested, ran the machine at speeds up to eighty miles per hour. "She was the fastest and steadiest engine I have ever run or seen," wrote Matthew, "and she worked with the greatest ease." The locomotive, which Jervis named the Experiment, was the first to deviate from a distinctively English design, and was America's first major contribution to locomotive technology.

Jervis was so impressed with his new design that he ordered both an old Stephenson-built Mohawk & Hudson engine to be altered and a new engine from the Stephenson works to be patterned after the Experiment. On its arrival from England Jervis rode on the Davy Crockett and deemed that it possessed "almost as smooth and steady a motion as a stationary engine." The 4-2-0 wheel arrangement became the standard for locomotive builders during the decade following 1833.

Although railroads were being built in New York by the early 1830s, the state was still in the euphoria of the canal boom. A number of lateral canals were being constructed to connect with the Erie, and the "Grand Canal" itself was scheduled for enlargement. One of the new laterals was a canal from Binghamton, on the Susquehanna River, to Utica, on the main line Erie. Named the Chenango Canal, it was built in fulfillment of a campaign promise made by John Tracy during the gubernatorial election of 1832. Jervis was selected as chief engineer.

Although the Chenango Canal held little promise of economic success, it did provide Jervis with another opportunity to demonstrate his ability for innovative engineering. The canal was an inter-

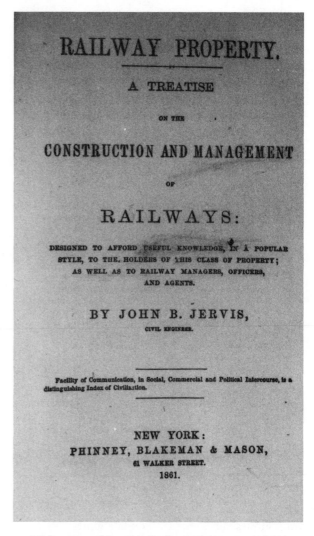

RAILWAY PROPERTY.

A TREATISE

ON THE

CONSTRUCTION AND MANAGEMENT

OF

RAILWAYS:

DESIGNED TO AFFORD USEFUL KNOWLEDGE, IN A POPULAR STYLE, TO THE HOLDERS OF THIS CLASS OF PROPERTY; AS WELL AS TO RAILWAY MANAGERS, OFFICERS, AND AGENTS.

BY JOHN B. JERVIS,
CIVIL ENGINEER.

Facility of Communication, in Social, Commercial and Political Intercourse, is a distinguishing Index of Civilization.

NEW YORK:
PHINNEY, BLAKEMAN & MASON,
61 WALKER STREET.
1861.

Title page of Jervis's Railway Property *(1861)*

basin canal; that is, a canal which connects two separate watersheds. Jervis's problem was finding an adequate source of water at the summit level between the watersheds. Jervis decided upon the use of man-made reservoirs even though other engineers were skeptical of the plan's ultimate success.

The reservoir system would depend on rainfall as its source of water. European experience revealed that reservoirs retained only about one-third of the total rainfall, and this would not be sufficient for the canal's needs. Jervis silenced his critics by developing a gauge which proved that 40 percent of the rainfall was retained in the artificial lakes, an amount adequate to meet the needs of the canal. Jervis's measurement of rainfall and runoff was a breakthrough in the field of hydrology.

The water supply system excepted, the Chenango Canal project was not particularly challenging to Jervis, and he resigned as chief engineer in

1836, about a year before the canal opened for business. His resignation was prompted by an offer from the New York State Canal Commission to return to the Erie.

The Erie Canal had been such a success that the New York legislature approved its enlargement in 1835. Construction started the following year, and Jervis became chief engineer of the eastern division, taking with him William McAlpine, his principal assistant on the Chenango. As usual, Jervis plunged into work immediately, recommending changes in the canal route, the elimination of two major aqueducts across the Mohawk River, and the construction of an aqueduct in order to improve the troublesome Schoharie Creek crossing. Though of his recommendations only the Schoharie Aqueduct was approved by the Canal Commission, it was constructed to Jervis's specifications, and a major portion of it stands today as a monument to Jervis's ability as a civil engineer.

Jervis had been with the Erie enlargement project for only a year when he was given the opportunity to build one of the first great urban water supply systems in the United States. The choice of Jervis to supervise construction of the Croton Aqueduct, a water supply system for New York City, apparently was based on his reputation and ability in constructing artificial waterways. While it was true that he lacked experience in the building of aqueducts, so did most American engineers. But this lack of experience did not deter Jervis from accepting the appointment as chief engineer. He saw the Croton as a new challenge and one that most certainly would enhance his reputation as an engineer.

For decades prior to the mid 1830s efforts had been made to provide New York City with an adequate supply of "pure and wholesome" water, but none of the efforts had been successful. In 1835 a Water Commission, appointed by the city's Common Council, reported in favor of the Croton River in northern Westchester County as a water source. After a public referendum endorsed the project in April the West Point-trained David Bates Douglass was hired to build the nearly 40-mile pipeline to mid Manhattan at an estimated cost of nearly $5.5 million. But Douglass was fired after little more than a year, ostensibly because of his inability to get along with the water commissioners. The hiring of Jervis set off a political controversy between the two men and their respective supporters that lasted for decades.

By the summer of 1837 work was underway on the aqueduct. During that time, Jervis visited Philadelphia to inspect its new water system and traveled to the nation's capital to observe the Potomac Aqueduct. The latter was of particular interest to him because of its similarity to the Croton. But neither project could provide him with models for the two most difficult structures of the Croton, the dam across the Croton River and the massive stone bridge over the Harlem River.

The dam across the Croton River consisted of a combination of masonry and earthen embankment. It was nearly completed on January 8, 1841, when disaster struck. Heavy rain and a snow melt caused an unprecedented amount of water to enter the new reservoir. The masonry spillway of the dam could not handle the unusually high level of water fast enough, and it rose to the level of the earthen section. Seepage between the frozen and unfrozen earth occurred, and, almost instantly, the entire embankment gave way. A wall of water swept down the Croton valley, taking three lives and causing much property damage.

Jervis was at the scene of the break within hours and quickly reported on the damage to the water commissioners. The chief engineer was not blamed for the collapse of the embankment. He was told to rebuild, this time replacing the earthen embankment with stone laid in cement. The second structure was completed within two years and stood until superseded by a larger dam in 1906. Jervis's rebuilt dam employed the first uses of a reversed curve spillway and a stilling basin, formed by a smaller dam 300 feet downstream from the main dam to contain the force of the water. This again demonstrated Jervis's ingenuity and placed him in the vanguard of hydraulic engineering. The use of the ogival spillway and the stilling basin became general practice in dam construction.

Although the dam was a new design, the High Bridge over the Harlem River was Jervis's greatest single achievement on the Croton project. Rising 138 feet above tide, the bridge was 1,450 feet long with 80-foot-wide arch spans over the river. Two parapet walls at the top of the bridge boxed in the four 36-inch cast-iron pipes needed to handle 50 million gallons of water each day. The cost of the structure was more than $900,000, or about one-tenth of the cost of the entire project.

The bridge's fifteen arches were unusual, Jervis wrote, in that "unlike most stone arches, the loads from above the arch ring were carried to the ring by a series of masonry walls instead of the usual earth fill." The purpose of this was to reduce the "dead load" between the side walls and to allow for "a more economical design." In addition to the new design for the bridge, Jervis also developed an ingenious method for testing the strength or bearing weight of the oak piles that were used to support some of the bridge piers. The test, described in detail by Jervis, "may well have been the first full-scale test of pile foundations in the United States."

Although the aqueduct was sufficiently complete to allow the passage of water by June 1842, the High Bridge required another seven years to finish. Temporary pipes were used in the interim. The New York City diarist George Templeton Strong called the bridge, upon its completion, "a very great piece of work." Apparently it was, as the piers and arches of the structure have been in use for nearly 150 years.

Jervis left the Croton in 1846. At fifty-one he had completed his greatest achievement as an engineer and was now considered by many to be the outstanding civil engineer in America. He had many great projects to his credit, but Jervis also had pursued interests other than engineering.

While in his teens, Jervis had joined the First Presbyterian Church in Rome. His deep religious commitment led him to attend meetings which brought him in contact with Charles Phinney, the greatest of the early nineteenth-century revivalists. It may have been the influence of Phinney and others that caused him to support the Free-Soil movement. A staunch Jacksonian, Jervis had refused to desert the Democratic party even when his beloved uncle John Bloomfield "went to the log cabin and drank hard cider" in 1840. But Jervis wavered in the 1850s and, finally, reluctantly joined the new Republican party which, as a purely sectional organization, could stand firm against the spread of slavery. Jervis remained a Republican for the rest of his life.

Perhaps one of the reasons for Jervis's support of the Democrats in the 1830s and 1840s was his considerable interest in banking, an industry with strong Democratic ties. He was financially involved in many banking institutions in New York State and also in the states of the old Northwest. John Bloomfield acted as his fiscal agent and regularly exchanged advice with his nephew on money matters. Jervis also speculated in property, particularly in

the proximity of his many transportation works. In addition he financed two of his brothers in several business ventures, all of which were less than successful. Jervis's support of his brothers was one of the rare instances of his miscalculation in money matters.

As successful as Jervis's financial affairs were in the 1830s his personal life was less fortunate. He was married in 1834 to Cynthia Brayton of Westernville, near Rome. But Jervis's work kept him away most of the time, and Cynthia was unable to accompany him because of poor health. A daughter was born to the couple on May 9, 1839, but she lived only a few hours. Five days later Cynthia died, apparently from the rigors of childbirth. Virtually nothing is known of Jervis's reaction to the tragic loss, but, now in his mid forties, Jervis did not want to remain alone. It was evident that loneliness had haunted him throughout his marriage when his work had kept him away from his wife. On June 16, 1840, Jervis married Eliza Coates. They remained together until Jervis's death but produced no children.

When Jervis returned to constructing railroads in 1846, he commenced a twenty-year phase of his life during which he was as much a manager as a builder. He accepted the chief engineer's job with the Hudson River Railroad and was an important force in convincing the line's backers that it could profitably compete with the Hudson River commerce. Jervis directed the completion of the line's New York City to Poughkeepsie stretch, the most difficult of the 140-mile route. Upon resigning his position with the railroad in 1849, he traveled to the British Isles to observe the opening of the famous railroad bridge across the Manai Straights. He was a guest of the English builder, Robert Stephenson.

On returning from Europe Jervis quickly plunged into railroads again, this time in the West. He became president and chief engineer of the Michigan Southern & Northern Indiana Railroad in 1850, which ran from Jackson to Chicago. It was routine work and posed none of the challenges he had encountered on the New York projects. An outgrowth of the Michigan Southern was the Chicago & Rock Island Railroad, of which Jervis was president from 1851 to 1858. During his tenure the line was pushed beyond Rock Island, Illinois, into Iowa, a move which required bridging the Mississippi. Although he did not design this first span across the river, Jervis did present a report or deposition on it,

Engraving of the Delaware & Hudson's Stourbridge Lion

apparently required in the famous "Effie Afton" case in which Abraham Lincoln was a defense counsel for the Rock Island Bridge Company.

Jervis's final position with the railroad completed his transition from engineer to manager. He was general superintendent of the Pittsburgh, Ft. Wayne & Chicago during the Civil War years. When Jervis took over the line was in default, but after little more than two years, Jervis had improved the railroad and its financial affairs to a point that a 10 percent stock dividend was declared. Jervis believed that railways should be managed by engineers and later wrote that "an engineering education fits a man best for the superintendence no less than for the construction of a railway."

After leaving the Pittsburgh, Ft. Wayne & Chicago in 1864, Jervis returned to Rome. At age seventy most people would be ready for retirement. He did not lack the funds to do so; he did, however, lack the inclination. In 1868 Jervis helped organize the Merchant Iron Works in his home community of Rome, New York, and served as secretary-treasurer of the company until his death in 1885. It also was in 1868 that Jervis was ac-

corded a well-deserved honor when he was made an honorary member of the American Society of Civil Engineers, a society he had been instrumental in founding.

Publications:

Description of the Croton Aqueduct (New York: Slamm & Guion, 1842);

Report on the Hudson River Railroad (New York: J. F. Trow, 1846);

Hudson River Rail Road Report on the Location of the Line Between Fishkill and Albany: with General Remarks on the Prospects of the Road (New York: Wm. C. Bryant, 1848);

Report on the Michigan Southern and Northern Indiana Railroads (New York: Van Norden & Amerman, 1850);

Letters Addressed to the Friends of Freedom and the Union ([New York]: Wm. C. Bryant, 1856);

Railway Property: A Treatise on the Construction and Management of Railways (New York: Phinney, Blakeman & Mason, 1861);

The Question of Labor and Capital (New York: Putnams, 1877).

Unpublished Document:

John B. Jervis, "Facts and Circumstances in the Life of John B. Jervis," Manuscript autobiography in Jervis Public Library, Rome, New York.

Reference:

Neal FitzSimons, *The Reminiscences of John B. Jervis, Engineer of the Old Croton* (Syracuse, N.Y.: Syracuse University Press, 1971).

Archives:

Material concerning John B. Jervis is located in the John B. Jervis Papers of the Jervis Public Library, Rome, New York.

James Frederick Joy

(December 2, 1810-September 24, 1890)

by John Lauritz Larson

Purdue University

CAREER: Teacher, Pittsfield, New Hampshire (1834-1835); attorney, Detroit, Michigan (1836-1890); legal counsel (1852-1857); director and solicitor, Illinois Central (1852-1857); director, Michigan Central (1852-1877); president, Chicago & Aurora (1853-1855); director, St. Mary's Falls Ship Canal (1853-1855); president (1855-1857, 1865-1871), director (1855-1874), Chicago, Burlington & Quincy; director, Burlington & Missouri River, Iowa (1859-1871); member, Michigan House of Representatives (1861-1862); director, Union Stock Yards (1865); president, Burlington & Missouri River, Iowa (1866-1871); director (1867-1870), president (1867-1876), Michigan Central; president (1867), chairman (1868-1870), director (1869-1877), Hannibal & St. Joseph; president, Leavenworth, Lawrence & Galveston (1869-1870); director and president, Kansas City, St. Joseph & Council Bluffs (1870-1874); director, Missouri River, Fort Scott & Gulf (1870-1875); director (1870-1877), president (1871-1872), Atchison & Nebraska; president, Detroit Post & Tribune Company (1881-1884); director and president, Wabash, St. Louis & Pacific (1884-1887).

James F. Joy practiced law in Detroit, but his real vocation lay in seizing opportunities for enterprise as they sprang up on the western edge of nineteenth-century America's expanding economy. One of the first men to visualize large interregional systems of railroad lines, Joy guided railroad expansion into the trans-Mississippi West in the decades surrounding the Civil War. Skilled at law and politics, Joy thrived in the heady atmosphere of the new country, then typically lost control to competitors who were more daring in speculation or more versed in the details of railroad operations. He was a "fixer" of deals who accelerated the progress of nineteenth-century railroad development on the Middle Border.

Joy was born on December 2, 1810, to James and Sarah Pickering Joy in Durham, New Hampshire. Joy took his early schooling in Durham, then went to Dartmouth College, where he graduated in 1833 at the head of his class. He studied law at Harvard in 1833-1834, then served one year as principal of an academy at Pittsfield, New Hampshire, and as a tutor at Dartmouth College, before finishing law school at Harvard in 1836. That year Joy moved to Detroit, where he was admitted to the bar. In 1837 he entered a partnership with George F. Porter that would last some twenty-five years.

Joy's association with Porter placed the Yankee newcomer directly in the midst of frontier Michigan's progress. Michigan had just joined the federal union and immediately adopted a program of railroad construction. George F. Porter served on the commission that guided this ambitious state system, but despite every effort Michigan's public works collapsed in the depression that followed the panic of 1837. By 1846 the economy had recovered, but debt, bad feeling, and physical deterioration still crippled the state's infant railways. Porter and Joy concluded that private enterprise should start the projects anew, and Joy wrote a series of newspaper articles advocating sale of the Central Railroad to willing entrepreneurs. John W. Brooks, a New York railroad engineer with high ambitions and wealthy friends, came to Detroit to investigate. It was Brooks who put Joy in touch with John Murray Forbes and the group of eastern capitalists who bought the Michigan Central Railroad and started rebuilding its tattered line. Joy's railroad career had begun.

The special expertise James F. Joy brought to pioneer railroading was a quick mastery of booster

James Frederick Joy

politics. Corporate charters and public works were controversial political issues requiring sensitive public relations work and vigorous tactical action. Joy proved a genius at both. His quick mind and excellent legal training gave him advantages over most rivals in frontier legislatures, while his connection to Forbes's financial networks gave him the money to accomplish what others only promised. With John W. Brooks in charge of construction and Forbes rounding up the funds, Joy, whose official title was "counsel," turned his attention to what lay ahead for this Michigan Central team.

The next step was not hard to see, but the pace of westward growth, which Joy already perceived, was not immediately apparent to investors in quiet Boston. Forbes found the expense and details of finishing a line across Michigan so absorbing that he balked when Joy presented him, in 1848, with plans for major extension. For only $50,000 Joy could deliver a valid Indiana charter to build a railroad around Lake Michigan toward the booming new city of Chicago. Forbes declined the bargain as "premature," and two years later it took all of Joy's political talents plus $500,000 to achieve the same result. Although Forbes stoically de-

fended his error, the race to Chicago fixed in his mind an almost unshakable confidence that James F. Joy understood western railroading as did no one else he knew.

By 1852, when the Michigan Central Railroad ran its first train into Chicago, Joy had worked out an excellent method for pushing rail lines into the frontier. Everywhere to the west local boosters clamored for transportation improvements that they hoped would ensure their fortunes. Local governments and state legislators eagerly courted promoters whose schemes met local approval and did not smack too much of absentee control. Working among these local interests and their politicians, Joy identified promising lines which offered both quick success for, and logical connections with, his existing railroad.

The Chicago, Burlington & Quincy (CB&Q) system grew out of this approach. In 1852 Joy directed Forbes to buy quietly into the Chicago & Aurora Railroad. John W. Brooks joined the board of this 12-mile road west of Chicago. Meanwhile three projects converging on Galesburg—the Peoria & Oquawka, the Central Military Tract, and the Northern Cross—all languished for lack of funds. Joy let it be known that "friends" in the East might have money, and representatives of each struggling company "turned up" in Boston one day to discuss their capital needs. Forbes listened, then sent them to Detroit where Joy laid down the terms of investment. Momentarily swollen with confidence, the locals contacted rival investors to see if better terms could be found. Joy promptly traveled to Galesburg with subscription books in hand and threw down a take-it-or-leave-it offer. Afraid to pass up a sure thing, the Illinoians signed for their shares. In 1853 Joy became president of the Chicago & Aurora, which he reorganized in 1855 as the Chicago, Burlington & Quincy. Joy continued as president through 1857, left the office in local hands until the end of the Civil War, then returned in 1865 to lead the railroad through another period of rapid growth.

Because railroading required special legislative permission to collect subscriptions, issue securities, contract debts, and condemn rights-of-way, Joy's political and legal talents gave Forbes and his friends a considerable edge in the West. When the federal government added land grants to the stock of inducements behind railroad expansion, James F. Joy immediately saw what could be made of this new resource. In 1852 the Hannibal & St. Joseph (H&StJ), a Missouri project touching the Mississippi River near Quincy, won a grant of federal lands; Joy urged his Boston friends to invest. By 1854 Forbes's group controlled the Hannibal's board of directors, and in February 1859 they completed the main line. Similarly the Burlington & Missouri River (B&MR) in Iowa, which ran west from Burlington, received a land grant in 1856 and saw a Forbes takeover the following year. All these connections were guided by Joy, who recognized land grants not as capital assests only, but as competitive plums that would go to others if he failed to grasp them first.

Even before the Civil War Joy concluded that competition would force major railroad lines into the western frontier far faster than local settlement required–or cautious investors preferred. While the struggle for victory in the war distracted most of his Boston colleagues, Joy watched the unfolding western business scene with care. Kansas City was stirring, and Joy entered negotiations with local boosters there to build a road to the Hannibal line and possibly to bridge the river as well for a through line into Great Plains cattle country. Congress had already passed the Pacific Railroad Act (1862) guaranteeing a transcontinental line from Council Bluffs to San Francisco. Once again local ambitions and politics laid the future at Joy's feet. In the CB&Q and the Hannibal, Joy controlled the earliest finished connection with the Missouri River Valley and potentially the first link to the transcontinental route.

As soon as the Civil War ended, the pace of development quickened. Again president of the CB&Q, Joy seized the Kansas City connection for the Hannibal-CB&Q combination. At the same time he took personal interests in the Kansas City Bridge Company and the West Kansas City Land Company (through which the stockyards would be built). Competitive pressures brought about by subsidies to the transcontinental line converged on this Kansas gateway, and Joy moved swiftly to secure several avenues of expansion at once. He demanded and got Kansas City's support for a land grant road heading south through Kansas toward the Cherokee Strip and Texas. He also entered a bid for the 800,000-acre Cherokee Neutral Tract, which he won through political clout. Joy hoped to push his Missouri River, Fort Scott & Gulf to the Cherokee border before any rivals, thereby gaining exclusive

rights to build across Indian lands into Texas. For defense against rivals on the cattle frontier he bought control of the Leavenworth, Lawrence & Galveston, a north-south Kansas competitor. He bought up various local fragments heading north from Kansas City and in 1869 reorganized them into the Kansas City, St. Joseph & Council Bluffs (KC StJ&CB), which would soon touch the Union Pacific (UP). By 1870 Joy's system boasted bridges across the Missouri and Mississippi and through lines radiating from Kansas City to Council Bluffs to the north, Chicago to the east, and Indian country to the south.

Railroading in a hothouse like Kansas City during the late 1860s required a fast and loose style that gradually estranged Joy from his more cautious Boston investors. When John W. Brooks fell gravely ill in 1866, John Murray Forbes neglected Joy with blissful confidence, causing the Kansas City connections to go unscrutinized for months. Joy plunged ahead in what were often reckless competitive ventures. Dirty tricks and even gunplay marred his race to the Cherokee Strip, where he lost the prize through uncharacteristic ignorance of legal details. Rapid investment in roads with little traffic to support them strained his financial reserves while cutthroat competition with rivals for the transcontinental interchange made that business more costly than profitable almost from the beginning. Finally, Joy's deep personal interest in Kansas City, and his more opportunistic style of development, contradicted the development vision of Joy's most influential backer, Forbes.

Forbes had always believed that western railroads ought to develop sequentially, following or closely preceding the advancing line of settlement. Only in this way, he reasoned, could the productivity of the country grow alongside the railroads and reward the investors of capital with revenues and profits. Federal land grants deranged this "natural" development and lured speculators into trunk-line adventures well ahead of demand. This was precisely what happened in Kansas City, and Joy insisted it was the only way to play the railroad game. Forbes began to wonder, and his young cousin Charles E. Perkins, who ran the CB&Q's Iowa feeder, poured a steady fire of complaint into his kinsman's ear when Joy's Kansas operations threatened to stop the Iowa line mid state. In 1867 Forbes accused Joy of bending the interests of the CB&Q for his own southwestern empire, and he demanded better treatment for the straighter Iowa line. Once the B&MR reached Council Bluffs in 1869, an immediate and bitter competition sprang up between it and Joy's southern route. Acting as president of the CB&Q, Joy pooled the Burlington traffic with three other Iowa roads, which sustained long-haul rates; but Kansas City was not in the pool, and Joy's personal interests there drew him into mischievous competition. While Perkins made trouble in Iowa, Jay Gould captured the Hannibal, and the Kansas City, St. Joseph & Council Bluffs failed to meet its interest payments. In late 1871 James F. Joy's southwestern system began to unravel.

Joy's approach to western railroading was brilliant in the short run, but his system was vulnerable in the end. He seized opportunities for innovator profits, special franchises, and exclusive privileges often without regard for their eventual profitability. Somebody would profit immediately, of course, whenever subsidies and charters abounded; but unless Joy could block the entry of later rivals, his gains were bound to be fleeting. Joy found himself constantly challenged by more efficient roads on the one hand and bigger gamblers on the other. In 1873 he complained to the stockholders of his failing KC.StJ&CB that none of his competitors' roads "were in contemplation when the road of this company was undertaken" and that nobody could have "predicted" that "all of them would be built." Coming from the wizard of Kansas City, this excuse seems incredibly naive. In truth a new generation of speculative roads forced pioneer builders like Joy to buy them up or lose them to the enemy, and when the original systems lacked the earning power to sustain this kind of burden, the structures collapsed. Joy's operations were seldom efficient, and his "dictatorial" personal style left local constituents more than ready to welcome competitors.

While his Kansas City system collapsed, Joy plunged steadily deeper into a parallel scheme that would finally end his close relationship with Forbes. A group of Iowa "River Roads" promised to link eastern Iowa with the Twin Cities, and Joy thought they could do for the CB&Q what the Council Bluffs road did for his Kansas City line. The CB&Q was fully extended helping its other family lines, so Joy organized construction companies in which he and selected stockholders invested. Six million dollars flowed out and securities proliferated, but the River Roads were never built. Eventually the CB&Q directors were asked to cover coupons for River Road bonds they held at Joy's recommendation. In 1874 Forbes asked to see the books on this venture. He learned to his horror that there were no books and that his old friends Joy and Brooks had taken profits from construction funds paid out of CB&Q advances to the bankrupt River Roads. Furious that such a "crédit-mobilier" was now attached to his name, Forbes launched a proxy war. In March 1875 he drove James F. Joy from the board of the CB&Q. Joy insisted he had done nothing wrong or new and that Forbes's own fortune over the last thirty years derived from precisely such affairs; but the old Bostonian believed he had been seriously betrayed.

Joy took refuge in the presidency of the Michigan Central, an office he assumed in 1867 when John W. Brooks retired. Although his Kansas City properties continued to thrive, his glory days were over, and he turned his attention more to things around home. Joy's fascination with frontier Kansas City never undermined his ardent feeling for Detroit, and many of his ancillary business ventures sprang from the interests of his hometown. Back in 1852, for example, Congress had passed a land grant for a ship canal at St. Mary's Falls that would facilitate water transportation from Lake Michigan to Detroit. Joy took the lead in managing the legislature and placed the charter and the land grant in the hands of Brooks, Forbes, and the eastern men who had rescued the Michigan Central. Some years later, in 1871, when his Missouri and Mississippi bridges had forged unbroken interstate railroad lines, Joy asked the Detroit city council for permission to dig a tunnel under the Detroit River to Canada and give his hometown better access to competing eastern routes. Crews dug for two years before leaking gas deposits forced abandonment of the task. In the 1880s Joy took an interest in the Detroit *Post and Tribune* and played a more active role in Republican politics than his time before had allowed. Near the end of his life, in the 1890s, he helped establish the railroad car-building industry that marked Detroit's economy until the triumph of the automobile.

It may have been Joy's interest in hometown prosperity that encouraged him in 1884 to accept the presidency of the bankrupt Wabash, St. Louis & Pacific and connect that line to Detroit. One of Jay Gould's recent conquests, the consolidated Wabash line from Toledo to Kansas City, had set off new wars among the trunk lines and then foundered on the rocks of falling income. Joy stepped in to arrange reorganization, but the old master was taunted in England with charges of being "Gould's man." Now seventy-four years old and perhaps tired of the game, Joy wrestled inconclusively with the Wabash for three stormy years, the connection to Detroit about his only reward.

James F. Joy married twice in his life. He married his first wife, Martha Alger Reed of Yarmouth, Massachusetts, in Detroit on August 12, 1841. Together they had four children before Martha's death in 1850. Joy married Mary Bourne of Hartford, Connecticut, on December 12, 1860, and three more children followed. Joy was said to be a bookish man, possessed of perhaps the finest personal library in Detroit. He built a grand three-story home fit for a mid-century business magnate, and he apparently never tired of the changes that whirled around him. Smarter and more successful than a typical local booster, Joy's business habits bore the marks of small-town enthusiasm long after more sophisticated New York and Boston styles ushered in the Gilded Age. His original vision, so fresh and innovative in the 1850s and 1860s, looked narrow in the company of huge consolidations from the 1880s onward. His contribution belongs to the transition period which first experimented with as-sembling the pieces in a wildly competitive environment. An early fixer of deals, Joy showed the way for the architects of America's national market system.

References:

Charles N. Glab, *Kansas City and the Railroads* (Madison, Wis.: State Historical Society of Wisconsin, 1962);

Julius Grodinsky, *The Iowa Pool* (Chicago: University of Chicago Press, 1950);

Arthur M. Johnson and Barry E. Supple, *Boston Capitalists and Western Railroads* (Cambridge, Mass.: Harvard University Press, 1967);

John Lauritz Larson, *Bonds of Enterprise* (Cambridge, Mass.: Harvard University Press, 1984);

Richard C. Overton, *The Burlington Route* (New York: Alfred A. Knopf, 1965);

Robert J. Parks, *Democracy's Railroads: Public Enterprise in Jacksonian Michigan* (Port Washington, N.Y.: Kennikat Press, 1972).

Archives:

Material concerning James F. Joy is located in the James F. Joy Collection of the Burton Historical Collections at the Detroit Public Library, Detroit, Michigan; in the James F. Joy Papers of the Michigan Historical Collections, Ann Arbor, Michigan; in the Michigan Central Railroad Archives of the New York Central System, Detroit, Michigan; in the Burlington Railroad Archives of the Newberry Library, Chicago, Illinois.

Theodore Judah

(March 4, 1826-November 2, 1863)

by Dan Butler

Colby Community College

CAREER: Various railroad and construction positions (1847-1854); chief engineer, Sacramento Valley Railroad (1854-1855); delegate, California Railroad Convention (1859); lobbyist, U.S. Congress (1859-1860); chief clerk, U.S. Senate and U.S. House Committee on Railroads (1861-1862); chief engineer, Central Pacific Railroad (1862-1863).

Theodore Dehone Judah was born in Bridgeport, Connecticut, on March 4, 1826, the son of Henry R. Judah, an Episcopal clergyman. Shortly after Judah's birth, the family moved to Troy, New York. Judah had been expected to follow his brother Henry into a military career but instead was allowed to develop his natural engineering talent at Rensselaer Polytechnic Institute. Early in his career Judah displayed a keen interest in railroads and soon moved from the engineering classroom to the railroad construction business.

In 1847 he married Anna Ferona Pierce, the daughter of a Greenfield, Massachusetts, merchant. After leaving school he was employed by several railroads, including the New Haven, Hartford & Springfield and the Connecticut River railroads. He was the engineer in charge of construction on the Vergennes Bridge Project in Vermont. Still later he helped plan and construct the Niagara Gorge Railroad and the Buffalo & New York Railroad, the last being part of the Erie system. He was also involved in the construction of a section of the Erie Canal.

In 1854 Judah was offered the position of chief engineer on a proposed railroad to be built in California, the Sacramento Valley Railroad. The president of the line, C. L. Wilson, wanted to construct a line from Sacramento to the mining areas in the foothills of the Sierras. California was not entirely unknown to Judah as one of his brothers practiced law in San Francisco. Upon his arrival in Sacramento he not only began to develop plans for

Theodore Judah (courtesy of the California State Library)

the line to the mines but also for one to the East.

Judah found a receptive audience. California was eager for more rapid communications with the East, and they now had a railroad engineer who had the vision and drive to work toward this end. Judah's initial goal, construction of the Sacramento Valley Railroad, was surveyed in less than one month. Traffic estimates for the line were made by counting freight and stage traffic along a parallel wagon road. In March 1855 the railroad laid the first rails on the Pacific Coast. Completed in February 1856, the line connected Sacramento with the foothills town of Folsom and reduced by a full day the travel time to the mining camps of California and the newly discovered deposits in Nevada. However, a decline in mining activity hampered the new company's operation. Judah left the Sacramento Valley Railroad in 1855 to survey a rail line between Sacramento and Benicia, a city which until recently had been the state capital. However, Judah's real interest focused on the building of a line eastward over the Sierras to Nevada and beyond. Once he completed the survey to Benicia, he turned all his attention to the mountains and located a passage through the range which became known as the Dutch Flat Route.

Judah made several subsequent surveys of the Sierras but always returned to his original line. Railroad construction in the difficult mountain terrain would prove extremely difficult; the mountains rise rapidly from the floor of the central valley of California, the canyons are steep, and the high peaks consist almost totally of granite. These natural obstacles did not dampen the Californians' desire for a rail line to the East, but they did convince many that, given present technology, a line built directly over the mountains was impossible. Judah's single-minded obsession with the line was also worrisome to many, and some actually doubted his sanity.

California had held its first statewide railroad convention in 1853 without much success. The second convention was held in San Francisco in September 1859 with Judah as a delegate from Sacramento. He proved to be a leading force both in the formulation of state plans for railroad construction and of proposals for the role of the federal government. Ten years of bitter debate coalesced as a concrete plan of action. Judah was selected to take the proposals to Washington and lobby for their approval, a job in which he proved to be well prepared not only in the technical aspects of rail construction but also in the areas of finance and legislation.

Judah had access not only to members of Congress and newspaper editors but also to cabinet officials. He was even allowed to present his plans directly to President James Buchanan. With the aid of Rep. John Logan of Illinois he was given office space in the capitol where he established what became known as the Pacific Railway Museum; the office became his headquarters where he expounded his railroad ideas to any who would listen. His efforts did much to bring the Pacific rail project to public attention, but Congress, preoccupied with slavery and the shadow of the Civil War, took no action. Judah, only temporarily discouraged, returned to California and again became active in surveying the Dutch Flat Route. By winter 1860 Judah had completed a detailed plan of the proposed line through the mountains and set about to raise necessary money to build the line. California law required $1,000 for every mile built within the state, and Judah estimated that the line would run 115 miles from Sacramento to the Nevada border. While the communities along the proposed route responded favorably to his request, San Francisco business interests turned a deaf ear. Disappointed at his rejection, the engineer returned to Sacramento where he met with a group of local merchants, including Charles Crocker, Collis P. Huntington, Mark Hopkins, and Leland Stanford. He was able to convince these men and some of their associates to finance the instrument survey of his mountain route. When that survey proved successful, Judah again returned to Washington to lobby for the necessary concessions from Congress.

The secession of the South provided Judah and his associates with a great opportunity. As the sectional controversy in Congress over the Pacific railroad was resolved by the war, Congress was much more receptive to the project. But despite the fact that Judah was able to argue that the railroad was necessary to hold California and Nevada for the Union, the government still remained slow to act. By now well-initiated to Washington politics, Judah was able to gain an appointment as a clerk to both the House and Senate committees on railroads. In this capacity he was able to push the bill forward. Despite opposition the Pacific Railway Act was passed in June 1862, and President Lincoln signed the legislation on July 1.

The Pacific Railway Act provided for two companies: one building east from California, the Central Pacific (CP), and the other building west from central Nebraska, the Union Pacific. Further, each line was granted a 400-foot right-of-way plus ten alternate sections of land for each mile of track built. The companies were also given loans on a first mortgage basis of $16,000 for each mile built on level ground, $32,000 for each mile built in the foothills, and $48,000 for each mile built in the mountains.

The major surveys for the Central Pacific (CP) had long been completed, and those still in the field made only slight changes to Judah's original route. Charles Crocker was awarded the first construction contract for the CP, an agreement to build the first thirty-two miles of line. Groundbreaking began in January 1863. By the 1862 law federal money would not become available until forty miles of track had been completed. Collis P. Huntington was sent to the East to sell stock while Leland Stanford, the governor of California, used his power to persuade the state and various county governments to contribute more than $1 million to the project. Even as the initial money was being raised, Judah and his partners had very different views on how it should be used. The four Sacramento partners, Crocker, Huntington, Stanford, and Hopkins, saw the forty miles as an obstacle to be overcome. Wanting the construction to advance as rapidly as possible with little regard for the quality of the work, the Big Four, as they were known, were eager to begin receiving government aid and also to corner the lucrative trade with the mining districts in Nevada. Judah, however, saw the first forty miles as the beginning of what he viewed as the most important railroad ever built, a road which would move goods and passengers between the Orient and Europe. He supported rapid construction, but only if it was at the highest level of engineering available.

The problem between the idealist and the speculators was their differing ideas about the significance of the railroad. The Big Four had come of age in California where quick profits were the rule, and they expected the railroad to be the catalyst in that direction. Judah himself had recognized that view when he tailored many of his early speeches to the quick profits that would be realized in controlling trade with Nevada. Everyone, Judah included,

realized that the railroad would generate large profits. The conflict arose over how these profits were to be obtained.

The slow pace of construction caused much protest and distrust in California. Many felt that the CP was simply a swindle engineered by a group of Sacramento merchants. Rather than a swindle, it was a power struggle which was causing the delay. Judah insisted on final authority on all matters of construction, and in this he was opposed by Charles Crocker. Several members of the board who supported Judah resigned over the conflict, but the four major stockholders remained united. Judah made little progress in his attempt to gain control of construction. The Big Four were strongly opposed to any effort which threatened their control of construction, which had been gained through the formation of a separate construction company that guaranteed large profits.

A resolution to the struggle required that one of the factions retire from the corporation. Judah, outnumbered and outmaneuvered, was the loser. The exact terms were never revealed, but it was assumed that Judah received an offer of $100,000, with the option to purchase the share of the other members for a like sum. Armed with this agreement, Judah left California in October 1863 to raise the necessary money. While traveling through the isthmus of Panama, however, he contracted yellow fever. The disease progressed rapidly, and Judah died on November 2, 1863, one week after reaching New York City. He was buried in Greenfield, Massachusetts. The line that Judah had envisioned was completed in 1869, but by that time the original engineer was little remembered.

References:

Maury Klein, *Union Pacific: The Birth of a Railroad, 1862-1893* (Garden City: Doubleday, 1987);
Oscar Lewis, *The Big Four* (New York: Knopf, 1938).

John S. Kennedy

(January 4, 1830-October 31, 1909)

by Saul Engelbourg

Boston University

CAREER: Partner, M. K. Jesup & Co. (1857-1860); partner, Jesup, Kennedy & Co. (1861-1867); senior partner, J. S. Kennedy & Co. (1868-1883); director, various railroads (1873-1909); director, vice-president, president pro tem, Bank of the Manhattan Company (1881-1909).

John Stewart Kennedy supplied and financed American railroads during the great age of railroad building, becoming James J. Hill's financial intermediary when Hill obtained control of the St. Paul, Minneapolis & Manitoba Railroad in 1878. From the early 1890s until his death, Kennedy was a director of the Bank of Manhattan Company and other financial institutions.

Born on January 4, 1830, he was the fifth son of John Kennedy and Isabella Stewart Kennedy of Blantyre, Lanarkshire, Scotland (in the vicinity of Glasgow). His family moved to Glasgow during his infancy. Leaving school at the age of thirteen, Kennedy worked as a clerk in a Glasgow shipping office. He remained there for four years while also attending classes both morning and afternoon. In 1847 he became a salesman for the Mossend Iron and Coal Company, a position he held for the next three years. Kennedy first visited the United States in June 1850 as a representative for William Bird and Company, a London firm which sold locomotive boiler tubing, and met his future partner, Morris Ketchum Jesup, a railroad commission merchant. In July 1852 Kennedy returned to the United Kingdom to head the Bird company's Glasgow branch office, a post he held until December 1856.

Kennedy returned to the United States in 1857 as a junior partner in M. K. Jesup and Company. For the next ten years Jesup and Kennedy participated in the enormous task of supplying, building, and financing western railroads. Jesup founded a branch in Chicago in 1859, in order to

John S. Kennedy

be closer to the construction frontier. Kennedy reorganized this branch in 1861 as Jesup, Kennedy and Company, specializing in railroad securities.

His partnership with Jesup terminated in 1867; and in 1868 Kennedy opened a railroad commission and private banking firm, J. S. Kennedy and Company, in New York. As a railroad commission merchant house, the company assembled orders for railroad supplies from diverse British and American manufacturers. These functions were more crucial for railroads during the construction phase than for those needing replacement equipment and for small rather than large railroads. J. S. Kennedy and Company helped finance these purchases and became a holder of railroad securities. Consequently, Kennedy and his competitors gradually shifted from supplying as commission merchants to financing as private (commercial and investment) bankers.

On October 14, 1858, Kennedy married Emma Baker, daughter of Cornelius Baker of Elizabeth, New Jersey. Like many other businessmen of his generation, Kennedy drew on his family for business associates. His first partner in J. S. Kennedy and Company was his brother-in-law Henry M. Baker, who served as the "inside" man. Family ties also played a part in John Stanford Barnes's joining the company as the "outside" man. Barnes's sister was married to Henry M. Baker.

As senior partner Kennedy supplied the capital. He owned one-half of the firm, with Barnes and Baker each holding a quarter. Baker's business association with Kennedy was relatively brief. After the worst of the panic of 1873 subsided, Kennedy and Baker had a falling out, and the junior partner departed in 1878. Then Kennedy constituted another partnership with Barnes, who handled the firm's business in the field. By increasing the value of various railroad properties, Barnes added to the wealth of Kennedy and such business associates as James Alfred Roosevelt of Roosevelt and Son and D. Willis James of Phelps, Dodge and Company. In 1885 Stephen Baker, a nephew on his wife's side, became Kennedy's private secretary, taking charge of all his interests until 1891.

The Kennedy firm functioned as the middleman between sellers of railroad supplies—representing, for example, such producers of rails as the Bowling Steel Company and the Cambria Iron Works—and the railroads. In 1870 J. S. Kennedy and Company (Kennedy, Baker, and Barnes) advertised itself as capable of performing all business connected with constructing and equipping railroads. Also, this firm served as a financial intermediary between those with capital to invest and the railroads—that is, as an investment banker. In an imperfect capital market, it was an agent and banker for railroads which frequently needed the endorsement of a commercial firm with a good credit standing to attract individual or institutional investors.

Private bankers flourished before the Civil War, but the needs of war finance and the railway boom encouraged others to enter the field. In an increasingly competitive atmosphere, Kennedy, like others in the business, attempted to protect his investment by taking a direct hand in the management of individual enterprises. In 1873 he became a director of the Cedar Falls & Minnesota (a branch railroad leased to the Dubuque & Sioux City and subleased to the Illinois Central); the Cincinnati & Indiana (leased to the Indianapolis, Cincinnati & Lafayette); the Indianapolis, Cincinnati & Lafayette; and the International & Great Northern. Kennedy also helped to reorganize the Indianapolis, Cincinnati & Lafayette; the Pittsburgh, Fort Wayne & Chicago; the New York, Chicago & St. Louis; the Cleveland & Pittsburgh; and the Central Railroad of New Jersey—among others.

The reorganization in 1878 of the St. Paul & Pacific Railroad Company proved to be Kennedy's most profitable and enduring investment. This developmental railroad had originated in 1857 as the Minnesota & Pacific to link St. Paul to the Red River. In 1862 the road was reorganized as the St. Paul & Pacific. It went bankrupt in 1872, leaving Kennedy (initially an agent of Dutch bondholders) to straighten out five years of legal and financial tangles. This particular transaction transformed him from being worth about $500,000, to being one of the richest Americans. Kennedy's previous railroad reorganizations had conformed to the norm: arranging financing, issuing securities, and transferring control to the new owners. Railroad bankruptcies, nominally a temporary and short-lived expedient, frequently had a way of lasting more or less indefinitely, especially during the distressed economic conditions after 1873. In this instance, Kennedy helped to convert the property into a more coherent system by supporting not-always-successful efforts to link the disconnected pieces of the railroad.

Essentially, J. S. Kennedy and Company provided the wherewithal for four railroad entrepreneurs, termed the George Stephen Associates, to buy the bankrupt St. Paul & Pacific. These four were two Canadians—George Stephen (president of the Bank of Montreal) and Donald A. Smith (chief commissioner of the Hudson Bay Company in North America)—plus Norman W. Kittson and James J. Hill of St. Paul. In addition to the purchase price, the men, whose entrepreneurial vision greatly exceeded their financial capacity, needed construction money, which they planned to obtain by selling "receiver's debentures." In the short run, Kennedy advanced a million dollars to finance the summer 1878 construction. J. S. Kennedy and Company was indispensable because Kennedy alone was willing to bear the risk by advancing seed money in excess of a million dollars to facilitate the transfer of the St. Paul & Pacific from the Dutch bondholders to the North Americans. Kennedy also profited because between 1877 and the foreclosure sale of 1879 he had been buying the bonds of the bankrupt railroad at deeply discounted prices.

Barnes retired as a partner in J. S. Kennedy and Company in 1880 after a dispute with Kennedy. The issue was the nature of the payment which the company could accept from George Stephen Associates. Barnes was more than willing, even eager, to accept the equity participation offered by the buyers. According to Barnes, Kennedy balked, wary of the possible imputation of conflict of interest. In 1882 Kennedy began to buy shares in the reorganized road. Kennedy owned 15,000 shares of the total 200,000 in 1889 and was second only to Hill as a stockholder. In 1901 Kennedy owned 96,000 shares, with only Hill owning more, although at times Kennedy was the largest holder.

When the City of Glasgow Bank collapsed in October 1878, the repercussions reached across the Atlantic. At its liquidation the bank owned securities of the Western Union Railroad Company plus stock in the Chicago, Milwaukee & St. Paul Railway Company. The liquidators invited J. S. Kennedy to become their representative in the United States. Kennedy thus had the responsibility of disposing of more than $5 million in securities, valued at par, at the best possible price. He negotiated in 1879 with Alexander Mitchell, president of the Chicago, Milwaukee & St. Paul, for an exchange of Western Union securities for those of the Chicago, Milwaukee & St. Paul. These were then sold through a Winslow, Lanier and Company syndicate in which J. S. Kennedy and Company participated. The liquidation realized much more than anticipated on the American assets of the bank. In part this was the result of capitalizing on the recovery of security prices, but it also resulted from Kennedy's negotiating tactics which combined persuasion and litigation.

As a result of his association with the St. Paul, Minneapolis & Manitoba, later the Great Northern, Kennedy in 1880 became one of the directors of the Canadian Pacific Railroad. He also joined the six-member $30-million syndicate which built that transcontinental. Kennedy acted as banker and fiscal agent for the Canadian Pacific. Conflict soon arose over both rates and routes between the St. Paul, Minneapolis & Manitoba and the Canadian Pacific. Hill and Kennedy sold their interests in the Canadian Pacific and resigned from its board in 1883. Ill health caused Kennedy to liquidate his firm on December 1, 1883. J. Kennedy Tod and Company became the successor.

Kennedy remained active, nonetheless. He worked with Hill as vice-president and director of the Manitoba; at the turn of the century he was a director of many railroads, including the Chicago, Burlington & Quincy; the Cleveland & Pittsburgh; the New York, Chicago & St. Louis; the Northern Pacific; the Pittsburgh, Fort Wayne & Chicago; and the Northern Securities. In 1886 and 1887 he had served as a receiver of the Central Railroad of New Jersey.

Kennedy's "retirement" broadened his role as a financier with diverse interests in leading New York financial intermediaries. He was a director of the Bank of the Manhattan Company from January 1881 until his death. Following the president's resignation under pressure, Kennedy held the post of president pro tem from December 1883 until February 1884, when he became vice-president until 1888; for a few months he became president pro tem again in 1893.

Kennedy also served as a trustee of the Central Trust Company from 1882 until he died. Benefiting from Kennedy's experience, the Central Trust was heavily involved in railroad securities as well as reorganizations. On several occasions, it acted as the trustee for the St. Paul, Minneapolis & Manitoba. Kennedy held similar positions with the National Bank of Commerce (1902), the New York Life Insurance Company (1903-1906), the Title Guaranty and Trust Company (1895-1909), and the United States Trust Company of New York (1896-1909). As a result of his varied banking activities, Kennedy became a seminal figure in the history of American banking and in the New York business community. Between 1875 and 1900 the trust companies of New York City grew faster than either the national or state banks. The trust companies lent to the emerging large industrial enterprises and assumed the function of trustees that had been performed by corporation lawyers and private bankers. In addition, they were chartered with perpetual life, an important advantage as the maturities of these bond issues lengthened.

Kennedy gave money away while alive rather than bequeathing it to charity in his will. His more important philanthropies included the New York Presbyterian Hospital, the New York Public Library, the Metropolitan Museum of Art, and the charity organization movement. The scale of Kennedy's benefactions dwarfed that of many of his contemporaries with comparable financial resources, perhaps because he had no children. Unlike many other philanthropists, Kennedy took an active part in the management of those institutions to which he entrusted any substantial amount of his money. He served as president of the New York Presbyterian Hospital for twenty-five years. As a trustee of the Metropolitan Museum of Art, his sophisticated taste influenced the collection of paintings. He liked the "old masters," but also such modern artists as Corot, Millet, and Rousseau. Although the magnitude of his gifts warranted it, he directed that no significant monument be erected to perpetuate his name. In 1891 Kennedy funded the one-million-dollar construction of the United Charities Building. Housing divergent charities in a single location was supposed to foster communication and enhance the efficiency with which those in need were helped. The establishment of the New York School of Philanthropy (affiliated later with Columbia University as the School of Social Work) was made possible by a grant from Kennedy in 1904.

John S. Kennedy died of respiratory failure in New York City on October 31, 1909, as one of America's richest men, with a $60-million estate. In his will Kennedy disbursed $2.5 million to Columbia and, as a demonstration of his commitment to higher education in general, he left $100,000 to each of nine institutions as well as lesser amounts to other colleges.

References:

John Stanford Barnes, "My Egotistigraphy," typescript autobiography, The New York Historical Society;

Heather Gilbert, *The Life of Lord Mount Stephen* (Aberdeen: Aberdeen University Press, 1976);

Gilbert, "The Unaccountable Fifth: Solution of a Great Northern Enigma," *Minnesota History*, 42 (Spring 1971): 175-177;

"In Memory of John S. Kennedy," *Survey*, 23 (November 27, 1909): 276-278;

Jesse P. Farley v. *James J. Hill et al.*, United States District Court, District of Minnesota, 1888. Transcript of the Record, St. Paul Public Library, St. Paul, Minnesota;

Albro Martin, *James J. Hill and the Opening of the Northwest* (New York: Oxford University Press, 1976);

Joseph Gilpen Pyle, *The Life of James J. Hill* (Garden City: Doubleday, Page, 1917);

R. E. Tyson, "Scottish Investment in American Railways: The Case of the City of Glasgow Bank, 1856-1881," in *Studies in Scottish Business History*, edited by Peter L. Payne (New York: Augustus M. Kelley, 1967), pp. 387-416;

Ronald B. Weir, *A History of the Scottish American Investment Company 1873-1973* (Edinburgh, Scotland: American Investment Company, 1973).

Archives:

Materials concerning John S. Kennedy are located in the James J. Hill Papers of the James Jerome Hill Reference Library, St. Paul, Minnesota; and in the Great Northern Railway Company Records of the Minnesota Historical Society, St. Paul, Minnesota.

Lake Shore & Michigan Southern Railway

by John F. Due

University of Illinois

The Lake Shore & Michigan Southern (LS&MS) Railway, as its euphonious name suggests, consisted of two major elements: the Buffalo-Cleveland-Toledo line of the Lake Shore, and the Toledo-Chicago lines of the Michigan Southern. The Michigan Southern itself consisted of two lines, the original line which crossed Michigan via Hillsdale and the "air line" which operated via Waterloo and joined with its counterpart at Elkhart. The LS&MS air line eventually became part of the main New York-Chicago route of the New York Central. While it was developed independently from the New York Central, the LS&MS came under Vanderbilt control in 1869. The LS&MS continued to operate autonomously until it was formally merged into the New York Central system in 1914.

The Michigan Southern was, in its initial stages, a product of efforts by the state of Michigan to speed economic development by constructing railroads. Under legislation enacted in 1837 the state built the "Central" line west from Detroit via Jackson to Kalamazoo in 1846, and also the "Southern" line from Monroe via Adrian to Hillsdale in 1843. Progress was slow on the Southern line in part because the state concentrated its efforts on the longer Central line, and in part because of the Southern line's unprofitable competition with the privately owned Kalamazoo & Erie, Michigan's first railroad which had reached Adrian from Toledo in 1836.

In the mid 1840s the state made the decision to sell the lines. In addition to escaping the heavy load of debt incurred during construction, state officials believed that private ownership would increase competition, heighten efficiency, lessen corruption, and avoid sectional disputes. The Central line, which became known as the Michigan Central, was sold in 1846 to a group of Boston investors and Michigan lawyer James F. Joy. The Southern line, known first as the Southern Railroad and later as

the Michigan Southern, was sold the same year to Michigan investors headed by Elisha Litchfield, a Detroit attorney and member of a prominent upstate New York family. The Michigan Southern was improved and steadily extended westward, reaching Coldwater in 1850. The newly energized Michigan Southern absorbed its old rival, the Kalamazoo & Erie, in 1849, and acquired franchises of the long dormant Northern Indiana Railroad in 1850, which it used to reach South Bend in 1851 and Chicago in 1852. The company jointly built and shared its Chicago station with the Rock Island Railroad from 1852 until 1971. In 1855 the Michigan Southern and the Northern Indiana were formally merged as the Michigan Southern & Northern Indiana (MS&NI) Railroad. Also in 1855 the MS&NI completed a direct line from Toledo to Elkhart, a line begun in 1852 by the Northern Indiana. The Litchfield family, John B. Jervis, and George Bliss were dominant in the leadership, but an 1857 financial collapse passed control of the MS&NI to New York financier Henry Keep. The Civil War contributed to a quick recovery.

The building of the Lake Shore between Buffalo and Toledo was a much more complicated affair and one very difficult to summarize. Plans for a line along portions of the Lake Erie shore had been formulated in the 1830s and, during the 1840s, several companies had been chartered to complete the project. Two major obstacles, however, stood in the way. The first was that the city of Erie, with support from the state of Pennsylvania, was determined to prevent service through the city. This attempt to ensure that all freight and passengers would transfer in Erie was a potentially expensive factor in the profitability of any line. The second obstacle was the state of Ohio's requirement that any rail line in their state use a 4-foot 10-inch gauge. Because the rest of the line would be constructed using the standard English gauge of 4 feet 8½ inches, the line would be forced to use the somewhat dangerous compromise gauge of 4 feet 9½ inches on its equipment. In time both these complications were eliminated, but not before causing substantial delays.

East of Toledo eight separately owned lines were merged one by one to form the through line to Buffalo. Two of these lines began construction west of Buffalo in 1852, the Buffalo & State Line from Buffalo to the Pennsylvania border and the Erie & Northeast between there and Erie. The Buffalo & State Line took over the operation of the Erie & Northeast in 1854 and in 1867 the two were officially merged under New York Central control as the Buffalo & Erie.

The line east from Cleveland to Erie was completed in 1852 by the Cleveland, Painesville & Ashtabula (CP&A) Railroad, long known as the Lake Shore, and officially named as such in 1868. The portion from Cleveland west to Toledo, incorporated as the Toledo, Norwalk & Cleveland (TN&C), was opened in 1853 and constituted the last link in the through route from New York to Chicago. The TN&C merged with the Junction Railroad, completed in 1853 from Elyria via Sandusky to Toledo, in 1855 to form the Cleveland & Toledo. The portion west of Sandusky was abandoned in 1858 and rebuilt in 1872 as part of the main line.

In May 1869 the Lake Shore and the Cleveland & Toledo merged under the name of the Lake Shore, which then in June merged with the MS&NI to form the Lake Shore & Michigan Southern. The new company absorbed the Buffalo & Erie in August 1869. The LS&MS operated 864 miles of track on its own line and, including its affiliates, could run over a total of 1,177 miles. The company was controlled by LeGrande Lockwood and Henry Keep, but was on reasonably close terms with Cornelius Vanderbilt's New York Central. After the merger Vanderbilt wasted little time in gaining control of the line, achieving this in November 1869 after the collapse of Jay Gould's and James Fisk's infamous Black Friday gold-corner scheme. Vanderbilt's son-in-law, Horace Clark, was installed as the head of the LS&MS and, being a risk-taker,

nearly brought the road into bankruptcy during the panic of 1873. Clark's overexpansion and speculations earned him Vanderbilt's displeasure and he was fired as president, dying shortly thereafter.

For the next four and a half decades the LS&MS operated as an autonomous road under New York Central ownership. Although both were Vanderbilt property the LS&MS competed with the Michigan Central for traffic on the Detroit-Chicago line. In 1869 the primary line of the LS&MS extended 522 miles from Buffalo via Erie, Cleveland, Toledo, Elkhart, and South Bend to Chicago and carried high levels of freight and passenger traffic. The second line, the old Michigan Southern main line, extended 131 miles from Toledo via Hillsdale and Coldwater to Elkhart. The entire system totaled 1,852 miles in 1914 when it was formally merged with the New York Central.

When this merger took place the LS&MS lost its identity. The lines, however, remained more or less intact until the 1960s. With the formation of Conrail and the passage of subsequent NERSA legislation, various segments have been abandoned. The main line from Buffalo to Cleveland and Chicago via Goshen remains a major Conrail and a secondary Amtrak route, but the old Hillsdale line has been severed in several places, part of it operated by the Lenawee County Railroad and part by the Hillsdale County Railway. The Fort Wayne-Jackson line is, except for small fragments, also gone, as are virtually all other branch line mileages except the Toledo-Detroit main line.

References:

A. F. Harlow, *The Road of the Century* (New York: Creative Age, 1947);

Lake Shore & Michigan Southern, *Annual Report* (1871-1914);

Robert J. Parks, *Democracy's Railroads: Public Enterprise in Jacksonian Michigan* (Port Washington, N.Y.: Kennikat Press, 1972).

Archives:

The records of the LS&MS are located in the Bentley Historical Library of the University of Michigan in Ann Arbor, Michigan.

Benjamin H. Latrobe

(May 1, 1764-September 3, 1820)

by F. Daniel Larkin

State University College, Oneonta, New York

CAREER: Architect and engineer, England (1787-1795); architect and engineer, Virginia (1796-1798); architect and engineer, Philadelphia (1798-1802); United States surveyor of public buildings, Washington, D.C. (1802-1812); chief engineer, Delaware & Hudson Canal (1804-1805); partner, Ohio Steam Boat Company, Pittsburgh (1813-1815); superintendent, rebuilding of the United States Capitol (1815-1817); architect and engineer, Baltimore (1818); architect and engineer, New Orleans (1819-1820).

Benjamin Henry Latrobe was the outstanding architect and civil engineer in the United States from his arrival in 1796 until his death in 1820. Latrobe combined talents as an artist, architect, and engineer to create an outstanding legacy for the American people. His drawings accurately captured American life and its flora and fauna, preserving Latrobe's era for succeeding generations. Latrobe also helped to build America in the literal sense. His architecture symbolized America's assertion of its complete independence from Great Britain and continues to provide the American people with a visible reminder of the emergence of their country as an independent nation. Latrobe's engineering works contributed to American greatness by helping to prepare the United States for the Industrial Revolution and by assisting in America's internal expansion. Although Latrobe died nearly a decade before the first locomotive made its appearance on an American railroad, he was responsible for training many of the engineers who later built the rail lines.

Latrobe's fifty-six years spanned the period during which the English colonies in America became restless under English rule, decided to separate from their European master, fought two wars to affirm and reaffirm their independence, and finally emerged with a feeling of nationhood. Latrobe helped them to achieve this spirit of

Benjamin H. Latrobe

nationalism, which had risen to a pre-Civil War high at the time of his death in 1820. A degree of irony lies in the fact that when he arrived in the United States in 1796, Latrobe had emigrated from his native England, the very nation from which the United States was seeking to finalize its independence.

Benjamin Latrobe was born in the Yorkshire village of Fulneck on May 1, 1764. His father, Benjamin, of French Protestant descent, was born in Ireland. His mother, Margaret Antes, was born in Pennsylvania, the daughter of a wealthy German Protestant. She met Latrobe's father when they both were in residence in the Moravian community of Fulneck, she there to study and he there to preach. In 1767 Latrobe's parents moved to London but, as was good Moravian practice, left their son at the Fulneck Moravian school where he boarded until 1776, when Benjamin was sent to Germany in order to finish his education. As the center of Moravian Protestantism Germany contained the most advanced Moravian schools. Latrobe studied at schools in Silesia and Saxony and remained in Germany until 1784 when, at age twenty, he returned to England. In Saxony Latrobe studied for the Moravian ministry, but by 1782 it had become apparent to his teachers that he was not sufficiently committed to the religion to become a minister.

When Latrobe returned to England, he moved in with his parents in London and, through his father's connections, was placed in the government Stamp Office (a tax department) in the summer of 1784. His employment there lasted until 1787 when he left to begin his engineering training under John Smeaton, a prominent engineer and friend of the Latrobe family. Latrobe developed his engineering skills while working with Smeaton and spent a portion of that time as a resident engineer on a section of the Basingstoke Canal. In 1790 he left Smeaton's tutelage for employment in the office of Samuel Pepys Cockerell, one of England's most renowned architects. Also in 1790 Latrobe married Lydia Sellon, daughter of William Sellon, a wealthy and well-known clergyman.

The next three years were bittersweet for Latrobe. He left Cockerell's business and opened an office of his own. For a time he experienced a meteoric rise in his reputation as an architect and received commissions for a number of houses, the design of which reflected the Greek style which Latrobe favored and used to a large extent in his later work. During this successful period in his career Latrobe and his wife had two children, a daughter, Lydia, and a son, Henry. But in November 1793 Latrobe's good fortune changed. His wife died in childbirth along with their third child. The following year he lost an important commission through the shelving of the Chelmsford Canal project. Latrobe had been retained to plan a canal between Chelmsford and the port town of Malden. His plans were accepted at the local level but rejected by the English Parliament due to concern over future expenditures resulting from an impending war with France.

These events caused the thirty-year-old Latrobe to decide to immigrate to America. He placed his children in the care of relatives and in November 1795 sailed for the United States. Following a voyage made more difficult by the shortage of food, Latrobe landed in Norfolk, Virginia, in March 1796.

The country in which Latrobe settled was still in its infancy. George Washington was beginning the final year of his two terms in the presidency, and the national Constitution was not yet a decade old. The United States was struggling to assert itself as a nation completely independent of Great Britain, from which it had been separated only thirteen years prior to Latrobe's arrival. As might be imagined, America of the 1790s continued to reflect the building styles of England, particularly the Georgian architecture in vogue since the beginning of the reign of George I in 1715. Although some alterations had been made in the Georgian type, the American Federal style that emerged for homes and public and commercial buildings was basically Georgian English. But America continued to seek a new form of architecture which would exemplify the young republic and its democratic foundations. Latrobe arrived at a fortuitous time, indeed, for America was ready to receive his new building style.

Latrobe began demonstrating his talents within days of his arrival. He took advantage of his contacts in Norfolk to obtain a commission to design a small residence for Capt. William Pennock, after which he drew the plan for the Virginia state prison in Richmond. While he was in Virginia, however, his engineering skills were in greater demand for canal work than were his architectural talents. Just as Latrobe arrived in the United States at a time when the nation was looking for architecture more expressive of its mission, so was the country also in the initial stages of constructing a system of internal improvements. Latrobe's European engineering experience made him an attractive candidate for waterway projects. For example, during a visit to Mt. Vernon in the summer of 1796, arranged by his friend and the president's nephew, Bushrod Washington, Latrobe was questioned by the president about improvement of the Virginia river system. His two-day visit to Mt. Vernon was documented by Latrobe's written observations on the Washingtons and their plantation.

In 1798 Latrobe's disappointment over the lack of monumental work available in Virginia in-

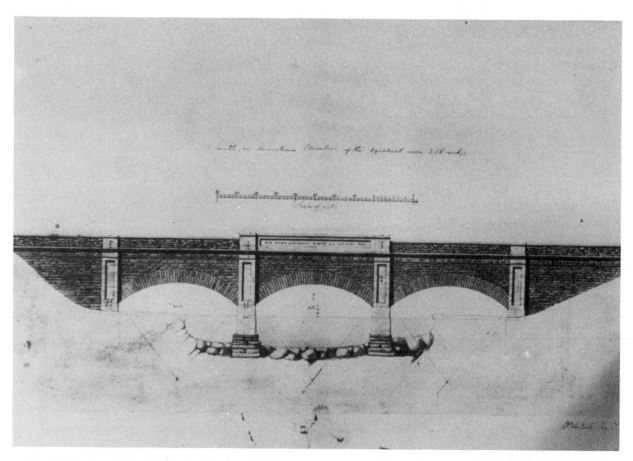

Latrobe's design for the Elk River Aqueduct of the Chesapeake & Delaware Canal (courtesy of Robert Brooke Papers, the New York Public Library, Astor, Lenox and Tilden Foundations)

duced him to travel to Philadelphia, a much larger city with greater political and commercial power than Richmond. Latrobe entered the Pennsylvania metropolis armed with letters of introduction, one of which was addressed to Samuel Fox, president of the Bank of Pennsylvania. Fox told Latrobe of the plans for construction of a new bank building, and Latrobe promptly submitted a design. His selection as the architect of the work marked the beginning of the Philadelphia phase of his career. The Bank of Pennsylvania was the first major American building designed in the Greek revival style and placed Latrobe in the vanguard of those builders who introduced classical Greco-Roman architecture in America. The classical design appealed to people in the United States because of its perceived relationship with the new country's political antecedent, ancient Greece. Construction on the Bank of Pennsylvania was started in April 1799 and was completed two years later.

Simultaneous with designing the bank Latrobe was retained to construct a water supply system for the city of Philadelphia. Following a severe outbreak of yellow fever in the mid 1790s the city fathers decided to build a system which would furnish a constant supply of pure water to Philadelphia's residents. At the time drinking water came from wells which were often contaminated. Officials planned to use the Schuylkill River not only for the new supply of drinking water but also to flush the city's streets, a measure they believed would help to prevent yellow fever and other diseases. Latrobe designed a system which employed the use of a large basin to allow impurities in the water to settle and a canal and tunnel to carry the water to the pump house. His design for the pump house contained the most novel departure from earlier water systems. The water was raised from the tunnel to an elevated reservoir by steam pumps, built in the Passaic, New Jersey, factory of Nicholas J. Roosevelt. The Philadelphia water system was the nation's first to use steam power and remained in use for nearly two decades until replaced by the larger Fairmont Works designed by Frederick Graff, a pupil of Latrobe's who worked with him on the first water system.

Although busily involved in the two Philadelphia projects, Latrobe found time to marry once again, this time to Mary Hazelhurst. The couple produced five children, two of whom died in infancy. Surviving were a daughter, Juliana, and sons, John H. B. and Benjamin H. Both sons were later employed by the Baltimore & Ohio Railroad, John as its general counsel and Benjamin as its chief engineer. During the period when Latrobe's second set of children were infants, they were joined by his first two children who had remained in England when Latrobe immigrated to the United States.

Both the Bank of Pennsylvania and the waterworks projects were completed in 1801. During the following eighteen months Latrobe's work was confined to designing several houses in the Philadelphia area, among which was the first built in the Gothic style in America, and planning navigation improvements for the lower part of the Susquehanna River. The river channel was cleared and deepened from a few miles north of the Pennsylvania-Maryland border to Chesapeake Bay. These projects were of lesser interest to Latrobe, who continued to search for positions of the magnitude of his first two Philadelphia commissions. In late 1802 President Thomas Jefferson invited Latrobe to Washington to submit plans for a naval drydock. Latrobe's ideas for the huge, covered structure impressed Jefferson, but the plan was rejected by Congress. Although Latrobe lost the drydock job, his acquaintance with Jefferson led directly to a presidential appointment in March 1803 to the newly created position of surveyor of public buildings. His first task was to build the House of Representatives wing of the United States Capitol. The Senate wing had already been completed, a fact which dictated the design of the House wing. Latrobe was not completely satisfied with the design of the Senate wing and fought to alter it against the objections of its designer, William Thornton, and others. But Latrobe had the support of the president and was able to complete the Capitol, incorporating the changes he had recommended, by the end of Jefferson's administration in 1809.

Latrobe also made design suggestions for the president's house, many of which were incorporated into the building after Latrobe's retirement in 1817. Unfortunately, much of Latrobe's early Washington work was destroyed when the British occupied the capital in August 1814. Upon the close of the war in early 1815 Latrobe returned to Washington to supervise the rebuilding of the Capitol. Although the outer walls survived the fire, the interior was totally destroyed, allowing for remodeling to Latrobe's design. The destruction and rebuilding of the president's mansion, also burned in 1814, opened the way for Latrobe's designs to be included in the building.

Latrobe managed to find time for other projects while working on the public buildings. The Roman Catholic Bishop of Baltimore, John Carroll, called upon Latrobe in 1804 to submit a plan for a cathedral. Latrobe drew magnificent designs in both the Gothic and Roman styles, the latter design being chosen. Latrobe contributed his expertise without charge for nearly a dozen years toward the completion of the church, the largest of his nonpublic architectural projects. Among the other buildings Latrobe completed during the first decade of the nineteenth century was the Gothic-design Bank of Philadelphia. Latrobe, with the support of the New Yorker Aaron Burr, then vice-president of the United States, also entered the design competition for the proposed New York City Hall. Despite the support of the powerful Burr, Latrobe lost the contest, a disappointment since he felt his was the best plan.

Also in 1804 Latrobe was appointed chief engineer of the Chesapeake & Delaware Canal, a waterway for which he had drawn plans as early as 1799. The canal was meant to connect the upper reaches of the two important bays of the mid-Atlantic coast. Work progressed on the waterway until 1805 when the canal company gradually sank into default. Latrobe was no longer paid in cash, but in worthless checks or in canal company notes. When the canal company finally went bankrupt later that year, the project was suspended. Latrobe had the fortunate luxury of relying on his government post for income. However, backers of the Chesapeake & Delaware project stubbornly persisted, and the canal eventually was completed in 1830, but not without federal support.

When the United States went to war against Great Britain in 1812, Latrobe's government post was suspended for the duration. As early as 1807 when the British frigate *Leonard* fired upon the American *Chesapeake* in one of the incidents that led to the war, Latrobe demonstrated that his allegiance was with his adopted country. His indignation over the unprovoked attack was such that in July 1807 he proposed to President Jefferson that he be given the post of military engineer to supervise the construction of coastal fortifications which could serve as protection against possible British attack. Jefferson, always mindful of excessive government expenditures, did not accept Latrobe's offer.

With his duties in Washington on hold, Latrobe was forced to seek alternate work. Latrobe moved his family to Pittsburgh in 1813 to take advantage of his involvement in a steamboat building venture with New Yorkers Robert Fulton and Robert Livingston. In 1807 Fulton had built and operated the first successful steamboat in the United States. Livingston provided the capital for the venture. The two men were predominant in the development of steam navigation of New York's lakes and rivers and by 1813 had expanded their interest to the Ohio and Mississippi rivers. The company that they formed, with Latrobe as a third partner, was called the Ohio Steam Boat Company. In addition to his engineering talents Latrobe contributed money to the company, an unfortunate investment since Latrobe eventually lost nearly all his savings and property in the company.

On his arrival in Pittsburgh Latrobe immediately began to design and construct the boats. Designed for the western rivers, they were wider and of shallower draft than the narrow, deep-draft eastern craft. Nicholas Roosevelt, Latrobe's friend from the Philadelphia Water Works, provided the steam engines for the boats. Almost from the beginning the infant company was beset by troubles. Inflation caused by the War of 1812 raised prices, resulting in significant overruns of the original cost estimates for the steamboats. Yet in April 1814 the first boat, the *Vesuvius*, was put into operation on the Mississippi between New Orleans and the Ohio River. The following month a second boat, the *Buffalo*, was launched. Latrobe was building boats in spite of the rising costs which, as it turned out, were not his major problem. By the time the *Buffalo* was launched, it was obvious that Fulton and Livingston had decided to terminate their partnership with Latrobe. Apparently Latrobe's one-third interest in the company, plus his $2,000 annual salary, were too much for Fulton and Livingston. Money to pay the shipyard workers in Pittsburgh and to complete the outfitting of the *Buffalo* ceased to arrive from the company offices in New York City. Latrobe tried to keep the Pittsburgh yards going by mortgaging his personal property and the unfinished *Buffalo*. Ultimately this was of no avail and

on September 1, 1814, he was forced to announce his insolvency. From then until the end of the year Latrobe supported his family by designing homes in the Pittsburgh area, but throughout the remainder of 1814 he sank deeper into despair and depression.

As it happened the 1814 destruction by the British of the principal public buildings in Washington was responsible for the rescue of Latrobe from his financial and psychological doldrums. Due largely to a letter-writing campaign conducted by his wife, her friends in Washington prevailed upon President James Madison to bring Latrobe back to Washington to rebuild the ruined buildings. Latrobe returned to the capital in April 1815, and by the end of June he had moved his family there. Latrobe directed the rebuilding of the Capitol and designed several private homes including one for the naval hero Commodore Stephen Decatur. During these Washington years he also provided suggestions to his old friend Thomas Jefferson for Jefferson's University of Virginia project, some of which were incorporated into the campus buildings. Although Latrobe's $4,000 annual government income was comfortable during this time, many old, unpaid debts continued to hound him. Also, his problems were compounded by a deteriorating relationship with Col. Samuel Lane, commissioner of the Capitol rebuilding project. Personality differences between the two men, coupled with Lane's frequent attempts to assert power, led to a final break in November 1817. Lane openly reprimanded Latrobe for not paying attention to Lane's orders and did so in the presence of the new president, James Monroe. Despite the fact that Lane was a cripple Latrobe physically attacked him, being restrained only by Monroe's presence. The attack on Lane, of course, made Latrobe's resignation inevitable. The cutoff of his government salary forced the sale of family possessions once again, and Latrobe moved to Baltimore in January 1818.

In addition to his work on the Capitol, Latrobe's final years in Washington resulted in a design for an arsenal in Frankfort, Kentucky. Latrobe planned the Frankfort arsenal to attain a more efficient utilization of the new process of manufacturing weapons using interchangeable parts, a technology pioneered by the arms maker Eli Whitney. Latrobe developed an interest in Whitney's process as he had for other new mechanical ideas and methods. For example, Latrobe had become an early advocate of railroads and, as early as 1808, had suggested to Treasury Secretary Albert Gallatin that wood-rail railroads be used instead of roads in swampy areas, particularly in the South where there existed an abundance of timber. Latrobe also favored the building of railroads as part of New York's projected central and western transportation project, which would connect the Hudson River with the Great Lakes, and he attempted to form a railroad company to transport coal from mines in Virginia to the James River. According to Latrobe's biographer Talbot Hamlin, evidence exists "that in the government quarry at Acquia an actual railroad of some sort, designed by Latrobe, was put into service," and in 1805 he also "used such railroads in the construction work of the Chesapeake and Delaware Canal." Although Latrobe pioneered the utilization of railways in the United States, none employed the use of steam locomotives.

Latrobe remained in Baltimore throughout 1818. While there he completed the Baltimore (merchant's) Exchange, his biggest commission other than the United States Capitol. Latrobe received $4,000 to design and supervise construction of the large, domed building with its classical lines. Before he left the city he executed the Baltimore Library, also designed in the Greek style. Latrobe's stay in Baltimore was limited by the fact that he had already accepted a post in New Orleans. He had taken on another waterworks and, in order to complete the job, left Baltimore for the southern metropolis in December 1818. After a sea voyage of nearly a month Latrobe arrived in New Orleans. He was captivated by the Crescent City, which was only then beginning to change its predominantly French character. He so liked New Orleans that within a year he returned to Baltimore to move his family south. Latrobe and his family traveled overland to the Ohio River and then continued by steamboat down the Ohio and Mississippi to their destination. Frequent stops were made along the route, and, at times, prominent local citizenry turned out to welcome the famous architect/engineer. The Latrobes arrived in New Orleans in April 1820.

Latrobe returned at once to the completion of the waterworks while simultaneously seeking additional work. His other notable commission in New Orleans was the Louisiana State Bank. The two jobs kept him very busy throughout the spring and summer of 1820, causing him to remain in New Or-

leans despite an epidemic of yellow fever. Latrobe should have been more mindful of the danger of the disease since his son Henry had died of the fever in New Orleans only three years earlier. But this fact did not deter Latrobe from his duties, and as the pestilence raged, Latrobe, too, was stricken. On September 3, three years to the day of his son's death, Benjamin Latrobe died of yellow fever. One of the most talented men in America succumbed at age fifty-six to the disease that his waterworks were meant to help eliminate.

Publications:

American Copper Mines (Philadelphia, 1798);

An Answer to the Joint Committee of the Select and Common Councils of Philadelphia, on the Subject of Supplying the City with Water (Philadelphia, 1798);

Designs of a Building Proposed to be Erected at Richmond in Virginia (Richmond, 1798);

Designs of Buildings Erected or Proposed to be Built in Virginia (Philadelphia, 1799);

Remark on the Address of the Committee of the Delaware and Schuylkill Canal Co. to the Committee of the House of Penna. as far as it Notices the "Views of the Practicability and Means of Supplying the City of Philadelphia with Wholesome Water" (Philadelphia: Zachariah Poulson, Jr., 1799);

View of the Practicability and Means of Supplying the City of Philadelphia with Wholesome Water (Philadelphia: Zachariah Poulson, Jr., 1799);

Design of a City Hall Proposed to be Built in New York (Philadelphia, 1802);

A Private Letter to the Individual Members of Congress, on the Subject of the Public Buildings of the United States at Washington (Washington, D.C.: S. H. Smith, 1806);

Plan of the Principal Story of the White House in 1803 (N.p., 1807);

Message from the President of the United States, Transmitting a Report of the Surveyor of Public Buildings of the United States, in the City of Washington (Washington, D.C.: A. & G. Way, 1808);

Anniversary Oration, Pronounced before the Society of Artists of the United States, by Appointment of the Society on the eighth of May, 1811 (Philadelphia: Bradford & Innskeep, 1811);

Opinion on a Project for Removing the Obstructions to a Ship Navigation to Georgetown, Col. (Washington: W. Cooper, 1812);

Designs for a Bank of the United States at Philadelphia, Pa. (Philadelphia, 1818);

Memorial of Benjamin H. Latrobe, Late Surveyor of the Public Buildings, in the City of Washington, in Vindication of His Professional Skill (Washington, D.C.: De Krafft, 1819);

Journal: Being the Notes and Sketches of an Architect, Naturalist and Traveler in the United States from 1796 to 1820 (New York: Appleton, 1905);

Impressions Respecting New Orleans; Diary & Sketches, 1818-1820, edited by Samuel Wilson, Jr. (New York: Columbia University Press, 1951).

References:

Edward C. Carter II, ed., *The Virginia Journals of Benjamin Henry Latrobe, 1795-1798* (New Haven: Yale University Press, 1977);

Carter, John C. Van Horne, and Lee W. Formwalt, eds., *The Journals of Benjamin Henry Latrobe, 1799-1820: From Philadelphia to New Orleans* (New Haven: Yale University Press, 1980);

Carter, Van Horne, and Charles E. Brownell, eds., *Latrobe's View of America, 1795-1820* (New Haven: Yale University Press, 1985);

Talbot Hamlin, *Benjamin Henry Latrobe* (New York: Oxford University Press, 1955);

Darwin H. Stapleton, *The Engineering Drawings of Benjamin Henry Latrobe* (New Haven: Yale University Press, 1980).

Archives:

The Benjamin Henry Latrobe Papers are located at the Maryland Historical Society, Baltimore, Maryland.

Locomotives

The earliest steam locomotives were developed in England. The first high pressure steam locomotive, built by Richard Trevithick, a Cornish mining engineer, began its service on iron rails in February 1804 and was able to pull a 10-ton load at an average speed of five miles per hour. By the early 1820s several steam locomotives had been operated successfully in England. The earliest master of steam locomotive construction was George Stephenson who, along with his equally illustrious son, Robert, constructed the Locomotion No. 1 for the Stockton & Darlington Railroad, the world's first modern railroad, in 1825. On its first run the locomotive successfully pulled a train of over thirty cars.

In 1826, shortly after the successful operation of the Locomotion, the first steam locomotive in the United States was operated by Col. John Stevens. He constructed the locomotive for experimental purposes and operated it on a loop of track at his home in Hoboken, New Jersey. Col. Stevens is sometimes called "the father of American railroads," partially because of this locomotive, and partially because he attempted to charter a railroad as early as 1812.

The first steam locomotive to operate on a commercial American railroad was the Stourbridge Lion, which ran over the Delaware & Hudson (D&H) Canal Company line from Honesdale to Carbondale, Pennsylvania. John B. Jervis, the chief engineer of the railroad, sent his assistant Horatio Allen to England in 1828 to purchase several locomotives for the new line. Jervis gave Allen precise specifications for the new locomotives: they should be able to operate at five miles per hour, the top of the stack should not be more than 10 feet in height, and the machine should weigh no more than 5½ tons. The last specification was the most critical because the new railroad had fragile wooden rails. Allen, unfortunately, returned with a locomotive weighing 7 tons, too heavy for the rails and trestles on the line where it was to operate.

The Stourbridge Lion was built by Foster, Rastrick & Company of Stourbridge, England, in 1829, before Robert Stephenson constructed his famous Rocket the same year. Locomotives are classified by their wheel arrangement in a system developed by Fredic M. Whyte of the New York Central Railroad about 1900. The first number represents the number of leading wheels, the second the number of driving wheels, and the third the number of trailing wheels. Thus a 4-4-0 is a locomotive with four leading wheels, four driving wheels, and zero trailing wheels. The Lion had four driving wheels (classed as an 0-4-0), vertical cylinders with power transmitted by what were known as "walking beams," a separate firebox, a multitubular boiler, and an exhaust pipe, all steam locomotive characteristics developed by the British. Three other locomotives were ordered at the same time, two from Foster, Rastrick & Company and one from Stephenson & Son. The fate of these other locomotives is unknown. As for the Stourbridge Lion it was of little value because of its weight and was never put into regular service, the D&H instead using it for a stationary boiler. Several parts of the locomotive still exist as an exhibit in the Smithsonian Institution.

Additional locomotives from British builders continued to be imported into the United States until about 1841. Orders declined rapidly after 1837, however, because of the downturn in business conditions caused by the panic of that year. John White of the Smithsonian Institution writes that the largest number of locomotives imported from England in one year was twenty-six in 1835. He further calculates that by 1841 only about 25 percent of the locomotives in service on American railroads were constructed in England. Several factors contributed to the decline of British influence on locomotive design. Because American railroads were constructed rapidly and without concern for permanence, they required locomotives which were more flexible than those built in England. In addition, the rolling terrain and numerous mountains of the United States required railroad systems to use much steeper grades than those common in England; thus American locomotives had to be more powerful for the same amount of traffic than British locomotives. Finally, because of the shortage of capital, American locomotives had to be less expensive than most of the locomotives constructed in England.

American locomotive manufacturers quickly began to build for these conditions. Some of them, like Matthias Baldwin and the Lowell Machine Shop, gained valuable experience by assembling British-built locomotives shipped to the United States in parts. Consequently, when these companies built their locomotives, their designs were heavily dependent on the British machines. The first commercial locomotive designed and constructed in the United States was the Best Friend of Charleston, built in 1830 by the West Point Foundry of New York City for the South Carolina Railroad. The chief engineer of the railroad was Horatio Allen, who had ordered the Stourbridge Lion in 1828. Clearly American builders could build locomotives, but they were not geared to build them quickly enough to satisfy the sudden demand for locomotives. Until American locomotive builders could do so, locomotives continued to be purchased from England.

As late as the end of the Civil War most of the American companies that constructed locomotives also constructed other products, a wise idea given the variable nature of the steam locomotive construction business. The major locomotive construction companies in the nineteenth century were the Baldwin Locomotive Works, which was found-

ed in 1832 and built about 17,000 locomotives; the Schenectady Locomotive Works, which was founded in 1851 and built about 5,700 locomotives; the Rogers Locomotive Works, which was founded in 1837 and built about 5,650 locomotives; the Hinkley Locomotive Works, which was founded in 1844 and built about 1,800 locomotives; and the Norris Locomotive Works, which was founded in 1834 and built about 1,400 locomotives. There were many smaller producers of locomotives, some of which built no more than one locomotive. A few individuals working in railroad shops, such as James Millholland of the Philadelphia & Reading and Ross Winans of the Baltimore & Ohio, also produced locomotives but the number from such sources is unknown.

Other well-known early American locomotives were the Tom Thumb, the De Witt Clinton, and the John Bull. The Tom Thumb, an experimental locomotive, was constructed by Peter Cooper in 1830 to convince the directors of the Baltimore & Ohio that a steam locomotive could pull their trains. On August 28, 1830, it was the first American locomotive to pull a railway coach with passengers, but it never operated in regular service because of its small size. The De Witt Clinton, built by the West Point Foundry, was the first locomotive to operate in New York State. The Clinton used a horizontal boiler, rather than a vertical one similar to the Best Friend of Charleston. The John Bull, constructed in England by Stephenson & Son, was shipped in parts to the United States on July 14, 1831. Isaac Dripps reconstructed the locomotive which had a boiler 6 feet 9 inches long by 2 feet 6 inches in diameter. Its grate area was 10.07 square feet, its firebox surface 34.8 square feet, and the flue surface 261.7 square feet. This locomotive was one of the first to be equipped with a "cowcatcher" to clear animals from the track, a piece of equipment not needed in England because most of the rail lines were fenced off from farmland.

Matthias W. Baldwin entered the locomotive construction business in 1831 when he was asked to construct a locomotive for the Philadelphia, Germantown & Norristown Railroad. The result was Old Ironsides, placed in regular service in November 1832, at a cost of about $4,000. The locomotive weighed 5½ tons and averaged about twenty-eight miles per hour on its first trip. Old Ironsides was followed by many other Baldwin-built locomotives in the nineteenth century, Baldwin

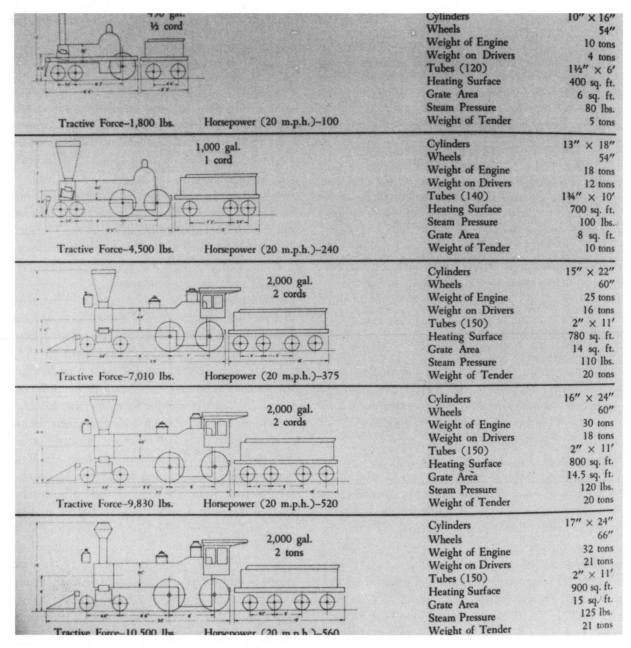

Cylinders	10″ × 16″
Wheels	54″
Weight of Engine	10 tons
Weight on Drivers	4 tons
Tubes (120)	1½″ × 6′
Heating Surface	400 sq. ft.
Grate Area	6 sq. ft.
Steam Pressure	80 lbs.
Weight of Tender	5 tons

½ cord

Tractive Force—1,800 lbs.   Horsepower (20 m.p.h.)—100

Cylinders	13″ × 18″
Wheels	54″
Weight of Engine	18 tons
Weight on Drivers	12 tons
Tubes (140)	1¾″ × 10′
Heating Surface	700 sq. ft.
Steam Pressure	100 lbs.
Grate Area	8 sq. ft.
Weight of Tender	10 tons

1,000 gal.
1 cord

Tractive Force—4,500 lbs.   Horsepower (20 m.p.h.)—240

Cylinders	15″ × 22″
Wheels	60″
Weight of Engine	25 tons
Weight on Drivers	16 tons
Tubes (150)	2″ × 11′
Heating Surface	780 sq. ft.
Grate Area	14 sq. ft.
Steam Pressure	110 lbs.
Weight of Tender	20 tons

2,000 gal.
2 cords

Tractive Force—7,010 lbs.   Horsepower (20 m.p.h.)—375

Cylinders	16″ × 24″
Wheels	60″
Weight of Engine	30 tons
Weight on Drivers	18 tons
Tubes (150)	2″ × 11′
Heating Surface	800 sq. ft.
Grate Area	14.5 sq. ft.
Steam Pressure	120 lbs.
Weight of Tender	20 tons

2,000 gal.
2 cords

Tractive Force—9,830 lbs.   Horsepower (20 m.p.h.)—520

Cylinders	17″ × 24″
Wheels	66″
Weight of Engine	32 tons
Weight on Drivers	21 tons
Tubes (150)	2″ × 11′
Heating Surface	900 sq. ft.
Grate Area	15 sq. ft.
Steam Pressure	125 lbs.
Weight of Tender	21 tons

2,000 gal.
2 tons

Tractive Force—10,500 lbs.   Horsepower (20 m.p.h.)—560

The development of the American locomotive from 1835 to 1875

becoming the premier locomotive builder in the United States. But even Baldwin did not survive without difficulty. Undertaking an expansion during the mid 1830s Baldwin sank into financial difficulty from which it took the company almost a decade to recover. Many locomotive construction firms did not survive at all.

By the late 1830s the builders were attempting to develop a few standard designs. In 1836 Baldwin refused to build a locomotive to a particular design, stating that he built several sizes of 4-2-0 locomotives and that he could not see the advantage of attempting to improve on these standard models. By

1841 William Norris offered what appeared to be four locomotive sizes ranging in weight from 7½ to 15 tons, all of them using a 4-2-0 wheel arrangement. Despite the fact that some of the fittings on the different types of locomotives were the same, these machines did not utilize interchangeable parts for such major components as boilers, fireboxes, frames, cylinders, and driving wheels.

The first two wheel arrangements that might be considered standard for locomotives were the 4-2-0 and the 4-4-0. The first 4-2-0 wheel arrangement was constructed in 1832 by the West Point Foundry and was the first to use John Jervis's en-

An 0-8-0 Camel locomotive designed for the Baltimore & Ohio Railroad by Ross Winans (courtesy of Baltimore & Ohio Railroad)

gine truck. Jervis's invention was a four-wheel truck that carried the weight of the front of the engine and used a three-point suspension system to enable it to operate over the uneven track of American railroads. Although this locomotive, called the Experiment, did not operate effectively because it was designed to burn anthracite coal, its wheel arrangement was the prototype for many similar locomotives. But the 4-2-0 soon proved too light for the increasing weight of American trains. Efforts to increase the adhesion of the locomotive, such as placing the firebox behind the driving wheels, did not solve the problem.

The 4-4-0 locomotive was first constructed in 1837. By 1840 it had proven itself to be approximately 60 percent more powerful than the 4-2-0 type, and the demand for 4-4-0s increased rapidly. Gradually, the 4-4-0 became the most popular wheel arrangement in the nineteenth century and, until the Civil War era, was virtually dominant on American railroads. By varying the size of the driving wheels and the weight of the locomotive, the 4-4-0 proved to be effective for both passenger and freight service. Because its three-point suspension made it flexible enough to operate over uneven

track, its initial cost was not much more than that of the 4-2-0, and it was not much more complex to maintain and repair, the 4-4-0 met the railroads' needs until the Civil War.

Not all locomotives constructed, however, were of the 4-2-0 or the 4-4-0 wheel arrangement. Railroads such as the Baltimore & Ohio and the Philadelphia & Reading, with extremely heavy coal transportation demands, needed heavier locomotives. In the early 1840s Ross Winans constructed an 0-8-0 with a vertical boiler for the B&O. Similar to Winans's earlier Crab locomotives, which were 0-4-0s, the new 0-8-0 was not very successful and was retired before 1850. Between 1844 and 1846 twelve horizontal-boiler 0-8-0s were constructed by Winans for use by the B&O. These locomotives used an unusual gear drive which caused the main and side rods to move in opposite directions when the locomotive was running. Equipped with small 33-inch driving wheels and side rods that almost touched the ground as they revolved, these locomotives were known as Mud-diggers. This locomotive design was greatly improved when Winans switched to a direct drive and increased the size of the driving wheels. Nonetheless, several of

231

the original Mud-diggers were still in switching service on the B&O as late as 1865.

The most prominent of the 0-8-0 type locomotives, however, were Winans's Camels, constructed between 1848 and 1860. These locomotives were extremely compact, having a wheelbase of only slightly over 11 feet and a weight of about 3 tons per axle. Utilizing a plate frame, stay bolts to mount the firebox, solid end rods, and a sloping firebox with the cab astride the boiler—the origin of the name camel—these locomotives were clearly at odds with standard American locomotive construction techniques. With a large grate area they were designed to burn coal rather than wood, and were the first large group of coal-burning American locomotives. To provide adequate grate area to burn coal the firebox was located behind the driving wheels and the frame. Consequently, the firebox could be as wide as the maximum width of the locomotive. Between 200 and 300 Camels were constructed. Ungainly looking and rough riding these locomotives were designed for slow speeds, typically under fifteen miles per hour, and they were designed to haul heavy freight trains. The Camels were successful, however, and the B&O did not retire its last one, Number 143 built in 1853, until 1898. The Philadelphia & Reading Railroad also made extensive use of 0-8-0 Camels.

One of the most fascinating periods of locomotive design was the 1850 to 1880 period when decoration became popular. Locomotives built during this period were finished in a variety of colors, often with pictures painted on the sides of the locomotive headlights, the tender, and parts of the engine as well. Locomotive crews assigned to these engines further adorned them with brass eagles, candlesticks, and bells all shined to the highest degree possible. Lithographs from that period testify to the endless variety of colors and shades of colors used on the locomotives. Lithographs of locomotives built by Baldwin, the Lawrence Machine Shop, the Hinkley Locomotive Works, Amoskeag Manufacturing Company, the Taunton Locomotive Manufacturing Company, the Rogers Locomotive Works, and, in particular, the Mason Machine Works show locomotives usually with red-spoked driving-wheel centers, green, blue, tan, or gray boilers, and trim in a contrasting color. Names were painted on the sides of locomotives because numbers were not commonly used until much later in the century.

The Ten-wheeler (4-6-0) was another popular wheel arrangement in the nineteenth century. The first locomotive constructed with this wheel arrangement is thought to be the Chesapeake, built by the Norris Locomotive Works for the Philadelphia & Reading in 1847. Other locomotives of this type built over the next decade were intended primarily for heavy freight service. Henry Tyson, master mechanic of the Baltimore & Ohio, improved this wheel arrangement in the late 1850s, and in the 1860s and 1870s it became an extremely popular locomotive for hauling both freight and passenger trains.

Another wheel arrangement that developed in the early 1850s was the 2-6-0. The first locomotives of this wheel arrangement were basically 0-6-0s with a pair of lead wheels placed in front of the driving wheels, but attached rigidly to the frame. James Millholland of the Philadelphia & Reading built the first locomotive with this wheel arrangement in 1852. While the lead wheels did not act as a true engine truck they did support some of the locomotive weight and must have had some "play" in them to allow adjusting to the radius of curves. Locomotives of this wheel arrangement were used successfully in heavy freight service in the 1850s. In 1858 Levi Bissell patented the swiveling two-wheel leading truck, which was not mounted rigidly to the frame and allowed the 2-6-0 (known as the Mogul) to be more flexible in adjusting to curved track. Although the first 2-6-0 with the swivel truck was delivered to the Louisville & Nashville, the first railroad to make extensive use of this wheel arrangement in powering most of its freight trains was the Erie Railroad.

Both the Ten-wheelers and the Moguls demonstrated a tendency to derail more frequently than the 4-4-0 or the 0-8-0 types. The suspension system was basically an extension of the Standard type (4-4-0) in which the drivers were equalized by four levers. Since the lead truck was not connected to the suspension of the six driving axles, there existed a five-point, rather than a three-point, suspension system. This system was not as flexible nor as stable as the suspension system of the 4-4-0. William S. Hudson of the Rogers Locomotive Works developed an effective three-point suspension system for six-driver locomotives in 1864, and the first 2-6-0 constructed with this suspension system was delivered in 1865. Since the Mogul had about 50 percent greater pulling power than the 4-4-0, by the mid 1870s it had become the standard freight locomotive for many railroads. Although popular, the 2-6-0 was soon challenged by another wheel arrangement.

The 2-8-0, or Consolidation, was a logical extension of the 2-6-0 for extremely heavy freight service. The first 2-8-0 type locomotive was designed by Alexander Mitchell, master mechanic of the Mahanoy Division of the Lehigh Valley Railroad, to move heavy coal trains over the grades of the division. The locomotive was constructed by the Baldwin Locomotive Works and was placed in service in July 1866. It was successful primarily because it could negotiate curves at a higher speed than could the cumbersome 0-8-0 heavy freight locomotives. The 2-8-0, however, could not pull any more than could contemporary 0-8-0s. Nonetheless, the first 2-8-0 was effective and continued in service until 1886. By that time the Consolidation was on its way to becoming the most popular steam locomotive in the United States. More than 33,000 of them were constructed from 1866 to 1950, a greater number than any other wheel arrangement of steam locomotive.

Eventually the major limitation of the 2-8-0 was the location of the firebox over the last set of driving wheels. Necessarily, the driver diameter had to be kept small, thus reducing speed, and the firebox had to remain shallow, thus reducing steaming capacity. Consequently, the Consolidation was used in the nineteenth century primarily for heavy slow-speed service, or in mountainous territory. In the twentieth century it became a favorite for branch lines and short lines. Many locomotives of this wheel arrangement remained in operation until the last days of steam in the early 1960s. Only one attempt was made in the nineteenth century to increase the steaming capacity of the Consolidation. In 1877 the Wootten firebox was introduced on the Philadelphia & Reading Railroad to increase steaming capacity and to allow the locomotive to burn anthracite coal. The firebox, by providing expanded grate area for the slower burning anthracite coal, also increased the steaming capacity of the Consolidation. As a result railroads in the coal regions, such as the Reading, the Delaware & Hudson, and the Western Maryland, developed the most powerful 2-8-0 locomotives.

In view of the success of the Consolidation it might appear that more wheel arrangements were not necessary. But the 2-8-0s had weight limitations

and the 2-10-0 (known as the Decapod) was developed to allow for greater power. Built as early as 1870 for the Lehigh Valley, again to haul heavier coal trains, the early decapods were not successful. They were not significantly more powerful than the Consolidation type and the long rigid wheelbase of the 2-10-0 experienced difficulty negotiating the sharp curves and staying on the inferior track common to nineteenth-century railroads. Although a modest number of these locomotives were built to fulfill the heaviest freight service requirements on a handful of railroads, it was not until the twentieth century, when they could be outfitted with larger boilers, that the 2-10-0 wheel arrangement came into its own.

By 1900 the dominant passenger locomotive was the 4-6-0 type and the dominant freight locomotive was the 2-8-0 type. The Standard (4-4-0) continued to be used in passenger service, but by 1900 was seldom found in freight service unless it was on a light branch line. The 2-6-0 continued to be used extensively, but after 1880 it was built with higher driving wheels for fast freight service, leaving the heavy freight duty to 2-8-0s or, in some cases, 2-10-0s. Switching locomotives were either 0-4-0s or 0-6-0s. Obsolete road locomotives of the 4-4-0, 4-6-0, 2-6-0, and 0-8-0 wheel arrangements were often reduced to yard service, and the 2-6-0s often lost their engine trucks, converting them to 0-6-0s.

Throughout the nineteenth century the improvement of the steam locomotive was dramatic, although the basic technology did not undergo a large number of new innovations. In 1835 the average weight of a locomotive was 10 tons, it could exert about 1,800 pounds of tractive effort, and 100 horsepower. By 1845 the average weight had increased to 18 tons, the tractive effort to 4,500 pounds, and the horsepower to 240. In 1855 the average locomotive weight was 25 tons, tractive effort was 7,010 pounds, and the horsepower was 375. At the end of the Civil War the engine weight had increased to 30 tons, the tractive effort to 9,830, and the horsepower to 520. By 1875 the weight was 32 tons, the tractive effort 10,500 pounds, and the horsepower 560. By 1900 the weight was at 60 tons and the tractive effort was 24,000 pounds.

The three major components of the steam locomotive were the frame, the boiler, and the engine (including wheels and running gear). The major change that took place in these components during the nineteenth century was an increase in size and a shift from iron and cooper to steel as the basic metal used in locomotive construction. The purpose of the frame was to provide a foundation for the boiler and firebox as well as the engine and running gear. Early American locomotives, however, used surprisingly light frames and actually depended on the boiler for primary stability with the frame acting as a secondary support system. The earliest American locomotives used wooden frames reinforced with iron plates and braces. Because the locomotives were light in weight and operated at slow speeds the easier-to-construct wooden frames were often preferred to iron frames.

But by the early 1840s the size of locomotives had grown to the point where new locomotives were too heavy for a wooden frame. As a result a switch to iron frames, constructed in three distinctive types, was inevitable. The bar frame was first used in either 1839 or 1842 and was composed of forged iron bars arranged in a top and bottom pattern tied together with pedestals and end bars or plates. Although the bar frame became the standard American frame, it was not widely used in England. Riveted frames attempted to copy the look of the wooden frames and were composed of iron plates riveted to two-inch-square iron bars. Riveted frames were used from the early 1840s to the late 1850s, although some locomotives were constructed with this type of frame as late as 1877. The slab-rail frame was a variation of the bar frame, substituting a single slab of iron for the boxlike bar frame. Few frames of this sort, or the common British plate, were used in the United States. The advantage of the bar frame was its flexibility and the strength of the boxlike structure resulting from the many braces and pedestals.

The American boiler was copied after the English boiler and was basically unchanged throughout steam locomotive history. It was composed of a separate firebox and smokebox, although in later years it appeared to be one structure. Small tubes running through the boiler connected the firebox at the rear of the boiler to the smokebox at the front. The gases released in the combustion process were drawn through the tubes, which were surrounded by water, to the smokebox where they were exhausted. As the gases moved through the tubes they assisted in heating the water in the boiler. There were several styles of boilers as well. The Stephenson boiler, of British origin, was favored because of

its simplicity. The Bury boiler provided more steam room. But the wagon-top boiler, developed in the 1850s, became the standard American boiler because it combined the simplicity of the Stephenson boiler with the enlarged steam-making space of the Bury. The wagon-top boiler got its name because the area of the boiler above the firebox was raised to allowed greater steaming room. Thus the diameter of the boiler was greater in this area, and it looked like it had a top almost like a Conestoga wagon.

Until 1870 boilers were constructed of wrought iron. Courses, or sections, of the boiler were constructed so that from front to rear the diameter was slightly larger with each course. Each course slid inside the other, overlapping for a short distance, and was then single-riveted. On some boilers the courses were only two sizes and were alternated. The result was a boiler of roughly similar diameter. After 1870 the increasing steam pressure required multiriveted joints between the boiler courses. The holes for the rivets were usually punched, although some mechanics preferred drilled holes. The most significant change in boiler construction came in the 1860s and 1870s when inexpensive steel replaced iron. This change allowed locomotives with much higher boiler pressure to be designed and built, and this led to more powerful machines.

The earliest boiler tubes (usually between 100 and 150 of them per boiler) were constructed of copper, rolled and lap-welded into tubes. Brass tubes were also used, but eventually iron tubes were necessary to endure the greater heat produced by coal-burning locomotives. Cheap steel tubes were introduced in the 1860s, but the cost and the difficulty in welding the steel tubes delayed their widespread use until the late nineteenth century.

To retain the heat of the boiler, particularly in cold weather, or if the locomotive was running at any speed, some form of insulation, or lagging, was used on most locomotives. The first lagging material was wood, and for many years it was the only material used. After about 1845 thin sheet-metal jackets were fitted over the lagging to protect the wood from the elements. Probably the most common nineteenth-century boiler jacket material was Russian iron, a metal that yielded a shiny gray surface. Although more combustible than wood, felt was also used for lagging, but it was not until the

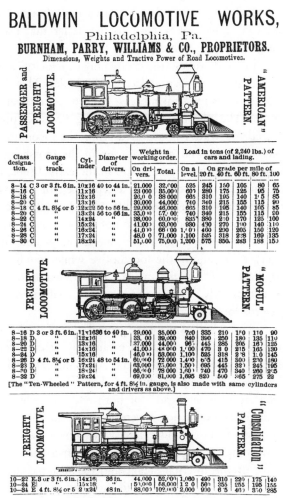

Advertisement displaying the locomotives offered by the Baldwin Locomotive Works, circa 1875

box (the top) was supported by a truss of crown bars (later staybolts). The wear on the firebox and the staybolts was heavy, particularly if the locomotive was a coal-burner, and the firebox required constant inspection, maintenance, and repair.

On wood-burning locomotives grates were simple, trouble-free devices composed of cast-iron bars. Rocking grates were not necessary because of the almost complete combustion of wood. Coal burning created problems, however. The heat was so intense that most cast-iron bars were melted in a short time. Furthermore, the combustion of coal resulted in substantial ash that had to be removed from the firebox at some point. The first problem was solved initially by water tube grates and later by steel grates. Water was forced through the hollow iron tubes that formed the water grate, thus preventing it from burning out. The second problem was solved by various forms of rocking or movable grates which could break up the unburned coal and the ash, dropping it onto the ash pan located beneath the firebox.

At the other end of the boiler was the smokebox which served as a chamber where smoke and gases from the combustion process and spent steam from the cylinders passed through and out of the smokestack. By the mid 1850s the smokebox also provided support for the cylinder saddle located beneath the smokebox. The exhaust pipe was located in the smokebox. This was an important device that helped to create the draft that made the steam locomotive successful. The exhaust pipe forced the steam that had been used in the cylinders out through small diameter nozzles into the smokebox and up the stack, along with the smoke and gases that were already there. The engineering challenge was to design the nozzle small enough to create the exhaust blast necessary to increase the power of the locomotive while not making it so small that excessive back pressure worked against the power generated by the powerful draft. Throughout the history of the steam locomotive the adjustment of the exhaust pipe was one of the most critical aspects of steam locomotive design and operation.

One of the most damaging aspects of a wood-burning locomotive was the abundant amount of sparks its operation generated. Without some spark-arresting device steam locomotives were always capable of starting fires. Until the development of larger coal-burning locomotives most of the spark-

last years of the century that asbestos and magnesium lagging materials were developed.

The firebox was a box within a box containing water between the two walls. The space between the two walls was about 2 inches on a wood-burning locomotive and 3 to 3½ inches on a coal-burning locomotive. It was in this space, the hottest in the boiler, that most of the water was converted to steam. Prior to the Civil War the firebox was constructed of wrought iron or copper, generally copper, and both materials were adequate for wood-burning locomotives. The move to steel fireboxes was accelerated by the higher temperature of coal-burning locomotives. The fireboxes of wood-burning locomotives were rather narrow and deep while those for coal-burning locomotives were wider and more shallow because of the different combustion characteristics of the two fuels. The inner and outer walls of the firebox were held rigid and separated by staybolts. The crown sheet of the fire-

arresting devices were located in the smokestacks of locomotives. The result was large balloon- or cone-shaped locomotive stacks that gave nineteenth-century locomotives their distinctive appearance. The smokestacks were not designed that way for the pleasure of viewers, however. Inside these stacks were metal plates and nets designed to break up and extinguish large sparks without reducing the efficiency of the draft process. Unfortunately, most effective spark-arresting devices restricted the efficient operation of the locomotive, and most locomotives that operated efficiently did not have good spark-arresting devices. Consequently, steam locomotives set many fires. While the problem was lessened with coal-burning locomotives, it still existed. Coal-burning locomotives, however, tended to have most of the spark-arresting devices inside the smokebox. Toward the end of the century the result was a reduction in the size of smokestacks and the disappearance of the balloon and bonnet stacks. Like the brake and the coupler, spark-arrester devices and designs were invented by the hundreds, but with little success.

One of the most important steps in the operation of a steam locomotive was the transfer of water from the locomotive tender to the boiler. Without water to be converted into steam the locomotive could not operate. The movement of water required some kind of pump. The earliest pump was a single-action force pump usually powered by the crosshead of the locomotive—the crosshead being the point where the piston rod was connected to the driving rod which was, in turn, connected to the main driving wheel. The most common system was to attach a pump to each crosshead. The crosshead pumps had two major disadvantages: they did not work when the locomotive was standing still, and they caused tremendous strain on the crossheads. When a locomotive was stationary it did not require much steam; thus, the fact that the feedwater pumps did not work in that situation was not a serious problem. When the locomotive was pulling a heavy train at a slow speed, thus requiring the maximum power of the locomotive, the feedwater pumps often could not supply an adequate amount of water—undoubtedly a more serious problem. Several other types of pumps were tried, but the most successful device was the injector developed in the 1850s.

The injector was one of the few railroad innovations that developed from a scientific background. A French engineer, using Venturi's law, designed a method of forcing water into the boiler that used steam from the boiler passing through a variety of nozzles and tubes to create high velocity and greater pressure than existed in the boiler. This device had many advantages over the feedwater pump. The injector had no moving parts, it pre-heated the water, it operated while the locomotive was standing, and it did not strain the crossheads. First used in the United States in the early 1860s, it did not gain widespread acceptance for almost twenty years because it was difficult to keep the injector operating properly. It was not uncommon to outfit a locomotive with two crosshead pumps and one injector (to supply the locomotive while standing). By the late 1880s the injector had been improved, and it quickly became the standard feedwater device for locomotive boilers.

The cylinders were the central part of the locomotive engine. Constructed exclusively of cast iron in the nineteenth century, the right and left cylinders were cast separately, and the ends were open. Separate cylinder heads for both ends were bolted to them. The valve boxes were also separate. The machining of the cylinder and valve boxes was the most complicated part of locomotive construction because of the internal steam and exhaust passages. Steam had to be channeled to each end of the cylinder in order for it to be admitted for expansion purposes. Another channel had to allow the spent steam to be exhausted. The admission and exhaust of the steam was controlled by the valve gear, and in the nineteenth century this was accomplished with the "D" slide valve. Pistons were hollow, constructed of cast iron, and packed with either wool or hemp. A form of beef fat, known as tallow, was the most common cylinder oil until petroleum products were first refined in the 1860s.

In the latter part of the nineteenth century, as the size of steam locomotives began to increase and fuel consumption along with it, a concerted effort was made to improve their efficiency. In 1874 the cost of fuel was about 30 percent of the cost of operating a steam locomotive. By 1892 the cost of fuel had risen to about 42 percent and was probably the single most expensive factor in operating a steam locomotive. One solution to poor fuel efficiency was an attempt to use the steam of a locomotive twice, an attempt that resulted in a "compound" locomotive. Although the first compound locomotive was constructed in the late

1860s, the common application of the principle did not occur until 1889 when Samuel M. Vauclain of the Baldwin Locomotive Works designed and built a locomotive copied after a British model.

A compound, or double expansion, locomotive, could realize more power from its steam than could a simple, or single expansion locomotive. In the average steam locomotive of 1890, steam was heated to a temperature of about 450 degrees Fahrenheit (achieving a pressure of about 200 pounds per square inch) in the water legs around the firebox. By the time the steam was drawn into the cylinders it had dropped to about 220 degrees (80 or 90 pounds per square inch). When the steam was exhausted it still had a pressure of about 30 or 40 pounds per square inch The compound answered this problem by first using the steam in a high-pressure cylinder and then reusing it in a low-pressure cylinder. The first cylinder in which the steam was used had to be smaller, because the pressure was higher, than the second cylinder where the steam was used at a lower pressure and temperature.

There were five forms of compound locomotives, three of which were developed at the close of the nineteenth century. The first type of compound, and the most successful in the United States, was the Vauclain compound. Vauclain's compound placed one cylinder on top of the other, a high-pressure and low-pressure cylinder on each side of the locomotive, with both pistons connected to a common crosshead. During a single cycle the main rod was driven one revolution by the high-pressure cylinder and one by the low-pressure cylinder. On passenger locomotives the high-pressure cylinder was usually on top, but on slow-speed freight locomotives the cylinders were reversed to provide room for the valve gear and rods. The second type of compound was the cross-compound developed about 1891. In this arrangement the high-pressure cylinder was placed on one side of the boiler with the low-pressure cylinder on the opposite side. Cutoff ports and timed crossheads allowed the two cylinders to work alternately. In 1893 the tandem compound was introduced (although it had been used experimentally in the 1860s), primarily for heavy freight service. The high-pressure cylinder was mounted slightly inside the low-pressure cylinder, but ahead of it. A double-headed piston (one in each cylinder) was used with a common rod connected to a single crosshead. The final two types of

compounds, the balanced (three or four cylinder versions) and the Mallet were not developed until after 1903.

Although the compound had a brief period of success it was eventually superseded by devices like the superheater that achieved the efficiency of the compound by heating the steam to a much higher pressure than was previously possible. The Mallet compound, however, did continue until the final days of steam. In fact the last steam locomotive constructed by the Baldwin Locomotive Works was a Mallet compound 2-6-6-2 for the Chesapeake & Ohio in 1949.

The engine trucks or lead trucks were originally constructed of iron with the frames made of wood reinforced with iron. At first the wheels in the engine truck were placed close together to make it easier for the locomotive to negotiate curves. In the early 1850s it was apparent that a longer wheelbase for the engine truck provided more stability and handled the weight of the cylinders and smokebox more effectively. By the middle of the decade the spread truck, with a wheelbase of between 66 or 72 inches, became standard. It was not until the 1860s that a separate two-wheel engine truck was devised. Few locomotives used a trailing truck in the nineteenth century. Trailing trucks would not become necessary until the demand for larger locomotives forced the firebox to be moved behind the driving wheels where it needed support.

Driving wheels were constructed out of wood, wrought iron, and cast iron. Many of the earliest locomotives, including the Stourbridge Lion, had wooden wheels with an iron hub and a thin iron tire. The value of iron, and later steel, for driving wheels could not be denied, and by the 1850s cast iron wheels were the standard in the United States. The reason cast iron wheels were so successful in the United States was because of the high tensile strength of the iron used and the care given to the casting process. Hollow hubs, rims, and spokes reduced the weight of the wheels. Steel was first used for the driving tire. A steel tire was desirable because it wore five times longer than an iron one. But because of steel's high cost, iron wheel centers did not become obsolete until the close of the century. Axles were originally made of wrought iron. By the 1870s steel axles were gradually replacing iron axles. One interesting note, however, is the extent to which nineteenth-century American mechanical engineers were suspicious of steel. They were familiar with the qualities of iron and, despite current perceptions of the superiority of steel over iron, tended to favor iron as the basic locomotive building material much longer than appears reasonable. The mechanics knew that iron in compression was as strong as, if not stronger than, steel. Steel, however, was more flexible, and it gained its initial success in the construction of fireboxes where flexibility was more important than strength. It is also worth remembering that steel was more expensive and until the late 1880s less consistent in quality than iron.

Perhaps the most complicated part of the locomotive was the complex valve motions developed to control the admission and exhaust of steam from the cylinders. While most mechanical aspects of the nineteenth-century American steam locomotive were admirably simple the valve motions were not. The objective of the valve motions was to cut off steam admission to the cylinders at a point where the expansion of the steam was complete and the thermal energy of the steam had been expended. In addition the motion had to provide the right amount of lead, that is, valve opening, when the piston was on "dead center." Lead was important because it cushioned the piston at the end of its stroke, and it helped to start the locomotive when one piston was on "dead center" (as one cylinder was "quartered," i.e., a quarter of a revolution ahead of the other; both pistons could not be on "dead center" simultaneously). A great deal of debate and experimentation continued throughout the existence of steam locomotives about the correct valve settings. What was the correct percentage of steam cutoff? What was the correct amount of lead? Separate and variable cutoffs were developed and used as were many forms of valve gear. The most common valve gear in the nineteenth century was the relatively simple Stephenson valve gear, developed by Robert Stephenson. Late in the century the Walschaerts valve gear was developed, and it became one of the predominant valve gears in the twentieth century.

Other components of the locomotive, such as cowcatchers, headlights, bells, whistles, and tenders, evolved as needed and were less complicated and critical in the mechanical development of the locomotive. Cowcatchers were crude wooden or iron devices designed to sweep obstructions, usually cows, off the track. Their shape was often similar to the moldboard of a plow. Many of the early cowcatchers were rather heavy and extended out in front of the locomotive in an unbalanced way. Improved fencing kept animals off the tracks by the latter decades of the century, and the cowcatchers became less formidable.

Headlights, uncommon in England, were much more important in the United States. Night operation was not common until the 1850s, however, so early locomotives were not outfitted with headlights. Often freight trains were operated at night, and at slow speeds, so as to clear the track for daytime passenger trains. The most effective early headlights were metal boxes with bright metal, usually silver-coated, reflectors mounted behind the oil lamp. The large size of these early headlights was necessary to contain the reflector and the oil source for the lamp. Although some electric headlights appeared in the 1890s, they were not common until the twentieth century.

Locomotive bells also became common in the 1850s as warning devices that were less disruptive than whistles. Bells were constructed of brass and by 1860 weighed anywhere from 60 to over 200 pounds. Whistles, a more commanding warning device, became common in the 1840s, somewhat before the bell. They were also constructed out of brass and had a tremendous variety of pitches and volumes.

Finally there was a tender, often ignored, but essential from the earliest days of steam locomotives. Because of the heavy water consumption of a steam locomotive–in the 1850s 1,000 gallons of water were required for a twenty-five-mile run–the tender was essentially a water tank. The problem with the tender was its weight. By the end of the Civil War it was not uncommon for a tender loaded with wood and water to weigh two-thirds as much as the locomotive. As the wood and water were consumed the weight of the tender declined dramatically creating a problem for the truck suspension system. A truck that rode well with a full tender was too stiff and inflexible when empty. The earliest tenders were four-wheeled. By 1850 most were either six-wheeled or, more commonly, eight-wheeled. The use of two four-wheeled trucks to support the tender worked best and was the standard configuration of most tenders by the 1860s.

In the nineteenth century steam locomotives ruled the rails. They replaced horses and sail cars quickly and were not challenged by another form of motive power until the 1920s. For some Americans they were seen as evil monsters scaring horses, setting fire to Sunday bonnets, and destroying the tranquillity of the American garden. For the majority of Americans, however, steam locomotives were seen as the most tangible form of progress the nation had to offer in the nineteenth century. They certainly performed a significant role in helping to bridge the tremendous distances of the nation. Few events in American history had more significance than the "golden spike" ceremony, which symbolized the linking of the Atlantic and Pacific oceans with bands of steel over which steam locomotives provided the motive power. Even today, for many people over fifty, the steam locomotive evokes an extremely positive sense of the past. Although steam locomotive preservationists are not as prominent in the United States as they are in Europe, nor are

their results as successful, in 1988 there are at least thirty steam locomotives operating in special service in many areas of the country. The continued support given to these obsolete machines is strong testimony to the important role of steam locomotives in the American consciousness.

References:

Alfred W. Bruce, *The Steam Locomotive in America* (New York: W. W. Norton, 1952);

Angus Sinclair, *Development of the Locomotive Engine* (Cambridge, Mass.: M.I.T. Press, 1970);

John H. White, Jr., *American Locomotives: An Engineering History, 1830-1880* (Baltimore: Johns Hopkins University Press, 1968).

–Robert L. Frey

Louisville & Nashville Railroad

by John F. Stover

Purdue University

The Louisville & Nashville (L&N) Railroad was chartered by the state of Kentucky in March 1850 for the purpose of diverting trade from the upper South to the river town of Louisville. The railroad's first president, Levin L. Shreve, a Louisville businessman, faced the twin problems of route location and finance. The city of Louisville subscribed $2 million, and Tennessee offered the normal $10,000 per mile for the route in that state, but progress was slow. Former governor John L. Helm succeeded Shreve as president in 1854 but was no more successful. By the fall of 1856 only thirty miles of line were fully in operation. In 1857 two men, James Guthrie and Albert Fink, joined the railroad, Guthrie as vice-president and Fink as construction engineer. Guthrie and Fink pushed construction, and the entire 185-mile main line to Nashville was put in operation in November 1859. The first through freight traffic was the shipping of supplies to the drought-ridden South. A branch line in the direction of Memphis gave the road a total line of 253 miles in 1860. James Guthrie became president in 1860, and Albert Fink was soon made general superintendent. The L&N, which was one of the few railroads built during the 1850s for a sum near

original estimates, on the eve of the Civil War had gross revenues of $716,000 and an equipment roster of 38 locomotives, 31 passenger cars, and 306 freight cars.

The track gauge of the Louisville & Nashville was 5 feet, the gauge that was used in much of Kentucky, all of Tennessee, and most of the South. At the outbreak of the Civil War the L&N was the only line running through neutral Kentucky that offered a direct connection between the rail network of the South and that of the North. The prosperity enjoyed by the L&N during the Civil War was due to the location of the line and also the careful and crafty management of the road's president, the eccentric and sometimes arrogant James Guthrie. Anticipating future scarcities, the Confederates feverishly bought supplies in the North and shipped them south over the L&N in the spring and early summer of 1861. This profitable traffic continued until September 1861, when President Guthrie rather reluctantly decided to support the Union. Throughout the war he received higher than normal rates for his federal business. His line was used in the early fall of 1863 when 30,000 men from the Army of the Potomac were moved to Tennessee to lift the

The Louisville, Kentucky, station of the L&N Railroad

siege of Chattanooga. The L&N also served as a major supply route for Gen. William T. Sherman's campaign in the South. The road's gross earnings increased fivefold during the war, the operating ratio never reached 50 percent, and good dividends were paid the stockholders (4 percent in 1863, 12 percent in 1864, and 8 percent in 1865). The mileage of the road did not increase during the war years, but motive power and equipment climbed over 50 percent.

Prosperity continued for the Louisville & Nashville in the early postwar years. Unlike most other southern lines, the L&N was not faced with the expensive problems of physical reconstruction. In 1868 the ailing Guthrie resigned the presidency and was replaced by his longtime friend H. D. Newcomb, a prosperous Louisville businessman who headed the L&N until 1874. Major extensions of the L&N were made during the Guthrie and Newcomb years. The L&N at the end of the war had three branches: a short one to Bardstown, a second one to Lebanon which during the next dozen years would be extended toward Knoxville, Tennessee, and a 46-mile line aimed toward Memphis but ending at the Tennessee state line. Two roads com-

pleted the L&N link with Memphis: the 82-mile Memphis, Clarksville & Louisville from the state line to Paris, Tennessee, and the 130-mile Memphis & Ohio from Paris to Memphis. In 1867 the L&N leased the Memphis & Ohio and purchased the road outright five years later, and in 1868 the L&N leased the connecting road, the Memphis, Clarksville & Louisville. President Newcomb was also interested in controlling two roads south of Nashville, the 120-mile Nashville & Decatur and the South & North Alabama, a 183-mile road between Decatur and Montgomery, Alabama. The Nashville & Decatur was leased in 1872, and in the same year the L&N acquired control of the South & North Alabama.

The expansion brought a modest increase in gross earnings, despite L&N freight rates that were declining in the postwar years. The L&N escaped receivership during the depression of the mid 1870s, but no dividends were paid in 1874, 1875, and 1876. By 1880 major expansions in mileage had been made at both ends of the system, in the South to Pensacola, Mobile, and New Orleans, and also in Kentucky. By 1880 the L&N was operating 1,840 miles of road with gross earnings of $7.4 million, an operating ratio of 57 percent, and an equipment roster of 284 locomotives, 222 passenger cars, and 5,200 freight cars. Yearly dividends between 1877 and 1880 ranged from 1 1/2 to 5 percent.

With the major expansion in mileage the financial control of the L&N shifted from Louisville to New York. In 1879 five of the twelve directors came from the North, four of those from New York City, and in that year about a third of the capital was held by New Yorkers. The rapid expansion in mileage had caused the L&N funded debt to increase from $17 million in 1879 to $48 million in 1881, with much of the new money from the North. By 1881 the board of directors included three men from Louisville, one from Nashville, one from Philadelphia, and six from New York City. The northern board quickly voted a 100 percent stock dividend, increasing the capital stock to $18 million. Edward H. Green was briefly president in 1880-1881 and was succeeded by Christopher Columbus Baldwin, both from New York City. Baldwin left the presidency in 1884 with the L&N burdened under a large floating debt and facing rumors of receivership. Receivership was avoided, but no dividends were paid from 1884 through 1887. Baldwin was succeeded by Milton H. Smith, a northerner who had been an L&N vice-president since 1882. Smith served as president from 1884 to 1886 and from 1891 to 1921. Eckstein Norton of New York was president from 1886 to 1891, but the operational control of the road remained with Smith during those years. Smith, while a gruff and stern man, was a prudent and honest manager who devoted himself wholeheartedly to the financial rehabilitation of the L&N. The mileage operated by the L&N increased only from 1,840 miles in 1880 to 2,200 miles in 1890, but gross earnings climbed during the same period from $7.4 million to $18.8 million.

Stock dividends of about 5 percent were paid in 1888, 1889, and 1890. Smith improved the road and, in one weekend in May 1886, had the entire trackage of the L&N converted to standard gauge.

While President Smith made every effort to increase freight traffic on his line, he hated passenger service and allowed his coaches to become antiques. Between 1884 and 1900 freight-ton mileage more than tripled and freight revenue nearly doubled, even though average freight rates declined from 1.3 to .7 cents per ton-mile in the same sixteen-year period. The Louisville & Nashville continued to expand its mileage in the 1890s and in 1900 was operating a system of 3,000 miles. The L&N also either leased or owned the majority of the stock in other railroads, more than 2,000 additional miles of line. In 1900 the total system of about 5,100 miles was located in every southern state east of the Mississippi except North and South Carolina, and served St. Louis, Cincinnati, Louisville, Nashville, Memphis, Birmingham, Montgomery, New Orleans, Mobile, Chattanooga, Atlanta, and Augusta. During the expansion of the 1890s Milton Smith followed a policy of general cooperation with the Southern Railway, the other major railroad in the South. After the panic of 1893 earnings on the L&N declined slightly, and no dividends were declared from 1894 through 1898. As Smith and his fellow officials celebrated the fiftieth anniversary of the incorporation of the L&N in March 1900, they could look back at half a century of solid growth and a remarkable degree of prosperity.

References:

Maury Klein, *History of the Louisville & Nashville Railroad* (New York: Macmillan, 1972);

John F. Stover, *The Railroads of the South, 1865-1900: A Study in Finance and Control* (Chapel Hill: University of North Carolina Press, 1955).

William Mahone

(December 1, 1826-October 8, 1895)

by E. Dale Odom

North Texas State University

CAREER: Teacher, Rappahannock Military Academy (1847-1849); chief engineer, president, general superintendent, Norfolk & Petersburg Railway (1851-1861); colonel, brigadier general, and major general, Army of Northern Virginia (1861-1865); Virginia legislature (1863-1865); president, Norfolk & Petersburg and Atlantic, Mississippi & Ohio railways (1865-1881); United States Senator from Virginia (1881-1887).

Virginia railroader and politician William Mahone was born on December 1, 1826, near Monroe in Southampton County, Virginia, the son of Fielding Jordan and Martha (Drew) Mahone. Fielding Mahone was a merchant and tavern keeper. Although information is scant about young Mahone's early education, it is known that his formal schooling lasted only two years before he entered Virginia Military Institute, from which he graduated in 1847 at the age of twenty-one. Mahone continued his study of engineering during 1847-1849 while teaching at Rappahannock Military Academy. His first work as an engineer came in 1849 when Mahone helped to construct the Orange & Alexandria Railroad. In 1851, two years after beginning his railroad career, he became chief engineer and constructor of the Norfolk & Petersburg, and within ten years had become president and superintendent of that line.

In February 1855 Mahone married Otelia Butler. They had three children, two sons and one daughter. Mahone was socially outgoing, especially liked to gamble, and was known as an accomplished poker player. Although there was no indication that he was especially interested in politics in his earlier years, any nineteenth-century railroad executive had to become interested in politics in order to protect his railroad line. He could have hired a lobbyist, but Mahone quickly exhibited the personality and inclination to do the task himself. He later

William Mahone

took up cooking as a hobby, but retained his interest in poker and politics throughout his life.

When Virginia seceded from the Union in 1861, the governor made the prominent young railroad executive quartermaster-general of Virginia. Very shortly thereafter, however, Mahone became colonel of the Sixth Virginia Regiment of Eastern Volunteers and was commander of the Norfolk district until it was evacuated in May 1862. He continued active service in the Army of Northern Virginia throughout the war except during a period when he was recovering from severe wounds received at the Battle of Second Manassas and during the few days he was able to spend fulfilling his duties as a Virginia state senator. Mahone was made a brigadier general in November 1861 and promoted to major general in August 1864. Mahone's attention to detail and his ability to acquire supplies made him well liked by his men and gave his unit a fine esprit de corps. Gen. Robert E. Lee considered Mahone among the finest of his younger generals. Early in the war Jefferson Davis was reputed to have offered Mahone the job of coordinating all the Confederate railroads.

When the war ended, the man who soon became known as the "poker playing railroad Bismarck" of Virginia quickly returned to his position as president of the Norfolk & Petersburg and energetically began refurbishing and expanding the railroad. Mahone was soon president of three railroads. The South Side, an adjoining railroad to the west, elected him to be its president in late 1865, and in the months following he acquired enough stock in the Virginia & Tennessee, a line still farther west, to be elected president of that company. Then, although he had some financial difficulties in achieving it, by 1870 he had acquired the state's stock in those lines and persuaded the legislature to consolidate the three railroads he controlled with a fourth line projected to the west into a new railway named the Atlantic, Mississippi & Ohio (AM&O).

Several of Mahone's critics, accusing him of treating the AM&O as if it were his own personal possession and angry that he drew a salary as large as President Grant's, said that the initials of the new railroad stood for "all mine and Otelia's." The new consolidated line ran 408 miles from Norfolk to Bristol, was a westward rival of the Baltimore & Ohio and the Pennsylvania, and in 1881, under new ownership, became the Norfolk & Western Railroad. During the early years of the 1870s Mahone was supported strongly by the state as he fought the Virginia railroad machinations of Tom Scott of the Pennsylvania. The struggle was at its peak in the spring of 1871; it became a literal fight when Mahone became involved in fisticuffs with John M. Lyon, attorney for the local interests that favored the Scott lines.

Debt, depression, and English capitalists soon proved to be even more formidable foes than the Pennsylvania interests that Virginians called the "bucktails." The problems originated in the summer of 1871 when Mahone refinanced the old debts of his company by issuing $15 million of new first-mortgage bonds. Nearly $6 million worth of

those 7 percent bonds were sold to English creditors. Hard times, brought on by the panic of 1873, ensued for the AM&O as well as for most other railways, and despite severe retrenchment by management, the company defaulted on its debts in 1874. Although President Mahone tried valiantly to stave off the collapse of the railway by negotiating with the line's European creditors, he lost, and in 1876 the company went into receivership. When Mahone failed in a bid to be named receiver, he turned to politics and made an effort to be elected governor of the state in hopes that as governor he might take political action to save his railroad. Although he lost a race for governor in 1877 and ultimately failed in his efforts to keep the line in the hands of Virginians, he managed to continue as president of the railroad throughout the period of receivership and supervised the sale of the line to northern railroad interests in 1881. They renamed the reorganized line the Norfolk & Western, and Mahone claimed $125,000 in back salary from the new company.

Meanwhile, Mahone had become increasingly involved in politics as organizer and leader of the Readjustors, a group which advocated reducing state debts and passing popular social and economic legislation. His organization succeeded in winning control of state government in 1879 and 1881 in their battles against the Bourbon Democrats of Virginia. In 1881, at the age of fifty-five, Mahone won election to the United States Senate. Largely as a result of his conflict with Virginia Democrats, he proceeded to vote with the Republican party in the senate. During his years in Washington he built a machine that controlled the Virginia Republican party for several years. Nevertheless, after 1882 his organization lost favor with the voters in Virginia, and Mahone never won another election, losing a race for the United States Senate in 1886 and a contest for governor in 1889.

In his latter days in Washington, the short, slight, long-bearded, blue-eyed Mahone was a familiar figure in his grey slouch hat and peg top trousers. He continued his love for poker playing and often joined his cronies for sessions at the Chamberlain Hotel in the national capital. He died in Washington on October 8, 1895, at the age of sixty-eight and was buried at Petersburg, Virginia. Although Mahone was buried without much fanfare for a man who had been so prominent in the history of Virginia, a few years later the United Daughters of the Confederacy erected a monument to him at Petersburg.

References:

Nelson M. Blake, *William Mahone: Soldier and Political Insurgent* (Richmond: Garrett & Massie, 1935);

Jack P. Maddex, Jr., *The Virginia Conservatives, 1867-1879* (Chapel Hill: University of North Carolina Press, 1970);

Charles C. Pearson, *The Readjustor Movement in Virginia* (New Haven: Yale University Press, 1917);

John F. Stover, *The Railroads of the South, 1865-1900* (Chapel Hill: University of North Carolina Press, 1955);

Washington Post, October 9, 1895, pp. 3, 10.

Archives:

William Mahone's personal documents are located in the William Mahone Correspondence of the University of Virginia Library, Charlottesville, and in the William Mahone Papers of the Duke University Library, Durham, North Carolina.

William d'Alton Mann

(September 27, 1839-May 17, 1920)

by John H. White

Smithsonian Institution

CAREER: Tavern operator (1859-1861); colonel, U. S. Army (1861-1864); petroleum speculator (c. 1865-c.1866); Internal Revenue assessor, newspaper editor, railroad promoter (c.1866-1872); railroad sleeping car promoter (1872-1888); president, Mann Boudoir Car Company (1883-1888); magazine publisher, *Town Topics* (c.1888-1920).

William D. Mann, a sleeping car operator and publisher, was born in Sandusky, Ohio, into a family of English colonists who settled in Massachusetts. While he was still in his middle teens, Mann's family moved west to Adrian, Michigan. Mann claimed to have received an education as a civil engineer, but this statement, like most other facts about his early life, remains undocumented. When he was nineteen years old, Mann moved to New York City, but he returned to the Midwest in 1859 in order to claim some meager property he had inherited in Ohio. Efforts to revive a tavern on the inherited property failed but a new opportunity presented itself two years later with the fall of Fort Sumter. Mann joined the First Michigan Cavalry as a captain and he moved to Washington. He formed his own Michigan regiment soon after reaching the capital city and was promoted to the rank of colonel, a title he adopted for the remainder of his life. Mann was no barracks soldier but was active in the field and fought at the Battle of Gettysburg.

In 1863 Mann, while still on active duty, took time to indulge in certain mechanical pursuits. He patented a sling for rifles and succeeded in selling a

William d'Alton Mann

considerable quantity of them to the U. S. Army. This device netted him enough capital to invest in the Titusville Oil Boom that began at the war's end. Mann's oil company proved to be more blue sky than black gold and several investors claimed he had falsely solicited money. Mann was arrested, released on bail, and then acquitted of the charges.

Mann did not linger in hostile territory but went south to seek his fortune among the army of like-minded northerners who traveled with satchels made of carpeting. Mann landed in Mobile, Alabama, and was appointed assessor of Internal Revenue, a position that hardly endeared him to the local inhabitants. He started a newspaper, the *Mobile Register,* and meddled in area politics but he grew less popular and was burned in effigy during an anti-carpetbagger riot. He next tried railroad promotion for the Mobile & North Western but by 1872 Mann decided the Deep South was not the most welcome place for a displaced Yankee.

He had developed a new interest in sleeping cars, perhaps inspired by his involvement in railroad promotion, and on January 9, 1872, Mann received a patent for his sleeping car design. Eschewing hostile and poor Alabama, Mann spent eleven years promoting his design in Europe. He endeavored to improve the conventional American sleeping car, with its makeshift convertible seat-beds and curtains, with compartment or room-style cars. The idea was hardly original with Mann as it had been tested some twenty years before his patent. Mann was nevertheless determined to make a fortune and saw the sleeping car as a means to this end. After failing to convince British rail managers of the merits of his plan, he went to the Continent where he met with greater success. By 1875 Mann had fifty-one cars in service on European lines. He was already in partnership with Georges Nagelmackers, the son of a Belgian banker, but the partnership was apparently an uneasy one and Mann was convinced to sell his interest in the International Sleeping Car Company to his Belgian partner in 1882 for $2 million.

Mann returned to New York in 1883 determined to introduce his room-style car to American travelers. That same year he formed the Mann Boudoir Car Company in competition with George Pullman and Webster Wagner. Most railroads were already under contract to Pullman or his smaller competitors; however, Mann attempted to squeeze into this crowded field. By 1885 he had forty-three cars in service. The public's reaction to his cars was mixed; many liked the size and comfort of the bedrooms but others distrusted the propriety of traveling in anything that sounded so spicy as a "Boudoir Car." And so the sleeping car business proved at best marginal; Mann never succeeded in landing any major contracts. He sold out in 1888 to the Union Palace Car Company that in turn was quickly absorbed by Pullman.

At age fifty Colonel Mann was still vigorous and ambitious. He was not about to retire but instead he decided to reenter the publishing business. New York was oversupplied with newspapers and so he decided to take over a magazine, *Town Topics,* already being operated by his brother. The magazine was essentially a society rag, though it touched upon many other subjects in a superficial way. It offered a weekly gossip column signed by "The Saunterer," a title soon taken over by Mann himself. The innocent chatter of this column grew ever racier under Mann's creative guidance, and few indiscretions or depravities of New York's first families failed to escape the notice of the Saunterer. In an age when the slightest deviation from a rigid moral code was cause for censure, the colonel's gossip column grew into a formidable instrument of reproach. Of course, one might escape unfavorable notice for a consideration. Loans or payments for a favorable write-up in projected volumes about the rich and famous could erase embarrassing revelations in the Saunterer's column. In simple language Colonel Mann and his staff were accused of operating a high-level blackmail operation. The scandal went public in July 1905 when the colonel's outrageous shakedown operation was exposed by an intended victim who told all to the district attorney. In the series of lawsuits that followed, the colonel was never convicted but his outrageous operation was exposed. The final trial ended late in 1906 when Colonel Mann was absolved of perjury. His editorial duties continued as before though the alleged extortion operation was closed down amid noisy protestations that it had never existed. In his eighty-first year, still active as editor of *Town Topics,* William d'Alton Mann died of complications following pneumonia.

Mann is important for his challenge (albeit unsuccessful) to Pullman's growing monopoly. He also provides a truer example than do some of the more typical targets of the less-than-honorable men who flourished in the late nineteenth-century business community.

References:

Andy Logan, *The Man Who Robbed the Robber Barons* (New York: W. W. Norton, 1965);

John H. White, *The American Railroad Passenger Car* (Baltimore, Md.: Johns Hopkins University Press, 1978).

Daniel Craig McCallum

(January 21, 1815-December 27, 1878)

by James A. Ward

University of Tennessee, Chattanooga

CAREER: Designed and patented bridge (1851); architect, bridge builder, engineer (1851-1854); general superintendent, New York & Erie Railroad (1854-1856); president, McCallum Bridge Company (1858-1859); military director and superintendent of railroads, Union Army (1862-1865).

Daniel Craig McCallum remains an enigmatic figure in nineteenth-century railway history. Variously described as cold, aloof, and strict, as well as warm, cheerful, generous, and genial, he was a rare combination of the romantic and the scientist, a curious blend of the engineer and poet. His major accomplishments, however, came as an engineer; he designed a much copied railroad bridge, devised a plan of organization for the first large railway, and commanded the Union military railroads. With a sharp, incisive mind, the habit of command, an ability to work with others, and a somewhat imperious nature, McCallum left his mark on his century.

Born to a tailor on January 21, 1815, in Johnston, Refrewshire, Scotland, McCallum immigrated with his parents to Rochester, New York. Due to his family's straitened circumstances Daniel received only an elementary education. Being a large, strapping youth he worked in construction as a carpenter and builder. A quick learner, he became interested in engineering design and architecture, talents that led him in 1851 to design and patent what he characterized as an "inflexible, arched, bridge." His design is described in his *McCallum's Inflexible Arched Truss Bridge Explained and Illustrated*, which was published in 1859. Over the years the bridge patent brought him a large income.

McCallum's life changed soon after the New York & Erie Railroad opened its 464-mile road from the Hudson River to Dunkirk in May 1851 and became the longest railway in the world. By 1854 the road enjoyed gross revenues of $5.3 million, operated over 200 locomotives and 300 cars,

Daniel Craig McCallum

employed over 4,700 workers, and posed new and difficult managerial problems for its administrative officers. McCallum joined the railway as superintendent of its Susquehanna Division in 1852 and in 1854 was promoted to general superintendent with responsibility for all its operations. He brought order to the line's administrative chaos and in the process set organizational and managerial precedents that were emulated across the country.

Superintendent McCallum established rigid lines of authority and a system of daily, weekly, and monthly reports that checked on everyone's performance. He drew up specific job descriptions for each position; erected a supervisory hierarchy to ensure that every employee knew to whom he reported; delegated authority to lower level supervisors and foremen, making them responsible for hiring and firing those under their command; enforced personal responsibility and accountability all through the ranks with regular reports; enforced discipline; and promised that pay and promotions would be based upon merit. To clarify the new chain of command, McCallum created one of the earliest organizational charts. Drawn in the form of a tree, the roots represented the board of directors, the trunk the president and general superintendent, and the five branches illustrated the road's divisions. Twigs and leaves defined each employee's position in the larger scheme. This organization of design helped the superintendent to coordinate the road's entire operation and to know where every train in the system was. McCallum stated his operating philosophy succinctly, saying that "the enforcement of a rigid system of discipline in the government of works of great magnitude is indispensable to success." While his plan made the Erie a more efficient and safe place to work, many employees resented losing their individual prerogatives and the more leisurely pace of operations. Engineers struck against McCallum's plan in 1854 and again in 1856. These two strikes cost McCallum his job in 1857, and the road fell prey to Daniel Drew and others who sapped its financial strength. Other large eastern trunk lines, however, most notably John Edgar Thomson's Pennsylvania, soon adopted a modified version of McCallum's organizational scheme. After leaving the Erie, McCallum went back into the bridge business, formed his own company in 1858, and prospered building bridges in the West and in Central America.

After the Civil War broke out and Union military leaders learned the importance of railways in modern warfare, Secretary of War Edwin Stanton appointed McCallum director of military railroads on February 11, 1862. His authority was extraordinary; he was empowered to seize and operate all private railroads and equipment necessary for the war effort. McCallum was circumspect, however, and became most valuable as a mediator between the government and railway presidents. In the wartime confusion McCallum's authority was eroded by another Stanton appointment, Col. Herman Haupt, who took to the field and actually ran the military roads. Although nominally under McCallum's authority, Haupt often acted without consulting McCallum; Haupt was also an engineering marvel,

and the two men soon clashed. Their relations did not improve when Haupt was breveted a brigadier general while still under the colonel's command. Their skills, however, complemented each other well; McCallum took care of the paperwork and smoothed ruffled feathers, while Haupt went out and moved men and materiel. Finally in 1863, when Haupt refused to sign his commission and left the service, McCallum's life was made much easier.

Using operational precedents Haupt had established, McCallum enjoyed his finest hour in the service of his adopted land when he coordinated the supply of Gen. William Tecumseh Sherman's 1864 Georgia campaign. With only a single-tracked road, McCallum sent an average of 160 cars a day to feed and supply 100,000 men and 60,000 animals. Before the war ended, General McCallum, who was breveted a brigadier on September 24, 1864, and a major general in March 1865, controlled 2,100 miles of road, employed a construction force of over 10,000 men, and had built or rebuilt almost 650 miles of road, 26 miles of bridge, 419 locomotives, and 633 cars. He spent nearly $40 million on the railroad war effort, but his close attention to detail and personal honesty spared his department any hint of scandal. The Scotsman could hold a grudge though; when he issued his final report, he failed to even mention Herman Haupt.

Although only fifty years old at the war's close, McCallum's postwar career was short. For a brief period he was an inspector of the Union Pacific Railroad, after which he retired with his wife, Mary McCann, and his three sons to Brooklyn, New York, and wrote poetry. In 1870 he published a volume of verse, *The Water-Mill and Other Poems*. On December 27, 1878, after a lengthy illness, McCallum died and was buried in Mount Hope Cemetery, Rochester, New York. Perhaps unwittingly he wrote what could stand as his own postwar epitaph in his poem "Water Mill":

> Possessions, power and blooming health,
> must all be lost at last,
> "The mill will never grind with water
> that is past."

Publications:
McCallum's Inflexible Arched Truss Bridge Explained and Illustrated (New York: S. T. Callahan, 1859);
The Water-Mill and Other Poems (Brooklyn, 1870).

Unpublished Document:

U.S. Congress. House, *Report of Brevet Brig. Gen. D. C. McCallum*, 39th Cong., 1st sess., 1866. H. Ex. Doc. 1.

References:

"Famous Firsts: Big Business Takes the Management Track," *Business Week* (April 30, 1966): 104, 106;

Thomas Weber, *The Northern Railroads in the Civil War* (New York: Kings Crown Press, 1952).

Otto Mears

(May 3, 1840-June 24, 1931)

by James G. Schneider

Kankakee, Illinois

CAREER: Merchant, road builder, freighter, investor (1864-1930); interpreter, Ute Indian Commission (1873); member, Ute Indian Commission (1881-1883); state representative, Colorado (1883-1885); president, Silverton Railroad (1887-1923); president (1889-1895), director, Rio Grande Southern (1889-1905); president, Silverton Northern (1895-1931); president, Chesapeake Bay Construction Company (1897-1899); president, Chesapeake Beach Railway (1899-1902); director, president, Mack Brothers Motor Car Company (1905-1906); director, president, Mack Brothers Manufacturing Company (1906).

The opening and early development of the area in and around the San Juan Mountains of southwestern Colorado were largely due to the indomitable spirit, native intelligence, and boundless energy of a Russian immigrant named Otto Mears. Many of the trails which he hacked or blasted into toll roads (and later railroads) are still serving the region today.

Otto Mears was born on May 3, 1840, of Jewish parents in the Russian province of Kurland, which later became the nation of Latvia. His father was English, his mother Russian, but her family, like many of the Jews then residing in Riga, had lived in Germany for nearly a century, thus accounting for the Germanic name of their child.

Both parents had died by the time Mears was three years old, so thereafter he made his home with a succession of uncles. After living with his mother's brother until he was nine Mears was sent to London to one of his father's brothers. From there he traveled to New York, where he took up residence with another uncle for a year. Mears then moved again, this time being sent, unaccompanied,

Otto Mears (courtesy of Colorado Historical Society)

to meet yet another uncle in California. His journey was by ship to Panama, across the Isthmus by horseback, and again by ship to San Francisco. His uncle, however, had already departed for the gold fields of Australia, leaving the eleven-year-old boy on his own.

Mears sold newspapers, learned tin-smithing, clerked in stores, and traveled about doing odd jobs in the mining camps of California and Nevada until Lincoln's first call for army volunteers from California came in mid 1861. He joined Company H of the First Regiment of California (infantry) Volunteers on August 17. His army experience took him to southern California in the fall, to Fort Yuma in the winter of 1862, and then in the summer of 1862 across the blistering deserts of Arizona and western New Mexico to the Rio Grande River. The rest of his army career was spent in western Texas, New Mexico, and Arizona. He was mustered out in Las Cruces, New Mexico, on August 31, 1864. The experience in the army provided Mears with the funds to start his entrepreneurial career.

After a short stint in Santa Fe as a clerk and then as the operator of a general store for a silent partner, Mears moved into southern Colorado, where in 1865 he opened a general merchandise store in Conejos and built the first sawmill in the area. He then constructed a gristmill to supply the army's nearby Fort Garland with its flour needs. After finding the local supply of wheat insufficient for his needs Mears moved north some fifty miles to the upper end of the fertile San Luis Valley. There, in the new town of Saguache, he opened a large general store and homesteaded on 200 acres which he planted in wheat, harvesting sixty bushels to the acre.

However, the army soon slashed the price it paid for flour, forcing Mears to seek other markets for his wheat. The miners working the diggings in California Gulch (near present-day Leadville) seemed to present his best opportunity. While heading northward to a gristmill on the Arkansas River, Mears's wagon load of wheat upset several times on the rude trail over Poncha Pass, spilling the loose wheat on the ground. While Mears was hacking out a passable road Territorial Gov. William Gilpin rode by and advised him to secure a toll road charter for the trail he was improving. Thus began the Mears System of Toll Roads, which eventually extended over 450 miles in southwestern Colorado. He did not build all of those roads, sometimes buying and then improving roads originally built by others. Those roads were the key to opening southwestern Colorado to commerce, and many are in use today as part of the Colorado highway system. The money he collected in tolls became

the cornerstone of Mears's success as an entrepreneur.

While expanding his toll roads Mears continued to operate his Saguache store, which became a stopping place for everyone heading westward. For a number of years it was the last place to secure supplies. He also served meals to travelers, always reserving the first seating for women and children.

The establishment of Saguache County in 1868 brought Mears his first public office. He became the county treasurer, and that was the start of his long, active interest in politics. During nearly all of his remaining Colorado years he was a force to be reckoned with on both local and state levels. Chosen as a Republican elector in 1876 the thirty-six-year-old Mears was selected to carry Colorado's three electoral votes to Washington in the presidential contest that saw Rutherford B. Hayes eke out a one-vote victory over Samuel J. Tilden.

While in the nation's capital the Colorado businessman secured a postal contract to deliver the mail once a week to the newly platted village of Ouray, which lay nestled in the San Juans at an elevation of 7,800 feet. Mears had previously won other mail contracts which fit nicely with his extensive freighting business, but none was quite so difficult as the one to Ouray. In the early spring, when the heavy snow cover was turning to slush and Mears's men said they could not get through, the sturdy pioneer strapped on snowshoes and carried the mail himself to keep from forfeiting the contract.

Mears's extensive travels in southwestern Colorado put him constantly in contact with various opportunities for development of the region. With others he founded such towns as Lake City, where, as he did in other communities, he began to publish weekly newspapers which were always boosters of the region and of their particular towns.

Because Mears learned to speak the Ute language, he became an interpreter for the Ute Indian Commission in 1873 and traveled to Washington with the delegation of chiefs and commissioners which was received by President Ulysses S. Grant. In 1880, following the so-called Meeker Massacre (when a group of Utes killed Indian Agent Nathan Meeker and other men at the agency and took the women and children captive), Mears was appointed a member of the new Ute Indian Commission. Following another trip to Washington with Chief Ouray and other tribal leaders, Mears was instrumental in securing Indian ratification of the Ute

Treaty. That led to the removal of most of the tribe to the Uintah Reservation in Utah. As the Utes were being settled on their new lands an attempt was made on Mears's life, but he escaped harm.

Turning again to politics Mears was elected from Saguache County to a single term in the Colorado legislature, where, as chairman of the House Committee on Counties, he was influential in drawing the boundaries for several new counties in the western part of the state. In 1889 he was named by Gov. Job Cooper to the Board of Capitol Managers, which oversaw the erection of the Colorado State House. Following the completion of the structure in 1901 the legislature ordered that a stained glass portrait of Mears be installed in the senate chamber in recognition of his key role in opening up the southwestern part of the state.

Following advice given him by Governor Gilpin, Mears sought to make the grades on all his toll roads gentle enough to be usable by the railroads which were destined to come. In 1881 he sold his Marshall Pass Toll Road to the Denver & Rio Grande (D&RG) Railway for its crossing of the Continental Divide on the D&RG route to Gunnison. Later Mears used parts of his other toll roads to build his own railroads in and around the San Juan Mountains.

Mears's first railroad was the narrow-gauge Silverton Railroad, which was incorporated in 1887. It headed north out of the town of Silverton at an altitude of 9,288 feet along Mears's toll road to Ouray. It was built to serve the prosperous Red Mountain mining district, allowing those mines to ship their low-grade ore to the smelters in Silverton and Durango. Its highest point was Red Mountain Pass at 11,025 feet. Construction was started in 1888 and the eighteen miles to Albany, past Red Mountain, were completed in 1889. The Silverton Railroad cost Mears $725,000 to build, which was considered a tremendous sum for one man to raise. The passenger fare on the line was twenty cents a mile, which was something of a record for that day. But considering the difficulties of construction and operation of a railroad at that altitude and over such formidable terrain, it was probably not unreasonable.

One of the notable features of the Silverton Railroad was the turntable at Corkscrew Gulch, about four miles from the northern terminus of the road. Even with the smaller turning radius of the narrow gauge, the topography could not accommodate a loop or a switchback, so a unique covered turntable was installed to allow cars to change direction, one car at a time, on the way to the Silver Bell and Joker mines and the towns of Ironton and Albany. The Silverton was a good revenue producer for several years.

Never at a loss for ideas, Mears developed plans to complete the rail connection from the end of his Silverton line to the town of Ouray, just eight miles away. Because of the steep grades through the precipitous Uncompahgre Canyon, Mears planned to accomplish that seemingly impossible task by building a cog railway. Although the company was incorporated, the cog road was never built.

Mears's most celebrated narrow-gauge railway was the Rio Grande Southern (RGS), which had the support of the Denver & Rio Grande Railway in connecting that line's tracks at Ridgway on the north with the terminus of its southern line at Durango. The success of the Rio Grande Southern would mean a great deal of connecting freight for the D&RG. The Rio Grande Southern was built to bring supplies into the booming mining towns on the west side of the San Juans and to haul the rich ore out to the smelters in Durango.

Mears also had other business interests which would benefit from the new railroad; he was a part owner of some of those mines and had an interest in a smelter in Durango, as well as in some commercial banks in several of the new towns. As he did in building the Silverton Railroad, Mears used some of his existing toll roads for the roadbed of the new railway, but he always built a replacement wagon road alongside the rails so as not to pass up future toll-road income.

Construction of the 162-mile RGS started in 1889 and the completion was celebrated on December 19, 1891, when the first train from Durango pulled into the thriving town of Rico. The crowning achievement of the RGS was the Ophir Loop, by which the line was able to ascend from the floor of the San Miguel River Canyon west of Telluride up the nearly sheer cliffs on the west side of the canyon to climb out at the southern end near the town (and mines) of Ophir. Competent engineers said that it was impossible to build a railroad along that route, but Otto Mears, without any engineering training and very little formal education of any kind, set out to accomplish it, and he did. At the south end of the canyon the switchback brought the tracks nearly directly above the high trestle of the previous leg. It was said that on one occasion with one train following closely behind another, the conductor on the higher train tossed an orange to the conductor of the lower one.

Referring to the Rio Grande Southern, railroad historian Lucius Beebe called it "a matchless triumph of imagination and daring," and in discussing its builder's place among the railroad greats, Beebe said: "Of them all . . . , Otto Mears is master and the Rio Grande Southern is his masterpiece. Of them all, only Otto Mears was, and is, incomparable."

What could have been Mears's most successful road became a victim of the virtual shutdown of mining in Colorado following the collapse of silver prices beginning in the spring of 1893 and culminating in the repeal of the Sherman Silver Act that October. The panic of 1893 was nationwide in extent, with many major railroads ending up, like the Rio Grande Southern, in receivership. Mears's fond hope of some day regaining control of the RGS never materialized. When the receiver took charge in August 1893, Mears lost control of the road. He was removed as president in 1895 but remained a director until 1905.

The line emerged from receivership in 1895, when the Denver & Rio Grande gained a controlling interest. Struggling along as a virtual subsidiary of that road (which had its own share of receiverships during the next fifty years), the RGS continued operating until 1952, when it was finally abandoned and the rails were taken up. But during World War II Mears's valiant RGS played an important role in hauling from that area some of the uranium ore used in making the first atomic bomb.

The repeal of the Sherman Silver Act also brought to an end the profitability of Mears's Silverton line. Placed in receivership in 1899, the Silverton Railroad was reorganized in 1904 as the Silverton Railway Company, with Mears as president of the new corporation. Although the Silverton continued to operate until the early 1920s, it never regained profitability. The right-of-way was deeded to the county in 1923 and the tracks were taken up three years later.

His Silverton Northern Railroad was originally planned as a branch of the Silverton Railroad, and construction started in 1893 on that basis, but the prospective financial difficulties of the Silverton road made it prudent to charter a separate corporation in 1895. The Silverton Northern ran northeast from Silverton to the rich silver mines at Eureka. The eight and one-half miles to Eureka (altitude 10,000 feet) were completed in 1896, and in 1905 the line was extended the final four miles to Animas Forks (altitude 11,200 feet), with much of the extension battling 7 percent grades. Only one loaded car of coal and one empty boxcar could be pulled up those grades to Animas Forks, and only three loaded ore cars could be handled on the way down. Although only a 12.5-mile narrow-gauge line, the Northern received national attention when Mears put into service a refurbished sleeper he had bought from the Denver & Rio Grande. It became a combination sleeper and diner named the Animas Forks, and its elaborate printed menus and wine lists are even today much sought-after collector's items.

Mears's daring in building a new mining railroad, at a time when the entire state of Colorado was severely depressed, well illustrates his eternally optimistic outlook. Despite the long odds, in this case Mears was right. The Silverton Northern was consistently profitable until the Great Depression of the 1930s, at which time Mears was no longer around to do battle. The Northern was finally abandoned in 1942, with the line's three locomotives ending up in Alaska on the White Pass & Yukon Railway, then busily hauling materials for the wartime construction of the vital Alcan Highway.

Always a master publicist for his own interests, Mears hit upon the idea of presenting unique passes to his biggest shippers and other important friends. He issued a variety of precious metal passes, including a very few in solid gold and a larger number in both solid silver and silver filigree. His passes, which were about the same dimensions as the paper ones then in use, are highly prized by collectors. Another time Mears presented to his guests at a party a sterling silver Otto Mears spoon. It was topped at the end of the handle by a bust of the promoter, while the stem and the bowl depicted scenes of his Silverton Railroad.

For the fifteen years after he lost the Rio Grande Southern, Mears, the eternal optimist, continued to investigate and sometimes participate in mining and railroad ventures in such disparate locations as British Columbia, North Carolina, New Mexico, and Louisiana. He also kept up a lively interest in mines around Silverton.

With things "very slow" in Colorado, as Mears wrote to a friend, he turned his attention to other projects. In 1897 he organized and became president of the Chesapeake Bay Construction Company, which planned to build a standard-gauge line from Washington, D.C., to a planned resort on Chesapeake Bay to be called Chesapeake Beach. The resort was expected to include major hotels, a racetrack, casino, fishing pier, and bathing beach, all of which would be great attractions for tens of thousands of government workers seeking relief from Washington's summer heat.

Construction of the Chesapeake Beach Railroad started in October 1897. Although the rails did not reach the beach until March 22, 1899, the Construction Company was dissolved and Mears became president of the railroad in October of 1898. Delays in acquiring some of the right-of-way, the difficulty of laying rails through swampland near the beach, and expensive bridge construction all added to the cost of the Chesapeake Beach line. An uncooperative Maryland legislature failed to legalize general gambling, so the casino was not built. The expected crowds of passengers failed to materialize, dooming the road to a dreary existence. Because of continuing losses Mears was removed from the presidency in 1902 by the majority owner, his longtime friend David Moffat, Denver banker and former president of the D&RG and later the builder of the Denver, Northwestern & Pacific Railroad.

Competition from the automobile in the 1920s was the final complication for the Chesapeake Beach Railway. In 1935 most of the tracks were taken up and today only a 2.9 mile vestige of the road remains as the East Washington Railway, mainly delivering carloads of coal from connecting carriers to an electric generating plant.

In 1905 Mears brought some new investors to the Mack Brothers Motor Car Company and was promptly elected president of the Pennsylvania firm. Mack had just moved to a new manufacturing facility in Allentown, Pennsylvania. The company was already building fourteen-passenger touring buses and Mears's attention was quickly attracted because the company was then equipping one of the vehicles with flanged wheels to operate on rails. At least two such motorized cars were turned out during Otto's brief presidency, one being delivered to the Uintah Railroad in western Colorado, where it operated for many years. The other was a twenty-three-passenger rail car which was destined for

Mears's own Silverton Northern, and was even named the "Mary M." in honor of Mrs. Mears. But it never arrived in Silverton.

Mears was not reelected to either the board of directors or the presidency of the Mack Brothers Motor Car Company at its annual meeting in January 1906, but early the next month he became a director and president of Mack Brothers Manufacturing Company, a New York corporation headquartered in Brooklyn. He resigned from that firm on November 30, 1906, in what appeared to have been an amicable parting. In return for his stock he received some cash, "a four-cylinder tonneau car which is about completed," and the title to the building then housing the Mack operation.

Soon Mears returned to Silverton, content to look after his interests in several local mines and to operate his Silverton railroads. In 1910 he leased from New England interests the 7.5-mile Silverton, Gladstone & Northerly Railroad, which had been built in 1899 by the owners of the Gold King Mine at Gladstone to serve their property located north of Silverton. In 1915 the Silverton Northern bought the SG&N at a foreclosure sale, but the line ran only intermittently and was abandoned in 1925.

Mears was living in Silverton in October 1911 when a flash flood of unequaled ferocity washed out more than fourteen miles of the Denver & Rio Grande's narrow gauge line between Durango and Silverton. With the severe mountain winter coming on, Silverton residents were in a state of near panic; they depended on the railroad to bring in their coal and food supplies. The D&RG started its own crews rebuilding the track from the Durango side of the washout and hired the seventy-one-year-old Mears to handle reconstruction from the north end. He secured 300 men from among the miners and others thrown into unemployment by the calamity and used his own locomotives to haul them to the site each day, returning them home at sundown.

As soon as Mears took charge of the rebuilding, the *Silverton Standard* ran a two-sentence editorial: "Otto Mears, the Pathfinder, is on the job. Confidence is restored and we all feel better." They felt even better on December 2, 1911, when the first train bringing supplies from Durango pulled into Silverton before heavy snows hit the region.

In 1917 Mears retired to Pasadena, California, residing at the Maryland Hotel, one of the area's premier hostelries. He served on the hotel's board of directors and he and Mrs. Mears were treated as local celebrities by both employees and guests. Mears also enjoyed daily afternoon poker sessions with other retirees in a room just off the lobby.

Mr. and Mrs. Mears were married on November 17, 1870 and raised two daughters. Although Mears lost a considerable portion of his fortune in the panic of 1893, the family was always able to live comfortably. Mary Mears died in 1924, and after her husband's death in 1931 their ashes were scattered in the San Juan Mountains at the site of Mears's Bear Creek Falls tollgate on his spectacular road from Silverton to Ouray. Today that route is U.S. 550 and is known locally as the "Million Dollar Highway." At the side of the road, at Bear Creek Falls, is a gray marble marker which reads:

IN HONOR OF
OTTO MEARS
PATHFINDER OF THE SAN JUAN
PIONEER ROAD BUILDER
BUILT THIS ROAD IN 1881

- - - - - - -

ERECTED BY A GRATEFUL PEOPLE
1926

The date on the marker is in error, Mears having taken over construction in 1883, but the sign illustrates the esteem in which Mears was held by his fellow citizens.

References:

Lucius Beebe, *Mixed Train Daily: A Book of Short-Line Railroads* (New York: Dutton, 1947);

"Chapter of Daughters of American Revolution," in *Pioneers of the San Juan Country*, volume 1 (Colorado Springs: Out West Printing, 1942);

Josie Moore Crum, *Three Little Lines* (Durango, Colo.: Durango Herald News, 1960);

Mallory Hope Ferrell, *Silver San Juan: The Rio Grande Southern* (Boulder, Colo.: Pruett, 1973);

Sidney Jocknick, *Early Days on the Western Slope of Colorado and Campfire Chats with Otto Mears, The Pathfinder, From 1870 to 1883, Inclusive* (Denver: Carson-Harper, 1913);

Michael Kaplan, *Otto Mears, Paradoxical Pathfinder* (Silverton, Colo.: San Juan County Book Company, 1982);

Ervan F. Kushner, *Otto Mears: His Life & Times, with Notes on the Alferd Packer Case* (Frederick, Colo.: Jende-Hagan, 1979);

Poor's Manual of the Railroads of the United States (New York: Poor's, 1892-1916);

The Silverton Standard, October-December 1911;

Robert E. Sloan and Carl A. Skowronski, *The Rainbow Route. An Illustrated History of the Silverton Railroad, The Silverton Northern Railroad and The Silverton, Gladstone & Northerly Railroad* (Denver: Sundance, 1975);

Ida Libert Uchill, *Pioneers, Peddlers, and Tsadikim* (Denver: Sage, 1957);

Ames W. Williams, *Otto Mears Goes East: The Chesapeake Beach Railway* (Alexandria, Va.: Meridian Sun Press, 1975);

Francis Wood and Dorothy Wood, *I Hauled These Mountains In Here* (Caldwell, Idaho: Caxton Printers, 1977).

Archives:

Material concerning Otto Mears is located in the Otto Mears Papers of the State Historical Society of Colorado Library, Denver, Colorado; and in papers at the Denver Public Library, Denver, Colorado.

Michigan Central Railroad

by John Lauritz Larson

Purdue University

The Michigan Central Railroad began before Michigan was admitted as a state. In June 1832 a group of Detroit boosters, led by land office clerk John R. Biddle, secured a charter to build the Detroit & St. Joseph (D&SJ) Railroad westward to Lake Michigan. Encouraged by a surveyor's report completed in 1834, the promoters collected subscriptions, acquired banking privileges from the legislature, and set to work improving the route. In 1837, after being admitted to the Union, the state of Michigan launched an ambitious program of internal improvements which absorbed the D&SJ as one of three main cross-state rail routes. Unfortunately the panic of 1837 ruined the state loan that was to finance the construction, and progress on most of the projects ground to a halt.

As funds dried up the state concentrated its efforts on the old D&SJ route, designated the Central line, and thirty miles quickly took shape. The railroad was of a wood and strap iron design and built on a raised earthen bed according to plans more economical than durable. But in 1838 it served Michigan's needs, and, despite the failure of the Michigan State Bank in February 1839, the commissioners optimistically forged ahead. Sections to Ann Arbor and Jackson were begun in 1839 and opened in 1842. By 1846 the Central stretched 143 miles to Kalamazoo. Unfortunately the success of the railroad led to its physical destruction. Heavy traffic pounded the lightweight track to pieces, locomotives and bridges proved inadequate, and services deteriorated as repair costs skyrocketed. A heavier and more durable road was needed, but Michigan, mired in debt, could not afford to invest in rebuilding. Arrangements were made to sell the road to a group of Boston and New York capitalists who hoped to finish and operate the Central as a private enterprise.

The new owners, headed by John Murray Forbes of Boston and including John E. Thayer, Erastus Corning, D. D. Williamson, and George Griswold, accepted a bargain hammered out by Detroit attorney James F. Joy and backed up by engineer John W. Brooks's detailed *Report on the Merits of the Michigan Central Railroad, as an Investment for Eastern Capitalists.* Paying $2 million for the railroad, much of it in depreciated Michigan bonds, the easterners rebuilt the line to more durable specifications. While quickly extending the line to the Lake Michigan shore in 1849, Superintendent Brooks simultaneously labored to re-iron the tracks with heavy rails and to upgrade the physical plant to handle the agricultural and passenger traffic that in 1849 already grossed nearly $500,000. The whole effort cost over $6 million–50 percent more than Brooks had estimated–but President Forbes assured his stockholders that proper investments in the present promised increased returns in the future.

Forbes, however, did not immediately understand the implications of the explosive growth of Chicago as a center of trade and commerce. The original Michigan Central functioned as a portage road, connecting steamers on Lake Michigan with boats on Lake Erie. Brooks, on the other hand, anticipated Chicago's role from the start, recommending in his 1846 *Report* that the terminus of the road be shifted southward to New Buffalo in order to position the railroad to take advantage of the growing Chicago traffic. Soon competitors backing the Michigan Southern line were plunging toward Chicago with an all-rail route which, when completed, was certain to slash the high passenger rates on which the Michigan Central thrived. James F. Joy had in 1848 attempted to buy for $50,000 an Indiana charter that provided access for the Michigan Central to Chicago, but Forbes had hoped to avoid the expense until the main line was profitable. The mistake proved costly; in 1851 the Michigan Central spent ten times that amount for the Albany &

Salem's Indiana charter and the next year charged into Illinois with no legal charter at all. On May 21, 1852, just one day ahead of the Michigan Southern, the Michigan Central entered Chicago. The 248-mile main line was complete, laid with heavy rail, and ready for heavy levels of traffic.

Beginning in 1848 the Michigan Central paid 8 percent dividends; in 1852, with the line completed, these rose to a high of 14 percent. But competition caused revenue levels to drop, and the company found itself in a constant struggle between maintaining rates and its traffic base. During the 1850s Forbes and Brooks's strategy was two-pronged. They improved the physical plant, rolling stock, and services while simultaneously attempting to gain control of feeder lines, steamers, and eastern connections. Brooks succeeded Forbes as president in 1855, promptly installed telegraphic communications, and soon ran the fastest passenger trains in the country. Brooks also proposed the nation's first rate pool in an attempt to suppress ruinous competition. Forbes pretended a leisurely retirement, but he was heavily involved in seeking financing, an increasingly important function. He and a group of Michigan Central investors bought properties in Illinois, Iowa, and Missouri and invested heavily in the Great Western of Canada to insure friendly connections each way for the Michigan Central. By 1857 total investment in the Michigan Central surpassed $10 million, and revenues reached $3.1 million, almost three times the 1852 figure. But the improvements and expansions raised floating debt to $1.5 million, and the panic of 1857 forced Forbes to place $3.6 million in bonds at a deep discount in order to cover the road's obligation.

For its first two decades the Michigan Central remained essentially a main line railroad. After the Civil War, however, traffic agreements and defensive investments entangled the company in a larger web that by 1877 had added 519 leased miles to the original operation. The Michigan Air-Line, for example, was leased from the Vanderbilts in 1871 and, running from Jackson to South Bend, cut short the old main line. Leases on the Grand River Valley, the Jackson, Lansing & Saginaw, the Joliet & Northern Indiana, and the Kalamazoo & South Haven protected and expanded the Michigan Central's natural territory. Most of these acquisitions took place after the empire-minded Joy replaced the

disabled Brooks as president in 1867. But system building was inevitable in the railroad environment of the nineteenth century, and the Michigan Central's independence suffered from its strategic importance as a link between eastern and western trunk lines.

In 1873 the securities market again collapsed, and the Michigan Central defaulted on its dividend and interest payments. Its stock price fell, and for the next four years speculators toyed with it. Moses Taylor of New York's National City Bank owned the largest block of shares, but Jay Gould, Sidney Dillon, and Cornelius Vanderbilt together held a majority. Joy stepped down in 1876, and Taylor's man, Samuel Sloan, came in as president. But in 1877 William H. Vanderbilt's settlement of a telegraph war with Gould resulted in the transfer of control of the Michigan Central to the Vanderbilts. A new board replaced the last of the Boston group, and Vanderbilt named himself president in 1878. In 1879 he picked up control of the bankrupt Canadian Southern to add to the Michigan Central's route; by 1883, when Vanderbilt retired, the Central's 1,101 miles in the United States and its 513 miles in Canada had been integrated into the loosely structured New York Central system. Henry B. Ledyard served as president during the balance of the century. At century's end the Michigan Central contained 1,650 miles of track, was valued at $48 million, and generated $16.7 million in revenues.

References:

Alvin F. Harlow, *Road of the Century* (New York: Creative Age, 1947);

Charles Hirschfield, *The Great Railroad Conspiracy* (East Lansing: Michigan State University Press, 1953);

Edward Hungerford, *Men and Iron* (New York: Crowell, 1938; reprinted, 1976);

Arthur Johnson and Barry E. Supple, *Boston Capitalists and Western Railroads* (Cambridge, Mass.: Harvard University Press, 1967);

John Lauritz Larson, *Bonds of Enterprise* (Cambridge, Mass.: Harvard University Press, 1984);

Robert J. Parks, *Democracy's Railroads* (Port Washington, N.Y.: Kennikat Press, 1972).

Archives:

Records of the Michigan Central are located at the Michigan Central Railroad Archives of the New York Central System in Detroit, Michigan, and at the Burlington Railroad Archives of the Newberry Library in Chicago, Illinois.

James Millholland

(October 6, 1812-August 1875)

by Robert L. Frey

Wilmington College of Ohio

CAREER: Apprentice to George W. Johnson (1829-1832); mechanic, Allaire Works (1832-1848); master mechanic, Baltimore & Susquehanna Railroad (1838-1848); master machinist, Philadelphia & Reading Railroad (1848-1866).

James Millholland is representative of the many outstanding mechanics working in the United States in the nineteenth century who were largely responsible for the rapid industrialization of the country at a pace even the British had difficulty comprehending. Like many of his contemporaries Millholland was not educated in an engineering school, but learned his trade via the apprenticeship system. Millholland's contributions were primarily in railroading, although he did develop a bridge design that came into common use in the late nineteenth and early twentieth centuries.

James Millholland was born in Baltimore, Maryland, on October 6, 1812. Little is known of his childhood or the type of education he received. His father, a machinist himself, encouraged his son's developing interest in mechanical matters and his gifted abilities in mathematics. With these tools Millholland entered an apprentice system designed to give him the mechanical skills needed for a career as a mechanic, machinist, or mechanical engineer.

Millholland served his apprenticeship under George W. Johnson of Baltimore, a fortuitous choice as, at the time Millholland joined Johnson, his mentor had been asked by Peter Cooper to complete the diminutive locomotive Tom Thumb. Cooper had designed this small steam locomotive in an attempt to convince the Baltimore & Ohio Railroad to use steam locomotives as motive power. Cooper, however, did not have time to finish the project and asked Johnson to complete it. Johnson, of course, involved his new apprentice in the effort, and thus James Millholland was a part of one of

James Millholland

the pioneer steam-locomotive projects in the United States. It is a small wonder that most of the remainder of his career was spent in railroads.

After approximately three years of apprenticeship, however, Millholland abandoned work on locomotives and accepted his first job with the Allaire Works, a firm best known for building marine engines. Although little information remains on this five-year period in Millholland's career, toward the end of his stint with the Allaire Works it is known that he worked for a short time in a sawmill in Mobile, Alabama. In 1837, at the age of twenty-five, he left the Allaire Works for the position of master mechanic with the Baltimore & Susquehanna (B&S) Railroad. For the remainder of his career he remained with the railroad industry, one of the fastest growing and most exciting fields in the country for a young mechanic.

A twenty-five-year-old master mechanic of a railroad might seem most unusual but the Baltimore & Susquehanna was not a Baltimore & Ohio. The 60-mile route of the B&S ran from Baltimore north to York, Pennsylvania, through rolling, hilly terrain that required numerous curves, bridges, and ascending and descending grades. The road's ten locomotives were poorly suited for the line. Three were British-made, but all were constructed on British engineering principles. The result was a fleet of locomotives too light for the undulating profile of the B&S and too rigid for the sharp curves. Millholland immediately set to work remodeling the locomotives in the company's Baltimore shops, which were unusually well-equipped for a fledgling line like the B&S.

In the decade Millholland remained with the B&S he made a name for himself as a mechanic by introducing three innovations. First was the development of the cast iron crank axle. Many locomotives in the 1830s and 1840s were "inside connected," that is, the main rods were connected to the driving wheel axles inside the frame rather than externally. The main rods from the cylinders to the axles of the foremost driving wheels were connected to a U-shaped crank axle. Most of the crank axles were machined out of wrought iron, a time-consuming and expensive process. Because of the inadequate quality controls of that day many crank axles were constructed out of inferior iron, which failed under operating conditions. Millholland insisted not only that crank axles be made out of cast iron, but also that they be of the best cast iron possible, the same kind used to make cannons. While this type of cast iron was more expensive the increased serviceability of the cast-iron crank axles justified the added cost.

A second innovation which contributed to Millholland's growing reputation was his insistence that freight cars be equipped with wooden springs. On the large six-wheel freight cars he built for the B&S, a type then in use only on the Baltimore & Ohio, wooden springs were required. His wooden-springed cars remained in operation long after he left the B&S, eventually being replaced by iron and steel springs as the weight of freight increased toward the end of the century. Wooden springs, how-

ever, were inexpensive, easy to fabricate and install, and were adequate for the loads hauled by freight cars in the 1840s and 1850s.

Finally, toward the end of his tenure on the Baltimore & Susquehanna, Millholland developed the plate-girder bridge. Fabricated from boiler iron, the bridge consisted of two huge plates set on end under the rails. Tied together with iron braces, the bridge could span small creeks and depressions, was extremely sturdy, and did not take exceptional skills to construct or install. The first plate-girder bridge was installed by Millholland on the B&S in 1847 and continued in use until 1882.

By 1848 Millholland, at thirty-six years of age still a young man, had gained a reputation as an innovative mechanical engineer. He had achieved as much as he could with the B&S, a railroad of limited financial resources and leadership. His reputation secured him an offer of the position of master machinist on the Philadelphia & Reading (P&R) Railroad, one of the best-built American railroads. Millholland accepted the position and moved to Reading. What he saw when he arrived was impressive. The P&R had been carefully laid out less than ten years earlier by Moncure Robinson, one of the best American civil engineers. Built to haul coal from the mines around Pottsville, Pennsylvania, the main line descended gradually from Pottsville to Philadelphia, the line's terminus. Laid with the high-quality T-rail and with generous curves, the P&R was the finest American example of a railroad built to British standards. Because of the heavy coal tonnage carried on the line the P&R demanded the most powerful locomotives available. The quality of the rails and roadbed encouraged Millholland to design and build such locomotives for the line.

Millholland's most significant career achievement was the design of a locomotive capable of burning anthracite coal. When Millholland came to the Philadelphia & Reading Railroad most American locomotives were wood-burners. The construction of the firebox mirrored this fact. Since wood burned quickly the fireboxes were narrow and high so the wood could be stacked for the most efficient combustion. Coal, and particularly anthracite coal, burned best when spread in a thin layer over a large area. Fireboxes were not designed for coal, particularly anthracite, and Millholland set about to correct this condition.

As with most problems the solution did not come quickly. Initial efforts to reconfigure the firebox so as to increase the grate area failed. Although Millholland increased the width of the firebox to 66 inches (the common maximum was 34 inches), that alone did not result in an efficient coal-burning locomotive. The intense heat generated by the burning of the anthracite coal was much greater than that of wood. The abrasive action of the cinders was also new to coal-burning locomotives. The net result was firebox failure at a rate greater than that in wood-burning locomotives. To overcome this problem Millholland installed cast-iron plates to protect the firebox walls and to reduce wear, but these only succeeded in restricting combustion. To increase combustion Millholland added a combustion chamber but instead of making it a forward extension of the firebox placed it near the center of the boiler. The combustion chamber was connected to the firebox by large-diameter tubes in the hope that gases not burned in the firebox would pass to the central combustion chamber to be burned prior to being exhausted. The added complexity of keeping the tubes from the firebox to the central combustion chamber from leaking, plus the inefficiency of the design (the gases cooled too much by the time they reached the central combustion chamber) did not lead to the type of performance Millholland desired.

Nonetheless, a significant number of locomotives were constructed with the wide firebox and the central combustion chamber. The fact that most of these locomotives had to mix wood with coal when in operation attests to the fact that they were not entirely successful as coal-burners. Millholland did not give up the idea of the central combustion chamber until 1855, or perhaps 1856. Eventually, however, he combined the large-grate-area firebox (about 25 square feet in comparison with the 17.5 square feet in most locomotives) with a superheater (to increase the heat of the steam) to develop a dependable coal-burning locomotive.

The problem of excessive wear of the firebox was controlled by the introduction of the water grate into the United States by Millholland. The water grate consisted of iron tubes laid across the bottom of the firebox. Water was circulated through these tubes, thus reducing the possibility of the iron bars melting from the increased heat generated by burning anthracite coal. The net result of these improvements was that the proportion of Philadelphia & Reading locomotives which burned coal increased from 23 percent in 1852 to 70 percent in

1857. By 1859 only four wood-burners remained (less than 3 percent). It is true that many of the locomotives were soft (bituminous) coal-burning machines, most constructed by the prominent Baltimore & Ohio mechanic Ross Winans. In 1855, however, the P&R stopped buying Winans locomotives. This is interpreted by John H. White as evidence that Millholland had developed a successful coal-burning locomotive.

Millholland was also responsible for other developments of importance to the railroad industry. He advocated solid-end connecting rods (for the driving wheels), which did not depend on regular and accurate maintenance and were thus less liable to failure. Millholland was also the first to make common use of the poppet valve throttle, using it as early as 1848 or 1849, some twenty years before it came into general use on American railroads. He developed and used round, turretlike iron cabs, and he followed Ross Winans in using some of the first examples of steel driving-wheel tires for locomotives. He also followed Winans in designing boilers that sloped from the front to the rear as they approached the locomotive cab. Since the fireboxes on coal-burning locomotives, anthracite-burning ones in particular, were exceptionally wide, the sloped boiler allowed the cabs to be positioned over the rear of the firebox and still allow adequate space for the engineer and fireman. Finally, James Millholland was one of the first to use injectors to put water from the tender into the boiler. Although he did not invent these devices he was always willing to try new devices or ideas.

Toward the end of his career Millholland designed some extremely large locomotives for the heavy coal traffic on the Philadelphia & Reading. One, known as the Pennsylvania, was the largest locomotive in the world when it was completed in 1863. The locomotive weighed fifty tons, had a 0-12-0 wheel arrangement, and was designed to push trains up a 1 percent grade near Philadelphia. The cab was mounted forward over the boiler (locomotives of this type were known as "camelbacks") and, although one set of driving wheels was removed in 1870, the locomotive remained in service until 1885. Locomotives weighing fifty tons were not common until the turn of the century.

Millholland resigned from his position on the Philadelphia & Reading in 1866. He was only fifty-four years old and there is no clear reason for his resignation. He reportedly wished to devote his attention to other business and community interests, but little is known of these other interests and little is known of Millholland's personal life. This lack of documentation is not an unusual characteristic in the careers of nineteenth-century mechanical engineers. Many of them appear to have had a single all-consuming passion for their work, and a significant number retired early to enjoy life with savings they had carefully laid aside. Also, they did not have to deal with the public in the same way that railroad presidents did. In fact, seldom did Millholland have any direct communication with the board of the P&R. The P&R's *Annual Report for 1859* is unusual as it contains a report from Millholland. The board usually received reports from the superintendent of the railroad, Millholland's superior, and as a result the press was seldom interested in talking with people in Millholland's position. Presidents were important figures and most of them received significant press coverage. The only place people such as Millholland received coverage was in the trade press of the day, in publications such as the *Railroad Gazette*, the *American Railway Review*, and the *American Railroad Journal*.

Millholland lived the remainder of his life in Reading, Pennsylvania, where he died in August 1875. At the time of his death he was only sixty-three, but his death was preceded by a long and debilitating illness. It is possible that the harbingers of this illness caused his early retirement from the P&R. James Millholland was a highly successful mechanical engineer who was partially responsible for the perfection of the steam locomotive in the nineteenth century. Although not as well known as the railroad presidents of the century, men like Millholland were responsible for the technological developments that made it possible for the American railroad system to move freight and passengers. Regardless of the importance of the maneuvering and dealing accomplished by the corporate presidents and the bankers, men like Millholland, as the builders of the physical realities of railroads, deserve to be remembered.

References:

Joseph Anton Fisher, *1833-1958: 125th Anniversary of a Pioneer Railroad* (New York: Newcommen Society of North America, 1958);

Angus Sinclair, *Development of the Locomotive Engine* (Cambridge, Mass.: M.I.T. Press, 1970);

John H. White, *James Millholland and Early Railroad Engineering* (Washington, D.C.: Smithsonian Press, 1967).

Archives:

Material concerning James Millholland's career with the Philadelphia & Reading Railroad is located in the Reading Company Records of the office of the Trustees of the Reading Company at One Plymouth Meeting, Plymouth Meeting, Pennsylvania; in the Reading Company Records of the Reading Terminal at 12th and Market streets, Philadelphia, Pennsylvania, and in the Reading Company Records of the Eleutherian Mills Historical Library, Greenville, Delaware.

Alexander Mitchell

(October 18, 1817-April 19, 1887)

by H. Roger Grant

University of Akron

CAREER: Secretary (1839-1854), president, Wisconsin Marine & Fire Insurance Company (1854-1887); president, Chicago, Milwaukee & St. Paul [and predecessor and satellite companies] (1865-1887); member, United States House of Representatives (1871-1875).

The architect of the mighty Chicago, Milwaukee & St. Paul Railroad (after December 1927, the Chicago, Milwaukee, St. Paul & Pacific) was an uprooted Scot, Alexander Mitchell. Mitchell was born on October 18, 1817, the sixth of seven children in Abberdeenshire, Scotland, where his father, John Mitchell, was an industrious and successful farmer. Although the family was not poor, young Mitchell received only a modest formal education, attending local schools in the parish of Ellon. He later worked for several years in a law office in Aberdeen and as a clerk in a banking house in Peterhead.

Contacts in the financial world prompted Mitchell to leave Scotland for the United States in May 1839. This bright, hard-driving immigrant became secretary of the infant Wisconsin Marine & Fire Insurance Company, which was founded by fellow Scot George Smith. In reality the insurance operation had only a minor interest in writing marine or fire policies; rather it sought to provide general banking services. (The company's Wisconsin charter, loosely interpreted, allowed it to function in this capacity.) Mitchell immediately demonstrated his business acumen, and the so-called insurance firm flourished. In 1854 Mitchell bought out Smith, and from then on his personal wealth increased dramatically.

Like other entrepreneurs who enjoyed access to pools of investment capital, Mitchell became interested in railroads. He seemed to enter the field because of his strong loyalty to Milwaukee, Wisconsin's premier city, rather than to enhance his

Alexander Mitchell

pocketbook. He realized that his home community needed to increase its railroad connections, particularly to the north and west. By the mid 1860s Mitchell and others could see how the aggressive Chicago & North Western (C&NW) Railway had constantly strengthened rival Chicago. Mitchell's chance to bolster Milwaukee came in 1865 when he became director and then president of the financially troubled Milwaukee & St. Paul (M&StP), organized in 1863 to link Milwaukee with La Crosse. Mitchell energized this property. Soon the M&StP, with Mitchell at the throttle, consolidated its hold over several other local carriers. These acquisitions included the debt-ridden but important Milwaukee & Prairie du Chien the December 1867.

Mitchell did not stop here in his quest for a giant Milwaukee-based railroad system. In 1869 he also headed the archrival Chicago & North Western. Commented the *Chicago Post:*

> History repeats itself. The tears of Alexander the Great, because he had not more worlds to conquer, are familiar to every school-boy, and here we have another Alexander, surnamed Mitchell, who starting out with the Milwaukee & St. Paul railroad, first gobbled the Old Milwaukee and La Crosse, then the Prairie du Chien, then half a dozen small railroads in Wisconsin, Iowa, and Minnesota, then the Western Union, and now, *eheu iam satis!* the Northwestern [sic], with all its branches, spurs, divisions, and ramifications! As there are still other lines to gobble, however, we suppose the weeping will not commence until such little sidetracks as the Union Pacific, New York Central, etc. are added to the inventory.

Yet "Alexander the Great" Mitchell did not retain the presidency of the Chicago & North Western for long. He stepped down in 1870, largely because he lacked the power to fuse it into the M&StP.

Mitchell knew that the Milwaukee & St. Paul (the Chicago, Milwaukee & St. Paul [CM&StP] or "St. Paul," after February 1874) needed to extend its lines into the trans-Mississippi West, and even perhaps to the Pacific Ocean. (That, however, would not occur until 1909.) Following the deadly depression of the mid and late 1870s the Chicago, Milwaukee & St. Paul pushed steadily through Iowa, Minnesota, and then into eastern Dakota. In 1882, for example, the road opened a 260-mile line between Marion, Iowa, and Council Bluffs, Iowa, which gave it a vital connection with the Union Pacific. A year later the CM&StP laid 145 miles of track in what became South Dakota, and in 1887 completed a 203-mile extension from Ottumwa, Iowa, to Kansas City, Missouri. Like most sister Granger roads the CM&StP served the principal midwestern gateways and cast a web of lines widely; its size reached a whopping 5,669 miles in 1887.

While he was a careful and conservative railroader ("[He] was not inclined to speculate in stocks") and the architect of Milwaukee's position as a major midwestern metropolis, Mitchell was not a particularly popular personality. For one thing he did not make friends easily. A dour Scot, he commonly walked away from a person who engaged him in conversation. Apparently Mitchell

had only a few close associates, mostly from the business community. Furthermore, the so-called Granger Movement that swept the Upper Mississippi River Valley, the heart of the Chicago, Milwaukee & St. Paul's operations, at times singled Mitchell out for its wrath. Spearheaded by a coalition of merchants, commercial groups, and farmers, the Grangers sought, most of all, to end long-and-short-haul discriminations and to reduce rates. Reformers pressed hard for the creation of state railroad commissions with powers to supervise carriers and thus guarantee consumer triumphs.

Initially Mitchell sought to educate the public—and most of all lawmakers—about the silliness of mileage-based rate controls. In one "Memorial" or white paper he joined Albert Keep, the conservative president of the Chicago & North Western, to argue with depth and soundness the two firms' position. These arguments, which addressed the notion that "Equal mileage rates are inexpedient," typify the Mitchell-Keep logic:

> (a) It would prevent railway companies from lowering their fares and rates so as to compete with traffic by sea, by canal, or by a shorter or otherwise cheaper railway, and would thus deprive the public of the benefit of competition and the company of a legitimate source of profit.
> (b) It would prevent railway companies from making perfectly fair arrangements for carrying at a lower rate than usual goods brought in large and constant quantities, or for carrying for long distances at a lower rate than for short distances.
> (c) It would compel a company to carry the same rate over a line which has been very expensive in construction, or which, from gradients or otherwise, it's very expensive in working at the same rate at which it carries over other lines.

Very likely Mitchell soon sensed the naiveté in his company's position. In response the St. Paul embarked on a direct lobbying campaign, especially in Madison, to repeal or modify various Granger statutes, particularly Wisconsin's Potter Law. While the C&NW took no extreme actions—or any that smacked of corporate arrogance—the St. Paul did act decisively. Mitchell flatly refused to allow his company to erect much-needed grain-storage facilities in Milwaukee until Grangers halted their attacks. Not surprisingly, Wisconsin lawmakers repealed the noxious law in 1876.

The respect Wisconsinites had for Mitchell's abilities and his personal philanthropy allowed him a minor political career. While originally a Whig and then a Lincoln Republican, he joined the Democratic party in 1868, mostly because he had favored the reconstruction policies of President Andrew Johnson. Although an unsuccessful candidate for Congress in 1868, he won a seat in the House of Representatives in both 1870 and 1872. When Wisconsin Democrats nominated him for governor in 1877, he refused to accept.

An intensely private person, Mitchell seemed to be a doting husband and father. He married Martha Reed, daughter of a prominent pioneer Milwaukee family, on October 7, 1841. They had one son, John L. Mitchell, who would represent Wisconsin in the United States Senate between 1893 and 1899. On Mitchell's death on April 19, 1887, due to pneumonia and heart disease, the bulk of his $20 million estate was left to John.

In addition to Alexander Mitchell's obvious genius for acquiring wealth, he did much to shape the structure of American railroading. Like William B. Ogden, John Murray Forbes, James J. Hill, and several other contemporary railroad leaders, he sensed advantages of fusing together short lines with little likelihood of financial survival into viable transport units. He was indeed a successful "system" builder.

Publication:

Memorial of the Chicago & North Western and Chicago, Milwaukee & St. Paul Railway Companies to the Senate and Assembly of the State of Wisconsin, with Albert Keep (Chicago: Metropolitan Printing, 1875).

References:

August Derleth, *The Milwaukee Road: Its First Hundred Years* (New York: Creative Age Press, 1948);

Milwaukee Sentinel, April 20, 1887;

New York Times, April 20, 1887;

A. M. Thomson, *A Political History of Wisconsin* (Milwaukee: E. C. Williams, 1900);

Ellis Baker Usher, *Wisconsin: Its Story and Biography, 1848-1913* (Chicago: Lewis Publishing, 1914).

Mobile & Ohio Railroad

by James H. Lemly

Atlanta, Georgia

The Mobile Road, as the Mobile & Ohio (M&O) was often called, was planned and promoted primarily by the citizens of Mobile, Alabama. The railroad was expected to bring trade from the Upper Mississippi, the Missouri, and the Ohio River basins to Mobile. The project was named the Mobile & Ohio because it was intended to connect its home city with the great river systems which converged near Cairo, Illinois.

Mobile had been hard hit by the panic of 1837, and its port activity was declining. Business leaders conceived the plan of restoring commercial might to Mobile by developing a railroad which would compete with the Mississippi River. For a number of years the plan was dormant, but by 1847 public subscriptions were enough to finance a reconnaissance trip to the Ohio River. When the survey showed the road to be feasible, the railroad became a popular project and garnered strong support from the citizens of Mobile. The M&O was chartered in 1848 in Alabama, Mississippi, Tennessee, and Kentucky; public interest was aroused throughout the entire territory.

The city of Mobile voted a special tax to provide seed money, and Mississippi bought stock in the project. Tennessee granted a loan based on the mileage in that state. Most of the counties along the right-of-way bought stock, and many towns granted aid. But the action which guaranteed construction of the road was the grant of federal lands. Sen. Stephen A. Douglas of Illinois introduced a land grant bill in 1848 to aid the Illinois Central; the M&O was included in the final version of the legislation which was passed by Congress in 1850. The federal land granted to Mississippi and Alabama, estimated to be worth at least $2 million, was transferred to the company and was thought to be enough to "iron" the road through those states. Tennessee and Kentucky received no federal land but assisted the M&O in other ways.

The land grant allowed the M&O to proceed with construction. The first section, the thirty miles from Mobile to Citronelle, Alabama, was opened in 1852. After many problems and delays, the line was completed to Columbus, Kentucky, on April 22, 1861, just days before the outbreak of the Civil War. River steamers connected the M&O terminal with other river ports and with the Illinois Central at Cairo.

The M&O management expected heavy traffic from St. Louis, which was upstream and on the west bank of the Mississippi. As there was no bridge at St. Louis, the Columbus location seemed to be an adequate northern terminus. Also, the St. Louis & Iron Mountain Railroad had plans for a terminal at Belmont, just across the river from Columbus. At this point the Mobile & Ohio felt proud of its accomplishments, as the annual report for 1866 shows:

> At the commencement of the war, the company was in good condition, had inspired universal confidence at home and abroad and had ample resources.... The road in its progress to completion had met and overcome opposition of the greatest magnitude. In Mississippi, it had been opposed by the friends of a rival road from New Orleans; in Tennessee it had met the violent opposition of the enterprising and energetic city of Memphis.... Towns and villages, a short distance from the track of the road, put themselves in hostility to it because it did not change its location and send its cars directly to their doors ... we were constantly met by opposition from these local and rival interests.
>
> But by energy and perseverance this great road was completed—when the last rail was laid in the track, the company had a road of the first class, built in the most substantial manner—unsurpassed in the United States and amply supplied with rolling stock.... It was safe to calculate that within two years ... we could commence payment of dividends on our stock.

Because of the long delay in construction, the M&O never had a chance to prove its real worth. Because the Civil War began almost immediately after the completion of the road, the northern terminal was in federal hands within months. Throughout the war the M&O served as a medium of transport and a target for both sides in the conflict. The railroad emerged from the struggle in terrible condi-

tion. The following, also from the annual report of 1866, is a brief statement of the havoc the war brought:

> The war came and the company has suffered largely by it. The Confederate government controlled ... the road ... transporting men and supplies.... The Confederate government became our debtors ... in the sum of $4,983,871.23.... We were not able to collect it because of alleged want of means of payment. Add to this Negroes costing $119,691.00 and Alabama state bonds ... $125,000.00 and it makes the round sum in Confederate currency of $5,228,562.23, all of which was lost to this company. But our losses did not stop.... All our bridges, trestle work, warehouses and station buildings between Union City, Tennessee, and Okolona, Mississippi, a distance of 184 miles, were destroyed. General Sherman's raid to Meridian destroyed north and south of that place all the warehouses, water stations, bridges and trestle work on 48 miles and on 21 miles of that distance; he bent, and as far as possible destroyed, the rails and fastenings. From a full supply of rolling stock of the finest quality, we were reduced to one-fourth of what was necessary and that was in bad condition.... We had, at the close of the war, neither tools nor materials to repair our little remaining rolling stock and keep it on the track. In this condition ... the road was delivered back to us by the United States military authorities.

The M&O in 1865 needed to be almost entirely rebuilt and re-equipped, and it was also confronted by past-due interest on its debt. The creditors of the road were sympathetic, but the road was unable to restore even a semblance of prosperity. Finally, in 1875 the road went into receivership and operated in that situation for eight years. In spite of its financial problems, the road did serve its territory as well as possible. A branch from the main line to Aberdeen, Mississippi, was completed in 1870. Also, the 14-mile Starkville branch was opened for service in 1875.

The Belmont terminus of the St. Louis & Iron Mountain, which the M&O believed would be finished by 1861, was not reached until 1871. By this time the M&O saw that the Belmont-Columbus transfer would not be very helpful, and it began preparations to extend the M&O from Columbus to East Cairo. The plan was dropped because of financial difficulties, not to be revived until 1880 when the M&O receivers proceeded with the line. The M&O established service to Cairo on May 1, 1882.

In 1886 the M&O acquired the narrow-gauge St. Louis & Cairo road, changing it to standard gauge to make possible a through haul from Mobile to St. Louis with ferry service at Cairo. In its quest for more traffic, the M&O decided in the 1890s to build a line from Columbus, Mississippi, toward the southeast and Florida. A line to Tuscaloosa and Montgomery, Alabama, together with the 9-mile Warrior Southern branch and the 11-mile Brocton branch, was opened for service on June 30, 1898. In 1899 the 38-mile branch from Mobile to Alabama Port and Bayou La Batre was opened.

Some of the lines added to the M&O were valuable to the company, but the road was never able to compete successfully with its two prosperous and aggressive competitors, the Illinois Central and the Louisville & Nashville. For this reason the board of the M&O recommended in 1900 that its investors accept a security exchange plan offered by the Southern Railway System, effective January 31, 1901.

This exchange plan was nearly universally accepted, and for practical purposes the M&O ceased to be an independent rail entity. Because of political opposition it was not merged officially into the Southern and remained a separate corporate body until 1938 when it was divorced from the Southern. In 1940 the M&O was merged into the newly formed Gulf, Mobile & Ohio by the managers of the active and aggressive Gulf, Mobile and Northern, led by I. B. Tigrett.

Reference:

James H. Lemly, *The Gulf, Mobile and Ohio: A Railroad That Had to Expand or Expire* (Homewood, Ill.: Irwin, 1953).

Archives:

The corporate records of the Mobile & Ohio are in Gulf, Mobile & Ohio corporate records held by the library of the University of South Alabama, Mobile, Alabama.

David Halliday Moffat, Jr.

(July 22, 1839-March 18, 1911)

by James W. Hipp

Columbia, S.C.

CAREER: Messenger, assistant teller, New York Exchange Bank (1841-1855); teller, A. J. Stevens & Company (1855-1857); cashier, Bank of Nebraska (1857-1859); book dealer, Denver, Colorado territory (1860-1866); adjutant general, Colorado territory (1865-1867); cashier, First National Bank (1867-1880); treasurer, Denver Pacific Railroad (1867-1880); treasurer, Denver, South Park & Pacific Railroad (1873-1880); owner, Colorado mining operations (1870s-1911); president, First National Bank (1880-1911); director, treasurer, Denver, Utah & Pacific Railroad (1880-1883); director, Denver Tramway Company (1885-1911); president, Denver & Rio Grande Railroad (1887-1891); director, Denver Union Power Company (1890-1911); director, Denver, Northwestern & Pacific Railroad (1902-1911).

David Halliday Moffat, Jr., a banker and railroad official, was one of the most important figures in the industrial development of late-nineteenth- and early-twentieth-century Colorado. Moffat was born on July 22, 1839, in Washingtonville, New York, the son of David Halliday and Eleanor Louise Moffat. At Washingtonville Moffat received his only formal education in the local country school. When he was twelve years old Moffat left the family farm for New York City where he was hired to be a messenger for the New York Exchange Bank. By 1855 Moffat had advanced in the bank to the position of assistant teller.

But the East did not hold any fascination for Moffat. Samuel Moffat, David's older brother, had earlier moved to Des Moines, Iowa, and he convinced Moffat to move west in 1855. Moffat took

David Halliday Moffat, Jr. (courtesy of Colorado Historical Society)

an initial position with A. J. Stevens & Company of Des Moines, joining the banking firm as a teller. In 1857 he moved to Omaha, Nebraska, where he was hired as a cashier at the Bank of Nebraska. While in Omaha Moffat engaged in land speculation, an activity already on the rise in the late 1850s because of the increasing anticipation of the transcontinental railroad. Moffat reputedly made over $1 million by his twentieth birthday in this manner but lost the largely unrealized fortune during a business downturn. In 1859 Moffat's employer at the bank retired, and Moffat began to look farther West for a place to fulfill his ambitions.

Moffat entered into a partnership in 1860 with C. C. Woolworth, a book dealer, stationier, and freight and mail business operator, to open a branch of Woolworth's business in Denver, Colorado. Arriving in the newly settled village in March 1860, Moffat quickly began to prosper. He sold subscriptions to eastern newspapers and served as a clearinghouse for local and national news to the hordes of men who had come to Colorado to take part in the gold rush. In this position he made many contacts and became a well-known figure in the still-developing township; his reputation and his wide circle of acquaintances would serve him well in the future. In 1861 Moffat returned East to Saratoga, New York, where he married Fannie Buckhout, whom he had known during his childhood. The two returned to Denver where Moffat continued in his business.

He kept the bookstore open until 1866, by which time he had already served a year as adjutant general of the Colorado territory. In 1867 he was named chief cashier of the newly reorganized First National Bank in Denver, a good position in which to take part in the post-war development of the Colorado economy. Moffat, as did most boosters in the West, believed that economic development depended on the railroads. When it appeared that Denver would have no link with the Union Pacific at Cheyenne, Wyoming, Moffat joined other community leaders in chartering the Denver Pacific (DP) Railroad & Telegraph Company in November 1867. The company reached an agreement with Thomas C. Durant and Sidney Dillon of the Union Pacific (UP) whereby the UP would lay the track if the DP completed the grading. When the grading was completed the UP refused to honor its agreement. Faced with bankruptcy, the DP contracted for the Kansas Pacific to complete the line to Cheyenne. In 1870 the first DP locomotive, named the David Moffat, rolled into Denver.

The opening of the railroad spurred the development of the mining industry and also of other railroads. In 1870 Col. William Jackson Palmer headed a group that founded the Denver & Rio Grande (D&RG) Railroad, which had as its goal a line from Denver southward toward Santa Fe. In addition to the D&RG, Colorado was also a destination of the Atchison, Topeka and Santa Fe (ATSF) Railroad, a line which saw the gold and silver mines around Leadville as a lucrative source of cargo. Moffat was not left out of the rail expansion. In 1879 the Denver, South Park & Pacific (DSP&P) Railroad, of which Moffat was treasurer, opened from Denver to Buena Vista. The DSP&P operated with the D&RG a joint track to Leadville over which both shared in the mining wealth. Moffat sold his railroad interests in 1880 for $3 million to Jay Gould, who was quickly becoming a major figure in western railroads. That same year Moffat became president of the First National Bank in Denver.

Moffat's interest in developing a railroad system to take advantage of Colorado's mineral wealth was not selfless. During the 1870s Moffat had been acquiring mining properties; he became one of the biggest mine operators in the state, reputedly controlling over 100 separate sites. The income from these mines ran well into the millions of dollars. Not only did the mines produce freight to be carried by his railroads, they also produced the wealth used to construct the lines. As with other Colorado roads, Moffat's lines were closely intertwined with the mineral wealth of the area.

After the sale of his railroad interests to Gould in 1880, Moffat wasted little time in planning and investing in a new venture. In December 1880 the Denver, Utah & Pacific (DU&P) Railroad was chartered to build from Denver through the Rockies to the Pacific Coast. Construction began almost immediately and had reached Louisville, Colorado, when the project faltered. The Chicago, Burlington & Quincy Railroad purchased the DU&P but abandoned the line in 1886. The most notable feature of the DU&P was that its proposed route was almost exactly that followed later by the Denver & Salt Lake Railway, the Moffat Road.

In 1887 Moffat was elected president of the D&RG, a position through which he intended to continue his experiments in railroad development and expansion. Moffat initiated an intensive maintenance and repair program on the D&RG, planned further expansions into the mining areas, and, most importantly, began the process of transferring the D&RG to standard gauge track. Of the 1,685 miles of track operated by the D&RG in 1887, only 123 miles were capable of carrying standard gauge traffic. By the beginning of 1892 total trackage had increased to 2,006 miles, 1,101 miles of which could support standard gauge. Despite the very tangible improvements to the D&RG and Moffat's elaborate plans for the road, the D&RG directors were apprehensive over the cost of such programs. Moffat resigned his position in late 1891.

Moffat's experience with the D&RG did not diminish his activities in the Denver area. As one of the state's leading bankers, Moffat was intimately involved in many of the large projects around Denver. He invested heavily in both the Denver Union Water Company, which completed the Cheesman Dam in 1895, and the Denver Tramway Company, which constructed and consolidated Denver's streetcar system during the 1890s.

His financial interest in the last led directly to the 1901 formation of the Denver & Northwestern

Railway, a planned electric line intended to extend the Tramway line to Hot Sulphur Springs. These plans soon mutated into a new proposal to build a steam railroad from Denver to Salt Lake City. This road, known as the Denver, Northwestern & Pacific (DNW&P) Railroad, was chartered on July 18, 1902. The DNW&P operated its first trains in 1904, but the line was constantly under pressure from financial problems, competition from larger, well-established lines, and adverse weather conditions on the line's scenic, mountainous route. In 1905 the DNW&P tracks reached Hot Sulphur Springs, but this effort, merely the beginning of the plan, cost Moffat much of his extensive fortune. Moffat's Denver business associates continued to provide funding, but the line, because of the small amount of freight on the DNW&P and the high construction costs associated with building through the spectacular and difficult Colorado landscape, was unable to generate sufficient revenues to pay for itself. When these problems were added to the fierce opposition to the road of E. H. Harriman and George Jay Gould, the Moffat Road, as the line was known, faced almost insurmountable difficulties.

These were years that Moffat spent in constant travel and negotiation, attempting to gain both financing from investors and banks and compromises from his competitors. By 1911 his fortune was gone and his health was broken. In New York City on a trip to arrange financing, Moffat died on March 18, 1911. Reputedly he died as a result of the stress incurred through the mysterious cancellation of a financing deal which would have at least temporarily saved the DNW&P. In fact, Moffat suffered from heart disease and at the time of his death also had pneumonia. Shortly after Moffat's death the DNW&P entered receivership and was reorganized as the Denver & Salt Lake Railroad. In 1927 the Denver & Salt Lake completed a tunnel through the Rockies which was named the Moffat Tunnel. The engineering marvel was an appropriate monument to Moffat's industry and vision.

Moffat lived such a busy and industrious life that to concentrate merely on his railroad interests seems narrow and unjust. He was a popular and powerful man in most all of Colorado and exerted a substantial influence over many aspects of Colorado life. He was trusted as a banker and was regarded as having the interests of Denver and the state at heart. In politics he wielded a great amount of power, largely behind the scenes, in the Colorado Republican party. During the mourning period following Moffat's death, activity in the state came to a virtual standstill. Although his involvement in the DNW&P ended in death and failure, Moffat's achievements over the course of his life demand that he ultimately be viewed as a success.

References:
Harold A. Boner, *The Giant's Ladder* (Milwaukee, Wis.: Kalmbach Publishing, 1962);
Edgar Carlisle McMechan, *The Moffat Tunnel of Colorado: An Epic of Empire*, 2 volumes (Denver: Wahlgreen Publishing, 1927).

Charles Morgan

(April 12, 1795-May 9, 1878)

by James P. Baughman

Stamford, Connecticut

CAREER: Partner, Charles Morgan & Company (1809-1878); principal, New York & Charleston Steam Packet Company (1833-1837); partner, T. F. Secor & Company (1838-1850); partner, Harris & Morgan (1847-1867); principal, Empire City Line (1848-1858); principal, American Atlantic & Pacific Ship Canal Company (1849-1858); principal, Morgan Iron Works (1850-1867); principal, Accessory Transit Company of Nicaragua (1853-1858); principal, Mexican Ocean Mail & Inland Company (1853-1858); partner, Garrison, Morgan, Fretz & Raleston (1855-1857); principal, Southern Steamship Company (1855-1867); principal, Louisiana Dry Dock Company (1856-1867); principal, Atlantic & Pacific Steamship Company (1859-1865); principal, American & Mexican Steamship Company (1864-1867); partner, Charles A. Whitney & Company (1867-1878); principal, New York & Charleston Steamship Company (1867-1878); principal, Morgan's Louisiana & Texas Railroad (1869-1877); principal, Atchafalaya Bay Company (1871-1877); principal, Gulf, Western Texas & Pacific Railway (1871-1878); principal, Buffalo Bayou Ship Channel Company (1874-1878); principal, Texas Transportation Company (1875-1878); principal, Houston & Texas Central Railroad (1877-1878); incorporator, Morgan's Louisiana & Texas Railroad & Steamship Company (1877-1878).

Charles Morgan (courtesy of New-York Historical Society)

Prior to World War II the red-hulled passenger liners and freighters of Southern Pacific's Morgan Line were familiar sights along the Atlantic, Gulf, and Caribbean coasts of the United States, Cuba, and Mexico. Business travelers, vacationers, and shippers who preferred a sea voyage to a train or plane trip or a dusty highway knew they could count on Morgan ships for comfort and convenience. There were competitors, to be sure—notably, the Mallory, Clyde, and Cromwell lines—but the

Morgan Line was the oldest and, arguably, the best.

A unique feature of the Morgan Line was its southern interconnection with Southern Pacific's Sunset Route rail line to California. A passenger or a shipment could travel by sea from New York to New Orleans or Houston, and then by rail to San Francisco (or intermediate points) all on a single ticket or bill of lading. No other rail-water service in the United States was as extensive or under single management.

The reality of 1941 was the product of Charles Morgan's nineteenth-century dream. Born in Connecticut in 1795 but based in New York from 1809 to 1878, Morgan's importance to American business history lies both in his classic example of individual entrepreneurship and in what he accomplished and triggered in others during his sixty-nine years of productive enterprise.

Morgan was the pioneer and premier builder-owner-operator of steamships in the American coastal trades during the first three-quarters of the nineteenth century. At his peak Morgan owned and operated 109 steamers. He played an important role in the development of the port of New York and in the expansion of trade routes from Manhattan to the Southeast, the Gulf states, the Republic of Texas, Cuba, Mexico, and Central America. In the process he made lasting improvements to navigable waterways, port facilities, and rail routes throughout the Gulf states. His importance in the early economic histories of Charleston, New Orleans, Mobile, Galveston, and Houston cannot be overstated. At the same time, as a builder of ships, marine engines, railroads, and rolling stock, Morgan was a pioneer in two fundamental technological shifts: first, from sail to steam at sea, and ultimately, from water to overland rail transportation.

Morgan was also one of the first American businessmen to specialize in ships rather than in the cargoes they carried and to deploy them in liner (i.e., regularly scheduled at posted rates) rather than tramp service. Morgan and Cornelius Vanderbilt (who was only one year older) were among the first specialists in marine "common carriage"—Vanderbilt in ferries and river and sound packets, Morgan in coastal liners.

Always a private businessman who never sought public office, Morgan still had continuous and far-reaching involvement with governments. While not assisting in their passage, he was a prime beneficiary of the cabotage policies that closed U.S. intercoastal trades to foreign competition. He was a pioneer "ocean-mail" contractor and a major government supplier of marine engines, naval warships, and sea transportation—especially during the Mexican and Civil wars. And during the 1850s, first as partner and then as adversary of Vanderbilt, he intrigued both with legitimate regimes and with "filibusters" to open and control shortcuts to California via Mexico and Central America.

At the state and municipal levels Morgan pursued private ends but built economic infrastructure in the process. To provide an alternative gateway to Louisiana and Texas in 1869, he purchased the New Orleans, Opelousas & Great Western, a bankrupt railroad operating from the port of New Orleans to Brashear City on Berwick's Bay, and turned that sleepy fishing village into the bustling port of Morgan City (renamed in his honor in the 1870s). To give the vast hinterland of south Texas better access to the Gulf, he developed such ports as Port Lavaca and Indianola in the 1850s and Rockport in the late 1860s and connected them by wagon road and then rail to western points. To bypass high wharfage and warehouse charges in the port of Galveston, between 1874 and 1876 he dredged the ship channel that brought deep water for the first time to the port of Houston.

Morgan also aggressively used litigation to further his projects in the Southwest. He initiated and won several landmark cases that helped confirm the supremacy of federal law in matters of interstate commerce—notably, overturning state and municipal taxation of interstate freight and passengers and the local use of quarantines to impede interstate voyages.

Morgan's forebears, whose Welsh surname prophetically identified them as "of the sea," came to Boston in 1636 and to Killingworth, Connecticut, in the 1730s. The family prospered as farmers, fishermen, and coastal traders and raised young Charles (the third of four children born to George and Elizabeth Redfield Morgan) in an atmosphere of comfort and enterprise.

In 1809 Charles was sent to New York City and apprenticed to the grocery and hardware trades. Upon his parents' deaths in 1830 and 1832 he inherited the Morgan and Redfield properties in Killingworth but never moved back to Connecticut. He treasured his roots, however, and in 1871 endowed the Morgan School in his hometown (which operates today as the public high school of Clinton, Connecticut).

In the thick of the Port of New York's burst to prominence, Morgan opened his own ships' grocery and chandlery in Peck Slip in 1815. In 1817 he married Emily Reeves, and five children were born to the couple between 1818 and 1832. As Morgan's fortunes rose he and his family moved from Peck Slip to Pearl Street (1821), Beekman Street (1824), and Henry Street (1832). Emily died in 1850. The following year Morgan married Mary Jane Sexton (twenty-five years his junior), and in 1853 the couple built a fine townhouse at 7 Madison Square, where they lived until Charles's death in 1878.

Morgan phased out his grocery and chandlery by 1832 as he reinvested profits in ships. He moved quickly from passive shareowner to managing agent—building, owning, and operating vessels. Between 1819 and 1846, for example, he was a principal in the construction and management of thirty-five sailing packets operating from New York to Charleston, Savannah, New Orleans, and Kingston, Jamaica.

While Morgan's degree of specialization in these sailing trades was unique, the investments themselves were typical for their day. But Morgan became the pioneer in coastal steamships. In 1832 in equal partnership with James P. Allaire (a business successor of Robert Fulton) Morgan opened the first steam-packet service between New York and Charleston. By 1836 service had been extended to Havana, Key West, and New Orleans, by 1837 to Mobile and Galveston.

Intensifying his commitment to steam, Morgan purchased in 1838 a one-third interest in T. F. Secor & Company, New York's leading marine-engine builder. His second son-in-law, George W. Quintard, became manager of Secor's in 1847; and in 1850 Morgan became sole proprietor of the renamed Morgan Iron Works. The plant was located on the East River, at the foot of Ninth Street. An advertisement of 1850 details the product line which supplied Morgan's own enterprises and catered to the needs of customers in the ports and hinterlands his ships served: "Iron Founder & Manufacturer of Land & Marine Engines of All Descriptions, Saw Mills, Sugar Mills, Grist Mills, Cotton Presses, Pipes, Screws, Geering [sic] of All Kinds, Castings of Iron or Brass, Including Bells of Every Size, High & Low Pressure Boilers, Smithing, Turning & Finishing in All Their Branches with All Kinds of Iron, Brass, and Copper Machinery."

While Morgan and Quintard managed the iron works, it was Morgan, his first son-in-law, Israel C. Harris, and his second son, Henry R. Morgan, who managed the steamships through a partnership formalized as Harris & Morgan in New Orleans in 1847. Dun & Bradstreet credit reports in the 1850s rated them: "Spr. men, as honest as the day. . . . The Texas trade is monopolized by them, out of wh. they are coining money . . . one of the most profitable lines in the U.S. & prob. the world."

Morgan's enterprises flourished during the Mexican War, the Gold Rush, and the Civil War. Thirty-four federal charters during the Mexican War, and additional postwar ocean-mail contracts, helped establish service to Brazos St. Iago (1846), Tampico and Vera Cruz (1847), Port Lavaca (1848), Indianola (1849), Sabine Pass, Apalachicola, Cedar Key, Tampa, and Manatee (1856). Nineteen long-term charters and fifteen naval contracts for marine engines during the Civil War added substantial profits.

It was Morgan's deep involvement in the "transit wars" during the Gold Rush that first brought him to nationwide prominence. Rumors of the January 1848 discoveries in California reached New York City in August. Official notice reached Washington in September and was confirmed in President James K. Polk's annual December message to Congress. The Gold Rush was on, but San Francisco was still 14,194 nautical miles around Cape Horn from New York and 14,314 nautical miles from New Orleans. Morgan was among the first to offer an alternative—4,992 nautical miles from New York to San Francisco via Panama. Two competitors opened the Panama route in December 1848; Morgan's Empire City Line and the combined service of the United States and Pacific Mail Steamship companies. Lack of a mail contract put Morgan at some disadvantage. By 1850 he had formed a profitable new alliance with Cornelius Vanderbilt and shifted his attention from Panama to Nicaragua.

Morgan and Cornelius Vanderbilt were the prime movers in the formation of the American Atlantic and Pacific Ship Canal Company (1849) and the Accessory Transit Company (1851). The former company was to dig a canal across Nicaragua, and the latter was to provide interim service from San Juan del Norte, up Rio San Juan by shallow-draught steamers to San Carlos, across Lake Nicaragua by larger steamer to Virgin Bay, then overland twelve miles to San Juan del Sur on the Pacific. If all went well this route would beat the schedules available via Panama.

While Vanderbilt concentrated on the technical, financial, and political aspects of the canal (which was never built), Morgan ran the steamship connections to New York, New Orleans, and San Francisco, and the river-lake-transit route across Nicaragua. Shares in the canal and transit companies became a speculator's dream on the New York Stock Exchange. Every new arrival from the goldfields, every record passage, every positive surveyor's report, every supportive political maneuver would kite the stocks. Every loss or breakdown of a ship, every overland hazard or delay, every political or engineering setback would trigger a plunge. Insider trading made millions for both Vanderbilt and Morgan but also drove them apart.

Early in 1853 Morgan joined forces with Cornelius K. Garrison of San Francisco to oust Vanderbilt from the presidency of the transit company. They succeeded while the Commodore was on a cruising vacation to Europe aboard his new yacht, *North Star*. On his return in September, he wrote them one of the most famous letters in American business history: "Gentlemen—You have undertaken to cheat me. I won't sue you for the law is too slow. I'll ruin you. Yours truly, C. Vanderbilt."

Vanderbilt opened lines of ocean steamers to the Gulf and to Nicaragua in opposition to Morgan's. After a period of intense competition Morgan relinquished the transit presidency to Vanderbilt in January 1856. At the same time, however, he and Garrison were secretly supporting the filibuster William Walker, who had entered Nicaragua in 1855. In return Walker promised (if successful in gaining control of Nicaragua) to cancel Vanderbilt's concessions and award them to Morgan. With this advance information in hand, Morgan and Garrison sold all of their transit stock to Vanderbilt and went heavily short. Walker succeeded, transit stock plummeted, Morgan and Garrison covered their short position at enormous profits, and Vanderbilt took heavy losses and was frozen out.

Vanderbilt retaliated by financing mercenaries of his own who seized the river and lake segments of the transit. When Walker fell in 1857, the game was over. Morgan, Garrison, and Vanderbilt settled accounts, and the "War of the Commodores" ended in amicable compromise. The Nicaraguan transit never reopened. Morgan and Vanderbilt became partners again and took over the Atlantic side of the Panama route, which they operated profitably until they sold it in 1865.

The Reconstruction years were years of consolidation and expansion for Morgan's southern enterprises. He exited Central America to concentrate on the Gulf and reopened in 1866 all of his coastal lines which had been closed by the wartime blockade. Quintard and Morgan's son Henry retired from the business and Harris died—all in 1867. The iron works was sold profitably in 1867, and Harris & Morgan was succeeded in the same year by a new firm, Charles A. Whitney & Company—composed of Morgan; his third son-in-law, Whitney; and Alexander C. Hutchinson, a veteran of the iron works and Nicaragua.

After the Civil War Morgan concentrated on his dream of a combined water-rail service from New York to the Southwest. The project had begun in 1857, when the New Orleans, Opelousas & Great Western Railroad reached Brashear City, eighty miles west of New Orleans. Morgan had immediately contracted to extend the route by steamer to Texas ports, and had done so successfully until service was closed by the Civil War.

He reopened the service in 1866, but in 1869 took the big step: he bought the railroad out of bankruptcy, reinvigorated its western terminus (subsequently renamed Morgan City), began construction toward Houston, renamed the road Morgan's Louisiana & Texas Railroad, and operated the line for the next six years as unincorporated sole proprietor.

Meanwhile, in Texas in 1867, Morgan opened Rockport on Aransas Bay as the leading cattle and processed-meat (beef and turtle) port in the western Gulf. In 1870 he bought and extended a railroad, which he named the Gulf, Western Texas & Pacific, from Matagorda Bay to Victoria and Cuero. In 1876 he dredged the first version of what became the Houston Ship Channel and linked that city's inland railroads to deep water. In 1877 he went further and bought the Houston & Texas Central Railway, which ran 343 miles from Houston to Denison and 162 miles from Hempstead to Austin and Bremond to Waco.

Morgan incorporated his holdings the year before his death as Morgan's Louisiana & Texas Railroad & Steamship Company. It fell to Whitney & Hutchinson to complete the system. At the time of its sale to the Southern Pacific Company in 1883, the Morgan Line consisted of 17 steamships, 1,193 miles of track, 139 locomotives, 82 passenger cars, and 3,309 freight cars and offered through service from New York to San Francisco via New Orleans or Houston.

Charles Morgan died in New York on May 9, 1878, in his eighty-fourth year. Packed memorial services were held at Rutgers Presbyterian Church, with burial in Green-Wood Cemetery. Obituaries were uniformly positive, with the *New York Herald* of May 9, 1878, summing up:

> His career has been a notable one in the business annals of New York. . . . in all his . . . residence there of nearly seventy years duration he lived a quiet, unostentatious life, following his business with energy and diligence, and consequent success. His ample fortune was the result of qualities which some may think are now more rare than when he started his career. His word was never broken. Prompt and fair in business, quiet and courteous in demeanor, liberal and kind to the very large number of men constantly in his employment, not a few of whom have passed from youth to gray hairs in his service, he has left an enviable record in the mercantile history of New York.

References:

James P. Baughman, *Charles Morgan and the Development of Southern Transportation* (Nashville: Vanderbilt University Press, 1968);

Baughman, *The Mallorys of Mystic: Six Generations in American Maritime Enterprise, 1814-1941* (Middletown: Wesleyan University Press, 1972);

Carl C. Cutler, *Queens of the Western Ocean: The Story of America's Mail and Passenger Sailing Lines* (Annapolis: U. S. Naval Institute, 1961);

John G. B. Hutchins, *The American Maritime Industries and Public Policy, 1789-1914* (Cambridge, Mass.: Harvard University Press, 1941);

John H. Kemble, *The Panama Route, 1848-1869* (Berkeley: University of California Press, 1943);

Wheaton J. Lane, *Commodore Vanderbilt: An Epic of the Steam Age* (New York: Knopf, 1942).

Archives:

There is no single archival source for Morgan. The most productive original sources are to be found in the Notarial Records of New Orleans, Louisiana; the archives of the Southern Pacific Railroad (Texas and Louisiana Lines); and in the manuscript collections of the National Archives, Mystic Seaport, New York Historical Society, Baker Library of Harvard University, and Tulane University. These are all summarized in Baughman (1968).

John Pierpont Morgan

(April 17, 1837-March 31, 1913)

by Robert L. Frey

Wilmington College of Ohio

CAREER: Clerk, George Peabody & Company (1856); clerk, Duncan, Sherman & Company (1856-1860); manager, J. Pierpont Morgan & Company (1860-1864); partner, Dabney, Morgan & Company (1864-1871); managing partner, Drexel, Morgan & Company (1871-1895); managing partner, J. P. Morgan & Company (1895-1913).

John Pierpont Morgan was born on April 17, 1837, in Hartford, Connecticut. His paternal family traced its origins back to Boston in 1636, when Miles Morgan and his brothers, John and James, arrived from England. Miles Morgan eventually moved west to what became Springfield, Massachusetts, and was a farmer and militia leader in the area. From Miles came a line of descendants that included Joseph Morgan (1780-1847), J. P. Morgan's grandfather. Joseph moved from the family farm to Hartford, where he is credited with beginning the family fortune through his ownership of hotels, stagecoach lines, and fire insurance companies. Junius Spencer Morgan (1809-1890), Joseph's son, entered the banking business at age sixteen.

Junius Morgan gained experience with A. M. Ketchum, brokers, in New York, and with Howe, Mather and Company in Hartford before he became a partner in the dry-goods firm of J. M. Beebe, Morgan and Company located in Boston. The Morgan family, with fourteen-year-old J. P., the oldest of five children, moved to Boston. Junius came to be known as an ethical and highly religious man who maintained a skeptical eye toward democracy. Joseph Morgan had been a more tolerant individual, having had to adjust his beliefs to the varying clients of his tavern and hotel trade. Junius, however, was a more inflexible, aristocratic person, sure of himself and the correctness of his attitudes.

Julia Pierpont, J. P. Morgan's mother, had a prominent heritage as well, her father being the Reverend John Pierpont (1785-1868), a flamboyant Uni-

John Pierpont Morgan (courtesy of the Pierpont Morgan Library)

tarian clergyman. Eccentric and vocal, the Reverend Pierpont preached fearlessly about the evils of wealth and demanded that the church pay attention to the poor and the outcasts. He was opposed to imprisonment for debt and did not believe ownership of property gave the proprietor the right to do as he pleased. Clearly his philosophy was in conflict with that of Junius and J. P. Morgan. But the Reverend Pierpont was most concerned with the struggle against slavery. His abolitionist stance brought him into conflict with members of his congregation and eventually resulted in a six-month-long ecclesiastical trial. Pierpont was vindicated and immediately resigned from his pastorate to lead abolitionist causes. At the age of seventy-six he entered the Civil War as a chaplain and lived to see slavery defeated. He died a pauper, apparently estranged from his millionaire daughter and son-in-law.

In 1853 Junius Morgan became a partner in the international banking house of George Peabody & Company. Peabody, one of the first major philanthropists, was quite different from Morgan, but he recognized in Junius a shrewd and successful businessman. Peabody himself was one of the first great international bankers who realized the capital needs of the emerging United States could not be met internally. His banking firm thus sought the needed capital by marketing American securities in Europe. On Peabody's death in 1863 Junius Morgan took over the company, renaming it J. S. Morgan & Company.

J. P. Morgan's young-adult years were spent in Boston, where he attended English High School. He graduated shortly after his father became a partner of George Peabody but was not a brilliant student and excelled only in mathematics. His personality was decidedly reserved and occasionally hostile, further restricting a social life already impaired by a series of lung infections, which compromised his health. Since his health was still weak at graduation, Morgan was sent to the Azores to recover. This vacation was followed by extensive travel in Europe, study at the Vevey School on Lake Geneva in Switzerland, and additional study at the University of Göttingen in Germany.

In 1856, two years after graduating from English High School, Morgan joined his father's banking house in London. He was soon sent to New York to work for Duncan, Sherman & Company, a firm in the process of being saved from financial ruin by Peabody & Company. The elder Morgan asked the management of Duncan, Sherman & Company to make his son a partner, but they refused. In 1860 Junius helped J. P. Morgan to organize his own firm, J. Pierpont Morgan & Company, to act primarily as the New York agent of Peabody & Company. Specializing in foreign exchange, the office of the new company was located on Exchange Place in the Wall Street district of New York.

Shortly after assuming leadership of his own company, J. P. Morgan met and fell in love with Amelia Sturges. Unfortunately, Miss Sturges was afflicted with tuberculosis. J. P. Morgan's first request for marriage was refused, but he did not relent. In October 1861 they were married at her parents' home in New York, but she died four months later at Nice, France. This tragic romance seemed to mark a watershed in young Morgan's life. Up to that point his father was constantly wondering if his son would amount to anything, wondering if he had the ability and motivation to accomplish anything of note. After Amelia's death young Morgan singlemindedly put his attention to acquiring wealth and power. His father had no need to wonder further.

Like most financially secure young men it was easy for J. P. Morgan to avoid military service during the Civil War. He was not conscripted because the modest sum of $300 enabled him to hire a substitute. Early in the war, however, Morgan was peripherally involved in an embarrassing scheme in which he financed another's purchase and resale of obsolete weapons to the U. S. government at a profit. The result was a congressional investigation which, although clearing him of any criminal guilt, resulted in unfavorable publicity. Morgan was also involved in speculation in gold, which, because of the unsettled political scene, would vary widely in price in response to particular events. Working with Edward B. Ketchum, the son of his father's former partner, Morgan quietly purchased gold, sending some of it abroad to his father's house. Congress and the American people became concerned about this "gold corner," and Congress even passed a Gold Bill, later repealed, to control speculation. Morgan acquired wealth in this endeavor but gained much public enmity as well. The Ketchums, unwilling to get out of the gold speculation business in time, saw their banking house crushed as the price of gold declined. Morgan was more prudent and survived the collapse.

In 1864 J. Pierpont Morgan & Company became Dabney, Morgan & Company when Charles H. Dabney, formerly of Duncan, Sherman & Company, became J. P. Morgan's partner. The new company became the American representative of J. S. Morgan & Company, the successor of Peabody & Company. From 1864 to 1871 the company continued to be involved primarily in foreign banking. Although it attempted to market some foreign bonds in the United States, most of the business involved the financing of commercial credit to facilitate overseas trade. In the seven years of the partnership, the firm not only netted approximately $1 million in profits but also became one of New York's leading banking houses. In this role Dabney, Morgan & Company began to be involved with railroad financing.

Generally, Morgan was not involved in attempts to build railroads and to profit from their construction. As a banker his primary concern was the maintenance of financial and corporate stability, which allowed securities to sell and business to prosper. Consequently, he usually entered the railroad picture after a great deal of turmoil had taken place and attempted to stabilize the situation. One example was the 1869 battle with Jay Gould and Jim Fisk over the Albany & Susquehanna (A&S) Railroad in New York. Samuel Sloan, president of the Delaware, Lackawanna & Western, recommended Morgan as a possible ally to Joseph H. Ramsey, the president of the A&S, in his fight to retain control of the line. Morgan was named to the A&S board and used his money and influence to help Ramsey maintain his position. The episode, which involved Ramsey's arrest and a complex court case, undoubtedly contributed to Morgan's understanding of the high costs of unbridled competition.

In 1871 Morgan allied with Anthony J. Drexel to form Drexel, Morgan & Company. The Drexel house was an old and respected firm, but it had been outmaneuvered by Jay Cooke & Company in the rush to help finance the Civil War. In the early 1870s Morgan and Drexel allied to oppose Cooke & Company. By this time the House of Morgan included Drexel, Morgan & Company in New York, Drexel & Company in Philadelphia, J. S. Morgan & Company in London, and Drexel, Harjes & Company in Paris. J. P. Morgan became the dominant figure in this empire during the 1870s. His leadership style was typical of the day and would today be seen as autocratic. As a young banker he was considered dull because he did not engage in group discussions or decisions. Although the role of his associates has been underestimated Morgan did make the final decisions in most matters. Above all things, Morgan appreciated order, efficiency, and stability.

Throughout the 1870s the House of Morgan was increasingly involved in creating syndicates to help the United States government refinance its Civil War debt in a more manageable way. The Mor-

gan firms' profits from the 1877 syndicate were reputed to have been $5 million, though the actual figure was probably 10 percent of that. By 1879 the House of Morgan was the dominant American banking house, having replaced the Cooke House, which had collapsed in 1873. The 1880s, however, brought great changes to Morgan's company. In 1880 the House of Morgan was an old-style bank dealing in foreign exchange, selling American corporate securities in Europe, and participating in government financing. By 1890 the company had added to these tasks the provision of capital to corporations, and with it a substantial amount of corporate control by Morgan. His style was to consolidate and stabilize, not to establish and speculate. The industrial capitalist, who had replaced the merchant capitalist, was now being replaced by the finance capitalist, the quintessential example of which was John Pierpont Morgan.

Morgan's involvement in railroads increased in 1879 when William H. Vanderbilt, owner of 40 percent of the New York Central (NYC), sought to dispose of much of his stock in an effort to lessen public criticism of his control of the railroad. In exchange for this service Morgan was awarded a position on the NYC board of directors. Morgan marketed most of the excess NYC stock in England with little public knowledge until the task was completed. The firm realized a profit of about $3 million on the sale, and he became the fiscal agent of the NYC. Shortly thereafter Drexel, Morgan & Company became fiscal agents for the Pennsylvania Railroad as well.

Morgan was interested in changing the way in which railroads were constructed and managed. A significant percentage of the money for railroad construction came from the local, state, or federal government. Inadequately regulated by the government and too frequently managed by individuals intent only on quick profits, the railroad industry had become chaotic and demoralized. Morgan, of course, was not in favor of extending government controls, but he was aware of the need for stability in the business in order for investors to have confidence in railroad management. If public confidence waned there would be no public investment in railroad stocks and bonds. J. P. Morgan's solution for this problem is usually called "Morganization."

Many, but not all, of Morgan's involvements with railroads resulted from reorganizations. For instance, in 1884-1885 the New York Central was

Morgan nearing the end of his career (Gale International Portrait Gallery)

challenged when the New York, West Shore & Buffalo Railroad built a competing line down the west shore of the Hudson River. Because of the public's dislike of the Vanderbilts the West Shore project was very popular. On his part Vanderbilt intended to destroy West Shore rather than buy it out. In a separate project Vanderbilt had allied himself with the Philadelphia & Reading Railroad to build a railroad from Harrisburg to Pittsburgh to compete with the Pennsylvania Railroad. Morgan disliked the cutthroat competition evidenced in both situations, and he attempted to negotiate a settlement. By using a variety of pressures Morgan was successful in convincing Vanderbilt to buy the West Shore instead of destroying it and also to give up the line across Pennsylvania to avert a costly struggle between the NYC and the Pennsylvania.

The more common point of entry into a company for Morgan, however, was via the reorganiza-

tion of a railroad after bankruptcy. On the heels of the West Shore incident came Morgan's 1886 reorganization of the Philadelphia & Reading (P&R), a company that had been in receivership since 1880. The P&R had been attempting to compete with the Pennsylvania, which is why it was involved in the South Pennsylvania project with the NYC. In exchange for $15 million in working capital, Morgan created the first of his famous voting trusts—that is, a group of financiers temporarily in control of a company and acting for all of the stockholders. In the case of the P&R, Morgan's trust lasted from March 1886 to December 1887. The reorganization of the P&R was followed by a successful reorganization of the Chesapeake & Ohio, again using a voting trust and a Morgan-approved president.

Basically three controlling maxims governed Morgan's reorganizations. First, the bankrupt railroad had money pumped into it by the House of Morgan while excessive fixed costs were eliminated and other cost reductions were enacted as necessary. Second, Morgan attempted to act as a disinterested mediator to reduce unnecessary competition between the bankrupt road and its competitors. Since he was not involved in the history of the company, it was relatively easy for Morgan to succeed in his attempt to establish a "community of interest." Third, Morgan, in some way, usually by a voting trust, maintained control of the company in order to maintain financial stability and to honor the community of interest concept. All "Morganizations" involved absolute control by Morgan and his business associates for a certain time, usually five years.

The 1890s witnessed a further growth of Morgan's influence, but public opposition to men of great wealth and power like Morgan also increased. In 1893 Anthony J. Drexel died, and two years later Drexel, Morgan & Company became J. P. Morgan & Company. The Philadelphia house retained the name Drexel & Company, the London house also retained the name J. S. Morgan & Company, but the Paris house became Morgan, Harjes & Company. American gold reserves were threatened several times during the 1890s, and each occasion gave the banking community an opportunity to profit. Morgan, being the leading banker in the United States, was always in the forefront of negotiations with the Treasury. In 1895 Morgan created a syndicate to sell $62 million in bonds to attract gold. While the muckraking press charged that profits ranged from $7-$18 million, Morgan's total profit was slightly less than $296,000. Morgan chose to emphasize his patriotism in defending the gold-bond syndicate, but the misinformed and increasingly hostile public thought otherwise. The election of 1896 was a bitter contest in which Morgan and the bankers and industrialists were pitted against the perceptions of many farmers and laborers represented by William Jennings Bryan. Morgan and associates were able to win the day, but the public's unfocused frustration against the "malefactors of great wealth," as Theodore Roosevelt called them, was growing.

Part of the reason for the public frustrations which appeared in the election of 1896 were the hardships spawned by the panic of 1893 and the depression that followed. Agricultural failures, overspeculation, labor unrest, and a weakening of European trade all led to the depression. The failure of several key railroads, among them the Union Pacific (UP) and the Northern Pacific (NP), was the immediate harbinger of the panic. In 1889 and 1890 Morgan had attempted several private meetings of western railroad presidents in an effort to establish a community of interest regarding rates. Only partially successful in this effort, the railroad industry had continued to engage in the cutthroat competition that, in part, led to the failure of the UP and the NP. By 1895 one-third of the American railroad mileage was in bankruptcy and the opportunities for "Morganization" were so great that it appeared possible for Morgan to impose community of interest settlements on the entire railroad industry.

One of the most dramatic reorganizations was the combination of more than thirty southern railroads into the Southern Railway System, the largest railroad in the South. Morgan and his associates labored mightily to produce sense and efficiency where waste and corruption had reigned. In 1893 a voting trust, including Morgan and George F. Baker, president of the First National Bank of New York, reduced fixed charges, improved the physical condition of the lines, collected cash assessments from the stockholders, and issued new stock on the more than 7,000-mile system. Between 1893 and 1895 Morgan reorganized the Erie, a reorganization not nearly as successful as the Southern and one that saw Morgan clash with Edward H. Harriman. Harriman maintained that the sacrifices Morgan's plan demanded of the Erie's second-

mortgage bondholders were too severe. Morgan, with support from most investors, triumphed in the courts and implemented his plan.

The second reorganization of the Philadelphia & Reading proved to be quite different from the Southern or the Erie. The P&R had been reorganized by Morgan in 1886 but was now under the direction of an anti-Morgan president named A. A. McLeod who said, "I would rather run a peanut stand than be dictated to by J. P. Morgan." By attempting to build a rail empire into New England and by attempting to monopolize coal production, the P&R antagonized the New York Central Railroad, the Pennsylvania Railroad, and J. P. Morgan. The P&R was forced to borrow money for its expansion plans, and the Morgan interests were in a position to force the company into bankruptcy. The reorganization plan, lasting from December 1895 to March 1897, placed the P&R in a voting trust. Morgan had crushed a rebel.

An attempt to reorganize the Union Pacific turned into one of Morgan's most serious defeats. Frustrated by the unwillingness of the company to accept Morgan's reorganization, he abandoned the UP. Eventually Kuhn, Loeb & Company tried to reorganize the railroad, but they were not successful until the UP allowed Edward H. Harriman (characterized by Morgan as "that little fellow") to preside over the reorganization. It was completely successful, and the UP became one of the most powerful railroads in the country. Eventually Standard Oil, the National City Bank of New York, and Kuhn, Loeb & Company combined forces with Harriman to form a powerful banking interest of their own, an interest that was to prove a serious challenge to the powerful House of Morgan.

Virtually no other major railroad reorganization in the 1890s was done without Morgan's involvement. The Northern Pacific reorganization was important because it temporarily counterbalanced the failure of Morgan to reorganize the UP. Morgan had been involved in the NP since 1883, but after the company failed in 1893 Kuhn, Loeb & Company attempted unsuccessfully to reorganize it. The Morgan interests eventually entered and worked out a reorganization in conjunction with a major German bank, a requirement since many of the NP bonds had been sold in Germany (under Henry Villard's presidency). This reorganization became inordinately complex because James J. Hill and the Great Northern gained a substantial interest in the NP. The NP voting trust included Morgan, August Belmont, and George F. Baker.

Morgan was not only involved in railroads, but also with companies that controlled coal production and distribution in the United States. He was one of the founding partners of General Electric, a director of the Western Union Telegraph Company, the National Cordage Company, and eventually the major steel companies. In 1901 he was instrumental in the formation of the United States Steel Company, the first billion dollar industry in American history. U. S. Steel was an example of a vertical cartel, producing over 60 percent of the nation's steel, owning over 1,000 miles of railroad, more than a hundred ore vessels, and tremendous reserves of iron ore, coal, limestone, and natural gas. From the location of the raw materials to the finished product, the huge U.S. Steel Company was in complete control. In Morgan's view it was the ideal rationalized industrial cartel.

Perhaps 1901 and the U.S. Steel combination mark the high point in Morgan's career. There are several reasons why Morgan was able to reach such a pinnacle in his spectacular career. One was the increasing complexity of business. As the size of plants and the use of new and complicated technologies increased, the average worker was unable to understand the process. Because of the cost of the new technologies, vast sums of money had to be secured to purchase or develop this technology. The only people able to rapidly provide this money were the huge banking houses who, because of their investment, received a certain amount of corporate control. Finally, because the vast increase in stock had attracted new stockholders, the old-fashioned control by investors was on the wane. Operation of the companies was turned over to newly created professional managers. Because of the size and complexity of the companies, stockholders could no longer remain familiar with the operation of the company and had to rely on the managers who increasingly turned to the financiers for advice.

Small bondholders, stockholders, employees of all sorts, and labor unions were generally dealt with arbitrarily by the new centralized managements. Efficiency might have been increased, but sensitivity to employees and stockholders was not a high priority in Morgan's reorganizations. As the wealthy financiers, like Morgan, increased their wealth in public view, and as newspapers documented this more provocatively, the rage of the

American people grew. One factor which helped to increase the desire for government control over the titans of business were the feuds that took place between them, such as that between Morgan and Edward H. Harriman.

The major disagreements between Morgan and Harriman took place from 1900 to about 1905, and several of them involved the Northern Pacific Railroad. In an attempt to gain an eastern terminal at Chicago, James J. Hill purchased the CB&Q railroad from under E. H. Harriman who had attempted to acquire it earlier. Fearing direct competition, and supported by Standard Oil and Kuhn, Loeb & Company, Harriman attempted to buy a controlling interest in the NP. Eventually Hill figured out Harriman's strategy and, with the support of Morgan, attempted to retain control of the NP by purchasing all outstanding shares of stock. The result was the panic of 1901 where many stockbrokers sold stock "short" with no shares available for delivery at any price. The object of Morgan and Harriman, of course, was not the price of the stock; it was control of the NP. The final result was a pyrrhic victory for Morgan as he and Hill retained control of the NP, but at a tremendous cost of public opprobrium.

Morgan's power, although far greater in myth than in reality, suffered some reverses after 1901. The tremendous decline in the stock of the overly capitalized U.S. Steel Company, the Supreme Court's reversal of the Northern Securities Company, and the rise of numerous state banks which tended to disrupt Morgan's community of interest in banking, all tended to show that Morgan was not as powerful as his allies and enemies perceived. The panic of 1907 further showed that no matter how powerful Morgan was perceived by the public to be, he could not prevent overspeculation and mismanagement in American business. Morgan did play a major role in channeling money into the stock market and into certain companies to save them during the panic of 1907, but he could not avert the panic itself.

After the panic of 1907 the expansion of government regulation appeared to curb the era of aggressive expansion, and an era of consolidation and stabilization appeared. Harriman died in 1909, and his developing empire was put on the defensive by increased government antitrust actions that were certainly not actively opposed by Morgan. Morgan tended toward détente with the Roosevelt and Taft administrations, recognizing the significance of the public's hostility toward business and banking interests. Nonetheless, Morgan's empire was significant. By 1912 Morgan & Company dominated three large national banks, three trust companies, and three insurance companies. It also controlled ten major railroad systems with 49,000 miles of track, and five large corporations: U.S. Steel, General Electric, International Harvester, Western Union, and AT&T. Morgan and his partners held seventy-two directorships with $10 billion in resources, and with allies in other banking houses the total resources controlled amounted to $22.5 billion. Morgan and his colleagues were a substantial force indeed.

Two events in the last year of Morgan's life conspired to end his days in disappointment. One was the debacle of the New York, New Haven & Hartford (NYNH&H) Railroad and the other was the investigation of the money trust by Congress. In the case of the NYNH&H Railroad, Morgan had allowed his business interests to overcome his analysis of the political and social tenor of the times. Becoming a director of the NYNH&H in 1892, Morgan increased his control to the point where he, George Baker, and William Rockefeller were the dominant voices in the company. In 1903 Morgan moved his protégé, Charles S. Mellen, from the presidency of the Northern Pacific to the presidency of the New Haven, and he, under Morgan's direction, embarked on a drive to monopolize the transportation of New England. NYNH&H money was recklessly spent purchasing railroads, streetcar, and interurban companies regardless of the cost or the value of the property. The eventual purchase of the Boston & Maine brought intense public outcries to which Morgan turned a deaf ear. As money was spent on acquisitions, the New Haven's own line deteriorated causing spectacular and devastating accidents. Led by Louis Brandeis, efforts were made to bring Morgan to an accounting. Morgan died before Brandeis was successful, but the NYNH&H struggle occupied much of the last year of Morgan's life.

The Pujo Committee, although unable to prove the existence of a money trust, was able to demonstrate the tremendous amount of power in the hands of bankers like Morgan. Both George F. Baker and J. P. Morgan, when called to testify before the committee, denied any control over the financial affairs of the country. Morgan, in particular, generated a great amount of curiosity in his testimony but said little if anything on the stand that could have hurt him. When asked if he thought he had any power over industry in the United States, Morgan modestly replied, "Not the slightest." Spectators were stunned by Morgan's answers, but recent historical analysis demonstrates that Morgan was not as powerful as most of the spectators at the Pujo Committee hearing believed. Nonetheless, to suggest that he had not the slightest power over industry was a distortion that does not survive subsequent historical inquiry.

In January 1913, shortly after testifying before the Pujo Committee, Morgan made his customary winter trip to Europe. Amid rumors of ill health, he traveled around the Mediterranean with family, friends, and servants. Toward the end of March, Morgan became ill and died rather suddenly in Rome on March 31, 1913. He was buried in Hartford, Connecticut, and he left an estate valued at about $125 million—not particularly large when one considers the financial power Morgan possessed at his height. In truth it was power, not money, that interested Morgan.

Morgan's religious beliefs were strongly Episcopalian, but he did not discuss them widely nor did he inquire into religious matters deeply. He did provide much of the money to build the Cathedral of St. John the Divine in New York City. He was also an ardent art collector whose personal collection was valued at more than $50 million at his death. Morgan's personality was always reserved, although he had a romantic side that he attempted to curb later in life. Four years after his first romantic attachment he married Frances Louise Tracey, and they had one son, J. P. Morgan, Jr., and three daughters.

During his lifetime J. P. Morgan was the financial aristocrat of the United States and in his travels abroad was treated as an American aristocrat. Certainly his personality and management style lended itself to the aristocratic characterization. In an era when financial centralization was possibly necessary, Morgan had the right combination of fortune (he was not a self-made man) and fortitude to take advantage of the age. The age did not last long, however, as by the turn of the century the age of government regulation was dawning. Enough historical analysis exists, however, to show that Morgan took advantage of regulation by allowing the government to create financial and industrial rationalization when his power began to ebb. The government's record, however, was not nearly so successful as was Morgan's.

References:

Vincent P. Carosso, *The Morgans: Private International Bankers, 1854-1913* (Cambridge, Mass.: Harvard University Press, 1987);

Lewis Corey, *The House of Morgan: A Social Biography of the Masters of Money* (New York: Grosset & Dunlap, 1930);

Clarence Cramer, *American Enterprise: Free and Not So Free* (Boston: Little, Brown & Company, 1972);

Matthew Josephson, *The Robber Barons* (New York: Harcourt, Brace & World, 1934);

Gabriel Kolko, *The Triumph of Conservatism* (Chicago: Quadrangle Books, 1963);

Albro Martin, *James J. Hill and the Opening of the Northwest* (New York: Oxford University Press, 1976);

Robert H. Wiebe, *Businessmen and Reform: A Study of the Progressive Movement* (Chicago: Quadrangle Books, 1962).

Archives:

Papers and records concerning J. P. Morgan and his career are located in the J. P. Morgan, Jr., Collection of the Pierpont Morgan Library, New York, New York, and in the Morgan Papers of Guild Hall Library, London, England.

Samuel F. B. Morse

(April 27, 1791-April 2, 1872)

by George H. Drury

Trains *Magazine*

CAREER: Artist, inventor (1810-1872); president, National Academy of the Arts of Design (1826-1845); professor of painting and sculpture, University of the City of New York (1832-1837); New York City mayoral candidate (1836).

Samuel Finley Breese Morse was born in Charlestown, Massachusetts, on April 27, 1791, the son of Jedidiah Morse, a Congregationalist clergyman, and Elizabeth Breese Morse. At the age of seven he was sent to Phillips Academy in Andover, Massachusetts, and in 1805 he began studies at Yale University. He was undistinguished in his studies–indeed, Morse seemed to be taking up a career as the family ne'er-do-well–and instead took up painting.

Just before he graduated from Yale University in 1810, Morse met artist Washington Allston and decided to travel with him to England to study painting. Morse's parents disapproved, and Morse began working as a clerk to a Boston book publisher in order to finance his painting. One of Morse's paintings, *The Landing of the Pilgrims at Plymouth*, gained the admiration of Allston and Gilbert Stuart and caused Morse's parents to relent in their opposition to his proposed trip. Morse sailed for England in July 1811.

Morse's four years in England were spent mostly in London studying under Allston and at

Samuel F. B. Morse (courtesy of Smithsonian Institution)

the Royal Academy. His 1812 statue, *Hercules*, won the gold medal of the Adelphi Society of Arts. His painting *The Dying of Hercules* won the Gold

Medal of the Royal Academy spring exhibition in 1813. When Morse prepared to return to the United States he expected to do so as a success.

But when he returned to Boston in 1815 to mount an exhibition of his work, Morse was confronted with failure. The only market open to him was portraiture, so in summer 1816 Morse reluctantly traveled through New Hampshire painting portraits. In Concord he met and became engaged to his future wife, Lucretia Pickering Walker, who was barely seventeen years old.

Frustrated by the lack of success of his painting, Morse began to consider a career in the Episcopal ministry, perhaps as a reaction to the rising tide of Unitarianism in New England. Morse's parents advised against it, arguing that Morse lacked the disposition of a student and, further, that he already had a profession that could support him. After another about-face Morse and his brother Sidney invented a pump for fire engines. It was unsuccessful for its intended use but proved workable for lesser tasks.

In 1817 Morse traveled to Charleston, South Carolina, where he stayed with relatives and once again painted portraits. He returned to New England the next year, marrying Lucretia Walker on September 19, 1818. The Morses sailed back to South Carolina soon afterwards, where their daughter Susan was born in the summer of 1819. During the following winter Morse painted a portrait of U.S. president James Monroe. He discovered he had exhausted the market for portraits in Charleston and in 1821 again returned north to join his parents, brothers, wife, and daughter in the Trinitarian stronghold of New Haven, Connecticut, where his family had resettled.

Morse continued his painting in New Haven. A second daughter was born there but died in infancy; his third child, a son named Charles, grew to adulthood. In New Haven Morse began and completed a painting of the U.S. House of Representatives, which was exhibited unsuccessfully in Boston. Morse soon after turned his talents to the invention of a marble-carving machine.

Morse moved to New York in 1823 and in spring 1824 applied for the post of attache to Mexico, thinking the country might be an inspiration to his painting. The appointment of the minister to Mexico was derailed in Congress and with it Morse's appointment to the delegation.

A second son, Finley, was born in 1825, and Lucretia died soon afterward, the latter event occur-

ring while Morse was in Washington painting a portrait of the Marquis de Lafayette. That same year Morse helped organize a group of artists who were discontented with the American Academy of Fine Arts, which was controlled by businessmen rather than artists. In an attempt to defuse the protest, Morse was elected to the board of the American Academy, but he rejected the post and in January 1826 established the National Academy of the Arts of Design (now the National Academy of Design). He was president of the organization until 1845. Both of Morse's parents died in 1826, and he funneled his emotional energy into completion of his portrait of Lafayette and the writing of poetry. He again went to Europe, this time to Rome to continue studying painting.

While in Paris in 1832 Morse saw a semaphore telegraph in operation, observed that it was faster than mail, and began to think about whether he might find an application for electricity in the transmission of words. Sailing home on the *Sully* he discussed electricity with tablemates over luncheon. From that point on Morse ruminated on his ideas.

His 1832 appointment as professor of painting and sculpture at the University of the City of New York (now New York University) enabled him to begin work on an electric telegraph. He conceived the idea of a relay, by which a small current operates a switch controlling a larger current, and by 1837 he was sending signals through ten miles of wire wound around the walls of his room. That year he formed a partnership with Alfred Vail, Leonard Gale, and Francis O. J. Smith, all of whom provided Morse with either capital, intellectual support, or moral support. Morse's 1837 patent application for his electric telegraph included a means of coding numbers, a dictionary of words and associated numbers, and an arrangement of serrated movable type that actuated an electrical switch. The switch was soon replaced by the familiar telegraph key, which opened and closed the circuit according to the movement of the operator's hand.

In early 1838 Morse demonstrated his telegraph to the Philadelphia-based Franklin Institute, the U.S. House of Representatives, and President Martin Van Buren. In May of that year Morse traveled to Europe again, this time in an attempt to secure patents. In England he saw Davy's and Wheatstone's electric telegraph, which relied on observation of the deflection of a needle to one side or the other to receive messages; Morse's instrument recorded the message as a series of dots, dashes, and spaces on a long strip of paper. Despite his efforts, Morse was denied patents in England and France.

During this period Morse's interests were not limited to his invention; he ran for the office of mayor of New York in 1836 as the candidate of the Native American Democratic Association but received less than 6 percent of the votes. He was nominated again in 1841 but withdrew because of discord in the party. He also began making daguerrotypes, one of the first Americans to experiment with that form of photography.

Morse, ever short of money, had no way to test the telegraph commercially; it took five years before he was able—and then only with federal financial assistance—to construct a telegraph line along the line of the Baltimore & Ohio Railroad between Washington and Baltimore. On May 24, 1844, the first message was transmitted: "What hath God wrought?" It was quickly followed by news of the progress of the Democratic convention in Baltimore.

Morse was soon embroiled in legal battles with other inventors over patent rights to various components of Morse's system. The U.S. Supreme Court upheld his claim in 1854, and Morse finally derived a measure of wealth from the invention by the sale of his patent rights.

Morse had set aside painting for years to work on the telegraph. He considered returning to art and earnestly campaigned for a commission to paint one of the panels in the rotunda of the Capitol in Washington. Congress decided on another artist though, and Morse finally gave up his painting and turned his full attention to developments in the telegraph industry.

In 1847 Morse settled in a house near Poughkeepsie, New York, with his daughter Susan and sons Charles and Finley. In August 1848 he married a cousin, Sarah Griswold, who eventually presented him with four additional children.

Unlike many writers, artists, and inventors, Morse's achievements were recognized during his lifetime. In 1858 representatives of ten European nations met to honor Morse and present him, at his suggestion, with a gift of money in recognition of his work. Morse's associates Vail and Smith asked for a share of the 400,000 francs; Morse's lawyers concurred, and Morse retained only approximately one-third of the gift. By the 1860s Morse's income was

sufficient for him to devote much of his efforts to gentleman farming and philanthropy. He was one of the charter trustees of Vassar College (he was among the early advocates of woman's rights), and he also contributed generously to Yale University and Union Theological Seminary.

In 1871 telegraphers across the country contributed to a statue honoring Morse. At the unveiling of the statue in New York's Central Park, poet William Cullen Bryant spoke of Morse's inventive genius. Morse, he said, analyzed the processes of painting to discover the rules they obeyed—rules of cause and effect. Morse's was an organizing mind, said Bryant, citing the creation of the Academy of the Arts of Design. The ceremony concluded with the singing of the Doxology. That evening Morse's message of greeting was sent by a woman telegraph operator to all the cities in the United States and Canada. Morse himself tapped out his signature. His last year was much as previous years had been: philanthropy, letter-writing, study, and visits with friends. Morse died of pneumonia on April 2, 1872.

Morse did not invent the telegraph in one stroke. He was presented with the phenomena of electricity and magnetism, and he recognized the need for a means of communication over long distances. He carefully thought about what those forces could do and drew on the ideas of others to assemble the devices that would accomplish his goals.

It took the railroads, the first great beneficiary of Morse's invention, some time to realize the potential of the telegraph. In 1851 Charles Minot, superintendent of the New York & Erie Railroad, was aboard a train that was waiting to meet a long-delayed train running in the opposite direction. Minot grew impatient and telegraphed an order to hold the oncoming train. The engineer of Minot's train refused to proceed, unwilling to trust the telegraph; Minot took the throttle himself. Thus was born the entire system of train dispatching based on telegraphed train orders.

In the 1940s and 1950s train-order dispatching gave way to centralized traffic control (CTC), in which the dispatcher controls turnouts and signals remotely and trains proceed on the authority of signal indications; later radio communication between the dispatcher and train crews replaced the use of telegraph and telephone on lines with too little traffic to justify CTC.

In Europe the telegraph systems were the property of the government, often an arm of the postal service. In the United States, though, private companies erected the lines and operated the service. The companies gradually merged until one company, Western Union, held a monopoly on telegraph service. The mechanization of long-distance telephone service in the 1950s and 1960s and the reduction of the price of long-distance calls made the telephone a better means of personal communication, and it generally has replaced the telegraph for most purposes.

References:
Oliver W. Larkin, *Samuel F. B. Morse and American Democratic Art* (Boston: Little, Brown, 1954);
Carleton Mabee, *The American Leonardo: A Life of Samuel F. B. Morse* (New York: Knopf, 1943).

Archives:
Materials relating to Morse are located in the Samuel F. B. Morse Collection of the Manuscript Division, Library of Congress, Washington, D. C.

New York Central Railroad

by F. Daniel Larkin

State University College, Oneonta, New York

On December 28, 1825, George W. Featherstonhaugh, a wealthy resident of Schenectady County, applied to the New York state legislature to incorporate the Mohawk & Hudson (M&H) Railroad Company. From this modest beginning grew one of the great transportation systems in the United States. The act was finalized on April 17, 1826; and the last of the great Hudson Valley patroons, Stephen Van Rensselaer III, was appointed as the first president. Aside from his reputation as a notable of Albany and its environs, Van Rensselaer contributed little to the company. On the contrary, the prime movers of the company were Featherstonhaugh; Lynde Catlin, president of the Merchant's Bank of New York City; and John Jacob Astor, the famous merchant and fur trader. James Renwick, a mathematics professor at Columbia, later joined the trio.

In January 1829, after nearly three years of relative inactivity, vice-president Featherstonhaugh, treasurer Catlin, and director Astor formed a committee to initiate construction. Peter Fleming, the company's first engineer, reported that $275,000 would be needed to build the 16-mile railway from Albany, on the Hudson River, to Schenectady, on the Mohawk. The line, running directly between the two cities, was meant to complement travel on the mighty Erie Canal, not compete with it. Passengers bound for the West were expected to board

canal boats at Schenectady. Early in 1830 Fleming left the railroad. His successor as chief engineer was John B. Jervis, until then employed in a similar position with the Delaware & Hudson Canal Company. Jervis had gained valuable experience building that company's 16-mile coal-carrying railway.

The actual construction began under Jervis and moved ahead rapidly. By August 1831 the railroad, with its 4-foot 9-inch gauge track, was open for business. At first, the M&H used both horses and the line's single locomotive, the Dewitt Clinton, to pull the cars. Soon other locomotives were purchased from England and from the West Point Foundry in New York City, the builder of the Clinton. The Jervis-designed and West Point-built Experiment, with its forward moveable guide truck, was tested on the Mohawk & Hudson before it went into service on the sister line, the Saratoga & Schenectady Railroad.

By the time the M&H began operation, it had cost double the original estimates and continued to pose financial problems for the company throughout its twenty-two year operation. During the last six years of business, it was called the Albany & Schenectady Railroad.

With the first 16 miles of railroad west of Albany in operation, the next 300 miles or so to Buffalo were built amazingly fast. Service on the next link, the Utica & Schenectady, began in 1836. Its

The first Grand Central Station, 1871

tracks paralleled the Erie Canal and so until 1844 was not permitted to carry freight. From then until 1851, when the prohibition was dropped completely, freight could be hauled during the winter months but was subject to an added cost equal to canal tolls. The state legislature had protected its own interest by safeguarding the Erie Canal's freight business. All lines, as did the Mohawk & Hudson, steered clear of the state's mighty canal.

By the time the next road west, the Syracuse & Utica, opened its fifty-three miles in the summer of 1839, the Auburn & Syracuse Railroad already had begun to run steam trains. Albany and Buffalo, the state's principal Lake Erie port, were close to being linked by iron. Only two gaps remained. Finished in November 1841, the seventy miles between Auburn and Rochester completed the rail line from Syracuse to Rochester. The road had been built away from the canal line through the Finger Lakes villages of Seneca Falls, Waterloo, Geneva, and Canadaigua. In 1842 the Attica & Buffalo Railroad opened and formed the final link in the chain of seven distinct rail lines which bound together New York's central east-west axis.

It had taken eleven years to complete the construction of the railroads across central New York; and it would require another eleven years before these roads and others could be brought together in a combination called the New York Central.

Only two of the seven rail lines across central New York came close to the banks of the Erie Canal. Because of its cheap freight rates and the protection afforded by the legislature, the canal was avoided by competition-conscious railroad men. Yet even when competition was unavoidable, the cross-state lines made money. But there was another waterway in New York that was regarded with even more trepidation than the "Grand Canal": the Hudson River. Since the first decade of the nineteenth century steamboats had been regularly reducing the travel time between New York City and Albany. By the 1840s speeds of twenty-miles-per-hour or more were common on the Hudson. The railroads thought that they could not match the high speed and low cost of river travel. As a result, most planned their routes well clear of the Hudson. The first railroad to venture north out of New York City, the New York & Harlem, built a route well east of the river but found it unprofitable because of the sparsely populated areas it traversed.

In the early 1840s, however, several Poughkeepsie businessmen cautiously decided to challenge the river by building a railroad between their city and New York. They wisely chose John B. Jervis to head the engineering department. Jervis planned a water-level route and demonstrated in several reports that the road could compete on the basis of both price and speed. The reports were correct. Although Jervis left the company in 1849 the Hudson

The Mohawk & Hudson's Dewitt Clinton (courtesy of New York Central System)

River Railroad reached Poughkeepsie in 1850. A year later the line was extended to East Greenbush, across the Hudson from Albany. It was the logical connection between the central New York lines and the port of New York. What remained to be achieved was a rational combination of the short lines crossing the state.

Officers of the Utica & Schenectady (U&S) line took the lead in arranging the consolidation of the seven short lines. Erastus Corning, president of the U&S, and John V. L. Pryn, the road's treasurer, were elected to similar posts when the consolidated line, known as the New York Central, came into being in 1853. Consolidation brought Buffalo to within seven hours of Albany and signaled the beginning of an era of mergers. Many smaller lines were absorbed to complete the Central's dominance of central and northern New York.

It was left to the great Cornelius Vanderbilt to accomplish the next important union of rails in the New York–Albany–Buffalo corridor. He brought the Hudson River Railroad under his control in 1865 and in 1869 adroitly achieved the same with the Central. As president of both lines, Vanderbilt achieved the formation of the New York Central & Hudson River Railroad with ease in 1869.

Vanderbilt looked toward Chicago as the logi-

cal western terminus of his expanding system. He was greatly encouraged and aided in the concept of westward expansion by his son William. The Lake Shore & Michigan Southern was acquired in 1869 to provide an almost-level route from Buffalo to Chicago. With the death of Vanderbilt in 1877, William H. Vanderbilt began his own short, but impressive, stint as the empire builder of the Central. More roads were acquired west of Buffalo, the Nickel Plate Road in 1883 and the West Shore line in 1885. Both were built parallel to existing New York Central routes, a principal reason behind their acquisition. But William H. Vanderbilt's untimely death in late 1885 brought a sudden end to his expansion efforts. Chauncey Depew, president of the New York Central since the Vanderbilts removed themselves from public control of the line in 1879, led the system until he became its chairman of the board in 1898.

Despite their lessened role, Vanderbilt influence in the New York Central was strong through the end of the century. One such area of influence was in the goals of expansion. More railroads west of New York state were obtained, and one of them, the Cleveland, Cincinnati, Chicago & St. Louis (The Big Four), brought the New York Central to the Mississippi River. The 1900 lease of the Boston & Albany completed the Central's nineteenth-century empire building, leaving a system that stretched from Boston west to Chicago and St. Louis and from New York City north to the Canadian border. It ranked as one of the most powerful corporations in the United States.

References:

Alvin F. Harlow, *The Road of the Century: The Story of*

the New York Central Railroad (New York: Creative Age, 1947);

Edward Hungerford, *Men and Iron: The History of the New York Central* (New York: Crowell, 1938);

Frank W. Stevens, *The Beginnings of the New York Central Railroad* (New York: Putnam's, 1926).

Archives:

Material concerning the New York Central is located in the Erastus Corning Papers of the Albany Institute of History and Art, Albany, New York.

New York, New Haven & Hartford Railroad

by F. Daniel Larkin

State University College, Oneonta, New York

In 1844 the state of Connecticut incorporated the New York & New Haven Railroad. Road building was started in the Long Island Sound community of New Haven and the railroad headed west toward the city of New York, some sixty miles distant. The first major hurdle the new company had to overcome was to obtain a charter from the New York legislature. Construction was halted at the New York State line until opposition from the Westchester Turnpike Company was ended with a cash payment to the turnpike operators. In 1846 a New York charter was granted. Within three years the New York & New Haven had entered New York City via the tracks of the New York & Harlem Railroad, a horse-car line built from southern Manhattan Island north into the adjoining county of Westchester. The New York & New Haven forged an agreement with the Harlem road in order to gain entry into the city; the pact called for the sharing of the New York & Harlem's present and future stations in Manhattan. This clause would eventually prove to be extremely beneficial to the line from Connecticut.

The New York & New Haven's first president was Robert Schuyler, descendant of the Revolutionary War general Philip Schuyler and, unfortunately, a man of flexible ethical standards toward the road's business. However, during the five years after the completion of the road in 1849, Schuyler enhanced the road's position relative to competing railroads in Connecticut. The Housatonic, for example, was outmaneuvered in its quest for the connect-

ing trade with Long Island Sound's steamship lines. The New York & New Haven entered into a pool arrangement with the Housatonic's chief steamship connection on the Sound, which gave Schuyler's line much of the Housatonic's business. This arrangement was facilitated by the fact that the steamship line's president was Schuyler's brother. The wily Schuyler, however, lacked such an advantage in his battle with another major competitor, the Hartford & New Haven.

The Hartford & New Haven, incorporated in 1833, ran its first track from New Haven to Meriden. Until 1839, when the line was extended to Hartford, stagecoaches were used to convey travelers to that city from the end of track in Meriden. Within a decade of the road's completion to Hartford, it had acquired steamboats to run between New Haven and New York City to successfully compete with the longer, all-water steamboat route of the Connecticut River Line. By then the Hartford & New Haven had also extended the rails of its growing transportation system north to Springfield, Massachusetts, over the right-of-way of its offspring company, the Hartford & Springfield. From Springfield rail connection was available to Boston over the track of the Western Railroad and the Boston & Worcester. This was the extent of the Hartford & New Haven's growth when the New York & New Haven was completed in 1849 between its two terminal cities.

Schuyler chose to challenge the Hartford & New Haven by leasing a road called the New Haven & Northampton, which only extended as far as Plainville, Connecticut, about thirty miles north of New Haven, but had the charter rights to build to Springfield. If completed to Springfield the Northampton line would provide the New York & New Haven with a shorter, all-railroad connection between Springfield and New York City than the Hartford & New Haven's land-and-water route.

Schuyler's challenge to the Hartford & New Haven began a dispute between the two companies which lasted most of two decades. But Schuyler did not see his plan to a successful conclusion. In 1854 he nearly destroyed the New York & New Haven through the sale of almost $2 million of phony company stock, followed by his sudden departure for Europe. It took the railroad several years to recover from Schuyler's "management," but its strong geographic position gave it an edge over its nearly equally strong Hartford & New Haven rival. Finally, in August 1872, the two roads ceased their maneuvering and litigation and became the combined New York, New Haven & Hartford Railroad. W. D. Bishop was named the first president of the new corporation.

While New Haven's roads were moving toward their merger, the master of railroad combinations was busily planning a New York City palace to house some of his own lines and, incidentally, the New York & New Haven. Commodore Cornelius Vanderbilt ordered work to commence in 1869 on the first Grand Central Station at its Forty-second Street location. One of Vanderbilt's roads, the New York & Harlem, was the actual owner of the terminal. Because of its original agreement with the New York & Harlem, the New York & New Haven received quarters in the building. In fact, due to an error in planning, the New Haven's location was on Forty-second Street, a site much superior to that occupied by either of the Commodore's lines that shared the building. The New Haven became a tenant in the second Grand Central Station, when constructed, and has participated in the lucrative New York Central property rights on Park Avenue. The New Haven's early agreement with the Harlem Line was profitable indeed.

The New York, New Haven & Hartford, or simply the New Haven, as it was called, prospered following the union of the two roads. Even during the depression years following the panic of 1873,

the New Haven was able to retire the New York & New Haven bonds that fell due in 1876. Dividends were paid at 10 percent, and the remaining surplus was reinvested in the road. Although on firm financial footing, the New Haven was not without problems following the merger. From 1872 until after the beginning of the twentieth century, the railroad's chief concern was the construction of parallel lines to New York. New Haven policy was dominated by the obsession of preventing such competition or even the thought of it.

The New Haven sought to control all potential competition between New York and Boston. It first moved to acquire, by pool agreement, the Air Line road from New Haven to Willimantic. The Air Line was looked upon as a railroad that eventually could connect with Boston and pose problems for the New Haven. In 1882 the New Haven completed its takeover by executing a ninety-nine-year lease of the Air Line. The only other independent road out of New Haven was the New Haven & Northampton. The New Haven line previously had leased the line to Northampton and, after allowing the lease to lapse, moved to regain control of the railroad in 1881. The Northampton provided a too convenient route into New Haven territory for the Boston & Albany.

In the midst of the railroad's expansion of the 1880s, Charles P. Clark became president of the New Haven. A skilled and aggressive administrator, Clark ran the New Haven from 1887 until his resignation in 1900. As president of the New York & New England prior to coming to the New Haven, Clark envisioned a merger of the two lines as a logical monopoly of southern New England rail transportation. Thwarted by his own board of directors on the New York & New England, he began a new campaign to achieve his merger goal through the New Haven. Clark changed New Haven strategy from one of defensive acquisition to offensive empire building in an effort to realize his dream of one railroad system which could control the New York to Boston traffic, with branch lines and feeders where necessary throughout southern New England.

In 1892 the New Haven took over the Housatonic rail system and, in a move toward a route of its own to Boston via Providence, Clark's railroad took over the New York, Providence & Boston. In order to close the existing gap between Providence and Boston, the New Haven moved to acquire the

Old Colony Railroad the following year. The Old Colony provided not only a right-of-way between the largest cities of Rhode Island and Massachusetts, but also a boat line on Long Island Sound. In 1898 Clark's goal was finally realized with the addition of the New York & New England, which was designated as the New England Railroad. With the New Haven's southern New England monopoly complete, it ended the nineteenth century in splendid financial condition ready to expand its empire elsewhere in New England and even into New York State. Not surprisingly, such a viable system had already attracted the interest of a quintessential railroad financier who was adding to his rail domain and who would dictate New Haven policy in the early twentieth century, J. P. Morgan.

References:

George Pierce Baker, *The Formation of the New England Railroad System* (New York: Greenwood Press, 1968);

Alvin Harlow, *The Road of the Century* (New York: Creative Age Press, 1947);

John L. Weller, *The New Haven Railroad* (New York: Hastings House, 1969).

Archives:

Minute books and other material of the New York, New Haven & Hartford Railroad can be found at the Office of the Trustee of the New Haven Railroad, New Haven, Connecticut. Additional material can be found at the Conrail Warehouse, New Haven, Connecticut; the Baker Library of the Harvard University Graduate School of Business Administration, Boston, Massachusetts; the Wilbur Cross Library of the University of Connecticut, Storrs, Connecticut; and the G. W. Blunt White Library, Mystic, Connecticut.

Northern Pacific Railway

by Rex C. Myers

South Dakota State University

The Northern Pacific (NP) Railroad linked the Great Lakes (Duluth) and the Mississippi River (St. Paul) with the Pacific Coast (Portland and Seattle-Tacoma), providing transcontinental railroad service in the states of Minnesota, North Dakota, Montana, Idaho, Washington, Oregon, and by a branch line to Winnipeg, the province of Manitoba. The Northern Pacific existed as a corporate entity from its creation by Congress in 1864 until its merger into the Burlington Northern Railroad in 1970.

Before the Civil War national interest in transcontinental railroads focused on possible southern, central, and northern routes. In 1854 Isaac Stevens, governor of the Washington Territory, led a survey of the northern route which documented the feasibility of a railroad from the Great Lakes area to the Pacific. A decade later, now-Representative Stevens helped secure congressional passage of legislation creating the Northern Pacific Railroad Company; President Abraham Lincoln signed the measure on July 2, 1864. The railroad received no direct federal subsidy, but Congress supported it through the largest land grant in United States history. The legislation granted the NP rights to land along the proposed route totaling nearly 60 million acres.

The land grant did not, however, provide the funds necessary to begin construction, and the project languished until 1869 when the banking firm of Jay Cooke and Company assumed financial control over the venture. Chief Engineer W. Milnor Roberts resurveyed the route from the Pacific to the Yellowstone River's headwaters, and actual construction began in Carlton, Minnesota, on February 15, 1870, on the Lake Superior & Mississippi (LS&M) Railroad, a route leased by the NP. By 1873 track had reached the Missouri River at Bismarck, North Dakota. Worsening financial conditions in the country in general and in the NP in particular led to failure of Jay Cooke and Company in September 1873. As the panic of 1873 ensued all construction on the NP ceased.

Frederick Billings and a team of eastern businessmen reorganized the NP in 1878, consolidated its interest in the LS&M (reorganized as the St. Paul & Duluth Railroad), and resumed construction of the railroad west from Bismarck and east from Wallula Junction in Washington. During the same period in which the NP was being reorganized, German financiers, who held a large investment in the bonds of the Oregon Steam Navigation (OSN) Company, sent Henry Villard to the United States to protect their interests. Villard quickly realized the importance of the northern Pacific coast connection to any transcontinental railroad. In 1879 he consolidated his holdings in the OSN into Oregon Railway & Navigation (OR&N) Company and worked out a cooperative agreement with the Union Pacific to provide that line with an outlet to the northern Pacific coast. As a result Villard was able to buy control of the NP in 1881, using his famous "blind pool" to secure financing. Villard, through the OR&N, also controlled right-of-way from Wallula Junction along the southern bank of the Columbia River to Portland and, with the NP, had a transcontinental connection to the upper Midwest. During Villard's tenure Minnesota businessman T. F. Oakes became the vice-president of the NP.

In August 1883 track-laying gangs met at Gold Creek, Montana, fifty miles west of Helena. The next month, on September 8, an official last spike ceremony was held with great celebration. Villard organized the extravagant event, which included four trains filled with dignitaries, European financiers, former President U. S. Grant, and Secretary of the Interior Henry M. Teller. Between 8,000 and 10,000 people attended the event.

The completion of the Duluth-Wallula Junction line, some 1,675 miles, did not end the NP's growth. The NP reached Portland, Oregon, on OR&N track from Wallula, then used its own line north to reach Puget Sound. In order to avoid dependence on the OR&N, which the Union Pacific would not control until 1886, the NP, during 1883-1887, constructed a line from Pasco to Tacoma over the Cascade Mountains at Stampede Pass.

Villard's freewheeling management style led to the collapse of his financial empire in 1884 and his removal as NP president. Villard continued to play a role in the railroad's development. He returned to the NP as a member of the board of directors from 1887 to 1893. The railroad's charter did not permit it to build branch lines, so the NP set up a series of separately incorporated companies along its right-of-way and held the first mortgage to each. The expansion caused the railroad to overextend itself

financially, and it was heavily dependent on unstable agricultural and natural resource product shipments. The NP could not withstand the downturns in financing and traffic which came with the panic of 1893, and the railroad went into receivership that fall.

The company was reorganized in 1896 as the Northern Pacific Railway with financier Edward D. Adams at its head and on September 1 acquired the rights, franchises, properties, and lands of the Northern Pacific Railroad. The new corporation eventually secured control of the St. Paul & Northern Pacific Railway, the St. Paul & Duluth, the Seattle & International Railway, and the Minnesota & International Railway. It leased its Winnipeg line to the province of Manitoba.

James J. Hill secured control of the Northern Pacific Railway in 1901 by outmaneuvering Edward H. Harriman, who already held the financial reins of the Union Pacific and the Southern Pacific. Hill's takeover of the NP, combined with his Great Northern (GN) Railway, gave him a virtual monopoly of the northern transcontinental rail corridor. To the continued consternation of Harriman, Hill and J. P. Morgan also secured 98 percent of Chicago, Burlington & Quincy (CB&Q) Railroad stock. With the GN, NP, and CB&Q, Hill controlled a network of strong railroads between the Midwest and the Pacific coast, and a direct link to Chicago.

Hill and Morgan consolidated management of their railroads in 1901 by forming the Northern Securities Company to hold the stock of all three lines. President Theodore Roosevelt saw the corporation as a trust and directed the attorney general to seek its breakup under provisions of the Sherman Antitrust Act. In 1904 the U.S. Supreme Court dissolved Northern Securities. As the GN and NP continued to control CB&Q stock the relationship among the three railroads, while competitive, was not antagonistic. The NP and GN cooperated in 1905 to build the Spokane, Portland & Seattle Railroad, a line which completed a right-of-way along the north bank of the Columbia River from Pasco to Portland.

The years between 1897 and 1917 were prosperous for the Northern Pacific. Lumber and wheat production—traditional staples of its freight traffic—boomed and the region's population grew. During the last decade of this period the Milwaukee Road extended a transcontinental line which paralleled much of the NP route. Modest NP branch line expansion met the Milwaukee challenge and increased total trackage to more than 6,000 miles. The railroad adopted the red and black "monad" as its corporate symbol and characterized itself as the "Mainstreet of the Northwest." Its two "name" transcontinental trains were the "North Coast Limited" and the "Mainstreeter."

As the original northern transcontinental line the NP opened up the resources of a vast region from the Great Lakes to Puget Sound. Its large land grant holdings made it a partner, albeit an often controversial one, in the economic development of the states it served. The Northern Pacific's association and eventual merger in 1970 with the "Hill Lines" played a vital part in the Northwest's business and transportation history.

References:

Robert L. Frey and Lorenz P. Schrenk, *Northern Pacific Supersteam Era: 1925-1945* (San Marino, Cal.: Golden West, 1985);

Siegfried Mickelson, "Promotional Activities of the Northern Pacific Railroad's Land and Immigration Departments, 1870 to 1902," unpublished M.A. thesis, University of Minnesota, 1940;

Louis Tuck Renz, *The History of the Northern Pacific Railroad* (Fairfield, Wash.: Ye Galleon, 1980);

Eugene Virgil Smalley, *History of the Northern Pacific Railroad* (New York: Putnam's, 1883);

Charles Raymond Wood, *The Northern Pacific: Mainstreet of the Northwest* (Seattle: Superior, 1968).

Archives:

The Northern Pacific Railroad Company Records are at the Minnesota Historical Society, St. Paul, Minnesota.

Thomas Fletcher Oakes

(July 15, 1843-March 14, 1919)

by W. Thomas White

James Jerome Hill Reference Library

CAREER: Purchasing agent, assistant treasurer, general freight agent, vice-president, and general superintendent, Kansas Pacific Railroad (1865-1879); general superintendent, Kansas City, Fort Scott & Gulf Railroad and Kansas City, Lawrence & Southern Railroad (1879-1880); vice-president, Oregon Railway & Navigation Company (1880-1881); vice-president (1881-1888), general manager (1883-1889), president (1888-1893), receiver, Northern Pacific Railway (1893-1895).

Thomas Fletcher Oakes was an important, if largely unrecognized, figure in far-western railroading. Born into a well-established Yankee family, he nonetheless worked up from an entry-level position to president of the Northern Pacific Railway. As a railroad executive he was often overshadowed by Henry Villard, but Oakes did make important contributions by actually completing the Northern Pacific's main line, thereby opening the interior Northwest to settlement. Oakes also reorganized the railroad and made it a more effective, efficient corporation, although his contributions did not

prove sufficient to save the road from bankruptcy following the panic of 1893.

Thomas Fletcher Oakes, railroad executive, was born on July 15, 1843, in Boston, Massachusetts, the son of Francis Garaux and Ruth Page Oakes. A member of a long-established New England family, he was educated by private tutors and at Boston's Eliot School. At the age of twenty he was hired by Samuel Hallett & Company to work on the construction of the Kansas Pacific, which was the eastern division of the nation's first transcontinental railway line, the Union Pacific Railroad. He married Abby Rogers Haskell of Gloucester, Massachusetts, and they had five children. In 1865 he began working directly for the Kansas Pacific as purchasing agent and assistant treasurer. Oakes proved a quick study and an industrious employee and, as a result, was quickly promoted to general freight agent, vice-president, and, in 1879, to general superintendent of the line.

Oakes distinguished himself well in his performance during the general disintegration and reorganization of the western railroads that occurred in

Thomas Fletcher Oakes

the late 1870s. James F. Joy of Detroit and prominent members of the Boston investing community particularly were impressed by Oakes's work, and consequently they worked to have him appointed general superintendent of the 600 miles encompassed by the Kansas City, Fort Scott & Gulf and the Kansas City, Lawrence & Southern railroad companies. He served in that capacity only one year, however.

In 1880 Henry Villard, after obtaining control of the troubled Oregon Railway & Navigation Company, which operated along the Columbia River, recruited Oakes to manage that enterprise. When Villard obtained control of the Northern Pacific Railway the following year, Oakes was named vice-president and director of the line which had yet to fulfill the terms of its congressional charter to link the Midwest with the Northwest coast. Working, essentially, as Villard's executive officer, Oakes played an important role in Villard's domination of river and rail traffic along the strategically vital Columbia River, the principal east-west thoroughfare in the Pacific Northwest.

When Thomas Oakes assumed his new duties, a gap of 1,000 miles of unconstructed railroad line remained on the Northern Pacific. From the west the railroad extended only to Sprague, Washington Territory, on the western slope of the Rocky Mountains. From the east the line had reached only to Dickinson, Dakota Territory, leaving much of the northern Great Plains and all of the Rocky Mountain cordillera yet to be traversed.

To complete the Northern Pacific's main line, which would make the railroad a transcontinental line and allow it to claim the massive land grant authorized by Congress, Oakes played a pivotal role. Within two years, at Oakes's direction, construction crews closed the 1,000-mile gap and laid an additional 1,000 miles of branch line for the Northern Pacific, Oregon Railway & Navigation, and Oregon & Transcontinental companies. In 1883 at Gold Creek, Montana Territory, Henry Villard orchestrated the last-spike ceremony as part of a system-wide celebration of the long-awaited completion of the Northern Pacific, which now ran from Lake Superior to Puget Sound. That fundamentally important new axis of trade and commerce which the Northern Pacific represented resulted in large measure from Oakes's efforts.

That same year he was promoted to vice-president and general manager of the newly-completed railroad, followed by terms as president and general manager (1888-1889) and president (1889-1893). In 1893 the Northern Pacific was forced into bankruptcy, a victim of the severe depression of that year that threw all transcontinental railroads, aside from the Great Northern, into receivership and generally ravaged the nation's economy. Meanwhile, Oakes confronted other challenges, including the ongoing dispute over the railroad's attempt to claim much of Montana's rich mineral lands—a claim hotly contested by mine owners, laborers, merchants, and nearly everyone else in the territory (after 1889, state). As president, Oakes did not resolve that dispute, which intermittently raged into the twentieth century, nor did he do so as one of the railroad's receivers. He was involved in other significant events that were resolved in the Northern Pacific's favor, however, and included the railroad's alliance with other roads and the federal government to combat the Coxeyite movement and to smash the industrially organized American Railway Union in the 1894 Pullman Boycott and Strike.

Two years later Oakes retired when a new management team took over, dominated by allies of the Northern Pacific's longtime rival, James J. Hill of the Great Northern Railway, and the House of Morgan. The records are vague, but Oakes seems to have retired from all active association in the railroad industry, moved to Concord, Massachusetts, and confined himself to working with the New York banking firm of Taylor, Cutting & Company and the directorships of various companies. On March 14, 1919, Thomas Fletcher Oakes died in Seattle, Washington.

References:

Thomas C. Cochran, *Railroad Leaders, 1845-1890: The Business Mind in Action* (Cambridge, Mass.: Harvard University Press, 1953);

Railway Age (March 21, 1919): 794;

Louis Tuck Renz, *The History of the Northern Pacific Railroad* (Fairfield, Wash.: Ye Galleon Press, 1980);

Eugene V. Smalley, *History of the Northern Pacific Railroad* (New York: Putnam's, 1883).

Archives:

Material concerning Thomas F. Oakes is located in the Northern Pacific Railway Company Records of the Minnesota Historical Society, St. Paul, Minnesota, and in the Henry Villard Papers of the Houghton Library of Harvard University, Cambridge, Massachusetts.

William Butler Ogden

(June 15, 1805-August 3, 1877)

by H. Roger Grant

University of Akron

CAREER: Sawmill operator (c. 1819-1835); postmaster, Walton, New York (c. 1826-1835); state senate, New York (1834-1835); real estate promoter (1835-1866); mayor, Chicago, Illinois (1837-?); president, Galena & Chicago Union (1846-1851); president, Chicago & North Western (1859-1868); president, Union Pacific (1862-1863).

One eminent mid-nineteenth-century railroad promoter and official was William Butler Ogden. Born on June 15, 1805, in Walton, New York, a village in heavily forested Delaware County, Ogden entered the business world in his early teens. Ogden's father was in poor health, which forced the young man to assume many of the responsibilities for the family's small sawmill. These pressing demands limited Ogden's opportunities for a formal education; yet, his early career convinced him that hard work made personal prosperity possible and likely. He proclaimed later in his life that "I was born by a sawmill . . . , christened in a mill-pond, graduated at a log-school-house, fancied I could do anything I turned my hand to, and that nothing was impossible and ever since . . . I have been trying to prove it, and with some success."

Ogden moved beyond his lumber business to become postmaster of Walton and in 1834 to win election on the Democratic ticket to the New York

William Butler Ogden

state senate. His most memorable speech before this august body involved his efforts to generate public sponsorship of the New York & Erie Railroad (later the Erie), a line projected to run from the Hudson River to Lake Erie via the isolated "Southern Tier," which included Ogden's home county. In his remarks to fellow lawmakers Ogden seemed to be almost clairvoyant; he foresaw "continuous railways from New York to Lake Erie, and south to Lake Erie, through Ohio, Indiana, and Illinois to the waters of the Mississippi, and connecting with railroads running to Cincinnati and Louisville in Kentucky and Nashville in Tennessee, and to New Orleans." And he added, "[They] will present the most splendid system of internal communication ever yet devised by man." Throughout his life this enthusiasm for railroads never flagged.

Ogden decided to leave the Empire State in 1835. His wealthy brother-in-law, Charles Butler, urged him to move to Chicago, Illinois, the Lake Michigan community of about 1,500 residents that was growing rapidly around old Fort Dearborn. Butler had become heavily involved in real estate speculation, and he wanted the bright, hardworking Ogden to oversee his interests in the American Land Company. He was not disappointed; Ogden excelled at his work. Later Ogden made his own real estate purchases and reaped a personal fortune from the land boom that came with the return of prosperity following the nasty panic of 1837.

A "natural leader" and a "natural orator," the well-to-do Ogden emerged as a popular figure in Chicago. When the community became incorporated in 1837 he won election as its first mayor. Throughout his tenure in that office he used his public powers to boost his adopted hometown. Not surprisingly, Ogden entered the field of transportation. His first concern was not a railroad project, but rather the languishing Illinois & Michigan Canal. Through his political and financial contacts he did much to push forward completion of this strategic waterway, which ran from Lake Michigan to the Illinois River at La Salle-Peru.

Railroads, however, had developed into a passion by the late 1840s. The iron horse had established itself fully by this time as the superior means of transporting people and most types of goods. Using the same enthusiasm he generated in support of the Illinois & Michigan Canal, Ogden served as a catalyst in turning the moribund Galena & Chicago Union Railroad into a thriving concern. Char-

tered by the state of Illinois in 1836 the company seemed destined to remain a "paper" project. But with Ogden as its president the railroad's status changed totally. When the Pioneer, a secondhand 4-2-0 Baldwin-built locomotive, pulled the first train over the Galena's iron-capped wooden track on October 28, 1848, this gala event was marked as a testimonial to Ogden's superb skills as a railroad promoter.

Ogden's handiwork functioned well. While the Galena & Chicago Union never reached Galena and the neighboring lead mining camps, it did tie Chicago with the nearby hinterland and by September 1, 1853, had reached Freeport, Illinois, 121 miles northwest of Chicago. In December 1855 the Chicago, Fulton & Iowa line opened from the Junction (West Chicago) to the Mississippi River at Fulton, Illinois, a distance of 135 miles from the Windy City. The Galena prospered almost nearly from the start. Its success attracted capital from the East and from Europe, capital used for the Galena's expansion and also that of midwestern railroad ventures, including the Illinois Central and the Chicago & Rock Island.

Yet Ogden was not at the throttle of the Galena when it moved rapidly away from Chicago and generated handsome dividends for shareholders. In 1851 he had resigned from both the presidency and the directorship of the road. The reason for his resignation involved neither a loss of faith in the company nor in railroading generally; it centered on a business transaction. Several Galena directors charged Ogden with misconduct; namely, they objected to the firm's purchase of ties and other construction materials from McCagg, Reed & Company, a concern in which Ogden served as a "special partner." Ogden was involved directly, but he simply used his contacts to assist the struggling road. Supplies were contracted *below* market price, and they were furnished on credit to the cash-starved Galena. In a subsequent trial, a court vindicated Ogden's conduct, and his reputation remained rightfully untarnished. "[Ogden] had given his time, his money and his credit to push on the Road," recalled Isaac N. Arnold, a Chicago lawyer. "[A]nd [he] had risked in it his private fortune, and I regarded as necessary the defense of this case, and the attack made upon his integrity as most unjust and ungrateful." Added Arnold, "I remember few, if any, cases in my professional life, in which I felt a deeper personal interest."

Difficulties at the Galena did not sour Ogden on railroad affairs. Rather he became more heavily involved in the industry. In 1853 he assumed a directorship in the Fort Wayne & Chicago (after August 1856, the Pittsburgh, Fort Wayne & Chicago, a future unit of the Pennsylvania system). In part due to his extensive lumber holdings in Wisconsin, he helped to develop railroads there. This led to his interest in the Chicago, St. Paul & Fond du Lac Railroad (Fond du Lac), the nucleus of the Chicago & North Western Railway (C&NW). After a rocky start the Fond du Lac was reorganized in 1859 as the C&NW and the property prospered. Its merger with the Galena five years later produced a powerful railroad enterprise.

Ogden served as the first president of the Chicago & North Western from June 7, 1859, until his retirement on June 4, 1868. He guided the road with care and skill. When he stepped down, the board passed this resolution that accurately reflects Ogden's involvement with the road:

> *Resolved,* That his [Ogden's] connection with this Company, dating back for a period of twenty-one years, his disinterested labors in its behalf without fee or reward during the whole time, the benefit he has conferred upon it and the country, demand our grateful acknowledgements.

By the time Ogden relinquished the presidency, the Chicago & North Western was an impressive property. The company operated six divisions (Galena, Iowa, Madison, Milwaukee, Peninsula, and Wisconsin) and sported 1,153 miles of mainline trackage. Its gross earnings totaled $12,614,846, and net earnings stood at a healthy $4,741,199.

Before Ogden left his post on the Chicago & North Western, he headed the "paper" Union Pacific Railroad between 1862 and 1863. Personal considerations induced him to make this involvement a brief one. Still, his presence gave considerable prestige to the project. Ogden's association with the emerging Union Pacific, moreover, revealed clearly his ongoing desire to see the country bound by a web of iron rails.

During the final decade of his life Ogden largely withdrew from business activities, including those that involved railroads. Although he sustained a personal loss of about $2 million as a result of the disastrous fires in Chicago and Preshtigo, Wisconsin, in 1871 (his lumber mills were destroyed in the latter conflagration), he nevertheless retained a large fortune, highlighted by his handsome villa at Fordham Heights, New York. On February 9, 1875, at the age of sixty-nine, he married Marianna Arnot, daughter of a prominent Elmira, New York, judge. Their marriage was short-lived; Ogden's health soon failed and he died on August 3, 1877.

William Butler Ogden possessed considerable vision and common sense. He correctly anticipated the need for railroads, even as early as the mid 1830s, and he knew they could effectively shatter the isolation of Chicago and the nation. Even the canal he backed–the 100-mile Illinois & Michigan–developed into a viable transportation artery and, in the 1850s and 1860s especially, contributed to Chicago's growth and overall well-being. The thoughts of diplomat Elihu B. Washburne, written in 1881, three years after Ogden's death, capture the essence of this railroad pioneer:

> Mr. Ogden was a man of education, intelligence, and refinement. As a businessman he had broad and enlightened views, a bold spirit, and unerring sagacity of courtly and polished manners. There is no society in the world he would not have adorned. As a conversationalist, I have hardly ever known his superior, or even his equal. If a public speaker is to be measured by results accomplished, there were few men ever more happy or more successful.

References:

Isaac N. Arnold, *William B. Ogden: Early Days in Chicago* (Chicago: Fergus Printing Co., 1881);

Thomas Wakefield Goodspeed, *The University of Chicago Biographical Sketches* (Chicago: University of Chicago Press, 1922);

W. H. Stennet, comp., *Yesterday and To-day: A History of the Chicago & North Western Railway System* (Chicago: Rand, McNally, 1910).

Archives:

The bulk of William B. Ogden's personal and business papers was destroyed in the Chicago fire of October 1871.

William Henry Osborn

(December 21, 1820-March 2, 1894)

by John F. Stover

Purdue University

CAREER: Director (1854-1877); vice-president (1855), president, Illinois Central Railroad (1855-1865); president, Chicago, St. Louis & New Orleans Railroad (1877-1882).

William H. Osborn, railroad promoter and president, was born December 21, 1820, in Salem, Massachusetts, the son of William and Anna Henfield (Bowditch) Osborn. His father was a farmer and came from an old New England family. The young Osborn, after a few years of attendance at the local rural elementary and high schools in Salem, gave up formal education at the age of thirteen to become a clerk in the East India House of Peele, Hubbell & Company of Boston. At the age of sixteen William Osborn was representing his company in Manila, Philippine Islands. While still in his twenties Osborn set up his own import-export firm in Manila. The firm prospered, and Osborn amassed a modest fortune by the time he was thirty-two. He left the islands, toured Europe, and returned to the United States in 1853.

In New York Osborn met Jonathan Sturges, a merchant with whom he had done business while in Manila. On December 14, 1853, Osborn married Sturges's daughter, Virginia Reed, and after a honeymoon in Europe the bride and groom established their home in New York City. Jonathan Sturges had been one of the original incorporators of the Illinois Central (IC) Railroad in 1851 and was still active in the affairs of the railroad. Sturges introduced his son-in-law to the directors of the Illinois Central, and he was elected a director on August 11, 1854, a position he would hold until 1877. Ten months later he was elected vice-president, and on December 1, 1855, he was elected president of the Illinois Central, an office he would retain until July 1865.

Even though the Illinois Central had been aided by an 1850 federal land grant, the IC's posi-

William Henry Osborn

tion in 1854 was precarious. It was a disconnected, unfinished line of 300 miles, had a floating debt of $2.5 million, and was trying to recover from a financial scandal involving its first president, Robert Schuyler. Osborn came to the Illinois Central without any railroad experience, but he learned quickly. He quickly showed an ability to master the management details of railroading and was particularly effective in financial matters. Osborn insisted on completing the charter lines of the IC with short-term loans rather than assessing shareholders up to the par value of the stock. By 1855 more than 600 miles of line were constructed, and late in September 1856 the last rails of the 705-mile road were spiked into place. The completed Illinois Central was the longest railroad in the world. When the panic of 1857 reduced traffic, the newly completed Illinois Central was faced with $4 million of short-term obligations that had little hope of being renewed. Osborn avoided receivership for the IC by reassuring the foreign bondholders, assessing the common stock up to par, and using his own credit to support the obligations of the railroad. In 1856 Osborn had made Capt. George B. McClellan the chief engineer for the IC with the understanding he would become vice-president once he was familiar with the line. With Osborn in New York City much of the time, Vice-President (after December 1857) McClellan was in charge of the effort to cut operating expenses wherever possible. The worst of the crisis was over by 1858 and 1859, and by 1860 freight tonnage on the Illinois Central had increased a third above that of 1857.

The dominant and controlling personality of William Osborn had managed not only to complete the IC but also to pull the line through the panic of 1857. William K. Ackerman, company secretary and treasurer during Osborn's presidency, later wrote that "the people of the state of Illinois have never known what a debt of gratitude they owe to Mr. Osborn for ... saving the road to the State." Osborn also led the Illinois Central during the four years of the Civil War. The north-south line of the Illinois Central became very busy with the coming of the conflict. Cairo, at the mouth of the Ohio, was one of the four railway gateways to the South, and its location almost made it like a pistol aimed down the Mississippi at the lower Confederacy. Soon the IC was crowded with troops and supplies as Gen. U. S. Grant planned his river campaign against Fort Henry and Fort Donelson.

Troops from Iowa, Minnesota, Wisconsin, and Illinois moved south through Cairo on their way to southern battlefields. Troop train revenue reached $410,000 in 1862, and total revenue on the IC increased from about $4 million in 1861 to nearly $8 million in 1865. Dividends, which were $4 a year in 1861 and 1862, rose to $6 in 1863, $8 in 1864, and $10 in 1865. The wartime prosperity permitted Osborn to pay off more than $2 million of the funded debt. During the war years, 1861 through 1865, Illinois Central land agents sold off more than 800,000 acres of their land grant for more than $9 million. Osborn wrote a fellow IC director to advise buyers "to take small parcels, thus ... the land actually sold will be cultivated and add largely to the value of adjoining lands." In midsummer 1865 William Osborn, worn out from his successes, resigned as president of the Illinois Central but retained his position on the board. For the next dozen years he continued to play a dominant role in guiding the policy of the railroad.

Since the completion of the charter lines in 1856 there had been no growth in the mileage of the Illinois Central. Osborn had far less interest in extending the IC into Iowa than some of his fellow directors. He was, however, interested in rail connections south of Cairo and in 1858 and 1859 had successfully urged George Peabody of London to help finance the completion of the 238-mile Mississippi Central, a road running from Canton, Mississippi, north to Jackson, Tennessee. South of Canton the connecting 206-mile New Orleans, Jackson & Great Northern gave service South to New Orleans. Both of the southern lines were badly damaged by the war, but by the late 1860s Gen. P. G. T. Beauregard was reviving the New Orleans, Jackson & Great Northern, while a northern carpetbagger, Col. Henry S. McComb, was in control of the Mississippi Central. By 1870 McComb had acquired the bulk of the stock of Beauregard's line and was in control of both roads. In 1872 Osborn inspected both of the southern roads and urged the IC to extend financial assistance to McComb, with some of the money to be used to build a 104-mile extension north from Jackson, Tennessee, to East Cairo, Kentucky. The depression following the panic of 1873 finally forced McComb's railroads into receivership in 1876. William Osborn was busy protecting the interests of the Illinois Central in the South and led the IC group, which purchased both lines during 1877. In November 1877 the two recently purchased southern lines were merged into the Chicago, St. Louis & New Orleans (CSL&NO) Railroad. Osborn was elected president of the consolidated line, and seven of the twelve board members were Illinois Central men. On a single day, July 29, 1881, James C. Clarke, IC vice-president and general manager of the southern line, directed the changing of the gauge of the 550-mile CSL&NO from the broader 5-foot gauge to the standard 4-foot 8½-inch gauge. Late in 1882 the Illinois Central negotiated a 400-year lease of the Chicago, St. Louis & New Orleans, and William Osborn retired as president of the southern line.

During his twenty-eight years with the line, Osborn was the dominant influence in the development of the Illinois Central. Though he was often not easy to work with, Osborn, more than any other figure, made the Illinois Central into a prosperous mid-American trunk line. Retiring to New York, Osborn devoted himself to philanthropy, bestowing gifts to the New York Hospital and the Bellevue Training School for Nurses. He died in New York City on March 2, 1894, survived by his wife and two of his four children.

References:
Thomas C. Cochran, *Railroad Leaders: 1845-1890* (Cambridge, Mass.: Harvard University Press, 1953);
Carlton J. Corliss, *Main Line of Mid-America: The Story of the Illinois Central* (New York: Creative Age Press, 1950);
John F. Stover, *History of the Illinois Central Railroad* (New York: Macmillan, 1975).

Archives:
Material concerning Osborn is located in the Illinois Central Records of the Newberry Library, Chicago, Illinois.

Asa Packer

(December 29, 1805-May 17, 1879)

by Richard W. Barsness

Lehigh University

CAREER: Farmer, carpenter (1822-1833); boat builder, shipper (1833-1843?); investor, operator, Pennsylvania coal properties (1839-1879); member, Pennsylvania house of representatives (1841-1842); associate judge, Carbon County, Pennsylvania (1843-1848); member, board of managers, Lehigh Valley Railroad (1851-1879); member, U.S. House of Representatives (1852-1856); president, Lehigh Valley Railroad (1854-1879).

Asa Packer was a mid-nineteenth-century Pennsylvania canal boat operator, merchant, and political figure who built the highly successful Lehigh Valley Railroad and achieved great wealth. Packer devoted an important portion of his fortune to philanthropic activities, the most notable of which was the establishment of Lehigh University.

Packer was born December 29, 1805, in Mystic, Connecticut, the son of Elisha, Jr. and Desire (Packer) Packer. Asa was a sixth generation direct descendant of John Packer, who, emigrating from England to the Massachusetts Bay Colony, had moved to Connecticut in 1651. The Packers were prominent in the community of Groton, Connecticut, for several generations, but this record of accomplishment did not carry through to Packer's father, who was unsuccessful in business. Packer also suffered

the misfortune of his mother's death in 1811, when he was only six years old.

Packer received only rudimentary schooling and became well acquainted with hard work at an early age. He obtained employment in a tannery and made excellent progress, but this arrangement ended when the owner died. He also experimented with farming, but found the results disappointing. In 1822, discouraged with prospects in Connecticut, the seventeen-year-old Packer set out on foot for remote Susquehanna County in northeastern Pennsylvania, which had been colonized by settlers from Connecticut some years previously.

Packer's objective was the home of a cousin, Edward Packer, a carpenter, who accepted Asa as an apprentice. He purchased land at nearby Springville, Pennsylvania, and built a cabin which served as his home for several years. He worked hard, cleared land, did some farming, and developed his carpentry skills, which he practiced briefly in New York City. On January 23, 1828, he married Sarah M. Blakslee, the daughter of a Schuylkill Township farmer. Asa and Sarah subsequently had two daughters and two sons: Lucy E. (1832), Mary (1839), Robert A. (1842), and Harry E. (1850).

Asa Packer was a man of simple tastes and straightforward virtues; he also possessed a high degree of energy, ambition, and foresight. In 1833 he

Asa Packer

moved his family southward to Mauch Chunk (now Jim Thorpe) on the upper Lehigh River. The newly developing anthracite coal industry and the completion of the Lehigh Canal in 1829 had transformed Mauch Chunk into a booming mining community. The superior qualities of anthracite had created a huge potential market for the fuel, and the Lehigh Canal, which connected with other canals at Easton on the Delaware River, made it economically feasible to transport anthracite to Philadelphia and other mid-Atlantic cities.

As a tradesman Packer quickly found employment building canal boats. Before long he chartered a boat for himself and began carrying coal from Mauch Chunk to Philadelphia. When this proved successful he chartered a second boat, and soon moved on to additional enterprises, including opening a general merchandise store in Mauch Chunk, establishing a boatyard for the construction and repair of canal boats, undertaking construction contracts for canal locks, and investing in mining properties. Packer's ability to expand his business activities was facilitated by successful collaboration with others, including his younger brother Robert W. and brother-in-law James I. Blakslee.

Asa and Robert Packer extended their operations to nearby Pottsville in 1838 where they built boats for the Schuylkill Canal and provided transportation service along that route to Philadelphia. The Packers were reputedly the first to send coal in unbroken cargoes from the Lehigh region into the metropolitan New York market. They also began leasing and working coal lands such as the Room Run mines of the Lehigh Coal & Navigation Company (the "Old Company") in 1839. The brothers parted ways (apparently in 1843 by mutual agreement), with Robert taking the activities centered around Pottsville and the Schuylkill Valley, and Asa remaining in the Lehigh Valley. By the time of Robert's death in 1848 mine production had increased significantly, and Asa had entered into new ventures with other parties.

By the early 1840s Asa Packer had become a leading citizen in Mauch Chunk. He was elected to the Pennsylvania legislature in 1841 and reelected in 1842. In Harrisburg he led the successful effort to establish Carbon County with Mauch Chunk as its county seat. In 1843 Packer began a five-year term as associate judge of Carbon County, thereby acquiring the title of Judge by which he was known for the remainder of his life.

As a businessman Packer was prepared to take physical as well as financial risks. One widely reported incident occurred in 1843 when boatmen on the Lehigh Canal tied up several hundred boats between Easton and Freemansburg and went on strike for higher wages. Packer and other contractors enlisted strikebreakers, the county sheriff, magistrates, and constables to reopen the canal. When Packer and others tried to untie a boat, a mob of angry strikers threw Packer into the river. While he swam to safety the rest of the party fled under a barrage of stones and other missiles from the strikers.

Although important technological improvements occurred in anthracite mining and transportation during the 1830s and 1840s, railroad promotion in the Lehigh Valley lagged due to the geography of the local fields, efficient operation of the Lehigh Canal, and the vested interests of the Lehigh Coal & Navigation Company (the dominant firm in the valley). However, the undeniable advantages of railroad transportation and successful development of such lines as the Philadelphia & Reading in the neighboring Schuylkill Valley attracted growing interest among a group of Lehigh Valley businessmen, including Asa Packer.

In 1846 the businessmen secured a charter from the legislature for a railroad along the Lehigh River to be called the Delaware, Lehigh, Schuylkill & Susquehanna. Five years passed, however, without serious efforts to proceed with the venture. In 1851, with the charter about to expire for lack of tangible progress, Packer moved decisively to the forefront. In April he became a member of the board of managers. In succeeding months he acquired much of the outstanding stock, promoted further subscriptions, and performed sufficient grading to save the charter. Construction activity moved into high gear late the following year.

Packer faced many difficulties during the construction of the railroad, which in 1853 was renamed the Lehigh Valley Railroad. Even though his own financial resources were entirely committed to the project, he found relatively little support from other investors. The terrain presented serious difficulties, cholera broke out in 1854 among the workers, and inflation and other factors caused major problems with subcontractors. The Lehigh Coal & Navigation Company presented further complications by its haggling over rights-of-way for connections and terminals. It took both Packer's firsthand knowledge of the construction business and his energy, determination, and willingness to risk everything to achieve success. Construction was completed in 1855 and regular service on the 46-mile main line between Easton and Mauch Chunk began in September 1855. At Easton the Lehigh Valley connected with other carriers reaching Philadelphia and New York.

As part of his transition from wealthy, small-town businessman into railroad leader, Packer spent considerable time in Philadelphia, New York, and Washington developing ties with financiers and other business interests important to the future success of the Lehigh Valley Railroad. These ties included valuable friendships with the leaders of the Jersey Central, the Camden & Amboy, and the Philadelphia & Trenton railroads, all of whom saw the Lehigh Valley's access to the anthracite region as mutually beneficial.

Probably the most paradoxical aspect of Asa Packer's construction of the Lehigh Valley Railroad was that he chose to resume active public service during this same period of time. Packer was elected to the U. S. House of Representatives in 1852 as a Democrat from the thirteenth District of Pennsylvania, and served two terms from 1853 to 1857. Why he wished to do so at a time of such intense business activity, and what he gained from the experience, are puzzles that remain to be solved. In any event his service appears to have been quite unremarkable. He was often absent from the floor of the House, spoke infrequently, and held only routine committee assignments.

In the course of his many business ventures Packer formed a cadre of capable assistants, several of whom were related to him by blood or marriage. The latter included his brother Robert, brother-in-law James I. Blakslee, son-in-law Dr. Garrett B. Linderman, nephew Elisha P. Wilbur, and sons Robert and Harry. These and other key lieutenants helped Packer move from one business success to another with few setbacks. In the case of the Lehigh Valley Railroad, business success meant upgrading and extending the original main line, acquiring and consolidating short lines, establishing interchanges with other important carriers, adding branch lines, and promoting the railroad's principal commodity, anthracite coal.

Packer encouraged a "fraternal spirit" among his employees and demonstrated a strong sense of community. Although his business success reputedly made him the wealthiest individual in Pennsylvania, he continued to work hard and live modestly in comparison with many of his industrial peers. Packer was also a deeply religious man. He served as vestryman in St. Mark's Episcopal Church in Mauch Chunk for forty-three years, was a generous benefactor of St. Luke's Episcopal Hospital in Bethlehem, and funded many other Episcopal activities in the region.

Asa Packer's most significant philanthropic enterprise, both in scale and impact, was the founding of Lehigh University in Bethlehem, Pennsylvania. Packer was motivated by a desire to provide educational opportunity and moral guidance for young men, to benefit the region where his business operations were centered, and to help develop the talent needed by the nation's new industrial enterprises. He sought the assistance of the Protestant Episcopal Diocese of Pennsylvania in developing plans and leadership for the new university, which received a state charter and opened for instruction in 1866.

The founder's gifts to Lehigh, which initially consisted of $500,000 and fifty-six acres of land, eventually totaled some $3 million in gifts and bequests. Packer's enlightened generosity was quite unprecedented in its day, yet he explicitly refused to allow the trustees to name the university after him, preferring that the university be named Lehigh.

At the 1868 Democratic National Convention the Pennsylvania delegation enthusiastically nominated Packer as a favorite son candidate for president. The delegation continued to support Packer until the fifteenth ballot, when it switched to Gen. Winfield Scott Hancock. A year later Packer became the Democratic candidate for governor of Pennsylvania. Although he did relatively little campaigning, he lost the election to incumbent governor John W. Geary by fewer than 5,000 votes. Perhaps the outcome was not wholly disappointing, for neither Asa nor Sarah Packer enjoyed society, and electoral success almost certainly would have required a radical change in lifestyle.

Primary sources regarding Asa Packer's life are scanty. He wrote few letters, spoke infrequently in public, and apparently made no effort to augment or correct accounts about his career which appeared during his lifetime. Notwithstanding occasional inconsistencies and gaps in information, both contemporary and subsequent accounts agree that Packer was a strong-willed individual with a high degree of integrity. He demonstrated outstanding initiative and determination, placed his own capital at great risk, and built his various enterprises from the ground up. Interestingly his high regard for "rugged individualism" co-existed with his paternalistic concern for family and community. Asa Packer became wealthy, but unlike many other new industrial leaders, indulged little in conspicuous consumption. He was a man of action whose work was his hobby as well as his vocation. He kept similarly close check on his philanthropic endeavors, particularly Lehigh University.

The centerpiece of Packer's long career unquestionably was the Lehigh Valley Railroad, of which he served as president for a quarter of a century. By the late 1870s the Lehigh Valley's 658-mile system extended from the seaboard in New Jersey through eastern Pennsylvania and into New York State. The company's capital account amounted to some $53 million.

In 1875, four years before his death, Packer prepared a last will and testament which reflected his determination that his achievement in developing the railroad be preserved far into the future by the five trustees of his estate (which included his two sons Robert and Harry and nephew Elisha P. Wilbur). Packer wanted the trustees to promote the further progress of the railroad and of the family and community interests with which it was affiliated:

> I have spent a large part of my life in projecting and building up the Lehigh Valley Railroad. It has been remunerative to me, the stockholders have given me their confidence and I have a deep interest in its future welfare and prosperity and in the welfare of those who have invested in it and have been associated with me in the enterprise.

When Asa Packer died at his Philadelphia residence in 1879, his legacy was a record of many business achievements: a railroad in sound physical and financial condition, a new university which blended classical education with the practical requirements of the new industrial age, and a capable group of associates whose responsibility was to use Packer's fortune to continue the progress of his various enterprises. The trustees of the estate did not disappoint him.

References:

Fred Brenckman, *History of Carbon County, Pennsylvania* (Harrisburg, Pa.: James J. Nungesser, 1913);

Milton C. Stuart, *Asa Packer, 1805-1879* (Princeton: Princeton University Press, 1938);

W. Ross Yates, *Asa Packer: A Perspective* (Bethlehem, Pa.: Lehigh University Press, 1983).

Archives:

Material concerning Asa Packer is located in the Asa Packer Memorabilia Collection of the Rare Book Room, Linderman Library at Lehigh University, Bethlehem, Pennsylvania; and in the Asa Packer Memorabilia of the Canal Museum at Easton, Pennsylvania.

William Jackson Palmer

(September 17, 1836-March 13, 1909)

by Jackson C. Thode

Denver & Rio Grande Western R. R.

CAREER: Brevet brigadier general of cavalry, U.S. Army (1864-1865); Congressional Medal of Honor (1865); treasurer and managing director, Kansas Pacific Railway (1865-1870); organizer and president, Denver & Rio Grande Railway (Colorado) (1870-1883); founder of Colorado Springs, Colorado (1871); organizer and president, Colorado Coal & Iron Company (1880-1884); organizer and president, Mexican National Railway (1880-1887); organizer and president, Denver & Rio Grande Western Railway (Utah) (1881-1889); president, Rio Grande Western Railway (1889-1901).

William Jackson Palmer, a daring Civil War Union cavalry commander while still in his twenties, after the war became the preeminent railroad builder in, and driving force in the development of, southern and western Colorado. In like fashion he wielded great influence on railroad construction and growth in eastern Utah and in northern Mexico. Born September 17, 1836, to Quaker parents, John and Matilda Jackson Palmer, on their farm in Kinsale, Delaware, Palmer died at Colorado Springs, Colorado, on March 13, 1909, at the age of seventy-two.

His early life was shared with two brothers and a sister; when he was five the family moved to the Germantown section of Philadelphia, where he was educated. Following primary schooling at the Friends' School and the Zane Street Grammar School, he entered the Boy's High School in February 1849 as the youngest member in his class. In 1853 William Palmer, seventeen years old, joined the engineering corps of the Hempfield Railroad, then locating its line through the Allegheny Mountains of Pennsylvania under the guidance of the distinguished civil engineer, Charles Ellett. With this elementary taste of railroading in his blood, he sailed to England in the summer of 1855 to study the railways and mines of that country. Palmer fi-

William Jackson Palmer (photograph by Harry L. Standley, courtesy of the Collection of Charles E. Tutt Library, The Colorado College, Colorado Springs, Colorado)

nanced his trip, in part, by an arrangement with the *Miner's Journal* of Pottsville, Pennsylvania, whose editor agreed to print and pay for any of the young man's interesting writings pertaining to English coal mines and mining methods. With some supplemental monetary help from relatives, and armed with letters of introduction from Friends in Philadelphia to Quakers in England, as well as from Charles Ellett to English businessmen and mine owners and engineers, the enterprising nineteen-year-old debarked from the sailing ship *Tuscarora* at Liverpool on June 21, 1855.

During the next two months Palmer toured on foot the industrial regions of northern England, visiting and studying the iron foundries, canal works, collieries, mines, and coking installations. His curiosity extended also to the English common folk encountered in his wanderings, and he came greatly to enjoy those contacts and experiences. In the evenings his articles for the *Miner's Journal* were assembled and roughed out or finished; twelve articles at $4 each would pay his fare home.

On August 20 he at last reached London and learned that his old Hempfield mentor, Charles Ellett, was in the city with his family. Enjoying the hospitality and friendship of these and other new American acquaintances during the next two weeks, he familiarized himself with the great city and its sights, then left for more investigations in the Midlands and Wales. Now he learned that his articles for the *Miner's Journal* were attracting attention. J. Edgar Thomson, president of the Pennsylvania Railroad, was sufficiently impressed with Palmer's writings to request the young man to investigate the use of burning coal in locomotives to replace the wood fuel then in use. Thomson also suggested that Palmer join the payroll of the Pennsylvania when he returned to the United States.

In visiting the vast workings of the South Wales mines and ironworks Palmer was introduced to the operations of the little 1-foot 11½-inch gauge Festiniog Railway serving the slate quarries above Porthmadog. The impressions and information gained there were to play a vital part in his introduction and development of the unknown and untried 3-foot narrow gauge in Colorado's Denver & Rio Grande Railway some fifteen years in the future.

In November and December 1855 he visited Paris where his letters of introduction resulted in rides on locomotives, one at night during which he noted the fireman saved steam and labor by leaning sleepily on the safety valve. Back in London in early 1856 Palmer's expanding acquaintance with influential citizens resulted in his attendance at meetings of the Royal Society, the Institute of Civil Engineers, the Geological Society, and the London Institution, witnessing appearances by such legendary professionals as Robert Stephenson, M. P., Sir John Rennie, and Isambard Kingdom Brunel. Visits to the tin mines of Cornwall followed, but after almost a full year the touring, studying, and writing came to an end. Departing Liverpool on the mer-

chant ship *Pam Flush* on April 18, 1856, he arrived at home near the end of May.

In July of 1856 he joined the Westmoreland Coal Company at a salary of $600 per year; the following December 15 he was elected secretary of the company. Resigning this position on May 19, 1857, he was hired to be the confidential secretary to Pres. John Edgar Thomson of the Pennsylvania Railroad, with a salary of $900 per year. Palmer remained with Thomson until mid 1861, much of his time devoted to successful experiments with burning coal in steam locomotives, leading to the adoption of coal in place of wood as the principal fuel on the railroad.

During all these early years of his working life Palmer continued his close association with the Society of Friends and the Quaker precepts under which he had been raised. But with the outbreak of the Civil War in 1861, his conscience, after weeks of pondering and deep contemplation, demanded his participation in the conflict as a Union soldier. In explaining his feelings to his mother she could only counsel, sadly, "William, if thee must fight, fight well!"

Palmer devised a plan for enlisting a troop of young men picked to serve as a light cavalry unit, to be offered for duty as escort and bodyguard to Gen. Robert Anderson (of Fort Sumter fame), now in command of the Army of the Ohio. Officers of Palmer's troop were to be elected by a fair vote of the members. He solicited his own friends to join, and asked for nominations for other volunteers. The ranks filled rapidly. Before the men here mustered into service, the election of officers for the troop was held, and Palmer himself was elected captain. He had just turned twenty-five.

Enlistment took place in September, and the Anderson troop mustered at Carlisle Barracks November 30, 1861. On December 2 they left for the West, arriving at Louisville, Kentucky, on December 6. A few days later the troop received its horses and settled down to the routine of training, drill, and discipline.

The service of the Anderson troop so pleased Gen. Don Carlos Buell, in command of the Army of the Ohio during the Shiloh and Corinth campaigns in the spring of 1862, that he gave a further assignment to Captain Palmer. Ordered back to Pennsylvania in late July, Palmer was to enlist a battalion of new men, selected in the same fashion as the original Anderson troop. So rapid was the success of this effort that Palmer requested, and was authorized, to enlarge the group to regimental size. The new men, carefully picked and primarily from educated, middle-class families, were enlisted "for special service." In ten days he raised a regiment of 1,200 men. As the 15th Pennsylvania Volunteer Cavalry they were mustered into U.S. service August 22, 1862. On September 8 Palmer was promoted to colonel and given command of the new cavalry regiment.

Palmer's promotion nearly coincided with the first Confederate invasion of the Union. At the awful battle of Antietam the rebels were halted. During the uncertain days following that bloody struggle, Colonel Palmer, in a "fit of injudicious patriotism," slipped through the opposing lines in an attempt to learn something of the enemy's course of action and report back. Before he could return, however, his hideout was discovered, and he was taken prisoner September 19.

Adroitly and successfully concealing his true identity, Palmer was imprisoned at "Castle Thunder," an old tobacco warehouse in Richmond, Virginia. During his incarceration there he again endured several narrow, nerve-wracking escapes from being truly identified to the Confederates. Exchanged, at last, for a Richmond civilian held by the North, Palmer returned to the federal lines on January 15, 1863. Early the next month he was able to rejoin his 15th Pennsylvania Cavalry, which had moved west the preceding November for assignment to the Army of the Cumberland, under the command of Gen. William S. Rosecrans at Nashville.

In the absence of their organizing commander, the new Pennsylvania enlistees had suffered. Lacking training and adequate leadership and with their "special service" status unrecognized by General Rosecrans, the eleven companies were dispersed throughout the army, and their morale was shattered. When ordered forward as foot soldiers in the Stone River campaign around Murfreesborough in January 1863, many refused to move, complaining that this was not the "Special Service" for which they had enlisted.

Such was the scene of insurrection, mutiny, and chaos confronting Palmer when he resumed command of the 15th Pennsylvania after his unwilling absence and imprisonment. By the end of May he had reorganized his regiment. Discipline was enforced, drilling and training diligently pursued. New officers were appointed, many later to become close associates in his ventures on the western frontier after the war.

By June 1863, to paraphrase the unit's published history, the regiment was ready to embark upon a career of activity and independent scouting which earned for it a name and fame that brought it renown throughout the Army of the Cumberland for fearlessness and bravery.

Following the Union victories at Chicamauga and Chattanooga in late 1863, Colonel Palmer was ordered east to Knoxville. His command was composed of only 175 of his own men who still had good horses, along with 100 men from the 10th Ohio Volunteer cavalry. The expedition, originally supplied with just ten days of rations, endured seventy days of severe winter campaigning and covered approximately 1,000 miles in day and nighttime operations. One foray in January 1864 resulted in the capture of Brig. Gen. Robert B. Vance, C. S. A., and his staff, along with 96 additional prisoners and many supply wagons, without loss of a single man from the Union force. The success of this exploit prompted the first recommendation for Palmer's promotion to brigadier general. Despite being enthusiastically endorsed to President Lincoln, the promotion was not confirmed by the U. S. Senate.

In the following year and a half Palmer's troopers earned much renown for their skill, fearlessness, and daring in cavalry warfare. Typical of their self-assured, brazen audacity in action was a predawn raid riding between two encamped rebel regiments, one on either side of the road. Holding their sabers to prevent noise, they passed through the sleeping enemy camps and broke into a trot. Suddenly a guard called out, "What are you fellers in such a hurry about?" A Palmer man, unseen in the darkness, answered, "We are always that way!" The guard, again: "What regiment is that?" The response: "The same old regiment with new clothes on!" By that time they were beyond their challenger and proceeded on their mission behind the enemy line at an even faster pace.

In October 1864 Palmer led seventy-five hand-picked men on a perilous cavalry venture from eastern Tennessee into Virginia and Kentucky, carrying dispatches and orders for Gen. Stephen Burbridge, whose whereabouts were unknown. In accomplishing its goal, the small Union command, constantly fighting off rebel guerrillas, bushwhackers, and a Confederate cavalry force, covered some 225 miles through an almost impassable region during a period of only seven days. Those of the 15th Pennsylvania left behind were anxious over their colonel's absence, one commenting in a letter home, "when he has to leave us we realize our loss, and all agree that no man can command us like he can."

After Confederate Gen. John B. Hood's Army of the Tennessee was routed by Gen. George H. Thomas's Army of the Cumberland at Nashville in December 1864, Palmer and his regiment were ordered to Decatur, Alabama, to join in blocking Hood's retreat by destroying his pontoon bridge over the Tennessee River. That objective failing, Palmer received permission to proceed at his own risk in an effort to find and capture or destroy the enemy pontoon boats and wagons. With less than 600 men operating in silence at night through hostile territory in freezing, nasty, winter weather, on New Year's Eve they found and burned 78 pontoon boats and 200 wagons, many loaded with plunder and supplies. The next night another train of 100 wagons was found, attacked, and destroyed.

When news of this successful engagement reached Gen. William T. Sherman during his march to the sea, his praise of the 15th Pennsylvania was unbounded: "They can ride faster, do more hard fighting and capture more wagon trains than any regiment in my command."

Almost immediately upon their return from that foray Colonel Palmer and 150 members of his unit were ordered to pursue a 300-man cavalry brigade of the notorious rebel general Nathan Bedford Forrest. The small Union force, worn and weary from its exertions just completed, was called to boots and saddles the night of January 11, 1865, to proceed on their new mission. At daylight on September 15 their quarry was found in camp at Red Hill, Alabama. The Palmer men, formed into three groups, each to attack from a different direction, charged immediately and captured or scattered the entire rebel force while the advance guard went on to the quarters of the brigade commander, Gen. Hyland B. Lyon. Upon capture this officer requested and was given permission to obtain his uniform; instead he procured his pistol, killed his Pennsylvania captor with one shot, and escaped. The prizes from this audacious six-day Union venture included six Confederate officers and over 100 enlisted men taken prisoner, a 12-pound artillery piece, "besides 100 good horses and a lot of plunder they had stolen in Kentucky...."

During those winter months Palmer came to his full stature as a soldier, revealing his quickness of decision, his eye for the country, and the drive and daring and power of his leadership. For these outstanding successes Palmer again was recommended for promotion by his commanding general, George H. Thomas, of the Army of the Cumberland. This time, effective November 4, 1864, seven weeks after his twenty-eighth birthday, Palmer was breveted brigadier general. Subsequently he was awarded the Congressional Medal of Honor for "distinguished gallantry in action near Red Hill, Alabama, January 14, 1865."

General Lee surrendered his Army of Northern Virginia to General Grant at Appomattox Court House on April 9, 1865, resulting in the collapse of the Confederate government. General Palmer, now in command of a brigade composed of the 15th Pennsylvania, 10th Michigan, and 12th Ohio cavalries, was ordered to join in the Union efforts to find and capture Confederate president Jefferson Davis and his 1,600-man cavalry escort as they attempted to escape and join still active rebel forces in Alabama.

The 12th Ohio captured C. S. A. Maj. Gen. Joseph Wheeler, leader of the cavalry, and his staff on May 9, 1865. The next day a small detachment of the 15th Pennsylvania captured Confederate Gen. Braxton Bragg and his wife. That southern lady, distraught and monumentally displeased, harangued her captors over her disgrace at having been taken captive by a Philadelphia fireman! That same day it all came to an end. The Confederate president, his wife, and remnants of his escort were captured by the 4th Michigan cavalry near Irwinville, Georgia.

The 15th Pennsylvania was mustered out and disbanded at Nashville, Tennessee, on June 19, 1865. General Palmer, termed by his old commander Gen. George Thomas as "the best cavalry officer in the service," was urged by that gallant old soldier to stay in the army. But Palmer's prewar interest and experience in railroading prevailed; after considering numerous offers in that field, in August 1865 he joined the Union Pacific, Eastern Division, as treasurer at St. Louis, Missouri.

As the line slowly progressed west from Kansas City across the prairies, Palmer became the prime factor in arranging and managing the necessary financing. In the spring of 1867, after the line had reached Salina, Kansas, 185 miles beyond the

Missouri, the directors arranged for surveys to determine the most feasible routes for the westward extension of the line. The expedition began in June; General Palmer joined the parties near Trinidad, Colorado, as leader in early August. Careful investigations of the passes over the southern Rocky Mountains were completed to Santa Fe and Albuquerque, then explorations on west to the Pacific Coast along both the 35th and 32nd parallels were undertaken.

After weeks of hair-raising, life-threatening adventure–attacks by Apache indians in ambush, loss of animals over edges of cliffs, hostile winter weather, days of hunger while lost in the barren, desolate wilds of Arizona and lower California–the parties reached San Francisco in late January 1868. On February 21 Palmer and two associates returned east, riding sleighs and stagecoaches across Donner Pass and the Nevada, Utah, and Wyoming deserts. On March 20 they completed the circle, reaching their original starting point in Kansas.

Palmer's *Report of Surveys Across the Continent,* published in 1869, discussed a total length of 4,464 miles of routes accurately surveyed, chained, and leveled by instrument during the nine-month campaign. Never utilized by the Kansas road, the surveys of the far western portions nonetheless proved of great value to other lines which later built through the country he had explored and mapped so carefully.

At the annual meeting of the railroad's stockholders on April 5, 1869, the name of the company was changed to the Kansas Pacific Railway, and Palmer was elected a director. Given his choice of positions as financial officer or construction manager, he chose to oversee construction of the line west toward Denver.

During the preceding six and one-half years the company had built 394 miles of road extending from Kansas City to Sheridan, Kansas. General Palmer, in his new position, established headquarters at Sheridan and promptly set to work, faced with constructing some 235 additional miles of railroad. Supplies of track ties, consumed at a rate of 2,500 per mile, became the greatest problem, for many had to be wagoned 400 to 600 miles from their sources. Keeping a sufficiently large force of laborers likewise presented difficulties in a region so remote from population centers. Raids by Plains Indians on surveying, grading, and track-laying crews further compounded his problems.

Construction east from Denver, which in June of 1870 achieved connection via the Denver Pacific with the Union Pacific at Cheyenne, Wyoming, was of great help in speeding construction. When the east and west extensions of the Kansas Pacific met on August 15, 1870, near present-day Strasburg, Colorado, little more than a year from the start at Sheridan, the road was completed. Close to the end of the project Denver's *Rocky Mountain News* said of General Palmer, that "It is his mind that has organized, his energy that has pressed and his enterprise that is completing the great work."

During the two years 1869 and 1870 General Palmer's attentions were thrust in yet another direction. In spring of the former year he met William Proctor Mellen, visiting the west with his nineteen-year-old daughter, Mary Lincoln, nicknamed "Queen." Mellen's prominence derived from his prewar law partnership in Cincinnati with Salmon P. Chase, who served as secretary of the treasury under President Lincoln and then as chief justice of the U. S. Supreme Court.

Palmer, now thirty-two years old, was smitten with the beautiful young lady accompanying her father. His avid pursuit for her hand was successful, and in a few weeks their engagement was announced. They agreed, however, that their marriage would be postponed until Palmer's work on the Kansas Pacific (KP) was completed.

The decision to build the KP directly to Denver disappointed Palmer. Having given so much to the earlier southwest surveys, he proposed a route southward to the Arkansas River to capture the trade on the Santa Fe Trail, then north to Denver. Unable to persuade the directors into such a scheme, he gradually developed in his mind the concept of a north-south line of his own, extending along the east base of the Rocky Mountains from Denver to El Paso, Texas, then on to Mexico City. To pursue his project Palmer resigned from the Kansas Pacific on May 4, 1870, to become effective August 15 when it was predicted the Denver extension would be completed.

No time was lost in the formation of Palmer's own company; on October 27, 1870, the certificate of incorporation for The Denver & Rio Grande (D&RG) Railway was filed with the secretary of Colorado Territory. The proposed line was to extend south from Denver, then west over the mountains to the Rio Grande del Norte in the San Luis Valley.

Following the river to Texas, the railroad would connect with another line built north-south in Mexico.

Two striking features were evident. The D&RG was to be the first railway west of the Missouri built without government subsidy. No federal land grants or bonds or guarantees were involved, but only a right-of-way 200 feet wide through the public domain, with 20 acres of ground every ten miles for station purposes. Second, a narrow-gauge 3-foot track was to be used, in sharp contrast to the standard 4-foot 8½-inch track most commonly used in the country. The narrow gauge was a new, daring, and untried idea, but it promised lower construction costs and much greater adaptability to its mountain environment than did standard gauge.

With such details settled Palmer journeyed east. On November 7, 1870, he and "Queen" Mellen were married at her father's home in Flushing, New York. The next day the couple sailed for England, where Palmer, to the neglect of his new bride, devoted a great deal of time to the successful solicitation of funds from wealthy British and Dutch investors for his railroad proposition.

Upon their return in March, Queen Palmer remained in the east while her husband proceeded on to Denver. Fifteen of his old 15th Pennsylvania cavalry companions, as well as several of his KP associates, were now involved in building the Denver & Rio Grande. Ancillary land and development companies were organized to locate and acquire town sites and natural resource properties along the proposed route. Stockholders in the railroad were entitled to subscribe to shares in the various satellite companies as construction progressed to yield outside profit and encourage continued financing until the railroad's earnings could provide funds.

First of the town companies was the Colorado Springs Company, incorporated June 26, 1871, even before construction of the railroad was started. The close ties and interest of British investors eventually brought the town such eminence that it became known as "Little London." It was the most successful of all such town-formation ventures originated by General Palmer.

The Denver & Rio Grande's first wrought-iron rails, imported from Wales, were spiked down at Denver July 18, 1871. On October 21 the track reached Colorado Springs, seventy-six miles south of Denver, and construction to Pueblo, another forty-three miles, was completed June 19, 1872. Numerous accounts of the history of the D&RG have

been published in recent years, detailing the many problems encountered in its early and later years of life. The financial panic of 1873 made construction funds scarce, and little progress was made. Palmer's cherished plan for a north-south line suffered defeat at Raton Pass, south of Trinidad, Colorado, in February 1878, when Atchison, Topeka & Santa Fe (ATSF) graders gained first occupancy of the ground, and the D&RG was forced to retire from the scene.

Two months later an almost parallel situation developed at the mouth of the Royal Gorge of the Arkansas River, just west of Cañon City, Colorado. ATSF and D&RG forces began work simultaneously in the narrow entrance to the chasm, resulting in the two-year-long conflict known as the "Royal Gorge War." The D&RG triumphed in court in this affair in 1880, and, under Palmer's guidance, the D&RG entered the period of its greatest expansion, extending its slim-gauge tracks throughout western and southern Colorado.

Because the Colorado company lacked charter authorization to build in Utah Territory, Palmer organized the Denver & Rio Grande Western (D&RGW) Railway July 21, 1881, filing the necessary documents at Salt Lake City. This new company completed its connection with Colorado's D&RG on March 30, 1883. Construction from Salt Lake City to Ogden was finished May 16, thus providing a through narrow-gauge main line, 771 miles in length, linking Denver and Ogden.

Palmer's activities during these four years of frenzied expansion of his two railroads soon brought him under fire. Rumors and inferences reflecting on his wisdom and honesty were leaked by recently elected, dissident members of the D&RG's enlarged board of directors. Outraged by these unfounded aspersions concerning his integrity, he resigned as president of the Denver & Rio Grande August 9, 1883. On June 24, 1884, he submitted his resignation as a director, finally severing all official connection with the line to which he had given birth, nurtured, and brought to full life during its fourteen years of existence.

Those two years were unkind to William J. Palmer in other ways, as well. The health of his wife had suffered from the altitude at Colorado Springs, and in 1883, with their three young daughters, Queen Palmer moved to New York City. Two years later she took up permanent residence in England, and though they never divorced, Palmer was left to carry on his various ventures alone, no longer with the possibility of any close family associations.

Early in 1880 Palmer and his associates had merged three of the D&RG's auxiliary land and industrial companies under their control to form the Colorado Coal & Iron (CC&I) Company. Palmer was elected president. Consolidating the resources of iron ore, coal and coking facilities, lands, and other physical assets of the former companies, the new CC&I began erection of a steel and iron works at South Pueblo, Colorado. The first blast furnace was fired on September 5, 1881; production of Bessemer steel commenced April 12, 1882. Rails, spikes, and nails became important products of the new steel mill, with the first rails going to the Denver & Rio Grande.

By late 1883 CC&I was faced with depressed markets, high expenses, and government legal challenges to its ownership of certain coal properties. In the fiasco that autumn over control of the Denver & Rio Grande, CC&I's most important customer, the same coterie of New York bankers who forced Palmer from the railroad also succeeded in gaining control of Colorado Coal & Iron, and he resigned the presidency of the latter when the board of directors met April 8, 1884.

Similarly in 1884 the Mexican National Railway, the product of Palmer's efforts dating from March 1872 to build a proposed southern extension of the D&RG, found itself in difficulty. Incorporated in Colorado October 22, 1880, and with construction of some 490 miles of narrow-gauge railroad to its credit in the following four years, the company was unable to meet its bond interest requirements due April 1, 1884. In the subsequent reorganization Palmer was replaced as president on July 9, 1887.

Only with his Denver & Rio Grande Western Railway, extending across eastern Utah from the Colorado border to Ogden, did Palmer enjoy truly enduring success. Maintaining its corporate independence his road reestablished "friendly" relationships with the D&RG in Colorado. But by 1889 the physical and economic handicaps of the 3-foot gauge mandated change. With Palmer continuing as president, the company was reorganized and refinanced under the name Rio Grande Western (RGW) Railway July 1, 1889. Relocated, built entirely new in many places, and converted over its entire length to standard gauge, the RGW joined in providing through service in connection with the D&RG (which also converted to standard gauge) and Colorado Midland on the east and the Central Pacific on the west beginning November 15, 1890.

Still headquartered in the stately mansion home named "Glen Eyrie," built for his bride in 1872 near Colorado Springs, Palmer managed to maintain contact with his family, making many trips to England during the late 1880s and early 1890s. In December 1894 the long-ill Queen Palmer died at age forty-four in her English home, and Palmer immediately departed for the funeral. After closing his wife's affairs he sailed back to America with his daughters, now twenty-two, fourteen, and thirteen years old. Palmer, too, changed–the lonely, remote, authoritarian father figure of the Colorado Springs area, held in awe by all, found a renewed love in family and friends with his lively daughters now so involved in his personal life.

In 1896, for the twenty-fifth anniversary of the founding of Colorado Springs, Palmer recalled the early days of the town in a long newspaper article. Again in 1901, his growing popularity and prestige in his adopted state were evident in the celebrations of the silver anniversary of Colorado's statehood.

In 1901 negotiations were successfully completed for sale of the Rio Grande Western to George Jay Gould who, shortly before, also had acquired control of the Denver & Rio Grande. Realizing more from Gould than he had expected, Palmer arranged to have the excess distributed among longtime faithful employees of the RGW.

This sale of his Utah railroad marked the end of General Palmer's active business life. From his years of work his holdings now had a net value exceeding $9 million, producing a steady income of some $30,000 a month without the necessity of his close and constant personal attention. In September 1901 he celebrated his sixty-fifth birthday. Palmer was still small and neat and wiry, carrying himself with military straightness, his long face tanned and weather-beaten. He still rode horseback with the same loose rein and long stirrup of his cavalry days in the Civil War. But now his attention could be given even more actively to programs of anonymous civic benefactions.

By 1907 a multimillion-dollar park system totaling 1,638 acres, acquired, developed, and landscaped under his direction and at his expense, had been donated to Colorado Springs. The Colorado

College, which he had fostered from the very beginnings of the town and which became the first degree-granting institution in the mountain West, was a further beneficiary of his largesse. In all, he gave away more than half his fortune, always shunning any personal publicity, honors, or display.

Tragedy struck in 1906. About noon on October 27 the seventy-year-old Palmer was returning from a morning ride through the nearby Garden of the Gods with his daughters Dorothy and Marjory and a friend. Drawing to a stop to open a gate, Palmer's small cow pony stepped on a rock and stumbled, throwing the rider to the ground. "The Civil War cavalry leader and explorer of the West, who had ridden half a million miles on horseback in every sort of violent, perilous circumstance, fell off a small walking pony who had merely stumbled. Palmer landed on his head on the road," explains Marshall Sprague, another of Palmer's biographers. The general's upper spine was broken in three places from the impact. The doctor's diagnosis noted that the victim could move his head and neck freely, move his shoulders, and bend his elbows slightly, but the rest of the body was paralyzed. The outlook was hopeless.

For more than a year Palmer survived in a specially developed waterbed. In May 1907 he received notice of the thirty-fifth reunion of his old 15th Pennsylvania cavalry outfit, to be held in Philadelphia in August. Having always maintained a close interest in and support of the Regimental Association and its members over the years, he planned to attend this special affair. When his doctor forbade such a long journey, Palmer brought the entire regiment to Colorado Springs for the celebration at his own expense.

A special ten-car Pullman train was chartered to depart Philadelphia August 17, collecting and carrying the veterans. On its arrival at Colorado Springs three days later, 280 of his old comrades joined their former commander in a week of reunion and celebration in which they were honored by crowds of local townfolk and treated to parades and sightseeing tours, concerts, parties, and banquets.

The heartening effects on Palmer of this happy event encouraged more activity. As he regained strength he directed his staff to purchase an electric automobile. This failing to meet his desires, he ordered a new White steamer on display at an automobile show in Chicago. When received at Glen

Eyrie it was a monstrous, gaudy affair, painted white, with bright red seats. A special padded case was formfitted to enfold the general's paralyzed body and fit the car, and soon he was visiting the local haunts of his horseback riding days once again.

On January 20, 1908, Palmer's oldest daughter, Elsie, married Leopold H. Myers of England at Glen Eyrie. The couple departed on a honeymoon to Italy, planning to meet the family the next September in England where daughter Marjory expected to wed. General Palmer decided he should be in attendance at that event as well, and after many preparations his entourage departed Colorado Springs on the last day of May. On the eastward ocean journey Marjory changed her mind, confessing to her father her love for Dr. Henry Chorley Watt, who had lived at Glen Eyrie as General Palmer's attending house physician ever since the accident. The English wedding was called off.

Undaunted, the family toured Europe that summer, returning to the United States in November. During the voyage home to New York Palmer suffered an accidental head injury, and thereafter his health deteriorated rapidly.

In the spring of 1909 Elsie and her husband returned to Glen Eyrie for a visit, and Palmer briefly saw his first grandchild. On the night of March 12, while asleep, he slipped into a coma. He died the next day, his three daughters gathered at his bedside.

The body was cremated, and the ashes interred under the yellow pines of Evergreen Cemetery in Colorado Springs. The funeral was attended by 600 students from Colorado College and more than 3,000 townspeople. Eighteen months later Queen Palmer's ashes, disinterred and returned from England, were laid to rest beside those of her husband.

The public's reverence, respect, esteem, and affection for this remarkable man have never dimmed. A plaque in his honor, signed by 480 survivors of his 15th Pennsylvania cavalry in 1910, is on display at The Colorado College. A monumental bronze equestrian statue, funded by popular subscription over twenty years, was unveiled in Colorado Springs September 2, 1929. The Liberty ship *General William J. Palmer* was launched at Richmond, California, in October 1943. In September 1986 people throughout Colorado celebrated the 150th anniversary of his birth, with his great granddaughter from England joining in the festivities. In the Union stations at Denver, Colorado, and Salt Lake City, Utah, at Colonia Railway Station in Mexico City, in Palmer Hall at The Colorado College, and at the Hampton Institute for Colored Students in Virginia can be found bronze memorial tablets commemorating the man and his work:

WILLIAM JACKSON PALMER
1836-1909

Union Cavalry General, pioneer railroad builder, prophet of Colorado's greatness. He mapped the routes of three transcontinental railways, supervised the building of the first road to Denver, organized and constructed the Denver & Rio Grande Railroad, stimulated the State's industries, cherished its beauties, founded Colorado Springs, fostered Colorado College, and served our Sister Republic of Mexico with sympathy and wisdom in developing its national railways.

Publications:

Map of the Route of the Southern Continental Railroad (Philadelphia: W. B. Selheimer, 1869);

Report of Surveys Across the Continent (Philadelphia: W. B. Selheimer, 1869);

The Westward Current of Population in the United States (London: Chapman and Hall, 1874);

The Monroe Doctrine (N.p., 1896?);

Letters, 1853-1868 [of] Gen'l Wm. J. Palmer (Philadelphia, 1906).

References:

George L. Anderson, *Kansas West* (San Marino, Cal.: Golden West Books, 1963);

Robert G. Athearn, *Rebel of the Rockies, the Denver & Rio Grande Western Railroad* (New Haven: Yale University Press, 1962);

William A. Bell, *New Tracks in North America* (New York: Scribner, Welford & Co., 1870, reprinted, Albuquerque, N. M.: Horn & Wallace, 1965);

John S. Fisher, *A Builder of the West, The Life of General William Jackson Palmer* (Caldwell, Idaho: Caxton Printers, 1939);

Charles E. Kirk, *History of the Fifteenth Pennsylvania Volunteer Cavalry* (Philadelphia: N.p., 1906);

George Foster Peabody, *William Jackson Palmer, Pathfinder and Builder* (Saratoga Springs, N.Y.: Privately printed, 1931);

H. Lee Scamehorn, *Pioneer Steelmaker in the West* (Boulder, Colo.: Pruett, 1976);

Marshall Sprague, *Newport in the Rockies* (Denver: Sage Books, 1961);

Rhoda Davis Wilcox, *The Man on the Iron Horse* (Colorado Springs: Dentan, 1959);

O. Meredith Wilson, *The Denver and Rio Grande Project, 1870-1901* (Salt Lake City: Howe Brothers, 1982);

Suzanne Colton Wilson, *Column South With the 15th Pennsylvania Cavalry* (Flagstaff, Ariz.: Northland Press, 1960).

Archives:

William Jackson Palmer's papers are located in the library of the Colorado Historical Society, Denver, Colorado.

Thomas Wentworth Peirce

(August 16, 1818-October 2, 1885)

by George C. Werner

Houston, Texas

CAREER: Partner, Peirce & Bacon (1843-1885); president, Galveston & Houston Junction Railroad (1866-1871); director, various railroads (1866-1885); president, Buffalo Bayou, Brazos & Colorado Railway (1870); president, Galveston, Harrisburg & San Antonio Railway (1870-1885); president, Galveston, Houston & Henderson Railroad (1871-1876).

Thomas Wentworth Peirce, shipowner, commission merchant, and southwestern railroad builder, was born in Dover, New Hampshire, on August 16, 1818. Colonel Peirce, as he was later called, was one of eleven children and the second oldest son of Andrew Peirce and Betsy Wentworth Peirce, both of whom came from colonial stock. Peirce's father and his uncle, James Wentworth, operated schooners between Dover and Boston, and his father and brother Andrew later expanded into the southern trade. Thomas was raised on the family farm at Dover. Although he was prepared to enter college at the age of thirteen, a change in his father's circumstances caused these plans to be abandoned. He was then appointed to a clerkship at Dover but continued to devote two hours a day to reading and other intellectual pursuits.

The severe New England weather was hard on Peirce's health, and, while still in his early teens, he was sent to Cuba for the winter. The following spring, not wanting to return to New Hampshire until June, Peirce came home via New Orleans. From there he made his first trip to Texas, which was then still a part of Mexico. Between the ages of fifteen and eighteen he worked in his father's shipping and commission business and later joined his brother's firm, A. Peirce & Company. The Peirce family was among the first to ship cotton from Houston to Galveston down Buffalo Bayou, the stream which later became the Houston Ship Channel. At nineteen Peirce was appointed to the staff of the governor of New Hampshire, where he was involved in the reorganization of the state militia, which resulted in his receiving the honorary title of colonel.

In the course of his business activities Peirce made numerous trips to Texas. On one of his early trips, probably in 1842, he traveled from Galveston to San Antonio and had his first view of the area through which he would later build the Galveston, Harrisburg & San Antonio Railway. With the expansion of the railroad system from Boston, the importance of small inland distribution ports such as Dover diminished, and in 1843 Peirce moved to Boston, where he and George Bacon organized the firm of Peirce & Bacon. The firm also engaged in southern trade, primarily in Texas, dealing in cotton, sugar, and hides. Peirce & Bacon grew into one of the largest commercial establishments in Massachusetts; Peirce's brother Andrew joined the partnership in 1851. The following year a branch house headed by Gen. E. B. Nichols was established in Galveston, and at the outbreak of hostilities in 1861 the firm had a fleet of fifteen packets operating between Boston, Galveston, and Liverpool. Although the firm of Peirce & Bacon remained in existence until the death of Colonel Peirce, it became a minor part of his activities as his railroad interests in Texas increased after 1865.

Peirce first became involved with the railroads of Texas in 1857 when Peirce & Bacon subscribed to $10,000 in stock of the Galveston & Red River, later the Houston & Texas Central (H&TC). Later in 1857 Peirce acted as a commission merchant supplying rails to the H&TC. By 1866 he was a director of the Galveston, Houston & Henderson (GH&H) and also president and director of the connecting Galveston & Houston Junction (G&HJ). The GH&H was an antebellum road which opened the first rail line between Houston and Galveston in February 1860, while the G&HJ opened a connecting link between the GH&H and the H&TC in

1865. Although Peirce was unsuccessful in his attempt to buy the GH&H at foreclosure in December 1871, he subsequently merged the G&HJ into the GH&H. Peirce continued as a director of the GH&H until 1881 and was president of the company between 1871 and 1876. He also remained a large stockholder in the company until it was reorganized by Jay Gould and Russell Sage in 1882. It was on the GH&H that Peirce found an able lieutenant in James Converse, who was to lead the colonel's subsequent railroad projects in Texas, Louisiana, and Mexico.

In 1868 Peirce acquired an interest in the Buffalo Bayou, Brazos & Colorado (BBB&C). This line was the first railroad to begin operating in Texas and by early 1860 had opened a line from Harrisburg (now a part of Houston) west to Alleyton near the left bank of the Colorado River. Although the company was originally promoted by Gen. Sidney Sherman of Texas, the line was largely built with Boston capital. The company had financial difficulties in the late 1860s and, as it could not pay various court-ordered judgments, was sold to William D. Sledge by the sheriff of Harris County, Texas, in July 1868. Sledge retained a quarter interest in the company and sold the balance to Peirce, Oakes Ames, Peter Butler, and Johnathan Barrett (who had been BBB&C president prior to the Civil War), all of whom were from Boston, and to John Sealy and John Hutchins of Galveston. The new owners bought equipment, rehabilitated the track, and built a permanent bridge over the Brazos River at Richmond, replacing a low-water crossing which had been in use for over ten years.

On January 24, 1870, the BBB&C was again sold, this time to satisfy the 1860 mortgage on the property. Peirce became president and a director, and in July the railroad was reorganized as the Galveston, Harrisburg & San Antonio (GH&SA). Peirce remained president and a director of the company until his death. Over the next several years Peirce bought out his associates and became the virtual sole owner of the GH&SA, the road being frequently called the Peirce Road in addition to its more formal nickname, the Sunset Route. The only early associate to remain with the GH&SA was Butler, who continued as a director as long as Peirce was alive. Although early plans were made to extend the GH&SA to San Antonio, the line did not reach the Alamo City until February 1877. While there were several factors which contributed to the

delay, a major cause was the disruption of the financial markets following the Chicago fire of 1871, which affected financing plans for the extension. The great Boston fire of November 9-10, 1872, also had an impact on the company, as it destroyed the local records of the GH&SA as well as those of Peirce & Bacon.

Peirce was also active east of Houston. The Texas & New Orleans (T&NO), another antebellum railroad, completed a 5-foot 6-inch gauge line between Houston and Orange, Texas, in April 1861. In addition work had begun on the Louisiana Division with the goal of connecting Houston and New Orleans by rail. The T&NO deteriorated during the war years and was reduced to handcar service before shutting down east of Liberty. An occasional freight train operated on the west end until 1872. The line was divided at Liberty and the two sections sold at foreclosure in 1871 and 1872 to John T. Terry and his associates, including Peirce and Ames. Peirce was named a director of the T&NO and, except for a few years in the early 1880s, remained in that position until his death. The T&NO was reconstructed as a standard-gauge railroad and reopened between Houston and Orange in August 1876.

The reopening of the T&NO did not complete a Houston-to-New Orleans route as the gap between Orange and Morgan City, Louisiana, still remained to be closed. In 1878 an agreement was reached between the T&NO, Morgan's Louisiana & Texas Railroad & Steamship Company (ML&T), and the newly organized Louisiana Western (LW) to complete the route. Peirce was a major stockholder in the LW, and James Converse surveyed the route of the new line. The ML&T extended its line from Morgan City to Vermillionville (now Lafayette), Louisiana, while the LW built between the Texas/Louisiana border and Vermillionville. When the route was opened for service in August 1880 as the Star and Crescent Route, Peirce owned or had interests in railroads running between San Antonio and Vermillionville, connecting there with a railroad for Algiers (New Orleans).

Although there were reports as early as 1878 of a community of interest between Peirce and the Big Four of California, C. P. Huntington, Charles Crocker, Leland Stanford, and the Hopkins interest, it is not known exactly when they agreed to join forces. However, surveying for the Mexican and Pacific extension of the GH&SA west of San Antonio began in early 1880 when J. E. Gray of the Southern Pacific (SP) and Converse jointly looked over the route to El Paso. In April William Hood of the SP left San Antonio to survey the line, and grading for the project began in January 1881 at San Antonio. The SP, building eastward to preempt a route claimed by the Texas & Pacific, reached El Paso in May 1881. Its forces continued eastward under the GH&SA charter, meeting the line from San Antonio just west of the Pecos River on January 12, 1883, where Peirce drove a silver spike marking the completion of the second transcontinental line across Texas.

In March 1881, shortly after work had begun on the extension of the GH&SA across west Texas, Peirce engaged surveyors to plan a route across Mexico from Eagle Pass, Texas. Later in the year a concession was obtained from Mexico for the Mexican International (MI), a road begun in 1883 and extended to Durango in 1892. C. P. Huntington, Charles Crocker, Leland Stanford, and Peirce were among the backers of the MI; and the GH&SA ran a branch to Eagle Pass and constructed a joint bridge with the MI across the Rio Grande. In June 1881 Huntington announced that the SP had purchased the T&NO, the LW, and the GH&SA. Huntington was named president of the T&NO and the LW, but Peirce retained at least nominal control of the GH&SA, remaining as its president and a member of its virtually unchanged board of directors. With the completion of the GH&SA across Texas in January 1883, the SP controlled a route from California to Vermillionville. The operation was extended to New Orleans a few months later with the purchase of Morgan's Louisiana & Texas Railroad & Steamship Company by Peirce, Huntington, Crocker, Stanford, and Mrs. Mark Hopkins. The acquisition included the railroad from Vermillionville to the Mississippi River, the H&TC, and the Gulf, Western Texas & Pacific, as well as the steamship routes from New Orleans to New York and Latin America.

In addition to his railroad interests Peirce had extensive landholdings in Texas, where his total acreage was larger than the combined area of Rhode Island and the District of Columbia. He also had a 10 percent interest in the Corralitos Hacienda in Chihuahua, Mexico, a ranch larger than the 1.25-million-acre King Ranch of Texas. Although Peirce was a lifelong Democrat, he was consulted by various secretaries of the treasury from both parties.

He was also offered official positions during the administrations of Franklin Pierce and Abraham Lincoln but declined, preferring to remain a private citizen.

Peirce's personal life was marred by tragedy. His first wife was Mary Curtis of Boston, whom he married on September 2, 1857. She died on July 23, 1862, only two months after the death of Thomas W., their only child. His second marriage, on September 2, 1873, was to Catherine Cornelia Cook of Cooperstown, New York. She was a niece of General Nichols. This marriage produced two children, Marion W., born in 1874, and Thomas W., who was born in 1877. At an early age Catherine Cornelia developed a mental problem which today would probably be diagnosed as Alzheimer's disease, and she died on July 7, 1881. Although he was frequently away from home for extended periods, several of Peirce's letters to his daughter survive and attest to his affection for his family.

In 1856 he bought Witch Hill Estate at Topsfield, Massachusetts, from the estate of Benjamin W. Crowninshield, James Madison's secretary of the navy. It is reputed that Peirce bought Witch Hill, which straddled the Newburyport Turnpike, so he could travel the twenty miles to Boston "on one change of horses." Witch Hill remained his primary residence, although he frequently wintered in San Antonio where he was preparing to build a home in 1881.

Peirce spent the winter following his second marriage in Europe, renting a house on the Isle of Wight where Marion was born. Before leaving for Europe he engaged a local builder to add a wing to the two-story ship captain's house at Witch Hill. On his return he found the wing added on the wrong side, which largely blocked his view of the Ipswich River Valley and the village of Topsfield. In 1879 Peirce employed Ernest Bowditch, a civil engineer who also practiced what is now called landscape architecture. Bowditch worked on Witch Hill for a number of years with a free hand and an unlimited budget. The only constraint seems to have been that all current projects had to be completed before the "old gent" returned from his winter in Texas. Bowditch carried out massive regrading projects, and his choice of planting materials, while limited, was chosen for the long term. A century later the basic elements of his plan are still visible at Witch Hill. Peirce enlarged the landholdings of the estate from about 120 acres to 440 acres and operated what was frequently called an experimental farm. He took a great interest in developing new farming techniques and improving old ones. Peirce was also interested in the breeding of Jersey and Holstein cattle and had a number of Hambletonian horses in his stable.

Peirce was generally treated with respect by Texas newspapers. He was available for interviews, and his philanthropy, which was of a local nature, was favorably noted. He made contributions to various religious and educational organizations and for civic improvements in towns along the GH&SA. His hometown was not forgotten. Peirce donated the land and building for the Peirce Memorial Church, which was dedicated at Dover in 1883 but which no longer stands.

The colonel died at the sanatorium at Clifton Springs, New York, on October 2, 1885, of congestive heart failure and is buried at Mt. Auburn Cemetery in Cambridge, Massachusetts. His estate was valued at $7.3 million, and, in addition to setting up trust funds for his children and his grandchildren, he also left varying amounts to the permanent school funds of nine towns along the GH&SA and $20,000 for the establishment of a hospital for the employees of that railroad as well as other charitable bequests. Unfortunately, due to the ineptness of his executors, not all bequests were carried out.

Today Peirce is remembered for the building of the GH&SA while his other activities are largely overlooked. However, during his lifetime his importance to the economic development of Texas was recognized as being much larger. In the late 1850s Texas senator Thomas Rusk stated that "Texas was more indebted to Thomas W. Peirce than to any other individual." Only one station, Peirce Junction, where the original GH&SA line to Houston branched from the main line, was named for the colonel, and the spelling was soon corrupted to Pierce Junction. Peirce's monument is the Sunset Route east of El Paso, which still remains the backbone of SP operations in Texas and Louisiana.

References:

Biographical Review Containing Life Sketches of Leading Citizens of Essex County Massachusetts (Boston: Biographical Review Publishing Co., 1898), XXVII: 9-11;

Frederick Clifton Peirce, *Peirce Genealogy* (Worcester, Mass.: Press of Chas. Hamilton, 1880);

Alonzo H. Quint, "A History of Dover," in *History of Rockingham and Strafford Counties*, compiled by D. Hamilton Hurd (Philadelphia: J. W. Lewis, 1882);

James L. Rock and W. I. Smith, *Southern and Western Texas Guide for 1878* (St. Louis: A. H. Granger, 1878).

Pennsylvania Railroad

by James A. Ward

University of Tennessee, Chattanooga

Pennsylvania fell behind in the early-nineteenth-century transportation revolution. New York stole a march on other eastern states with its Erie Canal (1817), Maryland followed quickly with its Baltimore & Ohio (B&O) Railroad (1828), and Massachusetts countered with the Boston & Albany Railroad (1830). Faced with mountainous western Pennsylvania, the state opted for a clumsy combination of canals, railroads, and inclined planes that was expensive and slow. Leading Philadelphia merchants sought to redress their trade disadvantages with a railroad connecting the state-owned Philadelphia & Columbia Railroad (1828) with Harrisburg and Pittsburgh. After holding a series of public meetings the merchants secured a legislative charter for the Pennsylvania Railroad (PRR) on April 13, 1846. An amendment stipulated that if the road did not raise $3 million with 10 percent of that amount paid in and put thirty miles of road under contract by July 30, 1847, the Baltimore & Ohio Railroad would receive permission to build to Pittsburgh.

The Pennsylvania was long blessed with excellent leadership. Its first president, Samuel Merrick, a Philadelphia manufacturer influential in that city's politics, acquired the necessary stock subscriptions, including $1.5 million from the city of Philadelphia. Merrick also hired an expert chief engineer, J. Edgar Thomson, from the Georgia Railroad. Thomson began locating the railroad only ninety days before the legislative deadline, but he quickly surveyed the first 100 miles of road and put thirty miles under contract in order to stymie the B&O. For the next two years he pushed construction ahead so quickly that the company was hard pressed to pay its bills. Moreover lines of internal corporate accountability were vague and bickering flared. Thomson disagreed with Merrick, who wanted to slow the work down, but the chief engineer eventually prevailed in the road's counsels. As a result, Merrick resigned in 1849 and was re-

placed with another Philadelphia merchant, William C. Patterson. Thomson stepped up the pace of construction, organized a transportation department, and operated the first revenue run on September 1, 1849. His relations with Patterson, who was also hard pressed to pay the bills, worsened, however. A confrontation between the two occurred at the 1852 annual meeting when, in a proxy fight, Thomson's forces ousted Patterson, and Thomson, the technical expert, assumed the presidency.

Faced with an empty treasury, Thomson was forced to use short-term loans to finally finish his road in 1854. Even then he continued to fight with state authorities, who controlled his access to Philadelphia, and who persuaded the state legislature to place a tonnage tax on the Pennsylvania's traffic to equalize competition with the state-owned system. The tax placed Thomson's road at a disadvantage with other regional trunk lines, and he responded in 1857 by buying the entire state-owned main line for $7.5 million; nevertheless, the tonnage tax was not repealed until 1861.

Thomson spent the 1850s upgrading his physical plant, double tracking parts of the main line, adding sidings, buying new equipment, and experimenting with coal-burning fireboxes and various braking systems. By the beginning of the Civil War he controlled a strong property that needed every ounce of strength it could muster to carry a wartime traffic that far exceeded its capacity. Despite inflation and physical deterioration, the road doubled its net profits during the conflict, laid steel rails, and vastly increased its equipment. By war's end the Pennsylvania was the largest corporation in the world, free of floating debt, and poised to expand.

With only enough postwar traffic to keep three of the four eastern trunk lines profitable and a new generation of railway entrepreneurs on the scene, competition intensified and took new strategic turns. When Jay Gould threatened the

The Pennsylvania Railroad's Market Street Station in Newark, New Jersey

Pennsylvania's western connections in 1868, Thomson acted with uncharacteristic haste. In January 1869 his board gave him carte blanche to acquire any necessary connecting roads, and he moved quickly. He had acquired the Northern Central before the war, the Philadelphia & Erie during it, and the Allegheny Valley afterwards, but in 1869 he suddenly expanded outside Pittsburgh, Pennsylvania, by leasing the Ft. Wayne & Chicago Railroad Company, and by purchasing roads to St. Louis, Louisville, Cincinnati, Vincennes, and Washington, D.C. Under a separate charter Thomas P. Scott, vice-president of the PRR, created a system of southern lines stretching from Washington, D.C., to New Orleans. The PRR expanded eastward in 1871 by leasing the United New Jersey Railroads, which gave the Pennsylvania a direct route to New York City markets. With their private funds Thomson and his Pennsylvania allies bought the Union Pacific in 1871 but lost it a year later along with large interests in the Northern Pacific, Kansas Pacific, and Texas & Pacific. On the eve of the 1873 panic the Pennsylvania system enjoyed gross revenues of over $70 million, a 1,090 percent increase over the 1860 figures.

The 1873 panic and the ensuing depression staggered the Pennsylvania, and the stress literally killed Thomson, who had been in poor health for years. When he announced a scrip dividend, stock-

holders named a special investigating committee that in 1874 demanded the Pennsylvania restrict its financial interests and make the company more accountable to its board and stockholders. On Thomson's death in 1874 his vice-president, Tom Scott, ironically one of the great expansionists of the age, became president and in a short, stormy tenure fought constant rate wars, tried to pool the important oil trade, paid off much of the road's floating debt, and withstood a strike and riots at Pittsburgh that left twenty-four dead and cost the PRR over $2.3 million. Although only fifty-seven years old in 1880, Scott's personal financial crises, and those of the PRR, impaired his health and he retired.

Scott's replacement was another Thomson protégé, George B. Roberts, who had started in the Pennsylvania's engineering corps and later became Thomson's assistant. As good times returned Roberts consolidated his road's financial position, fought rate competition, and resumed a cautious expansion to defend his markets. He acquired the Philadelphia, Wilmington & Baltimore Railroad in 1881, a road which gave the Pennsylvania an unbroken line from Baltimore to New York and also foiled Gould and the B&O interests, who had bid on the property. Roberts became nationally known when he defended his road against William Vanderbilt, who in 1883 decided to build the South Pennsylvania Railroad from Philadelphia to Pittsburgh. Supported by Pittsburgh interests, Andrew Carnegie, and the Reading Railroad, Vanderbilt began construction in 1884. Finally J. P. Morgan brought the Pennsylvania and New York Central parties together and, in a series of meetings, the most famous of which was on his yacht, convinced Vanderbilt of his foolishness and Roberts to buy the new road, portions of which later became part of the Pennsylvania Turnpike. Roberts also improved his terminals, expanded the road's New Jersey mileage, mollified labor, and weathered the century's greatest flood, at Johnstown, which caused almost $3.5 million in damages to the road. Roberts died of heart trouble in 1897 and was replaced by Frank Thomson, no relation to J. Edgar and another graduate of the road's engineering department, who died in office after only two and one-half years. Alexander J. Cassatt, who graduated from Rensselaer Polytechnic Institute with a degree in civil engineering and worked his way up through the Pennsylvania's engineering department, assumed the presidency. He inherited a railroad in 1899 that east of Pittsburgh had almost 46,000 employees, worked 3,715 miles of road, earned gross revenues of $88.5 million, and netted profits of $18.2 million. Moreover the company stood on the verge of tunneling into New York City and controlled lines radiating out to the Great Lakes and the Mississippi River. Widely regarded as "The Standard Railroad of the World," the PRR's greatest triumphs and failures lay in the future, but it had built a solid foundation which promised financial success in the approaching decades.

References:

George H. Burgess and Miles C. Kennedy, *Centennial History of the Pennsylvania Railroad Company, 1846-1946* (Philadelphia: Pennsylvania Railroad Co., 1949);

Patricia Davis, *End of the Line: Alexander J. Cassatt and the Pennsylvania Railroad* (New York: Neale Watson Academic Publications, 1978);

H. W. Schotter, *The Growth and Development of the Pennsylvania Railroad Company* (Philadelphia: Allen, Lane & Scott, 1927);

James A. Ward, *J. Edgar Thomson: Master of the Pennsylvania* (Westport, Conn.: Greenwood Press, 1980).

Archives:

The board of directors file along with records of some Pennsylvania Railroad subsidiary companies are located at the Eleutherian Mills Historical Library, Wilmington, Delaware. A small amount of material is located in the Pennsylvania Railroad Collection of the Pennsylvania Historical & Museum Commission, Harrisburg, Pennsylvania.

Charles Elliott Perkins

(November 24, 1840-November 9, 1907)

by John Lauritz Larson

Purdue University

CAREER: Cashier, Burlington & Missouri River Railroad (1859-1862); assistant treasurer and secretary, Burlington & Missouri River (1862-1865); general superintendent, Burlington & Missouri River (1865-1873); director, Burlington & Missouri River, Nebraska (1869-1879); director, Burlington & Missouri River (1871); vice-president and general manager, Burlington & Missouri River, Nebraska (1873-1880); director, Chicago, Burlington & Quincy (1875-1907); vice-president and general manager, Chicago, Burlington & Quincy (1876-1881); president, Chicago, Burlington & Quincy (1881-1901); president and director, Hannibal & St. Joseph (1883-1901); president and director, Kansas City, Council Bluffs & St. Joseph (1885-1886).

Charles Elliott Perkins lived the type of life nineteenth-century moralizers loved to tell about. He was born in Cincinnati, Ohio, on November 24, 1840, the son of a struggling Unitarian lecturer; he rose through "pluck and luck" and hard work to become president of one of the nation's great railroad corporations; and he died rich and well known as a businessman of consummate skill and integrity. His life seemed to verify those automatic truths about business and society that he, like so many of his generation, believed absolutely.

Perkins's immediate roots were humble, but he descended from early Boston's greatest families. His father, James Handasyd Perkins, died when Perkins was nine, leaving Sarah Elliott Perkins with five sons and no fortune. Charles, the eldest, stayed in public school until he was sixteen, spent a year with his uncle Stephen Perkins while attending high school in Milton, Massachusetts, and then returned to Cincinnati in 1857 as a clerk to a wholesale fruit grocer.

In the swirling dynamism of America's nineteenth century, marking fruit for neighborhood vendors understandably disappointed a young man

Charles Elliott Perkins

with dependents and a fortune to secure. In May 1859 Perkins wrote to John Murray Forbes of Boston, an older cousin who had earned one fortune in China and a second in western railroads, asking for help in selecting a career. "There is a great want of good, trustworthy businessmen for the management of our railroads," Forbes replied. "I can help you on better in that direction than any other . . . if you can fit yourself to manage such matters well."

Forbes had in mind a position on the fledgling Burlington & Missouri River (B&MR) Railroad, which in 1859 ran just seventy-five miles from the Mississippi River into the sparsely settled Iowa countryside. In 1857 Forbes's group of Boston capitalists seized control of this foundering local road, which had just secured a federal land grant. Charles Russell Lowell of Boston went to Burlington, Iowa, to set up the land office where Charles Perkins would start as clerk. In August 1859, for $30 monthly and a room in Lowell's cottage, Perkins took up railroading on the one line he would serve all his life.

In 1860 Lowell resigned from the B&MR, and Perkins took his place as land agent and assistant treasurer. Then the Civil War broke out, diverting everyone's attention away from railroads and the westward movement. As his peers won commissions and rode off to war and his superiors in Boston turned to matters of defense, Perkins grew bored in his isolation. By the summer of 1862 he grumbled to Forbes his intention to join the army "for $1,300 besides the glory," if he didn't get some recognition. Forbes smoothed his feathers and dealt him in on some Iowa land speculations. On September 22, 1864, he found further comfort by marrying his cousin and first love, Edith Forbes, a daughter of John Murray Forbes's brother Robert. Still, no personal diversion could quiet Perkins's growing concern that the distraction of the war would ruin the company's future prospects in Iowa.

Construction had stopped when the war began, and Boston capitalists were hardly inclined to pour labor and materials at wartime prices into an Iowa line going nowhere. Local people concluded that the absentee owners intended no good, and rumors spread that Forbes would never finish the road. The deadline for completing the Iowa road (in order to qualify for the federal lands) marched steadily closer, and competing lines threatened Burlington territory all around. In 1864 the Chicago, Burlington & Quincy (CB&Q) Railroad, a Forbes-group property connecting the B&MR with Chicago, began aiding construction with earnings, but that method of financing was much too slow. The Union victory finally meant new hope for the Iowa railroad, and by May 1865 Perkins, now general superintendent, was escorting CB&Q president James F. Joy through western Iowa to whip up excitement and financial aid.

Perkins's understanding of railroads owed something to his position not as an absentee owner but as a resident manager of a western railroad line. He also learned from his mentor, Forbes, the sequential approach to development. Perkins assumed, like Forbes, that east-west lines were the

natural thoroughfares; therefore, Iowa and Nebraska were the proper fields for CB&Q expansion. Joy, on the other hand, saw that quick profits could be taken from a roundabout route through Missouri on another CB&Q feeder, the Hannibal & St. Joseph, that connected with the transcontinental Union Pacific (UP). Perkins felt betrayed by Joy's Missouri connections, and he begged Forbes to see the danger. In an 1867 boardroom fight Forbes threw his money behind Perkins's Iowa line, beginning a contest for control of the CB&Q that dogged affairs for the next several years.

Perkins's idea for the CB&Q was to finish the Iowa line, build into Nebraska (where an 1864 land grant awaited them), and forge the shortest through route to the UP at Kearney, Nebraska. More costly in the beginning, such a plan promised long-run advantages when competition drove down profits on less efficient routes. Accordingly, Forbes and his friends among the CB&Q directors quickly completed the Iowa line in 1869, ran a short line north to the UP's Council Bluffs terminus, and chartered the Burlington & Missouri River Railroad in Nebraska to push their own extension westward. Perkins took charge of Nebraska land, construction, and colonization, though he refused to desert his home in Burlington. By the early 1870s Iowa challenged Missouri as the CB&Q's link with the western frontier.

The railroad troubles of the 1870s tested with fire the talents of young Charles Perkins. In that decade he developed from a provincial superintendent of a small western road into a major new system leader in a rapidly changing business world. He perceived four classes of problems that marked these years and shaped forever his views on business and railroad management. Reckless competition between rival lines was the first enemy of good business, and fraudulent construction deals ran a close second. Government regulation of the railroad business posed a third obstacle to success, and the rising temper of organized workers completed the difficult scene. Because Perkins was a resident manager responsible for detailed business and operations, yet still closely allied through kinship, influence, and investments with conservative outside capitalists, he developed a hybrid perspective that stood out in time as a model for professional corporate managers.

Perkins graduated in 1872 from general superintendent to vice-president of the B&MR, and in

Perkins about 1890

1873 to vice-president and general manager of the CB&Q's Lines West when the CB&Q absorbed the Iowa company. He clashed bitterly with James F. Joy, first over cutthroat competition in which Joy's Missouri lines cheated both Perkins's road and the famous "Iowa Pool" out of transcontinental interchange, and then over a construction scandal in Iowa (the so-called River Roads), in which Joy and several other CB&Q directors attempted a Crédit Mobilier-style scheme that collapsed. Joy was trying to "ride two horses in opposite directions at the same time," Perkins once complained, and this was bound to produce "some soreness." The solution for Perkins was to keep to a single mount and ride it for all it was worth. With more vigor than the Boston directors approved Perkins fought for his east-west conception of strategic development; more than any other director he was committed to a single railroad system.

In 1875 Forbes drove Joy and his allies from the CB&Q board, brought Perkins into the directory of the parent corporation, and began grooming his younger cousin for command. As a member of an awkward three-man Western Executive Committee from 1875 to 1878, Perkins sharpened his grasp of operating details, law, politics, and finance and stiffened his opposition to regulation and labor unions. He fought the Iowa Granger movement to a draw, and he crushed the 1877 railway workers'

strike within his jurisdiction by stopping the trains altogether until the men came back to work. By 1878, however, the committee approach to railroad management was obviously failing. But Perkins remained too inexperienced (or too headstrong) for some of the directors, so Forbes took the presidency himself for three more years. Finally in 1881 Perkins gained the position for which he had been training since the end of the Civil War, and he prepared to lead the CB&Q into a new decade of incredible growth and turmoil.

Charles Perkins now commanded a railroad that spanned much of three states and operated a network of local feeders in Illinois and Iowa that insured steady local traffic from the main line's "natural territory." In 1871 the CB&Q had lost the Hannibal & St. Joseph to Jay Gould, whose control of the Union Pacific, gained in 1875, made him Perkins's main strategic opponent. Forbes had never successfully forced open the western gateway at Kearney, which shrouded the future of the Nebraska lines; still, as a new boom took shape in the late 1870s, Forbes and Perkins planned a strategy that blended energy with caution. They decided to merge the Nebraska corporation into the CB&Q (claiming for the Iowa route all traffic that might otherwise have gone through Missouri), demanded once more free exchange with the UP at Kearney, and prepared to build their own line to the western city of Denver. "Perkins and I are not pugnacious," Forbes protested when competitors condemned this aggression, but "Jay Gould will be peaceful to the *strong* not the weak." Perkins believed that he sought only what was natural, that the "theoretically perfect Railroad system would be long and not very wide . . . with arms here & there reaching to great centers not within the system." There is no more succinct statement of Perkins's goals at the dawn of his presidency of the CB&Q.

When Perkins took office in October 1881 the Nebraska merger was recently completed and the Denver line was under construction, to be finished the following spring. With his own line across the Great Plains Perkins could afford to shun Gould's Union Pacific forces. He thus turned down an 1882 offer to buy back the Hannibal at a "fancy price" and got a better deal the next year for his patience. In 1885 Perkins launched the Chicago, Burlington & Northern line into St. Paul, which linked his main system with James J. Hill's new line to the Pacific Northwest, and he cast envious glances at possible routes between Denver and Oregon. By 1891 the CB&Q controlled over 5,000 miles of railroad from Chicago to the Rocky Mountains, with arms reaching to St. Paul and Kansas City. The "theoretically perfect" system was, for the moment, in place.

Through the dizzying boom of the 1880s Perkins never lost sight of what he believed were the essential principles of railroad management: economize operations and maximize earnings. Blending the theories of Adam Smith with those of Charles Darwin, Perkins argued that profits flowed to the fittest competitors and such competition best served the whole order of society. With a righteousness that frustrated his adversaries Perkins distinguished between his own competitive construction (done, he said, to stop Gould's unfair practices) and purely speculative projects like the Atchison, Topeka and Santa Fe's plan to cut diagonally through Burlington country with a new line to Chicago. Wherever cutthroat competition drove down revenues Perkins sought peace and pools, but he backed up cooperation with preparations for war. At home on the Burlington lines his message was always the same: keep the road and equipment in top shape, beat back all extraneous expenses, diligently seek traffic at paying rates, and charge all that the traffic will bear. With an uncanny eye for both minute detail and the big picture Perkins emerged as one of the most successful and intelligent railroad executives of the late nineteenth century.

With his aptitude for classification and his devotion to the firm (and not just his own fortune), Charles E. Perkins represents an early example of the professional corporate manager. He not only governed his company well but also wrote long explanations of how a company ought to be run. Experience, he thought, best proved ideas about managing the firm or behavior outdoors in the marketplace; yet the formalistic doctrines of natural law, so popular in his day, often distorted his reading of experience itself. Thus with each passing year he acquired more "proof" of what he already believed was the natural order of things.

A railroad corporation, argued Perkins, was a complex organization with an added problem of controlling men at great distances. Only a divisional structure broke the problem down into units small enough that responsible managers could do their work. Men worked best when they were completely responsible for their own jurisdictions, and since distant superiors could not know the details anyway,

Perkins spread authority downward. He loved hard information and authorized great expenditures for statistical departments that gave superintendents and top management abstract insights into the health of the whole machine. At the same time numbers alone were inadequate, and he insisted that a section superintendent "see his road every few days" on foot. Summarizing his rules in 1883 Perkins enjoined his staff to 1) delegate all you can, 2) trust subordinates to do their work, 3) avoid details, 4) don't listen to the "gossip of the camp," 5) require minute accounts of money, and 6) regard the feelings of others when managing men.

Perkins bitterly resented attacks on the free hand of management. Labor might organize for educational and social purposes, but class action to coerce employers simply broke the laws of nature. He openly supported collusion among railroad managers for mutual peace and profit, and he recognized that employment on a large railroad involved a "class of men," not the autonomous agents of free labor theory; still, he never comprehended collective bargaining by workers as anything but evil. The presidents of competing roads "should lunch together every day," he wrote in 1884, but strikes were "high-handed and absurd" and arbitration was an insult to the owners. When a strike crippled the CB&Q in 1888 Perkins suffered extended losses rather than surrender to false principles.

Government regulation carried the "error" of interference to more dangerous heights. Here Perkins's intellectual and practical faculties collided. Popular resentment of railroad practices mounted steadily, and he knew some regulation was inevitable, yet he could find no room in his system of commercial laws for the slightest concession to the enemies of laissez-faire. As federal legislation approached in the 1880s he denounced his colleagues who thought they could "modify public opinion by admitting the necessity of *some* legislation, hoping to be able to guide it." In a long and passionate response to Sen. Shelby M. Cullom's 1885 questionnaire Perkins denied unequivocally the need for and the wisdom of any regulation whatever. When in 1887 the Interstate Commerce Act outlawed pooling (the one kind of self-regulation Perkins approved of) he felt stripped of his only defense against predatory shippers and dishonest railroad agents. Perkins knew that the "question of political economy" turned, not on what was ideal, but on what was "expedient for society, for government, to do about the production, distribution, and consumption" of wealth. But his analysis stumbled on his formalistic assumptions; *all* regulations, he declared, were inexpedient, "as all experience proves." The "spirit of the age" was "communistic," he wrote to Forbes, and he could never understand that the public's desire to restrain trade perfectly mirrored his own yearning for restraint of competition.

Railroad managers never enjoyed the freedom Perkins craved; instead, they took refuge in ever larger combinations of lines that might protect them from cutthroat competition, local regulation, and commercial distress. Panic and depression between 1893 and 1896 forced most of the CB&Q's competition into receivership, and while Perkins's own road never missed a dividend, the reorganization of the industry surrounded his property with tough new rivals. Perkins's first response was aggressive; he toyed with buying the Northern Pacific, but his Boston directors held back. Immediately suitors paid him court, and Perkins set his mind to maneuvering the best possible sale of the CB&Q to one of the larger systems. To clear the stage he resigned from the presidency on February 5, 1901, and on April 20 he closed a deal with James J. Hill's Great Northern and Northern Pacific lines for $200 per share. The sale of the CB&Q capped Perkins's career and marked the end of an era in midwestern railroads.

Charles Perkins's business philosophy was bloodless and rigid, but the man himself was not. A gentleman of real intelligence and wit he was remarkably well read and well rounded in the great Victorian tradition. Perkins doted on his wife and seven children, who divided their time between the family's permanent home, The Apple Trees in Burlington, various residences around Boston, and long trips to resorts all over the continent. He loved hunting in the wilds of Kansas, he loved visiting with family near and far, but most of all he loved dinner, cigars, and conversation. His ready wit tempered the icy logic of his thoughts; when confronted with a new form of "fraud," the gas log, he quipped, "I shall simply throw things–cigar stumps, for instance–in the gas-log fire ... and say I thought it was what it pretended to be!" In Christmas distributions, presents to Kansas farmers where he hunted, relief to poor neighbors in Burlington, Boston, or almost anywhere along the CB&Q lines, Perkins's personal generosity openly contradicted his steel-edged

social theories. He even suffered large personal losses in a Lincoln, Nebraska, bank in order to protect depositors, who had trusted his name, from the inexorable forces of the marketplace. Still, he never saw in the hardships and suffering of individuals, towns, even whole regions, anything to shake his faith in the natural laws of trade.

At his death on November 9, 1907, Charles E. Perkins was hailed as a model businessman. "As a railroad builder he was perhaps as great a strategist as any man this country has produced," wrote one colleague, Frederick A. Delano, "and yet his name will never be connected with those who, in undertaking daring things, have brought ruin to themselves and their associates." It was "his brains that made the Burlington," added E. P. Ripley of the Atchison, Topeka and Santa Fe. Perkins's career seemed to document contemporary notions that business methods were "fundamentally sound" and that "corporations must be fairly conducted in order to survive." He had presided over what Delano called the "Burlington School" of railroad management, where his approval was "as good a diploma as a railroad man could ask for." James J. Hill said Perkins knew "more than anybody in the country about the right relations of business and government." In a sentimental tribute of which Perkins might well have disapproved, Hill stopped all activity on the CB&Q for five minutes November 11 while Charles E. Perkins was buried.

Whether or not Perkins knew the right relations between business and government he devoted more intellectual energy to the problem than any of his colleagues, and his endless writings on the subject (never published) stand as one of the most important windows historians possess into the mind of a working businessman in America's railroad age. In Perkins's life we find reflected both the character of that age and the peculiarities that make it difficult to understand today.

Publication:

Letter to Hon. S. M. Cullom (Cambridge, Mass.: University Press of John Wilson, 1885).

References:

Thomas C. Cochran, *American Railroad Leaders, 1845-1890: The Business Mind in Action* (Cambridge, Mass.: Harvard University Press, 1953);

Edith Perkins Cunningham, ed., *Charles Elliot Perkins: Family Letters and Reminiscences*, 2 volumes (Portland, Maine, 1949);

Frederick A. Delano, "Perkins of the Burlington," *Appleton's Magazine* (March 1908): 294-297;

Julius Grodinsky, *Jay Gould, His Business Career* (Philadelphia: University of Pennsylvania Press, 1957);

John Lauritz Larson, *Bonds of Enterprise* (Cambridge, Mass.: Harvard University Press, 1984);

Richard C. Overton, *The Burlington Route* (New York: Knopf, 1965):

Overton, *Burlington West* (Cambridge, Mass.: Harvard University Press, 1941);

Overton, "C. E. Perkins," *Business History Review*, 31 (1957): 292-309;

Overton, *Perkins/Budd* (Westport, Conn.: Greenwood Press, 1982).

Archives:

The majority of the extant papers concerning Charles E. Perkins are located in the Burlington Railroad Archives of the Newberry Library, Chicago, Illinois. The balance is located in the private collection of Richard C. Overton.

Philadelphia & Reading Railroad

by Robert L. Frey

Wilmington College of Ohio

The Philadelphia & Reading (P&R) Railroad was primarily a coal-hauling railroad located in the eastern part of Pennsylvania and in New Jersey. It is important because it hauled most of the early anthracite coal to Philadelphia, eventually connected Philadelphia and New York, and was a major factor in the development of the late-nineteenth-century American railroad system. In addition, the P&R was a railroad whose improvements in locomotive design and in coal transportation techniques marked it as one of the most innovative of nineteenth-century railroads. Many of these traits continued into the twentieth century as well, although the P&R lost its significant role in railroad history primarily because the nation moved west and the cities of Philadelphia and New York became less dominant in American business and commerce than they had been during the nineteenth century.

The Philadelphia & Reading was chartered on April 4, 1833, by Edward Biddle, a member of the Philadelphia banking family; Moncure Robinson, a prominent early civil engineer; Isaac Hiester; Matthias Pennypacker; and George deBenneville Keim. Biddle wrote: "We have concluded to apply to our Legislature for a charter for a railroad from Reading to unite with the Pennsylvania State Railroad at Peters Island. The Schuylkill Navigation Company are [sic] so slow in their movements, that we are tired of urging them on." The desire to ship anthracite coal from the eastern Pennsylvania counties of Lehigh, Wyoming, and Schuylkill in the 1820s had led to the construction of the Schuylkill Canal. The

canal, completed in 1825, was slow, taking seven days for a trip from the mines to Philadelphia, and was unusable during the frozen winter months. Efforts to encourage others to construct a railroad had not worked, so Biddle and his associates vowed to try.

The chief engineer for the proposed railroad was the extremely capable Moncure Robinson, who laid out a gradually descending line for the ninety-three miles from Pottsville through Reading to Philadelphia. Lack of funds forced Elihu Chauncey, the first president, to delay construction for several years and the line was not finished from Philadelphia to Pottsville until May of 1842. Some of the funds necessary to complete construction were raised by the sale of stocks and bonds to British investors. In return for this investment, some of the first locomotives and rolling stock were purchased from England.

The new railroad was favorably received by the public and soon began to repay the hopes of its builders. From the beginning, the P&R was a leader in technological developments. One of its first locomotives, the Gowan & Marx, established an early tonnage record when it moved a train of 101 loaded coal cars weighing 432 tons from Reading to Philadelphia at an average speed of 9.8 miles per hour. Edward Kirk, James Millholland, and John E. Wootten were well known as mechanical officers of the P&R: Kirk because he initiated locomotive construction at the Reading shops, Millholland because of his standardized locomotive designs, and Wootten because his wide firebox designed to burn anthracite coal led to the development of the "camel-back" or "Mother Hubbard" locomotives with the crew cab astride the boiler. In 1846 the P&R constructed one of the first iron bridges in the United States and, several years later, developed the famous Port Reading coal loading facility, which was considered one of the technological marvels of the nineteenth century.

During the 1840s several small coal-hauling lines in the Pottsville area were merged into the P&R. President John Tucker began to lease coal mines in 1851 and to acquire a shipping fleet to create a more integrated transportation system. The company helped to construct, then leased, and in 1858 acquired the Lebanon Valley Railroad, which ran from Reading to Harrisburg—an early central Pennsylvania rail center. The East Pennsylvania line from Reading to Allentown was acquired in 1869 and, with the Lebanon Valley Railroad, constituted a "crossline" to the Philadelphia-Reading-Pottsville main line. In 1870 the P&R acquired the Philadelphia, Germantown & Norristown Railroad, which had been chartered in 1831 and had operated the Matthias Baldwin, the first locomotive built by the famous locomotive manufacturer.

The most dramatic period of expansion of the P&R took place during the twenty-five years after Franklin B. Gowen became president in 1869. At thirty-four years of age, one of the youngest railroad presidents in the country, Gowen, who was in many ways a genius, set out to make the P&R a great system. He expanded the company into Bound Brook, New Jersey, by leasing the Central of New Jersey, which gave the P&R access to New York. Improved locomotives and larger coal cars were developed to increase the hauling efficiency of the railroad. Gowen also continued Tucker's practice of acquiring coal mines, but did so with little regard for the financial stability of the company. These purchases and several unwise attempts to expand the line beyond its financial limits drove the P&R into bankruptcy in 1880. With Gowen's purchases curtailed, the railroad emerged from bankruptcy within two years.

With the P&R again financially solvent, Gowen resumed his plan to purchase more coal mines. In addition he involved the P&R in regional "buccaneering" by allying it with W. H. Vanderbilt's New York Central (NYC) to build the South Pennsylvania Railroad from Harrisburg to Pittsburgh. The P&R wanted a western extension

and a strategy to curtail the monopoly of the Pennsylvania Railroad west of Harrisburg. The NYC was attempting to undermine the PRR—a powerful competitor. The P&R found itself in heady company when Standard Oil and J. P. Morgan became involved in addition to the NYC and the Pennsylvania. When Morgan, who did not like such cut-throat enterprises, pressured the NYC to abandon the South Pennsylvania project, the P&R was left without an ally. By this time, the company had already collapsed into a second bankruptcy on June 2, 1884, and Gowen was forced out as company president.

Disagreements stymied attempts to reorganize the P&R until 1887. Eventually J. P. Morgan reorganized the company, but at first his terms were considered unacceptable to key stockholders and sharp opposition developed. Slight modifications were made to the reorganization plan and Morgan advanced the company $15 million in 1896. The price was a voting trust, with Morgan as a member of the five-man committee, and an agreement that the railroad accept "harmonious relations," which meant an orderly division of the coal traffic between various coal-hauling lines and an end to cutthroat competition.

In 1890, after the trust ended, the company was controlled by a group of Philadelphia men, including George M. Pullman. Archibald Arthur McLeod, the president, gradually began a policy of expansion that challenged Morgan's concept of "harmonious relations." Morgan's attempts to blunt McLeod's plans were met with his famous comment: "I would rather run a peanut stand than be dictated to by J. P. Morgan." McLeod arranged leases of the Central of New Jersey once again and the Lehigh Valley, and he acquired several short lines connecting Pennsylvania railroads with New England lines. The crowning achievement was the acquisition by the P&R of the Boston & Maine and the New York & New England railroads. Next on McLeod's list was the Old Colony line, but already the P&R had control of rail lines from Boston to New York and Philadelphia. In acquiring this empire, McLeod not only stretched the financial resources of the P&R past the breaking point but also aroused the fear and antagonism of the New York Central, the Pennsylvania, and J. P. Morgan. Morgan dumped P&R stock, thus driving the price down and making it impossible for McLeod to borrow money, and entered the market to gain control of the Old Colony line for the New York, New Haven & Hartford. In 1893 the Reading collapsed into bankruptcy for the third time in less than fifteen years. Once again Morgan engineered a reorganization of the company that included a voting trust to control the company. This time Morgan made certain the president's views were more in line with his own.

Early in the twentieth century the Philadelphia & Reading Railroad again entered the national spotlight. The occasion was the coal strike of 1902. George F. "Divine-right" Baer, a vigorous anti-union man, was president of the company. He enacted wage reductions in company-owned mines and refused to deal with the nascent United Mine Workers. The resulting strike created a shortage of coal in Philadelphia, generated powerful attacks on the P&R in the press, and eventually led to intervention by Theodore Roosevelt, the president of the United States. Baer's statement that "the rights and interests of the laboring man will be protected and cared for—not by the labor agitators, but by the Christian men to whom God in his infinite wisdom has given control of the property interest of the country, and upon the successful management of which so much depends," certainly inspired the labor union and has been reprinted in many history texts as a classic example of the philosophy of the nineteenth-century capitalist.

After the reorganization of 1896, the P&R concentrated on hauling coal from the anthracite mines to market and on handling substantial bridge traffic moving to New York via the "crossline" from Hagarstown, Maryland, on the Western Maryland through Harrisburg and Reading to New York. In 1923 the coal mining properties were separated from the railroad by court order, and in 1924 the Reading Company became the operating unit of the old Philadelphia & Reading. Despite the compact regional nature of the railroad, it was a consistent money-maker until the 1960s, when anthracite mining virtually ceased and the "smokestack-industry" cities through which the Reading passed entered a long period of decline. The company once again entered bankruptcy in 1971 and ceased to exist as a separate corporate entity in 1976, when it combined with six other railroads to form the U.S. government-owned and operated Conrail System.

References:

George H. Drury, *The Historical Guide to North American Railroads* (Milwaukee: Kalmbach Books, 1985);

Joseph Anton Fisher, *1833-1958: 125th Anniversary of a Pioneer Railroad* (New York: Newcomen Society of North America, 1958);

Bert Pennypacker, *Reading Power Pictorial: From the Steam Era to Today's Diesels* (River Vale, N.J.: D. Carleton, 1973).

Archives:

The major depository for Philadelphia & Reading records is the Eleutherian Mills Historical Library at Greenville, Delaware. Records belonging to the trustees are located at the Reading Terminal, 12th and Market streets in Philadelphia, Pennsylvania. Minute books of the parent company may be found at the office of the trustees of the Reading Company at Plymouth Meeting, Pennsylvania. A list of the materials deposited in the Eleutherian Mills Library is in Duane P. Swanson and Hugh R. Gibb's, *The Historical Records of the Components of Conrail: A Survey and Inventory* (Greenville, Delaware: Eleutherian Mills-Hagley Foundation, 1978), pp. 48-53.

Henry Bradley Plant

(October 27, 1819-June 23, 1899)

by S. Walter Martin

Valdosta State College

CAREER: Various positions, New Haven Steamboat Company (1837-1854); superintendent, Adams Express Company southern territory (1854-1861); president, Southern Express Company (1861-1899); president, Plant Investment Company (1882-1899).

Henry Bradley Plant, northern developer of southern enterprises, was born in Branford, Connecticut, on October 27, 1819. His early ancestors came to this country in the 1640s and settled in Connecticut. Two of Plant's great-grandfathers fought in the American Revolution. Other Plants helped to repel the Indians from time to time, and others of the family made significant contributions to the early development of the United States.

Henry B. Plant's father, Anderson Plant, was the son of Samuel and Lorana Beckwith Plant; his mother was Betsy Plant, daughter of Levi Bradley. Anderson Plant was a farmer and a good father, but he died of typhus in 1825 when Henry was only six years old. Plant contracted the fever from his father and was not told of his father's death until he was nearly well. His sister also died from the illness. This double tragedy in the family left Plant and his mother alone until she married Philemon Hoadley of Martenburg, New York, several years later. The family relocated to New York but soon moved again to New Haven, which, being near Branford, brought them close to the Plants' original home. Plant's grandmother still lived in Branford, and he visited her frequently. She was a devout member of the Congregational Church, as were all the Plants, and much of Plant's devotion to the church came from her example. The strong influence of the Congregational Church remained with Plant throughout his lifetime. One of his ministers, Timothy P. Gillett, encouraged him to prepare to enter Yale University with hopes that he would study for the ministry, but Plant refused a college ed-

Henry Bradley Plant

ucation even though his grandmother offered to finance his studies. He did, however, attend a private academy in New Haven for a short time.

As a young man Plant drifted from one job to another. Finally in 1837, at the age of eighteen, he was hired as a deckhand by the New Haven Steamboat Company, which ran an express line between New Haven and New York. This job was much to his liking and led to the position which would eventually take him to the South and a leadership role in the transportation field.

Plant became familiar with the express business while working for the New Haven Steamboat

Company and was one of the company's most enter-prising young employees. His responsibilities increased when the company's capital was enlarged, and it was reorganized as the Adams Express Company. Adams Express began a vigorous program of expansion by buying out several smaller express companies. Plant became a key figure in these transactions and was transferred to New York, where the company's headquarters was located. Adams's biggest merger came in 1854 when it took over the Harnden Express Company, whose founder, William F. Harnden, was considered the father of the express business. He had begun a small line in 1839 and by 1854 operated the most far-flung agency in the country, serving the West and portions of the South. In 1854 the Harnden Company was the dominant express business in the Southeast.

Expecting to increase its business even further in this area, the Adams Company sent its brightest and youngest official, Henry B. Plant, to Augusta, Georgia, in 1854 to become superintendent of its new southern territory. Plant welcomed the move to Augusta because it meant greater opportunities for him in his business, and also that his sickly wife, Ellen Elizabeth Blackstone, whom he had married in 1842, could live in a warmer climate. She suffered from a lung ailment, and her doctor had advised that she spend some time in the South. She and her husband had already made two trips to Florida in 1853, and each time her health had improved in the mild temperature.

These days in Florida no doubt gave Plant some insight into the tremendous business opportunities in that state and in other undeveloped sections of the South, so he welcomed the 1854 opportunity to return to the South. After moving to Augusta Mrs. Plant continued to make occasional trips to Jacksonville, but nothing seemed to give her permanent relief from her lung disease, and she died on February 28, 1861.

Soon after Plant took charge of the Adams Express Company office in Augusta, he began to extend its routes over the railroads and navigable rivers south of the Potomac River. Offices were established in several principal cities, including Nashville, Memphis, Vicksburg, Louisville, and New Orleans. By 1858 he had pushed the business into Texas by merging with the New Orleans & Texas Express Company. The business developed rapidly under his guidance.

Plant was more concerned than most with the enmity between the North and South over slavery. Sensing that war was coming, he began to make plans for his business sometime before the actual fighting began. When fighting did break out in April 1861, the Adams Company, being a northern concern, feared that all of its southern holdings might be confiscated by the South. With this possibility in mind Plant was allowed to take control of all the southern routes of the Adams Express Company. For several weeks this arrangement prevailed while Plant waited for the Georgia authorities to act on an application to charter the company in that state. A charter was granted by the state of Georgia to the Southern Express Company on May 1, 1861, and immediately the signs above all Adams Express Company offices in the South were changed.

For the sake of his business in the South Plant made friends with many of the southern leaders, and on one occasion visited Pres. Jefferson Davis in Montgomery to assure him of his friendship and loyalty. While other northerners were leaving the South Plant remained and conducted his business without political affiliation or military involvement. President Davis admired the frank neutrality of the man and realized that the Confederacy could use the Southern Express Company to good advantage. Plant was given permission to move about in the South at will and to pass through army posts on business. His company transported mail and parcels throughout the South during the war and, in cooperation with the northern Adams Company, delivered packages and mail in the North as well. The United States post office did not handle mail from the South between 1861 and 1865, and the Southern Express Company filled this void. Many people, however, were suspicious of Plant and looked upon him as a Yankee playing "both ends against the middle."

As the war continued Plant's critics increased in number, and at times he was made to feel uncomfortable and even unwelcome. Pressures on him mounted, and in the summer of 1863 he suffered an attack of gastric fever and was advised to lessen the strain he had been under. Due to wartime restrictions and conditions his journey back to Connecticut, where his only child was living with his mother, was long and involved. In the fall he embarked on an extended European trip. He enjoyed traveling abroad and was determined to return to Europe. This he did in 1873, carrying with him his new wife, the former Margaret Josephine Loughman, his mother, and his son Morton. The second marriage was a happy one in every respect.

Plant lived in New York until the Civil War ended and returned to Augusta and the Southern Express Company in the spring of 1865. The company was reorganized, and northern capital was brought in to make it a bigger and stronger company. Plant was made president of the reorganized company, a position he held until his death.

With the construction of more railroads in the South after the war, the express business flourished, and by 1875 nationwide service was a reality. In 1879 Plant ventured into the railroad field himself, realizing that the future of the express business lay with railroads. He and a few associates purchased in 1879 the 350-mile Atlanta & Gulf Railroad, which extended from Savannah to the southwestern corner of Georgia, for $4,710,000. The intention of the builders of the road had been to connect Savannah with the Gulf of Mexico. After the purchase the road was rechartered by Plant under the name of Savannah, Florida & Western, and it soon became a significant link in all east-west transportation in Georgia and neighboring states. He next purchased a short line connecting Waycross, Georgia, and Jacksonville, Florida. In 1880 he bought and rebuilt the Charleston & Savannah Railroad line, which helped to facilitate travel between Florida, Charleston, and the North.

In order to unite all of his railroad investments and to attract additional capital, Plant formed a company, similar in structure to the Southern Express Company, called the Plant Investment Company. It was chartered in Connecticut in 1882 and not only operated the Plant railroads, but took as one of its purposes to purchase and develop other southern railroads. Plant owned most of the stock in the company, but other interested friends, including Henry M. Flagler, were invited to participate. Plant was president of the company until his death in 1899. From 1884 Plant's son, Morton F., was the elder Plant's chief business associate.

Plant's next move was to absorb several smaller railroads into the Savannah, Florida & Western Railroad, including the Live Oak, Florida & Rowland's Bluff; the Chattahoochee, Florida & East Pass; and the Live Oak, Tampa & Charlotte Harbor Road. These mergers added about 100 miles to the Plant system, giving it a total of nearly 500 miles. Plant's aim was to extend his business

into central and west Florida and to gain a terminus at Tampa. Like his rival on the east coast of Florida, Henry N. Flagler, Plant had dreams of tapping the rich South and Central American markets. He could do this with steamboat connections at Tampa. Working to this end, he extended the Du Pont–Live Oak line in 1884 to Gainesville, Florida, a distance of 110 miles, and then built a short line of twenty miles from Fort White, Florida, to Lake City, Florida, and also a line of twenty-four miles from Thomasville, Georgia, to Monticello, Florida.

In 1884 the Plant Investment Company purchased another strong link in its system, the Brunswick & Western Railroad. This road had been chartered in 1835 and connected Brunswick, Georgia, with Albany, Georgia, intersecting the Savannah, Florida & Western at Waycross, Georgia. At one time there was a proposal to extend the road to Eufala, Alabama, in order to connect with the Chattahoochee River, a main artery of transportation, but this plan was never carried out. The acquisition of the Brunswick & Western increased Plant's railroad system to nearly 1,000 miles in South Carolina, Georgia, and Florida.

Most of Plant's energies in the 1880s, however, were spent in acquiring and building portions of two other railroads in Florida which helped to complete his railroad system to Tampa and west Florida: the South Florida Railroad and the Florida Southern Railroad. The South Florida Railroad was under construction when Plant purchased controlling interest in it. The purpose for its construction was to connect Tampa Bay with the great commercial waterway, the St. John's River, at Sanford. The road was finished in 1886 to Sanford via Orlando and Lakeland. The completion of the road gave new life to Tampa and to an area which had been isolated from the northern portion of the state except by wagon or carriage line.

Plant's next venture was the completion in the late 1880s of the Florida Southern Railroad, which ran from Palatka via Gainesville and Ocala to Tampa. Arrangements were made for the road to work in cooperation with the Savannah, Florida & Western Railroad. Plant's steamers on the St. John's River also connected with the road at Palatka, making travel from north Florida and south Georgia to the Tampa area much easier. The Plant system covered 1,494 miles by 1890, extending from Charleston, South Carolina, to Tampa and Punta Gorda on the south, and from Savannah to Montgomery on the west. These roads serviced the best agricultural lands of four southeastern states. Farm products and naval stores were sent daily to markets and shipping points at Savannah, Charleston, Jacksonville, and Tampa.

The Jacksonville, Tampa & Key West Railroad, which connected Jacksonville and Sanford, was the last road to be purchased by the Plant Investment Company. Although the transaction took place in 1899, the road had been completed in 1886.

Plant established steamship lines on a number of rivers, including the St. Johns, the Chattahoochee, the Flint, and the Manatee. In 1886 he purchased a 200-foot steamer and established a line connecting Tampa with Key West and Havana, thus opening new possibilities for trade with south Florida and Cuba. All of his steamships made connections with his railroad for faster and more complete service.

In addition to his railroads and steamship lines Plant operated an extensive system of hotels for tourists, health seekers, and sportsmen. The largest and most elaborate was the Tampa Bay hotel, completed in 1891 at a cost of $2 million. Furnishings alone cost nearly $500,000. It was a huge Moorish structure which sat in the center of a 16-acre plot of ground in Tampa. Constructed of brick, the main entrance was flanked by sixteen polished marble columns. Inside, the guests were impressed by the beautiful staircases, the luxurious drawing rooms, and the expensive furnishings. Equally as comfortable and as luxuriant was the Hotel Belleview at Clearwater. Other Plant hotels included the Hotel Seminole at Winter Park, the Ocala House in Ocala, the Inn at Port Tampa, and Hotel Kissimmee at Kissimmee. These hotels were all widely known in the northern states from which winter visitors came to Florida.

Henry B. Plant died on June 23, 1899, after a life full of activity. A poorly executed will led to the 1902 sale of Plant's railroad properties and their consolidation into the Atlantic Coast Line Railroad. Nevertheless, Plant can be credited with building a large network of railroads, a well-run express business, a fine system of hotels, and a thriving steamship line.

References:

Karl H. Grismer, *A History of the City of Tampa and the Tampa Bay Region of Florida* (St. Petersburg: St. Petersburg Printing, 1950);

Henry V. Poor, *Manual of the Railroads of the United States for 1880* (New York: H. V. & H. W. Poor, 1880);

G. H. Smythe, *The Life of Henry Bradley Plant* (New York: Putnam's, 1898);

A. L. Stinson, *History of the Express Business* (New York: Baker and Godwin, 1881).

Morton Freeman Plant

(August 18, 1852-November 4, 1918)

by S. Walter Martin

Valdosta State College

CAREER: Various positions, Southern Express Company (1868-1882); vice-president (1882-1899), president (1899-1902); Plant System of railroads; vice-president, Plant Investment Company (1882-1899); director, Atlantic Coast Line Railroad (1902-1918).

Morton Freeman Plant was the son of Henry Bradley Plant, the founder of the Plant System of railroads, which later became a part of the Atlantic Coast Line Railroad. While the younger Plant was a competent businessman he did not have the same drive and determination as his father. Morton Plant is better known for his philanthropy than for his business acumen.

Plant was born on August 18, 1852, at the family estate in Groton, Connecticut. His mother, who was chronically ill, died of consumption in 1861, when Plant was ten years old; he spent much of his time with relatives. In 1868 Plant graduated from Russell College in New Haven and immediately began work in Memphis, Tennessee, with his father's firm, the Southern Express Company. From his first job with Southern Express, Plant worked himself through the ranks to earn his position of heir apparent. All of Plant's fortune and influence would ultimately derive from his father's businesses.

In 1882 Henry Plant formed the Plant Investment Company, the purpose of which was to build and acquire railroads and steamship lines. The Plant System of railroads, extending throughout Georgia and Florida, became Morton Plant's primary business responsibility. Plant remained as the System's vice-president until he became president upon his father's death in 1899. He remained as vice-president of the Plant Investment Company, Henry Plant being succeeded as president by Robert G. Erwin. Probate troubles with Henry Plant's will caused the Plant System to be sold in 1902 to the At-

Morton Freeman Plant

lantic Coast Line Railroad. Plant was named as a director of the railroad, remaining on the board until his death in 1918. In addition to these duties Plant served on the boards of numerous other companies and institutions, including the Southern Express Company, the National Bank of Commerce of New Haven, Connecticut, and the Peninsular & Occidental Steamship Company.

Despite his many business interests Plant cultivated many talents outside his occupation. For many years he was a leading figure in the world of yachting, in 1906 winning twenty-one prizes in twenty-five races in Europe. At one point he owned twelve racing yachts, the best known being the

320-foot *Iolanda*, which cost over $1,000 per day to operate.

Yet Plant is best remembered for his philanthropy. He gave well over $1 million to build and help operate the Connecticut College for Women, which opened in 1915. Plant also left $100,000 in his will for the Lawrence Hospital of New London, Connecticut. This was the second example of his giving to hospitals; in 1914 Plant pledged $100,000 toward the construction of a hospital in Clearwater, Florida. The hospital is still named for Morton F. Plant.

Plant was married in 1888 to Nellie Capron of Baltimore, with whom he had one son, Henry Plant II. After his first wife died in 1913, Plant married May Caldwell Manwaring in 1914. He adopted her son from a previous marriage. Morton

Freeman Plant died from pneumonia at his Fifth Avenue home on November 4, 1918. Although he inherited the bulk of his wealth he was a competent and shrewd businessman on his own accord.

Publication:
Cruise of the Iolanda (New York: Putnam's, 1911).

References:
Jan Kirby, *Giant Steps: The History of Morton F. Plant Hospital* (Clearwater, Fla.: Morton F. Plant Hospital, 1981);

Gertrude E. Noyes, *History of Connecticut College* (New London: Connecticut College, 1982);

Irene Nye, *History of Connecticut College* (New York: J. J. Little and Ives, 1943);

G. Hutchinson Smythe, *The Life of Henry Bradley Plant* (New York: Putnam's, 1898).

John Plumbe

(July 1809-July 1857)

by W. Thomas White

James Jerome Hill Reference Library

CAREER: Railroad surveyor and superintendent (1831-c.1835); publicist, lobbyist, and photographer (1836-1857).

John Plumbe, one of the first effective advocates of a transcontinental railroad, was born in Wales in July 1809. Little is known of his youth and upbringing other than that he immigrated to the United States with his family in 1821. In 1831 he was hired as surveyor, assisting Moncure Robinson, the famous civil engineer, in locating a route across the Allegheny Mountains. In 1832, after being recommended by Robinson, Plumbe was appointed to be superintendent of the Petersburg Railroad, one of the earliest lines in the region and which ran from Petersburg, Virginia, to the Roanoke River in North Carolina.

In 1836 Plumbe moved to Dubuque, in the Iowa Territory, which he called home for the rest of his life. Soon after the move to Iowa Plumbe began his activities calling for the construction of a Pacific railroad. It is not known why Plumbe became such a strong advocate of the project though plans for such an undertaking were widespread at the time.

His many lectures in Iowa, Wisconsin, and Illinois were popular, and Plumbe became well known as a railroad and town promoter. He also authored numerous resolutions and letters to newspaper editors under the pseudonym "The Iowan" urging the rail project.

Plumbe was able to secure in 1838 a $2,000 appropriation from the United States Congress to fund a survey for a rail route from Lake Michigan to the Mississippi River. The route, which was never built, was intended to run from Milwaukee to land which Plumbe owned near Sinipee, Wisconsin, near Dubuque. Although the rail line was never realized, Plumbe was able to publish in 1839 the results of his travels and surveys in his *Sketches of Iowa and Wisconsin Taken During a Residence of Three Years in Those Territories*. The book was significant in that it was one of the first descriptive accounts of the region's geography and included a map of the Iowa Territory.

Plumbe resumed his advocacy for a Pacific railroad in 1840, traveling that year to Washington, D.C., in order to lobby Congress directly. He was unsuccessful in his efforts, and much of Plumbe's activity during the rest of the 1840s revolved around his skills as a photographer. He moved to Philadelphia and opened a photography business, reputedly becoming so successful that by 1845 he had also opened stores in New York, Boston, Baltimore, Washington, Louisville, Cincinnati, St. Louis, and Dubuque. During this period Plumbe also developed a technique, which he called the Plumbeotype, of printing daguerreotypes on paper. The technique no doubt played a role in Plumbe's publication in 1846-1847 of a short-lived periodical known as both the *Popular Magazine* and *The Plumbe Popular Magazine*.

In 1849 Plumbe traveled to California via the South Pass, a trip which seems to have rekindled his interest in a Pacific railroad. Though he published many articles on the subject in the San Francisco newspaper *Placer Times*, Plumbe did not remain in California very long.

On his return to the East in 1850 Plumbe published an attack on fellow rail promoter Asa Whitney's plan for a transcontinental line. In his *Memorial against Mr. Asa Whitney's Railroad Scheme*, which was published in 1851, Plumbe

charged that Whitney's land grant proposal was merely an attempt to fleece the government. The effect of Plumbe's polemic and his activities after its publication are largely unknown. His fortunes seem to have taken a turn for the worse, for the next documented event in Plumbe's life is his suicide, which occurred in July 1857 in Dubuque. Although Plumbe was not directly responsible for the completion of the transcontinental railroad, he remains important as an example of the type of promoter and advocate who labored to realize the dream.

Publications:

Sketches of Iowa and Wisconsin Taken During a Residence of Three Years in Those Territories (St. Louis: Chambers, Harris & Knapp, 1839, reprinted, Ames: State Historical Society of Iowa, 1948);

The National Plumbeotype Gallery (Philadelphia: National Publishing, 1847);

Plumbe's Memorial (1850);

Memorial against Mr. Asa Whitney's Railroad Scheme (Washington, D.C.: Buell & Blanchard, 1851).

Reference:

John King, "John Plumbe, Originator of the Pacific Railroad," *Annals of Iowa*, 6 (January 1904): 289-296.

Henry Varnum Poor

December 8, 1812-January 4, 1905)

by Matthew A. Redinger

University of Montana

CAREER: Editor, *American Railroad Journal* (1849-1863); editor, *Manual of the Railroads of the United States* (1868-1890); editor, *Poor's Directory of Railway Officials* (1886-1895); editor, *Poor's Handbook of Investment Securities* (1890-1892).

Henry Varnum Poor was one of America's premier economic analysts and business journalists. In his ninety-three years he authored numerous books and articles and received national recognition as an authority on government and finance.

Henry Poor was born on December 8, 1812, to Dr. Silvanus and Mary Poor of Andover, Maine. The Poors' cheerful, busy home became the center of his early life and education. Henry's participation in the Andover Debating Society stimulated his

developing intellect. After leaving home in 1831, Poor attended Bowdoin College where Prof. Samuel A. Newman introduced Poor to political and economic theory. Poor graduated from Bowdoin in 1835 and entered his uncle Jacob McGraw's law firm in Bangor, Maine. Although he was admitted to the Maine bar and practiced law for fourteen years, Poor did not enjoy being a lawyer. As a result he looked for other interests to occupy him.

In September 1841 Poor married Mary Pierce after a three-year engagement. Mary, an intellectual in her own right, shared in her husband's ambition and offered moral support and intellectual stimulation in his Bangor business ventures. Bangor in the 1840s was in the midst of a booming lumber speculation. In 1845 Poor invested in timberlands which returned a substantial profit until those interests

Henry Varnum Poor

failed during the depression of the late 1840s. The failure had a long-lasting effect on Poor, as it both sharpened his business skills and taught him to avoid overoptimism.

On the completion of his brother's work on the Maine railroad system in 1849, Henry and John Alfred moved to New York City where they purchased the *American Railroad Journal*. It was as editor of the first commercially produced railroad journal that Poor made use of his talent and experience. John Alfred and Henry Varnum had entered into a partnership with John Schultz, a New York printer, to buy the journal. Shortly thereafter, Henry purchased John Alfred's interests. As editor Poor's responsibilities included preparation of copy, solicitation of advertisements, and the management of the paper's financial affairs.

Under Poor's editorship the paper changed as his idea of his own mission changed. In the first years of his association with the *American Railroad Journal*, Poor believed that the position as editor included an implicit role as spokesman for the railroad industry. In fact, from 1850 to 1852, he considered the paper's primary purpose as represent-

ing various railroad interests on Wall Street. However, in the last ten years of Poor's editorship, 1852-1862, he changed his tack. He began to see himself as a reformer. His biggest mission, as he saw it, was to warn railroads against reckless expansion of lines, the "foolish rivalry" which promised to bring collapse to railroading. Poor also used his editorials as vehicles for attacks on issues such as taxation, tolls, and other legislation that discriminated against railroads.

The first years of the 1860s brought a change of Poor's interests. The first (and only) of three planned volumes of his *History of the Railroads and Canals of the United States* reached the publisher in the summer of 1860. The next year, however, Poor became a writer for *The New York Times* editorial page. This work, the analyzing and recording of the nation's impending Civil War crisis, was more important, according to Poor, than his descriptions of the development of the railroad industry. Poor expanded his responsibilities and interests even further. In 1862, at fifty years of age, he accepted the editor's position at *Samuel Hallett's North American Financial Circular*. Later in 1863 Poor sold his interests in the *Railroad Journal* to devote more of his energies to the *Times* and the *Financial Circular*.

Poor became involved in the speculation craze of wartime New York, and did quite well in gold investments. His investments did so well, in fact, that he planned an early retirement. But Poor's plans crumbled when the panic of April 1864 caught him off guard. To rebuild his retirement reserves Poor took a variety of financial odd jobs, including the appraisal of railroad lands for financiers and the lobbying of Congress on behalf of railroad interests. Poor recognized that his cash reserves were dwindling, and that his retirement still seemed further and further away.

In 1867, on a suggestion from his son Henry William Poor, the elder Poor entered into a partnership with his son in the growing railroad insurance industry. The two called their company H. V. and H. W. Poor, and quickly began to prosper. In 1868, as his son managed the business, Poor wrote and published the first edition of the *Manual of the Railroads of the United States*. The *Manual* received immediate acclaim, and Poor planned future annual editions.

From 1868 to 1873 Poor divided his attention between lobbying Congress on key issues and his

Manual. He depended on his assistants and seldom wrote more than the volumes' introductions. After 1873 Poor turned away from the *Manual* and poured most of his energies into his lobbying efforts and writing for various journals. In spite of the small amount of time Poor spent on the *Manual,* he helped it become the authority on economics, railroads, and, later, various related industries. Both the *Manual*'s quality and quantity of information, compiled at first by Poor and later by his assistant Dr. Richard S. Fisher, were unprecedented. The annual's circulation grew with its reputation, from nearly 2,000 subscriptions in 1868 to over 5,000 by 1880.

In 1881, after eight years of near inactivity in the *Manual*'s publication, Poor took a new interest in his already successful annual. That year he formed Poor's Railroad Manual Company, of which he owned most of the stock. During his absence, Poor claimed, "the Manual had run pretty wild." He took on more of the writing responsibilities until he thought it had settled down. By 1886 Poor felt comfortable about giving the publishing responsibilities to the man who had replaced Fisher upon his death, John P. Meany. Poor continued to write the volumes' introductions until 1890, when Meany took over that job as well. After 1893 the volumes no longer carried Henry V. Poor's name as author.

Besides writing for the *Manual,* Poor spent his later years writing books and articles on money, banking, currency, and national economic policies. He published his magnum opus, *Money and its Laws,* a two-part financial history, in 1877. In 1878 Poor wrote *Resumption and the Silver Question,* a history of coinage and monetary policies.

Poor geared some of his later writings toward Republican partisan politics. In particular he wrote books for the presidential campaigns of 1888 and 1892. The first of these books, *Twenty-two Years of Protection,* was the more influential. In 1892 he revised and retitled the work as *The Tariff: Its Bearing Upon the Industries and Politics of the United States.* Besides these books, Poor produced a multitude of articles on railroads and finance for periodicals, including *North American Review, Railroad Gazette,* and *Bankers' Magazine.*

Henry Varnum Poor died on January 4, 1905. He left behind Mary, his wife of sixty-four years; three daughters; and a son, Henry William, of his seven children. Poor also left behind a reputation as one of America's foremost economists, business journalists, and political commentators.

Publications:

History of the Railroads and Canals of the United States of America (New York: H. V. & H. W. Poor, 1860);

The Influence of the Railroads of the United States in the Creation of its Commerce and Wealth (New York: Journeyman Printers' Cooperative Association, 1869);

Money and its Laws (New York: H. V. & H. W. Poor, 1877);

Resumption and the Silver Question (New York: H. V. & H. W. Poor, 1878);

The Pacific Railroads and the Relations Existing Between Them and the Government of the United States (New York, 1879);

Twenty-two Years of Protection (New York: H. V. & H. W. Poor, 1888);

The Tariff: Its Bearing Upon the Industries and Politics of the United States (New York: H. V. & H. W. Poor, 1892);

The Money Question (New York: H. V. & H. W. Poor, 1896; reprinted, 1897, 1898).

Unpublished Document:

With Israel D. Andrews: "The Trade and Commerce of the British North American Colonies and upon the Trade of the Great Lakes and Rivers," Senate Executive Document 112, House Executive Document 136, 32nd Congress, 1st Session.

References:

Alfred D. Chandler, Jr., *Henry Varnum Poor: Business Editor, Analyst, and Reformer* (Cambridge, Mass.: Harvard University Press, 1956);

Henry Varnum Poor; 1812-1905: List of His Writings and Maps (Washington, D.C.: Association of American Railways, 1942).

Archives:

The papers of Henry Varnum Poor may be found in the Charles Lyon Chandler Collection of Ursinus College in Collegeville, Pennsylvania; the library of the Maine Historical Society in Portland, Maine; the William Reynolds Collection of Allegheny College in Meadville, Pennsylvania; in the Baker and Widener Libraries of Harvard Business School in Cambridge, Massachusetts; and in the personal collection of Henry Poor Chandler in Washington, D.C.

Predecessors to the Association of American Railroads

Because railroads developed for the most part as discrete, privately owned enterprises, the designs and practices of the individual lines were not usually interchangeable. As railroads grew and the services they provided gained in importance, the need to coordinate among the different entities became generally recognized. Although the Association of American Railroads, the organization through which the railroads now coordinate their cooperation, was not founded until 1934, efforts to improve cooperation and efficiency were in place shortly after the Civil War.

The war had underscored both the potentialities and the deficiencies of the country's railroads. The ability to move quickly large numbers of men and great amounts of freight over long distances was a clear possibility for an efficient and well-linked rail system. The problem was that such an efficient and well-linked system was a myth. Too often, the efficiency of a railroad was limited to the length of the tracks it operated. At the beginning of the war more than 20 rail gauges, ranging from 3 feet to 6 feet, were in use throughout the country. Roads with differing gauges were unable to interchange cars and, in order to transfer freight, were forced to unload and reload cargo at the junction point between lines. Some major railroad lines even went to the expense of constructing multiple tracks with various gauges to facilitate interchange between lines.

Even when gauges were compatible between lines, problems with unstandardized car parts and the lack of rules governing the repair and return of cars on other line's tracks remained. To begin to resolve these questions, representatives of eleven railroads met in Adrian, Michigan, on September 16, 1866. The prospect of meaningful benefits growing out of these increased voluntary efforts at cooperation encouraged the railroads to direct more resources to the problem.

On September 18, 1867, representatives of at least twenty-nine railroads met in Altoona, Pennsylvania, to form the Master Car Builders Association. The organization's first goal was to solve the interchange problem; their agenda was the gauge discrepancy. The English had long ago adopted their 4-foot 8½-inch gauge as standard, and the many locomotives exported to the United States from England were of that gauge. Because of this English influence many, though not all, track gauges in the United States clustered around the English standard. The Master Car Builders Association recommended a standard gauge for trucks–but not tracks–of 4 feet 8½ inches that, with the wide-flanged wheels also recommended, would permit interchange between many lines in the United States.

Although the adoption of a standard gauge received a major boost when Congress required its use of the Pacific railroads, it was not until 1886 that the last major holdouts, several southern railroads, adopted the gauge and made it possible for a train to travel unencumbered over almost every railroad in the United States. In addition to their efforts to standardize gauge, the Master Car Builders Association also worked to encourage the development and installation of automatic air brakes and automatic couplers.

As the Master Car Builders Association worked to standardize track and rolling stock specifications, a second voluntary organization, the American Railway Master Mechanics Association (ARMMA), was formally established on September 30, 1868. This group was concerned with preventing the then common occurrence of locomotive boiler explosions. Explosions were reduced through the work of the ARMMA to standardize boilers, safety valves, and the composition of the steel used to build the boiler plates.

One of the best-known of the cooperative groups was the General Time Convention (GTC).

This group, first formed as the General Superintendents for the Arrangement of a Summer Time Schedule on May 14, 1872, took as its goal the resolution of one of the colossal problems facing the railroads in the nineteenth century: the chaos resulting from the use of more than seventy time zones in the United States. In some cases, where a city was serviced by multiple railroads, the traveler might be faced with timetables based on three different time zones, none of them corresponding to that of the city.

In 1886, with the absorption of at least one other group with the same objectives, the General Superintendents group changed its name to the General Time Convention. Although the GTC was the catalyst in persuading Congress in 1918 to establish the system of four time zones, it also pushed for the standardization of train signals, train orders, car movement reports, and car rental payment rules. Because of its quickly expanding list of interests, the GTC changed its name on April 18, 1891, to the American Railway Association (ARA).

Under this new banner the group dedicated itself to solving various rail management problems through standing committees which met at regular intervals. Owing to the fact that the railroad companies themselves became members of the ARA—other voluntary organizations were technical committees made of individuals—the ARA is regarded as the direct predecessor of the Association of American Railroads. It was not, however, the only one. Many other voluntary organizations were formed during the nineteenth century, most of them later joining forces with the ARA. These groups, along with the ARA, were later absorbed into the Association of American Railroads in 1934.

Unpublished Document:

Michael C. Douglass, "A History of the Association of American Railroads." Unpublished paper at the School of Finance and Commerce, University of Pennsylvania, May 1, 1962.

References:

William T. Faricy, *AAR: The Story Behind a Symbol* (New York: Newcomen Society, 1951);

Robert S. Henry, *This Fascinating Railroad Business* (Indianapolis: Bobbs-Merrill, 1946).

Archives:

The only publicly available documents of the Association of American Railroads are the association's annual reports.

—Frank N. Wilner

George Mortimer Pullman

(March 3, 1831-October 19, 1897)

by John H. White

Smithsonian Institution

CAREER: Store clerk (c.1845-c.1848); cabinet-maker (c.1848-1853); house mover and contractor (1853-c.1864); sleeping car promoter (c.1858-1897); gold field speculator (1862-c.1864); president, Pullman Palace Car Company (1867-1897).

George Mortimer Pullman was born on March 3, 1831, in Brockton, New York, the third of ten children of James Lewis and Emily Caroline Pullman. The steam railroad era was just dawning at the time of his birth. Though born into a modest family Pullman was to play a major role in American railroads and the associated supply industry. He came to dominate the profitable sleeping car business and was a major manufacturer of railroad rolling stock.

Pullman's father was a mechanic and sometime house mover. The family finances were such that Pullman was obliged to leave school at age fourteen to clerk in a country store. Within a few years he joined his brother in a cabinetmaking business at Albion, New York. In 1853 he took up one of his father's old trades and began moving buildings along the Erie Canal during one of its enlargement programs. He realized $6,000 from this enterprise and decided to expand his small fortune by going west. He settled in Chicago around 1857 and profited from a general rebuilding of the city that involved elevating buildings and streets. Pullman increased his capital to $20,000 in contracting to raise the level of several Chicago streets above the lake. His ambitions, however, were already beyond those of a general contractor and included wanting to make a fortune and becoming involved in some large enterprise. He began to cast about for some project of greater scope to match his ambition.

One secondary business venture involved the sleeping car business. Dozens of sleeping cars had already been put in service before Pullman became interested in the business. Theodore T. Woodruff was

George Mortimer Pullman

already active in the contract sleeping car business when Pullman began remodeling two coaches for sleeping car service on the Chicago & Alton Railroad in 1858. The cars were ready by the fall of 1859. Pullman joined in the enterprise with one of his friends from his Albion, New York, days, Benjamin C. Field, who had befriended him as a young man and helped him during his first years as a contractor. Field's experience, capital, and connections were valuable in establishing the fledgling sleeping car enterprise. Small contracts were made with several other Chicago-area railroads. Pullman replaced the dowdy remodeled coaches he had used to begin his business with new, commercially built cars.

As late as 1862 Pullman remained unsettled and unsure about what to pursue. He remained active in the contracting business and found time for banking and even a shirt factory. In the spring of 1862 he left Chicago for the Colorado gold fields and engaged in land speculation, mining, and the provision business. Meanwhile, Field continued to run the sleeping car business. Pullman returned to Chicago after about a year in Colorado. He was now thirty-two years of age and had amassed a respectable, if not great, fortune. It was time to concentrate on one line of work and make himself into a major capitalist. This was the ambition of a man who was clearly not a dreamer but a doer. Pullman decided to settle into the sleeping car business and make it his life's work.

In 1864 and 1865 he built a new luxurious car that incorporated all the best ideas of the builder's art. If not the best sleeping car of its day, as is often claimed, it surely equaled the finest cars produced by his competitors, notably Woodruff's Central Transportation Company (CTC), then the largest private sleeping car operation in the United States. During the next few years Pullman began producing other luxury cars. Most were built in the shops of contracting railroads, such as the Great Western Railway (Canada) and the Chicago & North Western Railway. By 1866 Pullman and his associates had forty sleeping cars in service on seven railroads. Pullman's goal to be a larger player in the expanding sleeping car field was advanced on February 22, 1867, when the Pullman Palace Car Company was organized with capital of $1 million. Pullman, through his new company, now had the support of prominent Chicago money barons such as Marshall Field. Just four months after incorporating the Palace Car Company, on June 13, 1867, Pullman married Hattie Sanger of Chicago. This union eventually produced four children who were raised in a grand style in a mansion on Prairie Avenue.

Pullman expanded his sleeping car business with considerable energy. His first efforts to break into the southern and far western market, while not notably successful, did enable him to find a valuable ally in Andrew Carnegie, who, upon meeting Pullman, became his champion, despite the fact that Carnegie was a stockholder in Central Transportation Company. In 1868 Carnegie helped Pullman win the sleeping car contract on the about-to-be-opened Union Pacific Railroad. He then started working within the Central Transportation organization to effect a Pullman takeover. Carnegie felt the CTC's management was overly conservative and that the potential of the sleeping car business could be more speedily realized by someone with Pullman's acute business sense and energy. A lease was completed early in 1870, and Pullman's relatively small firm in effect swallowed the giant CTC. In 1876 Pullman was operating 800 cars on about 30,000 miles of railroad. He also employed 2,000 workers and operated a large car repair and building shop in Detroit. In 1874 several cars were sent to England for service on the Midland Railway. More cars eventually went to Italy, Ireland, and even India. There was talk of a Pullman-operated transatlantic steamship line. But most of these schemes faded or expired. The British operation, never really a success, was sold to English investors in 1907. Pullman could not resist financial involvements with the New York Elevated, the Northern Pacific, the West Shore, and the Union Pacific railroads, and he, at one time or another, was a promoter or officer in all of these firms. But by the 1880s he came to understand that the sleeping car enterprise demanded all of his attention.

In 1880 the Palace Car Company, just thirteen years old, had grown beyond even Carnegie's expectations. The company operated cars over some 60,000 miles of railroad and its stock was worth $6 million. Actual earnings on investment were figured at better than 18 percent. Its cash reserve grew each year, reaching $6 million in 1890. Within seven years it grew to $25 million, and, while many businessmen worried over how to meet their obligations, Pullman's company fretted over how best to distribute its gigantic hoard of cash. Dividends were paid with the regularity of a government loan. Widows and orphanages were well advised to invest in Pullman stock.

As the Pullman monopoly grew and prospered, its ambitious leader looked for a new challenge and outlet. In 1879 Pullman decided to build a great, central car shop near Chicago which would not only maintain the company's numerous sleeping, dining, parlor, and rental private cars but would also produce cars for other railroads. The new plant would not be limited to the manufacture of luxury passenger cars but would also make ordinary coaches, baggage, freight, and even streetcars.

George Pullman (seated, center) with his family in 1897 (courtesy of Chicago Historical Society)

He purchased 3,700 acres of land fourteen miles south of Chicago bordering on Lake Calumet. Five hundred acres in the center of the tract were set aside for the car plant itself, the rest to be occupied by a planned city that Pullman envisioned as the finest model town in the world. It was carefully laid out with tree-lined streets, brick row houses, churches, schools, a shopping arcade, and parks. A fine hotel named for one of his daughters, Florence, helped to complete Pullman's vision for his industrial city. Pullman's detailed plans included a theater and a library. Solomon S. Beman was selected as the architect and was assisted by landscape archi-

tect Nathan Barrett in laying out the Pullman dream city. Construction began in April 1880, and the work moved so rapidly that the first family was settled in January of the following year. Pullman's involvement with the town and shops showed a wonderful enthusiasm, and he took an inordinate pride in its creation. For example, he purchased the giant and showy Corliss engine displayed at the 1876 U.S. Centennial Exhibition to power the machinery of the car shops. At its completion in 1881, 12,000 people lived in the town of Pullman. Its creator took great personal pleasure in escorting visitors from around the world on tours of his scientifically planned model town. The car plant itself was hardly secondary to the residential part of the town, being the largest railroad car plant in the world. The plant's 6,000 men produced 12,000 freight cars and 1,000 passenger cars per year. When production hit peaks employment more than doubled.

Early in 1889 Pullman bought the Union Palace Car Company, itself an amalgamation of the former Mann and Woodruff sleeping car companies. By the next year Pullman was operating over 2,000 cars on 120,000 miles of railroad, including lines into Mexico and Canada. Assets were calculated at $43 million at a time when the dollar was a hard currency backed by gold. Pullman, now approaching his sixtieth year, had surely surpassed his youthful ambition to be both rich and famous. His name was known and honored throughout the land. He was personally rich and traveled to and from his vacation homes aboard a fabulous private car named the P.P.C.C. The town of Pullman was a personal shrine. More honors came because of his support of the 1893 Columbian Exposition in Chicago. How could a man at such a pinnacle of triumph expect to be cast down almost without warning?

It started quietly in 1893, with no one, surely not Pullman himself, expecting disaster to follow. The national economy was faltering, and the car-building business began to fail. As orders dried up Pullman began to lay off car builders. As business grew worse Pullman decided to cut wages by 25 percent. The men walked out in protest and demanded restoration of wages, but Pullman would not relent. A union was organized with Eugene V. Debs's help, and an official strike was called on May 11, 1894. Late in the following month the American Railway Union went on a sympathy strike and refused to handle Pullman cars. When the strike grew violent, particularly in the Chicago area, U.S. troops were called out, the Illinois militia, deputy marshals, and sheriffs appeared, and, finally, the entire Chicago police force was ordered into the fray. The strike left $340,000 worth of railroad property destroyed, several men dead, and many others injured. Order was finally restored, and the trains were running again by late July, the Pullman car works reopening during the next month. But the strike was not over with the press and public. Why had Pullman refused to lower rents while reducing wages? Why had he refused to negotiate with his men? Why was he so rigid and unforgiving? Pullman reacted to

The interior of a Pullman sleeper (courtesy of Pullman Company)

these questions and criticisms in a defensive manner, forever tarnishing his image as an industrial statesman. Personally he was confused and embittered by what had befallen him so late in his career. Jane Addams likened him to a modern King Lear. Had he not always treated his men fairly? He was not operating a charity but a business. What of his duty to his stockholders? These and other questions tormented Pullman during the last few years that he outlived the end of the strike. He died at his Prairie Avenue home on October 19, 1897, of a heart attack. The *Railway Review* reported that: "In the gray dawn of the morning, ere yet the sun had risen, the man who has made railway travel a luxury and a delight to thousands, quietly said farewell to his labors and started out on the last long journey of all."

Pullman was such a public figure, especially during his later life, that both his personality and physical appearance were well recorded. In 1882 a Boston newspaperman described Pullman as being of medium height and weighing about 160 pounds. His face was described as calm and free of care lines. His eyes were bright brown and his mouth sensitive but firm. His abundant hair was tinged with gray, and his dress, as expected, was both conservative and immaculate. He was described as reserved, shy, and formal in demeanor. Some said he had a lordly manner, while another observer–none too kindly–described him as "hot as an ice crusher in winter." Yet he was forceful, strong, and farsighted. He worked with intensity and speed, loved order and ornament, and detested litter and confusion. Only such a strong, self-directed man could have accomplished what Pullman did in his lifetime.

Pullman should also be considered for what he did and what he did not do. He built a great business enterprise that endured long after his death, conceived and built a great industrial community, dominated the American sleeping car business and, for a time, the car-building trade. He managed his empire well and creatively, if he can be forgiven the 1894 strike. He did not, however, invent the sleeping car or the vestibule. Pullman was not an inventor or mechanic but could choose well those who were. Pullman did not really introduce luxury rail travel as is so often claimed but was instrumental in the spread of its popularity. For most of his career Pullman was praised for the artistry and refinement of his sleeping car decoration. But as popular taste began to turn against an overindulgence in ornament, Pullman's tastes were criticized as barbaric and excessive.

The Pullman company outlived its creator over eighty years. The sleeping car segment of the business grew and prospered in a manner that puzzled many economists. It seemed almost depression-proof, for in good times and bad the sleepers dependably rolled in a profit. In 1899 the last big competitor, the Wagner Palace Car Company, was absorbed, and, except for a few railroads that ran their own cars, the Pullman Company achieved its founder's goal, a monopoly of sleeping car travel in the United States. An antitrust suit in 1944 finally destroyed the monopoly, and Pullman sold off its sleeping cars in 1947 to an association created by various U.S. railroads. Actually, this turned out to be a good thing for Pullman, because the railroad passenger business was entering an irreversible decline, as the public turned to the automobile and airplane for intercity travel. In 1968 the railroad-owned Pullman Company suspended sleeping car service. The car-building side of Pullman, however, continued to prosper during the postwar boom. Pullman had, in fact, acquired a large number of car plants in the 1920s and so kept a large share of orders for new freight cars. The cyclical nature of this trade prompted Pullman to diversify into highway tractor trailers and oil-refining equipment. In 1980 Pullman, Inc. was taken over by Wheelabrator-Frye and was quickly dismembered. The car plants were closed or sold. What little that remains of the once mighty Pullman empire is now operated by Triniday Industries of Dallas, Texas.

References:

George Behrend, *Pullman in Europe* (London: Ian Allen, 1962);

Stanley Buder, *Pullman: An Experiment in Industrial Order and Community Planning 1880-1930* (New York: Oxford University Press, 1967);

Gerald G. Eggert, *Railroad Labor Disputes* (Ann Arbor: University of Michigan Press, 1967);

John H. White, *The American Railroad Passenger Car* (Baltimore, Md.: Johns Hopkins University Press, 1978).

Archives:

Papers concerning George M. Pullman are located at the Newberry Library, Chicago, Illinois.

Rails, Roadbed, and Track Gauge

The origin of the modern railway is shrouded deep in history. The Mesopotamian nation of Assyria hired stonemasons to build roads composed of two rows of stones, the center line of each being about 5 feet apart. The Greeks also used a self-guidance system for their wagons in areas where loads were heavy and traffic was frequent. Some evidence exists to suggest that the Greek "rut-roads" had a gauge of 5 feet 4 inches. Although most of these roads were single-lane affairs, they did have "turn-outs" at intervals where the wagons could pass. Power, of course, was provided by animals.

The Romans were the best known of ancient peoples to have railways. The Romans developed a standard width for their wagon wheels, which, although it appears to have been about 4 feet 9 inches, could have varied from 4 feet 6 inches to 5 feet. The Assyrian, Greek, and Roman systems, however, were not railways by modern standards. They had self-guidance systems but did not make use of any type of elevated rail. The first evidence of a self-guidance system on elevated rails appears in early sixteenth-century Germany. These small railroads, used for mining, possessed a gauge of no more than 28 inches and used human power to propel the carts. It appears that the carts had wheels with flanges on both sides so that the wheel sat on the wooden rail as does a pulley wheel on a rope.

The home of the modern railroad, however, is Great Britain. By 1560 railways to collieries had appeared in the north of England around the River Tyne. The evidence suggests that these railroads were surprisingly well built, a characteristic perhaps best explained by the heavy coal traffic in the area. Generally, an area 6 feet wide and 2 feet deep was prepared for the roadbed, which was then excavated and lined with pieces of oak 4 inches to 8 inches thick. Smaller pieces of wood were placed on top of these, and both were then covered by earth. On this base wooden rails were laid, usually without any type of cross-tie. The average individual rail was approximately 6 feet long and made of oak.

Although the early rails were primarily wooden, iron rails were used as early as 1716 on curves and other sections where friction was a concern. By 1738 the first cast-iron rails were in use but only at the points of greatest wear. The Coalbrookdale Railway, completed in 1767, was the first railroad to be laid entirely with cast-iron rails. By the latter part of the eighteenth century several noteworthy developments had been made in rail design. William Jessop developed a rail similar to the "T" rail in 1789 and may also have been the first person to use an iron-flanged wheel on an iron rail. His rail had an elliptical or "fish-bellied" under-edge that theoretically strengthened the rail.

Most of the early cast-iron rails were laid on blocks of stone or granite that served as risers, allowing the fish-bellied rail centers to stay above the ground. The Stockton & Darlington Railroad, the first public railroad in England, used a rail, designed by Robert Stephenson, called the "bullhead" rail. Although all of the rail types mentioned above were successful, the modern British rail developed as a variation of Stephenson's "bullhead" rail.

Railroad technology spread rapidly to the United States in the early nineteenth century. The first American railroad was the Quincy Railroad, built in Boston to carry granite from a quarry to Bunker Hill where a monument to the Revolutionary War battle was being constructed. The line was laid in 1826 and reached a length of four miles. Its rails were wooden and were spiked to granite blocks, used as sleepers and spaced at intervals of 8 feet. The wooden rails were 1 foot high and 6 inches wide with a flat iron strip 3 inches wide and 1/4 inch thick spiked to the inside edge of the rail. The roadbed was lightly cleared before the line was laid, but no excavations were made. The railroad lasted for twenty-five years but never saw anything more than light service with horse-drawn carts.

In 1827 the Mauch Chunk Gravity Railroad was constructed to carry coal from Summit, Pennsylvania, to the Lehigh River. This line was poorly graded, but it was the first railroad in the United

States to use bridge-type (inverted "U" shaped) rails. The road was also notable in that it used wooden cross-ties instead of stone, thereby increasing flexibility while continuing to hold the track in alignment.

The Carbondale & Honesdale (C&H) Railroad was built about the same time to carry coal to the Delaware River in northern Pennsylvania. This line used wooden rails similar to the Quincy Railroad, but the C&H gained permanent fame because it operated the Stourbridge Lion, the first steam locomotive used on an American railroad. Each of these early American railroads was constructed to carry coal or stone from a mine to either a river or the site where the material was to be used. All three were gravity lines; they originated at a higher elevation than they terminated, and it was possible to allow the loaded cars to drift down the hill by gravity. In the case of both the Mauch Chuck and the C&H the railroad provided the only support to the main mode of transportation: in both cases, a river.

The first trunk-line railroad was the Baltimore & Ohio (B&O). The B&O, chartered in 1827, utilized a roadbed laid with a more permanent mixture of broken stone and wood. Initially, however, the B&O used wooden rails strapped with iron. Eventually, the owners realized the advantages of iron and replaced the wooden rails. Interestingly, the builders of the B&O were concerned that turnouts would result in derailments, so they advocated the use of triple or quadruple track rather than turnouts and passing sidings. The construction of the B&O, although inferior to most British lines built at the same time, was superior to most American railroads, including some built as late as the Civil War. The Charleston & Hamburg (famous for The Best Friend of Charleston), for example, used wooden rails with iron strips until 1856.

The Camden & Amboy Railroad (a predecessor of the Pennsylvania Railroad located in New Jersey) was in the hands of Robert L. Stevens, one of the most creative of early American railroad engineers. Stevens was responsible for the development of the "T" rail, variations of which are used today on American railroads. He reputedly whittled the shape of the "T" rail, the general configuration of which was similar to Jessop's rail of 1789, from a block of wood while he was on an ocean voyage to England. The chief difference between the two designs was the shape of the railhead, Stevens's squarer design allowing greater contact with the

wheel and greater traction for the locomotive than Jessop's.

The "T" rail was not immediately accepted in the United States because it was too expensive to manufacture and because it provided more sturdiness than was needed in the 1830s. The British did not accept it until after the World War II, and the majority of British railroad trackage today remains laid with the familiar "bullhead" rail. At first Stevens spiked the "T" rail to stone sleepers, but he also realized that stone was too inflexible. Most of the Camden & Amboy was laid with either bridge rail (with the "fish belly") or wooden rail, however, since the cost of the "T" rail was too high even for the C&A.

The Pennsylvania Portage Railroad began using the English "bullhead" rail in the construction of its line in 1832. Bullhead rail, however, required a strong "chair" to support the rail, which in turn required strong anchoring on cross-ties located on a well-prepared roadbed. Roadbed preparation in the United States lagged far behind that in England.

By the middle of the nineteenth century there were significant differences between the American system and the English system of railway construction. American railroads were built more rapidly than their British counterparts and, as a result, were less sturdy. Because of the shortage of capital endemic to nineteenth-century America, American railroads were built at the lowest possible cost. While the British sought permanent right-of-way with broad curves and gentle grades, Americans paid scant attention to the curves and grades and accepted the fact that their railroads would require almost constant maintenance and replacement. Although British lines cost more money to build and took longer to complete, they were better built and lasted longer with less maintenance than American railroads.

Despite its cost and slow adoption the American "T" rail was an important advance. The earliest "T" rails were constructed of cast-iron but in the 1850s began to be made of steel. This change marked the true beginning of the modern rail. Virtually all major railroads were using the "T" rail by 1875. But some of the secondary lines and special purpose railroads, such as logging railroads, stuck to the other types of rail and, in some cases, old wooden rails.

Rail is weighed and classified by the yard in the United States. For example, a 32-pound rail is the weight of one yard of rail. The standard length of one unit of steel rail was 30 feet prior to 1893 and 39 feet thereafter. Iron rail normally weighed 26 to 28 pounds and ranged in length from 18 to 20 feet. Steel rail was capable of being heavier and stronger, the earliest rail weighing 32 pounds per yard, and 90-pound rail was common by 1900. In 1893 the dimensions of the "T" rail were standardized, thus contributing to the development of a national rail system.

In addition to rail design, inventors and engineers occupied themselves with track improvements. One of the most important pieces of trackwork is the turnout, the section of the track used for switching a train to another track. The turnout allows the railroad flexibility of operation and economy of construction. The fundamental problem of the turnout is that at one point the flanged wheels on one side of the train have to cross over the rail of either the main or diverging track. The earliest turnouts used a number of pivot points to move the rails. Realigning these points was time consuming and imprecise, leading to the derailments that the early B&O engineers had feared. Eventually the winged "frog" solved the problem of getting the flanged wheel across the diverging rail.

Another problem with rails was the joint where rail sections were joined. Most engineers considered the joint the weakest part of the railroad in the nineteenth century. As the weight of locomotives and cars increased, the joint became more and more important. Heavier rail, better quality plates to connect the rails, and improved roadbed eliminated most of the problems with the joint by 1900.

The cross-tie supporting the rail is also important in that it distributes the load to the ballast, holds the rail in line and gauge, keeps the rail from excessive transverse stresses, and provides elasticity. In the nineteenth century any hardwood was deemed appropriate for the material. The earliest wooden ties, however, were untreated and generally rotted quickly. The process of creosoting did not become common until the 1920s. On many lines, even in the nineteenth century, ties lasted for more than twenty years.

Supporting the cross-ties and the rail is ballast, which provides drainage so the cross-ties will be less subject to rotting and reduces dust and weeds. Many railroads in the United States did not use ballast, simply laying the rails on stone or wooden sleepers set on level and hastily cleared ground. But increased loads and higher speeds made the use of ballast necessary. The best form of ballast was, and remains, broken stone. In addition to being the only form of ballast that can be cleaned, it is also the most expensive. Slag, a product of blast furnaces, came into use as ballast about 1865, especially on railroads in Pennsylvania, West Virginia, and Maryland. Slag was clean and provided good drainage. Gravel was used as early as 1842 and, because it drained well, continued to be ballast material on many main lines throughout the century. Cinders and sand were also used because they were inexpensive and could be reworked easily. Neither, however, had the drainage qualities of broken stone, slag, or gravel.

In addition to turnouts, two other problems plagued the builders of early railroads–curves and grades. Straight or tangent track was not difficult to lay, but curves, particularly sharp curves, created problems. Curves are measured by the degree of turn made in 100 yards. Thus a 1-degree curve will have a radius of over a mile, while a 10-degree curve will have a 574-foot radius. A sharper curve, of course, increases wear on the rails. As the weight and speed of locomotives and trains increased in the nineteenth century the radius of the curves had to be increased. Spiral or compound curves where the radius gradually increased from 4 degrees, for instance, to 10 degrees, and superelevated curves came into existence about the time of the Civil War. They were not used extensively, however, until the 1890s and then only on the most carefully engineered main lines.

Grades also constituted problems to railroad engineers. Robert Stephenson recommended to the directors of the Stockton & Darlington (the first British common carrier) grades of no more than 0.33 percent (a rise of one foot in 330 feet). This was regarded as the limit by early British engineers. Since the United States was not as flat as England, Americans lacked the luxury of grade-limits. Although grades can cause increased rail wear, particularly if they are combined with sharp curves, the biggest problem is that grades limit the amount of weight a locomotive is able to pull. A heavy freight locomotive of the 1890s might have been able to pull 3,200 tons on level track. On a 1-percent grade this was reduced to 875 tons, on a 2-percent grade to 460 tons, and on a 3-percent grade to 210

Number of railroad companies	Miles of road	Gauge	Percentage of total mileage
14	1,777	6' 0"	5.3
21	2,896	5' 6"	8.7
2	182	5' 4"	.1 —
63	7,267	5' 0"	21.8
39	3,294	4' 10"	9.9
1	120	4' 9¼"	.1 —
210	17,712	4' 8½"	53.3

Railroad mileage by gauge in the United States and Canada, January 1, 1861 (from George Rogers Taylor, The American Railroad Network, 1861-1890)

tons. Even these figures assumed a train speed of about ten miles per hour and a temperature of 35 degrees Fahrenheit or higher. Colder weather reduced the tonnage even more.

Usually severe grades could only be resolved by rebuilding the line. This was an expensive practice that less affluent railroads could not always afford. Sometimes tunnels, such as the Hoosac Tunnel in western Massachusetts, could eliminate grades, but these were expensive projects that often taxed the technological abilities of nineteenth-century engineers. The only other solution was to run more trains or to provide "helper" service—more locomotives to power the train over the mountain.

But grades and curves were not the greatest impediment to the development of a national rail system. In the United States the largest problem was the lack of standard track gauge. The Stockton & Darlington was laid to a gauge of 4 feet 8½ inches. Several British railroads were built to other gauges, but an act of Parliament in 1830 required all British railroads to build to the standard gauge of 4 feet 8½ inches. In the United States no legislative act was ever passed, and the variety of gauges caused many problems. By the time of the Civil War there were at least seven gauges in operation in the country. Although the most common gauge was the English standard gauge, there were significant regional variations. Most of the New England lines were standard with the exception of the Grand Trunk line in Maine which had a 5-foot-6 inch gauge. There was more variation in the Middle Atlantic States where the Erie Railroad and the Delaware, Lackawanna & Western were built to a gauge of 6 feet, the widest used in the United States. The Camden & Amboy had a gauge of 4 feet 10 inches while the Delaware & Hudson originally had an odd 4-foot-3 inch gauge. Most of the

remainder of the railroads in Pennsylvania, Maryland, Delaware, New York, and New Jersey were standard gauge. In Ohio most of the railroads were built to 4-foot-10 inch gauge, but some were standard gauge and a few measured 5 feet, 4 inches. While Indiana and Illinois were more conventional, the major railroads in the southern part of the state, dominated economically by Cincinnati, were built to Ohio's 4-foot-10 inch gauge. West of the Mississippi River most of the railroads were built to a gauge of 5 feet, 6 inches, and southern railroads were laid to a 5-foot gauge, with the exception of Virginia and North Carolina where most of the lines were standard gauge. George R. Taylor's chart shows the number and relative importance of the various rail gauges.

In the post Civil War period the movement to construct narrow gauge railroads grew in the United States. Concentrated primarily in the mountainous areas of Colorado in the twentieth century, narrow gauge railroads were attempted in almost all sections of the country in the latter half of the nineteenth century. Pennsylvania, Ohio, Virginia, and other southern states all had narrow gauge railroads, most of which acted as "feeder" lines to the major railroads and were constructed primarily because they were inexpensive. Several efforts were made, however, to construct a long distance narrow gauge system from the Great Lakes to the Gulf of Mexico, from Toledo, Ohio, to Galveston, Texas. These efforts were doomed to failure because the trackage was in most cases redundant, the speeds were slow, and the costs of transporting freight and passengers were no lower than on standard gauge railroads.

Although American railroads were not built to the standards of their British counterparts, they served the needs of a new nation with limited capital and labor. By the late nineteenth century most of the major main lines of the country had been substantially rebuilt to eliminate sharp curves and steep grades. Improved tunnel boring skills and a new generation of bridges also helped to conquer the difficult topographical challenges faced by American railroads. By the end of the century the best lines consisted of 100-pound or heavier rail and well-ballasted lines with grades of less than 2 percent and curves of 10 degrees or broader. Less profitable roads and branches had lighter rail, little or no ballast, and steep grades and sharp curves, although wooden rails had disappeared.

References:

W. Bridges Adams, *Roads and Rails* (London: Chapman and Hall, 1862);

Cecil J. Allen, *Railway Planning and Making* (London: Longmans, 1928);

Thomas M. Cooley, *The American Railway* (New York: Scribners, 1897);

Paul Hamlyn, *Railways* (London: Westbrook House, 1963);

Lewis Henry Haney, *A Congressional History of Railways in the United States* (Madison, Wis.: Democrat Printing Company, 1908);

Rupert S. Holland, *Historic Railroads* (Philadelphia: MacRae Smith, 1927);

T. W. Metre, *Trains, Track and Travel* (New York: Simmons-Boardman, 1926);

William G. Raymond, *Elements of Railroad Engineering* (New York: John Wiley, 1947);

George Rogers Taylor, *The American Railroad Network, 1861-1890* (Cambridge, Mass.: Harvard University Press, 1956);

Slason Thompson, *A Short History of American Railways* (New York: Appleton, 1925);

Walter L. Webb, *Railroad Construction: Theory and Practice* (New York: John Wiley, 1932).

–Robert L. Frey

Railway Mail Service

The en route sorting of mail aboard specially designed rail cars began in the United States on a regular basis effective August 28, 1864, when service was established between Chicago, Illinois, and Clinton, Iowa, over the Chicago & North Western Railroad. Skeptics were legion. One critic argued that the Post Office Department would have to hire a regiment of soldiers to follow trains in order that mail flying out of the Railway Post Office (RPO) cars be retrieved. Nevertheless, the experiment succeeded, and for over a century the Railway Mail Service (RMS) represented the backbone of the country's intercity postal distribution system.

En route sorting evolved gradually. In 1810 thirty-five distribution centers were set up around the nation, and contracts were let by the postal service to move closed (locked) pouches from one to another of these facilities. The number of centers grew as the country expanded, and when railroad companies were formed, they predictably assumed some of the contracts. The Post Office Department assigned route agents to certain rail lines as early as 1837; these government employees opened pouches and made elementary distribution from them. Rather more sophisticated experiments using cars de-

signed for the purpose were conducted on the Illinois Central Railroad and on the Hannibal & St. Joseph Railroad during the early 1860s. All of it pointed to inception of the Railway Mail Service, which was established in July 1869 with George B. Armstrong as its first superintendent.

The purpose of the new system was, of course, to expedite and make efficient distribution of the mails for a growing country. As the system of rail lines expanded, so did the number of RPO routes. These were usually identified by the endpoints of the route—Boston & New York, Chicago & Minneapolis, and San Francisco & Los Angeles, for example—and not by the transportation company charged with hauling the RPO cars over its lines. As the process grew, sophisticated and integrated schedules were devised to facilitate connections and thus the movement of mail to and from all parts of the country. Mechanical advances even allowed for nonstop exchanges by way of a trackside mail crane and an on-board "catcher arm" that snatched the awaiting pouch as the train sped along.

The work of RPO clerks was tedious and demanding. The car had to be "dressed" (racks fitted with sacks and pouches and sorting cases labeled), the mail loaded and "worked" (sorted), and finally emptied during the tour of duty. The work was also dangerous—especially during the earlier years when wooden cars disintegrated and often burned upon collision.

Nevertheless, morale among the clerks was good. Pay scales were relatively high for these government employees who frequently perceived themselves among the elite of civil servants. Individual pride resulted from superior scores made on mandatory periodic examinations which measured speed and exactitude in sorting. In addition, crews assigned particular scorn to brother crews that "went stuck"—that is, failed to work all mail consigned.

The demise of en route sorting was collateral with the demise of the American passenger train. Routes assigned to interurban electric roads went early as did streetcar routes, branch lines, and then main line locals. Mail passed to over-the-road truckers, in some cases to Highway Post Offices, and to airlines. The end came for the Railway Mail Service with reliable jet aircraft, with the interstate highway system, with the removal of long-haul passenger trains, and with the Post Office Department's decision to revert to a "sectional center" concept. The last RPO route, the New York & Washington, rolled its final miles in 1977.

References:

Clark Ezra Carr, *The Railway Mail Service, Its Origin and Development* (Chicago: McClurg, 1909);

Bryant A. Long and William J. Dennis, *Mail By Rail: The Story of the Postal Transportation Services* (New York: Simmons-Boardman, 1951);

James E. White, *A Life Span and Reminiscences of Railway Mail Service* (Philadelphia: Deemer & Jaisohn, 1910).

–Don L. Hofsommer

Edmund Rice

(February 14, 1819-July 11, 1889)

by Robert M. Frame III

James Jerome Hill Reference Library

CAREER: Member, territorial House of Representatives (1851); director, Minnesota & Northwestern Railroad (1854-1856); president, Minnesota & Pacific Railroad (1857-1861); president, St. Paul & Pacific Railroad (1862-1872); president, St. Paul & Chicago Railroad (1863-1877); state senator, Minnesota (1864-1865, 1873-1874); state representative, Minnesota (1867, 1872, 1877-1878); mayor, St. Paul (1881-1883, 1885-1887); member, U.S. House of Representatives (1887-1889).

Edmund Rice, lawyer, politician, and railroad executive, was instrumental in the development of the first railroads in Minnesota, companies which were the predecessors to James J. Hill's St. Paul, Minneapolis & Manitoba Railway (later the Great Northern Railway). Contemporaries referred to Rice as the "father of the Minnesota railroad system."

Born on February 14, 1819, in Waitsfield, Vermont, where he attended common schools, Rice went to Kalamazoo, Michigan, in 1838 to study law and was admitted to the bar in 1842. Before coming to St. Paul, Minnesota, in July 1849, he served in the Mexican War as first lieutenant with a Michigan regiment.

In St. Paul he was the senior partner in the law firm of Rice, [William] Hollinshead, and [George L.] Becker, which became one of the most prominent firms in the Minnesota Territory. Their law office also served as the governor's office until the capitol building was constructed in 1853, revealing the extent and intimacy of the partners' political connections.

In 1851 Rice served in the territorial House of Representatives. With his older brother, Henry Mower Rice, who had been in Minnesota since 1839 and in the 1850s was a territorial delegate to Congress, he was active in the movement to secure railroads for the region.

Before finally abandoning his law practice in 1856 to devote more time to railroad projects, Rice served from 1854 to 1856 as a director of the Minnesota & Northwestern Railroad Company, an abortive effort to establish a land-grant line.

In Congress Henry Rice successfully labored to secure a railroad land grant to the territory in 1857. Minnesota, in turn, chartered the Minnesota & Pacific (M&P) Railroad Company and three others. Edmund Rice, at thirty-eight years of age, was the M&P's (later the St. Paul & Pacific's) president, an office he continued to hold until 1872. He was ably assisted by chief engineers David Chauncey Shepard and William Crooks. Two routes were authorized: the main line from Stillwater via the Twin Cities to the present community of Breckenridge and the branch line from St. Anthony (later Minneapolis) to St. Vincent at the Canadian border.

Despite Rice's optimism, influence, energetic leadership, and tireless pursuit of eastern investors, the company struggled with grave financial and legal difficulties. Finally, in early 1862 the state legislature (Minnesota had achieved statehood in 1858) transferred the M&P's rights and property to a group of associates under a new title, the St. Paul & Pacific (StP&P), thus wiping out all claims and liens. Work began anew, and in the summer of 1862 the first railroad mileage in Minnesota, ten miles between St. Paul and St. Anthony, was put into operation. The road's second locomotive, which had arrived by steamboat in 1861, was named the Edmund Rice.

Although his railroad had a good charter, Rice had not yet succeeded in financing the construction of many of the miles authorized under the franchise. The two original lines remained to be completed, along with new routes added by charter amendments in the 1860s. The railroad's situation was complicated considerably by the Civil War and, in Minnesota, the 1862 Dakota War involving Indians and white settlers. As president, Rice returned to his efforts to raise capital, using his terms as a state senator and state representative to gain extensions of time limits on construction and land grants.

Rice worked remarkably hard for the railroad. Through the 1860s he traveled to Chicago, New York, Philadelphia, Washington, and England in attempts to raise money. He attempted to instill in investors the same confidence in Minnesota's railroad future that he himself had. He suffered rebuffs from bankers and disappointments from contracts not ratified or fulfilled.

From 1863 to 1877 Rice was also president of the St. Paul & Chicago, whose franchise was attached to the St. Paul & Pacific charter. Unlike the StP&P, its line ran southeast, to Winona, and in 1872 was sold to the Milwaukee & St. Paul (later known as the Chicago, Milwaukee, St. Paul & Pacific).

Edmund Rice's essential role as railroad president evolved as one of a middleman between politics and business, between the legislature and investors. Endowed with what contemporaries reported as a "large, commanding figure," he was said to be affable, good natured, loyal, determined, and "imperturbable in the face of adversity."

Although his most active and creative years were spent developing railroads and their finances, he achieved wealth not through his companies but through fortuitous real estate investments. As his railroad involvement waned Rice, a lifelong Democrat, turned increasingly to political office and real estate dealings. Through the 1870s and 1880s he served terms, often multiple, in the state senate and house of representatives, as mayor of St. Paul, and finally as a representative in Congress from Minnesota from 1887 to 1889. He was defeated for reelection in 1888 and died at his home in White Bear Lake, Minnesota, on July 11, 1889.

References:

Ralph W. Hidy and Muriel E. Hidy, "Great Northern History Manuscript," 2 volumes, undated [c.1985]. Photocopy of typescript in James Jerome Hill Reference Library, St. Paul, Minn.

Ralph W. Hidy, Muriel E. Hidy, and Roy V. Scott, with Don L. Hofsommer, *The Great Northern Railway—A History* (Boston: Harvard Business School Press, 1988);

T. M. Newson, *Pen Pictures of St. Paul....* (St. Paul: Privately printed, 1886), pp. 153-155;

U. S. Congress, *Biographical Directory of the American Congress 1774-1971* (Washington, D.C.: USGPO, 1971);

George E. Warner, *History of Ramsey County and the City of St. Paul* (Minneapolis: North Star Publishing, 1881).

George B. Roberts

(January 15, 1833-January 30, 1897)

by Michael Bezilla

Pennsylvania State University

CAREER: Civil engineer (1851-1862); assistant to the president (1862-1869); fourth vice-president (1869-1873); second vice-president (1873-1874); first vice-president (1874-1880); president, Pennsylvania Railroad (1880-1897).

George B. Roberts left an imprint as much on the character of the Pennsylvania (PRR) Railroad as on its balance sheets. A sober, diligent but unexciting business leader, Roberts molded the PRR in his own image. Although the railroad had never been a speculative enterprise, during his presidency it became more than ever a model of no-nonsense capitalism. Under Roberts the Pennsylvania also reached its basic geographic limits while solidifying its position as the nation's largest and most prosperous railroad.

George Brooke Roberts was born on January 15, 1833, on his family's estate, Pencoyd Farm, in Montgomery County, Pennsylvania. His parents, Isaac Warner Roberts and Rosalinda Brooke Roberts, were fifth-generation descendants of Welsh settlers and heirs to considerable wealth and prominence in Philadelphia society. Roberts received his first formal schooling at nearby Lower Merion Academy before enrolling at Rensselaer Polytechnic Institute at Troy, New York, at age fifteen. He showed exceptional ability as a scholar, completing the three-year engineering course in two years and staying another year for postgraduate studies.

In 1851 Roberts became a rodman, or surveyor's assistant, under J. Edgar Thomson, chief engineer of the Pennsylvania Railroad. Roberts helped survey the PRR's main line through the Allegheny Mountains between Altoona and Pittsburgh. Once this task was accomplished a year or so later, Roberts left to join a PRR subsidiary, the Sunbury & Erie, as an assistant engineer in charge of locating that company's route between its namesake communities. In 1854 he joined the North Pennsylvania Rail-

George B. Roberts

road, later part of the Reading system, to survey a line from Philadelphia to Bethlehem. He then returned briefly to the Pennsylvania system as principal assistant engineer of the Northwestern Railroad of Pennsylvania. In 1857 he left again to serve successively as chief engineer for the Allentown & Auburn; the Mahanoy & Broad Top Mountain; and the Lorberry Creek railroads, all of which were soon incorporated into the Reading. He moved next to the West Jersey Railroad, which was then building from Camden to Cape May. Roberts viewed these frequent changes of assignment as a means of gaining experience and broadening his reputation as a professional engineer.

Meanwhile, J. Edgar Thomson had become president of the Pennsylvania Railroad in 1852. A distinguished engineer himself, Thomson appreciated Roberts's accomplishments and in 1862 appointed him special assistant in charge of systemwide construction. The Pennsylvania had built from Philadelphia to Pittsburgh in 1854 and was preparing to launch major extensions to Buffalo, Chicago, St. Louis, and Cincinnati. It was already the nation's largest railroad, having $8.5 million invested in road and equipment and annual gross revenues surpassing $1 million.

Roberts was elevated to fourth vice-president and elected to the PRR's board of directors in 1869, although he remained in charge of construction. He was promoted to second vice-president in 1873. A year later Thomson died and was succeeded by First Vice-President Thomas A. Scott. At Scott's request the directors elected Roberts to the first vice-presidency, a post of diverse responsibility that included supervision of finances, engineering, and operations.

Roberts's rapid advancement resulted mainly from his professional ability and willingness to carry out whatever tasks were assigned him. He does not appear to have been inordinately aggressive or ambitious. Indeed, contemporaries invariably noted his modesty, his consideration for subordinates, and his desire to hear all sides of an issue before acting. That he was a favorite of J. Edgar Thomson certainly boosted his career, but Thomson was not the kind of leader who tolerated mediocrity. Roberts was an obvious choice for the railroad's presidency, to which he was elected June 1, 1880, following Scott's retirement.

Roberts displayed a cautious and deliberate managerial style that endeared him to many directors who had been unhappy with Scott's flamboyance and impulsiveness. The new president considered the intense competition and consequent rate cutting among the railroads to be the most serious problem the industry faced. His solution was to make the PRR so lean and efficient that it could outlast its rivals in the rate wars and still deliver a steady profit. It was a philosophy based on survival of the fittest and left no place for government intervention or for speculative schemes that might yield only short-term gains. For George Roberts railroading was a long-term enterprise.

Improvements to the physical plant reflected Roberts's concern for future growth. The Trenton Cut-Off, for example, completed in 1892, allowed freight trains running between New Jersey and Harrisburg to bypass the congested Philadelphia area. Similarly, Roberts rebuilt the old West Penn line (later the Conemaugh division) to main line standards so that through-freight traffic could be routed around the busy Pittsburgh steel district. Major new yards were constructed at Conway and Pitcairn (in 1884 and 1888, respectively) to handle more efficiently Pittsburgh's ever-increasing industrial traffic. The most notable terminal improvement occurred in Philadelphia where the Broad Street Station opened late in 1880. The structure eventually ranked behind only City Hall as the community's most famous landmark. The railroad moved its general offices to the building in 1894. Two years later the PRR constructed its first bridge across the Delaware River at Philadelphia, giving it a badly needed direct connection with subsidiary lines running to the Jersey shore resorts.

Although route expansion slowed, as Roberts desired to add only those lines most likely to generate profits, significant additions were made nonetheless. The railroad grew from about 6,100 route-miles in 1880 to 8,900 in 1896. An extensive network of branch lines was developed in the western Pennsylvania coalfields, and the Schuylkill Valley division was built to tap heavy industry in that region. The Pennsylvania's most important acquisition came in 1881 when it bought the Philadelphia, Wilmington & Baltimore (PW&B) Railroad, which formed the middle segment of the PRR's New York-Washington line. The PRR had previously operated over the PW&B via a trackage-rights agreement. However, when the B&O attempted to gain control of the line, Roberts countered with a $14.9 million purchase of PW&B stock that assured its permanent inclusion in the Pennsylvania system. Ironically, the most publicized expansion never fully materialized. In the early 1880s the New York Central and the Reading railroads began building the South Penn Railroad as an alternative to the PRR's Harrisburg-Pittsburgh route. In response, Roberts increased the PRR's holdings in the New York, West Shore & Buffalo Railroad, which ran parallel to the Central's Hudson River line. He had no real interest in the West Shore, a property of dubious value, and took the action only to counter his archrival. Financier J. P. Morgan, recognizing the pointlessness of such overexpansion, brought Roberts and Central President Chauncey Depew together for a celebrated meeting aboard his yacht, the *Corsair*, in New York harbor on July 4, 1885. With Morgan acting as intermediary both sides agreed to drop their proposed ventures and return to the status quo.

Buoyed by America's unprecedented industrial growth the PRR's freight ton-miles increased by 125 percent between 1880 and 1896. In contrast, because of rate competition and falling prices, net income rose only 77 percent, and net revenue per ton-mile actually fell. This situation reinforced Roberts's conviction that the railroad had to plow back its earnings to improve operating efficiency. He adhered to this policy throughout his administration, unswerved by periodic criticism from stockholders—particularly a number of British financial houses—that the small dividends understated the railroad's prosperity. In 1880 earnings made available to shareholders totaled $7.6 million and did not rise above $9 million until 1890. By 1896 they had fallen to $7.2 million. The president's policies enjoyed the continuing confidence of the company's directors, however, and indelibly stamped the Pennsylvania as one of the most conservatively managed railroads in the nation.

Roberts shunned publicity and devoted most of his spare hours to his family and the Episcopal church. He made little attempt to act as a national spokesman for the railroad industry and declined to engage overtly in politics. (He had nothing of substance to say on the enactment of the Interstate Commerce Act in 1887, for example.) "If as many people knew me at sight as Mr. Depew, I should not be able to endure it," he once remarked. "As it is, I can go about as I please and no one points me out, so I am left in peace." Thus, when Roberts died of a heart ailment at Pencoyd Farm on January 30, 1897, the *Philadelphia Public Ledger* aptly noted that he was "less known personally than any other prominent man of his time." He was twice married: to Sarah Lapsely in 1868, and to Miriam P. Williams in 1874. He was survived by four sons and two daughters.

George Roberts's policies strengthened the Pennsylvania's reputation as the best managed and most financially sound railroad in America. He bolstered the precedent J. Edgar Thomson had set for holding the company's interests above those of any individual. Many contemporary observers, contrasting him with some of his more colorful counterparts on other lines, labeled him a plodder. Nevertheless, over the next half-century the Pennsylvania was to amply demonstrate the wisdom of his long-term approach to investment.

References:

George H. Burgess and Miles C. Kennedy, *Centennial History of the Pennsylvania Railroad* (Philadelphia: Pennsylvania Railroad, 1949);

Patricia T. Davis, *End of the Line: Alexander J. Cassatt and the Pennsylvania Railroad* (New York: Neale Watson Academic Publications, 1978);

"George B. Roberts—Sketch of His Remarkable Career," *Philadelphia Public Ledger*, February 1, 1897, pp. 1-2;

"George B. Roberts," *Railroad Gazette*, 29 (February 5, 1897): 98-99;

H. W. Schotter, *The Growth and Development of the Pennsylvania Railroad Company* (Philadelphia: Allen, Lane & Scott, 1927);

William B. Wilson, *History of the Pennsylvania Railroad Company* (Philadelphia: H. T. Coates, 1899).

Archives:

The records of the Pennsylvania Railroad, though currently uncataloged, are located at the Pennsylvania Historical and Museum Commission, Harrisburg, Pennsylvania.

Moncure Robinson

(February 2, 1802-November 10, 1891)

by William H. Patterson

University of South Carolina

CAREER: Survey volunteer, Virginia Board of Public Works (1818); chief engineer, James River Canal extension (1821); surveyor, Pottsville & Danville Railway (1828); surveyor, Allegheny Portage Railroad (1828); railroad builder, Heath & Mills Coal Fields (1830); railroad builder, Petersburg & Roanoke Railroad (1831); railroad builder, Richmond & Petersburg Railroad (1832); railroad builder, Richmond, Fredericksburg & Potomac Railroad (1832); railroad builder, Winchester & Potomac Railroad (1832); railroad builder, Philadelphia & Reading Railroad (1834); designer, Gowan and Marx locomotive (1838-1840); railroad builder, Little Schuylkill River Valley (1838); surveyor of New York Harbor, U.S. Navy (1842); retirement (1847); railroad builder, Palmetto Railroad (1886-1887).

Moncure Robinson, civil engineer, is hailed by R. W. Brown as a "Genius of America's Earliest Railways." Brown also states that Robinson "built *more* American railroads in the first two decades of their existence than any man." Robinson's railroad-building techniques were often novel for his time, but they were proven effective and used in subsequent constructions. His strong influence on railroads has been felt both at home and abroad; according to R. B. Osborne, "Robinson [was] . . . the first American engineer who received the recognition and appreciation of the rulers of Europe. . . ."

Moncure Robinson was born in Richmond, Virginia, on February 2, 1802, the eldest son of John and Agnes Conway (Moncure) Robinson. His father was a clerk of the district and circuit courts of Richmond, Virginia, and a merchant whose firm was active in foreign trade. The family was of a prestigious background.

When he was six years old Robinson entered Geradine Academy in Richmond. At thirteen he enrolled at William and Mary College, where by the

Moncure Robinson (courtesy of California State Railroad Museum)

age of sixteen he was not only the youngest student at the school but was also preparing to graduate.

His father wanted him to study law, but Robinson decided to make his career as a civil engineer, which at that time was hardly recognized as a profession in America. Robinson began his training in 1818. The Board of the Public Works of Virginia, under the general direction of Messrs. More of Maryland and Briggs of New York, wanted to make a topographical survey and a connected line of levels across the state from Richmond to the Ohio River. Robinson applied for a position on the corps of engineers but was refused because of his age. He was, however, allowed to accompany the group as a volunteer. R. B. Osborne states that on this expedition Robinson "made accurate notes of the coal deposits" in what is now West Virginia, which showed "the quantity of the undeveloped wealth of state." The next year, in 1819, Robinson returned to western Virginia to survey lands that his father owned but knew little about, a trip covering several hundred miles on horseback.

When Robinson was nineteen years old, he was hired by Governor Pleasants of Virginia to extend the James River Canal. As the chief engineer on the project he first widened the original canal and then lengthened it nearly thirty miles.

In 1821 he also visited the Erie Canal, which was then under construction. He was given complete access to the canal plans, which gave Robinson an opportunity to compare canals and railroads. Robinson came to believe that railroads were the wave of the future, that they were more efficient, more flexible, and cheaper. He tried to convince authorities in Virginia to build a railroad instead of further extending the James River Canal to Covington, as originally proposed. When they declined Robinson's railroad proposal, he resigned his position on the canal project.

Robinson traveled to Europe in 1825, and his early acquaintance with the French language enabled him to attend lectures in mathematics and science at the Sorbonne in Paris and to mingle with French society. While in Europe he studied public works in the Low Countries, Wales, and England, where he met many of the leading engineers including Robert Stephenson. In Europe Robinson received word that his father's mercantile firms had failed. Although saddened by the news, he persisted in his studies and did not return home until late in 1827.

In 1828 the canal commissioners of Pennsylvania asked him to make the surveys for the Pottsville & Danville Railway, one of the first railroads constructed in the United States, and a project intended for the development of the anthracite coalfields. The construction of the second tunnel on this railroad involved a new technique devised by Robinson; the men worked from both ends of the tunnel and met in the middle.

The commissioners also requested that he make surveys for the Allegheny Portage Railroad. His report called for a tunnel one mile long through Blair's Gap Summit. In 1830 Lt. Col. Stephen H. Long proposed the construction of a macadamized highway instead of the railroad and the tunnel. Although many argued that Robinson's plan

was the better one to follow, the tunnel was avoided. Some writers, including R. B. Osborne and Michel Chevalier, the noted nineteenth-century French engineer, have claimed that the absence of the tunnel lessened the economic value of the road and lowered the developmental potential of the region. In place of the tunnel, the Allegheny Portage Railroad devised a method for the transportation of loaded boats from the canal, over the mountains, and to another canal.

In 1829 Robert L. Stephens urged him to accept the offered position of engineer-in-chief of the proposed Camden & Amboy Railroad. Robinson requested that he have the appointment of all the officers of his engineering staff and be in full control of his department. Stephens did not agree with these conditions, and Robinson declined the offer.

Robinson was engaged in the construction of the Petersburg & Roanoke and the Richmond & Petersburg railroads in 1831. On the Richmond & Petersburg Railroad he built a bridge over the James River, which won him the attention of Michel Chevalier. The bridge, although considered expensive at the cost of $117,200 or $41 per lineal foot, was one of Robinson's great achievements. Apparent in the project is Robinson's ability to adapt expenditures to the means available to him. The structure, 2,844 feet in length with a grade line of 60 feet above the water, was built at Richmond over the James River. It had nineteen spans, which varied in length from 140 to 153 feet. It was a lattice bridge, chiefly composed of 2-inch plank, with 1,500 pounds of iron in the entire structure. It was completed September 1838. When the Confederate army abandoned Richmond on April 3, 1865, it burned the long bridge over the James River along with the depot in Richmond. The loss was estimated at $254,318, nearly one-third the capitalization of the Petersburg road. The bridge was rebuilt at a cost of $118,245 and reopened on May 25, 1866. The cost figure of the new bridge of $41.32 per lineal foot for the superstructure alone indicates the economy on the earlier Robinson bridge.

Michel Chevalier published full details of Robinson's bridge, including the plans and cost of the bridge, in his work *Histoire et Description des Voies de Communication aux États-Unis et des Travaux d'Art qu'en Dépendent* (1841). The bridge caught the attention of many engineers and served as a model for the iron lattice bridges in Europe.

Robinson proposed and built both the Richmond, Fredericksburg & Potomac (RF&P) and the Winchester & Potomac railroads in 1832. The Richmond, Fredericksburg & Potomac formed an important link in the rail system to the south and southwest. The Winchester & Potomac linked with the Baltimore & Ohio at Harpers Ferry.

Robinson's chef d'œuvre, the Philadelphia & Reading (P&R) Railroad, which he built and financed, was begun in 1834. Osborne writes that Robinson constructed the railroad so that "its capacity could be readily expanded to meet economically any increase of the demand." He regulated the alignment and gradients for the most advantageous transportation of coal, as well as for the economic conveyance of a large mixed traffic. Robinson formulated three rules for determining grades and curvatures to follow in the construction of this railroad: (1) "from the coal region to Columbia Bridge, over the Schuylkill, near Philadelphia, no grade should be adopted more difficult for the locomotive than a level. . ."; (2) "all other grades, which must therefore be descending with the grade, should not exceed nineteen feet per mile"; and (3) "the shortest radius of curvature on the main line should be eight hundred and eighteen and fifty-seven hundredths feet, or seven degrees." The second rule insured that an engine would be able to return to the region with the same number of cars, empty, that it had taken full to the terminus. In addition to the three rules, Robinson's plans included a stone bridge across the Schuylkill River at Black Rock Tunnel. With four spans of 72 feet, it was the first structure of its size and material to be built for a double-track railroad in the United States.

In 1836 Robinson went to England to negotiate a loan for the P&R at the request of Elihu Chauncey, the first president of the railroad. Robinson left two of his relatives, Wirt Robinson and Wilson Miles Carey Fairfax, as engineer-in-chief and principal assistant, respectively, in charge of the Philadelphia & Reading project. In London Robinson met Sir Francis Edgerton, who loaned the Philadelphia & Reading Railroad Company $2 million. The well-known London banking firm Gowan & Marx was chosen to negotiate the loan, and Thomas Hankey was appointed its custodian. This loan was the first foreign loan established for the Philadelphia & Reading Railroad Company.

In 1834 Robinson received a charter to extend the P&R from Reading to Pottsville. Within the charter was a clause which denied voting rights to foreign stockholders. While in England Robinson procured a second loan, for $1 million, to be given for the extension to Pottsville on the condition that the no-voting clause be removed from the charter. The passage was not repealed, and the loan was abandoned.

In 1838 Robinson was hired by Thomas Biddle, William Keating, and Edward R. Biddle of Philadelphia to construct a railroad to help develop the Tamaqua coalfield in Pennsylvania. The railroad line ran up the valley of the Little Schuylkill River and enabled the connection of the coalfields to tidewater by rail.

In honor of the London bankers who had negotiated the 1836 loan to the Philadelphia & Reading, Robinson began in 1838 to design a locomotive, which was built by the Philadelphia firm Eastwick & Harrison. On February 20, 1840, the locomotive "Gowan and Marx" had its first run from Reading to Columbia Bridge.

The performance of the locomotive, coupled with Robinson's other achievements, caught the attention of many people abroad, including the czar of Russia. The czar requested that Robinson serve as the engineer for the proposed railroad to be built from St. Petersburg to Moscow. Robinson declined the offer because of his health and disinterest in spending so much time away from the United States. He did, however, offer his counsel to the czar's commissioners and introduced them to the Eastwick & Harrison firm. The firm was offered a contract, which it accepted. They transported their shop to Russia and followed Robinson's plans for the "Gowan and Marx" engine and the Reading Railroad in their construction of the St. Petersburg to Moscow railroad for Czar Nicholas I.

In 1842 the secretary of the navy commissioned Robinson and others to survey and report on a suitable site for the construction of a dry dock in New York Harbor. The commission examined the harbor and determined Wallabout Bay to be the best site. The completion of this job marked the end of the major portion of Robinson's professional career.

After Moncure Robinson's retirement as a civil engineer in 1847 he continued as a director of various railroad companies, in which many of the chief executive officers were members of his family. Edwin Robinson was president of the Richmond, Fredericksburg & Potomac; Wirt Robinson was pres-

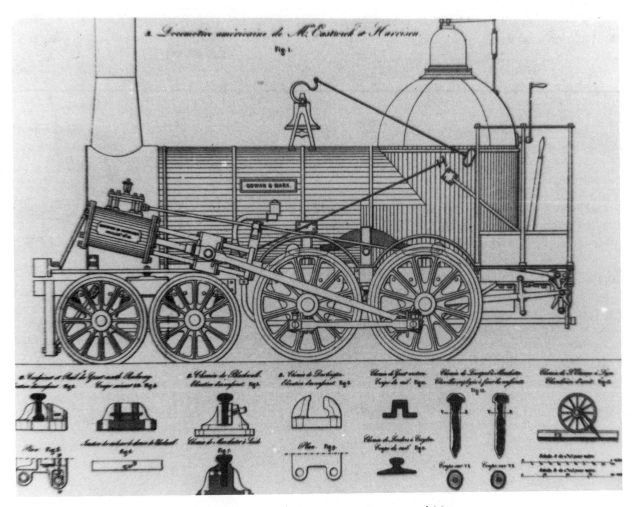

Sketch of Robinson's locomotive Gowan and Marx

ident of the Richmond & Petersburg; and his son, John Moncure Robinson, became president of the Seaboard & Roanoke (S&R), the Raleigh & Gaston, and the Baltimore Steam Packet Company. As financial agent of these companies and others, Robinson was associated with members of the family including Thomas A. Biddle, Enoch Pratt, and his son-in-law Charles Chauncey. Through his financial strategies he melded together railroads from Acquia Creek, Va., to Atlanta, Ga., and Cheraw, S.C., during his remaining years. These railroads included the RF&P, the Richmond & Petersburg, the Petersburg, the Raleigh & Gaston, the Raleigh & Augusta Air Line, the Georgia, Carolina & Northern (leased to the S&R), the Carolina Central, and the Palmetto railroads as well as the Baltimore Steam Packet Company. In 1900 most of these railroads formed the northern half of the Seaboard Air Line Railway Company.

The combination of railroads linked New York City through Philadelphia, Baltimore, Washington, Richmond, Petersburg (the projected Virginia & Carolina Railway would provide service to Ridgeway, N.C.), Raleigh, and Cheraw. Robinson was a longtime advocate of this route and came out of retirement in 1886 to construct and finance the Palmetto Railroad, which extended the line from Hamlet, N.C., to Cheraw. Further extension in South Carolina was assured as that state chartered additional lines south in 1889. William Moncure, Robinson's nephew, was the chief engineer.

Robinson married Charlotte Randolph Taylor on February 2, 1835. The couple moved to Philadelphia, where they established a home, had ten children, and led an active social life. Robinson was a strong Episcopalian who insisted on morning prayers and regular attendance at church. In the beginning he protested the running of trains on Sunday, although he later admitted the need for a seven-day-a-week schedule.

R. W. Brown made the following observation on Robinson's influence:

> ... within nine years after the first locomotive operated in America, the railroads he surveyed, constructed or on which he was consulting engineer, extended 721 miles—more than one-third of the entire railroad mileage in the entire country.... Of the grand total of 341 locomotives in the country at that time (1838), 129 ran on his railroads.

He was honored in 1833 by election to the American Philosophical Society. He received an honorary membership to the American Society of Engineers and was an honorary member of the Engineer's Club of Philadelphia.

Moncure Robinson died on November 10, 1891, in Philadelphia. He was survived by his wife, Charlotte, and eight children.

Publications:

Danville and Pottsville Railroad Company (Philadelphia: Clark & Raser, 1831);

Reports of Moncure Robinson, Esq. & Col. Stephen H. Long, engineers appointed by the Canal Commissioners for Examining the Different Routes for Crossing the Allegheny Mountains (Harrisburg, Pa.: Henry Welsh, 1831);

Philipsburg and Juniata Rail-Road Company (New York: G. F. Hopkins, 1833);

Report on the Continuation of the Little Schuylkill Railroad (Philadelphia: J. and W. Kite, 1834);

Report on the Philadelphia and Reading Railroad (Philadelphia: J. and W. Kite, 1834);

Obituary Notice of Michel Chevalier (Philadelphia, 1880);

Obituary Notice of Henry Seybert (N.p., 1883).

References:

Revelle Wilson Brown, *Moncure Robinson (1802-1891) Genius of America's Earliest Railways* (New York: The Newcomen Society, 1949);

Michel Chevalier, *Histoire et Description des Voies de Communication aux États-Unis et des Travaux d'Art qu'en Dépendent* (Paris: C. Gosselin, 1841);

Horace Edwin Hayden, *Virginia Genealogies* (Baltimore, Md.: Southern Books, 1959);

Richard Boyse Osborne, *Professional Biography of Moncure Robinson* (Philadelphia: Lippincott, 1889).

Archives:

A large collection of material concerning Moncure Robinson is located in the Earl Gregg Swann Library at the College of William and Mary, Williamsburg, Virginia.

The Rutland Railroad

by Charles J. Kennedy

University of Nebraska

The early history of New England railroads revolved around efforts on the part of several companies to build lines from the Atlantic Ocean to the Great Lakes or Canada. The Rutland Railroad was part of this picture. The Champlain & Connecticut River Rail Road Company was incorporated in 1843 to build a railroad in a north-northwesterly direction from Bellows Falls, Vermont, to Burlington, a distance of 120 miles. Reorganized in 1847 as the Rutland & Burlington Railroad, the line was finally completed to Burlington in December 1849. The southern end of the line had adequate connections to Boston, but the northern end of the line encountered competition with the Vermont Central which resulted in a struggle that did not end until 1898. Unable to gain an adequate northern connection and thus become a connecting route from tidewater to the Great Lakes at Ogdensburg, New York, the Rutland & Burlington's local traffic was inadequate to maintain profitable operations.

As early as 1854 the Rutland & Burlington had defaulted on its mortgage payments, but it was not reorganized into the Rutland Railroad until 1867. New management under John B. Page embarked on an aggressive effort to secure satisfactory connections from Burlington to Ogdensburg by acquisition or construction of connecting lines. Before the revitalized Rutland could accomplish this goal the Vermont Central leased it as a defensive measure in 1870. The terms of the lease, however, proved more profitable to the Rutland management than might have been the case if they had run the railroad by themselves.

The panic of 1873 forced the Vermont Central to reorganize as the Central Vermont (CV), but it still retained the lease on the Rutland. By 1887 a new player had entered the game. The increasingly powerful Delaware & Hudson (D&H) Railroad became a threat to the Central Vermont by purchasing controlling interest in the Rutland. In 1890 the

Central Vermont lease of the Rutland expired. At this point the Delaware & Hudson could have taken over the operation of the Rutland, but since the lease arrangement was so favorable to the Rutland (and consequently to the D&H, which garnered most of the profit) a new lease was approved with the Central Vermont despite the fact that the annual payment was slightly reduced.

Unwise business decisions like the lease of the Rutland, however, forced the Central Vermont into receivership in 1896. Consequently the CV notified the Rutland it was discontinuing the lease. In a strange chapter in railroad history, the management of the Rutland did not want the railroad back and went to court to force the CV to honor the lease. The court told the Rutland's president, Charles Clements, that he would have to take the railroad back whether he wanted it or not. Without the rental income from the CV, the D&H now had to subsidize the weak Rutland. The D&H escaped from this financial burden on October 22, 1898, by selling the Rutland stock it owned back to the Rutland's president. After twenty-eight years the Rutland was independent but still had no Ogdensburg connection. No longer forced to compete with a strong Central Vermont, the Rutland secured its Ogdensburg connection in less than three years.

The major component of the Ogdensburg connection had been completed in 1850 as the Northern Railroad of New York. It linked Ogdensburg with Rouses Point at the north end of Lake Champlain and then east to a connection with the Vermont & Canada. The Vermont & Canada, later a part of the Vermont Central, provided connections for the new line to the south through St. Albans, Essex Junction (several miles east of Burlington), and Brattleboro. In 1870 the Vermont Central leased the Northern Railroad of New York, which had been reorganized as the Ogdensburg Railroad in 1858 and the Ogdensburg & Lake Champlain

The Rutland engine J. Burdett waits to pull a funeral train in 1896

(O&LC) in 1864, as part of the plan to forestall the expanding Rutland as mentioned above. When the Central Vermont collapsed into receivership in 1896 the O&LC regained its independence.

Both the Rutland and the Ogdensburg & Lake Champlain were orphans in the northern New York-Vermont picture after the failure of the Central Vermont. The more aggressive, and perhaps more competent, Rutland management moved to close the gap between the Rutland and the O&LC north of Burlington. Chartering the Rutland & Canadian Railroad, a line was quickly constructed from Burlington to Rouses Point using the islands at the north end of Lake Champlain as "stepping stones." A three-mile causeway connected the islands with the mainland and the line was completed early in 1901. On September 27, 1901, the Rutland acquired the O&LC. The northern connection was finally complete, but too late to claim center stage in the tidewater-to-Great-Lakes traffic picture.

The final link of the twentieth-century Rutland ran south from its namesake city to Chatham, New York, and came to be known as the Chatham Division. It also had a complex and often colorful history. Chartered in 1845 as the Western Vermont Railroad, it was built south from Rutland to North Bennington and then west about ten miles to a connection with the Troy & Boston Railroad at White Creek, New York. Completed in 1853, it was eventually leased to the Troy & Boston as part of a through, but rather circuitous, route from the Hud-

son River to Boston. In 1865 the Western Vermont was renamed the Bennington & Rutland (B&R), and two years later the Vermont Central and the Rutland, in a rare show of unity, contested the Troy & Boston for control of the Bennington & Rutland. The result was termination of the Troy & Boston lease of the Bennington & Rutland and a colorful railroad war in which the B&R people attempted to seize Troy & Boston locomotives and rolling stock in Vermont. Several daring attempts to rescue the locomotives and cars were reminiscent of the famous "Great Locomotive Chase" of the Civil War.

The major result of the Bennington & Rutland and Troy & Boston "war" was to isolate the B&R from its east-west connections and to convert it into a road that went "nowhere." The company frantically sought another east-west connection or a southern connection to New York. A line with the quaint name of the Lebanon Springs Railroad had been built north from Chatham, New York, in the general direction of Bennington. Because of a lack of funds, it was languishing in the wilds of western Massachusetts with no firm plans for completion. Bennington area citizens aided the B&R in rushing the Lebanon Springs to completion by building to Bennington and then leasing it in 1869. The Lebanon Springs provided east-west connections with the Boston & Albany and a New York connection with the New York & Harlem line, both at Chatham. The Lebanon Springs and the Bennington &

Rutland were combined into the Harlem Extension Railroad in 1870 and leased to the omnipresent Vermont Central in 1873. Familiar financial problems forced the VC to relinquish its lease on the Harlem Extension in 1877, and a reorganization split the line once again into two separate railroads: the Bennington & Rutland and the Lebanon Springs Railroad.

The Bennington & Rutland maintained its southern connection with the Lebanon Springs, but it also mended relations with the Troy & Boston, thus opening an alternative east-west connection. As such the B&R managed to survive as an independent until it was purchased by the Rutland in 1900. The Lebanon Springs had a much more difficult time. It was reorganized at least three times, and finally, as the Chatham & Lebanon Valley, it was leased by the Rutland in 1899 and purchased outright in 1901. For about thirty years through trains operated from Ogdensburg via Rouses Point-Burlington-Rutland-Bennington-Chatham to New York despite difficult competition which had the advantage of shorter routes. The Bennington-Chatham part of the line was referred to as "the corkscrew" because of its hasty construction which resulted in steep grades and sharp curves.

Thus by 1901 the modern Rutland was assembled. Despite high hopes for gaining a major place in the tidewater-to-Canada or Great Lakes trade, by the time the Rutland was assembled other lines had well-established routes and service. Consequently the Rutland was never more than a local railroad with modest connecting traffic. Nonetheless it gained a certain appeal throughout the years and has remained a favorite among rail fans and historians. The fact that the Rutland was one of the first Class I railroads to be completely abandoned in 1961 (some parts were restored to service after 1964) only heightened the nostalgia and put the railroad in the same category as the Ontario & Western, abandoned several years earlier.

References:

George Pierce Baker, *The Formation of the New England Railroad Systems: A Study of Railroad Combination in the Nineteenth Century* (Cambridge, Mass.: Harvard University Press, 1937);

Thomas A. Bjorkman, "The Rutland Railway," M.B.A. thesis, Graduate School of Business Administration, New York University, 1964;

Edward Hungerford, David W. Sargent, Jr., Lawrence Doherty, and Charles E. Fisher, *Vermont Central–Central Vermont* (Boston: Railway and Locomotive Historical Society, 1942);

William Pletz, *History of the Rutland Railway* (Reading, Ohio: Privately printed, 1958);

Jim Shaughnessy, *The Rutland Road* (Burbank, Cal.: Howell-North, 1981).

Archives:

Records pertaining to the Rutland Railroad are located in the Charles J. Kennedy Railroad History Collection at the University of Nebraska in Lincoln, Nebraska. Other papers are in the personal archives of Charles J. Kennedy in Lincoln, Nebraska.

Thomas A. Scott

(December 23, 1823-May 21, 1881)

by James A. Ward

University of Tennessee at Chattanooga

CAREER: Retail clerk (1835-1841); clerk, Pennsylvania State Works (1841-1843); partner, sawmill and ice house (1843-1847); clerk, Philadelphia office of State Works (1847-1849); freight forwarder, Leech & Company (1849-1850); station agent, Hollidaysburg, Pennsylvania Railroad (PRR) (1850-1851); Pittsburgh agent, PRR (1851); third assistant superintendent, PRR western division (1852-1853); general superintendent, PRR western division (1853-1860); vice-president (1860-1874), president, PRR (1874-1880); colonel, District of Columbia Volunteers (1861-1862); assistant secretary of war (1861-1862); president, Union Pacific Railroad (1871-1872); president, Texas & Pacific (1872-1880).

Thomas A. Scott was among the most important railroad officials in nineteenth-century America. A self-made man, he rose quickly through the ranks of the Pennsylvania Railroad (PRR) and used its vast political and financial power to make his influence felt all over the United States. Before assuming the road's presidency in 1874, Scott represented the PRR's taciturn president, John Edgar Thomson, in public. Scott's classical good looks, confident bearing, and ebullient personality helped weld together an investment group, centered on the PRR front office, that included Andrew Carnegie, Herman Haupt, Drexel & Company, George Pullman, Jay Cooke, William Jackson Palmer, and Simon Cameron, which invested in railroads and industrial enterprises from Maine to New Orleans to Utah. In the late 1860s and early 1870s the group dominated a rail empire that reached into New England, throughout the South, into the Southwest, and across the northern Great Plains towards Oregon. And for one shining moment, in 1871 and 1872, the group came close to creating a true transcontinental system when the Pennsylvania interests gained

Thomas A. Scott

control of the Union Pacific (UP). Although he was far from the richest man in the investment group, Scott frequently was its most public figure, often serving as president of the group's properties. He was also the most politically astute of the group; he was known personally in dozens of statehouses, dominated the Pennsylvania state legislature for decades, and frequented the halls of Congress. Yet for all the reams of newsprint devoted to his activities, he remains an enigma. His estate evaluation, contrary to Pennsylvania law, was never made public, and his papers were destroyed after his death; to date no one has written a full-length biography of Scott.

This most public of men, who helped determine the economic shape of the United States, came from the most humble circumstances. Born on December 23, 1823 in the village of Loudon, Franklin County, Pennsylvania, to Thomas and Rebecca Douglas Scott, Scott possessed none of the advantages usually associated with wealth and fame. His father owned an inn on the turnpike between Baltimore and Pittsburgh, and most authorities think that Scott's congenial personality was shaped in the years he helped his father at home. Similarly, his lifelong interest in transportation matters may have been piqued as he talked to the wagoneers who stopped for the night; ironically, Scott later helped put them out of business.

Tragedy struck Scott's life when his father died in 1835 and his mother, struggling to support a large family, sent Scott to live with his married sister, whose husband operated a general store near Waynesboro, Pennsylvania. After a year and a half Scott moved in with his brother, James D. Scott, who owned a business in Bridgeport. Scott acquired the rudiments of a business education by working in these family businesses and at seventeen was proficient enough to become a clerk for his brother-in-law, Maj. James Patton, the tolls collector on the Pennsylvania Public Works at Columbia. Scott was an apt pupil, and Patton's successor, a Doctor Given, soon promoted him to chief clerk. In 1843 Scott and Given became partners in a sawmill which held a state lumber contract, but a flood wiped out their investment. Scott then entered into a partnership with James Vaugh to buy an ice house across the river from Columbia that sold its ice in Baltimore. When that venture failed in 1847, Scott returned to the State Works as a clerk in the Philadelphia tolls office. He was soon promoted to chief clerk, but after two years he quit and returned to Columbia where he took a job as a westward shipper for the freight-forwarding firm of Leech & Company.

For most of his life Scott parlayed aptitude and luck into good fortune. While Scott was with Leech & Company, Herman Haupt, the superintendent of transportation, received reports about him and recommended Scott for a position as the railroad's station agent at Hollidaysburg. Scott took the job on November 20, 1850, before the Pennsylvania line was completed to Pittsburgh. Hollidaysburg was the junction of the PRR with the state-owned Allegheny Portage Railroad, which the PRR was being forced to use temporarily. Scott's political experience with the State Works and his native business talents served him admirably as he sought to coordinate the two rivals' schedules and rates. In 1851 he was sent to Pittsburgh as the railroad's agent, where he employed a recent Scottish immigrant, Andrew Carnegie, as his personal telegrapher. Less than a year later Scott was promoted to third assistant superintendent of the western division, in which position he introduced the use of the telegraph to dispatch trains. In 1853 he was named general superintendent of the division, a position of great responsibility in which he oversaw all employees and traffic. Willing to try innovations, Scott introduced the smoking car and the Woodruff sleeping car to the PRR.

He was also involved in railway developments west of Pittsburgh; Scott handled negotiations with Ohio and Indiana railroads to attract feeder traffic to the PRR. He also extended financial and political aid to lines that eventually formed links from Pittsburgh to St. Louis and Cincinnati. In some cases Scott played a direct role in such affairs; he became vice-president of the Steubenville & Indiana Railroad in 1857 and also was president of the Western Transportation Company, which was created in 1856 to finish and operate the Pittsburgh & Steubenville Railroad.

Although he had been the chief lobbyist for the PRR at the state capitol in Harrisburg since 1853, Scott was unschooled in federal politics until acquiring these western interests. In order to complete his plan for an unbroken through route from Philadelphia to points west, a bridge over the Ohio River was required. But the point across the river from Steubenville was in Virginia, a state which denied permission for the bridge. Scott persuaded Pennsylvania Sen. Simon Cameron to introduce federal legislation to allow the crossing. Cameron failed to have the act passed, but he and Scott formed a lasting friendship and financial partnership that would bring them wealth, power, and public ignominy.

By 1860 Scott's responsibilities had reached a level that would leave him physically broken in less than twenty years. After William B. Foster, Jr., the Pennsylvania's vice-president, died unexpectedly in 1860, Scott was named to take his place. The new post relieved Scott from managing the road's day to day affairs and charged him with handling the company's political and financial affairs. He quickly showed that he was the right man for the job when he induced the state legislature to rescind its tonnage tax on the road's traffic. Initially introduced in 1846, the tonnage tax was designed to protect the State Works. Despite Thomson's buy-out of the State Works in 1857, the lawmakers refused to lift the tax. The railroad withheld its payments, and Scott stepped into the fray in summer 1860, buying newspaper advertisements, lobbying politicians, and bringing whatever economic pressure he was able in order to pass his commutation measure. Charges of bribery and payoffs flew throughout the session and, although never formally proven, tarnished Scott's reputation for years. He emerged victorious, however, and the tax was lifted on March 3, 1861, Scott achieving a compromise in which the PRR agreed to use its tonnage tax obligations to complete other railroads in the state. The PRR thus helped construct many of its feeder lines, most of which eventually were gathered under the PRR's corporate umbrella. With the tax commutation gained, the PRR finally felt able to compete with the New York Central, the Erie, and the Baltimore & Ohio (B&O).

Also in 1860-1861 Scott and Cameron teamed up with Thomson to gain control of the Northern Central (NC) Railroad, which served the Pennsylvania coal fields and provided a link to Baltimore and a potential extension to Washington, D.C. John Garrett, who took over as president of the B&O in 1858, sought to maintain his road's traffic monopoly to the capital. To accomplish this Garrett raised charges on traffic that entered Baltimore over rival lines destined for Washington. Scott and Cameron sought a federal law prohibiting such discrimination, but the bill failed. When financial troubles hit the country after Lincoln's election, however, the B&O was forced to sell some of its NC holdings. Scott and Cameron bought them and in March 1861 the two men and the Pennsylvania Railroad took control of the NC. Scott stood at the threshold of acquiring a southern rail empire but the enmity he, Cameron, and Thomson had earned in the B&O's front offices returned to haunt the Pennsylvanians when Cameron became secretary of war.

The outbreak of the Civil War on April 12, 1861, made men like Scott, who knew how to run railroads, invaluable to the Union; Scott was immediately drawn into the conflict. When the Confederates damaged the B&O's lines, Washington, D.C., was in danger of being cut off from the North. Moreover, the B&O's problems threw the burden of supplying the capital upon the PRR and the NC. Pennsylvania Gov. Andrew Curtin placed Scott in

charge of transporting all troops and military materiel through that state. Within a week the situation in Washington became more critical when Confederate sympathizers in Maryland attempted to stop Union troops moving through Baltimore and burned bridges on the NC and the Philadelphia, Wilmington, & Baltimore (PW&B) Railroad. Secretary Cameron summoned Scott to Washington to reopen the NC and the PW&B; when Scott reached the capital it was entirely isolated. On April 27 Cameron placed Scott in charge of all railways and telegraphs between Washington and Annapolis in an attempt to open communications to that port city. Within a few days Scott had the line running, and supplies flowed into Washington. A grateful President Lincoln presented Scott with a colonel's commission in the District of Columbia Volunteers on May 3; Scott used the title until he died. Three weeks later Cameron placed Scott in charge of all government railways and telegraphs, and, with this authority, he coordinated the military transportation during the First Battle of Bull Run. On August 1 Scott was named the first assistant secretary of war, although he still maintained his position on the Pennsylvania Railroad. In the meantime Scott oversaw the rebuilding of the B&O and extended its tracks through the city of Washington to Long Bridge to a connection with the Orange & Alexandria Railroad in Virginia.

Cameron, however, was coming under intense fire for his handling of defense contracts and the general laxity in his war department. Inevitably Scott became embroiled in the disputes. On July 12, 1861, Scott had issued a rate schedule for carrying military supplies and men, and Cameron's detractors in Congress attacked the rates as too high. They also accused Scott of favoring the PRR and the NC over the B&O. Cameron was eased out of office on January 11, 1862, and named ambassador to Russia. Despite Scott's testimony that his rates were only suggested maximums and that wartime necessity led him to route men and materiel over the PRR and NC, he resigned his war department position on June 1, 1862.

Scott was too valuable to the war effort, however, to remain idled for very long. When it became necessary to reinforce Gen. William Rosecrans at Chattanooga, Tennessee, in September 1863, Secretary of War Edwin Stanton placed Scott, temporarily recalled as a colonel, in charge of transporting two Army corps of 23,000 troops from Virginia to the western theater. Scott accomplished this task in just over eleven days over a flimsy rail network and saved General Rosecrans from certain defeat. Scott's feat stands as one of the great military troop movements in the history of war.

In 1865 Scott was the second ranking officer in the largest corporation in the United States. That same year he also married Anna Duke Riddle of Pittsburgh, with whom he had a daughter and son. His first wife, Anna Margaret Mullison, with whom he also had a daughter and son, had died in 1855. Scott was always remembered as a warm family man despite the heavy demands on his time. Even when his responsibilities increased after the war, as he oversaw expansion of the PRR and cultivated his own speculations from his personal railcar, Scott's devotion to his family remained.

Postwar competition among the four eastern trunk lines was keen, and in 1869 the PRR protected its western flank by leasing several Midwest lines, including the Pittsburgh, Ft. Wayne & Chicago Railroad and other lines to Cincinnati, Indianapolis, and St. Louis. Two years later the PRR leased the United Canal and Railroad Companies of New Jersey, which provided a route to New York City. Using his political clout, Scott maneuvered the state legislature to create two separate charters that he used to great effect. One, the Pennsylvania Company, organized with Scott as president in 1870, brought all the Pennsylvania's lines west of Pittsburgh under one corporate entity. The other, the Southern Railway Security Company, enabled the PRR to buy southern roads, the most important being the Richmond & Danville Railroad, that Scott hoped to merge into a continuous line from Philadelphia to New Orleans. His southern investments, however, were among his largest disappointments; the Pennsylvania divested itself of Scott's acquisitions in that region after the panic of 1873.

Scott's greatest postwar successes were in the West. After the war he and his Pennsylvania interests invested in Jay Cooke's Northern Pacific Railway and also tried to build the first transcontinental line, the Union Pacific, Eastern Division (UPED). When the UPED could not compete against the federally funded UP, Scott and his associates renamed the road the Kansas Pacific and linked it to the UP by means of the Denver Pacific. When the UP fell upon hard times following the Crédit Mobilier scandal, Scott, Thomson, Carnegie, and Pullman discovered they could gain control of

it for a reasonable investment. On March 1, 1871, Scott was elected UP president, replacing Oliver Ames. For a year Scott and his fellow investors stood astride a transportation empire that covered three-quarters of the United States. Scott was still not content; he was determined to reach the Pacific over his own rails. He took over the presidency of the Texas & Pacific (T&P) Railroad, a company chartered a year earlier to build from Vicksburg to San Diego. Scott counted upon federal and state land grants to finance the project, but Reconstruction politics and the public disdain for such aid after the Crédit Mobilier scandal ended Congressional support for this type of aid. Nevertheless, Scott continued to lobby Congress for Southwest land grants long after the 1873 depression made such gifts improbable. Scott invested so much of his own fortune and that of his Pennsylvania allies in the transcontinental plan that the Pennsylvania interests lost control of the UP in 1872 and were brought to the verge of bankruptcy by the 1873 panic. Scott barely survived the financial distress, and the panic severely curtailed his expansionary dreams. He did make one last try to resuscitate the T&P in 1877 when he helped to negotiate a political compromise that would give Rutherford Hayes the presidency and land grants to several southern railways. Hayes took the White House, but the southern lines never saw their land.

Three years earlier on May 27, 1874, Thomson, who had endured severe financial troubles in 1873 and worsening health, had died. Scott assumed the PRR's presidency and, faced with a stockholders' investigating committee, spent his years in office restoring his road's finances and selling its less-profitable extensions. For the first time in his life Scott retrenched, reduced mileage, and treaded warily. He even reduced dividends and in 1878 stopped payments for eighteen months, only the second time in PRR history that the road had skipped a dividend. The lapse was not Scott's fault entirely; the Pennsylvania had overexpanded in good times and was having difficulty meeting its bonded indebtedness.

Even in troubled times, however, Scott sometimes worked his old magic. Despite some notable lapses, he kept rates among the trunk lines fairly stable during the depression, introduced fast mail trains into the West, coped with the 1876 Philadelphia Centennial celebrations and their overwhelming traffic demands, and survived the labor riots that brought eastern railroads to a standstill in 1877. The labor strife began on the B&O when wages were cut 10 percent while dividends were maintained. The trouble spread to the PRR when workers in Pittsburgh took control of the PRR property. When the militia was deployed, violence erupted and the strikers destroyed over $2 million of the PRR property, leading Scott to pass his next dividends: He did, however, convince the state legislature that the state was responsible for the company's destroyed property, and the PRR secured $1.6 million in compensation from the state.

By 1878 Scott was exhausted and suffered the first of three strokes that would eventually kill him. The resulting paralysis was only temporary and Scott quickly returned to work, although he lacked his former enthusiasm. In his final two years with the PRR Scott established a trust fund to retire the road's debts, purchased stock in the West Chester & Philadelphia Railroad, bought 60,000 shares of his road's stock from Philadelphia, and started the Filbert Street Elevated Railway. Early in 1880 he suffered a second stroke and took a leave of absence to restore his health, but, aware that he lacked the strength to carry out his duties, he resigned his presidency on May 1, 1880. He also relinquished the T&P presidency and sold his holdings in that line to Jay Gould. He retired to his estate "Woodburn" near Darby, Pennsylvania, where he suffered a third stroke and died on May 21, 1881, at age fifty-seven. Although his assets were never made public, it has been estimated that he left a fortune valued at between $5 million and $15 million.

Scott was an example of the railway entrepreneur of vision and ambition who took advantage of the growing nation's dire need for national transportation. He combined a first-rate intelligence that quickly grasped and dealt with problems with an engaging personality and personal drive for power and wealth. He lived fast, knew virtually everybody worth knowing, and was an important figure in Congress, state houses, counting houses, and social circles. He left a strong Pennsylvania Railroad with connections to all the important cities east of the Mississippi River and north of the Ohio River, a southern transcontinental line that was later finished, and a vibrant industrial nation that rested upon the transportation infrastructure that he helped to build.

References:

Samuel Richey Kamm, "The Civil War Career of Thomas A. Scott," Ph.D. dissertation, University of Pennsylvania, Philadelphia, 1940;

New York Times, May 22, 1881, p. 2;

John F. Stover, *The Railroads of the South, 1865-1900: A Study in Finance and Control* (Chapel Hill: University of North Carolina Press, 1955);

Joseph Wall, *Andrew Carnegie* (New York: Oxford University Press, 1970);

James A. Ward, "J. Edgar Thomson and Thomas A. Scott: A Symbiotic Partnership?," *The Pennsylvania Magazine of History and Biography*, 50 (January 1976): 37-65;

Ward, *J. Edgar Thomson: Master of the Pennsylvania* (Westport, Conn.: Greenwood Press, 1980);

William B. Wilson, *History of the Pennsylvania Railroad Company: With Plan of Organization, Portraits of Officials, and Biographical Sketches* (Philadelphia: Henry T. Coates, 1899);

C. Vann Woodward, *Reunion and Reaction* (Garden City: Doubleday, 1956).

Samuel Sloan

(December 25, 1817-September 22, 1907)

by George M. Jenks

Bucknell University

CAREER: Importing house of McBride & Company, New York (1831-1856); president, Hudson River Railroad (1855-1865); New York state senator (1857-1859); commissioner, Trunk Lines (1865-1867); president, Delaware, Lackawanna & Western Railroad (1867-1899); president, Michigan Central Railroad (1877-1878).

Samuel Sloan had a twenty-five-year career in the importing business in New York before he made his mark as a railroad executive. Most of the rest of his life was involved in some way with the Delaware, Lackawanna & Western Railroad.

Samuel Sloan was born on December 25, 1817, in Lisburn, Ireland, the son of William and Elizabeth (Simpson) Sloan. The family moved to New York when he was a year old. He attended the Columbia College Preparatory School until he was fourteen, when his father died, and he had to leave school to help support the family of five children. He worked for two years for a merchant, and in 1831 found a job with the linen-importing firm of McBride & Company. He served that business in various capacities and in 1844 was made a partner in the firm. This experience served him well, enabling him to meet many important business and professional people.

In 1844 Sloan married Margaret Elmendorf and moved to Brooklyn, in 1852 becoming a supervisor of Kings (Brooklyn) County. Sloan foresaw the future of railroads and began investing heavily in railroad stocks. In 1855 he was elected to the board of directors of the Hudson River Railroad, which would later become a part of the New York Central system. That same year he was made president of the railroad and began his first experience in that field at the age of thirty-eight. He was also elected to the New York State Senate as a Democrat in 1856 and served one two-year term.

Samuel Sloan

As president Sloan set about to learn the business of railroading by talking with the men who ran the railroad: engineers, agents, switchmen, all those concerned with day-to-day operations. It was said that he knew every employee. He was a born leader and a progressive one as far as improving the operation of the railroad was concerned. He introduced the use of telegraphy in operating trains, improved the roadbed, and used heavier rails, all at a time when many railroad leaders were milking the company for all they could through hastily constructed roads and a "public be damned" attitude.

In 1858 Cornelius Vanderbilt gained control of the Hudson River Railroad and offered Sloan the presidency of his Harlem Railroad. Sloan declined because he did not think that he and Vanderbilt could work together. In 1865 he resigned as president of the Hudson River Railroad and took a position as commissioner of Trunk Lines in the middle Atlantic states.

A close friend of Sloan's was Moses Taylor, president of the National City Bank, who had invested in the Delaware, Lackawanna & Western Railroad. Through this acquaintance Sloan was elected in 1864 to the board of managers and in 1867 became president. The Lackawanna, as it was called, was one of the coal roads which served the anthracite regions of Pennsylvania. There was heavy competition between the several railroads, taking the form of shipping rebates, rate wars, and other cutthroat tactics. Sloan negotiated a rate agreement among the coal roads in 1870, but the agreement was broken in 1876, and two of the larger carriers, the New Jersey Central and the Philadelphia & Reading, went into bankruptcy. It was just this sort of chaotic competition which led to the formation of the Interstate Commerce Commission in 1887.

Sloan sought to expand the Lackawanna and make it into a general freight handler rather than just a coal road. One of the problems that prevented this was the old 6-foot gauge of the Lackawanna. Sloan recognized the problem and took action to change to the standard 4-foot 8½-inch width as quickly as possible to prevent any break in service. Not only did the rails have to be changed but the rolling stock had to be modified also. Sloan had construction crews lay a third rail on the line at the proper distance for standard gauge. On a Sunday in 1876 the switch was made, and within twenty-four hours the trains were running again. The cost was over $1.25 million, but it was worth it. Lackawanna stock went from 30 to 94 almost at once. Along with obtaining an entrance into Buffalo, the regauging helped to increase general freight business as well as coal shipments, and passenger increases were up over 85 percent from 1881 to 1890.

In 1877 Sloan was named president of the Michigan Central Railroad by William H. Vanderbilt as a gesture to the New York financiers. When Vanderbilt gained control of the road he had himself elected president instead of Sloan. Sloan served as president of several other railroads: the Fort Wayne & Jackson in Indiana, the International & Great Northern in Texas, the Pere Marquette in Michigan, and the Rome, Watertown & Ogdensburg in New York. He resigned as president of the Lackawanna in 1899 but remained as chairman of the board until he died in 1907. Sloan was a man whose middle and later life was devoted wholly to railroading. He seemed to have no other interests; for him the business of life was business. He was stern, but fair, and expected others to be likewise, and neither gave nor took quarter in competition.

Sloan served on the boards of many corporations: Oswego & Syracuse Railroad; Syracuse, Binghamton & New York; Utica, Chenango & Susquehanna Valley; Green Bay, Winona & St. Paul Railway; Louisville, New Albany & Chicago Railroad; Manhattan Railway; Wabash Railroad; Texas & Pacific Railway; Missouri Pacific Railway; Bank of Metropole; Bank of the Manhattan Trust Company; Consolidated Gas; Farmers' Loan & Trust; Mechanics Bank; Mt. Hope Mineral; National City Bank; National Insurance Company; New York Mutual Gas; National Security Company; Seamans Bank for Savings; Western Union Telegraph Company; and Queens Insurance Company of America.

Sloan and his wife were the parents of six children. He died on September 22, 1907, in Garrison, New York, at the age of ninety.

References:

Jules I. Bogen, *The Anthracite Railroads* (New York: Ronald Press, 1927);

Robert J. Casey and W. A. S. Douglas, *The Lackawanna Story* (New York: McGraw-Hill, 1951);

Thomas C. Cochran, *Railroad Leaders, 1845-1890* (Cambridge, Mass.: Harvard University Press, 1953);

Joseph Rankin Duryee, *The Story of Samuel and Margaret Sloan* (New York: H. J. Lucas, 1927).

Archives:

Materials concerning Samuel Sloan are located in the Erastus Corning Papers of the Albany Institute of History and Art, Albany, New York; and in the Michigan Central Railroad Archives, Detroit, Michigan.

John Gregory Smith

(July 22, 1818-November 6, 1891)

by J. Kevin Graffagnino

University of Vermont

CAREER: President, Vermont Central Railroad (1858-1872); governor, state of Vermont (1863-1865); president, Northern Pacific Railroad (1866-1872); president, Central Vermont Railroad (1873-1891).

John Gregory Smith, railroad executive and Civil War governor of Vermont, was born on July 22, 1818, at St. Albans, Vermont, and died there on November 6, 1891. He was the eldest son of John and Maria Curtis Smith and could trace his family roots in America back to early seventeenth-century Massachusetts. His father was a successful lawyer, state legislator, congressman (1839-1841), and pioneer Vermont railroad promoter. An 1838 graduate of the University of Vermont, Smith studied law with his father and at Yale University before joining his father's St. Albans law practice in 1841. On December 27, 1843, he married Ann Eliza Brainerd of St. Albans; together they produced six children.

The 1840s were a decade of considerable railroad planning and building in Vermont, and the Smith family was influential from the outset in the development of the state's rail network. In the late 1840s and early 1850s John Smith simultaneously promoted the Vermont & Canada (V&C) Railroad in northwestern Vermont and assumed a major role in the running of the Vermont Central (VCR) Railroad. John Gregory Smith worked with his father on the two railroads, and, on the elder Smith's death in 1858, John Gregory and his brother, Worthington C. Smith, became president of the VCR and president of the V&C, respectively. Maintaining the aggressive entrepreneurial style that had become the family trademark, the brothers made St. Albans the headquarters for the two lines, established a complicated pyramid of subsidiary companies and suppliers that brought them considerable personal wealth, and fought off the charges of rival

John Gregory Smith (courtesy of Vermont Historical Society)

stockholders that the financial benefits of the two railroads were flowing largely into the Smith family coffers.

Like his father, John Gregory Smith combined business with politics. He served two terms in the Vermont state senate (1858-1859), then three terms in the state house of representatives (1860-1862), the last two as speaker. On leaving the state legislature he distinguished himself during two terms as governor (1863-1865) by his staunch support for Abraham Lincoln's administration and his strong concern for the men in Vermont's Civil War regiments. Effective in his work for the national Republican cause, he also presided over the expansion of Vermont's small state government to meet the rapidly growing bureaucratic responsibilities of the war effort. After the war Smith declined all requests to run for additional public office, serving only as chairman of the state delegation to the Republican national convention in 1872, 1880, and 1884, but retaining a noteworthy measure of control over Republican party politics in Vermont for the rest of his life.

However, politics took a back seat to railroading for Smith after 1865. By the mid 1860s he had built the Vermont Central Railroad into an impressive system with dependent lines into Canada and New York, and in 1866 he moved to connect the VCR network to the West by succeeding Josiah Perham as president of the nascent Northern Pacific (NP) Railroad. Smith broadened the company's financial base, bringing in as investors many of the East's most prominent financiers. After several years of delays and false starts, he also got construction of the road off the drawing board, with some 500 miles of track laid during his years as president. Meanwhile, he soon came under attack for the same sort of financial tactics he had perfected in Vermont, as a growing number of observers charged him with extravagance and misuse of NP funds to enrich himself and his associates. In the face of this mounting criticism, and with the NP close to bankruptcy, Smith resigned as president in August 1872, turning control over to Jay Cooke and George Cass, who in turn presided over the NP's near demise in the panic of 1873.

After resigning from the NP helm, Smith devoted most of his energies to his Vermont financial and political empires. The Vermont Central Railroad controlled some 750 miles of track by the early 1870s, giving it the most extensive railroad network in New England and the seventh largest in the United States, but the perpetually shaky line collapsed in 1872-1873. Smith engineered a reorganization that created a new Central Vermont (CVR) Railroad, with himself as president, to replace the bankrupt company. Although the new CVR managed to keep its trains running in Vermont, Smith had to give up some of the subsidiary companies and leases outside the state. While his administration continued to attract charges of corruption, nepotism, and mismanagement, Smith weathered every storm and retained control. In state politics he remained a powerful and influential Republican leader, proving especially adept at protecting his railroads from unwelcome state regulation and legislation. At the local level St. Albans charities and institutions benefited greatly from Smith family largesse during the last decades of his life. He served as president or director of several local banks and corporations and helped ensure that St. Albans's position as one of Victorian Vermont's most prosperous communities remained secure. John Gregory Smith died in St. Albans on November 6, 1891, after a month's illness, at the age of 73.

References:

Lewis C. Aldrich, ed., *History of Franklin and Grand Isle Counties, Vermont* (Syracuse, N.Y.: D. Mason & Co., 1891), pp. 732-37;

Albert Ricker Dowden, "John Gregory Smith," *Vermont History*, 32 (April 1964): 79-97;

Robert C. Jones, *The Central Vermont Railway: A Yankee Tradition*, 1 (Silverton, Colo.: Sundance Books, 1981);

Jacob G. Ullery, comp., *Men of Vermont* (Brattleboro, Vt.: Transcript Publishing, 1984), p. 96;

Samuel Williams, "Our War Governors: J. Gregory Smith," *The Vermonter*, 2 (August 1896): 1-9.

Archives:

The Vermont Historical Society, Montpelier, Vermont, has fourteen boxes of Smith family correspondence, business records, etc., 1810-1899 (NUCMC 64-1590). Special Collections, University of Vermont Library, Burlington, Vermont, has thirteen boxes of Smith family correspondence and miscellaneous papers, 1797-1956.

Platt Smith

(May 6, 1813-July 12, 1882)

by Leland L. Sage

University of Northern Iowa

CAREER: Lawyer (1847-1882); chief organizer and solicitor, Dubuque & Pacific Railroad (1853-1860); vice-president, Dubuque & Sioux City Railroad (1860-1867); director and officer, various railroads (1860-1882); director, Dubuque Bridge Company (1868-1882).

If sometime Dubuquer John Plumbe was the dreamer of a railroad to the Pacific, Dubuque's Platt Smith was one of the hardheaded practical men who realized that one way for that dream to become a reality was to build it slowly and patiently, one short link at a time. Ultimately these links could be joined so as to form one continuous line. Of course the day would come when men could project and plan from scratch, as it were, one grand continuous line, say from Omaha to San Francisco, but this was done only after men had had years of experience in the short-link type of planning and construction.

There would seem to be a good explanation for Platt Smith's hardheaded practical approach to the problems inherent in railroad building: he was himself a graduate of the "school of hard knocks," and he developed a sense of practicality which was very beneficial to him as an organizer and builder of railroads. If one is looking for a prime example of a successful, self-made man, Platt Smith fits the model.

Born May 6, 1813, to desperately poor parents in or near the little town of Hoosick, New York, northeast of Albany, the family moved to Chenango County, New York, when Smith was only two years old. Here he grew up, working at a variety of odd jobs, growing in wisdom and stature over the years. The latter became more obvious than the former as his magnificent physique loomed up in any crowd. Schooling came only at short intervals and gave him little more than an ability to read and do simple sums. His tenure as a store

clerk was a learning experience which would stand him in good stead during his later years.

As a mature young man well into his twenties he worked his way to the West, eventually finding himself in Maquoketa, Jackson County, Iowa. With little more to offer than a strong back and well-developed muscles, he might have become nothing more than the little town's "handy man," but fate intervened in the form of a debilitating illness. For two years he was a victim of the ague. Fortunately, the young man had something in his nature which appealed to Maquoketa's hotel keeper and his wife, Mr. and Mrs. John E. Goodenow, who took care of him and saw him through this trying period. The Goodenows were truly the first family of Maquoketa, both literally and figuratively. The founder of the town, Mr. Goodenow had it platted and personally saw to it that the lots were given away or sold; a municipal government was organized, with himself as the first mayor; a school was provided; and churches were made welcome.

While the town was still young it happened that two men, named Harrington and Doolittle, became involved in a petty dispute over a piece of land. Harrington had built a cabin thereon and Doolittle, in anger, had destroyed the structure; Harrington retaliated by thrashing his opponent. Doolittle sued and Harrington asked Platt Smith to be his adviser. Smith, though not a lawyer, spoke in Harrington's defense and, with great effect, told the familiar Biblical story of Solomon's settlement of the argument between two women, each of whom claimed to be the mother of a baby. Smith reasoned that just as the woman who objected to Solomon's proposal to divide the baby and award each a half was deemed to be the rightful mother, so Harrington was the rightful owner of the land and cabin because even in a heated dispute he had not wanted to harm the cabin, whereas Doolittle had done his best to destroy it. The judge went along with Harrington's adviser and decided the case in his favor.

Smith found himself a local hero and even Doolittle, the loser, came to him and urged him to follow his apparent talent for the law, offering to procure law books for Smith to study. Smith accepted the offer, found a lawyer in nearby Bellevue who was willing to take him in as a helper and student, and, now twenty-nine years old, began his law studies. After overcoming many setbacks, including denial of his petition for admittance to the Dubuque bar, he was finally examined by Judge Joseph Williams, whose court was in session at Tipton, and admitted to practice in the courts of the Territory of Iowa in March 1843. At the age of thirty he had triumphantly vindicated the judgment of many friends who had urged him on in this experiment in adult education. His career would eventually take him all the way from the petty cases before a justice of the peace to the Supreme Court of the United States, which he was admitted to argue before in the winter term of 1852.

Smith first made his reputation as a criminal lawyer, but after the admission of Iowa as a state in December 1846, he moved along with the more orderly times into civil law. By 1847 he had won his way by hard work and phenomenal success into membership in the Dubuque bar that had earlier rejected him. Within the year he had formed a partnership and, for some years, was perhaps the busiest, hardest-working lawyer in Iowa. In 1853 and 1859 he participated as counsel in three important cases before the United States Supreme Court which established him as an attorney who could hold his own with the best. The cases were *Chouteau* v. *Moloney* (57 U.S. 203), *Fanning* v. *Gregoire* (57 U.S. 523), and *Dubuque & Pacific Railroad Co.* v. *Edwin C. Litchfield* (64 U.S. 66).

In the first of these he faced Reverdy Johnson, a former attorney general and soon to be one of the lawyers in the Dred Scott case. The chief justice was the redoubtable Roger B. Taney. Chouteau sued Moloney, who was represented by T. S. Wilson and his partner, Platt Smith. The Chouteau claim to lands in and around Dubuque was based on the will left by Julien Dubuque, in which he set forth the fact that the Indians had given him vast lands in return for his friendship. The Supreme Court held that the gift to Dubuque had given him only the right to *work* the lead mines, not a title to the property, therefore the titles held by Moloney

(and others) were valid, and the Chouteau claims were invalid. The *Fanning* v. *Gregoire* case involved the right to operate a ferry between Dunleith (now East Dubuque) and Dubuque. In this case Smith's opponent was his own senior partner, T. S. Wilson. Gregoire claimed he had a license to operate the ferry, a permit given him by the city of Dubuque after Gregoire had dropped his old territorial permit. Fanning had held on to his territorial permit and claimed it was older (and better) than Gregoire's license issued by the city of Dubuque. Smith, representing Gregoire, argued that Dubuque was the creature of the state of Iowa, therefore any act of Dubuque was really the act of the new state of Iowa, taking precedence over an act by the territory. The Court went along with Smith's argument. In the 1859 case involving title to certain lands along the Des Moines River, the Court held that title to these lands issued from the Congressional Act of May 15, 1856, which had granted them as an aid to the construction of a railroad from Dubuque to the Missouri River (as well as other roads from Lyons [Clinton], Davenport, and Burlington). Smith, representing the railroad, was opposed by the prestigious Burlington resident and attorney, Charles Mason, formerly chief justice of the courts of the Territory of Iowa. Justice John Catron spoke for the Court and upheld Smith's client.

Thrilling as it must have been to match wits and hold his own in the company of these intellectual giants, an equally exciting activity among businessmen at the time was railroad promotion. Platt Smith joined in this new mania, which soon consumed all of his energies and attention and would eventually lead to the virtual abandonment of his law practice. For several years business leaders had dreamed and talked of railroads from the Mississippi to the Pacific. Dubuque leaders, whose focus up to this time had been on Mississippi River traffic, now visualized Dubuque as a rail center. In 1853 Smith and friends turned talk into action by forming the Dubuque & Pacific (D&P) Railroad Company, for which they secured a charter from the general assembly of Iowa on April 28, 1853. The president of the company was Captain Jesse P. Farley, well known for his steamboat business on the Mississippi. One of Iowa's senators, Gen. George Wallace Jones, was made chairman of the board. Platt Smith, though the prime mover in the enterprise, was content with the office of solicitor; later he would be a vice-president and solicitor.

Thus began a career in railroading which would go well on into the 1870s. Other Dubuquers who invested in the new company were Lucius H. Langworthy and Gen. C. H. Booth. Morris K. Jesup, a New Jersey capitalist, was the principal eastern financier; his brother, Frederick S. Jesup, a Dubuque banker, was made treasurer, probably at the behest of his brother in order to monitor the Jesup interests. In addition to drawing up the articles of incorporation, Smith was in charge of procuring the right-of-way, and was the man on the scene who furnished the driving power which kept the project on course when others grew fainthearted.

Not much was done in 1853 and 1854 except to raise money by the sale of bonds. The Illinois Central provided the incentive to begin the actual construction by extending its line from Galena to Dunleith. This brought the rails from Chicago to a point which was only a trip across the river into Dubuque. Dubuque now became a thriving, growing city, and Galena began a recession into just another way station on the railroad from Chicago instead of an important terminus. Another stimulant to construction was the federal Land Act of May 15, 1856, which provided lands to aid in the building of four lines to the Missouri River. The actual grants were made to companies such as the D&P to help them in underwriting the expenses of construction of east-west roads across Iowa. The D&P and its westward successors, soon to be leased and ultimately sold to the Illinois Central, received over 1.2 million acres for sale to settlers along the line. The other lines out of Clinton, Davenport, and Burlington also fared well.

Slowly and surely the D&P inched its way to Dyersville, Earlville, Manchester, Independence (thus ruining the hopes of Quasqueton for greatness), Jesup, Waterloo, and Cedar Falls, the last greeting the arrival of the rails with a gala celebration on April 1, 1861, totally oblivious to the threat of war which proved to be less than two weeks in the offing. Platt Smith was one of the principal speakers at the Cedar Falls celebration.

Completion of the road up to this point was a personal triumph for the Dubuque attorney. The D&P was "his" railroad even though others provided the money. Without his management, driving force, and ability to cope with the inevitable difficulties, the job would never have been completed. Even before the road reached Waterloo it had been necessary to put through a complete reorganization,

emerging in 1860 with a new title, the Dubuque & Sioux City (D&SC) Railroad Company. In this new organization Smith was given more recognition than in the D&P. He was made a vice-president and almost by default was put in charge of planning and construction, not as an engineer but as a manager who knew more than anyone else about what was necessary to complete the project. Construction from Cedar Falls was resumed after the war. By the time the rails had reached Iowa Falls it was necessary again to reorganize and refinance. Some directors wanted to stop the line at Iowa Falls; others, including Smith, wanted to go on to the Missouri River (Sioux City). Smith's faction was victorious. A new financial angel was supplied in the person of John Insley Blair of New Jersey, who found the needed money and more than matched Platt Smith's great driving force. With great difficulty the road was pushed to Fort Dodge; crews were then started from Sioux City as well as Fort Dodge, saving much construction time, but not enough to prevent the company from being the last of the four trans-Iowa lines to reach the Missouri. Unfortunately Smith incurred the displeasure and diminishing respect of Jesup and the other D&SC leaders; they lost no opportunity to denounce him, and eventually he was dismissed from his vice-presidency on June 21, 1867, on the grounds that he no longer held the minimum amount of stock required to qualify as an officer.

Meanwhile, Smith had discovered the necessity of building feeder lines to serve the trunk line. His first effort in this direction was a line to serve the counties north of Cedar Falls with a road called the Cedar Falls & Minnesota Railroad. This road had already been organized when the D&SC reached Cedar Falls and Platt Smith was made its president. The Civil War slowed the project but it was completed after the war, along with several other feeder lines. These lines eventually formed part of a rail network which enabled the state's boosters to assert that no point in Iowa was more than twelve miles from a railroad.

All of this feverish activity excites the admiration even of those accustomed to the frenetic pace of the twentieth century. When one takes into account the sparse office facilities, poor communication systems, and the necessity of spending much time in the field to keep close watch on construction contractors, Platt Smith emerges as a veritable miracle worker. Little wonder that he sometimes displayed contempt for eastern financiers who could lead easy lives. He was always conscious of the monetary gulf that separated him from the "money-bags" of the East, or even his own Dubuque, but his abilities as a planner and field manager supplied certain talents that they did not have. In 1867, in spite of Blair's criticism, and in spite of his uneasy relationship with the city, his abilities were recognized by Dubuque and he was the guest of honor at a banquet in which his praises were sung and his talents recognized by his fellow workers and citizens.

As a self-made man Smith's business philosophy valued independence. He expected governors and legislators to help the railroads, mostly by leaving them alone. When, for example, a charter was needed for a new line or a permit for a new bridge, or approval for his wage policy, or the distribution of free passes as management saw fit ("where they would do the most good"), he expected cooperation, not an inclination to reform and regulate. Fortunately for him, his heyday was before state and federal commissions came into power. His death in 1882 spared him the agony of observing Governor William Larrabee of Iowa (1885-1889), who would come along to lead the fight for rate regulation—and win; he did not have to watch Governor Albert Baird Cummins (1902-1908) win the battle to abolish the free pass system. He expected state legislators and congressmen, even senators, to act as messengers and do his biddings, especially his fellow Dubuquer, William Boyd Allison, a representative for four terms and a senator for six terms. Allison was a small stockholder in several lines and was nominal president of the company which built the railroad bridge across the Mississippi from Dubuque to Dunleith. Smith held considerable stock in the company, and did not hesitate to give Allison orders. The Mississippi River bridge project of 1868 was the climax to Smith's career. He helped Andrew Carnegie persuade the company directors to buy the best grade of steel when Carnegie was in great danger of losing the sale. The bridge remains in use as of 1987, a monument to both men.

Smith's last years were filled with pain and illness, stemming from a series of paralytic strokes. His personal life was filled with sadness: his first wife, Caroline, whom he had met in his Maquoketa days, died in 1874; their son had died in infancy in 1845. His second wife, a member of a prominent Dubuque family, survived him for many years (until 1912), as did their one son. Smith died on July 12, 1882. He and all his family members are buried in Linwood Cemetery, Dubuque, as are many of his colleagues and coworkers. His Dubuque home at 961 Bluff Street still stands and is in use as a dance studio and residence. He did not amass a great fortune, but his investments and savings made him comfortable. His real legacies to his adopted state were a railroad from Dubuque to Sioux City, which became part of the Illinois Central, and the example of his life.

References:

A. T. Andreas, *Historical Atlas of the State of Iowa* (Chicago: Andreas Atlas, 1875);

Thomas C. Cochran, *Railroad Leaders, 1845-1890: The Business Mind in Action* (Cambridge, Mass.: Harvard University Press, 1953);

Carlton J. Corliss, *Main Line of Mid-America: The Story of the Illinois Central* (New York: Creative Age Press, 1950);

J. W. Ellis, *A History of Jackson County, Iowa* (Chicago, 1910);

Arthur Q. Larson, "Platt Smith of Dubuque: His Early Career," *The Palimpsest,* 58 (May-June 1977): 88-96;

Larson, "Railroads and Newspapers: The Dubuque Controversy of 1867," *The Annals of Iowa,* 48 (Winter/Spring 1986): 159-176;

Carolyn Curtis Mohr, *Guide to the Illinois Central Archives in the Newberry Library 1851-1906* (Chicago: Newberry Library, 1951);

Leonard F. Ralston, "Iowa Railroads and the Des Moines River Improvement Land Grant of 1846," *Iowa Journal of History,* 56 (April 1958): 97-128;

Ralston, "Railroad Interests in Early Iowa," *Annals of Iowa,* 41 (Winter 1973): 1129-1147;

Leland L. Sage, *William Boyd Allison: A Study in Practical Politics* (Iowa City: The State Historical Society of Iowa, 1956);

[Judge] Oliver P. Shiras, "The Dubuque Bar of the Past," booklet in the Dubuque Center for the Study of Area History;

John F. Stover, *History of the Illinois Central Railroad* (New York: Macmillan, 1975);

Robert M. Sutton, *The Illinois Central Railroad in Peace and War, 1858-1868* (Urbana: University of Illinois Press, 1948);

Mildred Throne, ed., "Mahony-Smith Letters on the Dubuque and Pacific Railroad," *Iowa Journal of History,* 54 (October 1956): 335-360;

John Rider Wallis, *Platt Smith, 1813-1882: A Brief Biography* (Dubuque County Historical Society, n.d.);

Archives:

There are hundreds of Platt Smith letters in the Illinois Central Archives, the Newberry Library, Chicago.

Southern Pacific Company

by Don L. Hofsommer

Augustana College

"Done." It was a simple but completely understood message that winged across the country from wind-swept Promontory, Utah, on May 10, 1869. The first transcontinental railroad–composed of two independent companies, the Central Pacific, building from the West, and the Union Pacific, arriving from the East–had been completed. Yet those who headed the Central Pacific realized that they could hardly rest on their laurels. Their work was not "done." Indeed, they and the company they headed were deeply in debt, and the future looked bleak. Completion of the Suez Canal in the same year drained traffic that the railroaders had counted on to the Orient, and business in Nevada declined as the silver mining boom passed into a lengthy depression. Moreover, their home state, California, was largely underpopulated and capital poor. On the other hand, they had little alternative than to plunge ahead.

The "Big Four," they were called–Charles Crocker, Mark Hopkins, Collis Potter Huntington, and Leland Stanford; these were the men who controlled the Central Pacific. And these were the men who built more trackage, who acquired existing lines, who began a ferry service on San Francisco Bay, and who built the Central Pacific into an integral part of a much larger concern–the Southern Pacific Company (SP).

The Central Pacific derived, in part, from the Sacramento Valley Railroad. In 1852 the sponsors of the road hired Theodore D. Judah to locate and build the line from Sacramento to Folsom and Placerville. The Big Four, all Sacramento businessmen, were recruited in 1856 as transcontinental aspiration took root in California. These aspirations were rewarded after years of lobbying by many transcontinental enthusiasts, including the Big Four and Judah, in 1862 when President Lincoln signed the Pacific Railroad Bill. The act authorized the Central Pacific, the company formed by Judah and the Big Four, to build east from California to a junction with another company, the Union Pacific, building westward from Iowa.

Progress on the line was slow in the beginning as financing was difficult to obtain. Judah became estranged from the other partners over these issues in 1863 and died later that year. The Big Four were in complete control. The Central Pacific reached the Nevada border in 1867, still two years and several hundred miles from the junction with the Union Pacific in Utah. But the completion of the Central Pacific's portion of the transcontinental railroad marked only the beginning of the transportation empire that the Big Four would consolidate under their holding company, the Southern Pacific.

Expansion. That seemed the watchword of the Big Four. It especially marked the philosophy of Collis P. Huntington, who emerged as majordomo. By the end of the 1870s lines owned or controlled by the Big Four pointed northward to Oregon, southward along the California coast, and southward through the San Joaquin Valley to Los Angeles. And by the summer of 1881 a major new route was pushed eastward from Los Angeles to Yuma and on to the Rio Grande at El Paso. Expansion followed in Texas and Louisiana as well as in California and Oregon. Ultimately the company fashioned a crescent-shaped system of lines from Portland to New Orleans in addition to the Overland Route segment from Ogden to Oakland.

The Big Four had created a truly prodigious enterprise. They transformed California and much of the West, and they did so in an amazingly brief span of time. Their operation opened incredible opportunities for the public at large and provided employment for thousands. And, not so incidentally, they became wealthy in the process.

Impressive as the Southern Pacific was at the turn of the century, it needed a constant and growing source of cash to fully develop the property.

That funding would not come from the Big Four. Mark Hopkins had died in 1878 and was followed in death by Crocker in 1888, and Stanford in 1893. On August 13, 1900, the most talented railroader of the four, Collis P. Huntington, joined them. Stock control passed during the next year to Edward H. Harriman. "We have bought not only a railroad, but an empire," he enthusiastically declared.

The Southern Pacific continued to grow under Harriman and thereafter. During the 1930s it acquired the St. Louis Southwestern, an important regional road on its eastern flank, and three decades later it would broaden its base by diversifying outside transportation. In 1983 the holding company would be merged with Santa Fe Industries to form Santa Fe Southern Pacific Corporation, and in 1987 the SP's railroads would be offered for sale.

Reference:

Don L. Hofsommer, *The Southern Pacific, 1901-1985* (College Station, Tex.: Texas A&M University Press, 1986).

Archives:

The Southern Pacific Company records are located at the corporate offices in San Francisco, California.

Southern Railway

by John F. Stover

Purdue University

The Southern Railway was chartered and organized in 1894 and would consist eventually of more than 125 earlier southern railroads joined through consolidation. The Richmond & Danville (R&D) Railroad was the original line of the rail network which eventually became the Southern Railway. Chartered in 1847, the 143-mile Richmond & Danville connected those two important Virginia trading towns when it was completed in 1856. The line paid modest dividends on the eve of the Civil War and played a major role in the Confederate war effort in that conflict. During the war the R&D built and controlled the 48-mile Piedmont Railroad which ran from Danville south to Greensboro, North Carolina. At Greensboro the Piedmont connected with the North Carolina Railroad, a 223-mile line completed in 1856, which ran in a flat horseshoe curve from Goldsboro via Greensboro to Charlotte.

In spring 1871 Tom Scott and his associates in the Southern Railway Security Company, which was controlled by the Pennsylvania Railroad, gained control of the Richmond & Danville. In September 1871 the R&D obtained a 30-year lease on the North Carolina Railroad. South of Charlotte, the R&D and the Southern Railway Security Company gained control of the 195-mile Charlotte, Co-lumbia & Augusta in 1872 and, at the same time, started to build the 263-mile Atlanta & Richmond Airline from Charlotte to Atlanta, Georgia. During the early 1870s Tom Scott and his Security Company gained control of other lines in North Carolina, Tennessee, and Alabama, giving the Pennsylvania indirect control of nearly 2,000 miles of southern railroads on the eve of the panic of 1873. Because of the havoc caused by the economic downturn, the Pennsylvania went into receivership in the mid 1870s, and by 1876 the northern railroad had sold off much of its southern rail holdings. Both the Richmond & Danville and the North Carolina escaped receivership in the 1870s, and the Richmond & Danville, still under Pennsylvania control, resumed its aggressive program of expansion.

Although the Pennsylvania sold the bulk of its southern lines in the mid 1870s, it still retained a controlling interest in the Richmond & Danville. However, in spring 1880 it sold its R&D shares to the W. P. Clyde syndicate, a group of northern and southern capitalists. With the R&D under its control, the Clyde syndicate obtained from the Virginia legislature in 1880 an act incorporating the Richmond & West Point Terminal Railway & Wharehouse Company, a holding company entitled to acquire by purchase, or otherwise, the securities of railroads in any of the southern states. The R&D held a majority of stock of the holding company, and the directors of the R&D were also directors of the holding company. In March 1881 the R&D leased the Atlanta & Charlotte Airline (formerly the Atlanta & Richmond Airline), which gave it a direct line from Richmond to Atlanta.

In the early 1880s the Richmond & West Point Terminal Company acquired three roads which had been in receivership in the 1870s: the Virginia Midland, a 405-mile road running from Danville to Alexandria; the Western North Carolina, a 203-mile line running west from Salisbury; and the Greenville & Columbia, a 294-mile road located in western South Carolina. The holding company also acquired a controlling interest in the Charlotte, Columbia & Augusta. By mid 1882 the R&D had a rail system of more than 800 miles, while the holding company controlled an additional 1,250 miles. Other lines added in Alabama, Mississippi, and Kentucky, including the Georgia Pacific and the East Tennessee, Virginia & Georgia, gave the R&D/Richmond Terminal by 1890 a combined southern rail system of about 8,000 miles. In the early 1890s the 1,200-mile Central of Georgia also came under indirect influence of the holding company. During the late 1880s internal bickering between the holding company and the R&D weakened the system, a problem exacerbated in the early 1890s by a growing amount of floating debt. As a result the various segments of the R&D/Richmond Terminal system were placed in receivership in June 1892.

The receivership and reorganization of the Richmond Terminal system was the most important financial development among southern railroads during the mid 1890s. There was a general feeling of satisfaction among northern financial circles when Drexel, Morgan and Company agreed in February 1893 to undertake the financial rehabilitation of the property. Complicated litigation concerning the Central of Georgia kept that line out of the reorganization, but the remaining properties consisted of about 6,000 miles. Morgan's first step was to ask for the deposit of all stocks and bonds with his company. This was an unusual practice, but it was approved and the great bulk of the securities were in Morgan's possession by May 1893. Morgan's agents and railroad experts at once began a detailed study of the various lines in the R&D/Richmond Terminal system. The investigation revealed that many of the roads were deteriorated, that much of the equipment was old, and that improper accounting methods were common on many of the lines. Morgan's plan of reorganization was delayed and modified because of a general decline in southern railroad revenue during the depression of 1893, but the final plan of reorganization was submitted in March 1894 and approved a few months later. Since several of the weaker properties were not included in the new company, the Southern Railway had a total mileage of about 4,600 miles. The new securities under the plan consisted of $140 million in mortgage bonds, $60 million in preferred stock, and $125 million in common stock. Cash assessments were levied against the original junior securities, and the proceeds were used to pay a $14 million floating debt and to provide for property betterment. The new Southern Railway was organized in June 1894, with Samuel Spencer as president and three members of the nine-member board coming from Drexel, Morgan and Company.

Born and educated in Georgia, Samuel Spencer entered railroad work in 1869, working his way through the ranks of the Baltimore & Ohio to be its president from 1887 to 1888. He became a railroad expert for the Morgan bank in 1889 and was active in the Richmond Terminal reorganization in the early 1890s. He remained president of the Southern Railway until his death in 1906. During the dozen years of his presidency, Spencer substantially increased the mileage, traffic, and net income of the Southern. The mileage of the line increased to 4,800 miles in 1897 and to 6,300 by 1900. Control of the Alabama Great Southern was obtained in 1895, the Memphis & Charleston in 1898, and several other lines were added by 1900. By 1900 the Southern Railway was serving most of the southern states with lines connecting Washington, Richmond, Norfolk, Charleston, Atlanta, Brunswick, Chattanooga, Mobile, Memphis, Cincinnati, Louisville, and St. Louis. The annual revenue of the Southern climbed from $16 million in 1894 to $19 million in 1897, and to $31 million in 1900. Net income increased from $5 million in 1894 to $6 million in 1897, and to $9 million in 1900. Between 1894 and 1900 the operating ratio dropped from 74 percent to 70 percent. In the early years of the Southern, most of the income was used for improvements in road and equipment. Dividends on the preferred stock were paid occasionally, but no common stock dividends were paid until after World War I. Instead, Spencer and his successors were preparing the Southern for solid prosperity in later decades.

References:

Stuart Daggett, *Railroad Reorganization* (New York: Houghton Mifflin, 1908);

Burke Davis, *The Southern Railway* (Chapel Hill: University of North Carolina Press, 1985);

John F. Stover, *The Railroads of the South, 1865-1900* (Chapel Hill: University of North Carolina Press, 1955).

Archives:

The corporate records of the Southern Railway are located at the company's headquarters in Atlanta, Georgia.

Samuel Spencer

(March 2, 1847-November 29, 1906)

by John F. Stover

Purdue University

CAREER: Superintendent, Long Island Railroad (1877-1879); assistant to the president (1879-1881), third vice-president (1881-1882), second vice-president (1882-1884), first vice-president (1884-1887), president, Baltimore & Ohio Railroad (1887-1888); railroad expert and partner, Drexel, Morgan & Company (1889-1894); receiver, Richmond & Danville Railroad (1893-1894); president, Southern Railway (1894-1906).

Samuel Spencer, railroad engineer and president, was born in Columbus, Georgia, on March 2, 1847, the only child of Lambert and Vernona (Mitchell) Spencer. His father, a cotton merchant and planter, was descended from James Spencer, who settled in Talbot County, Maryland, in 1670. Samuel Spencer was educated in the elementary schools of Columbus, and later at the age of fifteen he attended the Georgia Military Institute in Marietta. He left school in 1863 and enlisted as a private in Nelson's Rangers, a cavalry troop which included a number of boys from Columbus. Private Spencer campaigned in Mississippi and Alabama, served for a time under Nathan B. Forrest, and later served in the army of Gen. John B. Hood. After the war he returned to his father's plantation and when the University of Georgia reopened, he enrolled as a member of the junior class, graduating in 1867 with first honors. Even though he knew he was expected to enter the family cotton business, Spencer preferred the more active life of a civil engineer. He enrolled as an engineering student at the University of Virginia in 1867 and received the C.E. degree with high honors in 1869.

Samuel Spencer

Shortly after graduation Spencer started his railroad career as a rodman on the Savannah & Memphis Railroad, a short line in Alabama and later a part of the Central of Georgia. Spencer worked up to better positions and by 1872 was principal engineer on the road. He was married on February 6, 1872, to Louisa Vivian Benning, the daughter of Judge Henry Lewis Benning. Later in

1872 he worked briefly on the New Jersey Southern Railroad before shifting to the Baltimore & Ohio Railroad. On the B&O Spencer worked at various minor positions in both the transportation and traffic departments. In 1877 he was appointed superintendent of the Long Island Railroad at a salary of $5,000 a year. During his eighteen months in that position Spencer attracted the attention of J. Pierpont Morgan, whose bank held many securities of the Long Island Railroad. Morgan soon came to rely on Spencer's tact and general knowledge of railroading.

In October 1879 Spencer returned to the Baltimore & Ohio as assistant to Pres. John W. Garrett. In 1881 Spencer accompanied Garrett to Europe to secure a major loan for the B&O and, upon his return, was appointed third vice-president of the road. A year later he was elevated to second vice-president and in November 1884 was appointed first vice-president when Robert Garrett was elected president after the death of his father. As first vice-president Spencer was in charge of B&O operations. During his three years as president, Robert Garrett relied heavily upon the advice of Spencer and John K. Cowen, general counsel of the B&O.

Robert Garrett resigned the presidency of the B&O in the fall of 1887, and Samuel Spencer was elected to fill the vacancy on December 10, 1887. Spencer, in his single year as president, was a forceful and active executive. He reduced the nearly $9 million of floating debt by selling the line's private telegraph and sleeping-car services. Spencer felt that both rolling stock and railroad securities of other roads had been vastly overvalued on the company books. When his *Annual Report* for 1888 appeared, the *Railroad Gazette* was pleased with the Spencer reforms and wrote: "For the first time in many years we are given a straightforward account of the conditions of the Baltimore & Ohio R.R." The bulk of the B&O board of directors did not favor Spencer's reforms and feared that Drexel, Morgan & Company were seeking through Spencer to control the railroad. Spencer resigned the presidency on December 19, 1888.

In March 1889 Spencer joined Drexel, Morgan & Company, becoming first the railroad expert for the firm, and later, in December 1890, a partner in the banking house. In 1893 Spencer was appointed one of the receivers of the Richmond & Danville Railroad and also for some other lines of the failing Richmond Terminal System. In the past decade and a half the Richmond & Danville, with its holding company the Richmond Terminal Company, had gained control over a number of lines in half a dozen southern states from Virginia to Alabama. By 1892 the entire system was facing receivership, and early in 1893 Drexel, Morgan & Company agreed to undertake the financial rehabilitation of the system. In the final reorganization plan several of the weaker lines were not included, but the new Southern Railway had a total mileage of 4,600 miles. The Southern Railway was organized in June 1894, with Samuel Spencer as president.

From the outset Spencer was known for his conservative and efficient management of the new road. He had a capacity for detail, a quick grasp of problems, and the ability to present his views with directness. Having risen through the ranks, Spencer was able to get the best from those who worked for him. Spencer sought to promote the prosperity of the Southern Railway and also the region which it served. His traffic officials wooed furniture manufacturers, lumber mills, iron and steel companies, and others who would use the rich natural resources of the South. At the same time the new president urged greater diversification of agriculture and the promotion of greater trade with Latin America. Spencer also realized it would be wise to follow a policy of basic cooperation with the Louisville & Nashville (L&N), the other major railroad system in the South. In April 1896 he wrote Milton H. Smith, the L&N president, that the best policy "would be that neither of us would buy or promote lines which directly affect the interest or the territory of the other without consultation." For several years Spencer and Smith agreed to harmonize their interests as both of their railroads expanded.

Certainly the Southern Railway grew in the decade after its formation. Control of the Alabama Great Southern was obtained in 1895, and the Memphis & Charleston was acquired in 1898. Other lines were later added. By the turn of the century the Southern Railway was serving most of the southern states with lines reaching Washington, Richmond, Norfolk, Charleston, Atlanta, Chattanooga, Mobile, Memphis, Cincinnati, and St. Louis. In the dozen years after 1894 the mileage of the Southern had grown to 7,500, while the passenger and freight traffic had more than tripled. Annual earnings had grown from $17 million to $53 million in the period. Most of the net income was used for improvements in road and equipment, and no dividends on the common stock were paid until after World War I. Instead, Spencer was preparing his line for solid prosperity in later decades.

Spencer died on November 29, 1906, near Lynchburg, Virginia, in a rear-end collision of two fast passenger trains on his own railroad. He was survived by his wife and his two sons and a daughter. On the day of his funeral in Washington, D.C., all Southern Railway trains stood still for five minutes, and later 30,000 Southern employees made contributions for a monument in his memory. Samuel Spencer was an outstanding spokesman for both the railroad industry and the New South.

References:

Burke Davis, *The Southern Railway, Road of the Innovators* (Chapel Hill: University of North Carolina Press, 1985);

Maury Klein, *History of the Louisville & Nashville Railroad* (New York: Macmillan, 1972);

New York Times, November 30, 1906, pp. 1-2;

John F. Stover, *History of the Baltimore and Ohio Railroad* (West Lafayette, Ind.: Purdue University Press, 1987).

Archives:

Material concerning Spencer and the early years of the Southern Railway is located at the corporate headquarters of the Southern Railway in Atlanta, Georgia.

Leland Stanford

(March 9, 1824-June 21, 1893)

by Dan Butler

Colby Community College

CAREER: Attorney-at-law (1847-1852); businessman (1852-1861); Republican candidate, California state treasurer (1857); Republican candidate, governor (1859); governor, California (1861-1863); director (1863-1869), president, Central Pacific Railroad (1869-1885); U.S. senator, California (1885-1893).

Leland Stanford was born on March 9, 1824, in Watervliet, New York, the fourth son of Joshua Stanford and Elizabeth Phillip Stanford. He was christened Amasa Leland, but he dropped the first name before reaching adulthood. Stanford's father was quite wealthy; he owned a large farm and was involved also in the construction of roads and bridges in the local area. Stanford attended school until the age of twelve, after which he received instruction at home until he was fourteen. Later he attended both the Clinton Liberal Institute in Clinton, New York, and the Cazenovia Seminary in Cazenovia, New York. At age twenty he began to study law in Albany, and three years later, he was admitted to the bar.

Stanford established his law practice in Port Washington, Wisconsin, where his father had purchased for him a law library said to be one of the best in Wisconsin. In 1850 he returned to New York to marry Jane Elizabeth Lathrop, the daughter of a prominent Albany businessman. They returned to Wisconsin, but in 1852 Stanford's practice was destroyed by fire. Five of his brothers had preceded him to California, and the loss of his law practice compelled Stanford to join them. He left his wife in Albany and made his way to the West. Arriving in California in 1852, Stanford was set up in business by his brothers, who were already successful in a mercantile enterprise. Stanford opened his first store in Cold Springs in El Dorado County in partnership with Nicholas T. Smith, who would later become treasurer of the Southern Pacific Railroad. The store was moderately successful, but as the output of the mines which supported the area began to decline, Stanford moved his business to Sacramento in 1855. With the move to Sacramento, Stanford became involved with the businessmen who would be his partners in the Central Pacific (CP) Railroad: Charles Crocker, Mark Hopkins, and Collis P. Huntington. The group, known as the Big Four, became interested in railroad promotion and in 1860 helped to finance a survey by Theodore D. Judah for a rail line over the Sierras. Their real focus, however, was a Pacific railroad, a project in which Stanford would play a leading political role.

Leland Stanford

Stanford had long been interested in politics, a fascination probably born of his law practice. He also had the advantage of being involved in the early stages of the California Republican party, in which he soon became a major force. His involvement in the party, however, did not stem from any deep-seated hatred of slavery. Like the rest of the Big Four, Stanford saw the Republican party as a means of securing support for the Pacific railroad. Despite these factors Stanford's political career was slow in flourishing. In 1857 he ran for state treasurer as a Republican but was defeated. Two years later he was defeated in the race for governor. In 1860 he traveled to Chicago for the Republican convention, where he lobbied for the inclusion in the party platform of a plank supporting the Pacific railroad. After Lincoln's inauguration in 1861 Stanford went to Washington, where he promoted the railroad project to the president personally.

His efforts and those of other railroad activists and promoters paid off in 1862 when President Lincoln signed the Pacific Railway Act. The act authorized the federally subsidized construction of a railroad from Iowa to the Pacific coast. The Central Pacific Railroad, of which Stanford was a director, was to build from the West Coast while the Union Pacific was to build from Iowa.

Stanford was elected governor of California in 1861 and used his position to support and further the railroad project. His power and prestige attracted investors to the railroad and helped to garner other support in the state. In 1863 he led the successful campaign, amid charges of fraud and vote buying, to convince Placer and Sacramento counties to pledge large subsidies for the railroad.

Stanford was not renominated for a second term as governor in 1863 and instead turned his total attention to the CP. While he was not actively involved in the construction of the railroad, a task left to Charles Crocker, or in the raising of money through the sale of stock, which was handled by Collis Huntington, Stanford was heavily involved in gaining valuable concessions for the CP in Utah. Here he worked closely with Mormon leader Brigham Young to make sure that the railroad had access to the potentially prosperous front range of the Wasatch. It was also Stanford who suggested to Crocker that Chinese labor be employed in building the railroad, thus solving one of the most pressing construction problems faced by the CP.

Stanford and the rest of the Big Four reaped huge profits from the construction of the CP. They were also spared some of the turmoil suffered by the Union Pacific because of scandal, mismanagement, and government interference. On May 10, 1869, the transcontinental line was completed, Stanford helping to drive the gold spike marking the junction of the CP with the Union Pacific. Despite the completion of this major goal, the work of the Big Four did not cease.

Once the transcontinental line was completed, Stanford and his associates turned to consolidating their control over the state of California. Through the purchases of the California Pacific in 1878 and the San Francisco & San Jose in 1868, the Big Four were able to gain access to both San Francisco and Oakland. They also purchased important waterfront properties and expanded their holdings in northern California. In 1868 they gained the charter to build the Southern Pacific (SP) and in 1870 organized the SP to build the line from San Francisco to the Colorado River. Stanford and his associates were able to secure control of southern California by building not only to the Colorado River but also down the coast and through the San Joaquin Valley. The SP monopoly in California and Nevada allowed the line to charge the highest rail rates in the country.

Stanford took advantage of his role as a railroad executive. Shortly after the transcontinental line was completed, his wife presented him with a private railroad car. Traveling in it, Stanford insisted on all the respect he believed he was due as a company president. Work crews turned out as he passed, and revenue trains were placed on sidings to make sure that his train was not delayed. For all his perceived power, however, Stanford had already been moved to a secondary role in the management of the SP. His isolation became more noticeable in 1874 when the company headquarters was moved to San Francisco, where Collis Huntington assumed more and more control over the actual management of the company. When the Southern Pacific Company in Kentucky was incorporated, thus making its effective merger with the Central Pacific easier, Huntington had succeeded in concentrating most of the railroad power to himself.

There is little public evidence of Stanford's feud with his remaining business partners (Hopkins died in 1878). However, Stanford's limited role in SP affairs caused him some bitterness, and he began to retire more and more to his farm in Palo Alto and his ranch in Tehama County. On the ranch he was actively involved in developing highly prized racehorses. In addition to his property and his other interests, Stanford turned his attention to the education of his young son, Leland, Jr., who had been born to the couple after almost twenty years of marriage. He immediately became the center of his parents' life. The planning of their mansion on Nob Hill and the purchase of the land in Tehama County were, in part, to ensure the best possible opportunities for the boy. Stanford had received a relatively good education for the times, but he was determined that his son would receive an education suitable for a future prince of business. Leland Stanford, Jr., was tutored in languages and the arts, taken to Europe to cultivate his tastes, and given an education to prepare him for Harvard. In 1882, however, the young man, never in robust health, fell ill. His parents took him to Europe, but his condition continued to deteriorate, and he was eventually diagnosed as suffering from typhoid fever. The younger Stanford died in Florence, Italy, in March 1884; his death was a great loss to his parents, and they never fully recovered. Stanford did not, however, retire from public life.

His interest in politics had never fully waned; he was alarmed by the periodic rise of reform movements. Stanford had been eager to receive public aid for his railroad business but was extremely opposed to any attempt at regulation. For example, he had opposed the California Constitution of 1879 in the belief that it gave more power to the state in its attempt to control corporations. Although Stanford has often been pictured as somewhat ineffectual as a leader, he was an expert at protecting his own interests and those of his company. He viewed corporations as positive creations and government as a helpful ally to them, but only as long as they aided corporate aims. After his return to California in 1884, Stanford again became actively involved in the political arena. The California Senate seat was open, and he allowed his name to be presented to the state legislature.

Stanford's election to the United States Senate finally brought his quarrel with Huntington into the open. Huntington supported another Republican, Aaron Sargent, who had been a longtime supporter of the railroad. Huntington felt Sargent should be rewarded with the Senate seat. Stanford refused to give up his quest and was elected to the post over Huntington's objections. In 1890 Huntington publicly attacked Stanford for being not only an ineffective spokesman for the railroad and his state but also for being an opportunist. He claimed that Stanford had been absent from the Senate for the debate on such critical issues as the Silver Purchase Act and the Interstate Commerce Act.

Further problems between the two men revolved around Stanford's life-style. For many years Huntington had been cultivating the idea that the SP was financially weak and therefore needed relief from the required repayment of its government debt. Stanford was clearly not poor, and his open display of wealth in Washington made Huntington's task all that more difficult.

Stanford spent more than $20 million during his last years to establish Stanford University as a memorial to his son. Huntington, aware of Stanford's financial situation, was able to withhold SP money from Stanford by loaning it to other interests rather than dispersing funds to the directors. As a result, Stanford spent the last two years of his life attempting to protect not only the university but his vast holdings in real estate. The strain was too much. Stanford died at his home in Palo Alto on June 21, 1893, of a heart attack. His estate passed to his wife except for $2.5 million which was given to Stanford University. Most of his lands had to be sold to pay his debts and to fulfill the terms of his will.

References:
Matthew Josephson, *The Robber Barons* (New York: Harcourt, Brace, 1934);
Maury Klein, *Union Pacific: The Birth of a Railroad, 1862-1893* (Garden City: Doubleday, 1987);
Oscar Lewis, *The Big Four* (New York: Knopf, 1938).

Archives:
Some material concerning Leland Stanford is located at the Mariners Museum, Newport News, Virginia.

Amasa Stone

(April 27, 1818-May 11, 1883)

by Darwin H. Stapleton

Rockefeller Archive Center

CAREER: Builder and contractor (c. 1837-1876); superintendent, New Haven, Hartford & Springfield Railroad (c. 1845-1846); superintendent, Cleveland, Columbus & Cincinnati Railroad (1851-1853), president (1857-1858); president, Cleveland, Painesville & Ashtabula Railroad (1858-1869); managing director, Lake Shore & Michigan Southern Railroad (1873-1875).

Amasa Stone acquired considerable wealth as a railroad contractor, played a major role in consolidating early Ohio and other midwestern railroads, and became a major investor in banking and industry in the Midwest. He was born on April 27, 1818, in Charlton, Massachusetts, to Amasa and Esther Stone, who together operated a farm. Their son received a local education and worked on the family farm until his late teenage years, when he was apprenticed to a brother who was a carpenter. Buying out the last year of his apprenticeship in 1838, he moved into contracting for, and superintending the erection of, buildings and bridges. His brother-in-law William Howe was the inventor of an improved timber-truss bridge for which Howe received patents in 1840 and 1841. Stone assisted Howe in the development of the bridge, and in 1842 Stone formed a partnership with Azariah Boody to purchase Howe's patent rights.

The most important use for the Howe bridge was in railroad construction. Stone's initiation into this business occurred in 1839 when he assisted Howe in the construction of a bridge over the Connecticut River at Springfield, Massachusetts, for the

Amasa Stone

Western Railroad. Stone soon earned a reputation for his ability to construct Howe bridges quickly and inexpensively. In the following years, especially in his partnership with Boody, he is reported to have constructed hundreds of Howe bridges.

Stone first entered railroad administration in 1845 when he served as superintendent of the New Haven, Hartford & Springfield Railroad. The immense growth of midwestern railroading soon pulled him from New England, however, and in 1847, with partners Stillman Witt and Frederick

Harbach, he contracted to build the Cleveland, Columbus & Cincinnati (CC&C) Railroad. His success in that enterprise, and the investment which he acquired by accepting payment for his services in the stock of the railroad, led to his appointment as superintendent of the railroad in April 1851. Stone had already become a resident of Cleveland, apparently staking his career on the opportunities in the Midwest.

Though he had accepted the appointment "with much hesitation and reluctance," Stone's organizational talents became apparent during his term as CC&C superintendent when, with a primitive roadbed and a limited supply of rolling stock, the railroad successfully handled heavy business between the developing commercial-industrial centers of Cleveland and Cincinnati. Stone early initiated a strategy of establishing the CC&C as the preferred through route between Buffalo and Cincinnati, at first by planning regular connections between the Buffalo-Cleveland lake steamers and his Cleveland-Cincinnati trains. The strategy was so profitable that the railroad had virtually paid off its bonded indebtedness by the end of its third year of operation. Stone resigned his superintendency in 1853 but remained a director of the company.

In 1850 Stone had accepted a contract (with partners Witt and Harbach) to build the Cleveland, Painesville & Ashtabula (CP&A) Railroad eastward along Lake Erie from Cleveland. Completed in 1852, the line was extended to Erie, Pennsylvania, in 1854, where it connected with a line from Buffalo. This provided an all-rail route between Buffalo and Cincinnati, which the CC&C and the CP&A coordinated successfully. Stone served for many years as a director of both lines and was president of the CC&C in 1857 and 1858 and of the CP&A from 1858 to 1869.

While president of the CP&A Stone developed an aggressive strategy of line interconnection. He led the company to invest $500,000 in the stock of the Sunbury & Erie Railroad in 1858 because it offered the possibility of an alternate connection to the East Coast which would be competitive with the Pennsylvania, Erie, and New York Central lines. In 1863 Stone personally promoted the formation of the Jamestown & Franklin (J&F) Railroad in order to exploit the growing coal and oil fields of northwestern Pennsylvania, recognizing that that railroad's natural outlet was to Cleveland through

the CP&A. In 1866, the year after the J&F opened, it was leased to the CP&A.

Contemporary with these actions Stone was applying his skills to railroading farther west. With Stillman Witt as his partner Stone contracted in 1858 to build the Chicago & Milwaukee Railroad, and subsequent to its completion he became a director of that line.

Stone's concern for railroad consolidation impressed Cornelius Vanderbilt. In 1873, four years after the CP&A merged with Vanderbilt's Lake Shore & Michigan Southern Railroad, he asked Stone to serve as the line's managing director. Until 1875, when he resigned, Stone encouraged coordination among the merged routes as well as connecting lines. He wrote to the president of the Michigan Central Railroad that "the time will come when there will be little value in railroad property without general cooperation of competing lines," although Stone had no faith in government regulation to bring it about.

At the end of his tenure with the Lake Shore & Michigan Southern, Stone was determined to end his direct participation in business and turned to managing his investments and to carrying out philanthropic activities.

Stone became a major investor in railroads through his practice of accepting payment in company securities for his contracting. Records of his railroads indicate that he was not a passive investor, but traded and acquired stock freely, and experienced substantial capital growth. He put much of his accrued wealth into banking and iron and steel. He became president of the Bank of Commerce in Cleveland, the leading bank in the city during his era, and he was one of the founders of the Union Steel Screw Company of Cleveland in 1864. Later he was a chief stockholder in the Union Iron & Steel Company of Chicago.

Stone's chief acts of philanthropy were the building of a home for aged women in Cleveland, which was opened in 1877, and the financing of the cost of moving Western Reserve College from Hudson, Ohio, to Cleveland. In the latter instance, Stone was persuaded by his minister, the Reverend Hiram Hayden, to contribute $500,000 to construct new buildings in Cleveland (at a site later known as University Circle) and to enlarge the college's endowment. He bequeathed an additional $100,000 to the college at his death. One of Stone's stipulations was that the undergraduate part of the institution be named Adelbert College in memory of his deceased son, Adelbert Stone.

Stone's life ended by suicide on May 11, 1883. Some attributed the act to long-term bouts with insomnia and dyspepsia, others to a recent series of financial setbacks, and still others to chronic depression brought on by the Ashtabula bridge disaster. On December 29, 1876, an eleven-year-old bridge designed by Stone for the CP&A collapsed during a storm under the weight of a passenger train. Ninety-two people died and many were injured.

Subsequent investigations blamed Stone for ignoring the advice of bridge engineers and building the bridge with an untested Howe iron truss rather than the standard wooden truss. Nonetheless, the failure of the Ashtabula bridge was a significant factor in bringing American engineers' attention to the need to establish standards for the use of iron in bridges, a material which eventually made it possible to construct long-span bridges with greater strength and less expense than wood or masonry.

Stone married Julia Ann Gleason on January 13, 1842. His daughters Clara and Flora married prominent Clevelanders John Hay and Samuel Mather, respectively. Stone's most important contribution to American railroading was his early and continued promotion of coordinated service on connecting lines in Ohio and adjacent states, a key region for much long-distance traffic.

References:

"Amasa Stone," *The Encyclopedia of Cleveland History* edited by David D. Van Tassel and John Grabowski (Bloomington: Indiana University Press, 1987);

Amasa Stone: Born April 27, 1818. Died May 11, 1883 (Cleveland: De Vinne Press, 1886);

Annual Reports, Cleveland, Columbus & Cincinnati Railroad Company (Cleveland: Gray & Wood, 1852-1854);

Annual Reports, Cleveland, Painesville & Ashtabula Railroad Company (Cleveland: 1859, 1864-1865);

Thomas C. Cochran, *Railroad Leaders, 1845-1890: The Business Mind in Action* (New York: Russell & Russell, 1965);

John Hay, "Amasa Stone," *Magazine of Western History*, 3 (December 1885): 108-112;

Samuel P. Orth, *A History of Cleveland*, 1 (Chicago & Cleveland: S. J. Clarke, 1910).

Archives:

Material concerning Amasa Stone is located in the Lake Shore & Michigan Southern Railroad records of the Western Reserve Historical Society at Cleveland, Ohio.

William B. Strong

(May 16, 1837-August 3, 1914)

by Keith L. Bryant, Jr.

Texas A&M University

CAREER: Station agent and telegraph operator, general western agent of the southwestern division, Milwaukee & St. Paul Railroad, later the Chicago, Milwaukee & St. Paul Railway (1855-1865); assistant superintendent, McGregor Western Railway (1865-1867); general western agent, Chicago & North Western Railway (1867-1870); assistant general superintendent, Chicago, Burlington & Quincy Railway (1870-1874); general superintendent, Michigan Central Railroad (1874-1875); general superintendent, Chicago, Burlington & Quincy Railway (1875-1877); vice-president and general manager (1877-1881), president (1881-1889), Atchison, Topeka and Santa Fe Railroad.

William B. Strong (courtesy of Santa Fe Railway)

William Barstow Strong descended from colonial Massachusetts stock; his ancestors arrived in the Bay Colony as early as 1630. His parents, Elijah Gridley and Sarah Ashley Partridge Strong, settled in Brownington, Vermont, where their son was born in 1837. Like many New England families the Strongs moved westward, establishing their home in Wisconsin. William B. Strong attended the public schools of Beloit and then was sent to Bell's Business College in Chicago, graduating in 1855.

That year Strong began his successful career in railroading when he joined the Milwaukee & St. Paul Railroad as a station agent and telegrapher at Milton, Wisconsin. During the next twelve years he worked for that company or its subsidiaries as a station agent at Whitewater and Monroe, Wisconsin; general western agent at Jonesville, Wisconsin; and then assistant superintendent of an affiliate in McGregor, Iowa. Having progressed from agency work to operational responsibilities, Strong joined the Chicago & North Western for three years as a general agent in Council Bluffs, Iowa. He then moved to the Chicago, Burlington & Quincy (CB&Q), first as an assistant general superintendent in Burlington, Iowa, and then in the same capac-

ity in Chicago. Strong left the CB&Q for a year to serve as general superintendent of the Michigan Central in Chicago but rejoined the Burlington as general superintendent in 1875. His service on these granger roads and the Michigan Central provided a variety of experiences in managing growing railroad properties, and his success brought him to the attention of the Boston capitalists who dominated the Atchison, Topeka and Santa Fe (ATSF) Railroad. In 1877 they asked Strong to become the vice-president and general manager of this fledgling Kansas property that aspired to reach California and the Gulf of Mexico.

When Strong joined the ATSF it operated nearly 800 miles of track centered in Kansas with an extension west into southern Colorado. The company was founded in 1859 by Cyrus K. Holliday for the purpose of reaching Santa Fe in New Mexico territory from Topeka, Kansas. Control of the property had fallen into the hands of Boston capitalists who provided funds to construct a line across western Kansas to capture the cattle trade from Texas. Rival railways threatened the ATSF territory, particularly the Missouri Pacific, and the directors and stockholders sought to push the line west and south. They could not have found an executive more determined than Strong to build a rail empire.

Strong initiated a massive expansion plan that in a dozen years produced a system nearly 7,000 miles long. The dynamic and ambitious Strong brought together a team of men to expand the ATSF, and they made A. A. Robinson chief engineer for the construction of new routes. The ATSF moved quickly in 1877 to seize Raton Pass in northern New Mexico for a line into that territory. Strong then entered into a battle with William J. Palmer and the Denver & Rio Grande for control of Royal Gorge, the main pass for a line west from Pueblo, Colorado, to Salt Lake City. A protracted, violent fight for the gorge and lengthy legal problems ultimately led to an impasse, and the ATSF abandoned plans for a route through the gorge. Strong decided to drive his construction gangs southwest across the New Mexico and Arizona territories to California.

Named president of the ATSF in 1881, Strong persuaded the conservative Bostonians to launch a massive expansion program. As general manager he had pushed for new construction; now he threatened, cajoled, and urged them to accept his view that a railroad had to expand or die. Strong believed that expansion was success; a carrier that did not advance would lose ground to rivals.

The directors approved his plan, and using the land grant of the Atlantic & Pacific Railroad, which the ATSF had acquired in 1879, Robinson's forces reached Needles, California, in 1883. Collis P. Huntington's Southern Pacific (SP) Railroad desperately sought to keep the ATSF out of California. It had built a line east to Needles to block the indefatigable Strong just as it had built to Deming in southern New Mexico to thwart the ATSF's aggressive leader. Strong had constructed a line into northern Mexico to a port at Guaymas but traffic was poor.

Determined to reach a California port, he forced Huntington, whose line was vulnerable to Strong's plan to build a parallel line, to sell a portion of the SP trackage into Needles, and, with further construction and purchases of independent lines, the ATSF entered San Diego in 1885 and Los Angeles two years later.

With boundless energy Strong also launched an extensive expansion program in Kansas where ATSF agents encouraged immigration and the development of wheat farming. New branch lines generated traffic for agricultural exports, and Strong then sought a line to the Gulf of Mexico. The independent Gulf, Colorado & Santa Fe Railway (GC&SF) had built north from Galveston toward Dallas and Fort Worth in an effort to draw trade from Houston. Strong arranged for the acquisition of the GC&SF in 1886, and the ATSF drove a line south from Kansas across Indian territory to meet trackage the GC&SF was building north from Fort Worth. The through route to the gulf opened in 1887.

The ATSF brought freight and passengers eastward and northward to its terminal in Kansas City where connections took the traffic to Chicago and St. Louis. The ATSF and its rivals, mainly the Union Pacific, the Missouri Pacific, and the Missouri, Kansas & Texas, fought for westbound trade at Kansas City. Strong determined to build an independent line from Kansas City to Chicago in order for the ATSF to gain a larger share of the business. Chief engineer Robinson constructed a direct, high-speed route that opened in 1888. The railroad had to acquire new equipment, construct terminals in Chicago, and deal with intensified competition.

Strong's headlong expansion program created massive indebtedness for the ATSF and exacerbated tension between the carriers. Rate wars devastated revenues and traffic pooling agreements designed to stop the hemorrhage collapsed when there was open cheating. Strong had to defend the ATSF from Huntington, Jay Gould, and the leaders of such railroads as the Chicago, Burlington & Quincy. Yet even as competitive pressures grew, Strong had to build a new company headquarters, acquire a huge locomotive fleet, purchase thousands of cars, and engage in a modernization program to include new yards, shops, signal systems, and heavier steel rails.

ATSF traffic rose and fell with the output of Kansas grain farmers, but the requirements for dividends and interest payments on its huge debts were constant. To attract additional capital, dividends had been increased, and bond issues stood at $163 million by 1888. Some of the routes lost huge sums each year, and opposition to further expansion developed. Security holders were no longer enamored with Strong and his napoleonic plans. When ATSF stock plunged in 1889 the Boston financiers could no longer control the carrier. A new board of directors stripped Strong of his power, and he resigned as president in September.

The ATSF was largely Strong's creation. There was never any hint of scandal in its construction program, but overexpansion proved costly. Strong was blamed for the mounting losses that were the product of optimism, not stock manipulation or corruption. When the ATSF fell into bankruptcy in 1893, some financial observers pointed to Strong's expansion schemes as one factor in the company's failure. After reorganization, however, the ATSF prospered and the highly profitable system that emerged in the twentieth century was largely along the lines Strong had constructed.

Following his resignation Strong retired to a farm near Beloit, Wisconsin, with his wife Abby Jane Moore Strong, whom he had married in 1859. He took no further part in railroad activities but did pursue interests in local businesses. A Republican and a member of the Congregational Church, Strong moved to California in 1907 and died in Los Angeles in 1914. He was survived by two sons and a daughter.

References:

Keith L. Bryant, Jr., *History of the Atchison, Topeka and Santa Fe Railway* (New York: Macmillan, 1974);

Railway Age, 43 (August 30, 1889): 568;

L. L. Waters, *Steel Trails to Santa Fe* (Lawrence: University of Kansas Press, 1950).

Archives:

Material concerning Strong's years with the ATSF is located at the company's headquarters in Chicago and in warehouses in Topeka, Kansas.

John Edgar Thomson

(February 10, 1808-May 27, 1874)

by James A. Ward

University of Tennessee, Chattanooga

CAREER: Assistant engineer, Pennsylvania State Works (1827-1830); engineer, Camden & Amboy Railroad (1830-1831); engineer, various railway projects (1831-1834); chief engineer, Georgia Railroad & Banking Company (1834-1847); chief engineer (1847-1852), president, Pennsylvania Railroad (1852-1874).

J. Edgar Thomson, the quiet son of Quaker parents, rose through the technical side of the railroad industry to become one of the most important business figures in post-Civil War United States history. For one glittering moment Thomson came closer than anyone before or since to mastering a transcontinental rail empire when he controlled both the Pennsylvania Railroad and the Union Pacific in 1871. Although he lost the Union Pacific, he remained a powerful figure on Wall and Broad streets until his death. Thomson succeeded because of his careful, deliberate personality that prompted him to

frequently ponder financial decisions for long periods of time; when he finally made up his mind and gave his word to his associates, however, it was as good as gold. Also, as undisputed master of the largest corporation in the world, he often traded indirectly on the Pennsylvania's credit although he never directly used any of his company's securities for his own personal gain. Over twenty-two years Thomson put together a management team of great ability and, together with his outside financial allies, created an investment group, the Pennsylvania interests, that risked its credit from coast to coast and border to border. In the process Thomson amassed a considerable fortune still worth millions when he died during the depression of 1873.

Born on February 10, 1808, to Sarah Levis and her surveyor husband, John Thomson, in Springfield Township, Delaware County, Pennsylvania, John Edgar joined a family of two daughters, Anna and Mary Adeline, and a brother, Levis P. His par-

John Edgar Thomson (MG-286-courtesy of Penn Central Railroad Collection, Pennsylvania State Archives)

ents had been expelled from the Quaker meeting for marrying in the Presbyterian Church, but strict Quaker attitudes toward raising children still dominated the home. Nevertheless, in the rare moments J. Edgar reminisced about his youth, he spoke of his father fondly. The older Thomson took his son on surveying trips that honed J. Edgar's interest and enthusiasm for things mechanical. Young Thomson lived at home until he was twenty-four years old and drew upon his father's contacts for his early employment.

Given the family's middle-class farmer-mechanic status, it was strange that J. Edgar had very little formal schooling. Reputedly he wanted to attend West Point to become an engineer, but his poor academic background made that hope unrealistic. Instead, young Thomson learned the surveyor's trade, and, when Pennsylvania started construction in 1827 on a railway from Philadelphia to Middletown, Thomson's father used his influence to secure a job for his son on the project as a rodman for $30 per month. Thomson performed his routine tasks superbly and caught the eye of the Philadelphia & Columbia's chief engineer, Maj. John Wilson. Wilson promoted Thomson to principal assistant engineer and put him in charge of constructing the first twenty miles of railroad westward from Philadelphia. Just as J. Edgar started on his new task, the state ran out of funds and in 1830 laid off most of the engineers, including Thomson. Wilson became chief engineer of the Camden & Amboy Railroad and took Thomson with him to locate the road, a job Thomson finished in 1831.

For the next three years Thomson worked on various improvement projects in the Philadelphia region, mostly locating railways and estimating costs. His friends later recalled that he took a trip to England in the early 1830s to inspect railway technology there. Although there is no evidence that he did so, Thomson's almost manic fascination for technical subjects give the tale an authentic ring.

Southern railway developments, however, soon changed his life. Prominent Athens, Georgia, citizens met in 1834 to charter a railroad to connect the Charleston & Hamburg at Augusta with some unspecified western location (later Atlanta) to capture the upcountry cotton business. John Wilson was a native South Carolinian, and he probably recommended young Thomson to the Georgia promoters; they sent a director to Philadelphia to offer him the position of chief engineer with responsibility for locating and building the Georgia Railroad. Thomson accepted and arrived in Augusta on November 1, 1834, and by the first week in the coldest January on record he was in the field with a crew surveying the new line. By mid April he had drawn the profile maps and was ready to let the first construction contracts. In the heady financial days leading up to the 1837 panic Thomson pushed construction of his own line, made lengthy examinations of proposed connecting lines all over the South and as far north as Ohio, ordered rolling stock from his Philadelphia friend, Matthias Baldwin, and socialized with north Georgia's planter and merchant elite. At the same time he fought the rampant inflation that swelled his costs and the perennial southern labor shortage. Thomson's board of directors was so pleased with his sixty-five miles of finished road that it raised his salary to $4,000 per year in 1837.

Even Thomson, with all his technical expertise and energy, could not continue construction at such a hectic pace during the 1837 panic that devastated the region and bankrupted numerous connecting roads. His own crews shrank and slowed as the panic lengthened into a full depression in 1839. He managed to keep the work going during the first three years of the new decade, but financial problems led to a stockholders' revolt in which Augusta directors wrestled control of the company from the Athens group. Thomson's salary was cut 40 percent, and he resigned in protest only to be rehired with the promise that he would soon be allowed to finish the work. By 1842 he had crews locating the road to Atlanta, which Thomson named, and on September 11, 1845, the first train chugged into its new terminus. Thomson stayed with the road two more years, but his interest in routine operations was less than avid.

While in Georgia Thomson invested his salary in various nearby projects, often with success, and learned the intricacies of using money to make more. His southern investments were small in comparison to his later speculations but of the same type. He was interested in Georgia Railroad stock, local commodities markets, Central of Georgia bonds, municipal bonds, real estate as far west as Iowa, and new railroads such as the Montgomery & West Point Railroad, in which he had a controlling interest, and the Nashville & Chattanooga (N&C), which still operates over much of the road-bed he located. He would have stayed in the South had the N&C raised the funds in 1847 to build its road, for he would have been its chief engineer. Instead, he accepted an offer to construct the Pennsylvania Railroad.

Pennsylvania had lagged behind neighboring states after it built a combination of canals and railways across the state to compete with New York's Erie Canal. Its public works never captured the traffic originally envisioned for it, and Philadelphia slipped far behind its northern rival in the race for the western trade. Leading Philadelphia citizens met in 1847 and decided to build a railway to connect the Philadelphia & Columbia with Pittsburgh. The Pennsylvania Railroad's prospects were daunting, as it had to cross the Susquehanna River and some of the most mountainous terrain in eastern North America.

Thomson was hired in April 1847 and with characteristic energy put crews in the field almost immediately. He had only three months to let contracts before the Pennsylvania legislature would allow the Baltimore & Ohio Railroad to build a line to Pittsburgh. He barely met the stipulations; but by the end of the year he had all 134 miles of the first division from Harrisburg to the mountains under contract. Six months later he had the bridge under contract, but as in the South, his expenses outran the company's ability to pay them. The money shortage exacerbated tensions in the company. Pres. Samuel Merrick wanted Thomson to slow down while the chief engineer, who considered himself to be in charge, delighted in sending additional requests for funds to his board. Thomson considered quitting, but he did not want to leave before he finished the job. When in 1848 no provisions had been made for operating finished portions of the road, Thomson complained but was informed that his responsibilities included running the railroad in addition to building it through the mountains. Thomson selected one of his favorite engineers, Herman Haupt, and made him superintendent of transportation; on September 1, 1849, the Pennsylvania operated its first trains. Thomson's continued opposition to Merrick finally resulted in the president's resignation in 1849. Although William Patterson, a Merrick ally, assumed the presidency, Thomson continued to be a powerful force inside the company.

With his political problems temporarily solved, Thomson pushed construction work, and by early 1851 his rails entered Altoona, a town Thomson named after a north Georgia mountain pass. To gain a temporary connection with Pittsburgh, Thomson arranged to use the state's Portage Railroad over Allegheny Mountain until he could construct his own road around it. The agreement was a political thorn in Thomson's side. Moreover, the costs of pushing through the mountains were greater than the company's treasury could stand in 1851, and his relations with President Patterson worsened. Internal accountability within the company aggravated the conflict. Thomson, Haupt, and the treasurer all reported to the board rather than to the company's president. Various factions on the board supported one or another of the officers, thereby making every decision intensely political. The denouement came at the 1852 annual meeting where Patterson and his allies attempted to oust Thomson and his board friends. The electioneering in Philadelphia, where most of the stockholders lived, was intense; Haupt even locked some dissident shareholders in a room so that they could not vote. The outcome was a complete victory for Thomson and his friends. Patterson and most of his supporters resigned from the company, and the new board named Thomson president and made it clear that the other officers reported to him.

The new president's first task was to raise enough money to finish the western division and the Allegheny Mountain tunnel. Faced with a depleted treasury, Thomson floated a bond issue that he tried to sell in Europe, considered a second mortgage on the road, and finally settled for slowing construction and using earnings and short-term loans to finish the road. In February 1854 he ran his first train through the completed bore. Thomson was constitutionally unable to tolerate a physical plant not in first-class condition. When traffic rose tenfold on the opened sections, he started double tracking portions of the main line even before he finished construction of the whole road. Noting that his wood consumption was denuding nearby forests and making fuel more expensive, Thomson experimented with coal-burning fireboxes, converting many of his locomotives to coal by the eve of the Civil War. Ever the inveterate tinkerer, he tested numerous devices for stopping trains before he became the first president to adopt the Westinghouse air brake in 1869.

While Thomson watched technological details, he also took the larger view and kept an eye on his relations with his port city and other railway connections. Thomson was never a favorite of Philadelphia's merchant elite; Merrick and Patterson, who were politically active in the Quaker City, saw to that. But the road's chief officer courted the newly emerging manufacturers who depended upon the Pennsylvania for contracts and shipping and thereby allied himself with the rising generation of notables. With his growing regional importance and new financial allies, Thomson made the Quaker City's fortunes dependent upon his road's health.

To survive, Thomson knew his Pennsylvania had to gain secure western connections. Even before he finished his line, he convinced his board to invest in numerous feeder roads that gave him dependable connections to St. Louis, Cincinnati, and Columbus. When several of his western investments neared collapse in 1856, Thomson supported the creation of the Ft. Wayne & Chicago Railroad Company. After that corporation was crippled by the 1857 panic, Thomson had himself elected its chief engineer, advanced the Pennsylvania's and his own money to pay for its construction, and finished the road by 1858. Even as the first train

Thomson later in life (courtesy of John Edgar Thomson Foundation)

made a through run from Philadelphia to Chicago, however, the Ft. Wayne road was in desperate financial straits. Although the Pennsylvania was forced to let it go at auction in 1859, it retained 20 percent of its stock and a strong voice in the road's inner councils.

While occupied with his connections' problems and fighting the 1857 panic, Thomson overhauled his road's administrative structure. Drawing upon Daniel McCallum's innovations on the Erie, Thomson decentralized his own administration and created for the first time line and staff departments. The new plan delineated the lines of authority from the lowest trackwalker to the president's office in order to control the thousands of employees he had strung over the entire state and to safeguard the millions of dollars that flowed through their hands.

The panic year of 1857 also marked the end of his political fights with state works' commissioners, who had long argued that the Pennsylvania was driving the Main Line out of business and had convinced the legislature to levy a tonnage tax on the Pennsylvania to protect it. Thomson failed to free his road from the tax and finally decided his only hope was to purchase the entire Main Line. At a June 25, 1857, auction Thomson was the sole bidder with his offer of $7.5 million. The purchase saddled him with hundreds of miles of unremunerative and unwanted canals, but it also brought him the Philadelphia & Columbia Railroad that gave him a direct rail link from Harrisburg to Philadelphia. The addition to his road came none too soon, for the hard times at decade's end slowed traffic on all four eastern trunk lines, and rate wars broke out that relentlessly drove tariffs down. Thomson joined with his competitors in numerous meetings to set rates, allocate tonnage at competitive points, regulate speed and service on passenger trains, and outlaw free passes. The agreements rarely worked for very long, but they were rail executives' first attempts to ameliorate the worst competitive excesses in their business that would culminate in the creation of the Interstate Commerce Commission in 1887.

The Civil War ended trunk line bickering over rates and presented eastern roads with the new problem of carrying a huge influx of wartime traffic over lines designed for lower tonnages. Thomson had recoiled in horror at the very notion of the nation's breakup. He had no public position on the slave question, having bought and hired them for his southern projects, except to warn that it was tearing the nation apart. Moreover, his road profited from the cotton and textile traffic, and his port city had strong economic ties with the South. Thomson publicly supported the 1861 Crittenden Compromise that would have extended the 36-degree 30-minute line to the Pacific. When that failed and war broke out, Thomson was confident it would be short. When he realized it was not going to be over soon, the Pennsylvania's president became an avid Union supporter who helped in late April 1861 to open rail lines to ensure that Washington, D.C., would be adequately supplied and protected.

When Secretary of War Simon Cameron called Tom Scott and Andrew Carnegie into war service, Thomson was left without his closest corporate aides just as his road's tonnage dramatically rose. By the fall of 1862 the Pennsylvania received fifty cars a day in excess of its capacity, and Thomson drove his employees past their limits, working engineers as much as thirty hours at a stretch. The Pennsylvania's physical plant deteriorated, accident rates rose, and still Thomson's road could not carry all the traffic. He bought new locomotives, more rolling stock, and experimented with imported English steel rails to extend his roadbed's life. His subordi-

nates claimed he became obsessed with steel; he tried it in axles, fireboxes, and locomotive tires. He was so pleased with his results that he ordered as much as he could get. He could afford it; his net profits almost doubled during the war despite having to raise wages to keep up with inflation and issuing higher dividends to appease his stockholders. At war's end Thomson's policy of constant improvements financed from earnings made the Pennsylvania the largest corporation in the world and one of the most profitable. After doubling his rolling stock, increasing his locomotive roster almost 70 percent, laying new steel rails, and building a grain terminal in Philadelphia and oil storage facilities, Thomson estimated Pennsylvania assets at $55 million in 1865 with a debt of only $40 million. He would soon need that credit, however, for he was poised on the brink of an expansion spree.

Post-Civil War railway leaders who helped give the age its gilded image were a different breed than Thomson. They took huge risks in pursuit of great gains and flaunted their wealth; Thomson also took big risks but continued to live quietly with his wife, Lavinia Smith, whom he had married in 1854, on Rittenhouse Square in Philadelphia. Thomson may have been slow to act and more often reacted to dangers, but once he made up his mind he pursued his goals with an almost furious, though quiet, tenacity. Ironically, as Thomson aged he became more prone to taking greater risks with his own fortune and the Pennsylvania's resources. And he accomplished his greatest feats after the war in the face of his declining health, which, with increasing frequency, kept him away from his office.

With Jay Gould controlling the Erie, Commodore Vanderbilt ruling the New York Central, and feisty John Work Garrett determining the Baltimore & Ohio's fortunes, and with less eastern trunk line traffic, rate wars broke out anew. Strategy took a new turn in 1867, however, as Jay Gould attempted to win a tactical victory by purchasing the Pennsylvania's western connections. Thomson was slow to see this threat, but once he did he asked his board for carte blanche to purchase any connecting roads he thought necessary. Thomson walked out of that board meeting on a blustery January day in 1869 and moved to put together a rail empire with an energy that amazed even his closest associates. He purchased the Pan Handle route to protect his connections to Columbus, Cincinnati, and St. Louis, and then in May 1869 moved to protect his northern flank by leasing the Ft. Wayne road for 999 years. Not content to defend his western connections, Thomson moved in 1871 to gain a direct route to New York City. Philadelphia was no longer large enough to handle all the traffic he delivered there, and Thomson leased the United New Jersey Railroads, a combination that included the Camden & Amboy. Secure in the East, Thomson cast his eyes south where Tom Scott had put together a 2,000-mile system from Washington, D.C., to New Orleans. By 1873 Thomson's Pennsylvania spanned half the continent and handled $25 million in traffic on which he realized a net profit of $8.6 million, profits in the face of stiffened competition that had forced rates down by 50 percent.

When Thomson died in the depression year of 1874 his estate was valued at only $1.3 million; even before the depression, however, he probably was worth only between $5 and $10 million. With that modest postwar fortune he managed to secure control of assets worth between $750 million and $1 billion. His Pennsylvania accounted for $400 million, but he was also a major voice in transcontinental properties, coal businesses, oil firms, iron and steel companies, bridge concerns, real estate ventures, and manufacturing and construction companies. On a smaller scale he dabbled in life insurance, mining projects, the lumber business, and mineral explorations.

As he had done in the South, Thomson liked to speculate in advance of his or anyone else's rails. He favored projects located in developing areas that were about to be linked to the rest of the nation, or in scientifically novel fields, such as the steel industry, that promised high returns through future demand, or in projects that promised to eventually throw traffic across his Pennsylvania. Thomson also liked to ally himself financially with the brash, bright, young talent he attracted to the Pennsylvania, such as Tom Scott, Andrew Carnegie, Herman Haupt, George Washington Cass, Donald Cameron, John Scott, William Palmer, George Pullman, Jay Cooke, and the bankers at Drexel, Morgan. These Pennsylvania interests' major postwar activities were in trans-Mississippi railroads stretching from Duluth to Mexico. Thomson and his friends invested heavily in the Lake Superior & Mississippi River Railroad to connect Duluth with Jay Cooke's Northern Pacific (NP) at St. Paul. Drawn into Cooke's transcontinental scheme, Thomson supported the Philadelphia banker until his collapse in

1873. Thomson always had a weakness for transcontinental speculations; the sheer size and challenge of such undertakings combined with the possible profits that might accrue to his Pennsylvania attracted him. He signed the Union Pacific's (UP) charter in 1863 but after the war invested in the Union Pacific Eastern Division that promised great profits only if it could build faster than the government-aided Union Pacific. It failed, although as the Kansas Pacific (KP) it finally reached Denver, and Thomson helped build the Denver Pacific that joined the KP and UP. Later he bought into the Denver & Rio Grande (D&RG) and also backed Tom Scott's transcontinental schemes, buying into his Atlantic & Pacific (A&P) and his Texas & Pacific (T&P).

Thomson's greatest transcontinental success, however, came in 1871 when he and his friends captured control of the Union Pacific. Unable to pay the interest on its subsidy bonds, the UP directors approached the Philadelphia interests who agreed to supply funds in return for control of the road. By the smallest of margins the Philadelphians captured the road, and Scott became its president. For one short year in 1871 Thomson and his friends controlled the UP, NP, T&P, A&P, KP, and D&RG, a system that, if maintained, would have ensured Thomson's Pennsylvania national transport dominance for decades. It all came unraveled, however, when the Pennsylvania interests lost the UP in early 1872, and the rest of their shaky projects skirted bankruptcy in the next year's panic. Nevertheless, Thomson, in his quiet manner, had come closer than anyone before or after to putting together a truly transcontinental rail empire.

The 1873 panic killed Thomson. He spent the few remaining months of his life trying to shore up the Pennsylvania and his private fortune. Saddled with a $16 million floating debt incurred to finance his expansion program, Thomson had to advance money to many of his weaker acquisitions and declare a scrip dividend to Pennsylvania stockholders. The shareholders appointed an investigation committee that complained in 1874 that Thomson had too much power and recommended numerous internal changes in the company. He lost many of his private investments as each member of the Pennsylvania interests attempted to prop up his own position. Carnegie survived to finish his Edgar Thomson steel works, while Scott was almost bankrupted by his Texas & Pacific adventure. Thomson met all of his financial obligations, but his health continued to deteriorate; a pulmonary condition worsened, and he suffered numerous small heart attacks. On May 27, 1874, he died.

What portions of Thomson's estate not needed to support his wife and his wife's niece, Charlotte Foster, whom they had raised, went to establish the J. Edgar Thomson Foundation to care for female orphans of railway men. The foundation is still active and had helped 1,800 girls by 1980.

References:

George H. Burgess and Miles C. Kennedy, *Centennial History of the Pennsylvania Railroad Company, 1846-1946* (Philadelphia: Pennsylvania Railroad Co., 1949);

Joseph B. Cumming, *A History of the Georgia Railroad and Banking Company and its Corporate Affiliates, 1833-1958* (Augusta, Ga., 1971);

James A. Ward, "J. Edgar Thomson and Thomas A. Scott: A Symbiotic Partnership?" *The Pennsylvania Magazine of History and Biography*, C (January 1976): 35-49;

Ward, *J. Edgar Thomson: Master of the Pennsylvania* (Westport, Conn.: Greenwood Press, 1980).

John B. Turner

(*January 14, 1799-February 26, 1871*)

by Gerald Musich

National Railroad Museum

CAREER: Construction contractor, superintendent, Ransom & Saratoga Rail Road (1835); construction contractor, Delaware Division of the New York & Erie Rail Road (1835-1837); construction contractor, Genesee Valley Canal (1837-1840); construction contractor, Troy & Schenectady Rail Road (1841-1843); acting director (1847-1850), president (1850-1858), director, Galena & Chicago Union Rail Road (1847-1864); president, Beloit & Madison Rail Road (1853); organizer, Chicago's North Side Horse Railway Co. (1858); director, Chicago & North Western Railway (1864-1869).

John Bice Turner, one of the major figures in opening up Illinois and its neighboring states to railroad development, was born on January 14, 1799, in Colchester, Delaware County, New York. He died on February 26, 1871, in Chicago, his home for twenty-eight years. His parents were Elisha and Patience Coville Turner, who were of English and Dutch ancestry, respectively. Upon his father's death in 1801 Turner was adopted and raised by David Powers, a farmer and tanner of Dutchess County, New York.

Turner married Martha Volentine in 1819 and first tried his hand at farming, then as a mill and store owner. By 1835 he found his future career as a railroad builder. He first contracted to build seven miles of the Ransom & Saratoga Rail Road

and then was placed in charge of the line's operations. The company used horse-drawn railroad cars, but under Turner's guidance the Champlain, one of the country's earliest steam locomotives, was put into service.

Late in 1835 he and two partners contracted to build the Delaware Division of the New York & Erie Rail Road. The work was suspended by the panic of 1837, a crisis that nearly bankrupted Turner. He spent three years on a contract with the state of New York to build the Genesee Valley Canal but again was nearly bankrupted when the state suspended canal operations in 1840. From 1841 to 1843 Turner built a section of the Troy & Schenectady Rail Road and worked to complete the Genesee Valley Canal.

Having accumulated nearly $57,000 through his construction work, Turner and his wife set out in the spring of 1843 by way of the Great Lakes to look for a place to settle in Illinois or Wisconsin. They decided to cast their lot with Chicago, and on October 15, 1843, the Turners moved to that seven-year-old city. Turner bought 1,000 acres near what is now Blue Island, brought 3,000 sheep from Ohio, and embarked on sheep raising.

About the time the Turners settled in Illinois, several Chicago businessmen and developers were meeting to find ways of building the Galena & Chicago Union (G&CU) Rail Road. The G&CU had

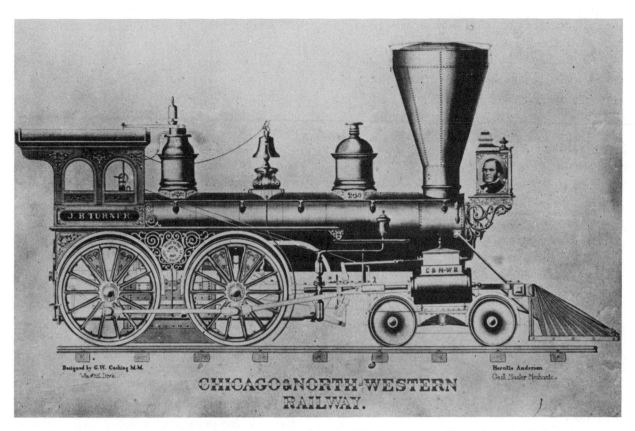

Drawing of the Chicago & North Western locomotive John B. Turner with Turner's portrait in front (courtesy of Chicago & North Western Transportation Company)

been chartered in 1836 with an eye to connecting Lake Michigan and the newly chartered city of Chicago with the older, lead-mining community of Galena, Illinois, near the Mississippi River. Construction of the line had been suspended by the effects of the panic of 1837. However, under the leadership of William Butler Ogden, Chicago's first mayor, various Chicagoans were anxious to revive the idea of the railroad.

Turner offered to put up $10,000 of the $300,000 believed necessary to build the G&CU's first division. When not enough others stepped forward to match Turner's offer, William B. Ogden and Turner set out to raise the money and revive the railroad. By 1847 the G&CU was reorganized with Ogden as president and Turner as acting (or executive) director. Ogden and Turner reasoned that eastern capitalists would not gamble money on the G&CU because of the disastrous record of Illinois' seven railroad ventures bankrupted in 1837. Therefore, the two men traveled throughout northern Illinois soliciting stock subscriptions from farmers and local businesspeople. They even persuaded several counties to impose a tax on local property, the proceeds going to buy G&CU bonds.

Ogden and Turner obtained hundreds of thousands of dollars of stock subscriptions, a remarkable feat in then sparsely settled northern Illinois. Under Turner's direction the G&CU built its first division, a 42-mile segment from Chicago to Elgin, between 1848 and February 1850; started operating revenue trains in October 1848; and turned a profit in 1850.

The success Ogden and Turner had in raising money locally and Turner's building of a railroad that became remarkably profitable in three years were two elements that touched off the midwestern railroad-building mania of the 1850s. Soon nearly every town in Illinois, Iowa, and Wisconsin set out to build its own railroad.

Turner became the president of the G&CU in 1850 when Ogden left the board of directors. He pushed the construction of the line, first to Rockford and then to Freeport, Illinois. In the spring of 1853 the G&CU faced the threat of a proposed railroad, the Chicago, St. Charles & Mississippi River Air Line Rail Road, which was roughly to parallel the G&CU from Chicago to the Fox River of Illinois, then head to Iowa on a straight or air line. Turner moved swiftly to crush this threat by building the G&CU's own air line from today's West Chicago to Fulton, Illinois, on the Mississippi.

Turner appears to have been a prudent and fiscally conservative railroad executive. Most notably he refused to have the G&CU engage in building branch lines, preferring instead to husband the G&CU's construction funds for pushing the mainline to the west. Turner seems to have had two motives behind this policy. In some instances he preferred to let local investors gamble their money on constructing risky feeder lines. If the branch line was a success the G&CU benefited from the business it generated. If it failed, the G&CU at its option could buy the bankrupt feeder line at a substantial discount. One branch line to the G&CU that defied the odds and became a major success on its own was the Aurora Branch. This 14-mile segment was built in 1850 to connect Aurora, Illinois, with the G&CU's line at today's West Chicago. The line quickly grew to become the Chicago, Burlington & Quincy, although it leased rights to use the G&CU line from West Chicago to Chicago until 1864.

In other instances, those in which the branch line looked to be a promising venture, Turner and his fellow directors preferred to organize the branch line railroad as their own company. In this way they benefited personally from the branch line's success, a success that was, of course, possible only because the G&CU served as the trunk line. For example, in 1853 Turner helped organize and became president of the Beloit & Madison Rail Road, now part of the Chicago & North Western (C&NW).

Turner stepped down from the presidency of the G&CU in 1858 but remained on the board of directors. Upon the merger of the G&CU with the Chicago & North Western in 1864, he became a director of the C&NW. He was, however, named as a defendant in a shareholders' suit against the G&CU on the claim that G&CU stock was acquired by the C&NW at too low a price.

Turner was a civic-minded individual. For example, owning a substantial portion of the town of Junction, Illinois (now West Chicago), Turner donated land for that community's first school and first church. In recognition of this charity, residents named the land adjacent to the town of Junction as the town of Turner, thus giving birth to Turner Junction. The community eventually was incorporated as the village of Turner in 1873, two years after Turner's death, and became West Chicago in 1896.

During his presidency the G&CU created Railroad Men's Reading Rooms along their line so as to provide employees with uplifting activities. Turner even had clauses added to the contracts of his personal land sales that stipulated that no alcoholic beverages may ever be dispensed from the land he was selling, apparently out of a concern over the drunkenness then prevalent among railroad employees.

Turner also served on Chicago's first Board of Water Commissioners and saw the laying of Chicago's first twenty-two miles of water pipes. In addition, in 1858 he organized the North Side Horse Railway Company in Chicago, his son becoming the manager.

Turner's first wife, Martha, died in 1853, and in 1855 he married Miss Adeline Williams. Upon his death on February 26, 1871, Turner left a family of three sons and three daughters.

References:

Album of Genealogy & Biography, Cook County, Illinois, thirteenth edition (Chicago: La Salle, 1900);

Biographical Sketches of the Leading Men of Chicago (Chicago: Wilson, Peirce, 1876);

Robert J. Casey & W. A. S. Douglas, *Pioneer Railroad: The Story of the Chicago and North Western System* (New York: McGraw-Hill, 1948);

W. H. Stennett, *Yesterday & To-day,* third edition (Chicago: C&NW Ry., 1910).

Ginery Twichell

(August 26, 1811-July 23, 1883)

by George M. Jenks

Bucknell University

CAREER: Assistant superintendent (1838-1849), superintendent (1849-1857), president (1857-1867), Boston & Worcester Railroad; U.S. congressman (1867-1873); president, Atchison, Topeka and Santa Fe Railway (1870-1873); president, Barre & Gardner Railroad (1873-1879).

Ginery Twichell was a self-made railroad leader and three-time Republican congressman from Massachusetts. Most of his career was spent in various capacities with eastern railroads, but it also included a four-year stint as president of the Atchison, Topeka and Santa Fe Railway.

Twichell (also spelled Twitchell in some references) was born in Athol, Massachusetts, on August 26, 1811, the son of Francis and Sally (Fish) Twichell. He had a common school education and at the age of sixteen left school to take a job in a mill. He held other minor jobs until the age of nineteen, when he took over a stage line from Barre to Worcester and established the first daily mail stages between Boston and Brattleboro, Vermont. He was the proprietor of several stagecoach lines and received many government contracts for carrying the mails. His success was apparently not due to his aggressiveness, since he is often referred to as "kind," "gentle," "mild," "honest," and "gentlemanly."

In 1835 the Boston & Worcester Railroad was opened. Twichell ran his stage lines in competition, but he soon became station agent for the railroad. This was his first railroad position. In 1838 the directors appointed him assistant superintendent of the line. He was promoted to superintendent in 1849 and finally rose to the presidency of the Boston & Worcester in 1857. During his ten years as president, there was a long controversy with the Western Railroad over freight rates. Business interests in eastern Massachusetts began to demand that Twichell and Chester W. Chapin, president of the Western Railroad, cease their quar-

Ginery Twichell

reling by merging the two lines. The merger was accomplished in 1867 as Twichell was leaving office.

Twichell had been a delegate to the Republican National Convention in 1864, which nominated Abraham Lincoln for a second term. In 1866 he was elected to the House of Representatives by a large majority, taking office in 1867 and resigning as president of the Boston & Worcester Railroad. He was twice reelected to Congress, serving until 1873.

While in Congress Twichell became interested, along with several Boston merchants, in controlling the Atchison, Topeka and Santa Fe (ATSF) Railway. After the Boston group attained financial control of the ATSF, Twichell accepted the presidency of the ATSF in 1870 and remained in that position until 1873. As president of the ATSF he saw the line extended from Florence to Newton, Kansas, but the ATSF had to complete the line to the Colorado border by March 3, 1873, or lose its land grant. Costs were high and the money market tight, but the job was completed ahead of schedule in December 1872. The ATSF had to postpone further building for several years or face bankruptcy. Despite the financial troubles Twichell had kept the railroad in operation.

On resigning the presidency of the ATSF and leaving Congress, Twichell returned to Massachusetts, where he was made president of the Barre & Gardner Railroad, serving in this capacity until 1879. He also served as a director of the Boston & Albany Railroad and had an interest in several western railroads.

Twichell shunned publicity and was regarded by friends and colleagues as an honest, efficient, and capable gentleman. He was married in 1846 to Theolotea R. Ruggles, by whom he had eight children, only one of whom survived him. He married again in 1877 to Catherine M. (Burt) Vinal. He was stricken with typhoid fever in 1883 and died on July 23 in Brookline, Massachusetts.

References:

Biographical Directory of the American Congress, 1774-1971 (Washington, D.C.: U.S. Government Printing Office, 1971);

Thomas C. Cochran, *Railroad Leaders, 1845-1890* (Cambridge, Mass.: Harvard University Press, 1953);

"Ginery Twichell," *New York Times*, July 24, 1883, p. 5.

Archives:

Materials concerning Ginery Twichell are located in the Erastus Corning Papers of the Albany Institute of History and Art at Albany, New York; other material is located in the Western Railroad Collection, Boston & Albany Railroad Company Collection of the Baker Library, Harvard Graduate School of Business Administration at Boston, Massachusetts.

Union Pacific Railroad

by Don Snoddy

Union Pacific Museum

The Pacific Railroad Act, passed by Congress in July 1862, granted the charter for the Union Pacific (UP) Railroad. As a means to secure the necessary capital to begin construction, this act provided for a land grant of odd-numbered sections of land for ten miles either side of the right-of-way and for the issuance of government loan bonds, repayable in thirty years. When the necessary funding did not materialize, because investors were already involved in the Civil War and were skeptical of potential profits to be made from a railroad through the wilderness, a supplemental act of July 1864 increased this land grant to twenty miles either side of the right-of-way, which would give UP over 11 million acres, and allowed the railroad to sell its own bonds in amounts equal to the government issue. The Pacific Railroad Acts also granted the railroad that first reached the 100th meridian of longitude the right

to continue construction as far west as necessary to link with the Central Pacific building east from Sacramento, California.

Ground was broken for the Union Pacific at Omaha, Nebraska, on December 3, 1863, and, with what limited capital could be raised during the Civil War, construction was pushed ahead completing a line by the end of 1865 to Fremont, Nebraska, some forty miles from Omaha. By 1866 the manpower shortage created by the war had ended, and money for investment was more available, although convincing investors that building a railroad through an uninhabited wilderness would prove profitable was still quite difficult.

Like many nineteenth-century railroads, a private construction company was employed to do the actual work. Originally chartered by the state of Pennsylvania as the Pennsylvania Fiscal Agency, the

Working on the railroad: (standing, from left) H. M. Hoxie and Samuel Reed; (sitting at table, from left) Silas Seymour, Sidney Dillon, Thomas Durant, and John R. Duff; the man seated at far left is unidentified (courtesy of Union Pacific Railroad Museum)

UP's prime contractor became known as the Crédit Mobilier of America (CMA) when Thomas C. Durant acquired a controlling interest.

Durant had been involved in railroad construction for several years prior to becoming involved in UP. He was an aggressive individual who moved from one project to another with lightning speed, sometimes without tying up the loose ends from the previous project. Durant served as president of the

Crédit Mobilier and also as vice-president and general manager of Union Pacific. A series of manipulations made the stockholders of Union Pacific also stockholders of Crédit Mobilier. This and the manner in which contracts were let and stock distributed caused an 1872 congressional committee (the Wilson-Poland Committee) to investigate Durant, the Crédit Mobilier, Oakes Ames, and, by default, the UP. The scandal resulting from the investigation was to plague UP for years.

In order to facilitate the construction CMA organized a Railway Bureau of five men to let contracts and oversee the daily operation of construction. As the contractors completed each 20-mile section of the railroad, which included laying the track, constructing shops, depots, side tracks, and furnishing necessary locomotives and cars, the government directors of Union Pacific, appointed by the president of the United States, approved the finished road. Union Pacific then assumed actual operation of the line and received the government land grants and bonds.

The Union Pacific Railway, Eastern Division, chartered by the Kansas legislature as the Leavenworth, Pawnee & Western Railroad Company in 1856, was an entirely separate company although Durant had a one-third interest. The Eastern Division was the UP's main competition in reaching the 100th meridian. The murder of its president, Samuel Hallett, by its chief engineer in a squabble over Hallett's authority, slowed them down.

The Eastern's problems and the UP's appointments in 1866 of Grenville M. Dodge as chief engineer, Samuel B. Reed as chief of construction, and the Casement brothers as chief track layers enabled the UP to pull ahead in the race.

The UP reached the 100th meridian in September 1866 and threw a grand celebration to commemorate the event. Durant arranged for everything an easterner would expect to see in the West: prairie fires, Indian battles, and buffalo and antelope hunting. In addition to caterers from Chicago and specially bottled wine, Durant arranged for the finest railroad cars available to bring guests all the way from New York to the end of the track in central Nebraska.

The railroad wintered in 1866 in North Platte, Nebraska, a point over 250 miles west of Omaha. Indians plagued the construction and survey crews, and Durant, whose absolute control was yet to be curbed by the Ameses, plagued the road from his New York office. Despite these problems the UP reached Cheyenne, Wyoming, in time to winter there in 1867. The Wahsatch Mountains of eastern Utah held the crews during the winter of 1868, as they worked desperately to beat the Central Pacific to Ogden, the entrance to the Salt Lake Valley. Finally, with winter behind them, the crews pushed on to Promontory Summit, Utah, for the joining of rails on May 10, 1869, which completed the first transcontinental railroad.

Durant had controlled the company during most of the construction period. He believed the only way to make money was in the construction of the railroad, while President Oliver Ames believed that colonization and its related businesses were the real key. Durant clashed with Ames over business decisions and Ames attempted to thwart his power by executive resolutions. Durant's attempts to control the line slowed construction significantly and allowed the Central Pacific many additional miles of track, something which made Durant very distraught. He was finally forced off the board completely in the spring of 1869, but by then the road was completed.

Jay Gould gained control of Union Pacific in 1874 and appointed Sidney Dillon as president and Silas H. H. Clark, his western representative, as vice-president and general manager of the railroad. By 1881 several lawsuits with the Wyoming Coal & Mining Company over lease arrangements had ended, and Gould took over control of the Wyoming coal mines as a means to provide revenue and fuel for the railroad.

Gould, in addition to overhauling the UP's management, also launched an ambitious expansion program. Because the charters of 1862 and 1864 prohibited UP from building branches, the expansions were built and operated as separate companies headed mostly by UP executives.

The consolidation of the Denver Pacific Railroad & Telegraph Company and the Kansas Pacific Railway into the UP was accomplished in January 1880. In 1882 UP began construction of the Oregon Short Line, which would connect with Union Pacific at Granger, Wyoming, and go to Portland, Oregon, providing access to Idaho, Oregon, and Washington. This line also gave competition to the Central Pacific and Great Northern railroads in the Pacific Northwest. Other major lines operated by UP were the Oregon Washington Railroad & Navigation Company and the St. Joseph & Grand Island Railroad Company.

The real push to recruit settlers to inhabit UP's huge land-grant holdings also began during Gould's tenure although over 800,000 acres had been sold by October 1873. Company land agents went east to entice the millions who crowded the large metropolitan areas to move west. To attract settlers from Europe the UP land department printed foreign-language pamphlets, encouraged émigrés to write to friends and relatives in Europe, and even employed some to return to Europe and recruit. By 1884 almost four million acres had been sold, including the land grants acquired with the Kansas Pacific-Denver Pacific acquisition, and every parcel for 200 miles west of the Missouri River had been sold.

Gould, "the most hated man in America," was not a popular individual with the press and the government. He selected Charles Francis Adams, Jr., of Massachusetts as president in 1884 to replace Dillon with the hope of salvaging the company. The government agreed on Adams, provided Gould completely divest himself from the Union Pacific. Adams's goal was to increase revenues and improve government relations. He was the father of the regulatory commission idea and was well liked in Washington because of his writings on railroad reform. While the system did expand, his success in bringing up revenues was mixed and better government relations escaped him. Adams also attempted to finance long-term obligations with short-term funding, a notion doomed to failure. Adams failed as president because, as Maury Klein writes, "of his repeated inability to put the right men in key positions." Even Adams admitted that "I fail because I cannot make up my mind on the instant and my reserves are not at my command."

Gould and Dillon returned to power in 1890 and attempted to bring economic recovery to Union Pacific. They both died in 1892, "thus," as Albro Martin notes, "saving themselves a great deal of trouble, and making way for fresh capital and new blood."

In 1893 a financial panic swept the country, and the Union Pacific went into the hands of receivers. The government foreclosed on the unpaid bonds it had issued to UP during construction. In 1897 a group of investors, headed by Edward H. Harriman of New York, bought Union Pacific at a foreclosure auction in Omaha for over $81 million.

After Harriman's purchase, he had his private car pulled over the whole system and then began a $25 million rebuilding program which included a double track main line. His efforts to reduce expenditures, including the standardization of locomotives, rolling stock, buildings, tools, parts or paint schemes, moved Union Pacific into the twentieth century as a first-class railroad operation.

Unpublished Documents:

Paul Rigdon, "Historical Catalogue of the Union Pacific Museum." Unpublished manuscript. Union Pacific Railroad, 1951;

Maury Klein, "Jay Gould and the Development of the American West," *Wheels & Deals: Railroads and the American West*. A symposium held at Omaha, Nebraska, December 7, 1985;

Albro Martin, "Morgan, Harriman and Hill and the First Great Railroad Consolidation Movement," *Wheels & Deals: Railroads and the American West*. A symposium held at Omaha, Nebraska, December 7, 1985.

References:

Charles Francis Adams, *An Autobiography* (Boston: Houghton Mifflin, 1916);

Charles Edgar Ames, *Pioneering the Union Pacific. A Reappraisal of the Builders of the Railroad* (New York: Appleton-Century-Crofts, 1969);

Robert G. Athearn, "A Brahmin in Buffaloland," *Western Historical Quarterly*, 1 (January 1970): 21-34;

Athearn, *Union Pacific Country* (New York: Rand, McNally, 1971);

Maury Klein, *The Life & Legend of Jay Gould* (Baltimore, Md.: Johns Hopkins University Press, 1986);

Klein, *Union Pacific: The Birth of a Railroad 1862-1893* (New York: Doubleday, 1987).

Archives:

Corporate records of Union Pacific are located at the Nebraska State Historical Society, Lincoln; the Oregon Historical Society, Portland; and at Union Pacific Railroad in Omaha.

Cornelius Vanderbilt

(May 27, 1794-January 4, 1877)

by F. Daniel Larkin

State University College, Oneonta, New York

CAREER: Operator, ferry and transport business (1810-1818); manager, Union Steamboat Line (1818-1828); owner, operator, Dispatch Line (1828-1830); operator, Hudson River Steamboat Line (1830-1834); operator, Long Island Steamboat Line (1834-184?); owner, Staten Island Steamboat Line (1838-1864); founder, Transit Company (1849-1853); president, Transit Company (1856-1864); president, Atlantic & Pacific Steamship Company (1859-1864); president, New York & Harlem Railroad (1863-1865); president, Hudson River Railroad (1865-1869); president, New York Central (1867-1869); president, New York Central & Hudson River (1869-1877); president, Lake Shore & Michigan Southern (1873-1877).

When Cornelius Vanderbilt, later known as the Commodore, was born in 1794, New York City was a bustling entrepôt of more than 50,000 people. Second only to Philadelphia in population, it was about to surpass that city in value of both exports and imports. New York City was, for a time, the capital of the state and, only four years before Vanderbilt's birth, had been the nation's seat of government, Washington being sworn in as president there in 1789. Although the money markets had made their appearance in the city by 1794, shipping still dominated New York's business. It was a good place for a future master of capital to be born.

But Vanderbilt was not born in Manhattan. His birthplace was in the sleepy, rural settlement of Port Richmond, located on the Staten Island side of the Kill Van Kull, the narrow sea link between New York and New Jersey. Today Staten Island is the southernmost outpost of New York City and the least populous of the five boroughs that make up the city. Then, although only five miles across the harbor from Manhattan, it was as remote and differ-

Cornelius Vanderbilt (courtesy of Brown Brothers)

ent from the commercial center as if it had been located 300 miles away on New York's frontier.

The Vanderbilts were a family typical of the early settlers of the colony. Unlike its English settled neighbors New York began as a Dutch colony called New Netherland. Clinging tenuously to the Hudson Valley, western Long Island, and what is now nearby New Jersey, the early inhabitants of the Dutch West India Company colony struggled to fend off the hostility of the climate, the original Indian inhabitants, and, finally, the English. Their attempt to remain a Dutch colony, lasting for a half century, ended in 1664 when the English simply took over. But New York was still Dutch when the first Vanderbilt arrived, probably in the late 1630s.

Settling first in what is now Brooklyn, the family later moved to New Dorp on Staten Island. It was there in 1764 that Cornelius Vanderbilt, the Commodore's father, was born to Jacob and Mary Sprague Vanderbilt. He tended to reflect more of his father's Dutch strain than the English characteristics of his mother. Like his father, he sought a bride from outside the Dutch community and married a Jerseyite, Phebe Hand, in 1787. The couple first eked out a living at Port Richmond, where Cornelius Vanderbilt was born on May 27, 1794. In 1795 the family moved to a larger house and more fertile land at Stapleton, which was located close to the edge of the Narrows, the channel between the upper and lower bays of New York.

The younger Vanderbilt was the fourth of nine children in the family of Cornelius and Phebe Vanderbilt. Since he grew up literally at the water's edge, Vanderbilt became an expert swimmer and was also adept at identifying various types of sailing ships. At an early age he was piloting his father's small sailboat to transfer farm produce to New York City. This work and the constant farm chores prevented him from obtaining little more than an introduction to reading and arithmetic. At age sixteen Vanderbilt ached to leave the lackluster farm life for adventure at sea. His parents did not permit it, but instead allowed him to earn the money to buy a small sailboat. As soon as the boat was his, Vanderbilt instituted a passenger and freight business between Staten Island and New York City.

By the time young Vanderbilt entered the transportation business in 1810, New York City contained nearly 100,000 people. It was already the largest city in the United States, and within a decade its future as the nation's premier port would be assured by the opening of the Erie Canal, the port's transportation link with the vast interior. But even as the principal American metropolis, the city's structures were confined to lower Manhattan Island, with most of the island remaining farm and forest. Yet, it was still a city on the move and the young boatman took advantage of New York City's growth. On fares as small as twenty-five cents per round trip from Staten Island, Vanderbilt was able to make well over $1,000 in his first year as a ferryman. His second year was even more profitable.

As Vanderbilt was struggling to build his business, the nation was about to boldly challenge Great Britain in a war fought, among other reasons, to prove the legitimacy of the United States. New York, because of its port, developed and voiced strong opinions about the impending conflict and the associated issues of free trade and sailors' rights. Many merchants and traders in New York City feared that the powerful British fleet would blockade the city, and these citizens formed the center of opposition to the War of 1812. But contrary opinions were not in short supply. Many were adamant that the British had no right to stop and search American shipping and conscript American sailors. These people and others who supported the war realized that New York was a border state and, as such, faced on two borders Britain's prize western possession, Canada. Because Great Britain was involved in a much larger European conflict, many thought Canada, defended by a garrison much too small for its responsibility, vulnerable to invasion and seizure. The governor was loyal to the prowar president James Madison, but the legislature, while willing to provide for the defense of the state, was less sanguine over the prospects for invading Canada. The diversity of opinions produced, if not an invasion of Canada, an impressive buildup of defenses around New York City.

The memory of seven years of British occupation of New York City was undoubtedly still vivid even though nearly thirty years had passed since the last royal soldier left in 1783. Construction of a system of fortresses, begun shortly before the War of 1812, was now pushed ahead at a frantic pace. Of particular importance were the partially finished forts on Long Island and Staten Island that were being built to guard the Narrows. Any British naval attempt to take the city would almost certainly come through this main approach to the river harbor.

Cornelius Vanderbilt was quick to exploit the opportunity, as workmen sought rides across the harbor and soldiers attempted to report to their new posts. Although competition was quick to pick up with the increased traffic, the eighteen-year-old held his own in the flourishing harbor trade.

In 1813 the British squadron blockading New York made an attempt to force its way past the forts. It was done, oddly enough, in the midst of a fierce gale. The guns of American batteries beat back the attack, but the garrison commander had to get word back to New York City requesting reinforcements, as the British were expected to renew their attack as soon as the weather cleared. Vanderbilt, alone, was willing to take his boat to New York. He piloted army officers through the gale to the city, and reinforcements were dispatched. This demonstration of bravery, combined with his reputation for honesty and reliability, landed Vanderbilt a government transport contract in 1814. In anticipation of a major British attack that year the harbor's forts were put on full alert, and Vanderbilt supplied six of them located in the Upper Bay area. Throughout it all he continued his regular ferry service between Staten Island and Manhattan.

Vanderbilt undoubtedly welcomed the added income, as on December 19, 1813, he had married Sophia Johnson. The couple had been acquainted for years, Sophia being the daughter of Vanderbilt's father's eldest sister. Nevertheless, both Phebe Vanderbilt and her husband Cornelius refused to permit the marriage between the first cousins. But the youngsters prevailed, and the wedding was held amidst a wild celebration.

The added obligation of supporting a wife proved to be a stimulus to the already industrious Vanderbilt. He used the money gained from his wartime activities to buy additional vessels and soon owned five coasters weighing twenty to thirty tons each. With these ships he expanded his territory to Boston and Delaware Bay and widened his business to include fish and fresh produce. The new operations plus the brisk ferry business brought Vanderbilt's cash savings to nearly $10,000 by 1817, in addition to the ownership of a small fleet of sailing vessels.

Ten years earlier an historic event had occurred on New York's waters which led in 1817 to changes in Vanderbilt's business operations. In 1807 Robert Fulton ran his first steamboat on the Hudson River, thereby serving notice to the users of sailing vessels. Awkward and only partially reliable at first, the steamboats were quickly improved and came to dominate trade on the Hudson and Long Island Sound. In 1817 a steam ferry appeared on the Staten Island run, and Vanderbilt's revenues dropped sharply. Steamboats could keep to their schedules indifferent to wind or weather. This advantage of steam over sail was not lost on Vanderbilt, and that year he decided to sell his fleet of sailboats.

When Robert Fulton began his steam venture he did so in partnership with New York's chancellor, Robert Livingston. The two partners secured from the New York legislature a monopoly on

steam navigation on all waters of the state. Entrepreneurs wishing to run steamboats on the state's waterways had to secure permission from the monopolists. One man who did so and became allied with the monopolists was Aaron Ogden, a former governor of New Jersey.

At first at odds with Fulton and Livingston over the legality of their monopoly, Ogden purchased the right to operate a steam ferry from near Elizabethtown, New Jersey, to New York City. Soon after Odgen's purchase Thomas Gibbons, a rambunctious, opportunistic lawyer from Georgia, also approached the monopoly to purchase the rights to operate a steam ferry from New Jersey. He was refused on the grounds that the monopoly had promised Ogden that he would have no competition. Gibbons, undaunted, simply decided to start a ferry service anyway and hired Cornelius Vanderbilt to captain his steamboat.

Vanderbilt began working for Gibbons, the only person he ever worked under, in 1818. He started with a small boat of 25 tons but soon convinced Gibbons that a larger craft was needed. Within a year Gibbons added the 142-ton *Bellona* to his growing fleet of steamboats and made Vanderbilt its captain. This ushered in a period during which Gibbons and Ogden battled over the latter's monopoly rights while Vanderbilt braved deputies and their writs by running the *Bellona* in and out of New York City. The young captain did his job of eluding the law so well that his salary was raised to $2,000 per season.

While employed by Gibbons, Vanderbilt moved to New Brunswick, New Jersey, to a small house located on Gibbons's waterfront property. It was there that his son and the successor to control of Cornelius's vast transportation empire, William Henry Vanderbilt, was born in 1821, the first of thirteen children. Sophia ran a portion of the house as an inn. Sophia's "Bellona Hall" was such a successful hostelry that Gibbons greatly enlarged it in 1824. Sophia's profit from the inn soon matched her husband's salary.

By the early 1820s the steamboat war in New York harbor was coming to a conclusion. Gibbons tried unsuccessfully to get New York's courts to rule against the legality of the monopoly. Unable to obtain satisfaction from the state courts, Gibbons vowed to get the United States Supreme Court to accept the case. He sent Vanderbilt to Washington with a retainer for Daniel Webster, whom, in association with U.S. Atty. Gen. William Wirt, Gibbons wanted to plead his case before the High Court. Finally the Supreme Court agreed to hear the case. In 1824, in *Gibbons* v. *Ogden,* Chief Justice John Marshall wrote one of the most famous decisions of his long tenure on the Court, ruling that New York's steamboat monopoly was unconstitutional. Shortly thereafter, the legislature repealed the privilege it had granted for all the state's waters. Marshall's decision was a landmark in that it sanctioned the power of Congress in the regulation of commerce between the states. Gibbons and Vanderbilt won a great victory, the reverberations of which continue to the present.

By the mid 1820s steamboat design changed from the earlier, shorter, more sluggish vessels to the sleek 200-ton side-wheelers that could make fifteen miles per hour and more in speed. They were the most comfortable mode of travel of the time, and travelers resorted to them wherever possible. Under Vanderbilt's management the Union Line of the Gibbons family prospered despite heavy competition. By the late 1820s the line was producing $40,000 in annual profit. Despite this profitability, William Gibbons, who had inherited the boats on his father's death in 1827, had no interest in keeping the line and advertised it for sale in 1828. Although Vanderbilt had about $30,000 in available capital at the time, it was not nearly enough to meet the asking price. As no buyers accepted Gibbons's price, the line remained unsold, and Vanderbilt continued to manage it. But by the end of 1828 Vanderbilt decided to strike out on his own. Even Gibbons's offer of a partnership did not stop him from leaving the Union Line.

Vanderbilt's determination to go independent meant that Sophia and their ever-expanding family had to move from their home of ten years. The family moved back to New York City to a small house near the Battery. A steamboat design by Vanderbilt was placed in service in 1829, and this formed, along with two boats purchased from Gibbons, Vanderbilt's Dispatch Line. The new line took passengers from New York to New Brunswick, New Jersey, via the Raritan River. From there Vanderbilt arranged with stage drivers to transport his passengers the twenty-five miles overland to Trenton, where another of the line's steamers completed the last leg of the journey to Philadelphia. Vanderbilt put himself in direct competition with the new owners of the Union Line. He proved to be such a formi-

dable rival in terms of cutting costs and providing comfortable, fast service that the Union Line offered to buy him out.

By 1830 the buyout was complete and Vanderbilt turned to a more glamorous and lucrative waterway, the Hudson River. Soon his new steamer, the *Cinderella,* was plying the river between New York City and Peekskill, about forty-five miles upstream. For a while Vanderbilt's swift vessel had a monopoly on that run, and profits piled up fast. But in mid 1831 a rival boat, owned by the crafty entrepreneur Daniel Drew, appeared. Drew and Vanderbilt entered into a contest of intense, cutthroat competition. Within a year Vanderbilt, aided by his younger brother Jacob, bought controlling interest in the competing boat from Drew. Jacob took the boat into service on Long Island Sound, leaving the New York to Peekskill run once again solely in Vanderbilt's hands. This success led Vanderbilt to expand his river operations to include Albany, 140 miles north of New York. For this grander undertaking he designed and had built the 230-ton *Westchester,* to that time the largest of his ships. The ship was put in service in 1832.

Cornelius Vanderbilt had been running the New York to Albany boats only a few months when he came into conflict with the combination that controlled many of the river's steamers. The Hudson River Steamboat Association dominated the river trade and was ready for war against the upstart Vanderbilt. Rate wars commenced, and Vanderbilt's resources were pushed to the limit. But his Elizabethtown ferry business managed to provide enough revenue to make up the Hudson River losses. While in the midst of the conflict, an incident occurred which nearly ended the rate war and Vanderbilt's life. In October 1833, while on a business trip to Philadelphia, Vanderbilt was seriously injured in a wreck on the Camden & Amboy Railroad. Barely surviving crushed ribs and a punctured lung, Vanderbilt spent the winter months convalescing and planning his offensive against the association. In the spring of 1834 he placed new boats on the run and was so effective in his onslaught that the association offered to buy him out. Vanderbilt agreed to remain off the Hudson for ten years, for which he received an estimated $100,000 and $5,000 per year for the term of the agreement.

Vanderbilt was not content to remain idle just because he had been "bought off" the Hudson. He quickly turned his attention to Long Island Sound where the New York to Providence route was becoming lucrative. Over 100 miles long and 25 miles wide in places, the Sound posed new problems for Vanderbilt. His boats had been built for river travel, not for the wind and waves of salt water. To meet the new conditions he commissioned the *Lexington,* a steamer weighing nearly 500 tons and especially designed to handle the rigors of the Sound. On its first voyage to Providence on June 1, 1835, the *Lexington* averaged a record-challenging speed of nearly seventeen miles per hour. The *Lexington* proved equal to the task of competing with the Boston & New York Transportation Company that dominated the passenger business on the Sound. At the end of 1835 the Transportation Company bought Vanderbilt's swift boat. This did not drive him from the Sound, however, since his other boats continued to ply the busy waterway.

When Cornelius Vanderbilt purchased half-interest in a Staten Island steam ferry line in 1838, he returned from whence he had started nearly thirty years earlier. Not yet forty-five years of age, he already was being called "Commodore" in recognition of his preeminence among the shipowners in and around New York. Within five years the Commodore's wealth would surpass $1 million, and his ownership of steamboats more than equal that of any man. At age fifty Vanderbilt, father of three sons and nine daughters and possessing a fortune rivaling most at the time, was about to enter that phase of his career which would bring him the most renown.

In 1844, when Vanderbilt was fifty years old, a presidential election was held that helped bring about new directions for Vanderbilt's career. The perennial presidential candidate Henry Clay ran on the Whig ticket against the Democrat James Knox Polk. It was an election that focused on expansion and the possibilities of annexing Texas to the Union. Vanderbilt actively supported Clay, but the expansionist Polk won. The Texas Annexation Bill was actually signed into law during the final days of his predecessor's term, and the new president welcomed the act even though it meant a possible war with Mexico, which was not happy about losing territory that it considered its own.

The expected war with Mexico erupted in 1846. By the late summer of 1847 American soldiers had stormed Mexico City, and peace talks commenced between the two nations. As part of the treaty signed the following March, not only was

Texas confirmed to the United States, but the present states of Colorado, New Mexico, Utah, Arizona, Nevada, and California were also included in the bargain. At the time California consisted of little more than a string of missions stretched along the coast road from San Diego to San Francisco. But at almost the same moment the treaty was being signed in 1848, the discovery of gold in California set off a wild transcontinental rush to collect the riches of the newly acquired territory. Among those who amassed gold from the rush without setting foot in the mining country was Cornelius Vanderbilt.

There were three routes to California in 1849: the arduous and adventuresome crossing of the American land mass, the all-water passage through the savage waters around Cape Horn, and the land and sea route across Central America. It was this third route that attracted Vanderbilt. Companies were already competing for the lucrative Panama trade, but Vanderbilt turned his attention to Nicaragua. Although wider than Panama Nicaragua had the advantage of a lake and a connecting river to the Atlantic by which passage could be made to within almost ten miles of the Pacific. Vanderbilt together with some associates speculated about the possibility of a series of short canals which would facilitate the all-water passage through Meso-America. The pliable Nicaraguan government proved no problem to the venture, but the presence of the British on the eastern Mosquito Coast of Nicaragua was a stumbling block. The British did not welcome the idea of an American canal, while Americans objected to a British protectorate over eastern Nicaragua which violated the Monroe Doctrine. The matter was settled by the Clayton-Bulwer Treaty of 1850, which essentially provided that neither nation would have exclusive rights in Central America.

Soon after the treaty was signed, Vanderbilt sailed for England to explore a joint venture with English bankers. The English were slow to commit themselves to a canal, and the Commodore returned home empty-handed. The bankers wanted facts and figures on the survey, so Vanderbilt left for Nicaragua on a steamship he had built for the ocean journey. It was a fast, comfortable coal burner that was to become the Atlantic link of Vanderbilt's new company. In Nicaragua he plied Lake Nicaragua in a smaller steamer and explored the shortest overland route from the lake to the Pacific. While Vanderbilt's engineers were completing the survey for the canal, he organized the Transit Company that would carry travelers from New York to San Juan del Norte by steamship, up the San Juan River and across Lake Nicaragua by steamboat, and then from San Juan del Sur to San Francisco by steamship. While the luxurious *Prometheus* operated in the Atlantic, the sparse *Pacific* was sent around the Horn for the Pacific run.

Vanderbilt's relationship with the Transit Company was of the on-again, off-again variety. When it briefly appeared that a canal might be built in Nicaragua, the company's stock soared, and Vanderbilt sold practically all of his holdings. Shortly thereafter, in late 1852, he offered to sell the company all the steamships which were in his name. The company officials accepted his price of $1.35 million for seven ships. Vanderbilt had temporarily lost his intense interest in business. His fortune was at $11 million and still growing. At age fifty-nine Vanderbilt decided to take a vacation.

Vanderbilt's idea of a vacation was a grand tour of Europe. He designed a yacht of 270 feet weighing 2,500 tons and had it built at a cost of $500,000. It would carry his traveling party, which consisted of most of his family, his physician and wife, his daughters-in-law, seven sons-in-law, and a few other friends. Christened the *North Star*, it took the party on a 15,000-mile voyage to Europe and the Mediterranean in the summer of 1853. By the time the entourage reached western Europe after their tour of the Mediterranean, Vanderbilt was being constantly treated to banquets and receptions. Many of his hosts wanted to establish business connections with an eye toward Vanderbilt's aid in opening a steamship line to Europe. In all the trip was deemed a success, and the Commodore returned ready to get back to the business of making money.

What he returned to was of major concern. While Vanderbilt was on his European voyage, Cornelius Garrison, the Transit Company's western agent, and Charles Morgan, a business colleague, joined together to snatch control from Vanderbilt. Morgan, during Vanderbilt's absence, was elected president, and when Vanderbilt realized what had been done behind his back, he naturally plotted revenge. He engaged in ruthless and ruinous competition with the Transit Company by placing the *North Star* on the New York to Panama run. In late 1855 Vanderbilt and his allies began to buy up

Transit Company stock. It was this stock that returned Vanderbilt as a director, and in February 1856 he replaced Morgan as president. Garrison followed Morgan out of the company later in 1856 when his contract as western agent was understandably not renewed.

Vanderbilt's Central American problems did not end with his recapture of the Transit Company. A major new problem arose in the form of the American adventurer William Walker, whom the Transit Company had helped to invade and conquer Nicaragua in May 1855. Walker, a Tennessean, who with a force of fifty-eight men captured the country from feuding rum factions, proceeded to establish a monomaniacal dictatorship which threatened to disrupt Vanderbilt's planned route across Nicaragua. When several Central American nations combined to support the president of Costa Rica against Walker, Vanderbilt sent guns and money to Costa Rica in order to assure the success of the move. One of Vanderbilt's agents, Sylvanus Spencer, personally led an attack on Walker and his forces. On May 1, 1857, President Mora and his forces defeated Walker, who then surrendered. Walker was allowed generous terms, and he returned to the United States. Although Vanderbilt achieved his goal of ousting Walker, his aid to the Central American forces did not gain him the influence he desired and needed to build the Nicaraguan Canal.

In the early 1850s two principal transatlantic steamship lines had emerged. One was the British-sponsored Cunard Line and the other the American Collins Line. On his return from Europe Vanderbilt also took a particular interest in Atlantic steamships and characteristically began to collect data on the business. When the outbreak of the Crimean War caused the British line to reduce its sailings to America because of the military need for steamships, Vanderbilt saw his chance to enter the transatlantic business. After an unsuccessful attempt to acquire the government mail subsidy, Vanderbilt entered into the competition by opening a passage between New York and Le Havre, eventually adding ports in England and Germany as destinations.

Vanderbilt had three ships in the Atlantic trade by 1857. With them he was able to capture less than 10 percent of the regular passenger trade for that year, falling short of Vanderbilt's expectations. Although his vessels, particularly the *Vanderbilt*, continued to set crossing records, it was difficult to turn a profit against lines that were subsidized. That Vanderbilt's line did make money was proof that successful transatlantic passenger business could be carried on if correct business methods were used. However, the profits were small, and increased competition appeared with new methods and technology. For example, fast and efficient iron ships with screw propellers were being introduced by the English. The Americans stuck to their wooden side-wheelers for a variety of reasons, the cost of iron being one. Finally, as it was a war that opened the way for Vanderbilt's entry into the Atlantic passenger business, so did a war put an end to that venture.

In spring 1861 the United States was torn apart by the Civil War. The outbreak of hostilities shut down Vanderbilt's transatlantic operations because of the demand by the government for large steamships to carry troops. Vanderbilt was a loyal Union man and offered his big ships to the navy. He was able to retain the smaller vessels of his Atlantic & Pacific Steamship Company formed in 1859, which had plunged him back into the tumultuous Isthmanian traffic to the West Coast. This time a railroad across Panama was the connection to the Pacific, and the Panama route prospered even during the war years. Vanderbilt armed his steamships against Confederate attack, but only one encountered serious difficulty when it became the unfortunate prey of the powerful rebel raider, *Alabama*. Even then Vanderbilt's ship was released on bond.

Vanderbilt's major contribution to the Union war effort was his gift of his greatest ship, the *Vanderbilt*, to the government. The fight between the *Monitor* and the *Merrimac* sparked the millionaire's generosity when a worried War Department sought his aid in destroying the feared *Merrimac*. On receipt of the telegram requesting his aid, Vanderbilt set out immediately for the capital. At a meeting with Lincoln, the president inquired if Vanderbilt could sink the Confederate ironclad. He confidently replied that he would ram it at high speed with his vaunted *Vanderbilt* and sink it, further informing President Lincoln that the steamship and his services would be given free of charge.

Vanderbilt immediately returned to New York to supervise the strengthening and arming of his ship. The bow was reinforced and a heavy ram added. Within a few days the ship, under the personal command of her owner, arrived at the mouth of Chesapeake Bay. Though the old captain was ready for war, the eagerly anticipated battle never oc-

curred. The *Merrimac* feared not the bellicose Vanderbilt, but instead the sturdy little *Monitor*, and failed to venture forth from its anchorage in Norfolk. The *Vanderbilt* served out the remainder of the war as a transport and later as an armed cruiser. In return for his contribution the Commodore received a vote of thanks from Congress and a large gold medal suitably inscribed.

In 1864 Cornelius Vanderbilt turned seventy. His decision to retire from shipping that year was prompted less by his age than by the high wartime prices paid for vessels. It was also brought on by the completion of his change of interest from steam-powered water transportation to steam-powered land transportation. Vanderbilt, who had for more than five decades made his considerable fortune in boats, severed his connections with steamships and turned to railroads.

In 1865 Vanderbilt's worth stood close to $30 million. With this backing he was ready to enter fully the arena of railroads. Actually, he had been dabbling in railways since the 1840s. At the time Vanderbilt retired from shipping, he was a director in the New York & Harlem Railroad, the New York & Erie, and had substantial interests in several other lines. Vanderbilt became the president of the New York & Harlem in 1863. As such he much improved the overall condition of the Harlem and put it on a sound financial basis by 1866. The following year Vanderbilt was still the Harlem's president, his son William H. vice-president, and William's son, Cornelius II, treasurer of the road. With the New York & Harlem securely under Vanderbilt control he turned his attention to a nearby line in which he held stock.

About the time that Vanderbilt began to show early interest in railroads, a group of capitalists from New York City and the mid Hudson River city of Poughkeepsie was preparing to challenge the mighty Hudson itself. They were planning a railroad that would run adjacent to the river at water level. Pessimists freely predicted that while the line might sustain itself in the winter when river traffic was at a standstill, the coming of the ice-free months would drive the railroad out of business. Nothing, in their opinion, could compete with the Hudson's swift steamboats and their low rates.

Nevertheless, the promoters of the Hudson River Railroad went along with the advice of their confident chief engineer, John Jervis, and commenced the daring project. They had built through to Poughkeepsie by 1849 and reached Albany (East Greenbush) in 1851. To the surprise of many the railroad succeeded in holding its own against the river trade. People were willing to pay the higher fares in return for the greater speed of the trains. The Civil War proved a great stimulus to the railroad, which profited from the increased wartime traffic.

In 1861 Vanderbilt already had stock in the Hudson River Railroad, but the New York & Harlem occupied his attention. However, at war's end Vanderbilt and his son William held large blocks of Hudson River Railroad stock. So much, in fact, that with the aid of other principal stockholders William was made vice-president of the road. As he also held the same office with the Harlem while his father was president, the two railroads became cooperative lines at the end of 1865. Soon Vanderbilt made the inevitable move, and, with an overwhelming majority of stock under his voting control, he became president of the Hudson River Railroad.

In 1853, two years after the Hudson River Railroad was built into East Greenbush across the river from Albany, the several lines that loosely tied New York's capital with Buffalo were brought together to form the New York Central. Under the direction of Erastus Corning and Dean Richmond the Central became a prosperous railroad. It had established itself as a trunk line but had to rely upon the river steamers or the Hudson River or Harlem Railroads for connection to New York City. Both railroads were controlled by Vanderbilt.

For a time the Vanderbilt roads and the New York Central cooperated and even exchanged some directors. But the haughty Central developed a habit of throwing its New York City business to the river in part to demonstrate its independence from Vanderbilt's lines. At first Vanderbilt considered his usual ploy of buying control in the troublesome railroad, but the Central's large capitalization made this impossible even for a man of Vanderbilt's millions. Then in January 1867 a dispute arose over the charges the Central paid to send its freight over the Hudson River Railroad, and the former road broke its agreement with the latter. As this occurred in the dead of winter when the ice was thick on the river, Vanderbilt used this as an opportunity to apply pressure on the Central.

From the moment that Vanderbilt posted notice that the Hudson River Railroad would no longer accept through passenger and freight from the New York Central, it was just a matter of time before that link with the west would become part of the Commodore's growing rail network. The Central tried to open a new route to the sea via the Boston & Albany, the Housatonic, and even the New Haven, but the New England roads would not cooperate. The Central was cut off from its port connection and, as such, could not continue to hold its position with the other major Great Lakes to Atlantic lines, the Erie and the Pennsylvania railroads. In November 1867 Vanderbilt received notification from prominent stockholders of the Central that they were ready to have him choose a new board of directors. When the Commodore went to the annual election the following month, he voted $18 million of the $28.5 million in company stock. The board and the company were his.

The New York Central's new president was Cornelius Vanderbilt. Vanderbilt's son-in-law was elected vice-president. Among the new directors were son William and two more in-laws. They were joined by the presidents of the Boston & Albany Railroad, the Cleveland, Painesville & Ashtabula Railroad, and the Michigan Central. The nucleus of a new, dominant system had been assembled in the Central's corporate leadership. Yet Vanderbilt was the undisputed master. He ordered money spent for improvements, revoked passes that had been so freely issued under the former administrations, and issued new ones where they would bring the best value–to politicians. He gave the order that the road's colorful locomotives were to become the standard black, that is, until an engine named the Commodore Vanderbilt appeared. Not only did it revive the colors and the shiny brass, it also carried his picture on the headlight. But few would deny that all this was the perfect right of the man the newspapers were now calling, the "Railroad King."

The next logical move on Vanderbilt's part was to combine his Hudson River line with his railroad from the Hudson to Lake Erie, which was accomplished on November 1, 1869. The New York Central & Hudson River Railroad that emerged did so with a capitalization that was expanded to more than twice the 1869 total for the two railways. By 1872 the total stock of the company was $90 million. In *Chapters of Erie,* Charles Francis Adams, Jr., described Vanderbilt's securities sleight as a maneuver in which "over $50,000 of absolute water has been poured out for each mile of road between New York and Buffalo." Nonetheless, the Commodore defended the stock increase with the claim that it was justified due to a gain in earnings. He stressed that the 8 percent paid on the old securities continued to be paid on the new stock, which held true even during the depression years following 1873. Of course considerable economizing was necessary to maintain the high rate of return because of income fluctuations during the hard times of the 1870s.

As soon as the New York Central & Hudson River Railroad was a reality, Vanderbilt decreed that a passenger terminal appropriate to the grandiosity of the new corporation was needed. The rail combine inherited the freight terminal built in 1867 for the Hudson River Railroad. It was a monstrous three-story structure, the first floor housing the loading docks with the second and third floors used as a warehouse. As if the size itself were not enough, the depot's facade was crowned with a pediment 150 feet long and 30 feet high at the center. Its bas-relief was a panoply of the Commodore's transportation history, central to which was a statue of appropriately gigantic proportion of the great mogul. The memorial drew mixed reviews depending, to no small extent, upon the commentator's feeling toward Vanderbilt himself.

Work on the original Grand Central passenger station was started only two weeks after the main line it was meant to serve became a reality. William H. Vanderbilt supervised its construction. The building's scale befitted its role. Covering some five acres, it ran nearly 250 feet along Forty-second Street and almost 700 feet from north to south. Park Avenue, running north from the terminal, was yet to become the fashionable boulevard which currently embraces the modern successor to Vanderbilt's original monument. However, even before the magnificent depot was completed, the public was hounding the politicians to have the tracks north of it placed beneath the street level. With the completion of the station in 1871 the clamor reached an intensity that city and state officials could not ignore. The Commodore and his Albany lobbyist, Chauncey Depew, fought hard against the added expense but were only partially successful. It was decided that from Forty-ninth Street north, the tracks would be below street level. But the city agreed to pay half the cost of the Park Avenue project, which was not completed until 1876. Vanderbilt was the butt of much criticism for the mess, detours, and delays caused by the digging, but after all was finished, the new upper Park Avenue ending

in the showcase terminal became a source of pride for New Yorkers.

Cornelius Vanderbilt's involvement with the New York Central in the late 1860s put him on a collision course with the New York & Erie Railroad. Completed in 1851 from the lower Hudson River in Rockland County to Dunkirk on Lake Erie, the Erie was a competing trunk line with the Central. In fact it was a rate war between the two roads in 1867 that contributed to Vanderbilt's election as president of the Central. The Central's stockholders wanted a fighter to help wage war against the Erie. Vanderbilt's strategy for winning was simple: end competition from the Erie by getting control of it.

The most powerful director of the Erie up to that time was Daniel Drew, the sometime competitor, sometime ally of Vanderbilt. Just as there was a Central election in 1867, so was there an Erie election the same year. Drew and his minions in Erie management were under fire. Vanderbilt saw this as a chance to increase his influence in the corporation. Drew realized that his position as Erie treasurer and director was being attacked from many quarters, so he struck a secret bargain with Vanderbilt. In return for the Commodore's support Drew agreed to act on Vanderbilt's behalf as an Erie officer.

Vanderbilt had no reason to trust Drew but went along with Drew's plan since he felt with Drew's cooperation control of the Erie would be easier. With Vanderbilt's help Drew was returned to the Erie board. There he was aided by two newcomers, James Fisk, Jr., and Jay Gould, brought into Erie management by Drew. Once back in office Drew, in league with Fisk and Gould, reneged on his promise of friendship and support toward Vanderbilt's interests in the Erie. Drew's reversal did not surprise Vanderbilt, who did not trust Drew in the first place. He simply reverted to his plan that worked so well with the Central. Vanderbilt would buy control of the Erie.

Drew, Fisk, Gould, and company anticipated Vanderbilt's next move. The Erie crowd decided to give Vanderbilt all the stock he wanted by simply printing thousands of shares of worthless certificates. Before Vanderbilt's brokers realized the swindle, so much stock had been purchased that it was necessary to keep buying in order to keep the price up. As soon as the Vanderbilt men bought the first 50,000 shares of the "new issue," the Erie gang printed another 50,000. When they heard that Vanderbilt had obtained an injunction and arrest warrants for them, they took their accumulated cash and fled to the safety of New Jersey, beyond the reach of New York law. Drew, Fisk, and Gould escaped with an estimated $7 million.

With the flight of the Erie directors, the trading in Erie stock subsided, but Vanderbilt and his supporters were left with about 150,000 shares which they could not sell. They had been purchased for an average of $75 per share. Most of the stock belonged personally to Vanderbilt. The New York Stock Exchange ruled against the Erie's most recent stock issue, but all that did was to prevent future sales of the stock. The scene of battle quickly shifted to a New York legislature eager to participate in what they envisioned as a lucrative boon to an otherwise dreary and unrewarding session. Jay Gould personally appeared in Albany to guide the Erie bill through lawmaking session. He was well supplied with cash in order to insure success. The bill was designed to legalize the stock issues and prevent Vanderbilt with his block of stock from becoming an Erie director by forbidding officers of the Erie from being an officer in the Central and vice versa.

The bill passed the legislature in 1868 after a sufficient amount of money was distributed and after a compromise settlement with Vanderbilt was negotiated. Vanderbilt eventually was able to get rid of 50,000 shares of Erie stock, but at only $70, somewhat less than he had paid for it. Vanderbilt's allies also were partially reimbursed for their losses. The settlement came at the expense of the Erie stockholders, but not necessarily the imaginative trio who were largely responsible for starting the war.

As for Vanderbilt he had been stung by the humiliating defeat. This was unusual, if not unique, for a man who for nearly sixty years had known success in his financial adventures. Now all he wanted was to forget the Erie war and have no further dealings with Fisk and Gould. The forging of the New York Central & Hudson River combination the following year helped him to put aside the memory of his one serious business miscalculation.

The year 1868 brought double misfortune to Vanderbilt. Not only did he lose the Erie war, but he also lost Sophia, his wife of fifty-five years. Within a year after Sophia's death, however, Vanderbilt remarried. His second wife was Frances Crawford, formerly of Mobile, Alabama. Some forty years younger than her husband the new Mrs.

Vanderbilt had a profound influence over her husband, causing him to turn toward religion and to provide monetary support to religious organizations. His $50,000 gift to allow the Church of Strangers to purchase their building on Mercer Street in New York City was but one example of his generosity.

Cornelius Vanderbilt was seventy-five years old when he consolidated the New York Central & Hudson River railroads. Most people would have considered it time to retire, particularly if they possessed a fortune equivalent to that of the Commodore. But Vanderbilt did not quit. Instead, he envisioned expanding the Central's empire, particularly to the west, where other trunk lines to the south of the Central were moving. The three lines that formed a direct route to Chicago from Buffalo were the Buffalo & Erie, to Erie, Pennsylvania; the Lake Shore from Erie to Toledo, Ohio; and the Michigan Southern & Northern Indiana Railroad from Toledo to Chicago. The Vanderbilt interests soon acquired control of these lines, and Horace Clark, another son-in-law of the Commodore, became Lake Shore president. On Clark's death in 1873, and with the added financial pressures of that year's panic, Vanderbilt took the presidency himself. The three lines were consolidated into the Lake Shore & Michigan Southern, which assured the Central a direct route to Chicago.

As insurance against the failure to acquire the fastest route, the Vanderbilt group already had bought blocks of stock in both the Michigan Central and Canada's Great Western. These two roads offered a line from Niagara Falls to Chicago via Windsor, Ontario, and Detroit. This, however, was not the preferred route since it included a ferry crossing of the Detroit River. But no chances were taken in the event that the hated Erie, also pursuing the Lake Shore, succeeded in acquiring control and blocking the Central from the hub of the Midwest.

With the continued expansion of the Vanderbilt railroad empire, the Vanderbilt fortune continued to increase. The second Mrs. Vanderbilt intervened once more in favor of altering Vanderbilt's aversion to giving away money. She introduced her husband to Bishop Holland McTyeire, then seeking money to build Central University near Nashville, Tennessee. Plans called for a seminary to be built as part of the project, and Vanderbilt agreed to give $500,000 to the proposed university. The trustees, in an expression of appreciation and undoubtedly with an eye to the future, voted to change the school's name to Vanderbilt University. When more funds were needed as the construction progressed, the pleased Commodore donated another $500,000.

As 1876 drew to a close it became obvious that Vanderbilt was dying. Weakened from a variety of causes which his doctors described as ulceration of the internal organs, Vanderbilt was unable to walk and spent his final months in a wheelchair. January 1, 1877, had scarcely passed when the old captain's relatives and his minister gathered at his home to wait for the end. It came on January 4. Vanderbilt was prepared, and his will dictated that the bulk of his $100 million estate, the majority of which was in New York Central & Hudson River Railroad stock, go to his son William and William's sons. He wanted his holdings to remain

nearly intact and as determined as Vanderbilt was in life, so was his intent carried out after his death. His favorite railroad was kept in the family, and his empire was enlarged and perpetuated.

References:

Charles F. Adams, Jr., and Henry Adams, *Chapters of Erie* (Boston: James R. Osgood, 1871);

Alvin F. Harlow, *The Road of the Century: The Story of the New York Central* (New York: Creative Age Press, 1947);

Wheaton J. Lane, *Commodore Vanderbilt: An Epic of the Steam Age* (New York: Knopf, 1942);

Gustav Metzman, *Commodore Vanderbilt (1794-1877): Forefather of the New York Central* (New York: Newcomen Society, 1946);

Arthur D. Smith, *Commodore Vanderbilt, An Epic of American Achievement* (New York: R. M. McBride, 1927).

Cornelius Vanderbilt II

(November 27, 1843-September 12, 1899)

by F. Daniel Larkin

State University College, Oneonta, New York

CAREER: Clerk, Shoe & Leather Bank (1859-1863); clerk, Kissam Brothers (1863-1864); assistant treasurer (1864-1867), treasurer, director, New York & Harlem Railroad (1867-1877); vice-president, New York Central & Hudson River Railroad (1877-1883); chairman, New York Central and Michigan Central Railroads (1883-1896).

Cornelius Vanderbilt II was born on November 27, 1843, the first son of William Henry and Maria Kissam Vanderbilt. At the time of Cornelius II's birth, his parents were living on a Staten Island farm, where Commodore Cornelius Vanderbilt had sent them until William Henry proved himself worthy of inheriting the family empire. The farm, near New Dorp, was described as "unimproved," and no doubt provided the younger Cornelius with many chores. His experiences on the then still rural island inculcated in him the work habits that would help him so greatly later in life.

Cornelius II was educated both in the common schools and in New York City private schools. As with his father and grandfather, Vanderbilt did

not attend college. He did, however, start work at the age of sixteen, joining the Shoe & Leather Bank of New York City in 1859. In 1863 Vanderbilt left that position to join the banking firm of Kissam Brothers at $50 per month.

That a grandson of the wealthy Cornelius Vanderbilt would begin work so young and in such relatively lowly positions is not altogether surprising. The elder Vanderbilt always held to the belief that his children and grandchildren would be better off if they worked early and hard in a position separate from the Vanderbilt empire.

The Commodore would wait until they proved themselves capable before he took them on in the family business interests. It was 1864 when William H. Vanderbilt gained his father's confidence and was offered a position as vice-president of the New York & Harlem Railroad. That same year Cornelius II joined the Harlem Railroad as assistant treasurer. If this were not measure enough of the elder Vanderbilt's confidence in him, then Cornelius II's appointment as treasurer and as a director of the line in 1867 was quite enough. His

Cornelius Vanderbilt II

growth into maturity was completed on February 4, 1867, when he married Alice Claypool Gwynne. They had seven children of whom three sons and two daughters survived to adulthood.

The next ten years were a time of learning and preparation for Cornelius II. In 1877 Commodore Vanderbilt died, leaving the bulk of the family fortune in the hands of William H. Vanderbilt. William succeeded his father as president of the New York & Harlem, and Cornelius II was promoted to vice-president. As the Commodore had prepared his son to assume control of the business, so did William Vanderbilt prepare his sons, Cornelius II and William K., to take over after him.

William Vanderbilt's control over the family empire was comparatively short. Although he was an able and successful leader, Vanderbilt was worn down by the pace and volume of the work. In 1883 he retired, leaving control of the rail empire to Cor-

nelius II, who was elected chairman of the board of directors of the New York Central & Harlem and Michigan Central railroads.

On his father's death in 1885 Cornelius became the titular head of the Vanderbilt family and exercised de facto control over its finances. Cornelius II, like his father, proved to be an able manager and successfully guided the lines under his control through the panic of 1893.

During his life Cornelius II was known as a hard worker, often arriving at his Grand Central Station office before any clerk. He was also known as a great philanthropist, serving as a trustee for many hospitals, seminaries, and museums. He gave over $1.5 million to Yale University. His reputation was almost unique among controllers of large fortunes in that he was regarded with approbation by many critics of wealth. Henry Claus, a contemporary of Vanderbilt and a critic of monopolies, assayed the Vanderbilt monopoly as beneficial:

> I regard the Vanderbilt property, however, in the light of a great trust, [Cornelius and William K. Vanderbilt] with Chauncey M. Depew as trustees, and I question very much if that eminent team of honest and able reformers, Henry George and Rev. Dr. Edward McGlynn, with other minor lights of the Anti-Poverty Society, could administer that trust with a greater army of well-paid, easy worked and well-fed men by any State of national supervision or management, or by breaking up a great corporation into a hundred or so small companies.
>
> The Vanderbilt system employs 200,000 people at better wages than they can obtain elsewhere, any place in the world.

Cornelius Vanderbilt II resigned most of his official posts in 1896 after suffering a slight stroke. He died in New York City from a cerebral hemorrhage on September 12, 1899, at the age of fifty-five.

References:

Wayne Andrews, *The Vanderbilt Legend; The Story of the Vanderbilt Family, 1794-1940* (New York: Harcourt, Brace, 1941);

Edwin P. Hoyt, *Vanderbilts and Their Fortune* (Garden City: Doubleday, 1962).

William H. Vanderbilt

(May 8, 1821-December 8, 1885)

by F. Daniel Larkin

State University College, Oneonta, New York

CAREER: Farmer, Staten Island (1842-1864); president, Staten Island Railroad (1857-1864); vice-president, New York & Harlem Railroad (1864-1877); vice-president, Hudson River Railroad (1865-1877); vice-president (1869-1877), president, New York Central & Hudson River Railroad (1877-1883); director, Vanderbilt rail empire (1877-1883).

William Henry Vanderbilt, the eldest of the thirteen children of Cornelius Vanderbilt, was born on May 8, 1821, in a small, waterfront house in New Brunswick, New Jersey, belonging to his father's employer, Thomas Gibbons. The feisty Gibbons had recently hired Cornelius Vanderbilt to captain his steam ferry on the run between New Jersey and New York City, which ran in competition with Aaron Ogden and in defiance of the Fulton-Livingston steamboat monopoly into which Ogden had bought. These were difficult times for the young Vanderbilt family. While Vanderbilt craftily evaded law officers to bring the Gibbons steamer in and out of New York, his wife Sophia opened part of their house as an inn in order to supplement the family finances. Her reputation as an innkeeper soon caused her income to rival that of her husband.

It was in this environment of hard work and determination that William Vanderbilt was raised. Unfortunately, he did not inherit the strength and stamina of his parents, and was a rather frail child. In 1829, when William was eight years old, the family moved to a small house near the Battery in New York City. While his father launched his own steam-ferry dispatch line, William was sent to the Columbia College Grammar School where he completed his basic education at age seventeen. As his father had little regard for more than a rudimentary knowledge of the three R's, William did not attend college. After a brief employment in a ship chandler's

William H. Vanderbilt

shop, William was placed by his father as a clerk in the banking house of Drew, Robinson and Company. Daniel Drew, a partner in the firm and a future archrival of the Commodore, provided William with the position in 1839 where he learned the business of finance at $16 per week.

In 1840, at age nineteen, William wed Maria Kissam, the daughter of a Dutch Reformed minister. His father disapproved of the marriage, maintaining outwardly that William was too young. However, since the Commodore had also married at nineteen, the real reasons for his objection may have been that Maria was a minister's daughter. At the time Commodore Vanderbilt had little regard for churchmen and, having made a sizable fortune already, little use for his eldest son marrying into a family lacking money. Nonetheless, the determined couple were joined in matrimony, and William diligently continued his work at Drew, Robinson. He performed so well at Drew, Robinson that he was about to be offered a partnership in 1842 when he fell ill, an illness attributed to the "close, indoor confinement" of his long working hours. While it may also have resulted from his physical infirmities as a youth, Vanderbilt was, in any case, unable to remain in his office position.

William's illness, coupled with his early marriage, was the last straw for the Commodore. Lacking patience and understanding for a son not as robust and vigorous as he, the disgusted father exiled William to Staten Island. The Commodore did not entirely disown William but instead gave him a parcel of seventy undeveloped acres near the old Vanderbilt family community of New Dorp, telling him to "make the best of it." William and his young wife moved to Staten Island in 1841 to become farmers.

Vanderbilt and his wife knew little about agriculture, but they worked hard to develop their holdings. (During the time they lived in New Dorp the couple produced nine children, of which four daughters and four sons survived.) Diligence and perseverance began to turn the land into a productive business, and William soon had the chance to add 350 acres to what his father had given him. Reluctantly, he approached his father for the $3,000 purchase price. The Commodore flatly turned him down, forcing William to turn to a bank to secure the loan with a mortgage on the land he owned. His father scolded him for his willingness to pay the high interest rate and told William that he would never amount to anything. But the Commodore closely followed William's progress and, pleased with the way his son worked the farm, provided him with enough money to close out the bank loan.

New York City was growing rapidly during the 1840s and 1850s, as new waves of Irish and German immigrants added to the city's burgeoning population. In 1850 the combined population of the cities of New York and Brooklyn was 612,000. By 1860 this figure had nearly doubled to almost 1.1 million. The market for farm produce was considerable and William Vanderbilt made the most of it. The fact that his neighbors on Staten Island respected his ability in making the farm a success and liked his affable manner led to William's involvement with a railroad even before his father left steamboats for railroads.

A short railway was constructed on Staten Island in the 1850s but suffered from mismanagement and was forced into receivership during the panic of 1857. The people of Staten Island prevailed upon Vanderbilt to take over management of the line. He did so and within two years the railroad paid its debts and became a successful enterprise. The line's success enabled Vanderbilt to purchase several ferries for the railroad which provided a direct connection to New York City. Vanderbilt was a successful railroader, a fact that did not go unnoticed by his father.

As a successful farmer William had another opportunity to demonstrate to his wily father that he was his equal as a businessman. As the story goes, the elder Vanderbilt was seeking to dispose of manure from the horses used to pull the Harlem Railroad cars in lower Manhattan, where steam locomotives were not used. The Commodore decided to sell the manure by the load, thereby gaining twice. He would get rid of it and the buyer would pay him to take the manure away. The Commodore did not, however, specify the size of the load, quite naturally thinking that a load was a wagonload. Bidding was held and William purposely topped all other bids in order to get the manure. While William was loading the manure on a scow to take it over to Staten Island, the Commodore went to the docks to chide his son and gloat over the high price per load that William had paid. The Commodore gleefully watched as the last wagons were unloaded onto the scow, and then asked William how many loads he could carry on the barge. His son calmly and assuredly replied, "Well, sir, I only take one load at a time." One can only wonder as to whether the old man was angry at being outfoxed, or proud of a son that was as astute a businessman as his father.

The Commodore undoubtedly felt a great sense of pride in 1864 when he offered William the vice-presidency of the New York & Harlem Railroad. Vanderbilt's twenty-two-year "exile" had ended and the Commodore accepted him as inheritor of the considerable Vanderbilt holdings. The Commodore evidently desired to make amends to his son by giving him a house on Fifth Avenue as a residence suitable to William's new status. The following year William added the vice-presidency of the Hudson River Railroad to his growing list of responsibilities. In his new positions William was strengthening his role as heir apparent to the Commodore.

Between the time William H. Vanderbilt assumed the Harlem office in 1864 and the Commodore's death in 1877, father and son worked together in forging a new rail empire. But as the elder Vanderbilt was already in his seventies, William assumed responsibility for many of the management details, making many important decisions subject only to his father's final approval. Throughout the late 1860s and until 1877 the Vanderbilts were a formidable team in railroading.

William Vanderbilt pushed for the 1869 consolidation of the Hudson River Railroad and the more recently acquired New York Central, envisioning the 700 miles of track of the two companies under one management. It was also William who was entrusted with the construction of the Vanderbilt's magnificent monument to their growing rail network, the Grand Central Station. And it was also William who looked to Chicago as the logical goal for Central's expansion, his father at first opposing the idea.

Before the Vanderbilts began their westward expansion they undertook the improvement of the Central. They needed to increase its capacity and prepare for competition from other railroads that were already under construction. The number of tracks was doubled from two to four in 1873 and 1874. Equipment modernization progressed with the retirement of the Central's last wood-burning locomotive in 1874, and new and larger engines needed to haul the increased traffic were brought on line. To achieve more efficient management the Central was divided into three divisions with a superintendent in charge of each. These reforms improved the line and made it more competitive. But the Vanderbilts still needed to look to the West if the Central was to hold its position as the preeminent trunk line. Vanderbilt had finally convinced his father to acquire access to Chicago.

The panic of 1873 brought hard times to most railroads. Hard-pressed by the depression, many formerly successful lines saw their stock plummet and were forced to suspend dividend payments. Some were brought only to the edge of bankruptcy and others dropped over. The aging Commodore was still mentally alert and, with his son as his adviser, moved into the western arena in earnest. By 1876 the Lake Shore & Michigan Southern and the

Michigan Central had fallen under Vanderbilt dominance and could provide links to the Northwest. On January 4, 1877, Cornelius Vanderbilt died and left his holdings almost completely intact to the man groomed to receive them, William H. Vanderbilt.

When Vanderbilt succeeded his father as New York Central president, he was fifty-six years old. He had already demonstrated that he possessed his father's love of hard work and his tendency toward thrift. Now, as unchallenged head of the Vanderbilt rail system, his charm, tact, and willingness to compromise when necessary and advantageous would be put to the most severe test. He had hardly taken over when his first trial occurred.

In the summer of 1877 reduced revenue brought on by rate wars led to a general reduction in pay on the railroads. The pay decrease varied but on the Central averaged 10 to 15 percent. The labor unrest stemming from the pay cuts was particularly destructive on the Baltimore & Ohio and the Pennsylvania railroads. Rolling stock was burned, stations and other buildings were destroyed, and many injuries and some deaths resulted. Federal soldiers were ordered by President Rutherford B. Hayes to restore order and protect railroad property. But little of the labor dissension and none of the rioting reached the Central. Although there was an interruption of some freight service, none of the passenger business was halted. Because of the loyalty of a majority of the Central's workers Vanderbilt ordered a bonus of $100,000 to be apportioned among them. Within three years after the wage decrease full pay was restored to all the Central's employees, illustrating the concern that Vanderbilt had for his workers and his railroad.

In attempting to change management-labor relations and the image of the New York Central, Vanderbilt was contending with a troublesome past. During the nearly ten years of his father's control of the railroad the Central was not well liked by the people who worked for it. Neither was it held in high regard by those who lived along its line and used the road. Many felt it skimped on service and equipment in the interest of lowering its operating expenses. Vanderbilt, unlike his father, saw the value in changing the public's attitude toward the railroad. One of his methods of accomplishing this was to hire a press agent to improve public relations. Of course, the bonus to the nonstriking employees in 1877 did no harm to the Central's image.

William Vanderbilt also must have recognized the value of a press agent in helping to stave off government regulation. In the early 1870s midwestern states began to regulate railroads with the Granger laws, sanctioned in 1877 by the Supreme Court in *Munn* v. *Illinois*. Congress flirted with railroad regulation in the mid 1870s and in 1869 Massachusetts took the lead by establishing a state railroad regulatory commission. By the time the New York legislature discussed the matter a decade later, ten more states had followed the Bay State's example.

When the Hepburn Committee of New York's lawmaking body took up state regulation of railroads in 1879, Vanderbilt was called to testify at the hearings. In view of what occurred regarding subsequent regulatory commissions, Vanderbilt's testimony was prophetic. He stated that his opposition to a state commission on railroads was based upon the belief that either the railroads would control the members of the commission, or the commission would control the railroads. He was convinced that equitable regulation by a public commission of a private-sector corporation could not be achieved.

Although William Vanderbilt spoke out against a state regulatory commission in 1879, he was sufficiently convinced by other testimony at the Hepburn hearings that the type of personal control of railroads which he exemplified was not popular. This recognition led him to dispose of a considerable amount of New York Central stock. He instructed J. P. Morgan to sell 250,000 shares of Central, primarily to European buyers. Not only was Central ownership diversified, but the securities eagerly snapped up by European investors brought new capital into the United States and helped spur the great railroad-building decade of the eighties.

When Vanderbilt took over the New York Central, the "railroad war" of 1875 and 1876 was foremost on his mind. Not only did it lead to the labor troubles of 1877, but rate wars resulted in lower revenues for the road. In the 1870s the railroads had yet to envision the opportunity that the federal regulatory legislation of the 1880s could provide for them, especially if they could influence the wording of the law. Their approach to ending the suicidal rate reductions in the seventies was to form "pools."

Briefly, a pool was an agreement by two or more railroads running between similar places to eliminate ruinous competition. As an example, for a short time the two major trunk lines running between New York City and the Midwest agreed to a pool on their westbound freight business. Their freight earnings were pooled and then divided based upon their respective income percentage of the total before the pool was organized. Theoretically, this allowed all pool members to maintain substantial rates and receive a share of the market based upon their prior record. The pool sounded reasonable, but in practice nearly all of them failed. Even so the new Central president seemed to like the idea of pooling. In a lengthy statement on the subject made in June 1878, Vanderbilt reiterated the situations that led to pools and outlined his support:

> That of all the plans yet suggested or tried, the division of tonnage under the present system has produced the most satisfaction and the most beneficial results. If any other scheme will work better, then I am in favor of that. High rates in the future are utterly impossible. The people are safe from extortionate charges. Stability of prices, fair rates for transportation, equitable dealings with shippers and general prosperity can only be had through some understanding embraced in what is generally styled a pool.

Although Vanderbilt supported the concept of pooling, evidence revealed that he was painfully aware of their abysmal record of failure. A year prior to his statement in support of pools, Vanderbilt took measures to prepare the Central for future rate wars by streamlining the road's upper level management to make it more efficient and effective. Three new offices were created: general traffic manager, general auditor, and general counsel. Also, the position of general ticket agent was changed to that of general passenger agent. Promotions to the traffic manager's post and that of general auditor were made from within the operating management of the Central. Chauncey Depew, the Commodore's lawyer-lobbyist, received the new counsel's job. It is difficult to determine the impact the more efficient organization had upon railroad earnings, but, notably, the annual report of 1877 showed the Central's first increase in earnings since 1873, although the black ink was confined to freight. Nonetheless, even after the passenger losses were deducted, net income was nearly $12.75 million on revenues of $29 million.

By 1880 Vanderbilt's reforms had resulted in a marked strengthening of the New York Central. He had put the company in a position to resist future rate cutting by his competitors. The railroad king did not have long to wait. In 1881 influential New York City merchants complained that cheaper freight rates on the Pennsylvania and Baltimore & Ohio were causing a shift in business to Philadelphia and Baltimore. New York was in danger of losing its premier port city position. A meeting was called in New York City but the attending trunk line representatives could not agree on a solution to the renewal of rate cuts.

Vanderbilt was quick to take the offensive and launched a severe rate war, which by September 1881 was grinding to a halt. One fact that was painfully apparent to all the combatants was that no matter how far the rates were driven down, the amount of freight traffic remained about the same as before the battles. Freight shipments were simply shifted around to the railroad with the lowest rates, which gained a temporary boost in traffic. But ultimately the total freight shipments did not increase with the inducements of lower shipping costs.

Peace returned by the beginning of 1882 and Vanderbilt turned once again to the West, this time in the direction of a railroad being built largely for promotional reasons. The New York, Chicago & St. Louis, more commonly called the Nickel Plate, was under construction between Buffalo and Chicago. It closely paralleled the Central's Lake Shore Railroad from Buffalo to Cleveland. From there it departed the Lake Shore line in order to reach Chicago by a route several miles shorter.

The Nickel Plate's nuisance value was not lost upon Vanderbilt. He recognized it for what it was and moved to acquire the property. By October 1882 he and his sons had completed their move upon the new railroad. With the coming of the new year the incumbent president of the road resigned and Vanderbilt was installed as president of the recently acquired property. The year 1883 saw the end of Vanderbilt's active participation in the management of the family enterprises.

When William Vanderbilt decided to relinquish his domination of the Vanderbilt holdings, he passed control to Cornelius II and William K., the eldest males of his eight surviving children. The son of the Commodore had succeeded his father for only six years, but had more than doubled the fortune he had inherited. Now perhaps with the premonition that he had little time left, he turned to his beloved horses and his philanthropies. But before he resigned, he established his sons firmly in power,

though this third generation of Vanderbilt millionaires would not be involved in the administrative details of running the transportation network. Cornelius II and William Kissam Vanderbilt became board chairmen of the various corporations and in that position oversaw policy.

The retired Vanderbilt spent his time vacationing, driving his renowned horses, and donating money to various charities. He was not miserly with his vast fortune, and gave away considerable sums. Five hundred thousand dollars was donated to the College of Physicians and Surgeons in New York City. A total of $1 million was presented to Vanderbilt University, the Metropolitan Museum of Art, and the Y.M.C.A. When the Khedive of Egypt offered an obelisk to the United States, Vanderbilt spent $100,000 to have it shipped and placed in New York City's Central Park. Even college students working at a resort benefited from his largess. Vanderbilt visited the Glenn House at the foot of New Hampshire's Mt. Washington in the summer of 1883 and upon his departure, he gave a $100 bill to each of the thirty students employed there. He was impressed with their manners and industry.

Vanderbilt built an impressive mansion at Fifth Avenue and Fifty-first Street, often entertaining there and proving to be a genial host and a stimulating conversationalist. He took an interest in public affairs while he continued to keep his hand in business. He may have been officially retired, but he was still looked to as the final arbiter. In fact, it may have been the pressure of the culmination of another struggle that brought on his untimely death in 1885. In early December the matter of the potentially competitive West Shore Railroad had finally been put to rest. The bankrupt New York, West Shore, & Buffalo had been sold to J. P. Morgan, Asbel Green, and Chauncey Depew, the Central's faithful attorney and its president. They organized the new West Short Railroad Company, all the stock of which was owned by the New York Central. The railroad itself was leased to the Central almost in perpetuity. With that running sore healed William should have felt relaxed and pleased. Perhaps he did, since on December 8, three days after the conclusion of the West Shore business, he appeared particularly fit. After lunch he was discussing some routine business with Robert Garrett, president of the Baltimore & Ohio, when he suffered a seizure and died almost instantly. The man who had spent so long proving his worthiness to continue the great Vanderbilt tradition ultimately had relatively little time to do so.

References:

William A. Croffut, *Vanderbilts and the Story of Their Fortune* (Chicago: Belford, Clark, 1886);

Alvin F. Harlow, *The Road of the Century: The Story of the New York Central* (New York: Creative Age Press, 1947);

Edward Hungerford, *Men and Iron: The History of New York Central* (New York: Thomas Y. Crowell Co., 1938);

Wheaton J. Lane, *Commodore Vanderbilt: An Epic of the Steam Age* (New York: Knopf, 1942).

John Van Nortwick

(April 5, 1809-April 15, 1890)

by Gerald Musich

National Railroad Museum

CAREER: Engineer, state of New York (1828-1845); chief engineer, Galena & Chicago Union (1847-1854); chief engineer, Aurora Branch Rail Road/Chicago & Aurora Rail Road (1850-1852); president, Chicago, Burlington & Quincy (1857-1865).

John Van Nortwick played an important role in the development of several early Illinois railroads. Over a nearly twenty-year period, he held key positions with the Galena & Chicago Union, oldest component of the Chicago & North Western; with the Chicago, Burlington & Quincy; and briefly with the Illinois Central.

He was born in Washington County, New York, on April 5, 1809, the only child of William and Martha (Flack) Van Nortwick. Given a thorough schooling in mathematics he was employed at the age of nineteen in the engineering department for the canals of the state of New York, his father being the canal superintendent at the time. He remained with the engineering department until 1845.

Van Nortwick married Patty Maria Mallory of Penn Yan, New York, on February 11, 1835. The next year he traveled to Batavia, Illinois, to visit his father, who had moved to that new community in 1835. Van Nortwick was impressed by his father's land and business investments, and, though he returned to New York, he became a partner in these ventures. The partnership, among other things, built both the Batavia dam on the Fox River and the community's first flour mill.

Van Nortwick lost his position with the state in 1845 when New York suspended all work on its system of public works. Secretary of War William L. Marcy, a former governor of New York, was impressed with Van Nortwick's talents and thus hired him as civil engineer for the construction of the U.S. dry dock at Brooklyn. Van Nortwick held that position for one year and then, in 1846, moved with his family to Batavia, Illinois.

Upon arriving in Batavia, Van Nortwick made a number of investments, including milling enterprises, a paper company, and landholdings. Virtually all of his investments appear to have been highly successful. His land acquisitions serve as an example of his foresight. He bought land that was covered with hardwood trees, knowing that Chicago was trying to expand its shipbuilding industry and was in need of hardwood. His only challenge was in finding a way to transport his wood the thirty-five miles to Chicago, with the solution being found in the Galena & Chicago Union (G&CU) Rail Road that Van Nortwick himself helped engineer.

Because of his civil engineering background, Van Nortwick was hired as chief engineer of the G&CU in 1847. To him fell the tasks of first laying out the course of the railroad, then overseeing the construction by private contractors. Under his management the G&CU built its lines from Chicago to Freeport, Illinois, and from Junction (West Chicago) to Fulton, Illinois.

In the midst of this construction, Van Nortwick played an important part in one of the G&CU's more difficult early decisions. In 1848, when construction started on the line, no communities except Naperville existed west of Chicago until one reached the Fox River, approximately thirty-eight miles west. Along the Fox River, however, were such small but thriving towns as Aurora, Batavia, Geneva, St. Charles, and Elgin. The land between the Fox River and Chicago was very marshy, so the trip by stage took sixteen hours. The railroad was to cut that time to three hours, so the residents of all the Fox River towns were especially anxious about the route the G&CU was to select. Locating the route through a particular town would bring it prosperity, while bypassing it could cause economic disaster.

The G&CU board tentatively chose a route crossing the Fox River at Elgin and bypassing Aurora, Batavia, Geneva, and St. Charles. Hearing this, the residents of the four spurned communities petitioned the board to reconsider and agreed to pay the costs of surveying a route that would serve all of them. Van Nortwick found himself in an unusual position. As chief engineer of the G&CU he was expected to evaluate this alternate route and recommend to the G&CU board what was in their best interest. But he was also a major landholder in Batavia, one whose personal investments were at considerable risk if Batavia were bypassed.

Whether he was sensitive to this moral dilemma or not, Van Nortwick became a strong proponent of the alternate route that would serve all five river towns. The G&CU board, however, rebuffed his recommendation and in 1849 decided to lay its route from Chicago thirty miles west to today's West Chicago and then northwest to Elgin. The board agreed, however, to work with the four bypassed communities if those towns built their own branchline railroads connecting with the G&CU.

Three branchlines were quickly formed. The St. Charles Branch ran from St. Charles to the G&CU at Junction, today's West Chicago. The Geneva Branch ran 1.8 miles from Geneva to St. Charles. And the Aurora Branch was constructed from the G&CU at Junction to Batavia and then to Aurora, a distance of 14 miles. Van Nortwick was hired in 1850 as the chief engineer of the Aurora Branch while retaining his post with the G&CU. The Aurora Branch quickly became the Chicago & Aurora Rail Road and later became the Chicago, Burlington & Quincy (CB&Q).

Van Nortwick eventually served as president of the CB&Q for eight years from 1857 to 1865.

His most significant contributions to that railroad, however, were probably those made in the early years of 1849 to 1852. Had his somewhat self-interested recommendation of rerouting the G&CU been adopted, the CB&Q may not have come into existence or at least would have taken a much different form. Quite likely as a result of his arguments, the G&CU agreed to the creation of the Aurora Branch, initially as a subsidiary of their operations. Van Nortwick then established the route of the Aurora Branch, oversaw its construction, and helped formulate the company's ideas of pushing west of Aurora as a major railroad in its own right.

The CB&Q elected Van Nortwick its president in 1857, shortly after the consolidation of the line with the Central Military Tract Railroad. During his eight-year tenure the railroad absorbed such smaller lines as the Peoria & Burlington; built major facilities in Chicago, including a twelve-stall enginehouse and a 30,000 sq. ft. freighthouse; and, in 1864, completed its own main line from Chicago to Aurora, thus eliminating its leasing of G&CU trackage from Chicago to Junction. When Van Nortwick took office as president in 1857, the CB&Q had a fleet of 54 locomotives, 39 passenger cars, and 760 freight cars. When he left office in 1865, the railroad had expanded to the point that it operated 105 locomotives, 71 passenger cars, and 1,930 freight cars.

Van Nortwick resigned as president of the CB&Q in June 1865, citing the fact that "my private affairs [are] requiring more of my time than would be consistent with a proper discharge of my official duties." These private affairs included numerous businesses that he owned, such as a milling concern, a water power firm, and the Van Nortwick Paper Co., a paper manufacturing company operating in Batavia and in Wisconsin.

Van Nortwick died on April 15, 1890. Surviving him were his wife, who died in 1893, and four children: William M., Eliza J., John S. and Mary E. Van Nortwick.

References:

Robert J. Casey & W. A. S. Douglas, *Pioneer Railroad: The Story of the Chicago and North Western System* (New York: McGraw-Hill, 1948);

Commemorative Biographical & Historical Record of Kane County, Illinois (Chicago: Beers, Leggett & Co., 1888), pp. 186-189;

Patrick C. Dorin, *Everywhere West* (Burbank, Cal.: Superior, 1976);

W. H. Stennett, *Yesterday & To-day*, 3rd Edition (Chicago: C&NW Ry. Co., 1910);

Gen. John S. Wilcox, ed., *Historical Encyclopedia of Illinois and History of Kane County* (Chicago: Munsell Publishing Co., 1904).

Archives:

Van Nortwick's diaries and several letters are in the collection of the Illinois State Historical Society, Springfield, Illinois. A microform copy of these documents is available through the State Historical Society of Wisconsin, Madison, Wisconsin. Occasional papers and letters are also included among the Chicago, Burlington & Quincy Railroad Company records, the Newberry Library, Chicago, Illinois.

Henry Villard

(April 10, 1835-November 12, 1900)

by John F. Due

University of Illinois

CAREER: Journalist (1857-1867); secretary, American Social Science Association (1868-1871); president, Oregon & California Railroad and affiliated companies (1876-1884); president, Oregon Railway & Navigation (1879-1884); president, Northern Pacific Railroad (1881-1884); principal owner, New York *Evening Post* (1881-1900); president, Edison General Electric (1889-1892); founder, North American Company (1890).

Henry Villard was one of the most important financiers and entrepreneurs of the last three decades of the nineteenth century; initially his interests were primarily in the railroad field, but they soon extended to industry and publishing. He was the dominant figure in the development of the railroad network of the Pacific Northwest.

Villard was born Ferdinand Heinrich Gustav Hilgard on April 10, 1835, of a distinguished Bavarian family, in Speyer, Rhenish Bavaria. His father, a lawyer and jurist, became a justice of the Supreme Court of Bavaria. Henry attended universities in Munich and Wurzburg but because of his republican sentiments became estranged from his father and immigrated in 1853, at the age of eighteen, to the United States. He changed his name to Villard, the name of a former classmate, in fear his father would force his return to Germany for military service. He traveled in the United States and in 1855 settled in Belleville, Illinois, where he remained for several years. The town of Belleville, some twenty miles southeast of St. Louis, had been settled in part by a group of well-educated Germans who, beginning in 1836, had left Bavaria for political reasons. One of these was Theodor E.

Hilgard, a first cousin of Villard's father and also a former jurist in Rhenish Bavaria. Villard lived with the Hilgards and became well acquainted with the youngest son, E. W., who became Villard's lifetime friend and personal business adviser. E. W. Hilgard returned to Germany for a Ph.D. in Chemistry and Geology and was one of the small group of scientists hired by the University of California at Berkeley in the 1870s who established the new university's reputation. He is regarded today as one of the founders of modern soil science. Hilgard helped Villard by later directing soil surveys for the rail lines in the Northwest. His work in demonstrating the fertility of arid soils in the West and in discovering a means of controlling alkali in the soil resulted in substantial agricultural traffic for the railroads.

Villard, during his stay in Belleville, learned English, read law, and edited a newspaper. In 1857 Villard began a ten-year stint as a journalist, reporting the Lincoln-Douglas debates and, after visiting Colorado, writing a guidebook to the Pikes Peak area. During the Civil War he served as a war correspondent for the New York *Herald* and the New York *Tribune*. In 1866 Villard married Helen Frances Garrison, the daughter of William Lloyd Garrison, the crusading abolitionist editor. They had two sons and a daughter. In 1868 he became secretary of the Boston-based American Social Sciences Association.

In 1871 Villard returned to Germany. Although he was suffering from poor health, Villard became active in German financial circles, some of which involved selling the bonds of the Oregon & California (O&C) Railroad. The O&C had been founded in 1870 by Ben Holladay, a pioneer stage-

Henry Villard (center in bowler) with friends in Oregon, 1883 (courtesy of Union Pacific System)

coach operator, as a consolidation of several Portland area railroads originally built by California promoters. The O&C built south from Portland, reaching Roseburg in 1872 on the way to California. Heavily in debt, the O&C defaulted on its bonds in 1873. Most of the bonds were held in Germany, and a bondholders protective committee sent Villard to Oregon to investigate the situation. An agreement that Villard reached with Holladay would have protected the bondholders, but Holladay did not implement it, and in 1876 the bondholders sent Villard back to finalize an agreement. He succeeded in persuading Holladay to transfer the O&C Railroad, the Oregon Steamship Company, and the Oregon Central Railroad to the creditors. Villard headed the enterprises and in 1879 made substantial personal purchases of their stock partly in an effort to end competition among them. During these same years, 1876-1879, Villard, as a representative of the bondholders, served as receiver of the Kansas Pacific Railroad.

For the next decade Villard was to play by far the dominant role in the development of transportation in the Pacific Northwest. An important background element in this development was the bitter rivalry that evolved between Portland and the Puget Sound cities of Tacoma and, later, Seattle. Portland had the advantage of being located on the Columbia River, the natural gateway to the east, and was

a well-established city by the mid 1870s. But navigation of the Columbia from Portland west to the ocean was difficult at best because of sandbars, whereas the Puget Sound points had excellent deepwater access to the Pacific. Villard was a strong believer in Portland and sought to develop a transportation system that would ensure the city's continued dominance of the trade to the inland and its participation in the transcontinental traffic.

There were two crucial elements in the picture. The first was the Northern Pacific (NP), chartered in 1864 to build a northern transcontinental line. The NP management soon became committed to the site that was to become Tacoma and bought extensive property at that location. The company was undecided as to whether initially to build on the north or south bank of the Columbia, but the ultimate goal was to build directly across the Cascades. Portland interests were, of course, greatly disturbed about the emphasis by the NP on Tacoma as the main western terminus.

The second element was the Union Pacific, which maintained an interest in building a line into the Northwest. The prime objective in Portland was to build its own railroad up the south bank of the Columbia River to a connection with the Union Pacific. But there was insufficient capital in Portland to attempt the project as the most likely source of funds, the Oregon Steam Navigation (OSN) Company, would have no part in financing a new competitor. Villard stepped into this picture in 1879 when he acquired the OSN by purchasing its stock from its Portland owners, Simon Reed and his associates. The OSN was absorbed into the Oregon Railway & Navigation (OR&N) Company, which was formed that year to build the rail connection to the Union Pacific. Jay Gould and Sidney Dillon, the leading figures in the Union Pacific, had agreed to the connection but, under pressure from Collis P. Huntington of the Central Pacific, backed out in the fear that Huntington would divert traffic to his Southern Pacific if the Union Pacific built to the West Coast. Accordingly, Villard sought to reach an agreement with the Northern Pacific for the NP to use the OR&N line to reach Portland. In 1881 the NP had gained access to sufficient funds to complete its line, and Villard concluded that he must gain control of the NP to ensure its use of the OR&N and to protect Portland. Accordingly, he commenced buying NP stock. Because he lacked sufficient funds of his own, he developed the famous Blind Pool and induced friends to put $8 million into a pool without knowing what it would be used for. This money enabled him to gain control of the NP, and he became its president in September 1881. His primary objective was to block the NP from building to Puget Sound and instead force it to use the OR&N for its connection to Portland.

The OR&N was completed to Dalles and Wallula in 1882. The Northern Pacific was pushed westward rapidly, and the two lines were joined at Wallula on September 8, 1883. Also in 1883 the NP completed the link between Portland and Kalama, joining Portland with Puget Sound. Villard expanded his control of transportation in the Northwest by acquiring the Oregonian Railway in the Willamette Valley and the Pacific Coast Steamship Company in 1882, and the Oregon & California in 1883. He persuaded the Union Pacific to build the Oregon Short Line to connect with the OR&N in eastern Oregon and not to build its own line to the coast. All of the lines Villard controlled were joined under a holding company, the Oregon & Transcontinental (O&T), which had been formed in 1871 and would have a varied and tortuous history.

The empire that Villard had built so quickly collapsed almost as fast. Completion of the NP involved tremendous cost overruns, and Villard, to maintain the confidence of his investors, had paid large dividends. By the end of 1883 the road could

not meet its obligations, and Villard resigned as president in January 1884.

He also resigned as president of the O&T and the OR&N, and the O&T lost the Oregon & California to the Southern Pacific, a fate Portland had always feared. In 1887 the NP completed its direct line to Seattle and Tacoma via the Yakima Valley and Stampede Pass; and the OR&N was leased to the Union Pacific. During the years 1884 to 1886 Villard was in Germany recovering from a nervous breakdown.

On his return, however, events were equally chaotic. By 1887 the Oregon & Transcontinental was in financial difficulties; Villard, now back in the Pacific Northwest, provided funds but refused the presidency. The O&T again gained control of the NP, and Villard was offered a position on the NP board to mediate the growing battle between the Northern Pacific and the Union Pacific for traffic in eastern Washington and northeastern Oregon. Portland, once Villard's strongest supporter, was now skeptical because of Villard's close ties to the NP and Tacoma. He worked hard to develop joint ownership of the OR&N by the UP and the NP and in 1888 again became president of the O&T as a result of German stock purchases. But his attempts to obtain approval of the joint lease failed, and unbridled building of competitive duplicating lines in the Palouse country of eastern Washington followed. Litigation and a battle for the O&T followed, and the Union Pacific lost to Villard in a proxy fight in 1889.

The UP then traded its O&T stock to the O&T in return for control of the OR&N. Financial commitments with regard to the OT and OR&N and traffic declines ruined the UP financially, leading to bankruptcy in 1893 and temporary loss of the OR&N. In 1893 Villard ended his activities in the Northwest railway picture as the NP also went into bankruptcy, and James J. Hill and Edward Harriman soon came to dominate the Northwest rail picture.

But Villard's business interests were not confined to railroads. He also played a role in developing the electric power industry and its many related uses. He was an early supporter of Thomas Edison, and the first nonexperimental incandescent electric plant was installed in the Villard-owned ship, the S S *Columbia*, in 1880. When Villard returned from Germany in 1886 with the backing of German banks and the major German electrical firm of

Siemens and Halske, he conceived of a plan to dominate the electric industry of the world through a giant cartel. As a first step he sought to gain control of the Edison enterprises, which were in urgent need of reorganization. In 1889, after his original plans were blocked by J. P. Morgan, he succeeded with Edison and Samuel Insull in consolidating the firms, including the Sprague Electric Railway and Motor Company, as the Edison General Electric Company. Villard was named president but did not concern himself with active management. He stressed the importance of growth through mergers and soon came to recognize that, in the immediate future, electric traction motive power offered the greatest potential, electric power offered more potential than electric lighting, and development of alternating current (AC) was essential, the latter a step anathema to Edison. He negotiated with Westinghouse, the dominant promoter and developer of AC, but dropped this and instead sought to acquire Thomson-Houston, the other major electrical manufacturing firm. He developed a plan which would have given the Edison interests control of the merged company, but J. P. Morgan again succeeded in besting Villard; Thomson-Houston gained control of the new company, called General Electric, and Villard was ousted as president in 1892. Villard did manage to make money on the deal, however.

Closely related to Villard's interest in Edison General Electric was his creation in 1890 of the North American Company, the first major public utility holding company, through the reorganization of the Oregon & Transcontinental. The previous year he had organized the Edison Electric Illuminating Company of Milwaukee, and under North American ownership he succeeded in consolidating both the competing electric power companies and the traction companies in the city into the Milwaukee Electric Light & Power Company. The company was headed by John I. Beggs, who stressed the traction properties and for two decades ran the system in an efficient but arrogant manner.

The North American Company, confined in Villard's day almost entirely to the Milwaukee area, later expanded to control the St. Louis transit system, the Illinois Traction Company, and the Washington (D.C.) Electric Railway & Light Company. But this was all long after Villard's death.

Villard's other activity was in journalism, following his earlier experience as a reporter. In 1881 he purchased a controlling interest in the New York *Evening Post* but refrained from influencing editorial policy.

Villard died in Dobbs Ferry, New York, on November 12, 1900, survived by his widow and three children. One son, Oswald Garrison Villard, served for many years as the distinguished editor of the *Evening Post* and the *Nation*.

Few persons have matched Villard's record for entrepreneurial activities in several major industries. He was the dominant figure in shaping the railway network of the Pacific Northwest, a major figure in the development of General Electric and the power and street railway industry in the United States, and played an important role in the publishing industry. In all fields he was a person of integrity and honesty, with a substantial breadth of vision. In terms of personal and social ethics among railroad promoters, Villard would be ranked close to James J. Hill; he was much less strictly short-term profit-minded than E. H. Harriman and far removed from the tactics of Jay Gould. Given his German background he was a strong believer in the efficiency of monopoly and always sought to curb competition, but not in an avaricious way.

Publications:

The Past and Present of Pike's Peak Gold Region (St. Louis: Sutherland and McEvoy, 1860; reissued, Princeton: Princeton University, 1932);
Memoirs (Boston: Houghton, Mifflin, 1904);
The Early History of Transportation in Oregon (Eugene: University of Oregon, 1944).

References:

James B. Hedges, *Henry Villard and the Railways of the Northwest* (New Haven: Yale University, 1930);
Forrest McDonald, *Insull* (Chicago: University of Chicago, 1962).

Archives:

An extensive collection of letters to and from Villard and copies of manuscripts and documents pertaining to his work in transportation are located in the Villard Papers of the Harvard University Library in Cambridge, Massachusetts.

Wabash v. Illinois

On October 25, 1886, the United States Supreme Court announced its decision in the case of *Wabash, St. Louis, and Pacific Railroad v. Illinois*. Taken in conjunction with other cases decided near the same time, such as *Santa Clara County v. Southern Pacific Railroad*, the Wabash decision crippled state railroad regulatory efforts. Consequently, many saw it as making federal regulation of interstate railroad practices necessary rather than merely desirable. The Wabash decision and federal railroad regulation have always been closely linked since the case was followed by passage of the famous Interstate Commerce Commission Act in the next session of Congress.

The impact of the Wabash decision was made more dramatic because it amounted to a virtual reversal of what had been the High Court's general position on state regulation of railways. In the Granger cases of the mid 1870s–*Munn v. Illinois*; *Chicago, Burlington & Quincy Railroad Co. v. Iowa*; and *Peik v. Chicago & Northwestern Railway*–all decided in 1876, the Supreme Court upheld state regulatory legislation, even where it had an interstate impact, as long as there was an absence of federal law on the subject. The language of the Munn decision, for example, was friendly in tenor toward the principle of state legislation to prevent railroads from discriminating, but the Wabash decision had the effect of questioning the right of a state to regulate when there was any incidental interstate impact, even in the absence of federal law dealing with the matter.

The basis for the Wabash case was an Illinois law passed in 1871, and revised in 1873, that prohibited railroads in that state from charging more for carrying the same class of goods for a shorter than a longer distance. The law said that doing so was prima facie evidence of unjust rate discrimination, provided for a penalty of up to $5,000 for an offense, and allowed the aggrieved party to recover three times the amount of the damages, court costs, and attorney fees. Litigation originated when an Illinois chartered company, the Wabash, St. Louis, and Pacific Railroad, charged Isaac Bailey and F. O. Swannell twenty-five cents per hundred weight for hauling freight from Gilman, Illinois, to New York City, while charging Elder and McKinney of Peoria fifteen cents per hundred weight for hauling the same class of freight to New York. As Peoria was eighty-six miles farther from New York than Gilman, the transaction on face violated Illinois law. The Wabash resisted paying the fine and the case was appealed to the Illinois Supreme Court, which upheld the state penalty and damages for Swannell and Bailey. But the Wabash appealed the case to the federal courts, and it reached the United States Supreme Court in the spring of 1886.

In its arguments the state of Illinois contended that its law applied as far as the state line, that the aggrieved party had the right to damages for shipment that far, and that Illinois had the right to collect the entire penalty for violation of the law. The Illinois attorney general also claimed the state law should be upheld since there was no federal law on the matter. The Supreme Court, in its decision, responded that each of the shipments was part of one contract, and that shipment in one state could not be separated from another. In other words, the freight was not shipped to the state line, unloaded, and reshipped to New York. The decision indicated that the Court would have upheld the state supreme court decision if the shipment had been entirely within the state and "disconnected from a continuous transportation through or into other states."

Unlike the earlier Munn decision, when the Court had generally spoken approvingly of state regulation of railroads, the majority in the Wabash decision stated that it was not its duty to speak about the principles involved in the Illinois law. The justices admitted that it might be equitable for Illinois law to deal with shipments that began and ended in that state. "But when it is attempted to apply to transportation through an entire series of States a principle of this kind, and each one of the States shall attempt to establish its own rates of transportation, its own methods to prevent discrimination in rates, or to permit it, the deleterious influence upon the freedom of commerce among the States and upon the transit of goods through these states cannot be overestimated."

Three justices viewed the same facts and the same background of cases and presented a minority report arguing that at stake was the right of the state to regulate, and that the state of Illinois had authority over the portion of transportation taking place within the state, regardless of whether it was all part of a single trip. The minority dissent cited a long line of decisions, but primarily rested its view on the fact that the state chartered the Wabash and therefore had authority over all its actions in the state of Illinois. The minority also argued that the inconveniences of transporting goods in interstate commerce through states with differing regulations had been "greatly exaggerated." Waite, Bradley, and Gray, the minority, essentially remained committed to the views expressed in the *Munn* v. *Illinois* decision of ten years before.

Although the Supreme Court did not strike down the Illinois law as unconstitutional, the principles enunciated in the Wabash decision effectively removed an immense portion of commerce from control of state legislatures. When the principles involved in that case were coupled with those involved in another case the same year, state railroad legislation was even more adversely affected. In the case of *Santa Clara County* v. *Southern Pacific Railroad* the Supreme Court held, in that case at least, that state regulation of railroad rates violated the due process clause of the Fourteenth Amendment, which prohibited any state from depriving a person of life, liberty, or property without due process of law.

When the U.S. Congress assembled late in 1886, advocates of various kinds of legislative approaches to federal regulation of railroads were under greater pressure than ever before to find some means of compromising on their plans. The Interstate Commerce Commission Act of 1887 was the outcome. Historians have generally agreed that it was a vague, poorly written, and myopic law that remained largely ineffective for many years. If so, then the decision of the Supreme Court in the case of the *Wabash, St. Louis, and Pacific Railroad* v. *Illinois* must bear some of the blame as well as the praise for hurrying federal railroad legislation.

—*E. Dale Odom*

Webster Wagner

(October 2, 1817-January 13, 1882)

by John H. White

Smithsonian Institution

CAREER: Wagon and furniture builder (1825-1843); railroad station agent (1843-1860); sleeping car promoter (1858-1882); president, New York Central Sleeping Car Company (1866-1882); representative and senator, New York State Assembly (1871-1882).

Webster Wagner was born on October 2, 1817, in Palatine Bridge, New York, the son of John and Elizabeth Wagner, whose German ancestors were pioneer settlers in the Mohawk Valley area. Wagner was raised on the family farm but learned the wagon-making trade and later set up a business in partnership with his older brother James. Both wagons and furniture were made but despite hard work the business failed, and Wagner eked out a living by operating an eating room. In 1843 he became station agent for the Utica & Schenectady Railroad at its Palatine depot and was thus able to observe railroad operations in all of its details.

Wagner's experience as a station agent convinced him of the need for sleeping cars. By 1858 Wagner had so improved his financial condition that he was able to implement his ideas on bettering sleeping-car service. In May of that year he and several partners contracted with the New York Central Railroad to operate Woodruff-designed cars between Albany and Buffalo. These were not, by any means, the first sleeping cars to operate in the United States; such equipment had been introduced some twenty years earlier. However, the growth of the American railroad system and the increase in long overnight journeys made sleeping cars more of a necessity than ever before. The commercial possibilities were also greatly enhanced, and Wagner's business prospered. By 1860 he had ten cars in operation and was able to offer service to New York City through an arrangement with the Hudson River Railroad. Wagner's operation grew so rapidly

Webster Wagner

during the next few years that he and his partners organized the New York Central Sleeping Car Company in 1866 with capital of $80,000.

In 1866 Cornelius Vanderbilt entered the railroad business. He soon controlled the several railroads using Wagner cars and made it clear he wanted a hand in all phases of railroad operations, including sleeping-car service. Wagner possessed no means to refuse him and in 1866 formed the New York Central Sleeping Car Company under terms dictated by Vanderbilt. As the Vanderbilt interests gained control of lines in the Middle West and New England, Pullman cars were banished in favor of Wagner cars. By 1870 the New York Central Sleeping Car Company's capitalization had ballooned to

Wagner Sleeping Car, the Commodore Vanderbilt

$600,000. In 1875 the old partnership business was reorganized as a joint stock company. The firm operated nearly 200 elegant sleeping and parlor cars; the latter style of luxury day car was introduced by Wagner in 1867.

As Wagner's operation grew in size and strength a conflict with George M. Pullman became inevitable. It broke out in 1875 when Pullman's contract with the Michigan Central expired. The Vanderbilt interests had gained control of the railroad and made sure that the new contract was given to Wagner. Pullman was furious and spent the next decade trying to punish the Vanderbilts and Wagner for this impertinent act. A series of lawsuits over disputed patents on basic sleeping-car hardware failed to destroy the New York Central Sleeping Car Company. As a result Wagner's operations continued to expand while Vanderbilt lawyers held Pullman at bay.

Wagner showed himself to be a man of many interests and unflagging energy, for he also found time for an active political career. He was elected to the New York State Assembly in 1871 and to the state senate in 1872. He was reelected each term to the latter office until the time of his tragic death in 1882. Wagner was also active in national politics and played a role in the nomination of James A. Garfield in 1880. His business interests made him a wealthy man, and his estimated annual income approached $1 million during his later years.

Webster Wagner was killed in one of his own drawing-room cars in a rear-end collision on the eve-ning of January 13, 1882, at Spuyten Duyvil, New York. The great enterprise he had created did not die with him, however. The management was temporarily entrusted to two loyal Vanderbilt lieutenants until 1885, when William S. Webb, a Vanderbilt son-in-law, was named to head the company. Webb had ambitious goals for the company and envisioned a greatly expanded operation. He meant to compete with Pullman more aggressively than had his predecessors. Webb enlarged the Buffalo car shops, began an ambitious building program of new rolling stock, and reorganized the old firm in 1886 as the Wagner Palace Car Company. Two years later Webb succeeded in doubling the capital of the firm. By the early 1890s the Wagner company employed 3,000 workers and operated about 600 cars over 20,000 miles of railroad. Yet Webb's expansion program was something of a failure, for profits actually declined and dividends were paid out of the company's surplus cash reserves. Pullman's operation was so large and so much more solid that Wagner could never hope but to be a poor, number two competitor. Negotiations to sell the company to Pullman began quietly sometime in the 1890s after both Webb and the Vanderbilts apparently agreed that the Wagner company was not worth saving. Pullman agreed to a very generous sale price of $36.6 million, and the Wagner Palace Car Company expired on January 1, 1900.

Reference:
John H. White, *The American Railroad Passenger Car* (Baltimore: Johns Hopkins University Press, 1978).

William Drew Washburn

(January 14, 1831-July 29, 1912)

by Robert M. Frame III

James Jerome Hill Reference Library

CAREER: United States surveyor general, Minnesota (1861-1865); founder, president, Minneapolis & St. Louis Railway (1870-1882); state representative, Minnesota (1871); member, U.S. Congress (1879-1885); founder, president, Washburn Mill Company (1879-1889); president, Minneapolis, Sault Ste. Marie & Atlantic and Minneapolis, St. Paul & Sault Ste. Marie railroads (1883-1889); member, American management committee, Pillsbury-Washburn Flour Mills Company (1889-1908); member, U.S. Senate (1889-1895); founder, president, Bismarck, Washburn & Great Falls Railway (1899-1904).

William Drew "W. D." Washburn, a lawyer, politician, and businessman, was one of the leading citizens of Minneapolis, Minnesota. Washburn's importance lies in his role as a developer of waterpower, railroads, and flour milling operations in the Minneapolis area. His success in these efforts expanded his influence to the entire upper Midwest.

Born in Livermore, Androscoggin County, Maine, on January 14, 1831, William Drew Washburn was the second youngest of Israel and Martha Washburn's eleven children and the youngest of seven sons. He was a descendant of John Washburn, who was secretary of the Plymouth Colony in England and arrived on the Mayflower. His paternal and maternal grandfathers were soldiers in the Revolutionary War, the latter serving under Washington at Yorktown. Several of Washburn's brothers also were notable, including Israel Washburn, Jr., Elihu Benjamin Washburn, and Cadwallader Colden, "C. C." or "Cad," Washburn.

Washburn was raised on the family farm in Maine and was educated in common schools and the neighboring academies of Gorham and Farmington. Entering Bowdoin College in 1850, he graduated with a bachelor's degree in 1854. Following college he studied law in the office of his brother Is-

William Drew Washburn

rael, then a member of Congress from Orono, and John A. Peters, later Maine's chief justice. Part of Washburn's time was spent in Washington as a clerk in the House of Representatives, where he became acquainted with the intricacies of Congress and its prominent members. He was admitted to the Maine bar in 1857 and promptly set out for the West.

Elihu Washburn had moved to Galena, Illinois, in the 1840s and was elected to Congress in 1853. Cadwallader Washburn had lived in Iowa and Illinois and ended up in Wisconsin in the 1840s, serving in Congress from 1855 to 1861.

Both men had interests in Minneapolis, where fellow Livermore natives had settled. In May 1857, following Cadwallader Washburn's advice, Washburn arrived in frontier Minneapolis, then a tiny village in the shadow of larger St. Anthony, located to the east across the Mississippi. Minneapolis was a town with no railroads and few mills, some two decades before achieving international dominance over the milling industry. Washburn opened a law office, just in time for the panic of 1857.

Despite the paucity of law business, Washburn did not have to worry. He was made secretary and agent of the Minneapolis Mill Company, a firm begun in 1856 by his brother Cadwallader, who had settled in La Crosse, Wisconsin; Robert Smith, who lived in Illinois; and Livermore native and Minneapolis resident Dorilus Morrison. The company was formed to develop the waterpower on the west (Minneapolis) side of St. Anthony Falls. With careful, farsighted guidance, the Minneapolis firm prospered while their east-side rival, the St. Anthony Water Power Company, floundered despite its more promising array of natural resources.

In October 1858 Washburn was elected to the Minnesota House of Representatives, although the 1858-1859 legislature (Minnesota's first since statehood was achieved in 1858) never met and he never took his seat. In addition he was treasurer of the city's new board of trade and chaired the founding of the First Universalist Society of Minneapolis. On April 19, 1859, Washburn married Elizabeth Muzzy of Bangor, Maine, the pair returning to Minnesota after the wedding.

In 1861 President Lincoln appointed Washburn U.S. surveyor general of Minnesota. He lived in nearby St. Paul for the next four years, receiving a thorough grounding in the state's timber resources, an education that resulted in his extensive involvement in the lumber industry. It also gave him the title "General," which friends continued to use throughout his life. In 1865 he returned to the mill company and permanent residence in Minneapolis. Now in his mid thirties, Washburn was elected to the Minneapolis school board in 1866 and the next year participated in the founding of the *Minneapolis Tribune*.

Although Washburn's involvement with flour and lumber milling in Minnesota was long and complex, he never was what was known as a "practical miller." Neither was his brother Cadwallader, the established milling entrepreneur who, in 1866, built

the first of Minneapolis's large flour mills. Both men were more interested in business administration and the public life of politics. Nevertheless, Washburn was involved in establishing both lumber and flour mills in Minneapolis and nearby Anoka during the 1870s. In 1877 he joined in the formation of Washburn, Crosby & Company with Cadwallader and John Crosby, who had married Washburn's sister-in-law. In 1879 Washburn was dropped from the Washburn-Crosby Company and he founded his own Washburn Mill Company to run the Minneapolis and Anoka flour operations. In 1889 his two mills, together with the three mills of Charles A. Pillsbury & Company, the Minneapolis Mill Company, and other entities, were bought by an English syndicate and merged into the Pillsbury-Washburn Flour Mills Company Ltd. The new British-owned company controlled the five mills that produced half of the flour made in Minneapolis, despite the fact that they were unable to buy the Washburn-Crosby Company. With Charles A. and John S. Pillsbury, William D. Washburn was appointed to the new company's Committee of Management in America. Washburn became chairman in 1901 when John S. Pillsbury died. In 1908 he retired at age seventy-seven from the committee, just as the company entered into a financial crisis and receivership.

Among Washburn's major achievements was the development of the Minneapolis & St. Louis Railway, a line intended to link Minneapolis millers and lumber dealers with the Lake Superior port of Duluth and a water route to the East, and also to provide a route south to St. Louis and from there via the Mississippi River to New Orleans. To accomplish this Washburn joined with Minneapolis entrepreneur and politician Henry Titus Welles in the late 1860s to purchase the 1853 charter of the east-west Minnesota Western Railroad Company, a planned line that had never laid a rail.

Late in 1869 Washburn and Welles gained control, and in May 1870 Washburn secured a resolution changing the road's name to the Minneapolis & St. Louis (M&StL) Railway Company. Additional charter changes allowed construction to extend to the south. To construct the northern connection Washburn and Welles incorporated the Minneapolis & Duluth Railroad in 1871, intending to connect with the Lake Superior & Mississippi just north of St. Paul, creating a shortcut to the lake port. Washburn was the president. That same year the southern line was completed to a junction near Carver, Minnesota, with the St. Paul & Sioux City. Washburn, as vice-president of the southern line, was especially proud of building the first railroad in Minnesota without the aid of a land grant.

Between 1871 and 1874 the M&StL was under the thumb of the Northern Pacific (NP), which controlled its finances. The economic crisis of 1873 bankrupted the NP and the M&StL reverted to local management with Washburn as its president. Under his guidance, despite rocky times, the line reached Albert Lea, Minnesota, in 1877, giving the M&StL the shortest route to St. Louis from Minneapolis. In 1878 it shipped half the Mill City's flour. Soon further expansion into Iowa allowed through-service to Fort Dodge. In 1881 a new corporation, still called the M&StL, consolidated its various lines: the old M&StL, the Minneapolis & Duluth, the Minnesota & Iowa Southern, and the Fort Dodge & Fort Ridgeley. In 1882 Washburn resigned the M&StL presidency, although he continued serving as a director for another decade.

Washburn enjoyed an unusual, albeit brief, steamboat rivalry with James J. Hill, launching in 1881 his *City of St. Louis* on Lake Minnetonka, west of Minneapolis, to compete with Hill's *Belle of Minnetonka*. The steamboats serviced the lakeside resorts each man's railroad had developed. Washburn's 1,000-passenger boat was reputedly the first inland vessel in the United States to be lighted by electricity. Hill's Lake Minnetonka Navigation Company soon controlled the lake trade and took over Washburn's concern.

Washburn's other rail venture also had its roots in the shipping interests of millers. In 1873, as president of the Minneapolis Board of Trade, Washburn had invited his brother Israel, then governor of Maine, to address local entrepreneurs. Israel urged millers to create their own direct rail route east, since the lake route was not open year round. A decade later, after departing the M&StL, Washburn led a group of Minneapolis mill owners and investors who incorporated the Minneapolis, Sault Ste. Marie & Atlantic (MSSteM&A) Railway, raising $1 million that year. The railroad's purpose was to give the millers the eastern rail line that they wanted by meeting Canadian lines at Sault Ste. Marie. Washburn was elected its president.

The great Minneapolis flour mills, however, also needed increasingly larger supplies of wheat to grind. Much of this wheat came from the fertile Red River Valley in western Minnesota, the Dakotas, and Manitoba. In 1884 Washburn joined with much the same group of investors to create the Minneapolis & Pacific (M&P) Railway, chartered to build west. Again Washburn was elected president. During 1887 the M&P pushed into Dakota Territory, while the MSSteM&A reached Sault Ste. Marie, meeting a Canadian Pacific branch built down from Sudbury, Ontario.

Pressed for funds, the two lines turned to the Canadian financiers George Stephen (later Lord Mount Stephen) and Donald Smith (later Lord Strathcona and Mount Royal). In return for their investment Stephen and Smith insisted that the Washburn lines be merged, a move accomplished in 1888. Stephen and Smith were Canadian Pacific backers who were also two of James J. Hill's associates in the formation of the St. Paul, Minneapolis, & Manitoba, which was then paralleled by the MSSteM&A's western extension. Washburn's line, a competitor financed by Hill's own Canadian bankers, caused Hill great consternation. The new, consolidated company was the Minneapolis, St. Paul & Sault Ste. Marie, also known as the Soo Line and as the "millers' road." In its first year the Soo Line carried nearly a million barrels of flour to markets in the East, about one-seventh of the Minneapolis output. In 1889 Washburn left the Soo for the U.S. Senate.

A lifelong Republican, Washburn had remained active in politics, both in and out of office, during the same years that he was busy organizing, financing, and administering railroads. He served in the Minnesota House of Representatives for the 1871 legislature, just when he was establishing the M&StL. Later, from 1879 to 1885, he went to Washington as a member of Congress, having bested agricultural spokesman Ignatius Donnelly in the millers-versus-farmers election of 1878. Once, in the heat of a campaign, the irascible Donnelly remarked that the two Washburn brothers (W. D. and C. C.) seemed to assume that they were born with "M.C." (member of Congress) stamped on the seat of their pants. In 1889 Washburn again defeated Donnelly, this time for the greater prize of legislative election to the U.S. Senate. While in the Senate Washburn was a member of the committees on commerce, post offices and post roads, and agriculture and was involved in restricting Chinese immigration. Washburn spent only one term as senator, however, for in 1895 the legislature chose instead the young Minnesota governor, Knute Nelson, who went on to a lengthy and distinguished national career.

Thanks to his experience with the Minneapolis waterpower at St. Anthony Falls, largely through the Minneapolis Mill Company, Washburn had long been aware of the critical water-supply situation involving the array of lakes at the Mississippi River's headwaters in north-central Minnesota. Proper damming and engineering control of these waters meant they could serve as vital reservoirs for the water-powered milling industry concentrated downstream in Minneapolis. Throughout his years in Congress Washburn labored for engineering appropriations so arduously that he became known as the "father of the reservoir system."

Retired from the Senate and in his late sixties, Washburn was not yet finished with the railroad business. In 1899 he was instrumental in the formation and financing in North Dakota of the Bismarck, Washburn & Fort Buford Railway, which became the Bismarck, Washburn & Great Falls in 1900. (The town of Washburn had been named for brother Cadwallader.) The road served the East Slope area of the Missouri River, which became Washburn country as towns and junctions were named for Washburn family members and friends. In 1904 the operation, including a small river fleet, was sold to the Soo Line, which had been behind the whole affair from the beginning. Washburn still had business interests, for in 1902 he had incorporated the Washburn Lignite Coal Company to mine the fields around Wilton, North Dakota. He remained involved with the North Dakota affair until his death.

Although Washburn was a man of enormous energy in business and politics, his involvement in social projects was relatively modest. Perhaps his major philanthropic work was the Washburn Memorial Orphan Asylum, established in 1883 by the will of Cadwallader, who had died the previous year. The orphanage was a memorial to their mother, Martha, and Washburn served as board president to the end of his life. Land for the orphanage in south Minneapolis was donated by Washburn, who had the surrounding 200 acres platted as Washburn Park, an affluent real estate development designed by landscape architect Horace W. S. Cleveland.

Washburn spent the last decades of his life at his Minneapolis mansion, Fair Oaks, where he died on July 29, 1912, leaving six children. Assessments of his demeanor and character are mixed. Most observers noted that he was slim, neat, fashionable, and elegant. Others added that he was aloof, mercurial, and opinionated. Some found him downright arrogant, domineering, and disdainful of any criticism. All would agree that William D. Washburn was a powerful and influential figure in the industrial development of the upper Midwest through the latter half of the nineteenth century.

References:

Thomas W. Balcom, *Washburn's Century of Helping Children: From Orphanage to Child Guidance Center, 1883-1983* (Minneapolis: Washburn Child Guidance Center, 1983);

Frank P. Donovan, Jr., *Mileposts on the Prairie: The Story of the Minneapolis & St. Louis Railway* (New York: Simmons-Boardman, 1950);

John A. Gjevre, *Saga of the Soo: West from Shoreham* (N.p., 1973);

James Gray, *Business Without Boundaries: The Story of General Mills* (Minneapolis: University of Minnesota Press, 1954);

Lucile M. Kane, *The Waterfall that Built a City: The Falls of St. Anthony in Minneapolis* (St. Paul: Minnesota Historical Society, 1966);

Charles B. Kuhlmann, *The Development of the Flour-Milling Industry in the United States* (Boston: Houghton Mifflin, 1929);

Albro Martin, *James J. Hill and the Opening of the Northwest* (New York: Oxford University Press, 1976);

William J. Powell, *Pillsbury's Best: A Company History From 1869* (Minneapolis: Pillsbury Company, 1985).

Archives:

Although some of the Washburn brothers left collections of papers, William Drew Washburn did not. Some of his correspondence is in the papers of his contemporaries at the Minnesota Historical Society.

George Henry Watrous

(April 26, 1829-July 5, 1889)

by George M. Jenks

Bucknell University

CAREER: Lawyer (1855-1879); counsel, New York & New Haven Railroad (1861-1872); counsel, Hartford & New Haven Railroad (1864-1872); chief counsel (1872-1879), president, New York, New Haven & Hartford Railroad (1879-1887); vice-president (1882-1884), president, Hartford & Connecticut Valley Railroad (1884-1889).

George Henry Watrous was first a prominent lawyer specializing in corporation law; he also served as counsel for the New York & New Haven, the Hartford & New Haven railroads, and their consolidated road. He later was president of the New York, New Haven & Hartford.

Watrous was born in Bridgewater, Pennsylvania, on April 26, 1829, the son of Ansel and Demis Luce Watrous. He attended the public schools in Conklin, New York, and then Homer Academy. He attended Yale University and received a bachelor of arts degree with honors in 1853. He went on to Yale Law School and received his bachelor of laws in 1855.

George Watrous began the practice of law in New Haven with Henry B. Harrison, later governor of Connecticut. He and former governor Henry Dutton formed a partnership in 1857 which lasted until 1861, when Dutton was appointed to the state supreme court. Their firm was counsel to the New York & New Haven Railroad, a retainer which led Watrous to specialize in corporate law.

Watrous was active in organizing the Republican party in Connecticut and held several public offices. He was New Haven's prosecuting attorney from 1862 to 1865, a member of the Connecticut House of Representatives in 1864, Connecticut road commissioner from 1866 to 1870, and also served as counsel to the city of New Haven and on the board of education. He also served as a director of the National Savings Bank, the City National Bank, and the New Haven Power Company.

George Henry Watrous

After Dutton left their firm in 1861 Watrous continued as counsel to the New York & New Haven Railroad and in 1864 became the counsel for the Hartford & New Haven Railroad. He lavished free passes on legislators, a common custom, so they "would feel kindly toward me." Helping in the merger of these two railroads, Watrous became chief counsel of the consolidated New York, New Haven & Hartford Railroad in 1872. He was made a director of the road in 1875 and in 1879 became president, succeeding William Darius Bishop. He remained until 1887, when poor health forced his retirement. From 1884 to 1889 he was also president of the Hartford & Connecticut Valley Railroad.

Watrous was part of that group of New England railroad executives who attended private schools and Ivy League colleges and possessed a certain status and wealth. They were some of the most able and influential leaders of the time. Under Watrous's direction the New York, New Haven & Hartford Railroad continued to prosper and expand. His philosophy of business might be summed up in his own words in a letter to James H. Wilson, president of the New York and New England Railroad, "your first duty and mine also is to the property with which we are respectively connected and we have no duty or right, even, to sacrifice that for anything or anybody." Watrous was married in 1857 to Harriet Joy Dutton, who died in 1873 after bearing three children. He was remarried in 1874 to Lily M. Graves, who bore him four children. He died in New Haven on July 5, 1889.

Publication:

A Correction of Some of the Errors of the Minority Report of the Parallel Railroad (Hartford, 1869).

References:

Thomas C. Cochran, *Railroad Leaders, 1845-1890* (Cambridge, Mass.: Harvard University Press, 1953);

Edward Chase Kirkland, *Men, Cities and Transportation*, 2 volumes (Cambridge, Mass.: Harvard University Press, 1948).

Archives:

Archives of the New York, New Haven & Hartford Railroad are in New Haven, Connecticut.

George Westinghouse

(October 6, 1846-March 12, 1914)

John H. White

Smithsonian Institution

CAREER: President, Westinghouse Air Brake Company (1869-1914); president, Union Switch & Signal Company (1881-1914); president, Westinghouse Electric Company (1886-1908).

George Westinghouse was an exceptionally talented and productive inventor, industrialist, and engineering visionary. He was particularly active in the fields of transportation and power, and personally perfected, or commercially introduced, such important systems as the air brake, alternating electric current, automatic railway signaling, and steam turbines for ship propulsion and electric generation. All of these devices or systems remain essential to daily life, especially in the western world.

George was the eighth of ten children born to George and Emeline (Vedder) Westinghouse. His father's German ancestors settled in Vermont after leaving Westphalia. The Vedders were Dutch-English. The senior Westinghouse, a mechanic and small-time manufacturer of agricultural machinery, moved his business and family to Schenectady, New York, in 1856. Five years later the Civil War started, and two of George's older brothers enlisted. Being a patriot, George, at age fifteen, ran away from home to join his brothers at the front, but he was sent home. His zeal to defeat the South only intensified, and eighteen months later he persuaded his parents to let him enlist; Westinghouse went on to serve in both the Army and the Navy. After the war he briefly attended Union College, near his home, but he found little appeal in its classical curriculum, having already been bitten by the urge to perfect and promote machinery.

His real education was obtained at his father's factory, and Westinghouse found inspiration among the lathes, mills, taps, and dies. While still in his teens he designed and built a small rotary steam engine. His first patent, issued in October 1865, was for the same type of engine. This device was followed by a more salable invention, a car replacer intended to rerail railroad cars that had jumped the track. The rerailer's sales encouraged Westinghouse to perfect a longer-lasting reversible cast-steel frog, a device which extended the working life of railroad switches by allowing wheel flanges to cross a convergence of rails. Feeling he was being cheated by his partners in Schenectady, Westinghouse moved to Pittsburgh early in 1868 to find a new supplier for his patented rerailer. In Pittsburgh the

*George Westinghouse (Gale International
Portrait Gallery)*

young inventor met several railroad officials who proved essential to the success of his best-known mechanical device, the air brake.

Still in his early twenties, George Westinghouse had already traveled many miles by railroad—a circumstance not unusual in the time when railway travel was the norm. But he was no ordinary traveler; to him the railroads were not just a conveyance, they were also a technology and one that cried out for improvement. He was inspired to create the rerailer after enduring a long travel delay because of a derailed train. In a similar way his thoughts were turned to stopping trains more expeditiously because of another delay of several hours caused by a train wreck in 1866. The young mechanic was surely aware of other wrecks where many lives were lost. The saving of time and lives could be remedied by the implementation of some form of continuous power brakes in place of the old system of hand brakes and brakemen. The idea was hardly original with Westinghouse, for countless inventors had already patented and tested a variety of power brakes, Robert Stephenson's steam brake of 1833 being but one example. Westinghouse appears to have been largely unaware of previ-

ous efforts to perfect an effective train brake, for he repeated the work of earlier generations in his fledgling attempts to devise a momentum, then a chain, then a steam, and finally, an air brake. All had been tried and many had performed reasonably well. Chain and spring brakes had in fact been rather widely adopted on a few major lines. The air brake was first patented in 1845 by an Englishman named Crawford. Cutler and Rapp of Buffalo patented an air brake system in 1852 that anticipated every feature of the Westinghouse brake system except for the steam air compressor.

And so when the Westinghouse patent was issued on April 13, 1869, he was not literally the inventor of the air brake. Nor was the brake produced by Westinghouse particularly sophisticated at least during its first several years. It was actually a very simple pressure brake that incorporated no notable technical features. As the years passed, however, the design would become more complex. Westinghouse placed his brake on the market when the railroad industry was at last ready to seriously consider power braking. Traffic was increasing and with it the density of train traffic. To move more goods and people, speeds were on the rise. To run more trains faster required the ability to stop more quickly. And so the air brake was introduced at a time when a friendly reception was likely. Local rail officials, impressed by the bright, energetic mechanic fresh from Schenectady, allowed him to install his equipment on their rolling stock. The first test train rolled out of Pittsburgh in September 1868 some months before the patent was issued. The first test involved preventing the train from striking a wagon stranded across the track. More tests were ordered. During one trial a train moving at thirty miles per hour was stopped in only nineteen seconds, a distance of 380 feet.

By 1870 eight railroads were applying Westinghouse brakes to their trains. Major sales followed, so that in less than two years 4,000 cars were outfitted with Westinghouse brakes. By 1876 nearly 75 percent of the passenger trains in the United States had air brakes. Such a rapid acceptance of the Westinghouse apparatus was a remarkable achievement. Freight cars, it should be noted, were not generally equipped with air brakes until after 1895 because of the costs involved.

The genius of Westinghouse the inventor was demonstrated in 1872 and 1873 when he perfected the automatic air brake. In the original 1869 air

Westinghouse with his wife

brake the system failed if a hose broke, the cars parted, or some other major leak occurred to drain the system of air. In the new scheme reserve air tanks were placed under each car. The brakes were actuated by a *reduction* of pressure in the train or main air line running the length of the train. Hence if a leak developed, the brakes would go on automatically. The normal workings of the system were governed by a cleverly designed, pressure-sensitive device called the triple valve. Westinghouse achieved what every other railway brake expert had dreamed of creating–a fail-safe brake.

The production of air brake sets kept apace with technical improvements and an expansion of the railroad network. By 1883 there were approximately 55,000 cars using Westinghouse brakes, most of these in the United States. A plant had already opened in England, with others planned for France, Italy, Russia, Austria, and Australia. The air brake business had outgrown the old Pittsburgh shop, and in 1890 a new plant was built some fifteen miles to the east, at Wilmerding, Pennsylvania. It was surrounded by a model company town much on the order of Pullman, Illinois. However, the managers of Westinghouse allowed workers to buy their

houses on a time payment program. Wilmerding continues today as the home of the Westinghouse Air Brake Company, which now calls itself WABCO.

Westinghouse was propelled into fame and fortune by the success of the air brake. Yet his heroic energy prompted him to plunge into other technical and business endeavors. Railway safety was as dependent on good signaling as it was on good braking, and Westinghouse saw this area of engineering as a logical adjunct to the brake business. An interest in developing an interlocking switching plant powered by compressed air also prompted Westinghouse to enter the signal business. The Union Switch & Signal (US&S) Company was organized in May 1881 to exploit Westinghouse's ideas and the patented schemes of others whose rights were purchased by the Pittsburgh entrepreneur. Westinghouse had a genius for selecting the best ideas of others to exploit. He bought rights to basic patents for interlocking plants from the British firm of Saxby and Farmer and the U.S. firm of Toucey and Buchanan. Interlocking plants were a coordinated system of switches and signals necessary for the safe operation of large railway terminals or busy junctions. Smaller interlocking facilities might be effectively handled by manual operation, but bigger plants needed power to shift the levers, switches, and signal apparatus. Under Westinghouse's guidance US&S was a pioneer in power interlocking. The first hydropneumatic plant was installed on the Reading system at Bound Brook, New Jersey, in 1883. Electropneumatic plants–which became the industry's mainstay–were introduced by US&S in 1891. The signal businesses grew so large that Westinghouse created another Pittsburgh satellite plant at Swissvale, Pennsylvania, in 1887. The enterprise flourished with little effective competition until 1904 when General Railway Signal Company was established at Rochester, New York. US&S survives to the present time, but it is no longer a Westinghouse-controlled corporation.

While Westinghouse was busy with the air brake and signal businesses he cast about for a project to fill his idle time. The man's capacity for useful employment was amazing. Deposits of natural gas were discovered in the Pittsburgh area and Westinghouse set out to find a way to effectively and cheaply transport gas by pipeline. He devised an ingenious high-low pressure transmission system that moved gas at high pressure over long distances but

Westinghouse with Lord Kelvin

then distributed it to homes and factories at the greatly reduced pressures necessary for safety.

Westinghouse was looking for new opportunities and challenges outside the railway supply industry. The natural gas adventure was too small to satisfy his needs for very long. His attention was drawn to steam turbines and electric power. The two technologies started as independent endeavors but in a relatively short time would merge and grow into a new giant industry that had a net worth of over $1 billion in 1900. Electric power made the steam engine obsolete and revolutionized life in homes and factories throughout the world.

Westinghouse had been interested in prime movers since the time of his boyhood rotary engine. He helped his brother manufacture a high-speed reciprocating engine that achieved considerable success. About 1895 Westinghouse learned of Charles Parsons, an English technician whose work with reaction steam turbines had been underway since 1884. Parsons had transformed the sluggish, wasteful rotary engine concept into a smooth, efficient, high-speed power unit. Parsons's turbine was one-tenth the size of an equivalent reciprocating engine and thus was ideally suited for limited space applications like ships, where bulky power plants occupied valuable cargo spaces. The turbine's high rotary speed made it ideal for driving electric generators. Westinghouse sensed a great commercial potential in turbines and bought the American rights to Parsons's designs. Turbines were installed in the Westinghouse Electric power plant in Pittsburgh to demonstrate the practicality of this form of steam power. The success of these three small units led to a 1,500-kilowatt turbogenerator for Hartford, Connecticut, which was installed in 1899 and 1900. A few years later Westinghouse's major competitor, General Electric, came to accept the superiority of the turbogenerator and installed a turbine large enough to drive 12,000 kilowatt generators at Chicago's historic Fisk Street power station. Westinghouse also promoted steam turbines for large-scale marine propulsion, an idea which became dominant on the high seas by 1915.

During his life the air brake was seen as Westinghouse's greatest achievement. This might be the expected perspective during the railway age but today it could be argued that Westinghouse's participation in the so-called "War of the Currents" was of more consequence. The predominance of alternating current (AC) is due largely to the leadership of George Westinghouse. Thomas A. Edison dominated the electrical world because of a series of spectacular inventions and technical advances in this

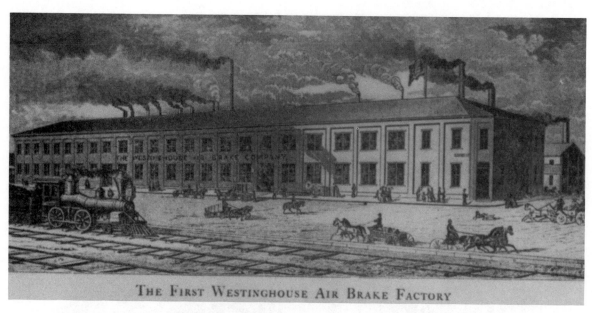

THE FIRST WESTINGHOUSE AIR BRAKE FACTORY

Sketch of Westinghouse's first air brake factory

field, but Edison was a passionate believer in direct current (DC) and as such promoted this form of power for all domestic and industrial purposes. For all of DC's merits there was no economic way to change its voltage. Safety demanded that the consumer not be subjected to potentials of more than 100 to 200 volts, but efficiency in transmission required higher voltages. This is true because the energy transmitted is the product of voltage and current, and resistance results in energy loss. However, by raising the voltage and lowering the current, the same energy can be conveyed with less heat loss. At relatively low voltages, such as those Edison employed, electrical transmission was limited to a radius of approximately a quarter mile.

Westinghouse and other technicians understood the problem though there was no single solution obvious to all. It was known that alternating current could be stepped up and stepped down in voltage by the process of induction in a non-moving-part transformer. A Frenchman, Lucien Gaulard, working with an English partner, John D. Gibbs, patented such a transformer in September 1882. Westinghouse bought the rights to their design a few years later. At first he was not convinced that AC and transformers were the solution to the electric power problem and so moved cautiously. He hired William Stanley to perfect a test system in Great Barrington, Massachusetts, during 1885 and 1886. Stanley proved equal to the task, and the results convinced Westinghouse that Edison was wrong and that the future belonged to AC. Whoever perfected

the system would reap a golden harvest while helping mankind at the same time. Westinghouse was naturally in favor of both.

On January 8, 1886, the Westinghouse Electric Company was incorporated. Though he was not an electrician Westinghouse quickly mastered the mysteries of harnessed lighting. He took direct hand in some of the design work and reshaped the Gaulard/Gibbs transformer so that it could be machine made, thus making it more commercially viable. Large-scale manufacturing of AC lamps, generators, and transformers was underway by September 1887. Edison maintained a noisy campaign against the "unsafe" Westinghouse AC system but to no avail. He was largely silenced in 1892 when Edison General Electric Company and Thomson-Houston Electric merged as the General Electric Company. The new firm quietly accepted the inevitability of AC power and in so doing vindicated Westinghouse's judgment on the subject. Direct current, however, in the future would maintain its hold on urban electric traction and elevator motors. Westinghouse contended and ultimately proved that long-distance electric railways were best served by AC motors. The high-speed trains operating today between New Haven and Washington are a result of Westinghouse's vision.

By 1890 there were 300 Westinghouse AC power plants in operation, yet most were small systems; Westinghouse believed a larger public demonstration was necessary. The 1893 World Columbian Exposition in Chicago was seen as the proper vehicle to demonstrate the wonders of AC. Westinghouse won a contract to install over 92,000 lamps and other smaller electrical exhibits, including Nikola Tesla's polyphase AC motor and an electric kitchen. Tesla's motor effectively solved the critical problem of producing mechanical power for AC users. Central to the exhibit was a hulking 750-kilowatt generator of the sort that inspired Henry Adams's essay about the Virgin and the Dynamo.

The 1893 Exposition display helped Westinghouse win a contract to install a very large hydro-electric plant at Niagara Falls. Three 5,000 horsepower generators were installed. The success at Niagara is credited with generating the commercial confidence that led to the large-scale investment necessary for a national power system. At the time of Westinghouse's death, over 14 billion kilowatt hours of electricity were being generated in the United States.

At age sixty Westinghouse could look back on a varied career replete with countless business and technical successes. Before he left this life he would hold 361 United States patents. He had gained a solid engineering reputation and was recognized as the founder of some seventy-two firms with aggregate assets of $200 million. He enjoyed a reputation as a captain of industry that other industrialists of his day must have coveted. This reputation was based in part on good labor relations. There were no ugly strikes like those at Pullman or Homestead to blemish the name of Westinghouse. To the contrary, Wilmerding really was a model city. Good wages were paid, and Westinghouse was a pioneer in granting a half holiday on Saturday as well as paid vacations. Additional benefits ranged from providing workers with turkeys at Christmas to organizing a special train to carry the shop men to the 1876 Centennial celebration. While such gifts today might be regarded as patronizing, Samuel Gompers was moved to say that if all employers were like Westinghouse, the American labor movement would expire.

Westinghouse gained recognition for his achievements while still young. In 1874 he was given the Scott Medal by the Franklin Institute. A decade later the king of Belgium awarded him the Order of Leopold. Medals and degrees also came from Italy, France, and Germany. He was given an honorary doctorate by the school he attended so briefly, Union College. The Fritz Medal came in 1905, followed by the Edison Medal seven years later. He was made president of the American Society of Mechanical Engineers in 1910. Even after his death, more honors came as an indication of the esteem due America's great engineer/entrepreneur.

For all the success and honors Westinghouse's world came crashing down unexpectedly. The bank panic of 1907 caught him unprepared. Several of his firms failed, and in the ensuing reorganization Westinghouse lost control. He was too forthright to deal effectively with the lawyers and financiers who pounded upon his faltering companies. All were solid businesses and did not fit the mold of the watered or blue sky enterprises that failed, predictably, at the first financial downturn. Because Westinghouse was intent on running his own businesses, he disliked dealing with the investors and bankers who wanted to share in the control of the companies. He dealt with a small circle of investors who were temporarily unable to provide the short-term working capital needed by great enterprises like Westinghouse Electric. After fourteen months the receivership ended, but a new board now governed the company, and the powers of the president were so restricted that Westinghouse resigned in 1908. He continued to head the always solvent but much smaller air brake and signal companies.

Although he lost control of the electric company Westinghouse was not personally ruined. He was comfortable financially and found solace in mechanical developments involving steam turbine reduction gearing and automotive air springs. But the loss of his companies was a severe blow, and he could not bear to ride by the gates of his Pittsburgh plant. More time was spent in residences in Washington and New York. Late in 1913 his health began failing, and he developed heart disease. The physique of iron and will of steel would no longer sustain him, and he died of heart trouble in his Manhattan apartment on March 12, 1914.

He was an imposing man, six feet tall and large of frame. Yet his manner was polite and not imperial. His associates found him cheerful and unaffected; one writer said he was as simple as a child. Yet he was surely not a fool. He was devoted to work, had no hobbies, never smoked, drank little, and ate sparingly. He married Marguerite E. Walker on August 8, 1867, and they had one child. Work clearly remained his principal interest. This man of broad talents, practical and intellectual gifts, ambition, energy, and vision was clearly destined for success. The historian's perspective may best summarize his life. Daniel Boorstin said he "combined a versatile inventive genius with a shrewd sense of how to exploit his inventions financially."

References:

Mary Brignano and Hax McCullough, *The Search for Safety: A History of Railroad Signals and the People Who Made Them* (Pittsburgh: Union Switch & Signal, 1981);

George Westinghouse Commemoration: A Forum Present-ing the Career and Achievements of George Westinghouse on the 90th Anniversary of His Birth (New York: American Society of Mechanical Engineers, 1937);

Thomas P. Hughes, *Networks of Power: Electrification in Western Society, 1880-1930* (Baltimore, Md.: Johns Hopkins University Press, 1983);

Francis E. Leupp, *George Westinghouse: His Life and Achievements* (Boston: Little, Brown, 1918);

Henry G. Prout, *A Life of George Westinghouse* (New York: Scribners, 1921);

John H. White, *American Railroad Passenger Car* (Baltimore, Md.: Johns Hopkins University Press, 1978).

Asa Whitney

(March 14, 1797-September 17, 1872)

by W. Thomas White

James Jerome Hill Reference Library

CAREER: Merchant, New York City (1817-1825); buyer and partner, Frederick Sheldon and Company (1825-1836); self-employed dry goods merchant (1836-1842); China agent for several New York trading firms (1842-1844); self-employed railroad promoter (1844-1852).

Asa Whitney, railroad promoter and merchant, was born on March 14, 1797, at North Groton, Connecticut, the eldest of nine children born to Shuball and Sarah Mitchell Whitney. Little is known of his early life, but he seems to have had an ordinary education and upbringing common to the sons of reasonably successful New England farmers. Farming held little appeal for Whitney, however, and around 1817 he moved to New York, where he immediately began his career as a dry goods importer and merchant.

Whitney's early career was a prosperous one. From about 1825 to 1836 he traveled extensively in Europe as a buyer and, later, a partner in the New York firm of Frederick Sheldon and Company. While in France he married Herminie Antoinette Pillet, who died in New York on April 1, 1833. Two years later he married Sarah Jay Munro, grandniece of John Jay. In 1836 Whitney organized his own firm but fell on hard times because of the depression of 1837.

The collapse of his fortunes, including the death of his wife in 1840, compelled Whitney to start over. In mid 1842 he sailed to China, where he remained for fifteen months as an agent for several New York merchant firms and as a speculator for his own account. During his brief sojourn in Asia Whitney amassed a great deal of money, although the details of how he did so remain unclear. With a fortune sufficient to allow him a life of leisure he left China in 1844, following the signing of the preliminary articles of the Treaty of Wang-hea, which granted the United States privileges similar to those earlier given Great Britain.

During his return voyage Whitney reputedly formulated his plan for the construction of a transcontinental railroad. Once in New York he drafted a formal proposal and presented the memorial to Congress in January 1845. In this initial plan Whitney urged a route from Lake Michigan's western shore to the south pass of the Rocky Mountains, from which one line would be built to San Francisco and one to the Columbia River. Construction would be financed by the sale of lands, set aside by Congress along a 60-mile-wide strip spanning the entire route. Later, presumably in response to critics' charges that he was attempting an enormous land grab, Whitney added that title to said lands should not vest in him, his heirs, or others until twenty years after completion of the railroad, although he did request a salary of $4,000 a year to supervise construction of the proposed railroad.

Whitney urged a northern transcontinental route for two primary reasons. First, access to San Francisco Bay and other ports on the northwest coast represented the shortest route to Asian seaports for freight shipped across country from the eastern trading and manufacturing centers. Next, the northern route traversed more thinly populated and more fertile lands than other, more southerly, routes. Consequently, the northern lands seemed to offer the better environment for heavy future settlement, which in turn would benefit directly the proposed railroad. In short, Whitney insisted that a transcontinental railroad, built along the route he proposed, would provide the necessary technological basis for the young nation's western settlement and its anticipated growing commerce with Asia. After 1846 and the war with Mexico the necessity of intercommunication among states and territories that spanned the entire continent became yet another powerful argument favoring a transcontinental railroad.

While Congress considered his memorial, Whitney, in 1845, undertook a personal reconnaissance of a part of his proposed route. He used the trip as the basis for a media campaign to mobilize popular support for his plan. He sent periodic reports, or long letters, to newspapers throughout the country and, consequently, led a national publicity drive in support of the northern transcontinental railroad, a campaign that he waged in various forms for the next seven years.

Powerful opponents of Whitney's proposal quickly emerged. Stephen A. Douglas of Illinois, who favored Chicago as a terminus, objected on various grounds, including the proposal that settlement precede construction of the road. Whitney responded in a pamphlet, *Reply to the Hon. S. A. Douglass* [sic], but the controversy continued to rage. Thomas Hart Benton led another faction that opposed the plan unless the road's terminus was St. Louis, while others insisted upon Memphis or other southern cities as terminals. Further, Benton insisted that a thorough survey be made of the western lands before construction of any railroad was authorized, while also remaining generally opposed to any legislation that would "set apart and sell to Asa Whitney, of New York, a portion of the public lands, to enable him to construct a railroad from Lake Michigan to the Pacific Ocean." Benton

charged that the cession would involve the transfer to Whitney and his partners of over 100 million acres of public lands. Critics also argued that the government, rather than private parties, should construct the road, while others, including fellow transcontinental advocate John Plumbe of Iowa, charged that Whitney's plan was nothing but a scheme designed to effect a colossal land grab from the national government.

Whitney continued to lobby for his plan by constantly roaming the country delivering lectures and writing letters. In 1849 he published a pamphlet entitled *A Project for a Railroad to the Pacific*, which restated his arguments. Frustrated by his attempts in the United States, Whitney journeyed to England in 1851 to urge a similar transcontinental route for Canada.

Unable to find support there, he returned to the United States, married Catherine (Moore) Campbell on October 6, 1852, and retired to Locust Hill, his estate outside Washington. The following year Congress appropriated funds for a survey of the proposed routes. Although sectional differences precluded any further action until the Civil War, Congress did pass the first Pacific Railroad Act in 1862. By the time of Asa Whitney's death from typhoid in 1872, the Union Pacific/Central Pacific railroad system was complete, and construction had begun on the Northern Pacific, Southern Pacific, and Santa Fe railroads. While Whitney is not credited directly with the construction of any transcontinental railroads, his promotional efforts, and those of others, did much to make the railroads a reality.

Publications:

Atlantic and Pacific Railroad: A. Whitney's Reply to the Hon. S. A. Douglass [sic] (Washington, D.C., 1845);

Memorial of Asa Whitney, of New York City, Relative to the Construction of a Railroad from Lake Michigan to the Pacific Ocean (Washington, D.C.: Blair & Rives, 1845);

National Railroad Connecting the Atlantic and Pacific (Washington, D.C., 1845);

To the People of the United States (N.p., 1845);

Memorial of Asa Whitney Praying a Grant of Public Land to Enable Him to Construct a Railroad from Lake Michigan to the Pacific Ocean (Washington, D.C.: Ritchie & Heiss, 1846);

Mr. A. Whitney's Address Before the Legislature of Alabama, on His Project for a Railroad from Lake Michigan to the Pacific (Washington, D.C.: J & G. S. Gideon, 1847);

Address of Mr. A. Whitney, Before the Legislature of Pennsylvania, on His Project for a Railroad from Lake

Michigan to the Pacific (Harrisburg, Pa.: I. G. M. & J. G. M. Lescure, 1848);

Memorial of Asa Whitney Praying a Grant of Public Land to Enable Him to Construct a Railroad from Lake Michigan to the Pacific Ocean (Washington, D.C.: Tippin & Streeper, 1848);

A Project for a Railroad to the Pacific (New York: G. W. Wood, 1849);

Plan for a Direct Communication Between the Great Centres of the Populations of Europe and Asia (London: W. Clowes, 1851);

Asa Whitney versus A. L. Mowry (Philadelphia, n.d.);

Bill, Answer & Complainants Proofs (N.p., n.d.);

Golden Wedding of Asa Whitney and Clarinda Williams, 1866 (N.p., n.d.).

References:

Margaret L. Brown, "Asa Whitney and His Pacific Railroad Publicity Campaign," *Mississippi Valley Historical Review,* 20 (September 1933): 209-224;

Nelson H. Loomis, "Asa Whitney: Father of the Pacific Railroads," *Proceedings, Mississippi Valley Historical Society,* 6 (1912-1913): 166-175.

Theodore Tuttle Woodruff

(April 8, 1811-May 2, 1892)

by John H. White

Smithsonian Institution

CAREER: Wagon builder and mechanic (c.1827-c.1854); railroad car builder (c.1855-c.1858); railroad sleeping-car promoter (c.1856-1864); partner, Central Transportation Company (1862-1864); banker (c.1865-1870); president, Norris Iron Company (1870-1875); independent inventor (1875-1892).

Theodore T. Woodruff, a railroad sleeping-car pioneer, was born on April 8, 1811, near Watertown, New York, the son of Simeon and Roxanna Woodruff. Young Woodruff worked on his father's farm and attended local schools until he was sixteen years of age. He then was apprenticed to a wagon maker in 1827 for a three-year term. Woodruff later worked as a pattern maker and developed into a practical mechanic and a part-time inventor. Like a number of other mechanics, he became interested in perfecting a sleeping car for overnight railway travel. This notion remained dominant–for Woodruff at least–until he became master car builder for the Terre Haute, Alton & St. Louis Railroad in about 1855. The chief engineer of the line, Orville W. Childs, encouraged Woodruff to perfect his sleeping-car ideas and helped him obtain two patents, one for a seat and the other for a couch, in December 1856. A number of overnight cars had been previously built and tested yet none remained in service for any extended period. In the first decades of American railroading most rail travel was too short

to require luxury service, but as the system developed by midcentury, so too grew a market for sleeping- and parlor-car travel. It was not so much Woodruff's inventive genius or vision as it was fortuitous timing that led to the successful introduction of sleeping cars. The traveling public, particularly its more affluent members, was ready to pay an extra fare for the comfort of a berth.

Childs helped Woodruff find backers, and the Wason Car Company of Springfield, Massachusetts, completed a demonstrator car in October 1857. During the day the car ran as an ordinary coach, but at night its convertible seats were made into beds. Additional berths were lowered from the ceiling. The test car created some interest, and contracts for more cars were made with several railroads, including the Illinois Central, the Galena & Chicago Union, and various individual operators such as Webster Wagner. In September 1858 Woodruff landed his first big contract when he signed on the Pennsylvania Railroad. Andrew Carnegie, an employee of the railroad at the time, sniffed out a good investment opportunity and bought a number of shares of T. T. Woodruff & Company at the time of the Pennsylvania agreement. In later years Carnegie called it the best investment he made as a young man and said that it was responsible for his later riches. Woodruff did not become so prosperous.

The sleeping-car business flourished, and in December 1862 the partners decided to reorganize the business as the Central Transportation Company. Capital was set at $200,000. Various patents and competitors, such as the sugar-baron-turned-sleeping-car-operator E. C. Knight, were consolidated into the new company. Luxurious cars began to appear at the same time; their fancy interiors, elegant bedding, and hot-air heating systems delighted the public and made the new Woodruff cars more popular than ever before. In 1865 it was necessary to increase the capital limit to $2 million. During the next year Central Transportation had eighty-eight cars in service and introduced the first Silver Palace cars. In 1869 return on investment was nearly 18 percent, and earnings reached $256,000. Central Transportation appeared destined to become a major corporation.

Behind the scenes, however, conditions were not so positive. Woodruff had already left the company in 1864 for reasons never explained. Carnegie, though a minor shareholder, decided the managers, including Woodruff's older brother, Jonah, were not capable of realizing the sleeping car's full potential. Carnegie favored a newcomer to the field, one George M. Pullman, and worked from the inside to help Central's rival succeed. In the late 1860s Carnegie helped Pullman wrest the valuable Union Pacific contract away from Central, and in February 1870 he assisted in arranging for a lease of the mighty Central Transportation to Pullman's fledgling sleeping-car operation.

Meanwhile, Woodruff strayed from the sleeping-car business into less profitable enterprises. He moved to Mansfield, Ohio, and dabbled in banking for several years. When he was sixty years of age, Woodruff decided to again become active in business. He moved east to Norristown, Pennsylvania, and purchased the Norris Iron Company in 1870. The firm made boilers, steam engines, rock crushers, and other heavy machinery. All went well for a few years until the effects of the 1873 panic overwhelmed Woodruff. He went bankrupt in 1875 and lost not only the machinery business but also his savings and a fine house on Broad Street in Philadelphia. Reduced to poverty, Woodruff and his wife moved in with their daughter. But the old mechanic's spirit was not broken, and he resolved to remake his fortune. During the last seventeen years of his life he developed and promoted a number of inventions which included a steam plow, a surveyor's compass, and a screw propeller. While on a business trip to sell the propeller he was struck down and killed by an express train at Gloucester, New Jersey. The poverty of his last months was relieved by a pension provided by Andrew Carnegie.

References:

Joseph F. Wall, *Andrew Carnegie* (London & New York: Oxford University Press, 1970);

John H. White, *The American Railroad Passenger Car* (Baltimore, Md.: Johns Hopkins University Press, 1978).

Selected Route Maps

Selected Route Maps

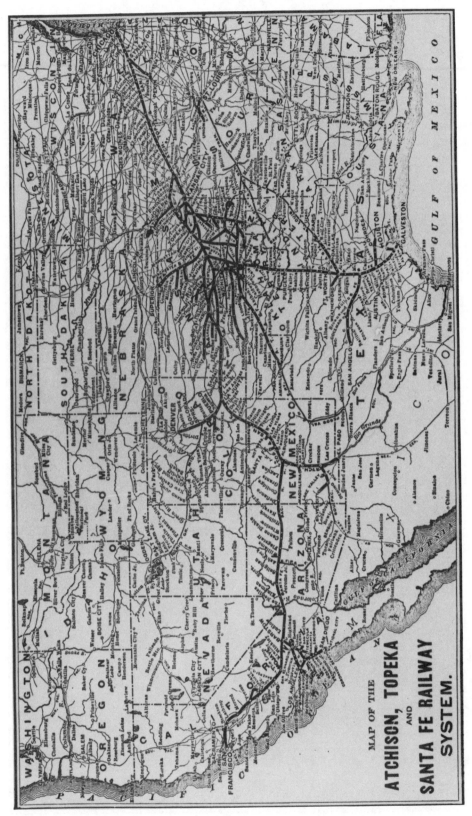

Route map of the Atchison, Topeka and Santa Fe Railroad, 1890s

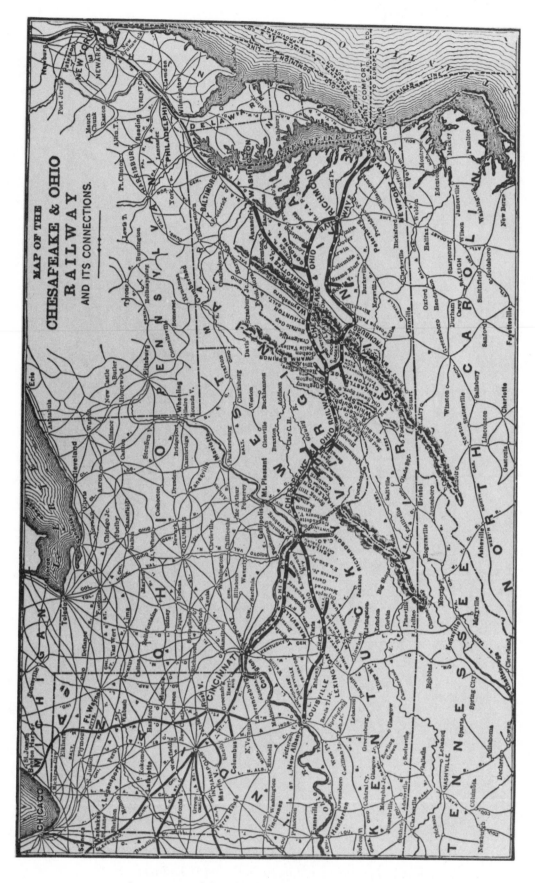

Route map of the Chesapeake & Ohio Railway, 1890s

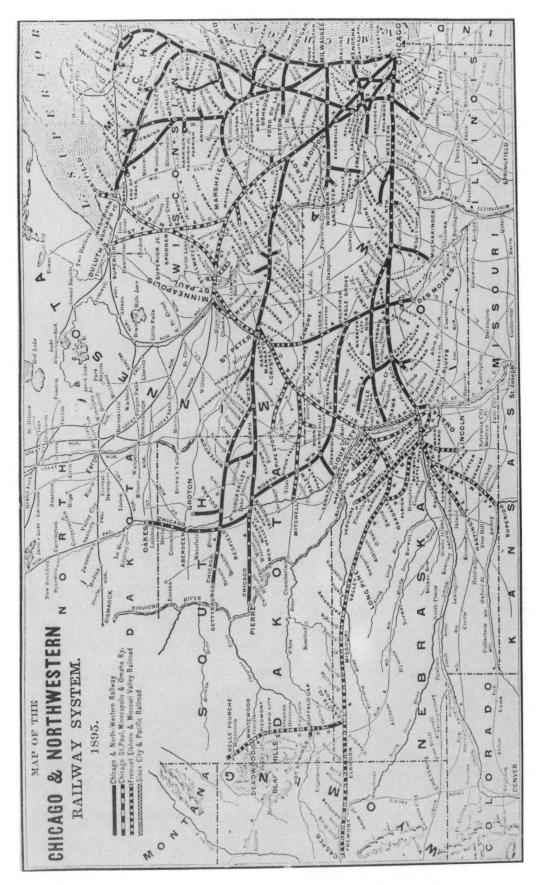

Route map of the Chicago & North Western Railway, 1895

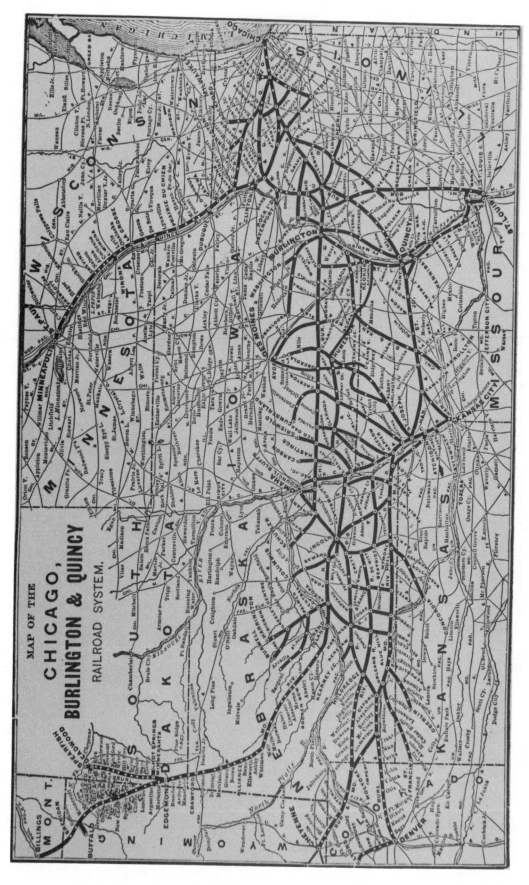

Route map of the Chicago, Burlington & Quincy Railroad, 1890s

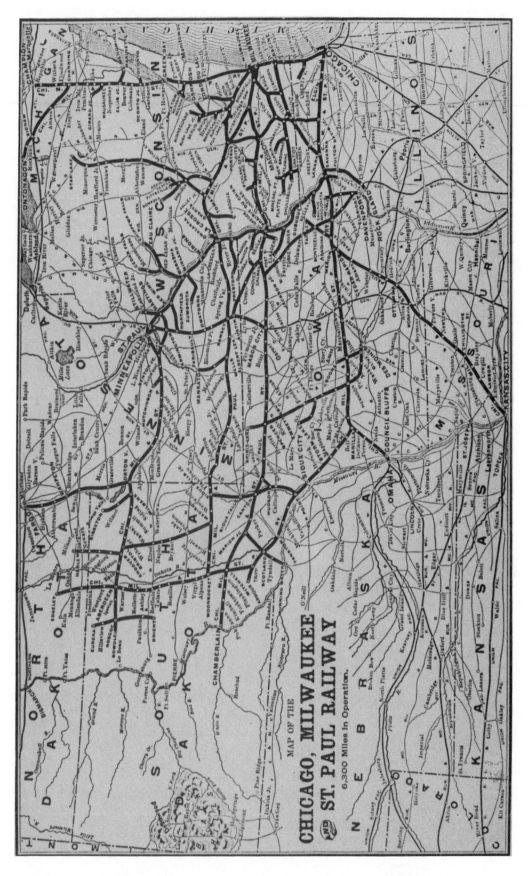

Route map of the Chicago, Milwaukee & St. Paul Railway, 1896

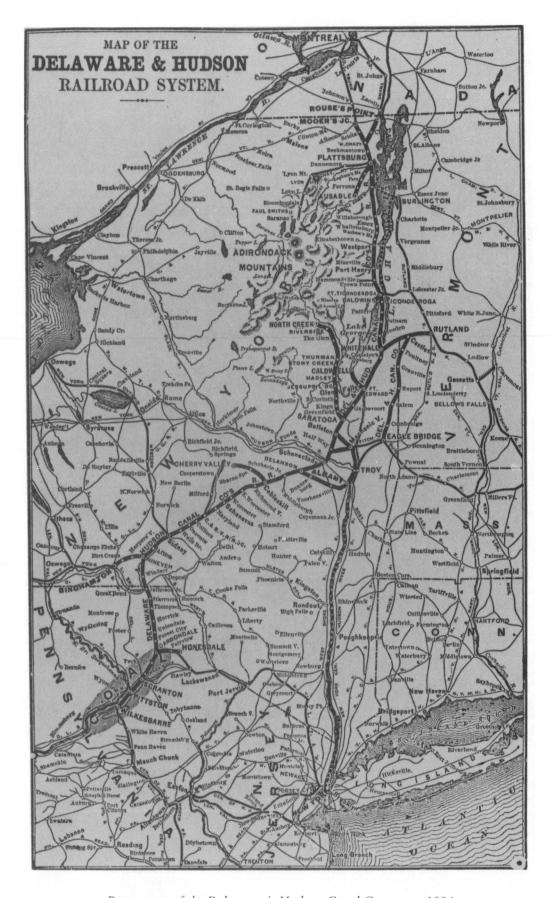

Route map of the Delaware & Hudson Canal Company, 1896

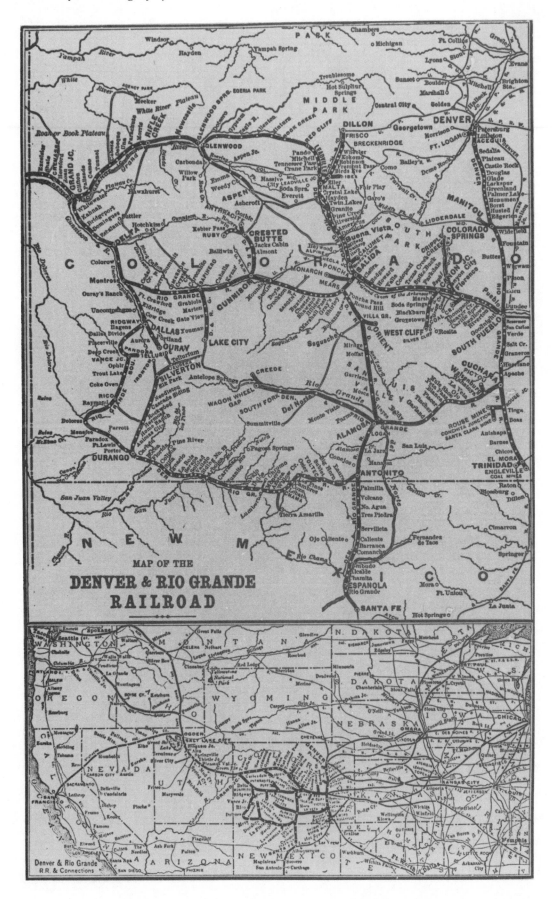

Route map of the Denver & Rio Grande Railroad, 1896

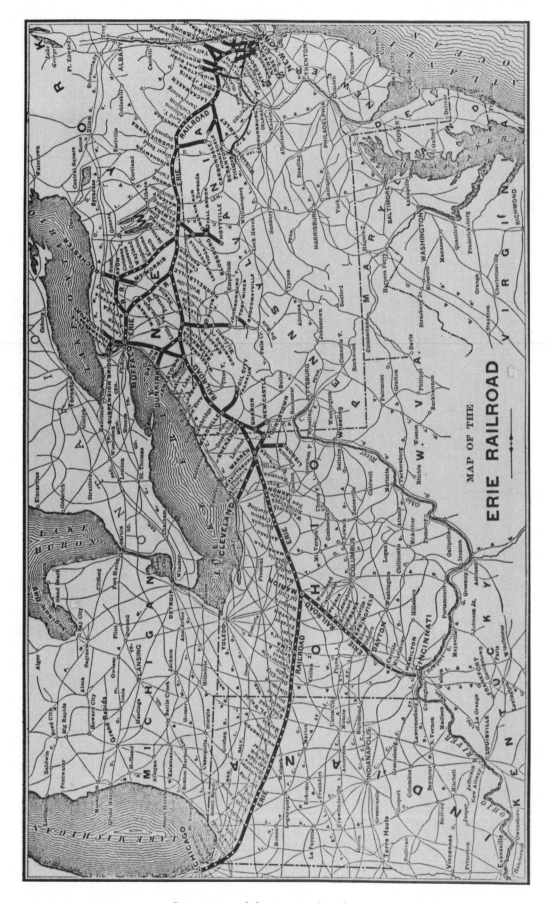

Route map of the Erie Railroad, 1890s

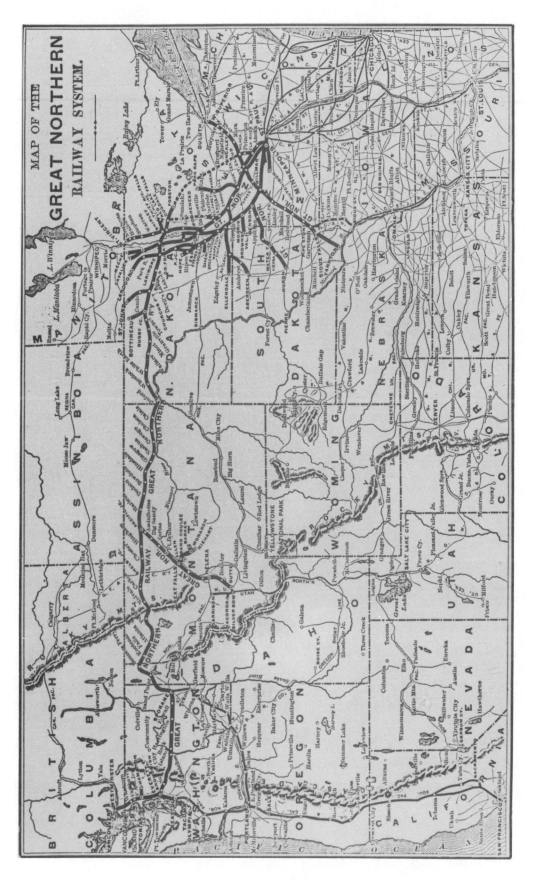

Route map of the Great Northern Railway, 1896

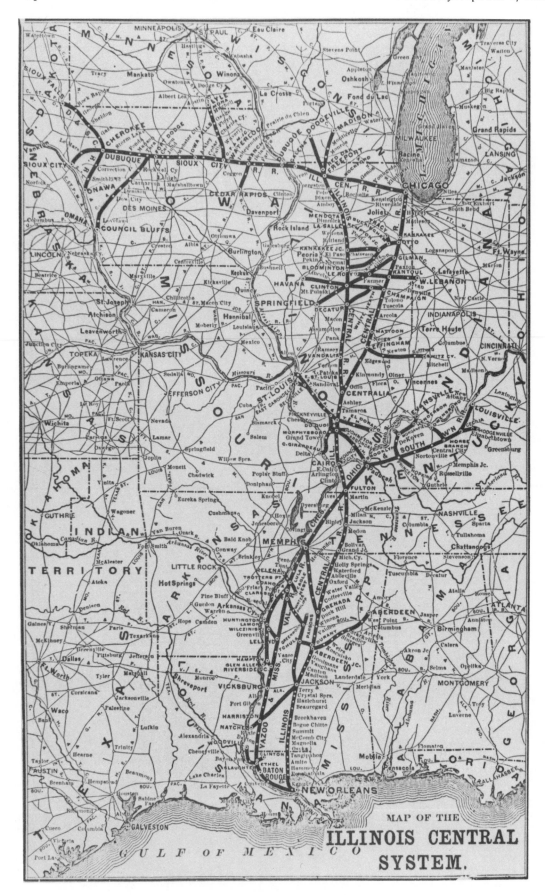

Route map of the Illinois Central Railroad, 1896

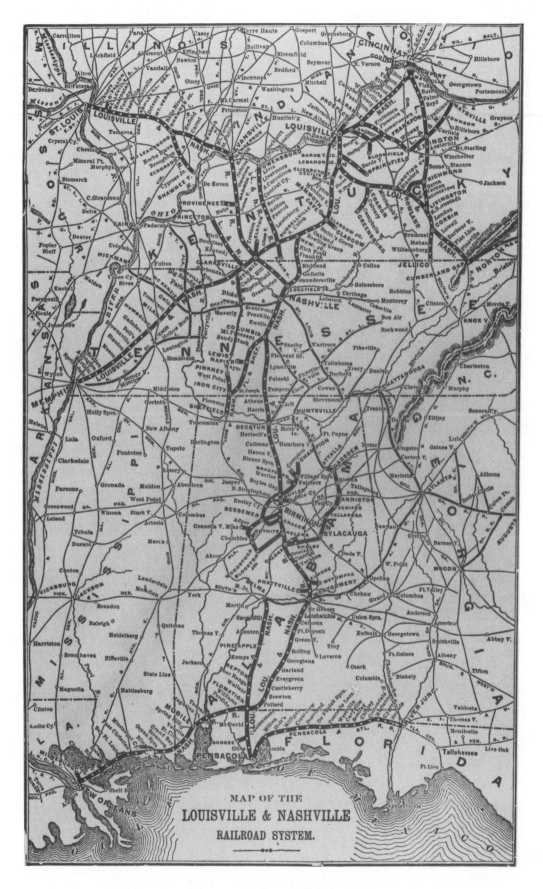

Route map of the Louisville & Nashville Railroad, 1896

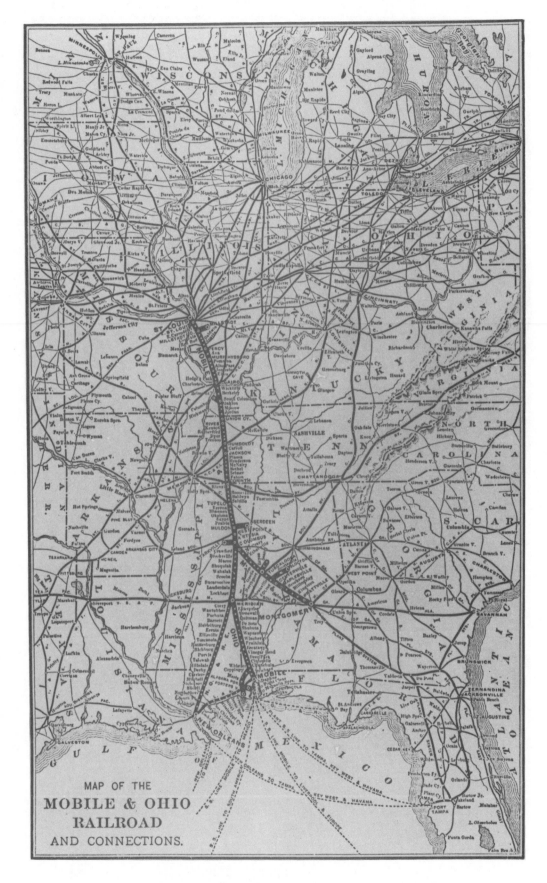

Route map of the Mobile & Ohio Railroad, 1890s

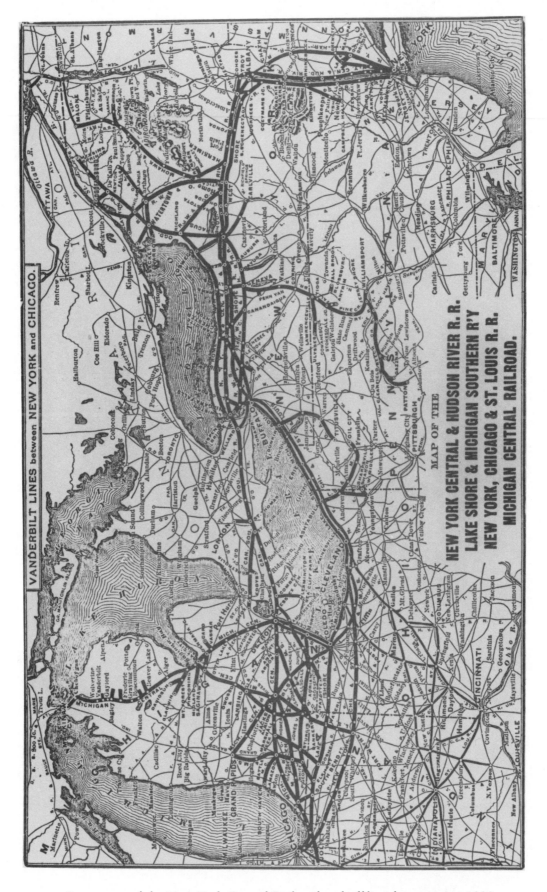

Route map of the New York Central Railroad and affiliated companies, 1888

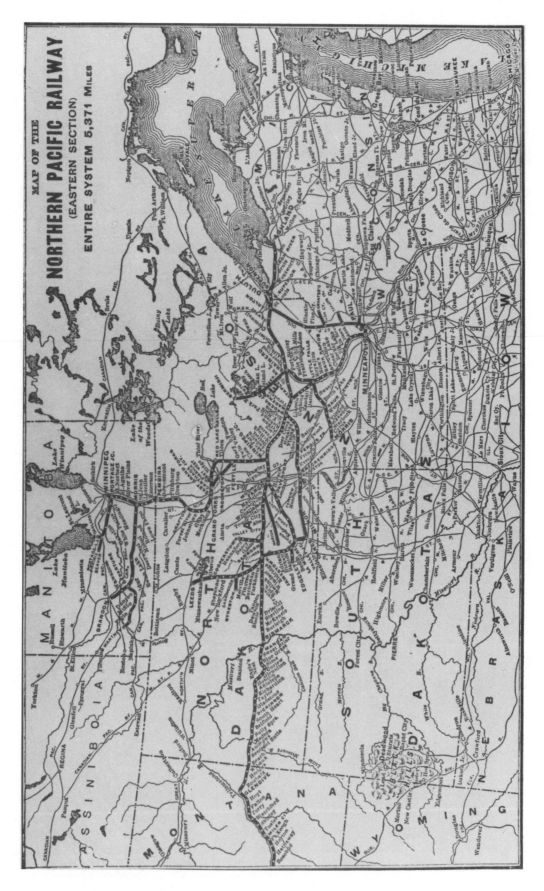

Route map of the Northern Pacific Railway (eastern section), 1904

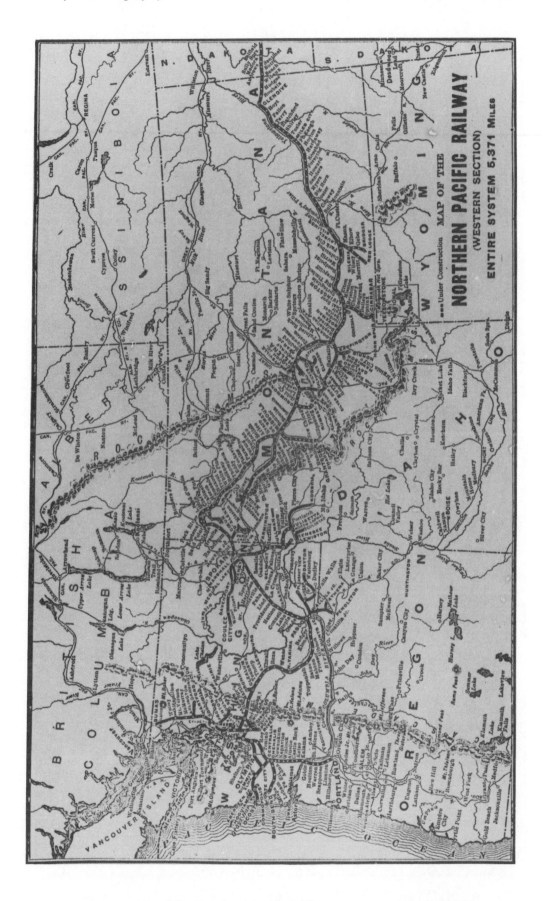

Route map of the Northern Pacific Railway (western section), 1904

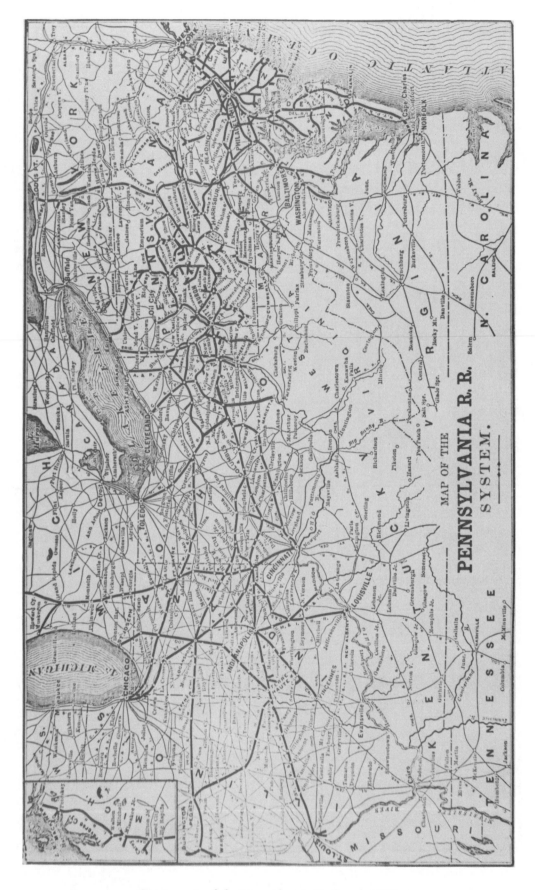

Route map of the Pennsylvania Railroad, 1888

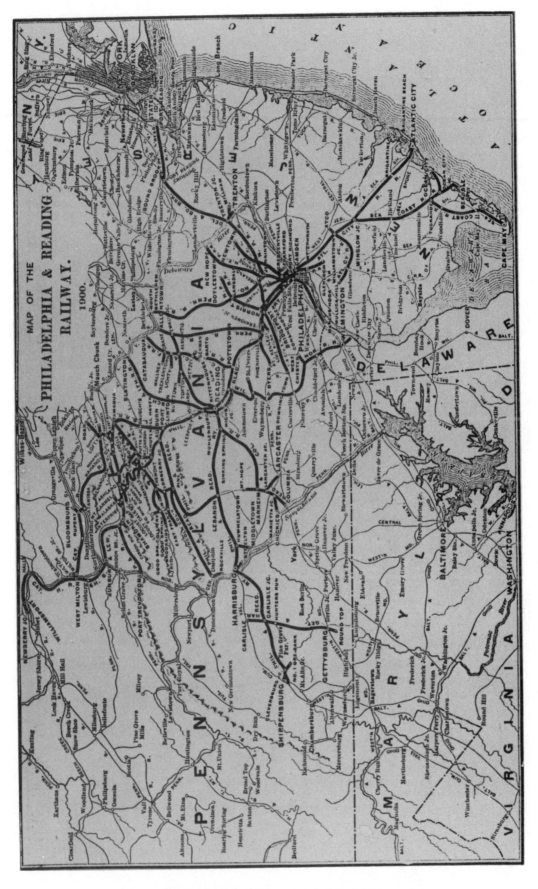

Route map of the Philadelphia & Reading Railway, 1900

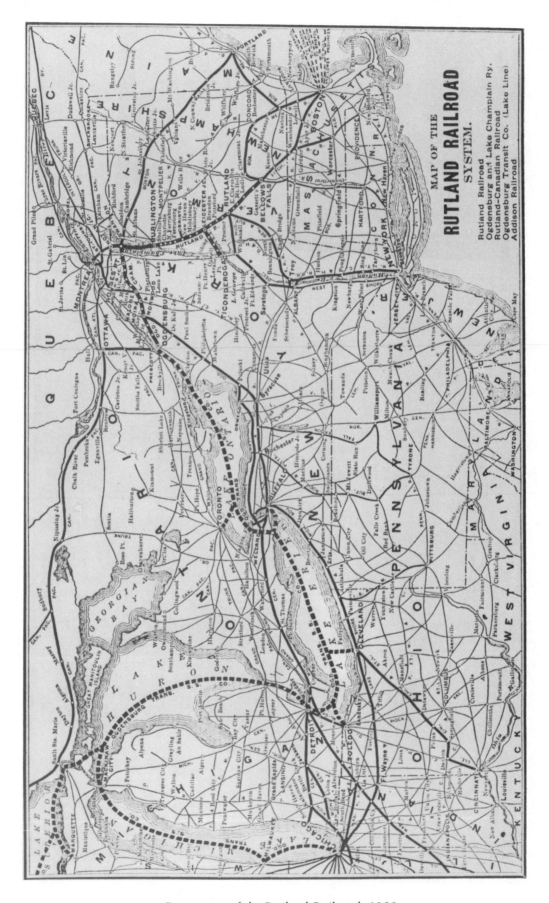

Route map of the Rutland Railroad, 1900

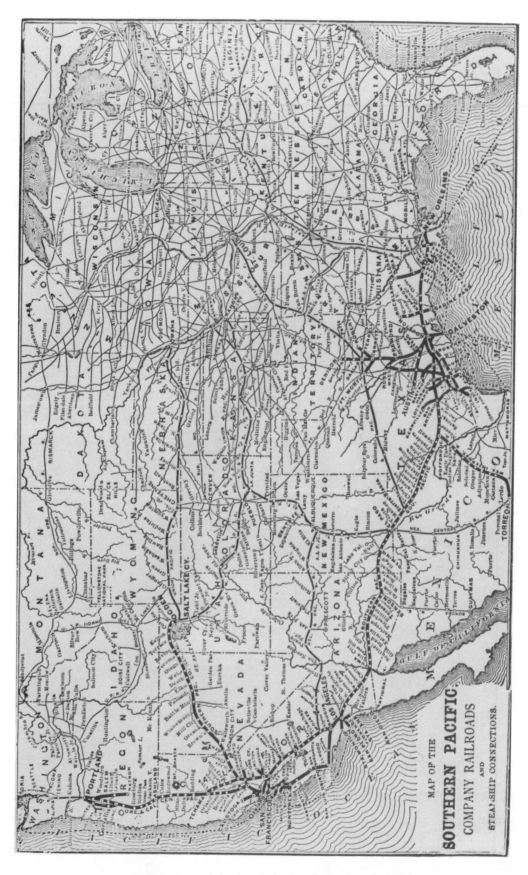

Route map of the Southern Pacific Railroad, 1896

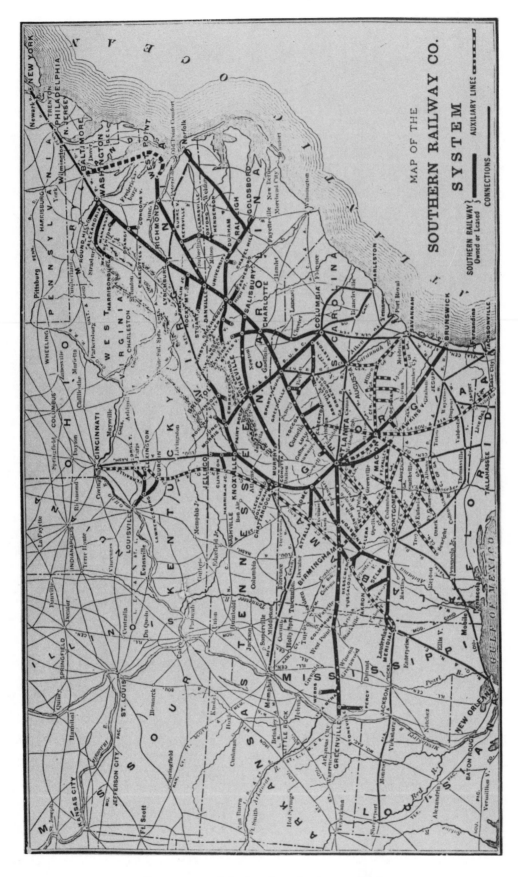

Route map of the Southern Railway, 1896

Contributors

Richard W. Barsness–*Lehigh University*
James P. Baughman–*Stamford, Connecticut*
Michael Bezilla–*Pennsylvania State University*
Keith L. Bryant, Jr.–*Texas A&M University*
Dan Butler–*Colby Community College*
R. Milton Clark–*Missoula, Montana*
George H. Drury–Trains *Magazine*
John F. Due–*University of Illinois*
Saul Engelbourg–*Boston University*
Robert M. Frame III–*James Jerome Hill Reference Library*
Robert L. Frey–*Wilmington College of Ohio*
J. Kevin Graffagnino–*University of Vermont*
H. Roger Grant–*University of Akron*
William S. Greever–*University of Idaho*
George W. Hilton–*University of California, Los Angeles*
James W. Hipp–*Columbia, South Carolina*
Don L. Hofsommer–*Augustana College*
George M. Jenks–*Bucknell University*
Charles J. Kennedy–*University of Nebraska*
Alec Kirby–*George Washington University*
Maury Klein–*University of Rhode Island*
F. Daniel Larkin–*State University College, Oneonta, New York*
Katherine Larkin–*Oneonta, New York*
John W. Larson–*Purdue University*
James H. Lemly–*Atlanta, Georgia*
Richard Lowitt–*Iowa State University*
Albro Martin–*Bradley University*
S. Walter Martin–*Valdosta State College*
Lloyd J. Mercer–*University of California, Santa Barbara*
Gerald Musich–*National Railroad Museum*
Rex Myers–*South Dakota State University*
Roger Natte–*Iowa Central Community College*
E. Dale Odom–*North Texas State University*
William Patterson–*University of South Carolina*
Matthew Redinger–*University of Montana*
Leland L. Sage–*University of Northern Iowa*
James G. Schneider–*Kankakee, Illinois*
Carlos A. Schwantes–*University of Idaho*
Don Snoddy–*Union Pacific Museum*
Darwin H. Stapleton–*Rockefeller Archive Center*
John F. Stover–*Purdue University*
Jackson Thode–*Denver & Rio Grande Western Railroad (Retired)*
James F. Ward–*University of Tennessee, Chattanooga*
Charles B. Weinstock–*Pittsburgh, Pennsylvania*
George C. Werner–*Houston, Texas*
John H. White, Jr.–*Smithsonian Institution*
W. Thomas White–*James Jerome Hill Reference Library*
Frank N. Wilner–*Association of American Railroads*

Railroads in the Age of Regulation, 1900-1980

The following is a list of entries in *Railroads in the Age of Regulation, 1900-1980,* edited by Keith L. Bryant, Jr. Provided as a cross-reference guide, it is intended to aid readers in their use of the railroad volumes in the *Encyclopedia of American Business History and Biography.*

Adamson Act
Akron, Canton & Youngstown Railroad
Alton Railroad
Amtrak
Association of American Railroads
Atchison, Topeka & Santa Fe Railway
Atlantic Coast Line Railroad
W. W. Atterbury
Gale B. Aydelott
Baltimore & Ohio Railroad
Bangor & Aroostook Railroad
John W. Barriger III
Bessemer & Lake Erie Railroad
Benjamin F. Biaggini
Boston & Maine Railroad
Robert J. Bowman
Alan S. Boyd
D. William Brosnan
William C. Brown
John M. Budd
Ralph Budd
Central of Georgia Railroad
Central Railroad of New Jersey
Central Vermont Railway
Chesapeake & Ohio Railway
Chicago & Eastern Illinois Railroad
Chicago & North Western Railway
Chicago, Burlington & Quincy Railroad
Chicago Great Western Railroad
Chicago, Milwaukee, St. Paul & Pacific Railroad
Chicago, Rock Island & Pacific Railway
Chicago South Shore & South Bend Railroad
W. Graham Claytor, Jr.
Martin W. Clement
Conrail

Thomas Conway, Jr.
D. C. Corbin
L. Stanley Crane
John W. Davin
Frederic A. Delano
Delaware & Hudson Railway
Delaware, Lackawanna & Western Railroad
Denver & Rio Grande Western Railroad
William N. Deramus III
Detroit, Toledo & Ironton Railroad
Dieselization
Lawrence A. Downs
Frederic C. Dumaine, Jr.
Albert J. Earling
Electric Traction
Electrification
Howard Elliott
Emergency Railroad Transportation Act
Erie Railroad
James H. Evans
John D. Farrington
Samuel M. Felton, Jr.
William W. Finley
Stuyvesant Fish
John P. Fishwick
Henry M. Flagler
Florida East Coast Railway
Donald V. Fraser
Francis J. Gavin
George J. Gould
Grand Trunk Western Railroad
Carl R. Gray
Great Northern Railway
Guilford Transportation Industries
Gulf, Mobile & Ohio Railroad

Fred G. Gurley
Fairfax Harrison
Edwin Hawley
Ben W. Heineman
Hepburn Act
Louis W. Hill, Sr.
Walker D. Hines
Hale Holden
Marvin Hughitt
Clark Hungerford
Henry E. Huntington
Illinois Central Railroad
Illinois Terminal Railroad
Samuel Insull
Interstate Commerce Act
Arthur Curtiss James
Downing B. Jenks
William J. Jenks
Wayne A. Johnson
Morgan Jones
Kansas City Southern Railway
John C. Kenefick
Julius Kruttschnitt
Lehigh Valley Railroad
Long Island Rail Road
Leonor F. Loree
Louisville & Nashville Railroad
Robert A. Lovett
Maine Central Railroad
Mann-Elkins Act
William G. Marbury
David O. Mathews
William Gibbs McAdoo
Wilson J. McCarthy
James McCrae
Harold J. McKenzie
Louis W. Menk
Microwave Communications
E. Spencer Miller
Minneapolis & St. Louis Railroad
Missouri-Kansas-Texas Railroad
Missouri Pacific Railroad
Monon Route
William H. Moore
Harry C. Murphy
Nashville, Chattanooga & St. Louis Railway
New York Central System
New York, Chicago & St. Louis Railroad
New York, New Haven & Hartford Railroad
Norfolk & Western Railway
Norfolk Southern Corporation

Ernest E. Norris
Northern Pacific Railway
Operating Ratio
Penn Central
Pennsylvania Railroad
Pere Marguette Railway
Alfred E. Perlman
Piggyback/Trailers-on-Flatcars
Pittsburgh & Lake Erie Railroad
Prince Plan of Railroad Consolidation
William J. Quinn
Railroad Land Grants
Railroad Unions and Brotherhoods
Ratemaking
Samuel Rea
Reading Company
Rebates
John S. Reed
W. Thomas Rice
Edward P. Ripley
Donald J. Russell
St. Louis-San Francisco Railway Company
St. Louis Southwestern Railway
Fred W. Sargent
Stuart T. Saunders
Henry A. Scandrett
Seaboard Air Line Railroad
Seaboard Coast Line Railroad
Perry Shoemaker
Matthew S. Sloan
John Walter Smith
Robert H. Smith
Soo Line Railroad Company
Southern Pacific Company
Southern Railway
Spokane, Portland & Seattle Railway
Lucian C. Sprague
William Sproule
Staggers Rail Act of 1980
A. B. Stickney
Arthur E. Stilwell
James M. Symes
Texas & Pacific Railway
Isaac B. Tigrett
William H. Truesdale
Walter J. Tuohy
Frederick D. Underwood
Union Pacific Railroad
United States Railroad Administration
Unit Trains
Valuation Act of 1913

Index

The following index includes names of people, corporations, government agencies, organizations, laws, and technologies. It also includes key terms such as *bridges, safety,* etc.

A page number in *italic* type indicates the first page of an entry devoted to the subject. *Illus.* indicates a picture of the subject. *Map* indicates the depiction of the route of a railroad at a given point in its history.

Index